P9-CKY-467

DATE DUE

			PRINTED IN U.S.A.

CLIFFS NOTES

HARDBOUND   LITERARY   LIBRARIES

EUROPEAN LITERATURE LIBRARY

Volume 3

<u>*Russian Literature*</u>

7 Titles

ISBN 0-931013-22-4

Library distributors, hardbound editions:
Moonbeam Publications
18530 Mack Avenue
Grosse Pointe, MI 48236
(313) 884-5255

MOONBEAM PUBLICATIONS
Robert R. Tyler, President
Elizabeth Jones, Index Editor

FOREWORD

Moonbeam Publications has organized **CLIFFS NOTES**, the best-selling popular (trade) literary reference series, into a fully indexed hardbound series designed to offer a more permanent format for the series.

Hardbound volumes are available in a **BASIC LIBRARY**, a 24 volume series. The current softbound series (over 200 booklets) has been divided into five major literary libraries to help researchers, librarians, teachers, students and all readers use this series more effectively. The five major literary groupings are further subdivided into 17 literary periods or genres to enhance the use of this series as a more precise literary reference book.

Hardbound volumes are also available in an **AUTHORS LIBRARY**, a 13 volume series classified by author, covering 11 authors and over 70 Cliffs Notes titles. This series helps readers who prefer to study the works of a particular author, rather than an entire literary period.

**CLIFFS NOTES HARDBOUND
LITERARY LIBRARIES**
1990 by
Moonbeam Publications
18530 Mack Avenue
Grosse Pointe, MI   48236
(313) 884-5255

Basic Library - 24 Volume
ISBN 0-931013-24-0

Authors Library - 13 Volume
ISBN 0-931013-65-8

Bound In U.S.A.

EUROPEAN LITERATURE LIBRARY

Volume 3

<u>Russian Literature</u>

CONTENTS

ANNA KARENINA

NOTES

including
- *Life of Tolstoy*
- *List of Characters*
- *Brief Synopsis of the Novel*
- *Chapter Summaries*
- *Critical Commentaries*
- *Analysis of Plot Structure*
- *Analysis of Tolstoy's Technique*
- *Analysis of the Novel's Themes*
- *Character Analyses*
- *Review Questions and Theme Topics*
- *Selected Bibliography*

by
Marianne Sturman

Cliffs Notes

INCORPORATED

LINCOLN, NEBRASKA 68501

CONTENTS

THE LIFE OF LEO TOLSTOY (1828-1910)

Leo Nicolaevich Tolstoy was the next to youngest of five children, descending from one of the oldest and best families in Russia. His youthful surroundings were of the upper class gentry of the last period of serfdom. Though his life spanned the westernization of Russia, his early intellectual and cultural education was the traditional eighteenth century training. Lyovochka (as he was called) was a tender, affection seeking child who liked to do things "out of the ordinary." Self-consciousness was one of his youthful attributes and this process of self-scrutiny continued all his life. Indeed, Tolstoy's life is one of the best documented accounts we have of any writer, for the diaries he began at seventeen he continued through old age.

In 1844 Leo attended the University of Kazan, then one of the great seats of learning east of Berlin. He early showed a contempt for academic learning but became interested enough at the faculty of Jurisprudence (the easiest course of study) to attend classes with some regularity. Kazan, next to St. Petersburg and Moscow, was a great social center for the upper class. An eligible, titled young bachelor, Tolstoy devoted his energies to engage in the brilliant social life of his set. But his homely peasant face was a constant source of embarrassment and Tolstoy took refuge in queer and original behavior. His contemporaries called him "Lyovochka the bear," for he was always stiff and awkward.

Before his second year examinations, Tolstoy left Kazan to settle at his ancestral estate, Yasnaya Polyana (Bright Meadow) which was his share of the inheritance. Intending to farm and devote himself to improve the lot of his peasants, Tolstoy's youthful idealism soon vanished as he confronted the insurmountable distrust of the peasantry. He set off for Moscow in 1848 and for two years lived the irregular and dissipated life led by young men of his class. The diaries of this period reveal the critical self-scrutiny with which he regarded all his actions, and he itemized each deviation from his code of perfect behavior. Carnal lust and gambling were those passions most difficult for him to exorcise. As he closely observed the life around him in Moscow, Tolstoy experienced an irresistible urge to write. This time was the birth of the creative artist and the following year saw the publication of his first story, *Childhood.*

Tolstoy began his army career in 1852, joining his brother Nicolai in the Caucasus. Garrisoned among a string of Cossack outposts on the borders of Georgia, Tolstoy participated in occasional expeditions against the fierce Chechenians, the Tartar natives rebelling against Russian rule. He spent the rest of his time gambling, hunting, fornicating.

Torn amidst his inner struggle between his bad and good impulses, Tolstoy arrived at a sincere belief in God, though not in the formalized sense of the Eastern Church. The wild primitive environment of the Caucasus satisfied Tolstoy's intense physical and spiritual needs. Admiring the free, passionate, natural life of the mountain natives, he wished to turn his back forever on sophisticated society with its falseness and superficiality.

Soon after receiving his commission, Tolstoy fought among the defenders at Sevastopol against the Turks. In his *Sevastopol* sketches he describes with objectivity and compassion the matter-of-fact bravery of the Russian officers and soldiers during the siege.

By now he was a writer of nationwide reputation and when he resigned from the army and went to Petersburg, Turgenev offered him hospitality. With the leader of the capital's literary world for sponsor, Tolstoy became an intimate member of the circle of important writers and editors. But he failed to get on with these litterateurs: he had no respect for their ideal of European progress and their intellectual arrogance appalled him. His lifelong antagonism with Turgenev typified this relationship.

His travels abroad in 1857 started Tolstoy toward his lifelong revolt against the whole organization of modern civilization. To promote the growth of individual freedom and self-awareness, he started a unique village school at Yasnaya Polyana based on futuristic progressive principles. The peasant children "brought only themselves, their receptive natures, and the certainty that it would be as jolly in school today as yesterday." But the news of his brother's illness interrupted his work. Traveling to join Nicolai in France, he first made a tour of inspection throughout the German school system. He was at his brother's side when Nicolai died at the spa near Marseille, and this death affected him deeply. Only his work saved him from the worse depressions and sense of futility he felt toward life.

The fundamental aim of Tolstoy's nature was a search for truth, for the meaning of life, for the ultimate aims of art, for family happiness, for God. In marriage his soul found a release from this never ending quest, and once approaching his ideal of family happiness, Tolstoy entered upon the greatest creative period of his life.

In the first fifteen years of his marriage to Sonya (Sofya Andreyevna Bers) the great inner crisis he later experienced in his "conversion" was procrastinated, lulled by the triumph of spontaneous life over questioning reason. While his nine children grew up, his life was happy, almost idyllic, despite the differences which arose between him and the wife sixteen years his junior. As an inexperienced bride of eighteen, the city bred Sonya had many difficult adjustments to make. She was the mistress of a country estate as well as the helpmate of a man whose previous life she had not shared. Her constant pregnancies and boredom and loneliness marred the great love she and Tolstoy shared. In this exhilarating period of his growing family, Tolstoy created the epic novels, *War and Peace* and *Anna Karenina,* while Sonya, rejoicing at his creative genius, faithfully turned his rough drafts into fair copy.

Toward the end of 1866, while writing *Anna Karenina,* Tolstoy entered on the prolonged and fateful crisis which resulted in his conversion. He recorded part of this spiritual struggle in *Anna Karenina.* The meaning of life consists in living according to one's "inner goodness," he concluded. Only through emotional and religious commitment can one discover this natural truth. Uniquely interpreting the Gospels, Tolstoy discovered Christ's entire message was contained in the idea "that ye resist not evil." This doctrine of "non-resistance" became the foundation of Tolstoyism where one lived according to nature, renouncing the artificial refinements of society. Self-gratification, Tolstoy believed, perverted man's inherent goodness. Therefore property rights—ownership by one person of "things that belong to all"—is a chief source of evil. Carnal lust, ornamental clothing, fancy food are other symptoms of the corrupting influence of civilization. In accordance with his beliefs, Tolstoy renounced all copyrights to his works since 1881, divided his property among his family members, dressed in peasant homespun, ate only vegetables, gave up liquor and tobacco, engaged in manual work and even learned to cobble his own boots. Renouncing creative art for its corrupt refinements, Tolstoy wrote polemic tracts and short stories which embodied his new faith.

But the incongruity of his ideals and his actual environment grieved Tolstoy. With his family, he lived in affluence. His wife and children (except for Alexandra) disapproved of his philosophy. As they became more estranged and embittered from their differences, Sonya's increasing hysteria made his latter years a torment for Tolstoy.

All three stages of Tolstoy's life and writings (pre-conversion, conversion, effects of conversion) reflect the single quest of his career: to find the ultimate truth of human existence. After finding this truth, his life was a series of struggles to practice his preachings. He became a public figure both as a sage and an artist during his lifetime and Yasnaya Polyana became a mecca for a never-ceasing stream of pilgrims. The intensity and heroic scale of his life have been preserved for us from the memoirs of friends and family and wisdom seeking visitors. Though Tolstoy expressed his philosophy and theory of history with the same thoroughness and lucidity he devoted to his novels, he is known today chiefly for his important contributions to literature. Although his artistic influence is wide and still pervasive, few writers have achieved the personal stature with which to emulate his epic style.

MAIN CHARACTERS

Note: Every Russian has three names: first name, patronymic, last name. The root of the middle name is that of the father, plus a suffix meaning "son of" or "daughter of." Thus Anna's middle name is "Arkadyevna," while that of her brother is "Arkadyevitch." Russians call each other by the Christian name and patronymic, rarely by surname. For the sake of clarity, however, English translators use the characters' family names wherever possible.

Anna Arkadyevna Karenina
High society heroine whose love affair keynotes the novel.

Alexey Alexandrovitch Karenin
Anna's deceived husband. He is a frigid, lonely man with an influential government position in St. Petersburg.

Sergei Alexeyitch Karenin (Seriozha)
Anna's son whom she is forced to leave for her lover's sake.

Count Alexey Kirillovitch Vronsky
Anna's lover, an honorable, rich, handsome aide-de-camp with a promising army career which he gives up in order to live with Anna.

Konstantin Dmitrich Levin (Kostya)
Autobiographical hero of novel.

Princess Katerina Alexandrovna Shtcherbatsky (Kitty)
The eighteen year old debutante who becomes Levin's wife.

Prince Stepan Arkadyevitch Oblonsky (Stiva)
Anna's brother who is a pleasure-loving socialite.

Princess Darya Alexandrovna Oblonsky (Dolly)
Stiva's long-suffering wife and Kitty's older sister.

Nicolai Dmitrich Levin
Levin's profligate brother who dies of tuberculosis.

Sergei Ivanitch Koznyshev
Levin's elder half-brother who is a famous writer and intellectual.

SYNOPSIS OF *ANNA KARENINA*

PART 1 (34 chapters)

A crisis develops in the Oblonsky household when Dolly finds out about her husband's affair. Stiva's sister, Anna Karenina, arrives to reconcile the couple and dissuades Dolly from getting a divorce. Konstantin Levin, Stiva's friend, arrives in Moscow to propose to the eighteen year old Kitty Shtcherbatsky. She refuses him, for she loves Count Vronsky, a dashing army officer who has no intentions of marrying.

Meeting the lovely Madame Karenina, Vronsky falls in love and begins to pursue her. He and Anna are so involved with each other at the grand ball that Kitty's hopes for Vronsky are shattered. Anna, followed by Vronsky, returns to her husband and son in St. Petersburg, while the disappointed Levin returns to his country estate.

PART 2 (35 chapters)

Kitty falls ill after her humiliating rejection by Vronsky. At the German spa where she takes a rest cure she tries to deny her womanly nature by becoming a religious do-gooder. Realizing the hypocrisy of this new calling, Kitty returns to Russia cured of her depression and ready to accept her ultimate wifehood.

Consummating her union with Vronsky, Anna steps into a new life with much foreboding for the future. By the time she confesses her adultery to the suspecting Karenin, she is already pregnant with Vronsky's child.

PART 3 (32 chapters)

Devoting himself to farming, Levin tries to find life meaningful without marriage. He expends his energies in devising a cooperative landholding system with his peasants to make the best use of the land. Seeing his brother Nicolai hopelessly ill with tuberculosis, he realizes he has been working to avoid facing the problem of death. He also realizes he will always love Kitty.

Vronsky's career ambitions rival his love, and as he has not chosen between them, he is still uncommitted to Anna. Having rejected her husband, but still unable to depend on Vronsky, Anna finds her situation desperate. Her life is in a state of suspension.

PART 4 (23 chapters)

Kitty and Levin are engaged to marry. Karenin, who has tried to maintain appearances of domestic tranquillity, finally builds up enough anger to hire a divorce lawyer. Anna is confined of a daughter, but dangerously ill from puerperal fever. At her deathbed, Karenin forgives her and feels sanctified by this surge of humanity and Christian charity. At this sudden reversal of their roles Vronsky feels so humiliated he attempts suicide. These incidents form the turning point of the novel. After Anna's recovery, the lovers go abroad and Anna refuses divorce (though Karenin agrees to it) for fear of giving up her son.

PART 5 (33 chapters)

Levin and Kitty, after some initial difficulties, adjust to being married. Nicolai's death affects Levin deeply, and he realizes that emotional commitment, not reason, enables one to overcome life's problems. As if to underscore his life-affirmation, they learn Kitty is pregnant.

After they honeymoon in Italy, Anna and Vronsky return to Petersburg. Violently affected from seeing her son again, Anna's love for Vronsky becomes more desperate now that she has no one else. Despite his objections, she boldly attends the theater as if to affirm her love before conventional society. Humiliated at the opera, she blames Vronsky for lacking sympathy with her suffering, while he is angry at her indiscretion. This keynotes the decline of their relationship, although it is temporarily restored as they go to live in the country.

PART 6 (32 chapters)

Among Levin's summer visitors is a socialite who pays so much attention to Kitty that Levin asks him to leave. Visiting Anna at Vronsky's estate, Dolly finds her own drab life preferable to the formal luxury and decadence of Anna's. Complaining that Vronsky is eager for independence, Anna tells Dolly she must rely on her beauty and her love to keep his interest. Vronsky feels especially burdened by the demands of Anna's love when she calls him home from a refreshing political convention.

PART 7 (31 chapters)

Kitty gives birth to a son. Karenin, under the influence of his fanatically devout friend, Countess Lydia Ivanovna, becomes religious and uses his hypocritical faith as a crutch to overcome his humiliation and loneliness.

Anna, seeing the irreversible decline of her love affair, has no more will to live and commits suicide.

PART 8 (19 chapters)

Vronsky volunteers for service in the Russo-Turkish war. Tolstoy uses this part of the novel to express his pacifist principles. Levin discovers "salvation" when he resolves to "live for his soul" rather than for selfish goals. He realizes the meaning of life consists in living according to the goodness inherent in every individual. Understanding death as part of a reality-oriented life, Levin is at peace with himself.

PART 1

CHAPTERS 1 to 5

Summary

The household of Prince Stepan Arkadyevitch Oblonsky is in a state of confusion that began three days ago when his wife discovered his relationship with their former French governess. Dolly Oblonsky says she can no longer live in the same house with her husband.

Stiva (as he is called) considers her attitude unnecessarily harsh, despite the gravity of the situation. Though she is a good mother to their five children and manages the household well, she is worn out and no longer young or good looking; whereas he feels himself in prime enjoyment of his powers. Meanwhile all the servants, painfully aware of the Oblonsky's problems, feel a separation is imminent.

On the third day, while the barber shaves his face, Stiva reads a telegram, announcing that his sister, Anna Arkadyevna Karenina, will arrive tomorrow to visit. Perhaps she might reconcile husband and wife.

Dressed and shaved, feeling fragrant and comfortable, Stepan Arkadyevitch reads his letters, some office papers, and peruses a liberal newspaper, one advocating the views of the liberal majority and satisfying to his truthful temperament. Interrupting his reading, he affectionately greets two of his children, treating them to bon-bons as he sends them off.

While his carriage awaits him, Stiva sees a petitioner and gives her advice. Taking his hat, he feels as if he forgot something. Lighting a cigarette, squaring his shoulders, he rapidly walks to his wife's bedroom.

Darya Alexandrovna is collecting her things and the children's clothes in order to pack up and leave for her mother's house. Regarding her husband out of startled eyes, prominent in her sunken and thin face, she scans his figure which radiates health and freshness. Though he tries to look pitiful and humble, she notes with disgust that good nature of his which everyone praises and likes so well.

The brief interview fails. Dolly shrilly insists she will leave the house, while Stiva pleads his guilt and begs her to forgive his one lapse of passion which could not belie their nine years of happy marriage. When he weeps in sympathy for her, Dolly becomes angrier than ever: she seeks his love, not his pity.

Dolly leaves the room to attend to a child crying in the nursery. Plunging into the duties of the day, she crowds the grief out of her mind for a time. Stiva slowly leaves the room. "Maybe she will come around," he tells himself.

Commentary

"Happy families are all alike," Tolstoy writes as the first words of *Anna Karenina,* "Every unhappy family is unhappy in its own way." Specifying this generalization the author details the life of a well favored aristocrat. Stepan Arkadyevitch has an excellent post in Moscow, is the head of a loving and smoothly run household. His wife, Darya, Stiva's feminine counterpart in the Russian class system, centers her life on raising the children and tending her husband. But his infidelity shatters their harmonious life and Dolly must confront the problem of how to repair her personal ruin. For Stiva, his marital life is of secondary value; his official duties, his social activities, and his pleasures are primary. Thus we see that the values of men and women in this society are oriented toward different goals and Stiva's affair with the French governess causes these different values to stand in clear relief.

In these chapters Tolstoy has set up a small working model which generates all the subsequent themes of *Anna Karenina.* Stiva's petty love affair prefigures the adultery of Anna with Vronsky, and serves as a negative comparison with Levin's successful marriage later in the novel. The individual's quest for meaning through personal relationships and through the details of ordinary life begins – though modestly – among the descriptions of domestic life in the Oblonsky household.

CHAPTERS 6 to 11

Summary

Stepan Arkadyevitch, one who "was born in the midst of those who has been and are the powerful ones of this world" is president of a government board in Moscow, part of a department in the ministry where his brother-in-law, Alexey Alexandrovitch Karenin, holds one of the most prominent positions. Stiva's kindliness and good humor have won him the respect and liking of all his subordinates as well as his superiors. Despite excellent abilities, Stiva did poorly at school for he was idle and mischievous. Yet he does a good job at the office; never getting carried away with his work, his indifference to the business at hand increases his objectivity and accuracy.

During his busy morning, Stiva receives the unexpected visit of his childhood comrade, Konstantin Levin, an intense, thoughtful man of the same age. Levin, modeled after Tolstoy himself, cares deeply for farming, raising livestock, and managing his ancestral estate. He despises town life for being superficial and frivolous, while Stiva considers Levin's affairs as trifling. Despite their differences, the two men have remained close friends. Levin's love for Dolly's youngest sister, Kitty Shtcherbatsky, also reinforces their friendship.

Konstantin Dmitrievitch Levin has come to Moscow specifically to make an offer to the Princess Shtcherbatsky. He regards Kitty as a perfect creature and feels unworthy beside her. Though he believes she deserved better than an ugly, ordinary man like himself, he feels he could not have a moment's rest until he made her an offer.

When Levin arrives at Moscow, he puts up at the house of his elder half-brother, Koznyshev. Sergey Ivanitch Koznyshev, a famous thinker and writer, concerned with intellectual problems and immersing himself in the political trends of Russia, is of an entirely different temperament than Levin. Rather than ask his brother's advice on his personal problem, Levin tells Koznyshev of his disenchantment with his local Zemstvo organization and they talk about provincial self-government in general. (Zemstvos are representative county councils founded in 1864 by Alexander II.)

Sergey Ivanitch remarks that their brother Nicolai had turned up in Moscow and shows Levin a hostile note he received. Nicolai, after Koznyshev had covered an I.O.U. for him, writes that the only favors he wishes of his brothers is that they leave him in peace. Half-brother to Koznyshev, and elder brother to Konstantin, Nicolai has dissipated the greater part of his fortune, quarrelled with his brothers, and lives in the strangest and lowest company. Levin at once wants to visit his ruined brother, but first drives to the place where he might meet Kitty.

Arriving at the Zoological gardens' skating rink, Kitty's presence dominates his thoughts and he sees no one but her. The expression of her eyes — soft, serene, thoughtful — and her smile transports him and he feels softened and tender as in his early childhood. An excellent skater, Levin works off some of his nervousness by executing a daring leap down the coffee house steps. While he and Kitty skate together, Levin responds so meaningfully to her casual questions that he constantly blushes. She asks how long he intends to stay in Moscow. "It depends on you," Levin says, and is horrorstruck at his inadvertent confession. Kitty stumbles, then hurries away from him toward her parents. Her mother, having higher hopes for her child, gives Levin a cold greeting but invites him to call on them. To offset her mother's coolness, Kitty bids him a friendly farewell and her smile throws Levin into ecstasy.

Stiva now arrives. After greeting his in-laws, he draws Levin off to dinner, intently planning their menu while they drive to the restaurant. Oblonsky is perfectly at home among the bronzes, starchy tablecloths, mirrors, obsequious waiters. In their private dining room, he selects their wines and courses with elaborate care. Levin feels almost sullied in this luxurious atmosphere. After the freshness of skating and his delight in the innocence and truthfulness of Kitty, his present setting seems stale and artificial. People in the country, he tells Stiva, order their lives around the goal of work, not idleness. City people, having lost touch with the functional aspects of life, are only prepared to seek pleasure. "Why yes," answers Stiva good-naturedly, "That's just the aim of civilization — to make everything a source of pleasure." Oblonsky, guessing why Levin returned to Moscow, declares he would be delighted to have him as a brother-in-law. He wonders if Levin knows Count Vronsky, for this handsome aide-de-camp is also in love with Kitty. Alexey Kirillovitch Vronsky, rich, brilliant, and well connected, is, according to Stiva "one of the finest specimens of the gilded youth of Petersburg." Levin pales at this news. He feels that Stiva's counsels and talk of rivalry profane his great feeling for Kitty.

Oblonsky tells Levin of his own domestic problems and Konstantin cannot understand that a man would go "straight to the bakeshop and steal a roll" when he has just dined on plenty. Fiercely monogamous, Levin says he has "a loathing for fallen women" but then recollects his own sins. Stiva points out that life does not consist of clear-cut principles; its variety, charm, and beauty is made up of "light and shadow" and that Levin is wrong to believe that one's work, one's relationships, one's thoughts must always correspond to a defined aim in life.

After dinner, the two friends part. Levin looks forward to his evening at the Shtcherbatskys where his fate will be decided.

Commentary

Levin enters the novel in a customary outburst of frankness and intense conviction. He tells Stiva he no longer participates in the Zemstvo, derides Oblonsky's bureaucratic job as a sinecure, and mentions Kitty, Immediately we learn of his main impulses: his quest for rural reform, his rejection of town life, and his passion for Kitty. Levin's character becomes further defined by a comparison to that of Koznyshev and Nicolai, and during his behavior in the episodes at the skating rink. The discussion between Levin and Stiva as they dine concentrates other themes of *Anna Karenina* which Tolstoy later defines, especially that of the conflict between monogamy and sexual freedom. Defending the undivided family, Levin cuts himself short as he recalls his own lapses. This moment keynotes the inconsistencies between personal ideals and personal behavior, a problem which Levin (and Tolstoy) struggles with and a problem which Stiva overlooks and rationalizes by his hedonism.

CHAPTERS 12 to 15

Summary

Tolstoy introduces Kitty, the eighteen-year-old girl, who was spending her first winter "out in the world" and who already has two serious suitors, Levin and Count Vronsky. Kitty's parents, having gone through the anxieties of getting their two elder daughters married off, have renewed arguments over their third. The old Princess Shtcherbatsky reflects how much easier it was in the older days when young girls did not demand their own freedom of choice in marriage. Nowadays it is hard for parents to know when to use their influence to protect their daughters against a rash or unsuccessful choice. The old prince prefers Levin for his plainness and honesty, while his wife prefers Vronsky for his dash and brilliance. She wonders why the young officer, openly flirting with Kitty at balls and calling on her at home, has not yet made an offer.

Kitty considers her feelings toward each of her suitors. While she feels "perfectly simple and clear" with Levin and somewhat awkward with Vronsky, she decides she prefers the dashing officer.

Kitty receives Levin in the drawing-room alone. He blurts out his proposal, his heart sinking as he gazes at her. "That cannot be," Kitty whispers, "Forgive me." The old princess arrives and guesses what has happened; pleased, she welcomes Levin cordially.

Vronsky arrives among the other guests, and Levin remains to see the man Kitty loves. He sees Vronsky as an agreeable, sincere, very calm and intelligent person. Levin soon finds an opportunity to slip quietly away.

As she gets ready for sleep, Kitty rehearses the events of the evening. Though elated at having received an offer, she weeps as she recalls Levin's kind eyes filled with dejection. Downstairs her parents argue. The old prince accuses his wife of debasing their child by catching "an eligible gentleman" for her and discouraging her feelings for Levin, by far the better man. If Kitty falls in love with Vronsky, a "peacock" and featherhead "who's only amusing himself," she might meet the same fate as their unfortunate Dolly.

Commentary

Kitty, although ready to love, is still not mature enough to discriminate. But she is flooded with happiness at Levin's proposal and does not know why. Vronsky is introduced in the most favorable way, and, at Kitty's unfeigned joy at his arrival, the theme of her indiscriminate love deepens.

As Kitty's mother reflects on the simpleness of matchmaking when she was a girl, Tolstoy telescopes the family history through his characteristic device of "interior monologue." This discussion also pinpoints a primary theme of the novel — the problem of marriage in a modern society.

CHAPTERS 16 to 23

Summary

Vronsky, after his luxurious and coarse life in Petersburg, finds a "great and delicate pleasure" in the affection of this "sweet and innocent girl," though he feels no urge to marry and sees nothing wrong in paying attention to Kitty. The next day, waiting at the train station to meet his mother, he meets Oblonsky, whose sister is arriving on the same train. When Stiva explains that Levin's depressed mood last night was the result of Kitty's refusal, Vronsky feels like a conqueror and a hero.

When the train arrives, his mother introduces him to her traveling companion, the charming Madame Karenina; something peculiarly "caressing and soft" in the expression of her face catches his attention. Countess

Vronsky explains this is the first time Anna has been away from her eight year old child and is somewhat anxious. "Yes," Anna smiles, "the countess and I have been talking all the time, I of my son and she of hers." Vronsky unable to take his eyes from Madame Karenina watches her walk lightly and rapidly with her brother to their carriage, carrying her "rather full figure with extraordinary lightness."

A sudden accident at the station draws a crowd. A guard, not hearing the train move back, has been crushed under the wheels of the car. Anna is horrified and even more impressed to learn that the man is the only support of an immense family. "Couldn't something be done?" she asks, and learns a few moments later that Vronsky had given 200 rubles for the benefit of the widow. Suspecting that this gesture has something to do with her, Anna frowns; it is something that ought not to have been.

In the carriage, Stiva wonders at her quivering lips and her tears. "It's an omen of evil," Anna says, and changes the subject. "Have you known Vronsky long?" she asks. "Yes," answers Stiva, "We're hoping he will marry Kitty." "Indeed?" says Anna softly, then with a toss of her head, "Come, let's talk about you and what you wrote me about in your letter."

Anna's kindness and warmth, as well as her accurate recollection of the names, ages, and past illnesses of the Oblonsky children win Dolly's confidence. Eventually Anna talks of the problem that brought her to Moscow in the first place. She points out how miserable Stiva felt at his infidelity and how repentant he is. "I don't know how much love there still is in your heart for him," she tells Dolly. "You alone know whether there is enough for you to be able to forgive. If there is, then forgive him!" Dolly won over by Anna's sympathy and understanding, feels much comforted.

Kitty calls on the following day, soon finding herself in love with Anna, "as young girls often fall in love with older and married women." Anna's eagerness, freshness, and the elasticity of her movements seem to be those of a girl in her twenties, while her seriousness and mournful smile attract Kitty to her maturity. Congratulating Kitty on behalf of Vronsky, Anna relates an incident where the young man had saved a woman from drowning, a story told her by Countess Vronsky. But she does not mention the incident of the 200 rubles; fearing something personal in that gesture, she does not like to think of it. Dolly's children, shrieking with delight to see their aunt, interrupt further conversation, while Anna runs laughing to meet them. After dinner, Vronsky unexpectedly passes by but declines to join them. Kitty assumes he comes to seek her but does not wish to intrude while they have a guest. The visit seems odd to all of them, but particularly to Anna and she is troubled.

The great ball is held the following evening, and Kitty, intoxicated by the elegance of gowns around her, the lighted chandeliers, the liveried footmen, feels her eyes sparkle and her lips rosy as young men constantly ask her to dance. She is certain that Count Vronsky will propose to her this night. Anna appears, beautifully elegant in a simple low-cut black velvet gown that brings out all her charm. Elated to see Vronsky, Kitty wonders why Anna deliberately refrains from answering his bow of greeting. Vronsky tells Kitty he has regretted not seeing her for so long. As they face each other during the pause before the dance, Kitty gives him a look "so full of love — that look, which met with no response, pierced her heart with unending shame for years after." During her quadrille with another partner, Kitty observes Anna and Vronsky dancing opposite. On Anna's expressive face appears the signs of excitement and success that she herself feels familiar with, while Vronsky's expression, always firm and independent, bears a look of "bewilderment and humbled submissiveness, like the expression of an intelligent dog when it has done wrong." Kitty's world crumbles; only her self-discipline allows her to continue dancing and smiling and talking.

Commentary

We first hear of Anna Karenina in Chapter 1, where she intends to arrive at Moscow to repair a broken marriage: indeed an ironic touch on the part of the author. The railroad station, the scene of Anna's first meeting with Vronsky, provides a symbol that concentrates the ideas of beginning, and, representing a point of departure as well. Alighting in Moscow, Anna confronts a new destiny and enters a foreign world. The "evil omen" which makes her shudder foreshadows her doom.

What is outstanding in Anna is her charm and fascination, apparent to Vronsky as their glances first meet. Capable of deep and strong passions, her whole being is directed toward love. Tolstoy writing that "her whole nature was so brimming over with something that against her will it showed itself..." indicates that her capacity for love has not yet been awakened.

Another outstanding quality is Anna's maturity. When she tells Vronsky that she and his mother have talked about their sons throughout the journey, Anna assumes herself a generation older than her future lover. This "age" difference between them underscores the essential duplicity and futility of their future relationship. The comparison of Seriozha with Vronsky also foreshadows Anna's later dilemma when she must choose between her child and her lover.

Anna becomes the object of fascination and love for everyone in her brother's household. She appeals to the children, wins Dolly's confidence; Kitty falls in love with her for her qualities of youth (denoting her peerage and future competition with Kitty) and maturity (denoting the emotional depth which charms Vronsky). But her charm is "diabolical and strange" at the same time. Kitty notices this during the ball when Anna regards her smilingly and with "drooping eyelids."

The key to Anna's personality and the quality which endears her to Tolstoy is her naturalness and emotional depth. She responds with her heart, not with applying social principles. Counseling Dolly to forgive Stiva, Anna argues, not from the standpoint of maintaining appearances to preserve a reputation before society, but from inner emotions. If you love him, then forgive him, Anna says. At the same time this quality provides the source of Anna's nobility, it also increases her susceptibility for a lawless passion.

In these episodes which reveal subtleties of individual character and relationships, a few of Tolstoy's narrative devices deserve brief mention. Though he is thoroughly an omniscient author, Tolstoy allows us to view the ball through the narrower—and more intense—viewpoint of Kitty, who watches Vronsky fall under Anna's spell. Kitty's suffering conveys to us the full quality of Madame Karenina's fascination.

Tolstoy also shows great dexterity in handling the psychological tensions and their physical relief. A good example of this occurs when Anna tells Kitty what a chivalrous nature Vronsky has. She relates how he saved a woman from drowning but refrains from mentioning the incident of the 200 rubles. In the pause, her frown keynotes the deceit which will enmesh her more and more; but at that moment, the children rush in and Anna, laughing, tumbles them to the ground.

CHAPTERS 24 to 27

Summary

Leaving the Shtcherbatskys, Levin walks to his brother's lodgings. He thinks how worthless he is, and Kitty is right to prefer Vronsky. He thinks of the ugliness of his brother's life, and how unfair it is for society to judge his outward achievements when his soul is as truthful and as full of goodness as anyone else's.

Thin and emaciated from consumption, Nicolai lives in squalor with his common-law wife, Marya Nicolaevna (Masha), whom he had rescued from a brothel. Finding his brother demoralized by illness, drunkenness, and a life of failure. Levin is too depressed to stay long. He has Masha promise to write him in case of need and takes the first train home, arriving toward evening of the next day.

Catching sight of his waiting coachman at the station, receiving the news of his estate — a cow had calved, the contractor had arrived — Levin feels his confusion and despondency drop away. He resolves to always help his brother, to abandon his dreams of happiness through marriage, and never give way to low passions, memories of which now torture him with unassuageable guilt. Like Dolly caught up in her household, the management of his large estate absorbs Levin's thoughts and temporarily soothes his disappointment.

His house represents his whole world, for here his parents spent their lives and here he and his brother were born. Although his mother died when he was very young, her image is sacred to him, and his future wife must satisfy the holy ideal of woman he conceives in his mother's image. Unlike his friends for whom marriage is merely one of the numerous facts of social life, Levin considers it the chief affair of life, basic to his entire happiness. He has always looked forward to the family he would have, then, secondarily, to the wife.

Sipping a cup of tea that evening, sitting with his faithful housekeeper, Agafea Mihalovna, reading a book, Levin daydreams. He finds all nature in unity and at peace. "One must struggle to live better, much better," he muses, happily concluding that "nothing's amiss, all's well."

Commentary

These chapters show Levin in his true element. His house, his land, his peasants represent his roots and the source of his nourishment. The happiness Levin feels upon returning to his estate after the suffering experienced in Moscow prefigures the salvation he finds at the end of the novel. Moreover, Levin's return to the country strikes a strong contrast with the events at the ball. This section emphasizes the thematic duality of the novel which unfolds more and more in subsequent parts: Anna and Vronsky and the social milieu of town life, Levin and Kitty and the natural life of the country.

CHAPTERS 28 to 33

Summary

Anna wants to leave Moscow the next day. Dolly finds her sister-in-law strangely nervous, always close to tears, but Anna is unable to tell her why, that she is leaving sooner than intended in order to avoid Vronsky. She confesses to Dolly that Kitty is jealous on her account and she had caused her misery at the ball. Dolly remonstrates soothingly, saying she is glad that her sister had no further hopes for Vronsky since he is so fickle. At parting the two women embrace and profess sincere affection.

Nervous and excited, Anna is relieved to be on the train journeying home to her son and husband and resume her nice comfortable way of life again. She thinks of Vronsky and wonders at her vague feeling of shame when there is nothing to be ashamed about. Still tense, she alights at the next station for a breath of cold air. Suddenly Vronsky appears at her side and she is seized by a feeling of joyful pride at his look of reverence and devotion. "You know that I have come to be where you are," he says, "I can't help it." Pausing before her answer, Anna feels this moment in the midst of a snowstorm has drawn them close together. She begs him to forget, as she had forgotten it, the statement he has just uttered.

Still in her tense mood, Anna cannot sleep for the rest of the trip. Meeting her husband at the station, she feels dissatisfied with "his imposing and frigid figure, his high pitched voice, now noticing how his ears stick out. What she suddenly recognizes for the first time, is "an intimate feeling, like a consciousness of hypocrisy, which she experienced in her relations with her husband."

As her son dashes downstairs to greet her at home she feels that even he is somewhat less delightful in reality than in the image she had of him while away. But her pleasure in his caresses, seeing his plump little shape, his curls and blue eyes soothes her. After a visit from Karenin's friend, the Countess Lydia Ivanovna, and after unpacking and dining with her son, Anna feels resolute and irreproachable as she assumes the habitual conditions of her life.

Karenin appears for dinner precisely at five o'clock, and leaves for a meeting afterwards. Every minute of his life is portioned out and occupied, for Karenin adheres to the strictest punctuality in order to accomplish what he requires himself to do. "Unhasting and unresting" is his motto.

When Alexey Alexandrovitch returns, at exactly half past nine, Anna chats with him, recounting everything about her visit to Moscow while refraining from mentioning Vronsky. Karenin flatly denounces Oblonsky's extra-marital dalliance, and Anna thinks what a truthful, good-hearted man her husband is. In her thoughts she defends him as if someone said he is someone she cannot love.

Commentary

Anna's journey back to her home represents her retreat from the emotional stimulation she experienced through Vronsky. Her attempt at flight, however, is interrupted by the presence of the young officer who takes the same train. The snowstorm in which they meet corresponds to the stormy state of their emotions.

Anna's suddenly perceived dissatisfaction with her husband's appearance and manner, and her slight disappointment upon first seeing her son, shows her perceptions of the life she has been familiar with have already been changed under the influence of this passion to which she is still unawakened. But her feverish state passes when she reassumes her old habits and the "causeless shame" she felt during her journey vanishes.

The character of Karenin, with its compulsiveness and dullness, shows that he is a poor foil for Anna's vivacity and love of life. Tolstoy also shows their relationship is routine and erotically incomplete as "precisely at twelve o'clock," Karenin bids Anna to bed. She follows, "but her face had none of the eagerness which, [in Moscow] fairly flashed from her eyes and her smile; on the contrary, now the fire seemed quenched in her, hidden somewhere far away."

CHAPTER 34

Summary

Vronsky returns to his Petersburg apartment and finds his favorite comrade, Petrivsky, there with some friends, including Baroness Shilton, Petrivsky's current companion. Amidst the slightly drunken chatter and gossip of his gay, broad-minded companions, Vronsky drops back into the light-hearted pleasant world he has always lived in. He has a bantering discussion with Baroness Shilton about divorce. Her husband, she says, wants to keep her property by way of retribution for her unfaithfulness.

Vronsky dresses himself in his uniform to report to his regiment. He plans, among other visits, to pay his cousin Princess Betsy Tverskoy a call. Related to Anna through marriage, Betsy would bring him into that society where he might meet Madame Karenina. As he always does in Petersburg, Vronsky leaves home, not meaning to return until late at night.

Commentary

In this chapter Vronsky returns to his familiar habits, just as Dolly, Levin, and Anna have gone back to their "starting points" after confronting their respective crises. Vronsky's light talk with the baroness about divorce preludes his more intense arguments with Anna later on, and the behavior attributed to Baron Shilton suggests the nature of Karenin's response to the same problem.

Part 1 ends on a note of departure, as Vronsky leaves to form connections which will give him further chances to see Anna. This lightly undertaken departure, however, represents one with grave consequences for Vronsky: he is really departing from his old way of life with its facile relationships to embark upon a new existence and a relationship of unimagined intensity.

PART 2

CHAPTERS 1 to 3

Summary

Kitty is ill, and the prominent specialist who examines her, finding nothing specifically wrong suggests she be taken abroad to a health spa. Her father and Dolly both realize that Kitty's nervous irritability is due to a broken heart. The old prince blames his wife for influencing Kitty's affections in the first place, while Dolly explains to her mother that Kitty had refused Levin whom she might have accepted had she not counted on Vronsky's proposal. Princess Shtcherbatsky finally realizes the sin she committed against her daughter.

Tearful and miserable when Dolly comes to her room, Kitty does not divulge what her sister has already guessed: that she is ready to love and accept Levin and detest Vronsky. Instead Kitty rages. She says she is ashamed and humiliated at discovering herself to be a marketable commodity, that all the eligible men are free to look her over, that her parents are only interested in marrying her off. She only feels free with Dolly and the children, Kitty says.

Dolly's difficulties at that time were no better. Besides suspecting further infidelities of Stiva, Dolly is always short of money and her large family is a constant source of worry. Besides a new baby in the house, Dolly has to care for the children ill with scarlet fever. Kitty goes home with her sister to nurse the youngsters through their illnesses, and still unwell six weeks later, she and her parents go abroad during Lent.

Commentary

Kitty's first venture into womanhood, resulting in failure, makes her retreat back into a dependence on her family. Having suffered deep humiliation on the very occasion she was intoxicated by her attractiveness and femininity (the moment when she looked with love at Vronsky) her reaction is to deny her womanhood. Kitty's physical illness expresses the violence of her denial. Kitty's immaturity is shown by her choice of Vronsky over Levin; still influenced by her mother, she lacks the self-knowledge which would prompt her to choose accurately.

Kitty's crisis confuses her mother's sense of duty. While realizing she was wrong to influence her child, Princess Shtcherbatsky feels it is wrong not to guide her daughter. Besides touching on the difficulty of communication between generations, Tolstoy shows that judgments based on social principles rather than emotional values lead to disappointment and disillusion.

CHAPTERS 4 to 11

Summary

Three social spheres form subdivisions of Petersburg's top society: one is composed of Karenin's government officials, another that of elderly, benevolent, pious women and their learned, ambitious husbands. Centered around the Countess Lydia Ivanovna, and called the "conscience of St. Petersburg", this set is the one through which Karenin built his career and the one Anna has been closely connected with. Of late, feeling bored and ill at ease in this group whom she suspects of hypocrisy, Anna prefers the third circle of society proper—the world of balls and dinner parties. Her link with this group is through the Princess Betsy Tverskoy. In this circle, Anna and Vronsky frequently meet.

At one of Betsy's dinner parties, they are engrossed in talk. Anna begs him, if he loves her as he says, to leave her in peace. But Vronsky, his face radiant as he pleads his love, says it is impossible for him to live separately from her. Anna is unable to reply. As she looks into his face with eyes full of love, Vronsky is ecstatic.

Karenin arrives, and glancing toward his wife in her animated conversation with Vronsky, talks with Betsy. While seeing nothing improper or peculiar in his wife's behavior, Karenin notices the disapproval of the other guests. Leaving before dinner, though Anna insists to remain, Alexey Alexandrovitch resolves to mention the matter this evening.

Thinking it over, Karenin decides a talk is not such a simple matter after all. For the first time he tries to imagine what his wife thinks and feels, whether she could possibly stop loving him and turn to another man. The irrational and illogical feeling of jealousy throws him into confusion. Having always lived for his work in official spheres — a reflection of life — Karenin is horrified to suddenly confront life itself. While composing the speech he would deliver to Anna, he tries to soothe himself. But the sound of a carriage driving up, then the sound of her light step on the stairs, frightens him.

Anna pretends surprise at his request for a talk. Inwardly marvelling at her confident answers, she feels herself clad in an impenetrable armor of falsehood and wonders how easily she can lie. Karenin notices the change immediately. The depths of her soul, always open to him before, now close against him. Looking into her laughing eyes, alarming with their impenetrability, Karenin feels the utter uselessness and idleness of his words.

He warns that her thoughtlessness and indiscretion might cause herself to be spoken of in society, her "too animated conversation" with Count Vronsky this evening which attracted attention, to give an example. Anna responds cheerfully and seems sincere. Reminding her of her duty, for their lives have been joined "not by man but by God" Karenin says this concerns not himself, but Anna and their son. "I have nothing to say," she answers, restraining a smile, "and it really is bed-time."

Their talk marks a new life for Karenin and his wife. Though outwardly unchanged, their intimate relations completely alter. Forceful when dealing with affairs of state, Karenin feels helpless dealing with his wife. "Like an ox with bent head" he waits submissively for the axe which he feels raised above him.

Vronsky satisfies his one desire which absorbed him for nearly a year. Overcome by her sense of degradation, Anna sobs and does not speak. Her shame infects him, and he feels a "murderer's horror before the body of his victim." Realizing "the murderer must make use of what he has obtained by his crime" Anna sadly submits to his kisses for "these are what have been bought by my shame." "Everything is over," she says, "I have nothing but you left. Remember that."

The shame, rapture, and horror she feels upon stepping into a new life drives all other feelings from her. She has no calm left in which to reflect on what occurred, but in her dreams she has to face her ugly position. She dreams she is the wife of Alexey Alexandrovitch as well as of Alexey Vronsky. As both caress her, she explains to them, laughing, that what had seemed impossible before is now simply and satisfactorily arranged. Both men are contented and happy. Anna's dream is like a nightmare and she awakes from it in terror.

Commentary

Anna's awakening passion changes the pattern of her social life. She avoids the serious group because its members are hypocrites, and attends the brilliant functions of Betsy's set. Her sudden awareness of hypocrisy reflects her awareness of her own deceit. This deceit, however, is two fold. Anna suspects that her emotionally incomplete existence as the faithful wife of a man she realizes now she does not love was basically hypocritical. The other source of deceit is adultery, a condition of fraud defined by society. At the same time, adultery provides the only means by which Anna can redeem her false marriage: through Vronsky she can achieve a truthful love relationship. This conflict between emotional truth and formal truth is the basis of Anna's tragedy.

At the point of Karenin's talk with Anna, however, there is no conflict. While her husband points out the social consequences of "indiscretion" and "tactless behavior," Anna can barely suppress a smile. Social convention, her smile says, is a trivial matter compared with emotional values, and her feelings for Karenin are trivial compared with her passion for Vronsky.

The tragic consequences of "stepping into a new life" suddenly loom large and real when Anna and Vronsky consummate their relationship. A life with two husbands is that of an outlaw; having broken one of the most forceful social conventions, Anna denies herself the protection society offers. She has no one left but her "accomplice."

Vronsky's position is less serious than Anna's, and he has pursued his conquest with more frivolous intentions. Though his love is deep — deeper than he realizes — his officers' code of behavior sets a prestige value on seducing married women: the higher her social standing, the higher the man's prestige. Tolstoy shows Vronsky's awareness of these values as Betsy and her cousin chat during intermission at the opera.

Only when he sees Anna's shame and when she rejects his platitudes about "moment of happiness" does Vronsky gain insight into the seriousness of his crime against her. Tolstoy's analogy of a murderer and his victim underscores the extent of Vronsky's commitment to Anna and forecasts her doom and his culpability.

CHAPTERS 12 to 17

Summary

In the early days of his return to the country Levin suffers deeply. Gradually the bitter memory of his rejection disappears as the daily incidents of his country life absorb him. With the coming of spring and his plans for many improvements on his estate, he is quite happy.

Stepan Arkadyevitch appears one evening for he is to sell a forest on his wife's property nearby. Stiva and Levin enjoy an excellent day of stand-shooting, returning with a good catch of snipe. While Oblonsky and the prospective purchaser, Ryabinin, haggle over the price of the forest, Levin fumes. Stiva, hungry for cash, settles for a much lower price than Konstantin thinks the property is worth.

Later on, the two friends talk of the Shtcherbatskys, and Levin learns of Kitty's illness, of Vronsky's rejection. Stiva says Kitty had only a "superficial attraction" for the young officer, that Vronsky's being "such a perfect aristocrat" impressed her mother but not Kitty. Levin's anger at Ryabinin, the fraudulent sale of the forest, and at Vronsky focusses on the concept of "aristocrat". Those like Vronsky or like Ryabinin who gain success by currying favor are not aristocrats, he says. Russia's aristocracy consists of people produced through generations of landowners, not those parasites who deplete and devalue her land and resources for their own gain (like Ryabinin). "I prize what's come to me from my ancestors or been won by hard work," pursues Levin, rather than maintaining myself "by favor of the powerful of this world." He and Stiva part as friends despite the painful subject which could have caused a rift.

Commentary

In these episodes we gain insight into Levin's way of life as a landed proprietor. His dislike of Ryabinin, a land speculator, and his anger at Stiva's cheap sale of the forest derives from a threat to his basic values. This devaluation of valuable property, by a destructive agent who deals in money rather than in values, is a devaluation of resources, tradition, rootedness. Stiva, by his desire for momentary gain, becomes an unwitting tool for undermining the source of Russia's strength and, indeed, the whole existence of "aristocracy", defined by Levin as those who have a vested interest in protecting the basic values of national life. If the peasants cheat landowners out of their property, then at least the land goes to those who deserve it because it is their mainspring of existence. Ryabinin, on the other hand, represents the irresponsible overthrow of the old order; appreciating no values but those of cash and material gain, he intrudes chaos and impoverishment where constructive change and enrichment is required. Vronsky who, like Ryabinin, is uncommitted to the land and basic traditions, whose career is socially and politically oriented, contributes no values to stabilize either himself or other human beings. Kitty's illness, her "devaluation" by Vronsky, proves Levin's point.

Through Levin's arguments, Tolstoy states a general system which generates his philosophy. Human beings must be committed to deeply-rooted values — a personal need corresponding to love — in order to maintain their humanity. Without a source of inner strength, an individual's life becomes empty of meaning and frivolous, capable of destroying other lives besides perverting his own.

CHAPTERS 18 to 25

Summary

While Vronsky's life runs its normal course with its social and military obligations, his passion absorbs his entire inner life. "Society" has various reactions. The younger men envy him; his brother, who enjoys his own extramarital affairs, disapproves because "those whom it was necessary to please" disapprove. His mother thinking an affair in the highest society is "a finishing touch" for a promising young man, disapproves when she hears Alexey refused an important post in order to remain in Petersburg, and when she learns the affair is based upon a desperate, not graceful and worldly, passion. Meanwhile the women of Anna's circle await the turn of public opinion before falling upon her with the full weight of their scorn.

Besides his regimental and social interests, Vronsky is passionately fond of horses and racing. At this time, he has purchased an English thoroughbred and anticipates winning the officers' steeplechase. On the morning of the race he checks his mare, Frou-Frou, and, satisfied she is in the best possible condition, he drives to Anna's house. He resolves to put an end to their impossible position which demands so much lying and deceit. Anna's thoughtful pose impresses him anew with her beauty and grace, and he gazes enraptured until she feels his presence and turns to greet him. Vronsky perceives something new troubling her, but she is reluctant to answer his inquiry. Finally whispering, "I am with child," Anna brings the matter to a head. Vronsky insists that only divorce will "put an end to the deception in which we now live. Our fate is sealed." For fear of losing Seriozha, Anna refuses to consider divorce, but does not mention this to Vronsky. The sound of her son's voice ends their talk, and Vronsky drives to the race.

With mounting excitement, Vronsky watches as the English groom leads Frou-Frou in. Lean and beautiful, she moves as if on springs. Nearby a groom tends a strong, exquisite stallion, the lop-eared Gladiator who is Frou-Frou's chief competitor. Vronsky approaches the starting gate, following his rival Mahotin, Gladiator's rider. They are among seventeen officers competing in the nine hurdle race which runs a three mile elliptical course.

The white-legged Gladiator takes the lead. Frou-Frou, without any urging, increases her speed and draws up to the other horse on the outside, just as Vronsky would have asked her to. His affection for this responsive mount increases. Leading Mahotin's stallion, Vronsky knows he will win, for Frou-Frou's last reserve of strength is more than a match for the final jump. Increasing her speed, the mare clears the ditch. But at that instant, Vronsky makes a dreadful, unforgivable blunder: he drops back — too soon — in the saddle. The white-legged stallion flashes by, while Vronsky, with one foot on the ground feels the mare sink beneath him. Not realizing his clumsy movement has broken her back, he tugs at the reins. Fluttering, she is unable to rise. In a sudden passion, he wrenches the lines, then savagely kicks her belly. A doctor and some officers run up, quickly deciding to shoot the mare. Vronsky leaves the race course; for the first time in his life he knows the bitterest kind of misfortune — misfortune beyond remedy, caused by his own fault.

Commentary

It is significant that Anna's announcement of her pregnancy occurs at the same time Vronsky's passion for horses bears fruit, his imminent victory at the steeplechase. Both situations demand all the resources of which Vronsky is capable in order to meet the challenge. Both crises are confrontations with destiny.

With obvious significance, Dostoevsky remarks that Anna and Vronsky appear to him as a fine mare and full-blooded stallion (an analogy which other critics have also pointed out). Mahotin's stallion wins the race, but the sensitive mare loses her life. The close relationship between rider and mount is akin to Vronsky's bond with Anna. The intensity of their unlawful love is like the intensity of the steeplechase with their life running a course of obstacles which both, as one, must overcome until their race against moral law is won.

But Frou-Frou's entire being exists for racing, Anna's for loving; that the mare breaks her back in fulfilling the purpose of her existence prefigures Anna's subsequent doom. Vronsky, however, does not share his horse's commitment to the race. Though he loves Frou-Frou while they are in the run, his passion for racing is basically frivolous and self-indulgent. The analogy applies to his love affair, where Vronsky, though deeply in love, is not committed to Anna as she is committed to him. That Vronsky's lack of commitment can make him destructive when his mount flounders (he kicks the mare) presages his hostility to Anna when their relationship becomes irritating.

Although Vronsky's horsemanship is unexcelled, Frou-Frou required a perfect rider. And Vronsky had missed perfection by a fatal blunder at the most critical moment. Anna as a sensitive, responsive woman, demanding all-consuming love from her lover, finds Vronsky unequal to meet her exacting requirements. This fatal, irreparable flaw in their relationship drives her to destruction.

The tragedy of the steeplechase, as well as of the doomed liaison, is not a function of Vronsky's horsemanship nor of an inability to love. It is rather a moral tragedy, implicit in human life, occurring whenever an individual confronts crisis. The critical moment provides an "historical necessity" whereby man's imperfectibility defines his destiny.

CHAPTERS 26 to 29

Summary

Despite their changed relationship, Karenin maintains appearances, visiting Anna each week at their summer villa. When they talk, she chats lightly and rapidly, while Karenin, no longer observing the deceit in her entire attitude, responds only to the literal meaning of her words. His hostility, however, expresses itself by an especial coldness to his son. More shy than ever before in front of his father, Seriozha is reduced to silence as Karenin addresses him with an ironical "young man" whenever he speaks to him.

At the race, Karenin watches his wife gaze after one rider, her eyes never observing how horse after horse falls while many officers receive injuries. After Vronsky's fall, Anna weeps with relief to learn he was not killed and accepts Karenin's arm as he leads her from the pavilion. Driving home, Alexey Alexandrovitch remarks on her "unbecoming behavior" in public, repeating his request that she conduct herself to preserve appearance. "I was and I could not help being in despair," replies Anna. "I hear you, but I am thinking of him. I love him, I am his mistress."

His face assumes the solid immobility of the dead. When they arrive home, he informs her in a shaken voice that she must conform to outward propriety until he decides the measures "to secure my honor." Relieved at having spoken, Anna looks forward to meet Vronsky that evening.

Commentary

In these chapters Tolstoy shows how Karenin runs his own "race". by plunging himself deeper into his official work he attempts to escape his thoughts about Anna. However he cannot avoid the obvious truth as he observes Anna at the steeplechase. Karenin finds himself not only at the sidelines of the race course but at the sidelines of a situation which engrosses Anna and Vronsky.

Anna's confession, besides relieving herself of an unstated lie, aims at destroying her husband since she only declares what Karenin already knows but fears. Having told Vronsky, "He (Karenin) doesn't exist," Anna's words seem to carry out her wish, for her husband's face assumed the "solid immobility of the dead." Symbolically ridding herself of him, Anna joyfully anticipates her meeting with Vronsky.

CHAPTERS 30 to 35

Summary

At the German spa, Kitty is strongly attracted by a Russian girl who arrived with an invalid lady named Madame Stahl. She observes how this Mademoiselle Varenka, an adoptive daughter to her companion, makes friends with all who are seriously ill. Varenka's dignity and her absorption in her work — that of performing charitable services for the patients around her — inspire Kitty to emulate her. Despite her pretty face and nice figure, Varenka lacks sensuousness: this is one source of her appeal to Kitty.

Soon after the Shtcherbatskys arrive, two newcomers who provoke "universal and unfavorable attention" appear regularly at the springs. They are a bony Russian man and a pock marked, peasant faced woman named Marya Nicolaevna. When Kitty learns this is Levin's brother Nicolai, she feels disagreeably inclined toward the couple.

Becoming friends with Varenka, Kitty begins to plan her life according to the example of Madame Stahl and her companion. Helping those in trouble, distributing and reading the Gospel to "the sick, and criminal, and the dying" is a career of peace, happiness and goodness for Kitty. Through Varenka, Kitty realizes that to live an exalted life, one must only forget oneself and love others.

Her life's plan backfires humiliatingly. The wife, in one of the families she assists, blames the husband for being infatuated with the young Princess Shtcherbatsky; the woman acts cool, almost rude, to Kitty. Through her father's ironic, critical attitude toward the Pietists (as he calls Madame Stahl and her followers) Kitty realizes the potential hypocrisy of this religious enthusiasm. Her confusion causes her to be disagreeable to Varenka, and after she begs forgiveness of her friend, she gives up this new life's calling. But Kitty does not give up everything she learned from this experience. She becomes aware of her self-deception in "supposing she could be what she wanted to be." She also becomes aware of "all the dreariness in the world of sorrow, of sick and dying people" among whom she lived, and suddenly feeling this oppressive atmosphere, she longs for the fresh air of Russia, of Yerhushovo where Dolly and her family are spending the summer. Kitty returns home cured, no longer carefree and light-hearted, but at peace. The misery she experienced in Moscow is only a memory.

Commentary

Kitty's sojourn at the German spa is the story of her maturation. This period of reflection and purification allows her to accept fulfillment through marriage and family life. Because she violently rejected her womanhood at first, Varenka was Kitty's ideal of perfection. Tolstoy describes Varenka as lacking precisely what Kitty had too much of — "a suppressed fire of vitality and a consciousness of her own attractiveness" — qualities of sensuousness, in other words. As Kitty attempts to live a "soulful" life as Varenka does, she learns it was impossible to deny one's own nature. This became apparent to her when she is accused of turning the head of a married man, although the reader learned this sooner when Kitty immediately rejected the very ill Nicolai Levin. Varenka, Kitty's opposite, learns the same lesson in a different way: later in the novel she is unable to achieve the love of Koznyshev. Both girls submit to their peculiar destiny, Varenka by remaining single and living selflessly, and Kitty by accepting her womanly nature.

PART 3

CHAPTERS 1 to 6

Summary

Koznyshev, deciding to take a vacation, goes to visit his brother, Konstantin Levin. Nothing is more relaxing for Koznyshev than this rural atmosphere; whereas Levin, engulfed in the full tide of summer work, is annoyed at his brother's attitude. Farms and peasants and livestock are part of Levin's life work, while Koznyshev regards this sphere of being merely a refreshment from heavy intellectual labors.

At mowing time, Levin is strongly tempted to join the mowers, but he fears his brother would laugh at him. Finally overpowered by his desire for work and exercise — refreshment from the tiresome intellectual brilliance of Koznyshev, Levin, as casually as possible, orders his scythe sharpened. Working between two peasants, Levin finds it difficult to equal the efforts of the mowers with their untiring muscles. Swinging the scythe with his arm and entire body, Levin concentrates so intensely that all concept of time vanishes. At the noontime break he stays with the peasants, sharing a meal of salted bread with an old man and drinking of the warm river water. Exhausted and exultant, Levin feels at peace.

Koznyshev notes his brother's restored spirits when Levin returns. As they talk together, Levin suspects that Koznyshev's interest in politics, in progressive trends, in the education of the peasants (whom he likes as a class, not as individuals whose experience differs from his own) are only subjects for intellectual exercise. He feels his brother lacks emotional force in all his beliefs.

Koznyshev sums up: "Our differences amount to this," he says, "that you make the mainspring self-interest while I suppose that interest in the common weal exists in every man of a certain degree of advancement." Agreeing with Levin's point that "action founded on material interests would be more desirable," Koznyshev understands that Konstantin, with his own intense, almost primitive, nature requires "intense energetic action or nothing." Appreciating one another's differences, the brothers part affectionately when Koznyshev leaves.

Commentary

Besides defining the differences between the brothers, their arguments represent Levin's own struggle for meaning as he strives to discover the "key to life" first through science, then philosophy, finally concluding that the answer lies in living a "natural life," that is, seeking a universal identity of his soul and that of nature. Koznyshev's emptiness and sterility derive from his dependence on intellectual processes, while Levin's "salvation" derives from his emotional commitment. The exultant feeling of health and peace Levin achieves from mowing prefigures his anti-intellectual solution to life's ultimate meaning.

Levin's "materialism" is based on his confidence in the importance of individual needs. Education, for instance, means nothing to him unless it furthers one's emotional development and deals with increasing one's awareness of basic life goals. For him, peasants do not require education since they understand the basic relation between an individual and his purpose in life. To Koznyshev, education is important for its own sake and must be universally applied so that everyone has intellectual tools with which to understand the complicated problems of an advanced society.

CHAPTERS 7 to 11

Summary

While Oblonsky goes to Petersburg on business, Dolly and her six children move to the country estate at Yergushovo which was part of her dowry. By moving out of Moscow, she avoids the pressing bills of the tradesman which lack of funds prevent her from paying, and her children completely recuperate from their various winter illnesses. Now that her husband no longer loves her, Dolly finds her greatest life pleasure through her children. Meeting Dolly and the youngsters returning from church one morning, Levin exclaims she appeared as "a hen with her chicks" and admires this group of an ideal family. Hearing that Kitty will spend the summer with her sister, he blushes and falls silent. Later he tells Dolly he will not call on her, since Kitty's refusal was final, and any mention of the matter is only a source of pain.

One day in July, Levin drives to the village on his sister's estate to supervise the division of the hay harvest. When it is satisfactorily apportioned, he sits on a haycock to observe the meadow teeming with brightly clad peasants. A young peasant lad loading hay with his pretty bride catches his attention. As the young couple laugh together, he is struck by the strong, young, freshly awakened love which shows in their faces.

Engulfed in this sea of cheerful toil the idea enters his mind that he could, if he wanted to, renounce his artificial, selfish existence with its utterly useless education for this busy, honorable life of simple toil. Deep in thought, Levin leaves the meadow while a chilling night breeze springs up. As a four-in-hand drives by, he sees the serene, thoughtful expression of a girl's face in the window, and then Kitty's candid eyes fall on him. Her face lights up with wonder and surprise, but she does not look out again. As the carriage passes and daylight brightens the sky, Levin makes his decision. "No," he says, "However good that simple life of toil may be, I cannot go back to it, I love *her*."

Commentary

Just as Kitty discovered she could not be untrue to her inner nature, Levin realizes he must follow his destiny. Despite the temptations of the agreeable, natural life of his peasants, he resignedly concludes that he must first find truth and meaning within the bounds of his given nature. As Kitty passes by on her way to Dolly's estate, Levin recognizes his commitment to the life he now leads. Before he can change his career, he must first wrestle with his present way of life and discover its basic values. Thus, on an individual level, Tolstoy shows how Levin struggles for meaning within the bounds of his own "historical necessity."

CHAPTERS 12 TO 23

Summary

At Anna's confession, Karenin remins still and deathlike. After seeing her home, he is better able to examine the problem. Like a sufferer who has had the bad tooth extracted, he feels relief at his wife's outburst. Despite his deep cowardice, he first considers challenging Vronsky to a duel. Karenin decides that, being indispensable to the ministry, he should allow nothing to interfere either with his duties or his reputation; no, a duel would solve nothing. Legal divorce, or even separation, is also not feasible, since the resulting scandal would injure only himself and the guilty parties would be united; they should rather suffer from their crimes. His only recourse is to keep his wife with him, conceal from the world what had happened, use every measure in his power to break off the intrigue, and above all (though he does not admit this) to punish her. His decision pleases him, and he feels satisfied that religious sanction coincides so conveniently with his self-interest. He resolves to write Anna a letter announcing his decision to maintain the status quo.

When he arrives home in Petersburg, Karenin first writes to Anna, then turns to an official matter, the business of setting up a commission to inquire into the work of the Native Tribes Organization Committee. Having accomplished both important items of work, Karenin retires, well pleased with himself.

Despite contradicting Vronsky when he said their position was an impossible one, Anna too desires above all to put an end to her false and dishonorable marriage. But where would she turn if put out of her husband's house? In her distress she imagines that Vronsky, loving her less, already finds her a burden. No, she cannot offer herself to him. Besides miserable, Anna is frightened: in her new spiritual condition she feels everything in her soul is double, each part claimed by conflicting loyalties to the two men in her life. If her relations to Vronsky and Karenin are in question, there is no ambivalence about Seriozha. Her aim and only support in life is her son. But she must act quickly to secure his helpless position. Ordering her things packed, she decides to leave with him for Moscow.

Then she reads Karenin's note which just arrived, and feels her plight more awful than ever. Shuddering at his threat that he would take her son if she persists in her unlawful ways, Anna finds her husband's insistence to lead the same life they always live further evidence of his willingness to exist by lies and hypocrisy. Enraged and frustrated, she realizes she is not strong enough to escape this intolerable situation. Never able to know freedom in love, she would remain the guilty wife constantly threatened with exposure, deceiving her husband for a disgraceful liaison with a man whose life she could not share. Weeping unconstrainedly, Anna cannot conceive how it will end. Later that afternoon she attends Princess Betsy's croquet party, leaving early to meet Vronsky at six o'clock.

As he does four or five times a year, Vronsky spends that day figuring his accounts and putting all his affairs in order. Despite his frivolous life, he hates irregularity and always manages his finances with care. He calls this day of reckoning a *faire de lessive,* and at this point, Tolstoy also reckons up the course of Vronsky's life.

Throughout his career, Vronsky has lived by a code of principles which answers problems in his life: "gambling debts must be paid, the tailor need not be; one must not lie to a man but might to a woman; one must never cheat anyone but may a husband; one must not pardon insults, but one may insult others, and so on." Lately, however, Vronsky finds these rules do not withstand the present contingencies of his intense love. Now that Anna's pregnancy means their lives must be joined, he wonders if he is prepared to make the necessary sacrifices. Ambition in his career rivals his passion for Anna, and he envies his good friend and school comrad, Serpuhovskoy who had become a general and now expects a command with great political influence. When they meet at a party, Serpuhovskoy tactfully tells Vronsky that women are the chief obstacles to a man's career. Marriage clears the path, however, and he begs Vronsky to give him *carte blanche* permission to use his influence in advancing his friend. Russia needs men like you in her service, he tells the officer. Promising to think it over, Vronsky goes to meet Anna.

When he reads Karenin's note to Anna, and she tells of her confession, he joyfully thinks "a duel is now inevitable" and pictures that honorable moment when, after firing into the air, he awaits the shot of the outraged husband. Serpuhovskoy's advice flashes through his mind — that it is better not to bind oneself — and he knows he cannot mention this thought to Anna. Seeing the lack of determination in his face, Anna loses hope.

"Things cannot remain as he supposes," says Vronsky, thinking of the duel but saying something else. She must leave her husband. "But my son!" cries Anna, "I should have to leave him and I can't and won't do that." To Vronsky the choice is simple: she must leave her child or maintain this degrading position. "To whom is it degrading?" says Anna. The only thing important in her life is Vronsky's love, and "if that's mine, I feel so exalted...that nothing can humiliate me." As she sobs, Vronsky, himself close to tears, feels helpless knowing he is to blame for her wretchedness. Sadly, Anna realizes her fears: everything will remain the same.

That Monday, at the usual sitting of the Commission, Karenin emerges victorious. His motion carried after a fight, even against the arguments of his rival Stremov, three new commissions are appointed to investigate the Reorganization of the Native Tribes. Petersburg society talks of nothing else but Karenin's latest victory.

The next day Anna arrives in Petersburg, her visit marring Karenin's satisfaction from yesterday's triumph. Demanding his wife's conduct to be above the suspicions of even the servants, Karenin forbids Anna to meet her lover. In return, he allows her all the privileges of a respectable wife without fulfilling the duties of one.

Commentary

These chapters define the characters of Karenin and Vronsky, and with Anna Arkadyevna caught "double-souled" between them, they have reached a stalemate. Both men have gone as far as their characters and experiences allow them to go. Until a crisis, the situation is to remain static.

Vronsky is a representative character of the milieu of army and court nobility which has made his career. His motivations are socially conditioned according to his social role and function as a promising career man in the military. Guided by his "code of behavior" Vronsky concludes a duel will occur, thus solving the problem of his honor. With confusion, he realizes that a duel will not solve Anna's disgrace. Now that her condition demands his assuming responsibility for her future, a resolve he has not yet decided, Vronsky's imagination stops.

Karenin, shown as almost the very symbol of bureaucracy, approaches his domestic problems the same way he meets problems at the office. Tolstoy tells us this as Alexey Alexandrovitch first dispatches a letter to Anna, then turns to the business of the Native Tribes Commission. Karenin sees Vronsky as an enemy like Stremov, a rival to be overcome through political, rather than personal, application. Human impulses are sunk deep within him. Religion, whose principles he applies as an afterthought, is for Karenin just a set of highly institutionalized rules. Since a duel solves no problems for a bureaucrat, Karenin issues no challenge. He must compromise emotional problems and avoid their poignancy through the principle of expediency.

38

CHAPTERS 24 to 32

Summary
    The after effects of Levin's evening on the haycock destroy his pleasure as a squire and make him dissatisfied with farming. He is additionally annoyed because Kitty is spending the summer merely twenty miles away. Seeking a change, Levin visits his friend Sviazhsky who lives in a remote part of the district with splendid snipe marshes nearby.

    Although the hunting is poor, Levin's discussions with Sviazhsky and another guest about the state of the Russian peasant and the inefficient use of the land inspire him to devise a new system of agriculture. After a few days, he hastens home to put his plan into action. Levin wants to increase the peasants' interest in the success of their work, even if it means, temporarily, that new methods and new machinery be sacrificed. He plans that he and the peasants work as shareholders in the estate. One stumbling-block is that summer farming is in full swing. Another is the insurmountable distrust of the peasants; they cannot believe that the master has any other aim than to squeeze all he can out of them. Some of the peasants grasp the idea of cooperative land plots and parts of the farm are divided accordingly, the rest of the estate remaining as before. Problems arise, of course, and some of the peasants do not put in the improvements they had agreed upon. These matters, along with managing the rest of the estate and writing a book on the subject occupy Levin until well in September.

    Late one evening a visitor arrives. Hearing the familiar sound of coughing, Levin runs downstairs to greet his brother Nicolai. He has come, as Levin requested, to receive his share of a recently sold family estate. Although happy to see him, Levin feels frightened as he kisses the dry skin and looks into the unnaturally glittering eyes. Death, since it marks his own brother, confronts him for the first time and with an expecially irresistible force.

    Despite their deep affection, their conversation is insincere and disagreeable. Though Levin knows his brother is trying to hide his fear of death, he is stung by the bitter criticisms the sick man makes of his new system. Nicolai accuses him of being communistic, that Levin lacking conviction just reorganizes the peasants to flatter his self-esteem. After Nicolai leaves, Levin sees death or the advances of death in everything. He works harder than ever to realize his scheme, feeling this the one thread to guide him through the ever impending darkness.

Commentary

Levin's farming scheme is an "action founded on material interests," to quote Koznyshev, aimed at the efficient use of available resources of land and labor so that the peasants, as well as the master, gain profit. Unnecessary waste is repulsive to Levin (exemplified at his disgust over Stiva's careless sale of the valuable forest) who believes that long-term reforms and basic life goals are based on materialist considerations. Levin's passion for agronomic reform satisfies his need for arduous work and expresses his search for meaning through emotional commitment rather than through intellectual inquiry. Criticizing his brother's reforms for showing his lack of conviction, Nicolai echoes Levin's deep-seated anxieties. Konstantin suspects himself of the same fault, fearing his zeal for reform merely as an avoidance of a deeper issue. Nicolai is right; Levin attempts to avoid the "deeper issue" of death, and with his brother's condition forcing him to confront the problem, Konstantin begins to struggle with this grave threat.

Levin's materialism derives from his attachment to sensual reality. His intense nature drives him to search for the meaning of his life through the everyday actions of his human individuality. Levin's desire for marriage and family is also based on this search. Love and his future offspring are essential to his self-fulfillment as a human being. As a further tie to his immediate world, marriage increases his sense of reality. But death has no part of Levin's life-seeking scheme and his attempt to come to terms with this threat becomes an obsessive struggle that carries him through the rest of the novel.

PART 4

CHAPTERS 1 to 23

Summary

Although totally estranged, the Karenins live as before. Anna continues to meet Vronsky but always away from home and her husband knows about it. All three endure their misery only because they hope for a change. Karenin expects this passion to pass with the lapse of time, while Anna hopes "something" will turn up to settle the situation. Vronsky, submitting to her lead, waits for the problem to clear up of itself without his taking any action.

In the middle of winter, Vronsky spends a tiresome week showing a foreign prince the sights of the city. A "true gentleman," the visitor is a stupid, self-satisfied, immaculate person. Dignified and poised with his superiors, free and simple with his equals, contemptuously indulgent with his inferiors, the visitor is a disturbing mirror-image of Vronsky himself. When the foreigner finally leaves, Vronsky so relieved to be delivered from this distasteful self-reflection, engages in an all night revel to purge himself.

Returning home, Vronsky finds a note from Anna asking him to see her while Karenin is at a meeting. At her gate, Vronsky alights from his sledge only to come face to face with Alexey Alexandrovitch just entering his carriage. As they bow coldly to one another, Vronsky feels like a snake in the grass, a position foreign to his nature which angers and frustrates him.

Having heard about his latest revel, Anna feels more wretched than ever and scolds him in one of her more and more frequent fits of jealousy. Though he knows she is prompted out of her great love for him, Vronsky takes fright at her outburst. At these moments his love vanishes, and he notes her increasing stoutness, her somewhat faded beauty and the new spiteful expression which sometimes crosses her face. Yet he feels the bond between them can never be broken. Asking her what the doctor had said, Vronsky learns their child shall arrive soon. Their position will then be resolved, says Anna, but not as they expect. Tears well in her eyes and she feels sorry for him. "Soon we shall be at peace and suffer no more," she says. "And I shall not live through it."

Karenin storms directly to Anna's rooms when he returns. Furious that she dared see Vronsky at their home, he declares he will see a lawyer and begin divorce proceedings. Seriozha is to remain with his sister until the case is decided. "Leave me Seriozha," Anna pleads, "You don't love him. You want him in order to hurt me." "Yes," answers Karenin in his fury, "I associate my son with my loathing for you." Anna begs that Seriozha remain until after her confinement; at that Karenin loses his temper completely and flings from the room. The next day he engages a famous Petersburg lawyer to take the case.

Karenin's previous victory at the last sitting of the commission turns into defeat. With full information about the condition of the native tribes (gathered through all the administrating officials in these remote parts) his enemy, Stremov, goes over to his side, carrying other members with him. Not only agreeing with Karenin, Stremov proposes even more radical solutions to the problem so that, carried to an extreme, the measures prove ridiculous. The commission divides in confusion, no one knowing whether the native tribes are flourishing or impoverished. All the indignation of public opinion and of officialdom falls on Karenin. Owing to the contempt of those who know Karenin's domestic life, as well as this last blunder, his position is somewhat precarious. To remedy matters, Karenin resolves to travel—at his own expense—to the distant provinces and investigate for himself the condition of the native tribes.

Stopping in Moscow for three days, Karenin meets Oblonsky. To get rid of his brother-in-law, Alexey Alexandrovitch agrees to dine at the Oblonskys the following evening. Stiva is delighted to have Karenin as the most distinguished guest for his party where Kitty and Levin are also to attend. This occasion emphasizes his recently happy life. Although still short of money, he manages to provide fine gifts for the pretty actress he has recently taken under his protection, and Dolly has been quite cheerful for a time.

Returning from church, Karenin sets to work. He writes to the lawyer, enclosing some of Vronsky's letters to Anna as evidence, and then receives a deputation for the native tribes on the way to Petersburg. Then the servant announces Oblonsky. Stiva begs Alexey Alexandrovitch to reconsider the divorce. At least Karenin must talk to Dolly before going any further with proceedings.

One of the last to arrive at his home, Oblonsky perceives at first glance that his guests are not yet brought together. In a moment he has introduced everyone to everyone else. Bringing Koznyshev and Karenin together on a talk about the russification of Poland, Stiva has the conversation lively and his company relax and begin enjoying themselves.

At Levin'a arrival, Kitty's face lights up with joy and she almost bursts into tears. To Levin her every word holds unutterable meaning and his whole being is filled with tenderness for her. While everyone else discusses women's right, Levin and Kitty talk softly together, delighted at their perfect understanding.

Meantime Dolly draws Karenin off for a talk. She begins by protesting Anna's innocence, but Karenin's response cuts her short. She tries to change his mind—"anything but a divorce," she pleads—appealing to his sense of Christian charity. But even after the intense discussion, Karenin's opinion remains the same.

Levin and Kitty talk at a card table while she scribbles with a chalk. He is amazed that their minds are in such perfect agreement. However badly he expresses a thought, she always understands. Taking the chalk from her, he writes only the initial letters of his question: "When you told me it could not be—did that mean never or then?" Pointing to the "n," Kitty says, "That means 'never' but it's not true." A few more sentences pass between them with the chalk, and then Levin writes the initials for, "I have never ceased to love you." With this device he asks her to marry him and Kitty answers "Yes" before he finishes writing. When the Shtcherbatskys leave. Levin feels so forlorn without her that he can hardly await the next morning to call on them.

After the dinner, Levin accompanies his brother Koznyshev to a meeting. Filled with joy, he finds everyone splendid and good-hearted. Levin listens to the debate on missing sums of money and the laying of sewer pipes. He concludes that the subject is unimportant to the debating members and that they merely enjoy themselves.

Levin's excitement allows him no rest that night. Toward noon the next day he arrives at the Shtcherbatskys and Kitty runs to meet him. The old prince and princess are kind and affectionate; both have tears in their eyes. Then the servants offer congratulations, and then relations begin to arrive. This is the beginning of the "blissful hubbub" which never diminishes until the wedding.

Levin feels Kitty has much to forgive. One matter is his lack of faith, but his betrothed does not care. She says she knows his soul and in it sees the goodness she values. The other item concerns his past life, and Levin regrets he is not as chaste as she. Wishing to share all his secrets, he gives her his diary, and Kitty weeps bitterly over the notebook. This confession is the one painful episode of their engagement. When she forgives him, Levin feels more than ever unworthy of her love. Morally bowed before her, he prizes his great undeserved happiness more highly than before.

Returning to his lodgings, Karenin recalls his talk with Dolly. Annoyed at her reminder of Christian forgiveness—"love those that hate you"— Karenin turns to consider his tour of inspection in the provinces. First he reads his two telegrams. One contains news that Stemov received the very appointment he had coveted for himself. The second is from Anna. "I am dying," she writes. "I beg, I implore you to come. I shall die easier with your forgiveness." Realizing her confinement is near, he decides the note is not just a trick. He will leave for Petersburg right away, perform his last duty to her, retaining his self respect despite everything. But he cannot drive away the reflection that her death would solve his most pressing problem.

At home Karenin learns she had been safely delivered yesterday but she is very ill now. Entering Anna's room he finds Vronsky, face in hands, weeping at her writing table. Karenin's appearance confuses him. "She is dying," Vronsky says, "The doctors say there is no hope. I am entirely in your hands, only let me remain here." Turning from his tears, Karenin approaches Anna's bed. With flushed cheeks, glittering eyes, she talks rapidly in a ringing voice. She speaks of Seriozha, and of her husband who does not himself know how good he is. Karenin's face quivers as he sees her gaze at him with such tender and ecstatic affection as he has never seen in her before.

"Don't be surprised at me," Anna says. "There is another woman in me (who) loved that man and tried to hate you...Now I'm my real self, all myself. I'm dying now. Only one thing I want: forgive me, forgive me completely..."

Suddenly Karenin gives way to an emotion which gives him a new happiness he has never known. Kneeling, with his head against her arm which burns like fire through his sleeve, he sobs. She calls Vronsky, who, seeing Anna, buries his face in his hands. "Uncover your face!" she orders. "Look at him! He is a saint!" To her husband she cries, "Uncover his face, Alexey Alexandrovitch, I want to see him!" Karenin draws Vronsky's hands away, uncovering a look terrible in its agony and shame. "Give him your hand," says Anna, "Forgive him." Karenin stretches out his hand," while unrestrained tears stream down his cheeks. "Thank God, thank God," murmurs Anna. Then the pains begin again. Crying for morphia, she tosses about on the bed.

Anna had puerperal fever, the doctors said, and ninety-nine cases out of a hundred are fatal. In a coma, Anna's end is moments away. Toward morning she regains consciousness, then sleeps again. The doctors are hopeful.

That day, Karenin comes to Vronsky in the boudoir. The luminous, serene expression of his tear filled eyes impresses Vronsky. "The happiness of forgiving has revealed to me my duty," the husband tells him. "Should the world hold me a laughing-stock, I will never forsake her and will never utter a word of reproach to you." Promising to call should Anna wish to see him, Karenin suggests that Vronsky leave.

As if in a stupor, Vronsky stands on the steps. All the rules of his familiar world now seem false and inapplicable. Anna had raised her deceived husband to an elevated position from which that despised creature proves himself, not ludicrous or false, but kind, straightforward, and dignified. Their positions are reversed: Karenin exalted, magnaminous, himself debased, petty, and deceitful. Feeling further dejected since his love for Anna had increased during her illness, Vronsky has been humiliated before her at the very pinnacle of his love and has now lost her forever. Returning to his brother's house, Vronsky finds rest impossible even after his vigil of three days and nights. Out of desperation and wretchedness he aims his gun at his heart and fires. With consciousness dropping from him, Vronsky is suddenly aware that he has missed.

In the following weeks, Karenin basks in his feeling of inward peace. Now that he freely loves and freely forgives, he finds life so simple. He has a great affection for the newborn daughter and visits the nursery many times a day. Yet he feels the world will not understand him, that something more is expected of him. Though realizing his relations with Anna are still unstable and unnatural, Karenin does not want the situation to change.

The "misunderstanding world" for Karenin is best represented by the stylish Betsy Tverskoy who has just arrived with a message for Anna. Vronsky had written to beg Anna to see him once more before he departs to a new post at Tashkent, a distant province. A little afraid of her husband, Anna asks his advice, but Karenin cannot express himself under Betsy's contemptuous gaze. He is relieved when Betsy leaves them. Karenin is aware of Anna's irritation in his presence. His physical proximity repulses her. Deciding never to see Vronsky again, Anna feels the misery of her false position with full strength. "Oh God, why didn't I die," she sobs.

Realizing Anna's hatred of him, and realizing that the world demands their divorce, Karenin is in a dilemma. Divorce would place Anna in a helpless position, disgrace both children, and deprive himself of everything he cares for. Yet he realizes that the world would prevail against what he thinks is right and proper.

Oblonsky arrives while the Princess Betsy is leaving. Finding his sister in misery, Stiva tries to convince Karenin to consent to divorce. After they discuss the matter, Alexey Alexandrovitch gives Stiva permission to arrange matters as he sees fit.

Vronsky hovers between life and death in the days following his attempted suicide. His action solved one source of his misery and he can confront Karenin's magnaminity without humiliation. Resolving that he would no longer come between the repentant wife and her husband, he accepts a post which Serpuhovskoy found for him and asks Betsy to arrange a final meeting with Anna before he leaves for Tashkent.

Betsy arrives with news that Karenin has consented to a divorce. Vronsky dashes to Anna's house. Without looking to see whether they are alone or not, he showers kisses on her, while Anna trembles with emotion. Finally able to speak, Anna tells him she wants no divorce, that she is worried about Seriozah. Tears flow down her cheeks, and she is unable to smile.

Vronsky refuses his Tashkent post, and, noting the disapproval from high quarters at this action, quickly resigns his commission. A month later Karenin and his son are left alone in the house. Anna goes abroad with Vronsky, not having obtained a divorce and having resolutely refused one.

Commentary

This section presents the parallel careers of Levin and Anna in striking contrast. As Levin embarks to fulfill his life through his courtship and marriage to Kitty, we see his career as an affirmation of his life. This part of his story already points to the happy ending in his struggle to overcome death. Anna's imminent death in this section, however, portends disaster.

Just as death reverses life, Anna's deathbed crisis reverses the process of her love affair. From this point on, we see the slow-motion deterioration of her relationship with Vronsky and its corresponding effect on her lover and husband.

As Vronsky and Karenin exchange roles during this crisis, they both achieve an emotional intensity neither have previously experienced. At the point of losing Anna, Vronsky rises to the pinnacle of his love but finds himself unable to cope with his humiliation and debasement. With Karenin exalted, Vronsky's "code of prescribed behavior" offers no solution to his present crisis. His life based on regimented social values to sustain his ego, Vronsky cannot countenance this sudden loss of honor. He responds by trying to destroy his suddenly meaningless life now that it can no longer conform to formulistic interpretation. Tolstoy shows us that Vronsky is too rigid to sustain the intensity of his passion. The attempted suicide tells us of the ultimate futility of Vronsky's attempt to maintain the emotional depth of love that Anna demands from him.

For Karenin, Anna's deathbed crisis acts as a catalyst releasing his latent emotions of love and forgiveness—emotions which he has spent his life trying to repress. His exaltation results from his sudden discovery of universal love and the truth of "turning the other cheek," a basic tenet in Tolstoyan Christianity. No longer resisting evil, Karenin's confrontation with evil allows him to overcome it. Death for Alexey Alexandrovitch becomes the basic truth which makes him a living human being capable of love.

With a masterful touch of irony, Tolstoy also brings Anna to a point of reversal when she is near death. In her fever, Anna's "real self" begs forgiveness while she gazes with tender affection at her husband. However, when she returns to health, Anna chooses in favor of Vronsky. Tolstoy's device here is a Dostoevskian twist to show how the moment of death illuminates life's truths, whereas the state of health provides the conditions for illusion.

This awareness of life-in-death provides the climax of the novel, with the main characters perceiving truth from the heights of their emotional intensity. Hate and deceit no longer exist in the presence of death, and Anna, Vronsky, and Karenin live a moment of pure innocence. From the point of Anna's recovery, however, the novel portrays the human condition as if after the Fall of Grace. Karenin, despite his ennoblement, finds Anna cannot love him. Vronsky pursues his ill-fated love, while Anna follows through toward her already doomed destiny.

Thus Tolstoy provides a crossroad in this section of the novel, defining the direction his main characters will take from now on. Levin's path ascends toward light and love, while Anna's career points to tragedy.

PART 5

CHAPTERS 1 to 6

Summary

Stiva tells Levin he needs a certificate of confession before he can be married. Levin appears in church, confessing to the old priest his sin of doubting everything, even the existence of God. After receiving absolution, he ponders over the priest's questions as to how he will provide for his children's "spiritual advancement in the light of truth."

Levin dines with his bachelor friends the night before the wedding. Koznyshev points out that a wife interferes with her husband's pleasures. But Levin considers his greatest happiness is being with Kitty and following her wishes.

Suddenly unsure of what her wishes are, he is even jealous of Vronsky all over again. Seeking Kitty, Levin asks her if she is sure she wants to marry him. She bursts into tears, and when calm again, explains why she loves him: because she understands him perfectly, because she knows what he would like, and everything he likes is good.

The wedding takes place the next day, and the young couple leave for the country that evening.

Commentary

With communion, the bachelor party, the long church ceremony, Levin undergoes the rites-of-passage into this new phase of his life. He is happy from a feeling of freedom — not the type of egocentric, intellectual liberty Koznyshev defends — but a freedom derived from the emotional satisfactions of his new relationship with Kitty. Levin's last minute doubts, Kitty's mixed feelings as she anticipates her new life, their fumbling during parts of the church ceremony, are minor adjustments which prefigure the major adjustments both Kitty and Levin undergo during their first period of life together.

CHAPTERS 7 to 13

Summary

During the three months that Anna and Vronsky travel abroad, they are sensitive to the reactions of their acquaintances. Avoiding contact with Russians, they discover that most people they know are tactful about their illegal relationship.

In this first period of freedom and rapid return to health, Anna feels "unpardonably happy," and her illness, the crisis of Karenin's attitude, leavetaking from her son, seem like parts of a fevered dream. Vronsky's presence is a continual delight for her. He is constantly attentive, showing no regret for sacrificing a promising career for her sake. Although seeking imperfections in Vronsky, Anna can find none.

Vronsky, however, soon learns that happiness "does not consist merely in the realizing of one's desires." After a period of contentment, he feels ennui. To fill sixteen leisure hours each day, he devotes himself to a succession of intense interests: first politics, then books, now painting. Although finding himself somewhat talented, his study and practice of art is brief. Vronsky realizes how shallow his talent is when they become acquainted with a Russian painter living in the same Italian town.

Abandoning his own portrait of Anna, he commissions the artist to paint her picture. Without this occupation, their life suddenly becomes boring. They decide to return to Russia and settle in the country. Anna plans to visit her son in Petersburg, while Vronsky intends business with his brother and divide their property.

Commentary

Despite the happiness of her honeymoon, Anna is threatened by memories of her past as well as by the insecurity of her future. This insecurity is represented by the careful way in which Anna and Vronsky choose their circle of friends, for Vronsky's nature is dependent upon society for his fulfillment. Although he bravely represses his regrets for the past, Vronsky's feelings are implicit in his restless search for a calling beyond the demands of his love. The basic frivolity of his pursuits underlines once more the basic frivolity of his love. Tolstoy implies that Vronsky and Anna can be happy and at peace if they are away from the pressures of urban society. But the test of their relationship is yet to come when they return to the city and try to settle accounts with the past they have left behind in Petersburg.

CHAPTERS 14 to 20

Summary

Despite their great love, the first period of Levin's married life is a trying one. Not knowing what is important to each of them, they have frequent arguments. After each quarrel, however, they experience a renewed tenderness and reaffirmation of their love. Only during their third month of marriage, after a four week stay in Moscow, does life begin to run smoothly.

Working on his book explaining his system of land reform, with Kitty embroidering near him, Levin recalls how he used to write in order to subdue the feeling of all-pervading death. Now he works to subdue the feeling of "unspeakable brightness" and joy. Having always believed that marriage was the time one started the business of life most seriously, Levin marvels at his months of idleness, for he has not done farm work or touched his book since his wedding. He does not understand Kitty's idleness and lack of "serious" interests derive from her instincts of nest building. Tolstoy explains that Kitty is preparing herself for the time when housekeeping and child raising become the total significance of her life.

Levin receives a letter from Marya Nicolaevna which tells that his brother is dying, and prepares to leave for Moscow. Kitty insists to accompany him, despite Levin's reluctance to have his wife confront a "fallen woman."

They arrive at the dilapidated, dirty country inn where Nicolai Levin and Masha are staying. Levin is repulsed by the dirt and disorder of the sickroom, by the writhing and groaning of the living corpse which is his brother. Kitty sits by Nicolai's bed, holding his hand and comforting him by sympathetic, unoffending words. She orders a better room for Nicolai, supervises the maid at dusting and scrubbing, has fresh linen put on the bed, fresh clothes for the patient, sends for the doctor, the chemist, summons the waiter. Nicolai has a new expression of hope on his face as he is freshly attired, resting comfortably in a sweet smelling orderly room. At Kitty's urging, he agrees to receive the sacrament and extreme unction. But his only faith, he whispers to Levin, rests in the phial of opium which releases him from his constant pain. For three days, Nicolai hovers on the brink of death. The long vigil is a terrible physical and emotional strain on those around him. When his brother finally dies, Levin is in utter despair at the enormity of death. He must cling more strongly than ever to life, to love. At this point, he learns that Kitty is pregnant.

Commentary

Out of more than two hundred chapters, only the one dealing with Nicolai's last illness has a title. This chapter—Chapter 20—called "Death," had great significance for Tolstoy, wherein he records the death of his own brother. The moment holds tremendous significance for Levin as well. He discovers more poignantly than ever that the mysteries of existence are not revealed to the intellect. Only an emotional experience can provide an individual with tools to accept the fact of death. While Levin finds himself still blocked at confronting death, Kitty is able to handle the situation. Marveling at his wife's intuitive ability to confront sickness and death, Levin remarks to himself, "Thou hast hid things from the wise and prudent and hast revealed them unto babes." Until he can renounce intellectual seeking to life's problems, Levin will still lack self-fulfillment. Kitty, on the other hand, fulfills her human destiny because she has no intellectual orientation.

CHAPTERS 21 to 33

Summary

Karenin finds himself alone and despised by all, as a sick dog left by the pack to fend for itself. At the deepest point in his misery, Countess Lydia Ivanovna enters his study unannounced and offers herself as his confidante and helper. Doing what she can to "lighten his burden of petty cares" the countess begins to run Karenin's household. Despite having considered her religiosity excessive and distasteful, Karenin is comforted by her prayers and exhortations. Lydia Ivanovna begins her management by telling Seriozha that his father is a saint and his mother is dead. Then she attends to the practical household affairs, though proving herself inept. Karenin's valet, Korney, quietly corrects her impossible orders, and things run smoothly under his guidance.

Lydia Ivanovna is given to excesses. She frequently falls in love, especially with people connected with the court, and now directs all her affections at Karenin. She is especially proud of having converted Alexey Alexandrovitch from an apathetic believer into a fervent Christian. With her usual blindness, she does not realize his belief is merely a convenient way for him to overcome his humiliation and misery. She is, of course, very jealous of Anna, and gives no answer to Madame Karenina's request to see Seriozha.

Karenin takes great care to provide his son with an excellent education. Hiring outstanding tutors in each discipline, he himself gives Seriozha lessons in the New Testament.

Seriozha, meanwhile, does not believe that his mother is dead. His favorite occupation during his walks is to look for her. Every comely, dark-haired woman sends such a rush of tenderness through him that his eyes fill with tears. He imagines how his mother would come to him, her smiling face revealed as she raises her veil to kiss him.

Arriving at Petersburg, Anna thinks of nothing but her son and how to meet him. Humiliated at the countess' lack of response, Anna's shame turns to wrath when Lydia Ivanovna does write, saying that Seriozha's ideals would be shattered by his mother's presence.

She enters the house early one morning and goes to her son's room. Seriozha has become a young boy since her absence, thinner, taller, more mature. Aching with love, Anna hugs him while he is still asleep. Finding his mother is a reality, not a delicious dream, Seriozha wriggles in her arms and presses closely against her.

Anna returns to her hotel room so dazed she does not know why she is there. Despite her intense longing, and having prepared her emotions for the meeting, she has been unable to foresee how violently the encounter would affect her. Now the nurse brings in the newly dressed baby girl, whose round pink face wreathes in smiles when she sees her mother. Yet Anna feels her love for little Ani is nowhere as intense as that reserved for her son, the first child on whom she lavished all the affection she could not give its father.

Gazing at her son's photograph, she sees a picture of Vronsky on the same page of the album, suddenly remembering he is the cause of her present misery. Along with a surge of love for Vronsky, she reproaches him in her mind for not being here to share her unhappiness. Perhaps he does not love her, she thinks, and finds all sorts of evidence to prove it: their separate hotel suites, the guest Vronsky brings with him rather than seeing her alone.

When Vronsky and Anna meet for dinner that evening, he finds her in an unusual reckless mood. She has invited guests to dine with them, flirts with the men, and, suddenly, decides to attend a benefit performance at the opera that night where all Petersburg will be there to see her. Your presence will acknowledge your position as a fallen woman, Vronsky wants to say to Anna. Begging her not to go, he tries not to look at her beauty, now heightened by the gown she will wear to the theater. Anna cries out that for her nothing matters but her love for Vronsky, that she does not regret what she has done.

Arriving when the performance is in full swing, Vronsky goes to Anna's box at intermission. He learns that she has been insulted by the countess in the next box, and her name is on everyone's lips as people throng the halls. Only at home does Anna succumb to the emotions her humiliation has aroused. She blames him for her shame, and Vronsky can comfort her only by repeated assurances of his love. Her dazzling beauty irritates him, and in his heart he reproaches her action. The next day, fully reconciled, they leave for the country.

Commentary

Anna's heart-rending visit to her son affects her the same way as his brother's death affected Levin: both cling more intensely to their love and life after experiencing a loss. Strengthened in her love according to the amount of suffering she paid for it, Anna defends her rights to happiness against the very society opposed to it. She declares the truth of her status by appearing in public. Quoting Steiner, "the ironic intensity" of the scene derives from its setting: "society condemns Anna precisely in that place where society is most frivolous, ostentatious, and steeped in illusion."

She blames Vronsky for her humiliation because he lacks the depth of soul to understand her torment at giving up Seriozha. Anna feels her challenge would have been a triumph had Vronsky been proud of her public declaration. Instead, like Karenin before him, Vronsky, perplexed at her wilful neglect of propriety, thinks only to hide his disgrace from the members of his social set. The moment of disagreement reveals Vronsky's limitations. At her public and proud affirmation of her love for him, he loses respect for her. He is even regretful of being attracted by her beauty, as if her physical charms were to blame for this embarrassment.

Thus Tolstoy shows the fateful differences between Vronsky and Anna. For Vronsky, love is not an absolute quality, but one which must be reinforced through its environment. Unfavorable circumstances wear love's intensity while Anna's love, under the same conditions, becomes more intense and desperate. This is another example of Tolstoy's concept of "historical necessity" which molds the human condition. Once Anna and Vronsky are isolated from Petersburg society, however, their lives run smoothly and the failing balance of their relationship is restored.

PART 6

CHAPTERS 1 to 5

Summary

Levin's household at Pokrovskoe is filled with summer guests he calls the "Schtcherbatsky element" although Koznyshev is also there. These include Dolly, her children and governesses, the old princess (supervising Kitty's pregnancy), Kitty's father, and Varenka who finally fulfills her promise to visit when Kitty is married.

Koznyshev's interest in Varenka causes everyone to hope for their marriage. Koznyshev was once betrothed to a girl when Levin was a child. When she died, Koznyshev vowed never to fall in love again. On this occasion, however, he decided to ask Varenka in marriage and the moment of declaration arrives when they find themselves alone during a mushroom hunting expedition. Nervous in the pregnant silence, Koznyshev and Varenka talk about the difference between two mushroom varieties. Their tension subsides, and each is somewhat relieved. "I cannot be untrue to the memory of Marie," thinks Koznyshev as they walk quietly and slightly abashed toward the rest of the company.

Commentary

Tolstoy implies that intellectuality leads to a self-centered sterility. Koznyshev's rational approach to life, and Varenka's abstract piety, prevent them from experiencing an intense human relationship. As these passion-denying individuals accept their lonely destiny, Tolstoy compares their empty existence with the flesh and blood love Kitty and Levin experience and which enriches their lives with significance and self-fulfillment. The emphasis here is on the "natural life" where one loves and procreates, as opposed to the "unnatural life" where one lives by abstract principles. Natural man, says Tolstoy again and again, grasps life through all its realities and can then understand death. Intellect and spirit merely bypass essential truths.

CHAPTERS 6 to 15

Summary

Stepan Arkadyevitch arrives that afternoon with another guest named Vassenka Veslovsky. Good-natured and handsome, brilliant in society, the newcomer has just spent some time at Vronsky's estate fifty miles hence. Although Vassenka makes a favorable impression on everyone else, Levin dislikes him, for he seems to pay especial court to Kitty. When Dolly, the old princess, and Kitty eagerly listen to Vassenka's stories at dinner, Levin's jealousy intensifies. He imagines that Kitty is already in love with Vassenka and perhaps has even planned a rendezvous. Later, Levin blurts out his suspicions to Kitty. She explains that she listened so intensely to Vassenka because he told them of Anna's life with Vronsky. Levin feels guilty for suspecting dishonorable intentions of such a "capital fellow."

Intending to be cordial, Levin with Vassenka and Stiva sets off for a two-day shooting expedition. Through Vassenka's heedlessness, many small reversals occur throughout the outing. Veslovsky's bungling prevents Levin from a successful catch of snipe. Nevertheless, Levin overcomes his hostility and concludes that, after all, Vassenka is simple, good-hearted, and congenial.

At home once more, Levin's jealousy flares up again. Kitty, as well, is made miserable by Vassenka's attentions. Despite acknowledging his guest's basic guiltlessness, Levin asks Veslovsky to leave. Everyone finds this ridiculous; Levin has no right to indulge his hypersensitivity to needlessly insult a guest. But Kitty and Levin are much relieved to be rid of Vassenka's bumbling presence.

Commentary

This petty incident lasts for ten chapters, although one is devoted to a discussion of economics among the three sportsmen. Innocent and bungling though he is, Vassenka has just been with Anna and Vronsky and, being naive and impressionable, has carried some attitudes from one host's house to the other. Thus the relationship between Anna and Vronsky has polluted the purity of Levin's home; Vassenka has become the "worm in the Garden of Eden." Newly married, Levin and Kitty are particularly sensitive to the narrow bounds between lawful and unlawful love. Their irritability on this point shows, not only the depth and intensity of their own love, but an implicit sense of guilt they feel being so happy together. Their attitude implies that married love is too transient and delicate a matter for basing one's life upon it. This foreshadows the moment when Levin finds supreme solace in religion rather than in sensual and material happiness.

Petty and insignificant though the situation may be, Tolstoy uses it as a vehicle — unconsciously or not — to suggest his own strict views of marital conduct. Later in life, especially in the story *The Kreutzer Sonata,* Tolstoy affirms the extreme position that sexual relations between men and women are basically evil. Levin, who considers Kitty "sacred" while she is pregnant, reflects Tolstoy's potential puritanism and rejection of profane love. Vassenka, on the other hand, superficial and unselfconscious, would be willing to effect a liaison with Kitty were she disposed. Usually sympathetic and compassionate towards Anna, Tolstoy here asserts his moralistic viewpoint as he presents, through Vassenka, the possibility — in parody — for another Anna-Vronsky affair.

CHAPTERS 16 to 25

Summary

Dolly keeps her promise to pay Anna a visit. Driving along, she ponders on the problems of married life. She sighs, considering her whole existence is spent either being pregnant or nursing babies, caring always for children and sometimes losing one despite the cares and worries. She wonders why is everyone so against Anna? Anna has someone who loves her, whereas she (Dolly) has a husband who loves others. Thinking of her life if it included a love affair, all sorts of passionate, impossible romances appear to her fancy. "Anna did quite right," Dolly concludes, "at least she is happy and is making another person happy. I certainly have no reproaches for her."

As her carriage approaches the manor house on Vronsky's estate, Dolly meets Anna on horseback with Veslovsky, Sviazhsky, the Princess Varvara (Anna's aunt), and Vronsky. Anna's face lights up as she recognizes Dolly, and Vronsky warmly greets her. Dolly finds everything about Anna brightened by her love; she is now more beautiful than ever.

Admiring the estate, Dolly is impressed by many new buildings. Those are the servants' cottages, Anna explains. She points out the stud farm, the stables, the new park, and "Alexey's newest passion," a brand new, partly constructed hospital Vronsky built for his peasants. Anna brings Dolly into the well appointed nursery, furnished with modern and expensive

English goods. Impressed by the healthy dark-haired little Ani, Dolly remarks how well she crawls, how pretty she looks.

We always have visitors, Anna says. Men need recreation and Alexey needs an audience. "I must make it lively here or Alexey will look for something fresh. That is why I like all this company," explains Anna, partly to apologize for her free-loading aunt, Princess Varvara Oblonsky. When Dolly calls on the old lady, the Princess says she is here to stand by her niece now that everyone else has thrown Anna over. "They live like the best of married couples," says the aunt, "it is for God to judge them, not for us."

Anna suggests a walk before dinner to show Dolly around the estate. Finding herself with Vronsky, Dolly feels ill at ease for she has never liked his proud manners. But as he enthusiastically explains about his building plans, their architectural design, his intentions for the new hospital, Dolly begins to warm toward him and understands the qualities Anna loves. Drawing her out of earshot of their friends, Vronsky begs Dolly to use her influence and persuade Anna to obtain a divorce. We have one child now, he says, and might have others. Yet they legally belong to Karenin: "unless she can obtain a divorce, the children of the woman I love, will belong to someone who hates them and will have nothing to do with them." Deeply moved, Dolly promises to talk to Anna.

Dinner is elegant and well-prepared; Vronsky is responsible for the excellent choice of food and wine. Anna appears in the third gown Dolly has seen her in that day, while Dolly feels ashamed to wear the one good frock she brought along, and that already patched. She is disturbed at the flirtatious exchanges between Anna and Veslovsky, which Vronsky seems to enjoy. Dolly recalls how Levin dismissed Vassenka for the same behavior. The impersonal atmosphere of this everyday, yet elegant, dinner makes Dolly uncomfortable. Her feelings intensify during the after dinner game of lawn tennis which to her has the "unnaturalness of grown-up people playing a child's game in the absence of children." In this idle atmosphere she suddenly misses the maternal cares and worries after only a one day holiday from them.

While Dolly prepares for bed, Anna comes to her for a private talk. She asks what Dolly thinks of her life. Though looking forward to the end of summer when she and Vronsky will be alone together, Anna says everything shows that "he will spend half his time away from home." Dolly advises divorce so Anna and Vronsky can marry and legitimize Ani and future children. When Anna firmly declares "there will be no more children" because she wishes it so, an unheard-of world presents itself to Dolly for the first time. My only ties to Alexey are those of love, continues Anna, and she must always be fresh and lovely to keep his interest. Dolly feels an impassable gulf of questions separate her from Anna, questions they can never agree on and which remain better unspoken.

Divorce would mean she permanently loses Seriozha, Anna explains to Dolly. Loving her son and her lover equally, "but both more than myself," she continues, is an impossible dilemma. "I cannot have them both, and that's the only thing I want... Nothing else matters," Anna concludes.

Filled with pity for Anna's suffering, Dolly sees her own life with renewed charm. She is eager to go home the next morning, while Anna is sad to see her go. She realizes that with Dolly's departure the feelings aroused in her will never be stirred again.

Commentary

The comparison between Dolly and Anna in this section shows the judgment of Tolstoy the moralist who finds a woman's happiness and source of fulfillment is through raising children. He portrays Anna in her luxurious idleness as if she is one of the guests at Vronsky's estate. Implying she is kept as a high class courtesan where everything is arranged according to Vronsky's tastes and interests, Tolstoy shows that even in daily life Vronsky does not include Anna as an integral part of his career. Confronting Anna's insecurity and suffering, Dolly finds her own routine life with her unloving husband preferable to Anna's life of frivolity. Dolly is also shocked that Anna denies the birth of future children. Her wonderment expresses for Tolstoy the decadence and immorality of Anna's relationship with Vronsky

Yet this is what Vronsky demands, although he is unaware of it. Considering himself as a resolute family man, Vronsky tells Dolly he would like to marry Anna and legitimize his children. But Anna is aware he would become bored with her if she became a housewife like Dolly: Dolly is very nice, says Vronsky, but "too much *terre à terre.*" With this understanding, Anna must remain attractive, avoid pregnancy, and live only for her lover. Though she is honored as a married woman, her position is yet that of a courtesan. The hopeless dilemma is complicated by her inability to choose between Seriozha and Vronsky. Since nothing else matters unless she can have them both, Anna can recklessly live a day by day existence. Her new habit of flirting is a guilt acknowledging gesture which exercises the charm that ties her to Vronsky. Tolstoy thus shows how Anna is already on the road to self-destruction. Dolly's departure, representing Anna's leavetaking of her virtuous past, shows her further commitment to the course of decadence and eventual suicide.

CHAPTERS 26 to 32

Summary

Vronsky and Anna live on in the same way and have much to occupy them. Besides reading many novels, Anna studies in architectural and agricultural journals to keep up with Vronsky's interests. Her knowledge and her memory amaze him, and he frequently discusses problems with her and finds her suggestions helpful. Appreciating all she does out of love for him, he nevertheless chafes at the loving snares she holds him in. Were it not for having scenes each time he attends a civic meeting or a race, Vronsky's chosen career as a progressive landowner would satisfy him entirely.

In October occur the nobility elections in the Kashin province where Vronsky's, Sviazhsky's, Koznyshev's, Oblonsky's, and some of Levin's estates are located. Vronsky is amazed how calmly Anna takes the news of his departure. Not daring to question her deeper responses, he leaves for the elections as a gesture of independence and to allay his boredom.

Since September, Levin and Kitty live in Moscow awaiting her confinement. Bored in the city, Levin agrees to accompany Koznyshev to the Kashin elections. This election is particularly important, Koznyshev explains, for the province marshal exercises tremendous power over education, use of public funds, and appointments of trusteeships. It is now necessary to elect a young, up-to-date progressive marshal to further provincial self-government. Kashin, wealthy and in the vanguard of progress, might serve as a model for other provinces to copy.

Levin does not understand the political power wrangles among the noblemen gathered at the assembly, nor does he attach much importance to the debates, speeches, or voting. He is glad to meet the old landowner he met last year at Sviazhsky's and their conversation expresses what Levin's friends would call a reactionary viewpoint. As the two talk of their loyalty to their farms, despite low profit and much work, Levin recognizes that he and this old landowner represent an ancient tradition of land owning that newcomers, like Vronsky, are changing by turning agriculture into an industry. Levin and his friend work more for love than for capital gain.

Sviazhsky draws Levin toward their group of victorious liberals. Unable to avoid meeting Vronsky, Levin speaks to him with unconscious animosity and tactlessness, displaying his total ignorance of the election proceedings. Vronsky is the host of the victorious election party. He has become so interested in provincial politics, and has actively participated in advancing the winning candidate. He even thinks he might run for office himself at the next election. In this happy frame of mind, Vronsky receives a note from Anna, explaining their daughter is ill with pneumonia and she is very worried. Bitterly, Vronsky contrasts the innocent election festivities with the "sombre burdensome love" to which he must return.

Anna has had no peace of mind since Vronsky left her so coldly. She knows he will be displeased to be asked to return home, and Ani is no longer seriously ill. As usual when Vronsky demands his rights to freedom, Anna concludes with the sense of her own humiliation. "He can go where he pleases, while I can not," she thinks. His cold look shows his love is cooling, but even so, their relationship can never change. Only her love and charm can hold him. She quiets these thoughts with morphine each night so she can sleep. Only marriage will guarantee Vronsky's felicity, Anna decides, and writes Karenin for a divorce. Toward November, they move to Moscow and set up house like a married couple. Each day they expect a reply from Karenin, then a divorce.

Commentary

Even while Anna becomes a worthy helpmeet for Vronsky, advancing his interests with her own efforts, he still feels his freedom restricted. His desire to be responsible only to himself, not to her, reflects his basic irresponsibility.

The election proceedings, seen as frivolous through Levin's eyes, underscore Tolstoy's anarchic demand that human beings must seek personal meaning first. Working for the public good is merely an avoidance on the part of political adepts like Koznyshev to face the basic problem of self-fulfillment.

PART 7

CHAPTERS 1 to 12

Summary

Kitty's delivery is long overdue and Levin, despite himself, settles into the expensive routine of Moscow life. He attends concerts, receives and returns pointless social calls, attends the English Club to dine, drink, and even plays some of the idle games his set indulges in. The club atmosphere of luxury, peace, and conviviality makes him even feel friendly toward Vronsky.

Oblonsky convinces Levin to meet his sister Anna who would be glad to see him. Her position is a trying one, Stiva tells him in the carriage, for none of Anna's women friends call on her. Despite her loneliness, she keeps herself occupied. Besides writing a promising children's book, Anna is taking charge of the destitute dependents of Vronsky's English groom who has ruined himself through drink. She is coaching the boy for school and has taken the girl into her house.

Levin's introduction to Anna is through the portrait he sees in the study. He is charmed by the picture of a woman of almost perfect beauty. Seeing Anna, he realizes the artist had caught her qualities, but finds the reality fresher and more seductive, though less dazzling.

Completely won over by Anna, Levin is touched not only by her charm and cultivation and intelligence, but by her deep sincerity.

When he returns home, Kitty flares up in jealousy noting the "peculiar brilliance of his eyes" from his visit with Anna. Kitty says Anna has bewitched him, that he has fallen in love with her. They become finally reconciled after a long talk.

Home alone, Anna wonders how she cannot refrain from wielding her charms on even a married man in love with his wife. The only one unaffected by her seems to be Vronsky and she blames him for lack of sympathy with her suffering. Vronsky returns home late, happy and cheerful from an evening at the club. His face becomes cold and set when Anna scolds him. She tells him she is "near disaster" when he acts so coldly. Alarmed, Vronsky becomes tender but seems to resent the surrender.

Commentary

Anna's "bewitchment" of Levin is further evidence of her perdition and ultimate doom. Confronting Vronsky's coldness, she feels that "side by side with the love that bound them there had grown up some evil spirit of discord" which neither will be able to overcome.

Levin's sympathy for Anna underlines their similar natures, for each seeks a deeper life meaning than that defined by their social milieu. Tolstoy seems to imply that they might have become lovers under different circumstances. But after this brief coincidence of their parallel careers, Levin and Anna pursue different paths. Hers ends in death while Levin discovers the key to life.

60

CHAPTERS 13 to 22

Summary

Early one morning, Kitty wakes her husband to inform Levin that the birth pangs have begun. Panicked, Levin rushes to the doctor, to the pharmacist and wonders why everything seems to move with unbearable slowness while Kitty's life is in danger. Later that evening, his son is born. He is awestruck at the strange way of life of women, seemingly so superior and important to that of men. He feels a sense of apprehension at his son — at this new helpless life coming from nowhere that suddenly asserts itself as part of humanity.

Oblonsky, finding his affairs in a bad way, seeks a more lucrative post. He goes to Petersburg to connect with influential people, especially his brother-in-law Karenin. He intends to speak with Alexey Alexandrovitch about Anna as well as about a new position. When Stiva brings up the matter of divorce, Karenin says he will seek "guidance" and give a final answer in two days. On his way out, Stiva visits with Seriozha. He asks if the child remembers his mother. Blushing, the boy murmurs "No," and leaves the room. Mention of his mother has aroused painful memories which Seriozha always tries to repress.

At one of the parties Stiva attends at Betsy Tverskoy's he learns that Karenin is not only influenced by "that half-witted Lydia Ivanovna" but by a "mystic nobody" named Landau who has been so taken up in Petersburg society that one woman has adopted him as her son. Karenin and the countess do not take a step without seeking the advice of this charlatan. Oblonsky calls on the Countess Lydia Ivanovna to ask her to recommend him among her influential friends. There he meets Karenin and Landau, the mystic. The countess and Alexey Alexandrovitch talk only about their new faith which they assure Stiva is the Sacred Truth. Then Landau goes into a trance, and from this state requests Oblonsky to depart. Stiva receives a note from Karenin the next day, a flat refusal for divorce. He realizes this decision is based on what the Frenchman said in his real or sham trance.

Commentary

Levin's mystical wonderment at the birth of his child and women's destiny contrasts ironically with Karenin's mysticism. Levin is on the way to self-realization while Karenin is at a spiritual decline. His new found religious adherence is a way for him to avoid the pain of his humiliation and to save face. Allowing himself to be guided by the ridiculous mysticism of Landau and by the countess' excessive religiosity Karenin no longer assumes personal responsibility. This new belief offers him an even better way to avoid self-confrontation than that offered by his bureaucratic position.

CHAPTERS 23 to 31

Summary

In the suspended condition of awaiting divorce, Anna and Vronsky find their relationship at a standstill. Both are irritable with each other: Anna feels his love is cooling, Vronsky is reproachful that instead of her trying to ease this position he placed himself in for her sake, Anna makes it harder to bear. Without discussing their problem, each seizes every opportunity to prove the other one wrong. Faced with his declining love, Anna assumes his affections belong to someone else. Her jealousy makes her quarrelsome although Vronsky remains faithful. Despite the bitterness, they enjoy brief moments of tenderness.

Their last quarrel begins when Vronsky puts off their journey back to the country because he must see his mother about some property. Anna refuses to let him go, assuming Vronsky wants to visit the attractive Princess Sorokin who lives with the old countess. "You will be sorry for this," she threatens as Vronsky steps into the carriage. Immediately regretful, Anna dispatches a servant with a note begging Vronsky to come back and talk things over. When the note misses him, she writes a telegram to him at his mother's home, and the suspense of waiting makes her desperate. Anna decides to seek Dolly for comfort and advice. Her thoughts during the drive are bitter and distracted. What a dreary business love is, she thinks. She has lost Seriozha and now Vronsky.

Dolly's hall porter informs Anna that Kitty is here, and she is immediately jealous of Vronsky's former love. Unwilling to meet her at first, Kitty's hostility vanishes when she sees "Anna's dear lovely face" again. The three women chat about the baby until Anna, rising, announces she has come to say good-bye, for they are to leave Moscow soon. Smiling, Anna expresses gladness at having seen Kitty again, she has heard so much about her, even from her husband. "He came to see me and I liked him very much," adds Anna with obvious ill intent. Dolly later remarks she has never seen Anna in "such a strange and irritable mood."

Feeling worse than before, conscious of "having been affronted and rejected" by Kitty, Anna feels that all human relationships are based on hate. At home, she reads a telegram from Vronsky: "I cannot return before ten," She would try to meet him at the railway station, she decides; if he is not there, she would go to his country home. In consequence of the scene there, she vaguely considers, she would take the train along the Nizhny line and stop at the first town she comes to. On the way to the station, her impressions crowd her mind—Kitty, Vronsky's cooled passions, her son. First we were irresistibly drawn together, and now we are irresistibly drawn apart, she thinks. My love grows more passionate and selfish while his is dying. It is not jealousy that makes me hateful but my unsatisfaction. As I demand that he give himself entirely up to me, he wants to get further and further from me. I know he is always faithful, but I want his love, not his kindness inspired by a sense of duty. That is much worse than having him hate me. Where love dies, hate begins. Anna glances at the houses she passes, where live people and "more people, and all hating each other." Would things change if she gained her divorce, Anna wonders, and concludes "No." That would not bring them happiness, just "absence of torment." I cause his unhappiness and he mine, she thinks. "Life is sundering us." Love is transient, but hate is everywhere. She loved Seriozha, but exchanged him for another love and did not complain while this other love satisfied her.

Alighting at the station, Anna takes her place in the corner of the train to avoid other people. A porter brings a note from Vronsky saying he is "very sorry" to miss her note but will return at ten. "No, I won't let you torture me," Anna thinks, her words addressed not to Vronsky but to the "powers that made her suffer." At the next station she walks to the edge of the platform in a daze. As a freight train approaches, Anna ducks her head and hurls herself directly under the wheels of the second car. "And the candle by which she had been reading the book filled with trouble and deceit, sorrow and evil, flared up with a brighter light, illuminating for her everything that before had been enshrouded in darkness, flickered, grew dim, and went out forever."

Commentary

As Anna, in her long soliloquy, traces the career which drives her to suicide, she reaches the same conclusion that Tolstoy mentions in *My Confessions*. "It is possible to live only as long as life intoxicates us;" he writes, "as soon as we are sober again we see that it is all a delusion, a stupid delusion." "Love" is the implicit idea in the term "life intoxication;" when Anna finds her love turned to hate, her life becomes a "stupid delusion" and death provides the only alternative. As spontaneously and naturally as Anna once confronted her love, she now accepts death. Always accepting full responsibility for her actions, Anna's suicide is an affirmation of her deep commitment to life. That death is the final truth of her career is expressed by Tolstoy's analogy of Anna's lighted candle which illuminates her life even while she extinguishes the light.

PART 8

CHAPTERS 1 to 5

Summary

Having recently published a book which was poorly received by the public, Koznyshev devotes his energies to promote the cause of the Serbian War which engages the sympathy of the slavophilic newspapers and the entire nation. After working for this cause throughout the spring and summer, he looks forward to a fortnight's rest at his brother's country estate. Koznyshev and his friend Katavasov take a train almost entirely occupied by a load of volunteers on their way to the front. Vronsky and his mother are at the station. Famous not only for his terrible misfortune of two months ago, the Count is known for volunteering himself and a whole squadron which he personally outfitted for the Serbian War. Chatting with Oblonsky, Koznyshev then goes to greet the Countess Vronsky. She describes her son's condition after Anna's death, how he would not speak for six weeks, and only accepted food when she forced him to eat. Begging him to speak with Vronsky, she says he is still miserable and suffers from a toothache as well.

Koznyshev feels dutybound to acclaim Vronsky for what he is doing for the sake of "all Slavic peoples." Lined with suffering, Vronsky's face has aged and his expression is of stone. Since my life is loathsome to me and useless, he tells Koznyshev, I am willing to waste it in this way as in any other. An approaching switch engine reminds him of his pain, and he tries to recall his best moments with Anna. Memories of his cruel and vindictive love poison his recollections. He can clearly picture the mangled body, with her beautiful head still intact, and the expression on her face as if she repeated that dreadful threat—that he would be sorry—she had uttered in their last quarrel. His face distorted by sobs, Vronsky turns from Koznyshev until he masters himself. At the ringing of the bell, they take their respective places on the train.

Commentary

Fiercely pacifist during the sentimental pan-Slavic fervor which brought Russia into the Serbian war against the Turks, Tolstoy's anti-war views implicitly undercut Vronsky's heroism and self-sacrifice. Thus we see Vronsky's gesture is another surrender to impulses which are basically frivolous. When he explains this is as good a way as any other to waste his useless life, Vronsky admits his self-indulgence. The incident underscores his limited morality. Vronsky thus disappears from the novel, hopelessly seeking a goal in life to replace the void left by Anna's death.

But his pilgrimage is doomed to fail. Finding an excuse in the war gives him a chance to avoid the basic confrontation with death, a confrontation which would be his means of salvation.

CHAPTERS 6 to 19

Summary

Nursing the baby, Kitty reflects on her husband's unceasing search for belief. Since the death of his brother, Levin examined the questions of life and death through reading philosophy and through modern scientific concepts which replaced the religious faith of his childhood. Though these ideas are intellectually interesting, Levin thinks, they provide no guidance for life. Feeling like a man "unprepared for life who must inevitably perish because of it." Levin reads tirelessly, but still finds no explanation. "Without knowing what I am and why I am here, life's impossible," he thinks. If I am just a little "bubble-organism" in the immensity of time and space which lasts a little and then bursts, then life is not just a lie, but the "cruel jest of some evil, hateful power to whom one could not submit." Death is the one way to escape this power, and Levin hides gun and rope for fear of committing suicide.

But he exists happily, he discovers, when he ceases worrying about the meaning of life. Absorbed among the thousand daily tasks of his existence—farming, livestock, his family, his hobbies and shooting and bee-keeping—Levin finds satisfaction, but he does not know why.

On an especially busy day, Levin chats with one of his peasants. Remarking on the differences among people, the old man explains why some extend credit and why other don't. "Some men live for their own wants, nothing else," he says, "while some like Fokanitch (an upright old peasant) live for their soul. He does not forget God." Suddenly inspired, Levin asks how one lives "for his soul?" "Why that's plain enough," answers the worker, "It's living rightly, in God's way. Like yourself, for instance. You wouldn't wrong a man..." Feeling wonderfully illuminated, Levin finds the ideas he struggles with so clear they "blind him with their light." And he has been solving the problem of life's significance all along without having realized it, he thinks. One must live with "the greatest goodness possible," and reason and intellect have merely obscured this simple, natural, irrational truth. In light of the truth of "natural goodness" Levin finds everything clear and simple. He returns home with a joyful heart.

While Kitty, the nurse, and the baby are still walking in the woods, Levin gets drawn, against his will, into an argument with Koznyshev and

Katavasov about the Serbian war. Levin believes that a man would sacrifice himself for the sake of his soul, but not for murder. He does not agree that Russia's entry into the war expresses the "will of the people," since a common peasant, for instance, is interested in his immediate material needs. Changing the subject, Levin observes the gathering storm clouds and suggests they all seek shelter.

At the height of the storm, Levin struggles through the forest to search for Kitty and the baby. He finds them drenched, but safe. Fear and relief having torn him from the world of sophistic argument, Levin feels restored by nature and this atmosphere of family love now that the thundershower has passed.

As he and Kitty stand on the terrace, gazing into the clear night sky, Levin feels at peace. My life will still be the same despite my new realization, he thinks. He will still quarrel with Kitty, scold the coachman, express himself tactlessly, and feel remorse afterwards. Though I am still unable to understand with my reason why I pray, he thinks, I will go on praying. But my life is no longer meaningless as it was before. Now "it has the positive meaning of goodness which I have the power to put into it."

Commentary

Book 8 can be considered, on one level, as Tolstoy's polemic against the Russo-Turkish war which broke out in April, 1877 while he was completing the novel. The author's view was so unpopular at the time that Tolstoy's publisher refused to accept the manuscript even though its tone was softened in two successive versions. Levin expresses Tolstoy's pacifist views, based on the idea that the "general welfare" can be achieved only by the strict observance of "the law of right and wrong which has been revealed to every man." The argument with Koznyshev convinces Levin he must pursue his own moral code despite the views of knowledgeable intellectuals. The imminent thunderstorm—an act of nature—turns his thought from these irritating transient matters to his more meaningful concentration on his family. As a literary device, the storm clears Levin's thoughts, while the same storm—that of the war—is merely a vehicle whereby the other characters avoid self-scrutiny and submerge their individual life quests by repeating of cliches like "fighting for freedom," "brotherhood of all Slavs," "national honor," and "upholding Christian faith."

Though *Anna Karenina* concludes with Levin's salvation, Tolstoy has raised many problems he leaves unanswered, and characters who must still confront unresolved lives. Vronsky is embarked on a course of atonement whose end is uncertain, Karenin remains a pitiable cuckold, and Levin, newly inspired by a love of God, remains at the beginning of a long and difficult career.

ANALYSIS OF PLOT
STRUCTURE AND TECHNIQUE

In the middle of his work on *Anna Karenina,* Tolstoy experienced his own moral "conversion" just as Levin does at the novel's conclusion. This was the time when Russia's greatest artist begins to despise art for being an idle, voluptuous, immoral luxury; where Tolstoy discovered life's significance must be self-denying so that one lives "for one's soul" by loving others in the image of God.

With these anti-art commitments, *Anna Karenina* became a tiresome, repellent work for the author. The novel may never have been completed at all were it not that its serialized publication obliged Tolstoy to fulfill his contract with the publisher. Levin reflects Tolstoy's own moral struggle and the novel progresses according to its author's evolving philosophy.

A. Parallel plot

The complexity and sweep of *Anna Karenina* derives from Tolstoy's use of the double plot. While Anna is the central symbolic figure of the story, Konstantin Levin is its hero. Anna and those around her derive their life experience from the highly developed standards of urban civilization, while Levin is a product of the less rigid, individualistic circumstances that obtain in the country. His values derive from his deep-rooted attachment to his ancestral property, while Anna's depend upon her social role as a high society matron. Despite their opposite backgrounds, both protagonists seek a deeper meaning for life beyond the socially defined restrictions of contemporary society. Primarily, Anna and Levin seek love as their basic fulfillment.

Through the vehicle of their parallel careers, Tolstoy seeks to relate and contrast the opposing values of urban life and country life. This dualism lies at the center of his art. For him, the distinction between city life and life on the land represents the fundamental tension between good and evil, between "the unnatural and inhuman code of urbanity" and the "golden age of pastoral life" (quoting Steiner). Developing *Anna Karenina*

in terms of this duality, Tolstoy investigates two planes of human experience: the personal and the cultural. This allows him not only to provide
insight into the day by day experiences of human beings, but to present a
panorama of Russian life at that time.

B. Anna Karenina as epic

Despite the basic structure of a multiple plot, *Anna Karenina* is essentially amorphic, lacking what Henry James called a "deep-breathing
economy of organic form." Considering, then, the novel as epic prose,
we must analyze its temper by contrasting Tolstoy with Homer, rather than
his contemporaries like Flaubert or James.

Tolstoy's pagan spirit—his sensual immediacy, his primitive attachment to nature—reflects the Homeric more than the Christian spirit. He
himself stated the comparison, remarking of his first works, *Childhood,
Boyhood, Youth,* "Modesty aside, they are something like the *Iliad.*"
Tolstoyan and Homeric epic have these characteristics in common,
writes Steiner:

"the primacy of the senses and of physical gesture; the recognition
that energy and aliveness are, of themselves, holy; the acceptance of a
chain of being extending from brute matter to the stars and along which
men have their apportioned places; deepest of all, an essential sanity...
rather than those dark obliquities in which a genius of a Dostoevsky was
most thoroughly at home."

As an epic intrudes "alien materials" among the main themes without
disturbing the artistic equilibrium, *Anna Karenina* embraces excess details, ignoring novelistic form where particulars must all ramify into the
main theme. "All things live their own life" in the epic, creating the "proper
'finish' and roundedness out of their own integral significance," writes
Steiner. *Anna Karenina* provides many examples of this epic technique.
Vividly describing Laska, Levin's pointer, Tolstoy shows an uncanny
insight into a dog's experience. The detailed childbirth scene, his sensual
awareness of Anna's "beautiful ring-adorned hands," the sympathetic
narrative of Seriozha's daydreams, all testify to this voracious appetite
for sensual experience—his "genuine epic temper" in other words. Minor
characters also live independently, as do minor characters of Homer.
Though Karenin's steward, Korney, for example, appears briefly, we sense
he has a past and future as much as his master has. This reverence of life
for its own sake, not for the sake of the novel, drives Tolstoy to describe
with pagan matter-of-factness whenever his characters dine, sweat, bathe,
or think sublime thoughts. These epic qualities generate the power of
Tolstoyan novels, allowing them to elude the structural bounds which dis-
distinguish the "artistically successful" novel from the more imperfect one.

"The truth is we are not to take *Anna Karenina* as a work of art," Matthew Arnold concluded in a criticism; "we are to take it as a piece of life...and what his novel in this way loses in art it gains in reality." Tolstoyan epic, basically a reflection of life, seems a titanic re-creation of life that stands by itself.

C. Technical devices

What inspires literary historians to classify *Anna Karenina* as a psychological novel is Tolstoy's use of "interior monologue." Each major character, through self-discourse, exposes his inner life by recapitulating his motivations, his previous experiences, his plans for future action. The interior monologue gives verbal definition to the semi-articulate processes of a character's consciousness. Anna's soliloquy as she drives to the place of her suicide is an example of this dramatic device.

By his use of stock epithets and recurrent phrases Tolstoy enables us to distinguish among the confusing number of characters. Anna's "dark curls" and "light step" appear frequently. Stiva's "handsome, ruddy face," Kitty's "truthful eyes," and Karenin's "deliberate, high-pitched voice" provide a few examples of this device. These verbal motifs not only suggest points of association, but provide us with indelible impressions of each person's appearance and character.

Tolstoy uses many symbolic devices throughout the novel, too many to enumerate. A partial list follows: the storm corresponding to the stormy state of one's soul; the symbolic value of the train station; the horse race as a working model of the Anna-Vronsky affair; the symbolism of the ball and the theater; Anna's "drooping eyelids" as the first sign of her witchery; her symbolic state of having a "double soul;" the "little man" of death in Anna's dream which echoes the ill-omened railway accident.

Watch for other symbols as you read. Use the Notes' analysis for a guide as you read the book. Notes are a supplement, not a substitute for the book. The Notes are an aid in the same way that an instructor's lectures are intended to enrich your viewpoint.

ANALYSIS OF THEMES

THEMES

A. Marriage

Containing a discussion of at least three marriages, rather than just one as in *Madame Bovary, Anna Karenina* provides an authoritative and thorough, if not definitive, treatment of the subject.

Stiva's relationship with Dolly suggests the incomplete relationship between Karenin and Anna. The Oblonskys' problems only seem lighter because of the double standard: it is less serious for a husband to stray than for a wife, since family unity depends on the woman. Tolstoy shows us that men's primary interests are outside the home, whereas women, like Dolly, center their existence on the family. Stiva, Vronsky, and Karenin, unlike Levin, divide their lives sharply between their homes and amusements, and they are each startled, through the incidents of the novel, to confront the previously ignored feelings of their wives. The divided pattern of these marriages, moreover, allows the dissatisfied partner to seek outside filfillment of social, emotional, or sexual needs. Anna exemplifies the divided nature of an unfulfilled spouse: during her bout of fever, she admits her affection for Karenin though another part of her soul desires Vronsky. Without solving these marital problems, Tolstoy develops his characters so they adjust to their incomplete relationships. Dolly dotes on her children, Anna gives Seriozha the love she cannot express toward Karenin (conversely lacking deep affection for her love-child Ani), while the husbands commit themselves either to work (like Karenin) or pleasure (like Stiva and Vronsky).

Tolstoy thus depicts the hopeless marriage patterns in urban society. Despite showing the blissful union of Kitty and Levin, Tolstoy ultimately states that marriage, and other sexually-based relationships, weaken the individual's quest for "immanent goodness." He prefigures this later doctrine as the love between Anna and Vronsky deteriorates and by the lighthearted intrusion of Vassenka Veslovsky.

While Tolstoy wrote *Anna Karenina*, however, he still exulted in the success of his own marriage. The result is that Levin and Kitty have the only mutually complete union of the novel. Their marriage is a fulfillment, not a compromise, because Levin's family represents an integral part of his search for essential reality. His outside interests and his love are vehicles which aid him to discover the truth of inner goodness. Because Levin's life is more meaningful than the succession of superficial interests which comprise the lives of Stiva, Vronsky, Karenin, his marriage is more meaningful.

From Tolstoy's scheme of Levin's salvation, we must conclude that women are secondary and not individuated. Since a woman's happiness derives from her family, then the wife of a soul satisfied husband will find emotional satisfaction. Tolstoy seems to say that if either Dolly or Anna loved Levin, they, too, would find personal significance in their marriage.

B. Historical necessity

Although Tolstoy has provided an exhaustive discussion of historic causality in *War and Peace,* his concept of "historical necessity" informs the destiny of characters in *Anna Karenina.* The term expresses the conditions in which human consciousness operates: "necessity" provides the form, "consciousness" provides the content. This is merely to paraphrase the thesis that history describes the dynamics of personality (or culture) responding to environmental challenge.

"Historical necessity" is illustrated in *Anna Karenina* according to the personal destinies of the main characters as they react to changing circumstances. Anna's adultery, for example, provides the necessity — that is, the structure — in which Anna, Vronsky, Karenin must retrench their values to overcome the crisis they face. How they meet the challenge of their situation generates the dynamics of the story. Levin's "necessity," how to come to terms with death, forces him to evolve a personal philosophy — a "moral consciousness" — in order to fulfill his life demands.

The nature of each one's response to his particular challenge, however, is defined by the heredity, education, environment which limits his nature. These factors explain why Vronsky remains selfish and fails in love, why Anna commits suicide, why Karenin succumbs to Lydia Ivanovna's influence, why Kitty cannot be like Varenka.

Historical necessity, therefore, is merely a verbal construct which helps us to explain the context in which human awareness operates. In *War and Peace* Tolstoy gives special attention to the forces of mass consciousness and cultural change. *Anna Karenina,* on a much more intimate level, illustrates the forces which allow individuals to confront challenges. They must, like Levin, overcome the crisis, compromise through stagnation, like Karenin and Vronsky, or succumb through death, like Anna.

C. Minor themes

The minor themes, as well as the major ones, all stem from Tolstoy's single-minded morality. His controversial anti-war views, expressed in Part 8, became formalized among the doctrines of Tolstoyan Christianity. A Christian's first duty, Tolstoy later stated, is to abstain from living by the work of others and from participating in the organized violence of the state. While all forms of violence are evil, any government compulsion shares this taint, since the individual must be free to follow his own inner goodness, seeking for himself what is right and wrong. These as yet unformalized doctrines motivate Levin's disinterest in the "Slavonic question" and make him challenge why Russian soldiers should murder Turks.

Despite Tolstoy's anarchic morality, he believes that God's judgment operates the sanctions of moral law. The Pauline epigraph which appears at the novel's title page expresses this fatalism: "Vengeance is mine and I shall repay, saith the Lord" (Romans, 12:19). In other words, the good character gains reward, the bad one is punished; Levin achieves salvation, Anna finds death. Only God judges, not men, says Tolstoy. Depicting the gossiping members of Anna's social set with pitiless irony as they glory in the scandal, Tolstoy chastises these human judges.

ANALYSIS OF MAIN CHARACTERS

KONSTANTIN LEVIN

Levin, on two levels, represents that part of Tolstoy's duality which defines country life as the environment where one may achieve salvation.

On a historic plane, Konstanin Levin speaks for the educated landowners, the backbone of Russian aristocracy in Tolstoy's terms, who defend the traditional national values. If Russia is to discover her modern destiny in an increasingly westernized world, she must depend on individuals like Levin to maintain a core of national identity. Depending from this source of inner strength, the processes of change and progress will effect a cultural enrichment as Russia carries herself firmly through the flux of history.

On a personal level, Levin represents the individual's quest for the meaning of life. This is where Tolstoy autobiographically records Levin's search. Living each moment with great intensity, Levin finds farming, manual work, his relationship with the peasants, a source of satisfaction. He is essentially a realist, not a mystic, and his sense of identity derives from a sensual, tactual communication with the world. Thus we see his feeling of peace after a day's mowing, and his unrest during political meetings. Though his intense nature seeks definition in love, Levin's ideal of family happiness represents, not only immortality, but his quest for roots and substantiality.

Corresponding to his profound hunger for reality, death is his greatest threat. Levin finds death a cruel joke if a life of suffering and struggle suddenly ceases to exist, like that of his brother Nicolai. In order to live at all, Levin discovers, he must come to terms with non-living. Anchored to life by his new family, he begins a head-on confrontation with death. Death is merely part of life, Levin concludes; if one lives "for one's soul" rather than for illusory self-gratification, the end of life is no longer a cruel trick, but a further revelation of life's truths.

What drives home this truth is Levin's sincere belief in God, for God is the source of goodness immanent in everyone's nature. To live without depending on selfish pleasures in order to feel alive, one must act according to this inner goodness. Thus Levin sublimates his selfish demands for love into a generalized love of being, a love of God. The "intoxication with life" which generates his depth and sensitivity, gives way to a "moral intoxication" (to use the term of James T. Farrell). The novel ends on this note of salvation.

ANNA KARENINA

Anna, the other part of Tolstoy's dual scheme, symbolizes the effects of an urban environment on Tolstoy's "natural man." Like Levin, Anna seeks a personal resolution between spontaneous, unreflecting life and the claims of reason and moral law. Being a woman, however, whose human destiny is to raise children and be mistress of her household, Anna is more victimized by culture and society than her male counterpart and is more sensitive to the social restrictions on her quest for personal meaning. Because she is claimed primarily by her position in an advanced — therefore corrupt — society, Anna is doomed at the outset.

Responding only to her inner emotions, she is the most natural character of all the urban noblemen in the novel. The strength of her inner nature enables Anna to cast off from conventional society and seek love as her basic definition.

Tolstoy makes it obvious that Anna's marriage will never satisfy her passionate nature. Karenin, an outstanding example of an individual dehumanized by sophisticated, rational society, is the first one Anna must reject. She must seek the love of a freer, yet honorable, individual. Presenting her with a military man for lover, Tolstoy develops Anna's tragedy with a cruel logical consistency.

Vronsky's brilliant promise in his career implies he has honor, daring, and a sense of life and death any good soldier requires. Opposed to these good qualities is his limited imagination, the military virtues of sacrificing individuality for a sense of corpsmanship, a frivolous attitude toward women, and his rigid code of behavior according to his military standards of "honor" and "prestige." We see the same values that attract Anna to Vronsky provide limitations which doom their liaison to failure. Tolstoy seems to say that Anna's search for love is hopeless: neither Karenin nor Vronsky have the inner power to respond to her emotional intensity. Had Anna fallen in love with Levin, a possibility Tolstoy presents in Part 7, she would have affirmed her love commitment through her children and husband in Levin's country environment.

The specific machinery of Anna's downfall derives from Tolstoy's basic moral philosophy: unselfish seeking of goodness obtains a state of grace, whereas a predatory self-assertion results in damnation. We see how Anna becomes cruel, vindictive, and self-destroying as she exists according to her single goal—to maintain her love relationship. This becomes harder to maintain as Anna loses, one by one, the outside values of the social order which structure not only her existence, but Vronsky's as well. Shut off from her son, her friends, her protective status, Anna's love provides her with the only source of vitality. Under the pressure to live only through her love, she denies her femininity as the vehicle of bearing children; her charms have become the singular weapon of the witch. Thus we see why Vronsky shrinks from her heightened beauty; it is to her witchlike metamorphosis that Vronsky responds so coldly, driving Anna, in her turn, to a state of jealous desperation which further repels him.

Tolstoy shows how Anna, seeking self-gratification in love, drives herself from salvation, away from God, toward satanism and self-destruction. Unlike Levin who had discovered love of God, Anna's search concludes at the dead end of hate, and death is her only recourse.

COUNT VRONSKY

Implying Vronsky's attractiveness as well as his rigidity, Stiva characterizes him as "a perfect specimen of Petersburg's gilded youth." Despite having intense interests—horse racing, politics, his regiment—Vronsky's life depends on various self-gratifications. He has no inner core of identity as Levin has, for his career depends on winning favors from the "powerful in this world." Though he resigns his commission out of what appears to be his principles and pride, he does so merely to pursue a substitute gratification—his passion for Anna. Vronsky's lack of self-scrutiny means he lacks primary self-responsibility; thus he is incapable of responsibility to others. It is his limited depth which sets up his conflict with Anna. Lacking a sense of personal significance, he cannot make his love significant. At the end of the novel, Vronsky, now realizing his guilt at Anna's death, faces a life made tragic by his own limited nature.

ALEXEY KARENIN

Priding himself on his rational, intellectual nature, Karenin symbolizes the very bureaucracy which governs Russia from its capital seat in St. Petersburg. But institutionalized procedure provides no answer to basic life problems. Tolstoy makes this clear when Karenin faces not only his domestic difficulties, but must directly confront the life conditions of Russia's "native tribes." Tolstoy thus symbolizes Karenin on a personal as well as cultural plane.

Becoming humanized with the emotional release he experiences at Anna's deathbed, Karenin has the opportunity to realize himself through love and Christian truths. But in order to adjust to the society that laughs at a cuckold, Karenin reverts to another form of superficial egoism. Perverting his humanizing insights to embrace a hypocritical mysticism, Karenin saves face but loses his personal significance. His new attachment to Countess Lydia Ivanovna symbolizes his pathetic failure.

KITTY SHTCHERBATSKY

Kitty bears a resemblance to Sonya, Tolstoy's wife, and the courtship scene in Part IV is autobiographical. While Kitty's character lacks the interest of Anna's, she is important as an example of a successful woman. Like Karenin, Kitty once embraced a spiritualistic religion to overcome the humiliation of unrequited love, but then came to accept her feminine destiny. Her womanliness, directed at the goals of family happiness, never descends to the witchlike level of Anna's.

Kitty's ill-timed infatuation for Vronsky serves the dramatic function of allowing her to recognize Levin as her true love. Vronsky's rejection at the height of a significant social event allows Kitty to reject the deceit and illusion of town life and follow Levin into the country.

DOLLY OBLONSKY

Although she is a successful woman, in Tolstoyan terms, Dolly fails to retain her husband's love. Compensating this lack by a redoubled interest in the children, Dolly maintains her equilibrium. After her visit to Anna, she is definitively reassured that living like a "hen with her chicks" provides more meaning to life than an existence based on desperate love.

STIVA OBLONSKY

Stiva seems to typify the corruption of human values that Tolstoy blames on city refinements. His "natural goodness" perverted by a life of pleasure seeking, he fails to appreciate his wife's worth and destroys a significant part of her life. His unwitting powers of destruction are echoed in the incident where he is the tool for devaluation of Russia's forest resources.

Stiva shares many qualities with Anna, though they lack the intensity of her quest for emotional commitment. But it is this very lack which makes Stiva a corruptive influence in the nation and in his intimate circle, while Anna's intensity makes her destroy only herself. Like Anna, Stiva responds to emotions, not conventions, while, by contrast to his sister, his superficiality allows him to satisfy his needs within his social environment.

MINOR CHARACTERS

Anna Karenina provides a catalogue of minor characters, each representing many aspects of Tolstoy's thematic duality, the conflict between urban and country based values. There is not space enough to mention the significance we can attach to each one, and a few suggestions have been previously made, especially referring to Koznyshev, Varenka, Vasenka Veslovsky, Nicolai Levin, and Ryabinin.

REVIEW QUESTIONS AND THEME TOPICS

1. Why do Tolstoy's characters have to come to terms with death in order to understand life? (See "General analysis," commentaries in Part 3.)

2. Discuss Tolstoy's philosophy in terms of the "natural life" of the country and the unnatural life of the city. (See "General analysis" and commentaries in Part 3.)

3. Why does Tolstoy attach equal importance to the everyday occurrences of individual life as to large happenings like war, politics, intellectual currents? (See subsection on "historical necessity" in General analysis; mostly though, you must consider your own impressions of the novel itself.)

4. Try to describe Anna's tragedy in your own words. Consider her career if she remained faithful to Karenin and then consider the rewards of her guilty existence with Vronsky. Is there a right and wrong in her choice of destiny? Does Anna have a choice?

5. What is the significance of the scriptural quotation on the novel's title page: "Vengeance is mine and I will repay, saith the lord."? (See General Analysis.)

6. Consider the ironic significance of the following incidents: Anna's attendance at the theater (Part 5); Dolly's renewed attraction to her own life after she visits Anna (Part 6); the contrasting reactions of Levin and Vronsky to Vassenka Veslovsky (Part 6); the reversed roles of lover and husband while Anna lies ill (Part 4.)

7. If you have read *Madame Bovary,* compare Flaubert's treatment of marriage with Tolstoy's in *Anna Karenina.*

8. Discuss the epic qualities of *Anna Karenina* which made Henry James criticize Tolstoyan novels as "loose and baggy monsters." (See General Analysis.)

9. What is significant about Stiva's sale of the forest property to Ryabinin the speculator? (See Commentary in Part 2.)

10. What is the significance of Anna's deathbed scene? (See commentary in Part 4.)

11. What is the significance of the horse race? (See commentary in Part 2.)

12. What significance do the following characters have in the novel: Koznyshev, Varenka, Betsy Tverskoy, Lydia Ivanovna, the old peasant of Part VII.

13. Discuss Anna's power of fascination and her capacity for cruelty that Kitty suspects in Part 1. (See commentaries in Part 1 and elsewhere.)

14. What characteristics do Anna and Levin share?

15. What characteristics do Vronsky and Karenin share?

SELECTED BIBLIOGRAPHY

James T. Farrell, "Introduction to *Anna Karenina,*" in *Literature and Morality.* New York: Vanguard Press, 1947.

Thomas Mann, "Goethe and Tolstoy," in *Essays of Three Decades;* New York: Alfred A. Knopf, 1948.

Thomas Mann, "Anna Karenina," in *Essays of Three Decades,* New York: Alfred A. Knopf, 1948.

D. S. Merezhkovsky, *Tolstoy as Man and Artist, with an essay on Dostoevsky;* London: 1902.

Earnest J. Simmons, *Leo Tolstoy,* 2 vols. Vintage Press (paperbound division of Random House.)

George Steiner, *Tolstoy or Dostoievsky, an Essay in the Old Criticism;* New York: Alfred A. Knopf, 1959.

Alexandra Tolstoy, *Tolstoy: A Life of my Father;* trans. by E. R. Hapgood; New York: Harper Brothers, 1953.

NOTES

NOTES

NOTES

THE BROTHERS KARAMAZOV

NOTES

including
- *Life and Background*
- *General Plot Summary*
- *List of Characters*
- *Summaries and Commentaries*
- *Character Analyses*
- *Chronological Chart*
- *Review Questions*
- *Selected Bibliography*

by
Gary Carey, M.A.
University of Colorado
and
James L. Roberts, Ph.D.
Department of English
University of Nebraska

NEW EDITION

INCORPORATED

LINCOLN, NEBRASKA   68501

Editor	Consulting Editor
Gary Carey, M.A.	*James L. Roberts, Ph.D.*
University of Colorado	*Department of English*
	University of Nebraska

ISBN 0-8220-0265-5
© Copyright 1967
by
C. K. Hillegass
All Rights Reserved
Printed in U.S.A.

1990 Printing

Cliffs Notes, Inc.   Lincoln, Nebraska

CONTENTS

The Brothers Karamazov Notes

LIFE AND BACKGROUND

Fyodor Mikhailovich Dostoevsky was born of lower-middle-class parents in 1821, the second of seven children, and lived until 1881. His father, an army doctor attached to the staff of a public hospital, was a stern and righteous man while his mother was the opposite — passive, kindly, and generous — and this fact accounts perhaps for Dostoevsky's often filling his novels with characters who seem to possess opposite extremes of character.

Dostoevsky's early education was in an army engineering school, where he was apparently bored with the dull routine and the unimaginative student life. He spent most of his time, therefore, dabbling in literary matters and reading the latest authors; the penchant for literature was obsessive. And, almost as obsessive was Dostoevsky's interest in death, for while the young student was away at school, his father was killed by the serfs on his estate. This sudden and savage murder smouldered within the young Dostoevsky and, when he began to write, the subject of crime, and murder in particular, was present in every new publication; Dostoevsky was never free of the horrors of homicide and even at the end of his life, he chose to write of a violent death — the death of a father — as the basis for his masterpiece, *The Brothers Karamazov*.

After spending two years in the army, Dostoevsky launched his literary career with *Poor Folk*, a novel which was an immediate and popular success and one highly acclaimed by the critics. Never before had a Russian author so thoroughly examined the psychological complexity of man's inner feelings and the intricate workings of the mind.

Following *Poor Folk*, Dostoevsky's only important novel for many years was *The Double*, a short work dealing with a split personality and containing the genesis of a later masterpiece, *Crime and Punishment*.

Perhaps the most crucial years of Dostoevsky's melodramatic life occurred soon after the publication of *Poor Folk*. These years included some of the most active, changing phases in all of Russian history and Dostoevsky had an unusually active role in this era of change. Using influences acquired with his literary achievements, he became involved in political intrigues of quite questionable natures. He was, for example, deeply influenced by new and radical ideas entering Russia from the West and soon became affiliated with those who hoped to revolutionize Russia with all sorts of Western reforms. The many articles Dostoevsky wrote, concerning the various political questions, he published knowing full well that they were illegal and that all printing was to be controlled and censored by the government.

The rebel-writer and his friends were, of course, soon deemed treasonous revolutionaries and placed in prison and, after nine months, a number of them, including Dostoevsky, were tried, found guilty, and condemned to be shot by a firing squad.

The entire group was accordingly assembled, all preparations were completed, and the victims were tied and blindfolded. Then, seconds before the shots were to be fired, a messenger from the Tsar arrived. A reprieve had been granted. Actually the Tsar had never intended that the men were to be shot; he merely used this sadistic method to teach Dostoevsky and his friends a lesson. This soul-shaking, harrowing encounter with death, however, created a never-to-be forgotten impression on Dostoevsky; it haunted him for the rest of his life.

After the commutation of the death sentence, Dostoevsky was sent to Siberia and during the years there, he changed his entire outlook on life. During this time, amidst horrible living conditions – stench, ugliness, hardened criminals, and filth – he began to re-examine his values. There was total change within the man. He experienced his first epileptic seizure and he began to reject a heretofore blind acceptance of new ideas which Russia was absorbing. He underwent a spiritual regeneration so profound that he emerged with a prophetic belief in the sacred mission of the Russian people. He believed that the salvation of the world was in the hands of the Russian folk and that eventually Russia would rise to dominate the world. It was also in prison that Dostoevsky formulated his well-known theories about the necessity of suffering. Suffering became the means by which man's soul is purified; it expiated sin; it became man's sole means of salvation.

When Dostoevsky left Siberia, he resumed his literary career and soon became one of the great spokesmen of Russia. Then, in 1866, he published his first masterpiece, *Crime and Punishment*. The novel is the story of Raskolnikov, a university student who commits a senseless murder to test his moral and metaphysical theories concerning the freedom of the will. The novel exhibits all the brilliant psychological analyses of character for which Dostoevsky was to become famous and incorporates the theme of redemption through suffering.

Most of Dostoevsky's adult life was plagued with marital problems, epileptic seizures and, most of all, by creditors. Often he had to compose novels at top speed in order to pay his many mounting debts, but by the end of his life, he was sufficiently free of worry so that he was able to devote all his energy to the composition of *The Brothers Karamazov* and at his death, only a year after the publication of this masterwork, he was universally acknowledged to be one of Russia's greatest writers.

GENERAL PLOT SUMMARY

By his first wife, Fyodor Karamazov sired one son — Dmitri — and by his second wife, two sons — Ivan and Alyosha. None of the Karamazov boys, however, was reared in the family home. Their mothers dead and their father a drunken fornicator, they were parceled out to various relatives. Fyodor could not have been more grateful; he could devote all energy and time to his notorious orgies. Those were the early years.

Dmitri comes of age, as the novel opens, and asks his father for an inheritance which, he has long been told, his mother left him. His request is scoffed at. Old Karamazov feigns ignorance of any mythical monies or properties that are rightfully Dmitri's. The matter is far from ended, though, for Dmitri and his father find themselves instinctive enemies and besides quarreling over the inheritance, they vie for Grushenka, a woman of questionable reputation. Finally it is suggested that if there is to be peace in the Karamazov household that the family must go together to the monastery and allow Alyosha's elder, Father Zossima, to arbitrate and resolve the quarrels. Ivan, Karamazov's intellectual son, accompanies them to the meeting.

At the monastery there seems to be little hope for a successful reconciliation. Fyodor parades his usual disgusting vulgarities, makes a dreadful scene, and when Dmitri arrives late, he accuses his son of all sorts of degeneracy. Dmitri then retorts that his father has tried to lure Grushenka into a liaison by promising her 3,000 rubles, and in the midst of their shouting, Father Zossima bows and kisses Dmitri's feet. This act ends the interview. All are shocked into silence. Later, old Karamazov recovers from his astonishment and once again he makes a disgraceful scene in the dining room of the Father Superior. He then leaves the monastery and commands Alyosha to leave also.

It is now that Dostoevsky reveals that Karamazov perhaps has fathered another son. Years ago, a raggle-taggle moron girl who roamed the town was seduced and bore a child; everyone, naturally, assumed that the satyr-like Karamazov was responsible. The child grew up to be an epileptic and now cooks for Karamazov. He is a strange sort, this Smerdyakov, and lately his epileptic seizures have become more frequent. Curiously, he enjoys talking philosophy with Ivan.

The day after the explosive scene in the monastery, Alyosha comes to visit his father and is stopped midway by Dmitri. The emotional, impulsive Karamazov son explains to Alyosha that he is sick with grief — that some time ago, he became engaged to a girl named Katerina, and has recently borrowed 3,000 rubles from her to finance an orgy with Grushenka. He pleads for Alyosha to speak to Katerina, to break the engagement, and to help him find some way to repay the squandered money so that he can feel free to elope with Grushenka. Alyosha promises to help if he is able.

The young man reaches his father's house and finds more confusion: Smerdyakov is loudly arguing with another servant about religion, spouting many of Ivan's ideas. Later, when the servants are ordered away, Karamazov taunts Ivan and Alyosha about God and immortality, and Ivan answers that he believes in neither. Alyosha quietly affirms the existence of both. Dmitri then bursts into the room crying for Grushenka and when he cannot find her, attacks his father and threatens to kill him.

Alyosha tends his father's wounds, then goes back to the monastery for the night. The next day he goes to see Katerina, as he promised Dmitri, and tries to convince her that she and Ivan love each other and that she should not concern herself with Dmitri and his problems. He is unsuccessful.

Later that same day, Alyosha comes upon Ivan in a restaurant, and they continue the conversation about God and immortality that they began at their father's house. Ivan says that he cannot accept a world in which God allows so many innocent people to suffer and Alyosha says that, although Ivan cannot comprehend the logic of God, there is One who can comprehend all: Jesus. Ivan then explains, with his poem "The Grand Inquisitor," that Jesus is neither a ready nor an easy answer-all for his questionings—that He placed an intolerable burden on man by giving him total freedom of choice.

When Alyosha returns to the monastery, he finds Father Zossima near death. The elder rallies a bit and lives long enough to expound his religious beliefs to his small audience, stressing, above all, a life of simplicity, a life in which every man shall love all people and all things, and shall refrain from condemning others. This is Zossima's final wisdom and when he finishes, he dies.

Next day many people gather to view the holy man's corpse, for popular rumor has whispered for years that upon Zossima's death, a miracle would occur. No miracle occurs, however. Instead, a foul and putrid odor fills the room and all of the mourners are horrified. Even Alyosha questions God's justice and, momentarily yielding to temptation, he flees to Grushenka's house. But after he has talked with the girl, he discovers that she is not the sinful woman he sought; she is remarkably sensitive and quite understanding and compassionate. Alyosha's faith is restored and, later, in a dream of Jesus' coming to the wedding of Cana, he realizes that life is meant to be joyously shared. Now he is absolutely certain of his faith in God and in immortality.

Dmitri has meanwhile been frantically searching for a way to raise the money to repay Katerina. He has even gone to a neighboring town to try and borrow the sum, but even there he fails. Returning, he discovers that Grushenka is no longer at home and panics, sure that she has succumbed to Fyodor's rubles. He goes first to his father's house; then, after discovering that she is not there, he tries to escape but is cornered by an old servant. He strikes him aside, leaving him bloody and unconscious, and returns to Grushenka's house. He demands to know her whereabouts and at last he is told that she has gone to join a former lover, one who deserted her five years before.

Dmitri makes a final decision: he will see Grushenka once more, for the last time, then kill himself. He travels to the couple's rendezvous, finds Grushenka celebrating with her lover, and joins them. There is resentment and arguing, and finally Grushenka is convinced that her former lover is a scoundrel and that it is Dmitri whom she really loves. The two lovers are not to be reunited, however, for the police arrive and accuse Dmitri of murdering his father. Both are stunned by the circumstantial evidence, for the accusation is weighty. Dmitri indeed seems guilty and is indicted to stand trial.

Alyosha, in the meantime, has made friends with a young schoolboy, the son of a man brutally beaten by Dmitri in a rage of passion and gradually the youth has proven his sincere desire to help the frightened, avenging boy. Now that the youngster is dying, Alyosha remains at his bedside, where he hopes to help the family and also to reconcile the young boy with many of his schoolmates.

Ivan, the intellectual, has neither the romantic passion of Dmitri nor the wide, spiritual interests of Alyosha, and when he learns of his father's murder, he broods, then decides to discuss his theories with Smerdyakov. He is astonished at the bastard servant's open confession that he is responsible for the murder. But Smerdyakov is clever; he disavows total responsibility and maintains that Ivan gave him the intellectual and moral justification for the murder and, furthermore, that he actually permitted the act by leaving town so that Smerdyakov would be free to accomplish the deed. Ivan is slow to accept the argument but after he does, he is absolutely convinced of Smerdyakov's logic. The transition is disastrous. His newfound guilt makes him a madman and the night before Dmitri's trial, he is devoured with burning brain fever. That same night Smerdyakov commits suicide. Dmitri's situation becomes increasingly perilous.

During the trial, the circumstantial evidence is presented in so thorough a manner that Dmitri is logically convicted as Fyodor's murderer. He has the motive, the passion, and was at the scene of the crime. Perhaps the most damning bit of evidence, however, is presented by Katerina. She shows the court a letter of Dmitri's in which he says that he fears that he might be driven to murder his father.

After the conviction, Dmitri agrees to certain plans for his escape but says that it will be great torture and suffering for him to flee from Mother Russia, from Russian soil, and to live in exile.

As for Alyosha, his future holds the promise of hope and goodness (qualities that were once never associated with the Karamazovs), for after young Ilusha dies and all his schoolmates attend the funeral, Alyosha gathers them together and deeply impresses them with his explanation of love and of friendship. Spontaneously, the boys rise and cheer Alyosha and his wisdom.

LIST OF CHARACTERS

KARAMAZOV FAMILY

Fyodor Pavlovitch Karamazov

The father, who is a cynical, immoral, and depraved sensualist dedicated only to the fulfillment of his carnal desires.

Dmitri (Mitya)

His oldest son, who develops an intense hatred for his father and who is convicted of murdering him.

Ivan

The second son, who develops into the extreme intellectual and who questions all values of life.

Alyosha (Alexey)

The youngest son, who is deeply religious and who functions as the central figure in the novel.

Smerdyakov (Pavel Fyodorovitch Smerdyakov)

Old Karamazov's illegitimate son, whose last name was assigned to him by Fyodor and whose first names were merely adopted. He grows up in the Karamazov house as a servant.

Adelaida

Karamazov's first wife and the mother of Dmitri.

Sofya

Karamazov's second wife and the mother of Ivan and Alyosha.

OTHER CHARACTERS

Andrey

The driver who takes Dmitri to his meeting with Grushenka in Mokroe.

Trifon Borissovitch

The innkeeper at Mokroe who testifies that Dmitri spent all of the three thousand rubles during his orgy.

Fenya

Grushenka's maid, who lies to Dmitri about Grushenka's whereabouts.

Father Ferapont

The acetic and deranged monk who is a bitter opponent to Father Zossima.

Fetyukovitch

The brilliant defense attorney brought in from Moscow to defend Dmitri.

Gorstkin (also known as Lyagavy)

The merchant who is interested in buying some property belonging to Karamazov.

Grigory Vassilyevitch

The old Karamazov servant who takes care of the children and who adopts Smerdyakov.

Grushenka (Agrafena Alexandrovna)

The lady of so-called loose morals who attracts the attentions and consequent jealousies of Dmitri and Fyodor.

Herzenstube

The old town doctor who gives favorable testimony in Dmitri's behalf.

Madame Hohlakov

The wealthy widow at whose house many of the scenes of the novel take place.

Lise

Madame Hohlakov's young daughter, who becomes engaged to Alyosha and then capriciously breaks the engagement.

Ilusha

The young boy whose illness brings all of his friends together with Alyosha.

Father Iosif (Joseph)

The librarian at the monastery.

Kalganov (Pyotr Fomitch Kalganov)

A casual friend who is present at Dmitri's party in Mokroe.

Katerina (Katya) Ivanovna

Dmitri's fiancée, whom he deserts upon falling in love with Grushenka.

Ippolit Kirillovitch

The public prosecutor who conducts the trial against Dmitri.

Kolya (Nikolay Ivanovitch Krassotkin)

The young boy who influences the other boys and becomes Alyosha's disciple.

Madame Krassotkin (Anna Fyodorovna)

Kolya's doting and widowed mother.

Lizaveta Smerdyastchaya

The town's deformed idiot, who is seduced by Karamazov and then gives birth to Smerdyakov.

Lyagavy

See *Gorstkin.*

Makarov (Mihail Makarovitch Makarov)

The district police inspector who questions Dmitri about the murder

Marfa Ignatyevna

Grigory's wife and another of the Karamazov servants.

Marya Kondratyevna

The daughter of Dmitri's landlady who is in love with Smerdyakov.

Maximov

An old destitute landowner who lives off the generosity of others especially Grushenka, in the closing chapters of the novel.

Miusov (Pyotr Alexandrovitch Miusov)

A cousin of Karamazov's first wife, who was instrumental in having Dmitri taken away from Fyodor.

Mussyalovitch

Grushenka's ex-lover, whose return precipitated Dmitri's strange behavior on the night of the murder.

Father Paissy

The learned theologian and devoted friend of Father Zossima who tries to console Alyosha.

Pyotr Ilyitch Perhotin

The young civil servant from whom Dmitri borrowed money on the night of the murder.

Mihail Ospovitch Rakitin

A young seminarian who professes to have very liberal and advanced ideas and who betrays his friendship with Alyosha.

Samsonov (Kuzma Samsonov)

A wealthy landowner who befriended Grushenka.

Captain Snegiryov

Ilusha's father, who is destitute and broken by misfortunes. He was attacked by Dmitri one night because he earned money from Fyodor.

Varvinsky

A district doctor who testifies as to Dmitri's mental condition.

Vrublevsky

Mussyalovitch's companion on the night of the orgy in Mokroe.

Father Zossima

The revered elder at the monastery and the spiritual guardian for Alyosha, whose teachings become central to all the ideas in the novel.

SUMMARIES AND COMMENTARIES

PART ONE

BOOK I

Summary

Karamazov: the name is well-known in Russia; it carries a taste of violence and dark Slavic passion. And there is much truth in the rumors and whispered tales told of Fyodor Karamazov. In his youth he was a loud profligate. His drinking and high living were notorious; he seemed insatiate. And marriage did not tame him. His marriage, true to form, was scandalous. But initially it was not scandalous because of its melodramatic elements — that was to be expected; life with Karamozov could not be otherwise. Initially, Karamazov's marriage was scandalous because it was romantic: he was penniless yet he wooed and married an heiress.

Adelaida Ivanovna believed in her young rebel-husband. Perhaps his spirit was bold and irrepressible, but he was the new breed of liberal Russian manhood. She believed it firmly. She tried to believe it for a long time. Then she was forced to face the ugly reality that instead of a rich-blooded idealist she had married an opportunist who was physically cruel and usually drunk. She also was forced to face another unpleasant truth: she was pregnant. She bore the baby, a son — Dmitri, or Mitya as she often called him — and when she could no longer endure her husband's viciousness, she abandoned both her son and husband and eloped with a young student.

Karamazov, ostensibly, was staggered by her rejection and, still the overly dramatic sort, like a loud tragedian he spent many of his days driving through the country, lamenting over his wife's desertion. But even that pose grew wearisome and soon he returned to his life of debauchery. When he received the news of Adelaida's death he was in the midst of a drunken orgy.

Young Dmitri was neglected and finally taken in by a cousin and when the cousin tired of him the child was given to other relatives; thus the baby grew up with a variety of families. But he was always told about his real father, that the man still lived, and that he held a rather large piece of Adelaida's property that was rightfully Dmitri's. The boy never forgot these tales of land and money and when he reached maturity, he visited his father and asked about the inheritance. He was unable, of course, to get any information from the old man but he began receiving small sums of money and, convinced that the property did exist, he revisited his father. Again the old man evaded his son's questions.

But if Karamazov was able to evade Dmitri, he could not evade other matters so successfully — the problems of his other sons, for example. For after the four-year-old Dmitri was taken away, Karamazov married a second time. This wife, Sofya Ivanovna, was remarkably beautiful and her loveliness and her innocence attracted the lustful Karamazov. He convinced her to elope with him against her guardian's wishes and quickly took advantage of her meekness. He began having loose women in the house and even carried on orgies of debauchery in her presence.

During Karamazov's years of cruelty and depravity, Sofya Ivanovna gave birth to two sons, Ivan and Alyosha. But she was not well and did not feel loved despite the attentions of old Grigory, the servant who did his best to comfort her and protect her from Karamazov. In spite of his care, she soon fell ill and died. When her former guardian heard about her death, she came and took the two boys, Ivan and Alyosha, with her and upon her own death she left a thousand rubles to each boy for his education.

Ivan Karamazov developed into a brilliant student who helped support himself by writing for journals and he slowly began to make a name for himself in literary circles. One of his articles, for instance, dealt with the function of the ecclesiastical courts; it attracted widespread interest and even the monastery in his native town spoke of it. Alyosha, the youngest Karamazov, developed into a devoutly religious person, his faith based on reality and untinged by mysticism or fanaticism. He was universally well liked, never criticized anyone, and seemed to love everyone.

As the action of the novel begins, Alyosha returns to his father's house and meets his brothers. He and Dmitri rapidly become good friends, but he feels puzzled by Ivan's reserve and intellectuality. As for his father, Alyosha openly loves him; he has never criticized or condemned his father's way of life. Alyosha has always been generous and forgiving, thus it was that Karamazov was not surprised when Alyosha first told him that he wanted to become a monk, the disciple of the renowned elder, Zossima. In those days, incidentally, an elder was often controversial. "An elder," it was said, "was one who took your soul, your will, into his soul and his will." But elder, by also setting exemplary models of holiness in their own lives, often attracted large numbers of followers.

The Karamazovs are reunited and the reason for their reunion deeply concerns Alyosha. The discord between Dmitri and his father has reached such a point that one of them, apparently the father, has suggested a meeting in Father Zossima's cell, where they can discuss differences under the conciliating influence of the elder. Alyosha, who understands his brothers and his father better than most people think, greatly fears the meeting.

Commentary

The Brothers Karamazov is often considered one of the world's most complex novels. Dostoevsky examines many different facets of life, investigates many problems of lasting importance, and is able to do so successfully in this novel because the mere size and bulk of the book allows him to proceed with deliberate slowness in introducing and in developing his ideas. Attempting in these Commentaries, however, to isolate some of the main ideas and to analyze them, destroys the essential unity of the novel. Part of its greatness is the manner in which Dostoevsky is able to integrate all the divergent elements into one unified whole. Each idea borders upon another and is somewhat vitiated when isolated from the remainder of the novel.

In the complex spirit of the novel and in the leisurely nineteenth-century fashion of giving the intricate background of the main characters, Dostoevsky begins his book, then immediately establishes its tone. He first announces the element of mystery in the novel—the "gloomy and tragic death" of Karamazov—then begins defining the elements of tragedy—especially, the Karamazov tragedy.

The older Karamazov is depicted as base, vulgar, ill-natured, and completely degraded and his "tragic" death will be revealed to be tragic only because his sons are implicated in the death—not because Karamazov himself arouses tragic emotion. In fact, in the trial scene later in the book, it is pointed out that the murder is not a parricide in the truest sense because Fyodor Karamazov never has functioned as a proper father. And, to support this idea, Dostoevsky begins at the very outset of the novel to show the blackness and vulgarity of the man who is to be murdered.

To emphasize the monster within Karamazov, Dostoevsky illustrates the lack of any paternal instincts. Karamazov did not discard his children from hatred or malice; he simply forgot about their existence. Furthermore, he was pleased each time that strangers came and took the children and therefore released him from responsibility; this allowed him to devote all his energy to his various orgies. One of Dostoevsky's ideas, prominent throughout the novel, then, concerns the place of the child in society and this theme receives its first expression in the chapter dealing with Fyodor Karamazov's treatment of his children.

In Chapter 2, Dostoevsky tells us that Dmitri "was the only one of Fyodor Pavlovitch's three sons who grew up in the belief that he had property and that he would be independent on coming of age." This idea is established early in the novel because it becomes the source of the antagonism existing between father and son. Dostoevsky carefully avoids making a direct statement about the full extent to which the father has cheated his son, but by the manner in which he arranges his descriptions of the father, we can assume that Fyodor has indeed cheated Dmitri out of a major portion of the inheritance. It is also noteworthy that of the three sons Dmitri is the only one whom the father intensely dislikes. This is easily explained: the other two sons make no financial demands upon the father; only Dmitri insists upon having his inheritance.

Following his thorough characterization of the older Karamazov, Dostoevsky devotes the next several chapters to the offspring—the brothers Karamazov, as different from one another as can be imagined.

Dmitri, throughout the novel, develops into the extreme sensualist, the emotional son. He did not complete his education; instead, he worked his way up through the military ranks to become an officer. He lacked discipline, however, and soon became involved in a duel and was demoted. Later he gained promotion again. But his deeds and emotions are fluid and fluctuating. He has, for instance, an instinctive dislike for his father but forms an immediate friendship with his brother Alyosha. He is the fiery-hearted, fierce, and emotional person who is easily swayed by his feelings.

Ivan, on the other hand, is the cold intellectual. At an early age he developed his propensity for study and his unusual aptitude for learning. He is the very proud son, always conscious that his early training was at someone else's expense. He began, therefore, as soon as possible, to write reviews in order to support himself, and before arriving in his native town, he has published a widely read, widely discussed article about the ecclesiastical courts. This article is the subject of a conversation in the next book between the monks and Ivan.

In contrast to his two brothers, Alyosha has none of Ivan's pride, nor is he as fiery as Dmitri. He is "simply an early lover of humanity," one who always tries to see the best side of everyone. He possesses an implicit trust in all people and, in all his relationships, he never judges others. Beneath his modest exterior, however, is a penetrating and understanding mind that detects many subtleties and distinctions. Alyosha is of course deeply religious but he is not the fanatical sort who bases his faith upon miracles. He is the complete realist who arrived at his beliefs concerning immortality and God through reasoning.

While presenting the characteristics of the three Karamazov sons, Dostoevsky introduces another principal theme — the conflict between faith and disbelief. Alyosha and Ivan represent the two opposite poles of acceptance and it is only natural that they do not become intimate friends at first. Alyosha, however, is perceptive enough to understand Ivan's problem. He knows that "Ivan was absorbed in something — something inward and important that he was striving toward, some goal, perhaps very hard to attain and that was why he had no thought for him." Looking forward, we realize that Ivan will forever struggle with the idea of belief and immortality and that this struggle will form one of the most dramatic sections of the novel. In contrast, Dmitri will slowly become a person of faith. He and Alyosha, consequently, become intimate friends from the very beginning.

In all his writing, Dostoevsky was interested in the psychology of actions. Particularly he was interested in the nature of contradictory actions. Many of his characters therefore perform actions that do not seem consistent with their personalities. Dostoevsky often investigates this idea in an attempt to understand why a person who acts in a certain manner will often perform an action that seemingly contradicts his nature. In the character of the father, for example, he shows Fyodor visiting the grave of his first wife and being so touched by her memory that he gives a thousand rubles to the monastery for requiems. For a man usually so miserly with money and not professing a belief in God, this action is strange and contradictory. Dostoevsky comments that "strange impulses of sudden feeling and sudden thought are common in such types." Later he also writes that Fyodor "was wicked and sentimental," and, even though the question of contradictory actions is never solved by Dostoevsky, it does occupy portions of the novel and the reader should be aware of the investigation.

The introduction of Zossima concludes the first book, the brief introduction being a transitional device. Zossima, one should be aware, will hold stage center in the following section. His role is important because he is antithetical to all but one of the vigorous Karamazov clan. He is a passive sort, yet he influences the decisive actions of Alyosha and thus influences the course of the novel. Dostoevsky attempts, in the character of the elder, to present the almost perfect person, and his characterization is convincing. So convincing, in fact, is it to Alyosha that his beliefs are shaken at Zossima's death. He has convinced himself that after the elder's death Zossima would bring extraordinary glory to the monastery. Death is rarely that simple. The fact that Zossima decomposes so rapidly weighs heavily on Alyosha and he is tempted to question, therefore, the validity of God's justice.

Summary

On the day scheduled for the meeting between the Karamazovs and the elder, Zossima, Fyodor and Ivan arrive accompanied by a former guardian of Dmitri's, Miusov, and a relative of Miusov's, Kalganov. Dmitri Karamazov, however, is not at the monastery and all wonder, naturally, if he will come; he was certainly notified only the previous day. The meeting takes on a certain air of mystery.

A very old monk emerges, greets the guests, then leads them to Father Zossima's cell. All are invited to have lunch with the Father Superior following the interview, he says. First, however, they must wait for Zossima.

The wait, though not long, seems interminable for Miusov. Uncontrollably, he finds himself growing increasingly irritated at the crude jokes that Fyodor Karamazov unleashes concerning the monastic life.

Father Zossima at last arrives, accompanied by Alyosha, two other monks, and Rakitin, a divinity student living under the protection of the monastery. The monks bow and kiss Zossima's hand and receive his blessings; the guests, however, merely bow politely to the elder. Deeply embarrassed by his family's austerity, Alyosha trembles. Now, more than ever, he fears that the meeting will be calamitous.

Karamazov apologizes for Dmitri's absence, then nervously begins a non-stop monolog of coarse anecdotes. At this, Alyosha is even more deeply embarrassed; in fact, everyone except the elder is distressed. The tension mounts and when Karamazov falls climactically to his knees and begs the elder, "what must I do to gain eternal life?" it is difficult to tell whether or not he is still playing the loud-mouth clown. No one but Zossima dares speak. The elder tells Karamazov that he must cease lying and, above all, he must cease lying to himself. At first, Fyodor is impressed by the advice but then resumes his joking and clowning until Zossima excuses himself. He must meet with an assembly of people outside the monastery.

The group outside are all peasant women — all but two. At one side, in a section reserved for the wealthy, are Madame Hohlakov and her partially paralyzed daughter, Lise, waiting to be blessed by the elder and to receive his advice on their problems. Zossima moves among the peasant women listening to their problems and offering them advice, emphasizing always the healing effect of the love of God. "Love is such a priceless treasure," he says, "that you can redeem the world by it and expiate not only your own sins but the sins of others."

Madame Hohlakov confesses to Zossima that, for her part, she suffers from a lack of faith; she can grasp neither the Christian idea of immortality nor any type of life beyond the grave. She says furthermore that if she does a charitable act that she wants to receive thanks and praise for it. Zossima tells her that if she practices active, honest love that she will grow to understand the reality of God and the immortality of her soul. "Attain to perfect self-forgetfulness in the love of your neighbor," he counsels her, "then you will believe without doubt." Ending the interview, he promises her that he will send Alyosha to visit Lise.

Commentary

Book II is largely devoted to a study of Zossima and his teachings. This saintly ascetic influences all of Alyosha's actions and to thoroughly understand this youngest member of the Karamazov clan, one must understand the man to whom he zealously attaches himself.

Zossima seems to have come to terms with life; he lives with perfect contentment and understanding—basically, a quiet and reserved man. He is not, for instance, visibly disturbed by Fyodor Karamazov's buffoonery; his quiet mien allows him to see deeply into the personality of Karamazov—of any person with whom he speaks. With Karamazov, he knows that the old man is intentionally trying to overact, to clown and, later, with Madame Hohlakov, he knows that she makes her confession in order to gain his personal approbation for her frankness. A large part of Father Zossima's greatness, therefore, is this perceptive understanding of mankind, his comprehension of the psychological factors and motivations that prompt human actions; his advice is therefore unusually sound.

Zossima's dignity is unique and, coupled with his extreme humility, most readily impresses a visitor. Alyosha, in contrast, is embarrassed when the Karamazovs do not ask for the elder's blessing, but Zossima shows no outward concern. He merely asks his guests to conduct themselves naturally and to be comfortable; their lack of reverence and discretion in no way offends him. His wisdom encompasses all aspects of life.

In general, Zossima's philosophy is based on the positive rather than on the negative. This is not immediately evident, however, for he tells Karamazov, in terms of negatives, to avoid drunkenness and incontinence, to defy sensual lust, and to realistically value the ruble. But Zossima also offers Karamazov a thoroughly positive view of living, the very simplicity of which should not mislead the reader into thinking that Dostoevsky is being oversimple. Extreme simplicity, in fact, is the key to Zossima's way of life. His is a philosophy founded on a simplicity so basic that it consists of only two concepts: the value of loving and the value of being honest and respecting oneself.

Zossima tells Fyodor, "Above all, don't lie to yourself. The man who lies to himself and listens to his own lie eventually comes to such a pass that he neither distinguishes the truth within him nor around him and so loses all respect for himself and for others." Later, he tells Madame Hohlakov that she cannot be helped so long as she speaks only to impress. "Above all," he says to her, "avoid falsehood, every kind of falsehood, especially to yourself." Zossima is convinced that if man is completely honest with himself, he can evaluate the evils within himself and overcome all such propensities, but when a person is dishonest, he is unable to detect good and righteous impulses; as a consequence, such a man ceases to have any respect for himself and begins, like Karamazov, to play the part of a ridiculous clown. In time such a man will lose all dignity. He will be of no value to himself or to others.

The high premium Zossima places on love is at the heart of this philosophy concerning honesty. When a person ceases to respect himself, he also ceases to love; he "sinks to bestiality in passions and coarse pleasures." Only through love, Zossima believes, can man gain the much-sought-after peace that makes life vibrant. This is essentially Zossima's message to the peasant women. He sends them home with the admonition that "love is such a priceless treasure that you can redeem the whole world by it and expiate not only your own sins but the sins of others." To Madame Hohlakov, who has trouble understanding the concept of immortality, he says, "by the experience of active love" man can be convinced of an afterlife — "strive to love your neighbor actively and indefatigably. In as far as you advance in love you will grow surer of the reality of God and of the immortality of your soul." If a person, he concludes, devotes himself completely to love — love of God, love of the individual – then that man can learn to believe in immortality without doubts.

While such summary statements of Zossima's views seem, on the surface, to be simple, they echo in a large degree the teachings of Jesus and the concepts by which Alyosha tries to live. Throughout the remainder of the novel, Alyosha attempts to practice Zossima's concept of love; he responds lovingly to every character and possesses no animosity for any – not for the small children who ridicule him nor even for Lise, who delights in tormenting him. Moreover, Zossima knows that Alyosha is the one person who can put into practice all of his teachings. And, as the elder sees that Katerina has sent a note for Alyosha and that Lise needs him to come visit her, it is such requests as these that support his decision to send Alyosha to live in the world rather than in the cloister.

Chapters 5-8

Summary

When Father Zossima and Alyosha return to the elder's cell, Ivan is discussing, with two of the monks, his article on the position of the ecclesiastical courts. He explains that he opposes the separation of church and state primarily because when a criminal needs to be punished, the public should not have to rely on the state to administer such punishment. Ivan states that if the church had the authority to punish and also to excommunicate the criminal, then a vast number of crimes would be diminished. To a degree, Father Zossima agrees but he points out that the only effective punishment "lies in the recognition of sin by conscience." According to the elder, the church has no real authority to punish the criminal and, therefore, withdraws "of her own accord" and relies upon "the power of moral condemnation." The discussion continues but is interrupted as Dmitri unexpectedly bursts into the cell.

Breathless, the overwrought Karamazov apologizes for being late, explaining that he was incorrectly informed of the time. He then goes forward, receives Father Zossima's blessing, and sits quietly in the background. As the discussion resumes, Ivan begins to detail his views on immortality and virtue, but is interrupted by Miusov, who scoffs at Ivan's hypothesis that if immortality does not exist then there can be no reason for virtue in the world. Dmitri is deeply disturbed by his brother's theory, especially by his suggesting that without immortality any crime could be committed without fear.

When Ivan and the monks grow quiet, Fyodor nervously resumes his crude verbal antics, then begins to insult Dmitri. In particular, he accuses him of duplicity in his relationships with Katerina Ivanovna and also with Grushenka, an unconventional young woman. Dmitri snaps that Fyodor is only being nasty because he is jealous; he too is infatuated with Grushenka! As the argument mounts and everyone grows more dreadfully embarrassed, Father Zossima suddenly rises from his place and kneels at Dmitri's feet. Then, without uttering a word, he retires to his cell. Everyone is confused as to the meaning of this mysterious act and they comment upon it as they leave the elder's cell to join the Father Superior for lunch. But there is one who cannot remain with the party. Fyodor explains that he is far too embarrassed to accompany them; he says that he is going home.

Alyosha accompanies Father Zossima to his cell and is told by the Father that he must leave the monastery. It is the elder's wish that the young Karamazov rejoin the world. Alyosha does not understand Zossima's request; he desires especially to remain in the monastery — most of all because he knows that Zossima is seriously ill. He desires, as long as possible, to be near the elder.

On the way to the Father Superior's house, Alyosha and Rakitin discuss Zossima's reverent bow before Dmitri. The seminarist says that the bow means that the elder has sensed that the Karamazov house will soon be bathed in blood. The bow, he says, will be remembered and people will say that Zossima foresaw the tragedy for the family. Rakitin continues, tossing out disparaging remarks about the Karamazovs, and teasing Alyosha about Grushenka's designs on him. Alyosha, unaware of Rakitin's motives, innocently refers to Grushenka as one of Rakitin's relatives, and is surprised when the young seminarist becomes highly indignant and loudly denies such relationship.

Meanwhile, Fyodor has changed his mind about attending the luncheon. He returns and unleashes his vicious temper on all present. He delivers a vulgar tirade about the immorality and the hypocrisy of the monks and elders, making the most absurd and ridiculous charges he can conjure up. Ivan finally manages to get the old man in a carriage but the father is not yet subdued. As they are leaving he shouts to Alyosha and orders him to leave the monastery.

Commentary

In a novel of ideas, the views of a certain character will often indicate the deep, essential quality of the personality far more thoroughly than any other device that an author might use. In these chapters, for instance, Ivan's character is revealed through his ideas, especially his views concerning the ecclesiastical courts and the relationship between church and state.

Ivan, unlike many people, does not believe in the separation of church and state on the grounds that the church has no business dealing with criminals. Ivan is, in fact, an unbeliever in the Christian sense but, as a practical matter, he believes that the vast amount of crime in Russia can be curbed by a simple solution. He believes that the state should use the church as a tool in all criminal procedures. Criminals have altogether too easy a lot, he believes. The criminal who steals, for instance, does not feel that he is committing a crime against the church when he steals because the church does not punish him. But, were the church incorporated into the state, any crime would be, besides against the state, automatically against the church. If a potential criminal were threatened with excommunication then crime would virtually be nonexistent.

Besides his views on church and state, Ivan also greatly stresses the power of immortality; without it, there would be no need for man to behave virtuously. Without the matter of immortality, man could commit any crime with no fear of eternal punishment. A belief in immortality, consequently, acts as a deterrent for the potential criminal and restrains him from committing crimes against society that otherwise he would have no compunction about committing. Such extreme views are central to many of Ivan's later struggles and they will have to be reconciled with new concepts following the death of old Karamazov.

After Ivan finishes, Father Zossima, who does not argue with him, penetrates into Ivan's inner self and senses that Ivan is indeed troubled about the problem of faith. The elder is aware that perhaps Ivan does not even know whether or not he actually disbelieves in immortality; perhaps he is only being ironic. This penetrating insight on the part of Father Zossima again attests to his unusual understanding of human nature. Later, of course, it develops that Ivan's madness results from his dilemma over belief and disbelief.

Earlier in the novel Father Zossima's humanity and his simple faith in the healing power of love were stressed. Now, another dimension is added. In these chapters we see that he can easily maintain an intellectual argument. He is no simple mystic; he has an active, alert mind that proves to be a deft opponent for Ivan's parryings. Also, Father Zossima's view of the criminal buttresses his earlier concepts of the power of love. He feels that the worst punishment for a criminal lies in what he calls the "recognition of sin by conscience." The state, according to him, can punish the criminal, but physical punishment does not reform a man nor does it deter future crime. A criminal must realize that crime is a wrongdoing by a son of a Christian society. Only in this realization can a criminal be deterred.

Father Zossima's deep understanding of human nature is recognized by Ivan, for after their discussion, he goes forward to receive the elder's blessings. When he came to the cell, remember, he did not go forward to either greet the elder or to receive a blessing.

The much-discussed bow of Zossima can be explained as being a part of his instinctive understanding of Dmitri's nature. He knows that Dmitri will suffer immeasurably but that his basic nature is honorable. Also, remember that unlike the others, Dmitri arrived and immediately went forward to receive a blessing from the Father. Zossima noted the act and later was keenly aware of Dmitri's dismay when he heard Ivan's theory on immortality and its relation to crime. In Dmitri, Zossima sees great love, great suffering, and ultimately, a great redemption.

Karamazov's flagrantly vulgar behavior is best explained in terms of Dostoevsky's purpose. The author is creating a portrait of a totally repulsive profligate for whom one can feel no sympathy. In this way Dostoevsky alleviates much of the horror that might otherwise accompany the murder.

In this book we are given our first reports about Grushenka. We hear, for example, that she is brazen enough to openly say that she hopes to devour young Alyosha. These reports, however, are hearsay; they vary from the character whom we eventually meet.

BOOK III

Chapters 1-5

Summary

Long ago a child with six fingers was born to Grigory and Marfa, Karamazov's servants; it lived only two weeks but was immediately replaced by a foundling, discovered under rather curious circumstances. On the night of his baby's burial, Grigory thought that he heard an infant crying in the yard. He investigated and found a dying young girl and, lying beside her, a newborn child. The mother was an idiot girl, commonly known as "stinking Lizaveta." But in spite of her abominable appellation, almost everyone liked the harmless feebleminded waif; many even provided her with food and clothing. Lizavetta grew up like the town's stray pet and, naturally, the townspeople were outraged when it was discovered that she was pregnant. It was unthinkable that someone would molest a helpless idiot, a girl who could not even talk — could not even identify her seducer. Rumors as to the father's identity, however, finally agreed on a culprit: old Karamazov. The baby, meanwhile, was adopted by Grigory and Marfa, and they called it by the name Karamazov assigned to it: Smerdyakov.

After Alyosha leaves the monastery, he finds himself growing increasingly fearful of his interview with Katerina Ivanovna, even though he knows that the girl is trying to save Dmitri from disgrace. But he has promised to see her, so he departs. He takes a shortcut to Katerina's house and is stopped by Dmitri. His brother insists upon talking, explaining that he can tell only Alyosha everything that troubles him. Immediately he begins an anguished confession of his baseness and sensuality. Painfully he recounts his history and particularly he ponders over this quirk in his sordidness: whenever he is in the very depths of degradation, he says, he likes to sing Schiller's "Hymn to Joy." He tells Alyosha of his irresponsible life as an army officer and describes his first encounter with Katerina Ivanovna. Then, she was the proud and beautiful daughter of the commanding officer of the camp and, for some time, she ignored Dmitri's presence and remained at a proper distance. But when Dmitri secretly discovered that her father had lent 4,500 rubles to a scoundrel who refused to pay them back, he sent a message saying that her father was about to be arrested. He would, though, lend her the money if she would, as payment, come to his room. He hoped to use the promise of a loan to seduce the proud and beautiful Katerina.

When Katerina arrived, Dmitri suddenly changed. He felt like such a blackguard before the frightened and beautiful girl that he gave her the money without trying to take advantage of her. She bowed down to the floor, then ran away. And, sometime later, after her father died, she came into a large inheritance from a distant relative. She returned the money and offered to marry Dmitri. He agreed and such were, he explains to Alyosha, the circumstances of the engagement.

Following his engagement, Dmitri returned to his father's town and became madly infatuated with Grushenka. But, though she heard much of the gossip about Dmitri, Katerina remained faithful and devoted to him. On one occasion, she even trusted him with 3,000 rubles to send to her half-sister; characteristically, Dmitri squandered the money on an all-night revel. His companion that night was Grushenka.

Now, Dmitri can no longer endure the burden of Katerina's love. He asks Alyosha to be understanding and to go to Katerina and break the engagement. He also has one other request of his brother: he asks him to go to their father and ask for enough money to repay Katerina the 3,000 rubles. The money exists, Dmitri assures Alyosha; he knows for a fact that Fyodor has 3,000 rubles in an envelope intended for Grushenka if ever she spends one night with him. If Alyosha will do this, Dmitri swears that he will repay Katerina and never again ask for money.

Commentary

In the opening chapter of this section, we receive much information about the Karamazov servants. Dostoevsky is not being needlessly thorough; these servants will play a significant role in the murder of old Karamazov and it is well that we become acquainted with them early in the novel. We learn that Grigory was a determined and an obstinate man, for example. "If once he had been brought by any reasons to believe that it [his viewpoint] was immutably right," Dostoevsky tells us, "then nothing can make him change his mind." Consequently, some of the damaging evidence at Dmitri's trial is given by this old servant, a man who would never change his story even though the reader knows that the servant's evidence is false.

Besides the character of Grigory, Dostoevsky also deals with the relationship between Alyosha and his father. "Alyosha," he says, "brought with him something his father had never known before: a complete absence of contempt for him and an invariable kindness, a perfectly natural unaffected devotion to the old man who deserved it so little." We, of course, understand that Alyosha is only following the dictates of Father Zossima, who advocates that one must love indiscriminately, even those who do evil to us.

Also dealt with in this section is one more highly individual character in this Karamazov tangle of personalities—the village idiot, "stinking Lizaveta," whose depiction grandly displays Dostoevsky's greatness in capturing the essentials that round out and animate his cast of minor characters. Here, in a few sure strokes, he creates a grotesque to whom we respond as a human being. Lizaveta is strikingly real; we believe in this creature who sleeps in barns and in passageways and whose appearance is so repulsive that some people are actually appalled. And, we learn that it was Karamazov who fathered her child; now all of his noxious qualities suddenly become putrescent. To dare think that anyone might embrace her is shocking, but to think Karamazov satisfied his lust upon her is to equate him with a barbaric and sordid savage; the man is bestial. He later tells Ivan and Alyosha that "there are no ugly women. The fact that she is a woman is half the battle."

Smerdyakov, then, the fourth son of Fyodor Karamazov, is the offspring of an idiot and a sensualist—little wonder that he is one of the most disagreeable persons in the novel, resenting even the kindness of his foster parents.

In addition to his introduction of Smerdyakov and the boy's background, Dostoevsky also presents the first lengthy, analytical description of Dmitri. And with this Karamazov son, Dostoevsky elaborates upon one of his favorite themes: the contradictory impulses within a personality. Often this idea is referred to as the "Madonna-Sodom" opposition, meaning that radical and diametrically opposed feelings exist at the same time within a person. Dmitri uses this concept to help explain his position, saying, "I can't endure the thought that a man of lofty mind and heart begins with the ideal of the Madonna and ends with the ideal of Sodom. What's still more awful is that a man with the ideal of Sodom in his soul does not renounce the ideal of the Madonna."

Dmitri wallows in his emotional mud and mire but, at the same time, longs to imbue his life with utmost purity. He is especially attracted to purity as represented by the Madonna image but, at the same time, finds himself helplessly trapped in a life of orgies; these he equates with the city of Sodom, destroyed by God because of its corruptness.

He says further that when he sinks "into the vilest degradation," that he always reads Schiller's "Hymn to Joy," and "in the very depths of that degradation I begin a hymn of praise. Let me be accursed. Let me be vile and base, only let me kiss the hem of the veil in which my God is shrouded. Though I may be following the devil, I am Thy son, O Lord, and I love Thee, and I feel the joy without which the world cannot stand."

The poem Dmitri refers to tells of the Goddess Ceres' visit to earth as she looked for her daughter. She found man, instead, "sunk in vilest degradation" and displaying total "loathsomeness." In the chorus of the poem Schiller suggests a remedy: "if man," he says, "wants to purge his soul from vileness" he must "cling forever to his ancient Mother Earth." It is to this poem that Dmitri's soul is attracted; the poem is his credo as he seeks the good and beautiful as a refuge from his periods of degradation. But Dmitri seems damned; there is no ready haven for him. He finds that "beauty is a terrible and awful thing." Beauty, for Dmitri, is especially trying when it is embodied in a woman; it evokes his most saintly emotions and simultaneously arouses his most sensual desires. He cannot reconcile this polar madness; he feels washed with purity and, at the same time, sloshed with torrents of base and vile emotions; his sanity is shielded by only a single thought: he is not totally dishonorable. And it is for this reason, to prove to Alyosha that he is honorable though at times low and base, that he narrates the story of his relations with Katerina Ivanovna.

He tempted her to his apartment when she was desperate for money. He planned to use her poverty to satisfy his own needs; he failed. A dramatic reversal occurred and he gave her the money and made not a single demand upon her body.

Dmitri's confusion is compounded by the fact that he knows that his father has offered Grushenka 3,000 rubles for one night of pleasure. He will not allow this to happen. If ever Grushenka accepts the invitation, for whatever reason, Dmitri tells Alyosha that he is forever doomed because he cannot accept the "leavings" from his father. If she does come to the old man, Dmitri warns his brother, he will be forced to kill their father. In fact, he confides, he hates old Karamazov so much that he is afraid "he will suddenly become so loathsome to me" that he will provoke his own murder. Such statements naturally forewarn us that Dmitri is ripe for murder. He is sensually frustrated, financially troubled, and romantically threatened; all these, coupled with his explosive nature, are ample reasons for us to realize that Dmitri is indeed capable of spilling his father's blood.

Throughout Dmitri's narration and throughout many other scenes of this type, Alyosha functions as a so-called father confessor figure. Dmitri is only one of many characters who will confess to Alyosha. His dress, his priest-like attitude, and his willingness to listen without condemnation make him an ideal person to receive such confidence. But he is much more than a Dostoevskian device for the reader. His personality evokes confession. He has an intense need to listen and learn, and understand mankind, and it is this that matches the other characters' powerful urge to talk, to confess, and to be understood.

Chapters 6-11

Summary

Arriving at the Karamazov house, Alyosha finds his father almost drunk, but still at the table with Ivan. They are listening to old Grigory and Smerdyakov arguing, and it is at this point that we learn more about the bastard Karamazov son. Smerdyakov is rather taciturn, somewhat morose, and naturally resents his position. Strangely, however, he even resents his foster parents. Smerdyakov is an enigma, plagued by jealousy, hatred, and epilepsy. In the household, he works as a cook. Years ago old Fyodor sent him off to Moscow for training and since he returned he has functioned only in that capacity. He is a trustworthy sort, all believe, regardless of his sullenness, for they remember that he once returned 300 rubles to Fyodor which the old man lost while drunk.

Smerdyakov, at present, is arguing with his foster father as Alyosha arrives. He asserts that it is permissible for a man to renounce his faith in God in order to save his life. And, to prove that man cannot function by faith alone, he says that no man has enough faith to tell a mountain to move to the sea. He thinks, therefore, that this is reason enough to realize that man may deny God to save his life and later ask for repentance. Curiously, throughout the argument, he seems particularly anxious to please and impress Ivan.

After Karamazov tires of the argument, he sends the servants away, but the conversation manages to return to the subject of religion and in answer to their father's queries, Ivan insists that there is no God. Further, he says, there is no immortality. Alyosha, of course, maintains that God does exist and that through Him man can gain immortality. Karamazov changes the subject. He talks now of women and begins a long, drunken, and cynical narration, centering upon Alyosha's mother. The attack is depraved. Karamazov delights in mocking his late wife's religious beliefs. He is so vicious, in fact, that Alyosha collapses and succumbs to a seizure exactly like the one that Karamazov described as afflicting Alyosha's mother. Ivan bitterly reminds his drunken father that the woman of whom he has spoken so crudely was also Ivan's mother, and, for a moment, old Karamazov is confused, but recalls then that Ivan and Alyosha did indeed have the same mother. The two are attempting to revive Alyosha as Dmitri dashes into the house.

Karamazov is startled and runs for protection and when he hears Dmitri shout that Grushenka is in the house, the old man grows even more excited and fearful. Dmitri runs frantically through the house trying to discover Grushenka, then returns to the dining room, where old Karamazov begins screaming that Dmitri has been stealing money from him. Dmitri seizes his father, flings him to the floor, and kicks him in the head; then before leaving, he threatens to return and kill the old man, shouting, "Beware, old man, beware of your dreams, because I have my dream too." And he dashes out to continue his search for Grushenka.

After Ivan and Alyosha bandage their father's wounds and put him to bed, Alyosha remains with him for a while, then leaves to go talk with Katerina Ivanovna. He stops in the yard and talks a bit with Ivan and this is the first time that Ivan has been cordial to his brother.

Alyosha arrives at Madame Hohlakov's home and asks for Katerina. The girl is anxious about Dmitri and promises to help save him, although he seems not to want her help; she is positive, though, that his infatuation for Grushenka will pass. Alyosha is greatly surprised to hear Katerina call Grushenka by name and he is even more surprised when he discovers that Grushenka has been hiding behind a screen, listening to their conversation. Katerina explains that Grushenka has just confessed to her that she will soon be reunited with a man whom she has loved for five years. Obviously Katerina is overjoyed at the news and, as she explains the new turn of events to Alyosha, she impulsively kisses and fondles Grushenka, calling her endearing names. She asks Grushenka to affirm what she has just said but Grushenka surprises them all. She becomes capricious and says that she just might change her mind. She also informs Katerina that she does not return the embraces Katerina has bestowed upon her. Katerina fumes. She has humbled herself in gratitude before Grushenka and is furious at the girl's flippancy. She lashes out with stinging, angry insults, but Grushenka merely laughs and walks out, leaving Katerina in hysterics.

Alyosha also leaves the house but on the way out, he is stopped by a maid, who gives him a letter. She tells him that it is from Lise. Alyosha continues his way back to the monastery but is stopped once more, this time by Dmitri. His brother is lighthearted and seems wholly unconcerned about the earlier events of the evening. He listens now to

Alyosha explain what has happened between Katerina and Grushenka and seems delighted. He laughs at Grushenka's actions and calls her affectionately his "she-devil." But suddenly his face darkens and he moans that he is a scoundrel. Nothing, he swears to Alyosha, "can compare in baseness with the dishonor which I bear now at this very minute on my breast."

The events of the night have been unnerving and, back at the monastery, Alyosha receives more bad news: Zossima's condition has worsened; he has only a short time to live. Deeply saddened by his family's sorrows, Alyosha nevertheless decides to remain close to the elder, for this man is also his father. And having made his decision, he begins to prepare for bed, then remembers Lise's letter and reads it. It is a love letter; she says that she loves Alyosha very much and hopes to marry him when she is old enough. She apologizes sincerely for making fun of the young priest and implores him to come visit her.

Commentary

Dostoevsky carefully details in this book the special sort of characterization needed for the enigmatic Smerdyakov, the son who will murder Karamazov. We learn, for example, that he "seemed to despise everybody," including his real father and also his foster father. It is clear that he could conceivably murder either one, and in cold blood, and furthermore we learn that in childhood that "he was very fond of hanging cats," certainly a sadistic and perverse pastime. As a complement to his psychological ills, he is physically sick; epilepsy overtakes him on occasion, a disease he inherited from his idiot mother. Of late, nervous fits have attacked him increasingly and it is one of these attacks that he later shams as his alibi when his innocence is questioned.

In his argument with Grigory, put forward to impress the intellectual Ivan, Smerdyakov uses the most basic semantic logic to prove his point. But the argument shows that he is interested in questions similar to those that disturb Ivan. And it is in this way that Dostoevsky sets up conflicting emotions within Ivan. Because of their like interests he is drawn to his half-brother, but at the same time, with a Dostoevskian duality of emotion, he is repulsed and sees him as a "mean soul."

The vulgarity of old Karamazov is once more emphasized in this section. This time, in the presence of Alyosha, he crudely ridicules his son's mother. This is a particularly painful scene because we have been told that Alyosha remembers his mother with deep love and respect.

The father's attack, then, believably brings on Alyosha's convulsions. Karamazov commits a verbal murder on Alyosha's memories and it is significant, following Alyosha's collapse, that Karamazov does not realize that the same woman gave birth to both Ivan and Alyosha. In other words, the two sons are so different that the old man has completely forgotten that they had the same mother.

In Chapter 9, when Dmitri unleashes an uncontrollable fit of anguish and knocks down first Grigory and later his father, Dostoevsky is tempering our credence in Dmitri's being a potential murderer. Both father and son are victims of powerful emotions and both are passionate sensualists; their antagonism and hatred has, at present, collided over the same woman. It is likely that such viciousness as we witness might result in murder.

Even Alyosha realizes the possibility of parricide within his family when he questions Ivan as to a man's right to assess another man and decide whether or not he is worthy to live. And Ivan too realizes the potential of parricide as it smoulders, for he answers Alyosha that "one reptile will devour the other."

In Chapter 10 we are introduced finally to the beautiful and the paradoxical Katerina Ivanovna. Several times we have heard of this lovely and haughty woman, willing to devote herself to Dmitri in spite of his barbarous forays. Now we see her. She absolutely refuses to accept Dmitri's breaking of their engagement. And the extremity of her resolve is so resolute that she even humbles herself before Grushenka.

As for Grushenka, she turns out to be far more interesting than gossip suggests. She may or may not be waiting for a scoundrel who deserted her five years earlier. And it is his return, incidentally, that precipitates the pivotal action of the novel. Grushenka's mercurial qualities are quite thorough; she is whimsical and mischievous and does seem as though she might be, as Dmitri laughingly tags her, a "she-devil." She is more than a tease, however, and immediately after the murder she realizes that she, in large part, is to blame for keeping both Dmitri and his father in suspense as to what she actually intends for them.

Dmitri's confession of baseness to Alyosha is in reference to his retention of the 1,500 rubles that he saved from the night of the Grushenka orgy; this money he has not yet returned to Katerina. And his keeping it burdens his scheme of values with far greater dishonor than the fact that he spent the other half of the sum. Later it is this anguish of

Dmitri's over the money he did not spend which convinces many people that such a man could not commit a murder.

At the monastery, Alyosha still does not know why Zossima has ordered him to go into the world. "Here was peace. Here was holiness"; one can easily lose one's way in the world, Alyosha realizes, and go astray. It is, though, exactly for these reasons that the elder has asked him to go into the world. Alyosha is the one person who will be able to walk through confusion and darkness and not lose his footing. At this moment, his father, Katerina, Lise, Dmitri, and Grushenka are all waiting to talk with him again; his life's work is among the people of the world who need his quiet example of love and respect.

PART TWO

BOOK IV

Summary

Nearing death, Father Zossima rallies a bit and gathers his friends and disciples around him. He speaks to them of the necessity of loving one another and all men and urges them to remember that each human being shares a responsibility for the sins of all others.

Alyosha leaves the cell, aware of the tense sorrow that hovers over the monastery. All members of the holy community, he is sure, anticipate some sort of miracle, one occurring immediately after the elder's death. There are, in fact, already rumors of Father Zossima's being responsible for a recent miracle. Not quite all, however, share Alyosha's idealization of Zossima. Living in the monastery is another very old monk, Father Ferapont, "antagonistic to Father Zossima and the whole institution of elders." Ferapont believes in a religion based upon severe fasting and upon fear of Satan, a belief totally opposite to the doctrine of love advocated by Father Zossima. Ferapont sees the devil at work in all things and frequently has visions of lurking devils, waiting to ensnare innocent souls. He is admired by only a few people because of such severity, but he does have a coterie of staunch followers.

After Father Zossima has retired to his cell, he calls for Alyosha and reminds the boy that he hopes Alyosha will return to the town in order to fulfill his responsibilities to his father and to his brothers. Alyosha acquiesces.

On his return, Alyosha finds his father alone. The old man insists that he plans to live a long time, but that he needs much money to attract young "wenches" to come to him in his later years, when he has lost much of his vigor. He vehemently proclaims that above all other things, he will remain a sensualist until he is forced to bed down with death.

Alyosha listens, then leaves his father's house. Outside he encounters a group of schoolboys throwing rocks at an outcast young lad, a frail young child about nine years old. Despite his fraility, however, the boy returns the violence and flings back sharp rocks at the squadron of young hoodlums. Then suddenly he breaks and runs. Alyosha dashes after the boy, anxious to discover what lies under such antagonism. But when he catches him the youngster is sullen and defiant. He hits Alyosha with a rock and lunges at him, biting his hand. He escapes once more and leaves Alyosha perplexed as to the meaning of such corrosive bitterness.

Alyosha's next stop is at the home of Madame Hohlakov. There he is surprised to learn that Ivan is also a visitor, upstairs at the moment with Katerina. Dmitri's presence might have been in order, but certainly Ivan's is unexpected to the young Karamazov. He asks for some cloth to bandage his hand and when Madame Hohlakov goes in search of medication, he is immediately set upon by Lise. She implores him to return her letter; it was a bad joke, she says. But Alyosha refuses to part with the letter. He believed its contents, he says, but he cannot return it; he does not have it with him. Alyosha then leaves Lise and goes to talk with Ivan and Katerina.

Katerina repeats to Alyosha what she has just told Ivan — that she will never abandon Dmitri, even if he marries Grushenka. Furthermore, she intends to help and protect him even though he does not appreciate it. Ivan agrees with her, though he admits that in another woman such behavior would be considered thoroughly neurotic. Alyosha can no longer retain himself. He tries to convince them that they love each other; they are only torturing themselves by their theorizings. Ivan admits that he does love Katerina, but says that she needs someone like Dmitri because of her excessive self-esteem. Then he says that he is leaving the next day for Moscow and excuses himself.

After Ivan leaves, Katerina tells Alyosha of a poor captain, a Mr. Snegiryov, who was once brutally beaten by Dmitri while the captain's young son stood by and begged for mercy. She has never forgotten the incident and asks Alyosha to take 200 rubles to the captain as a token of her deep sympathy. Alyosha says that he will do as she asks and leaves.

The captain in question lives in a ramshackle old house with a mentally deranged wife, two daughters (one of whom is a crippled hunchback), and his young son, Ilusha. Coincidentally, Ilusha turns out to be the outcast who earlier bit Alyosha's hand. Before Alyosha can explain why he has come, the boy cries out that the young Karamazov has come to complain about the hand-biting. And it is then that Alyosha understands why the boy attacked him so savagely: he was defending his father's honor against a Karamazov.

The captain takes Alyosha outside and tells him the story of his encounter with Dmitri and how terribly the episode affected his young son. He further emphasizes the family's poverty, and Alyosha—overjoyed that he can relieve the old man's poverty—explains that he has come to give him 200 rubles. The captain is delighted by such unexpected good luck and speaks of the many things he can now do for his sick and hungry family. But suddenly he changes his mind. With a proud gesture, he throws the money to the ground, saying that if he accepts the sum he can never gain his son's love and respect. Alyosha retrieves the money and starts back to Katerina to report his failure.

Commentary

At the end of Book III, Alyosha wonders why Father Zossima has asked him to leave the monastery. Book IV is Dostoevsky's explanation. From chapter to chapter, Alyosha moves among the characters as they grapple with their assorted problems. He fast becomes the living embodiment of the elder's teachings. Each chapter illustrates Alyosha's influences. In Chapter 2 he travels to his father's house and listens to the frustrations that plague the old man. Then he goes to Madame Hohlakov's and tries to pacify young Lise by calmly accepting her hysterical outcries. While there he makes an effort to bring Ivan and Katerina together as lovers. Next, he goes to the cottage of the destitute Captain Snegiryov. Obviously Dostoevsky intends us to see that Alyosha is meant for a life of activity, not for the quiet passivity of the monastery.

The message of Father Zossima is of particular importance in this book. Earlier he has emphasized the value of love and has admonished his adherents to love one another, to love all of God's people. Now he reminds his followers that simply because they have assumed a monastic life does not imply that they are more blessed than other people. In fact, "from the very fact of coming here, each of us has confessed to himself that he is worse than others." He also reminds his listeners that each man is responsible for every other man and "that he is responsible to all men for all and everything, for all human sins, national and individual." This speech alone contains all the reasons for Alyosha's leaving the monastery. A life of seclusion does not test one's strength if he is to be a representative of Zossima's theories. The elder's ideas can be tested only in the midst of busy society.

Father Zossima's ideas concerning the responsibility of one man for another can take on added weight in the conversations that Alyosha has with Ivan. Ivan refuses to take the responsibility for Dmitri's sins and tells Alyosha that he is not his brother's keeper. And later, Zossima's concept of responsibility triggers Alyosha into considering his own responsibility for Karamazov's murder.

At the end of Zossima's talk, rumors are spread of a forthcoming miracle, one that will coincide with the elder's death. Alyosha is intrigued by the rumors, especially since he believes Zossima to be saintlike, but he is sorely tested when his beloved elder's body rapidly decomposes.

As Alyosha begins his journey through the complex world of society, he goes first to his father's house and listens to all kinds of vulgar and disgusting stories. His father tells him that he will need much money in later years to tempt young "wenches" to sleep with him and suggests that Ivan is trying to marry Katerina so that Dmitri will have to marry Grushenka; thus old Karamazov will be prevented from remarrying and leaving his fortune to a new wife — in other words — to Grushenka. All these wild accusations color more darkly Dostoevsky's portrait of Karamazov as a repulsive and bestial type. Throughout the confession, Alyosha is able to retain his peaceful mein and never compromises his inner nature of dignity and love.

In the scene with young Ilusha, Alyosha still remains the perfectly self-contained individual. He does not even use any violence when Ilusha bites him so viciously. It is a bitter entrance into the world — stoned and bitten only because one is a Karamazov; none of this, of course, would have happened if Alyosha had remained in seclusion at the monastery.

But Alyosha has made his choice according to Zossima's wishes and according to the dictates of the elder who told him that he must marry and become one with the world. He, therefore, tells the young invalid Lise that when she comes of age they will marry.

As for another marriage — one between Ivan and Katerina — the solution is not quite so simple. They are apparently in love with each other, but both are so arrogant that they cannot come to an understanding. Part of the difficulty lies in Katerina's fantastic personality. She feels the need to suffer or to be humiliated by Dmitri and her statement that she will never abandon Dmitri, even if he marries Grushenka indicates the fanatical degree to which she plans to carry her suffering and martyrdom. Ivan well sums up her peculiar nature when he says that she needs Dmitri "so as to contemplate continually your heroic fidelity and to reproach him for infidelity."

For the present, then, Katerina's declaration results in an impasse; her views toward the two brothers will not be resolved until the trial and even then real objectivity will be impossible. Nevertheless, it is true that she feels the need to be humiliated by Dmitri. Proof of this lies in her deep sympathy with Captain Snegiryov, a man who has been humiliated by Dmitri. She asks Alyosha to take him 200 rubles "as a token of sympathy," but her sympathy is far greater than token value.

Alyosha fast becomes involved in social intrigues. But one should be aware that there is no rancor or bitterness in his new role. Alyosha has no resentment, even following the Ilusha incident. Quite the contrary, he has great compassion for a young boy who will try and defend his father's honor. Book IV, then places the neophyte Alyosha in a variety of new situations and the boy's skill in dealing with them suggests the future potential that Father Zossima sensed in him. Looking ahead, however, one might note that success is not total. Further along, it will become apparent that Alyosha often fails with adults. But it is with children that he most succeeds; with the younger generation his qualities of quiet love and devotion find the most fertile sympathy. This, of course, is part of Dostoevsky's vision — children represent the future of all hope and salvation and in this novel Alyosha entrusts Zossima's ideal of love and honor to the new generation.

BOOK V

Chapters 1-4

Summary

When Alyosha returns to Madame Hohlakov's to report his failure with the captain, he learns that Katerina has developed a fever following her hysterical outburst and is now upstairs, unconscious. To Lise, Alyosha explains the nature of his mission and his failure, and analyzes the captain's character for her. As he talks, Lise becomes very impressed with such deep insight and such warmth and love of humanity. She confesses that she indeed meant what she wrote in the letter. The revelation is startling and she and Alyosha discuss their feelings for each other and begin to make plans for marriage. For his part, Alyosha admits that he has told a white lie concerning the letter. He did not return it, not because he did not have it, but because he valued it too much.

Meanwhile, Madame Hohlakov, who has eavesdropped on the conversation, stops Alyosha as he is leaving and expresses deep disapproval of the match. Alyosha assures her that the marriage is yet far in the future, that Lise is much too young to presently marry.

Alyosha then, puzzling over Dmitri's actions of the previous night, decides to try and find his brother. It is more important, he believes, to "have saved something" of Dmitri's honor than to flee back to the monastery. The summerhouse seems a likely place to find his brother; this is where he often watches for Grushenka and dreams of her. As Alyosha waits, he overhears Smerdyakov singing and playing the guitar for the housekeeper's daughter. Alyosha interrupts, with apologies, and asks Smerdyakov if he has seen Dmitri. The cook is able to help Alyosha and says that Ivan has made an appointment to meet Dmitri at the Metropolis restaurant. Alyosha rushes there but Dmitri is not to be found. Instead, Ivan is dining alone. Ivan beckons to his brother and Alyosha accepts his brother's invitation to talk. Ivan admits, first off, that he is anxious to know Alyosha better; he has come to respect and admire the boy. Ivan also admits that he has an intense longing for life even though he constantly encounters only disorder and injustice. Alyosha, however, is more concerned about Dmitri and what will happen to him and what will happen to Fyodor if Ivan leaves the family. To this, Ivan insists that he is absolutely not his brother's keeper, nor his father's keeper, and confesses finally that he is dining at the restaurant for only one reason: he cannot bear the presence of his loathsome father.

That settled, Ivan begins to tell Alyosha of his views on "the existence of God and immortality." He says that he does not reject God but, on the other hand, he cannot accept Him. If God does exist and if he indeed created the world, the human mind should be able to fathom the deed and understand the purpose of creation. Ivan cannot and therefore rejects the world God created. If, he adds, this means that he must reject God, then that is another problem. Alyosha queries more closely, asking Ivan to be more specific as to why he cannot accept the world. Ivan answers by saying that he can love man at a distance but that he is unable to love his next door neighbor. For him "Christ-like love for men is a miracle impossible on earth." That which makes it especially difficult to accept the world, as it is, is the vast suffering and brutality in the world. If God exists, says Ivan, how can this horror be accounted for? He singles out the suffering of children as prime evidence of the world's indifferent cruelty. Children have had no time to sin, but they suffer. Why? Certainly not because of sin — supposedly the cause of suffering. He then recites several horrible examples of atrocities inflicted upon children by other human beings. Because such injustice is allowed to happen, Ivan simply cannot accept the mythical "harmony of God," or accept a universe where one who is tortured embraces his torturer. Such "harmony," says Ivan, "is not worth the tears of one tortured child." He concludes that if truth must be bought at the price of the suffering of children, then such truth is not worth the price. He tells Alyosha: "It's not God that I don't accept, Alyosha, only I most respectfully return Him the ticket."

Alyosha is horrified and tells Ivan that these thoughts constitute rebellion. Ivan offers Alyosha a further example: suppose, he says, one could create a perfect world for man but it could only survive by torturing to death "one tiny creature." Would Alyosha be the architect of such a world? As an answer, Ivan is reminded that there is One who can forgive everything "because He gave His innocent blood for all and everything." Ivan assures his brother that he has not forgotten "the One without sin," and recites a prose poem which he wrote several years ago. He calls his poem "The Grand Inquisitor."

Commentary

As Alyosha tells Lise of his encounter with the captain, we see that he, like Zossima, has a deeply penetrating mind and understands the inner workings of those whom he is trying to help. It is this understanding of human nature that proves Alyosha much more than a simple person of simple faith.

Zossima, remember, has commanded Alyosha to marry and, because of the elder, Alyosha has chosen Lise; no one, he believes, will make him a better wife. But for all of Zossima's influence, he is not a puppet-master. Alyosha is objective about the wisdom of his mentor's teachings and although he knows that Zossima is dying, he feels that it is a higher duty to find Dmitri than go to the elder's deathbed. Thus

Alyosha matures into a man of worldly responsibility and makes other men much more than only of spiritual concern.

In Chapter 3, Dostoevsky makes clear the earlier ambiguities of Ivan's character. Previously, the brother has maintained a distance from Alyosha because he has been evaluating him to see if he is merely an empty-minded religious fanatic. Now, however, Ivan has learned to respect and admire Alyosha because "you do stand firm and I like people who are firm like that, whatever it is that they stand by." Ivan is now ready to thoroughly discuss his beliefs with his brother. In addition, Ivan also feels that his impending departure makes it imperative to explain himself to Alyosha. But if he is concerned with Alyosha, he is certainly not concerned for Dmitri; he absolutely refuses to be either his brother's keeper or the "keeper" of Fyodor. He is quite adamant concerning this and his vehemence is easily recalled when the idea of Fyodor's being vulnerable for murder is discussed.

Preluding his views on religion, Ivan announces that he has a strong desire to live. He loves life even though he finds it illogical. Such an acknowledgement of a love of living is important because Ivan, with a philosophy seemingly nihilistic, might too easily be categorized as a suicidal cynic. Ivan is morally much stronger and is deeply committed to the business of living.

Both brothers, Ivan and Alyosha, agree that "for real Russians the questions of God's existence and of immortality ... come first and foremost and so they should." And, in its largest context, this is the subject of the novel. These ideas are central not just to the characters, but to an understanding of Dostoevsky's entire point of view.

Ivan surprises Alyosha by announcing "perhaps I too accept God," reminding his brother of the saying, "If God did not exist, it would be necessary to invent Him," because for Ivan the astonishing factor of Christianity is that man is basically such a "savage, vicious beast," that it is illogical that he could conceive of an idea so noble and magnificent as "God." Ivan is, of course, leading into his views about the baseness of most humans and the difficulty of believing man sufficiently noble to conceive of something so totally transcending his own vicious nature.

Most of all, Ivan desires a world in which his human intellect can fully comprehend the logic and purpose of life. He uses the analogy of two parallel lines which, according to Euclid, can never meet. Ivan's mind can comprehend this concept because he has a "Euclidian earthly mind." But if someone tells him that two parallel lines might meet somewhere in infinity and even if he sees it himself, he still cannot accept the theory. Therefore, even though he is willing to accept God, His Wisdom, and His purpose, he cannot accept "this world of God's... it's the world created by Him that I don't and can't accept."

To explain further why he does not accept the world, Ivan examines the brutality found in the world, saying that he cannot love his neighbor. It is easy to love man in the abstract sense, certainly, but when one looks into the face of a man, it is impossible to love him. For Christ, to love men was easy because He was God; but for ordinary men to love one's neighbor—the idea is ridiculously impossible. Later Ivan will elaborate upon this in his poem "The Grand Inquisitor."

Ivan uses the suffering of innocent children as his principal grounds for the world's unacceptability. The idea of the suffering innocent, of course, has plagued philosophers since time's beginning; it is the subject of such great works as the Book of Job. But Ivan does not concern himself with the sufferings of adults. For them, a philosophical justification is possible: the adult has sinned and his suffering is a punishment for his sins. Children, however, have not yet sinned and therefore Ivan cannot understand a world created by God which justifies their suffering. And regardless of whether one agrees or disagrees with Ivan, one must recognize the logic at work in this system of thinking. Life, for Ivan, must be rational—it must especially be rational if one is to appreciate God's wonder and love Him as one should.

So well has Ivan considered his philosophy that he is even amused by the term "bestial cruelty," for this, he believes, is an insult to beasts. An animal kills only for food and kills rapidly, but man kills slowly, deliberately, and often only for the sadistic pleasure of watching his victim suffer.

As Ivan speaks, he is quite aware that he is causing Alyosha to suffer; he knows well of Alyosha's fondness for children. But, although he is not his "brother's keeper," he is far from heartless and, for him, children are revered. He can find no logic that justifies their suffering. And he asks Alyosha what would be the basis of an eternal harmony if a victim would "rise up and embrace his murderer." If this higher harmony would, even in part, be based upon such suffering, then Ivan must renounce it. Truth is not worth such a price. In reference to the story of the general who had his dogs kill a peasant boy, Ivan states, "I don't want the mother to embrace the oppressor who threw her son to the dogs! She dare not forgive him! Let her forgive him for herself, if she will, let her forgive the torturer for the immeasurable suffering of her mother's heart. But the sufferings of her tortured child she has no right to forgive; she dare not forgive the torturer, even if the child were to forgive him!" Ivan rejects such monstrous injustice; he would rather remain with his "unavenged suffering and unsatisfied indignation."

When Alyosha tells Ivan that his view is that of rebellion, Ivan presents Alyosha with the following hypothesis: "Imagine you are creating a fabric of human destiny with the object of making men happy in the end, giving them peace and rest at last, but that it was essential and inevitable to torture to death only one tiny creature... to found that edifice on its unavenged tears, would you consent to be the architect on those conditions?" This analogy of Ivan's offers the same view as that expressed throughout the chapter—that a world created for men should not be founded on innocent suffering. As a humanist, Ivan cannot accept happiness or eternal harmony at the expense of any "unexpiated blood."

Alyosha reminds Ivan that he has forgotten the one Being Who "gave His innocent blood for all" and that it is because of Alyosha's objection that Ivan is provoked to narrate his prose poem, "The Grand Inquisitor."

Chapter 5

Summary

During the sixteenth century in Spain, at the height of the Inquisition, someone resembling Christ appears unannounced in the streets. The people recognize Him immediately and begin to flock about Him. But, as He is healing several of the sick and lame, an old cardinal also recognizes Him and orders the guards to arrest Him. Once again Christ is abducted.

That night, He receives a visitor. The Grand Inquisitor enters the darkened cell and begins a severe reprimand of Christ for appearing again and hindering the work of the church. The Grand Inquisitor explains to Christ that, because of His rejection of the three temptations, He placed an intolerable burden of freedom upon man. The church, however, is now correcting His errors and aiding man by removing their awful burden of freedom. He explains that Christ erred when He expected man to voluntarily choose to follow Him. The basic nature of man, says the Inquisitor, does not allow him to reject either earthly bread or security or happiness in exchange for something so indefinite as what Christ expects.

If Christ had accepted the proffered bread, man would have been given security instead of a freedom of choice and if Christ had performed a miracle and had cast himself down from the pinnacle, man would have been given something miraculous to worship. The nature of man, insists the Inquisitor, is to seek the miraculous. Finally, Christ should have accepted the power offered Him by the devil. Because He did not, the church has now had to assume such power for the benefit of man. And since Christ's death, the church has been forced to correct the errors made by Him. Now, at last mankind willingly submits its freedom to the church in exchange for happiness and security. This balance, says the Inquisitor, must not be upset.

At the end of the monolog, the Grand Inquisitor admits that of necessity he is on the side of the devil, but the challenge that Christ placed on mankind allows only a few strong people to be saved; the rest must be sacrificed to these strong. The Grand Inquisitor's scheme, at least, provides an earthly happiness for the mass of mankind even though it will not lead to eternal salvation. On the other hand, Christ's method would not have saved these same weak and puny men either.

When he finishes, the Grand Inquisitor looks at Christ. He has remained silent the entire time. Now He approaches the old churchman and kisses him on his dry, withered lips. The Grand Inquisitor frees Him suddenly, saying that He is never to come again.

Ivan finishes his story and wonders now if Alyosha will reject him or will try to accept him as a brother. As an answer, Alyosha leans forward and kisses his brother. "You are plagarizing my poem," Ivan cries in delight. The brothers leave the restaurant together, but they then part, each going his separate way.

Commentary

In the chapter preceding "The Grand Inquisitor," Ivan has struggled with the problem of suffering humanity and the injustice of this world. Now he turns to one of the major philosophical questions — one which has worried the Western world for centuries: the awesome burden placed upon man by his having complete freedom instead of church-directed happiness and security.

Dostoevsky achieves his dramatic impact in this chapter by having the two antagonists embody the two ideas in question—the Grand Inquisitor pleading for security and happiness for man; Christ offering complete freedom. Furthermore, the advocate for freedom—the reincarnate Christ—remains completely silent throughout the Inquisitor's monolog; his opponent does all the talking. Yet the old Inquisitor is no mere egotist. His character is one that evokes our respect. We consider his position in the church, his intellect, his certainty, and above all, his professed love for mankind. All this he does in spite of the fact that, as he finally admits, he has aligned himself with Satan.

The complexity of the Grand Inquisitor increases when we realize that he, like his divine opponent, has been in the wilderness and could have stood among the elect, but deliberately chose to take his stand with the weak and puny mass of mankind. And just as Ivan, in the preceding chapter, declared that even if God could justify innocent suffering, he would refuse to accept the explanation, so the Grand Inquisitor also affirms this stand. The two—Ivan and the Grand Inquisitor—are in close accord and much of the Grand Inquisitor is also seen in Ivan's questioning and perplexity. The two are also kissed by their opponents, Christ and Alyosha.

In the tale, when Christ reappears, the Grand Inquisitor has begun to build a world upon the concepts of authority, miracle, and mystery. And, as a cardinal, he speaks and commands with unquestionable authority. When he sees Christ performing miracles among the people, he has merely to hold out his finger and bid the guards take Him. The townspeople are cowed by him; they tremblingly obey him.

The church-conceived way to salvation and its strong-arm authority are targets for Dostoevsky and, through Ivan, he builds up a case of condemnation against the Roman Catholic church. The Grand Inquisitor, for example, visiting Christ in the night says to Him, "Thou hast no right to add anything to what Thou hadst said of old." That is, Christ has said all that was necessary. Since then the church has taken over with its great authority and established what should—and what should not—be believed. The church, not Christ, is the supreme authority in matters of faith and conduct. "Why hast Thou come to hinder us," he asks Christ and, to make sure that He does not overthrow the centuries of authority of the church, he says that he will "condemn Thee and burn Thee at the stake as the worst of heretics."

The argument between the Grand Inquisitor and Christ is made especially effective because Dostoevsky arranges their meeting on ancient terms: Christ is once again the prisoner, the accused, yet He does not defend Himself. Ironically, it is the executioner who must defend himself. The prisoner never utters a word. But it is wrong to see them as hero and villain. Both men—one silently, the other verbosely—argue for the best way in which man can achieve happiness. Both have humanistic motives and love for the mass of mankind. Their end result—happiness for man—is identical; only by definition and method do the men vary.

The Grand Inquisitor criticizes Christ for wishing to set man free, asking "Thou hast seen these 'free' men?" For fifteen centuries the problem of freedom has weighed heavily on both the church and mankind but now, says the Inquisitor, the church has "vanquished freedom and has done so to make men happy." His pity for the weakness of man has made him realize that man cannot handle such a burdensome problem as freedom and, to prove this point, he reminds Christ of the temptations He was tested by.

The source for the Grand Inquisitor's view is found in St. Luke, 4:1-13—

And Jesus being full of the Holy Ghost returned from Jordan, and was led by the Spirit into the wilderness,

Being forty days tempted of the devil. And in those days he did eat nothing: and when they were ended, he afterward hungered.

And the devil said unto him, If thou be the Son of God, command this stone that it be made bread.

And Jesus answered him, saying, It is written, That man shall not live by bread alone, but by every word of God.

And the devil, taking him up into a high mountain, showed unto him all the kingdoms of the world in a moment of time.

And the devil said unto him, All this power will I give thee, and the glory of them: for that is delivered unto me; and to whomsoever I will, I give it.

If thou therefore wilt worship me, all shall be thine.

And Jesus answered and said unto him, Get thee behind me, Satan: for it is written, Thou shalt worship the Lord thy God, and him only shalt thou serve.

And he brought him to Jerusalem, and set him on a pinnacle of the temple, and said unto him, If thou be the Son of God, cast thyself down from hence:

For it is written, He shall give his angels charge over thee, to keep thee:

And in *their* hands they shall bear thee up, lest at any time thou dash thy foot against a stone.

And Jesus answering said unto him, It is said, Thou shalt not tempt the Lord thy God.

And when the devil had ended all the temptation, he departed from him for a season.

An important question evoked by this passage is whether or not Christ was refusing the temptations — security through bread, authority, and miracle — for Himself alone, or whether by refusing He was doing so for all mankind and placing a burden too tremendous upon such a frail creature as man. If Christ refused solely for Himself, His refusal does not carry such heavy implications because He was divine and could easily afford to resist such temptations. But if He was refusing for all mankind, then it follows that He expects man to believe in something intangible even while He does not have enough to eat.

To complicate the matter, the Grand Inquisitor places his questions in the terms of being asked by "the wise and dread spirit," who offers Christ three things. Christ is clearly the rejector, but not for Himself alone — for all mankind. And when the Grand Inquisitor states, "The statement of those three questions was itself the miracle," he means that Satan is so wording his questions that the future fate of all mankind will be determined. He asks Christ to "Judge Thyself who was right — Thou or he who questioned Thee."

The first question is viewed in terms of freedom versus security. By refusing the bread, Christ is insisting that man must have freedom to choose to follow Him without being lulled into a sense of security by being provided with bread. If bread is provided, then man loses his freedom to choose Christ voluntarily. "Thou wouldst not deprive men of freedom and didst reject the offer, thinking what is that freedom worth, if obedience is bought with bread." The Grand Inquisitor feels that what Christ wants for man is impossible. "Nothing," he says, "has ever been more insupportable for a man and a human society than freedom." By denying bread or security for man and by giving man in its stead the freedom to follow Him of his own volition, Christ failed to understand the human nature of men who are "weak, vicious, worthless, and rebellious." To promise the bread of heaven to a man starving for earthly bread and to expect him to choose the former of his own volition, puts an insufferable weight upon mankind who must, by nature, reject Christ in favor of whoever offers earthly bread. The Grand Inquisitor cries, "Feed men and then ask of them virtue."

Instead of freeing all mankind, Christ (charges the Grand Inquisitor) succeeded only in freeing the strong. The tens of thousands who have the strength to voluntarily accept heavenly bread follow Him but what, asks the Inquisitor, is to become of the tens of millions who are too weak to accept, responsibly, the dreadful freedom of choice? Are the weak to be condemned for the sake of the elect who have the strength to follow after the heavenly bread?

The Grand Inquisitor says that he has corrected Christ's errors. He has done so because he loves the weak who hunger after earthly bread. Man is now fed by the church and, in return, has willingly relinquished his former freedom for security. "Man seeks to worship what is established beyond dispute" so that he will not have to face the dreadful "freedom of choice." If Christ had only chosen the bread, He then would "have satisfied the universal and ever-lasting craving for humanity – to find someone to worship." Christ erred in rejecting earthly bread for the sake of freedom. "Instead of taking men's freedom from them, Thou didst make it greater than ever! Didst Thou forget that man prefers peace and even death to freedom of choice in the knowledge of good and evil?"

Also, by His rejection of earthly bread, Christ forced man to choose between solid security as opposed to something that is "exceptional, vague, and enigmatic. Thou didst choose what was utterly beyond the strength of men. Instead of taking possession of man's freedom, Thou didst increase it and burdened the spiritual kingdom of mankind with its suffering forever." Now each individual man must decide for himself "what is good and what is evil, having only Thy Image before him." Had Christ truly loved mankind, He should have had more compassion and should have understood man's inherent weaknesses.

The Grand Inquisitor explains then that he (the church) has compassion and understanding for man and has given him "miracle, mystery, and authority." The church tells men what to believe and what to choose and thereby relieves him of choosing for himself. At last man has a sense of security which Christ denied him.

By miracle, the Grand Inquisitor explains that when Christ rejected the second temptation – the refusal to cast Himself down – he was rejecting one of the essential characteristics man expects from religion — the truly miraculous. Of course, Christ, as divine, could reject the miraculous, but He should have understood that the nature of man desires a miracle. "But Thou didst not know that when man rejects miracles he rejects God also; for man seeks not so much God as the miraculous. And as man cannot bear to be without the miraculous, he will create new miracles of his own for himself and will worship deeds of sorcery and witchcraft." In other words, man's basic nature is to seek that which transcends human existence; he worships that which is superhuman, that which has a sense of the miraculous.

"We are not working with Thee," the Inquisitor says, "but with *him* — that is our mystery. It's long — eight centuries — since we have been on *his* side and not on Thine. Just eight centuries ago, we took from him what Thou didst reject with scorn, that last gift he offered Thee, showing Thee all the kingdoms of the earth. We took from him Rome and the sword of Caesar."

The church has taken the kingdom of earth — that which Christ rejected. Here the church has established its plan for the universal happiness of man. "Freedom, free thought, and science" will create such insoluble riddles and chaotic disunity that soon, all men will gladly surrender their freedom, saying "You alone possess His mystery . . . save us from ourselves."

The future world of happiness will be based on a totalitarian state, organized on the principle of total obedience and submission and "they will submit to us gladly and cheerfully . . . because it will save them from the great anxiety and terrible agony they endure at present in making a free decision for themselves." The church will even allow certain people to sin so long as they are obedient and submissive. Man's happiness will be the happiness of children who have no responsibilities and no choices; all questions will be answered by the church. The only person unhappy will be, ironically, those few who will "guard the mystery." That is, only the members of the church who understand the above concepts will suffer because they will be the "sufferers who have taken upon themselves the curse of the knowledge of good and evil."

Like Ivan, the Grand Inquisitor is unwilling to become one of the few elect when it means that "millions of creatures have been created as a mockery." Only a few people in the world can prize or understand the freedom given them by Christ; these are the strong and the powerful. Out of pity for all mankind, the Grand Inquisitor, who could have been on the side of the elect, repudiates the system that would doom millions of the weak. Such a system is unjust and thus he chooses to accept a system designed for the multitudes of the weak rather than for the few of the strong.

At one point, the Grand Inquisitor says that he must burn Christ so that "man will not have to be plagued with that horrible burden of inner freedom." He is a martyr in a special sense because he reserves the privilege of suffering for the few strong people; in this way, the mass of mankind will not have to undergo the terrible suffering associated with absolute freedom. Christ consequently has no right to interfere in the church's organized happiness; He must be punished as an enemy of the people.

At the end of the discussion, Christ responds to the Grand Inquisitor by giving him a kiss on his withered lips. This paradoxical ending undercuts the soliloquy, leaving us to wonder what is right. The reader, however, should remember that Dostoevsky has created two opposite poles of response; man is seldom faced with such clear-cut opposition.

When Alyosha re-enacts the poem and kisses Ivan, it is partly because he recognizes that a man cannot come to such opinions as he has just heard unless he has given them considerable thought; they are obviously the most important questions of mankind. Furthermore, Ivan, like Alyosha, does have a deep love for humanity, a quality that makes anyone worthy of redemption.

Chapters 6-7

Summary

Ivan leaves Alyosha and feels greatly depressed. He cannot understand his depression until he realizes that perhaps it is because of his deep dread of meeting Smerdyakov. He does, however, go home, but seeing the cook sitting in the yard, hopes to pass him without speaking. Strangely, however, he cannot and finds himself greeting his half-brother with great cordiality.

Smerdyakov confesses to Ivan that he too is troubled because of the rivalry between Fyodor and Dmitri for Grushenka. He also fears that the strain of worry might bring on an epileptic seizure. Furthermore, he says, he knows that Dmitri has learned the secret signals that Grushenka is to use if ever she decides to come to Fyodor. If such a meeting occurs, the results could well be tragic: both Grigory and Marfa are ill and Smerdyakov fears that he is ripe for a seizure, and Fyodor will be left alone to face Dmitri's wrath. Ivan wonders why Smerdyakov told Dmitri the secret signals and suggests that perhaps Smerdyakov has arranged matters so that Dmitri will have access to old Fyodor as soon as Ivan leaves for Moscow. Ivan, however, cannot be a watchdog for Karamazov, so resolves to leave the next day for Moscow as planned. Smerdyakov insists that he not go to Moscow, however, that he go to a nearer town, but Ivan is firm and goes to bed without further discussion. The talk has left him exhausted, however, and he finds that he cannot sleep.

Next day, Fyodor pleads with Ivan not to go to Moscow, but to a town close by to sell a copse of wood for the old man. Ivan finally agrees and, as he is leaving, he admits to Smerdyakov that he is not going to Moscow. The servant whispers mysteriously that "it's always worth while speaking to a clever man." Ivan is puzzled.

A few hours later, Smerdyakov falls down the cellar steps and an attack of epilepsy seizes him. He is put to bed and, as predicted, Fyodor is alone. He locks all the doors and windows, then begins his wait for Grushenka. He is certain that she will come to him tonight.

Commentary

Leaving Alyosha, Ivan feels morose and dejected, emotions probably related to the guilt that he feels by associating with Smerdyakov. For even though Ivan does not realize it, he is subconsciously beginning to feel a certain duplicity in his relationships with the servant; the last two chapters, in particular, show how certain actions on Ivan's part implicate him in the murder of old Fyodor.

This fact is also important: Ivan feels a distinct loathing for Smerdyakov. He has entered into many philosophical discussions with him and we learn that they have discussed such questions as how there "could have been light on the first day when the sun, moon, and stars were only created on the fourth day." Smerdyakov, in turn, has discussed things that would impress Fyodor, hoping to make an impression on him and contradict old Grigory. He has, we discover, however, taken most of his ideas from Ivan. Even the idea of the murder came from Ivan.

When Ivan meets the cook, he has planned to say to him, "Get away, miserable idiot. What have I to do with you," but instead he says,

"Is my father still asleep?" This reversal suggests that Ivan is repulsed by this creature but is, at the same time, drawn to him. And, by the same analogy, Ivan is repulsed by the idea that his father will be murdered, but seems also to acquiesce in readying the scene for the hypothetical murder.

In these last chapters one can easily see how completely Smerdyakov has planned the homicide. We hear, first of all, that Dmitri has heard of the secret signals by which Grushenka is to come to the old man. There could, of course, be no reason for Smerdyakov to tell Dmitri about these signals except to lay suspicion on Dmitri when it is known that he was aware of such signals; furthermore, Ivan's ready acceptance of Smerdyakov's explanation indicates that Ivan is also anxious to accept such an alibi. Second, Smerdyakov announces that he feels that he will have an epileptic seizure on the following day—the day that Ivan will be absent from the house. Third, Smerdyakov announces that old Grigory will be doped with some strong medicine which Marfa gives him and always saves a bit of for herself; soon both will be in a heavy sleep. Consequently, Smerdyakov has conceived a perfect setting for murder; he has even created perfect alibis. As he announces later to Ivan—everything had to go just as he planned it; otherwise, the murder could never have been accomplished. Ivan even recognized this when he said earlier, "But aren't you trying to arrange it so?" and tried to remove himself from direct responsibility. But ultimately Ivan must take his share in the moral guilt for his father's death.

At the end of Book V most of the machinery is arranged for the murder. Smerdyakov pretends to have his seizure, old Grigory is laid up with illness, Marfa prepares the medicine for them both, and Fyodor anxiously awaits Grushenka.

BOOK VI

Summary

Father Zossima is propped in bed, surrounded by his friends and followers when Alyosha returns to the monastery. The elder is weak but is still quite alert and anxious to talk with his audience. He greets Alyosha affectionately and asks about Dmitri; he says that the bow made to him was an acknowledgment of the intense suffering he foresees for the boy. Alyosha, however, he says, has quite a different future and again he counsels the young monk to return to the world to look after his brothers. In this way, he says, Alyosha will learn to love all of life, to bless life, and to teach those who suffer to love and bless life.

These pleas to Alyosha are Father Zossima's last requests. Now he tells all assembled the reasons why Alyosha is so very special to him. Once, the elder says, he had an older brother who influenced him tremendously. Alyosha bears a particularly strong resemblance to that brother—physically and spiritually. Then Zossima begins to reminisce.

He was born to a noble family of only moderate means. His father died when he was only two years old and he was reared with his mother and the brother he spoke of. The brother, eight years older than Zossima, came under the influence of a freethinker and was soon a source of sorrow to the mother. He ridiculed her religious observances and her devout beliefs. Then, at seventeen, he contracted consumption and the family was advised that he had but a few months to live.

During the months he waited for death, a tremendous spiritual conversion took place in the boy. He became extremely pious and spoke continuously about the need to love all of God's creatures, even the little birds in the garden. He asked the servants to feel that they were his equal and often said that he wished he could be a servant to the servants.

Besides his brother, Zossima says that there has been another influence on him: the Bible. This book, he says, is a testament of the extent of God's love for all men. Zossima mourns for those who cannot find the vast love that he finds contained in the Bible.

But Zossima's affection for the Bible has not been lifelong. As a youth, he was sent to a military academy in St. Petersburg and soon neglected both the Bible and his religious training. After graduation, he led the carefree life that a typical young officer might. He courted a beautiful lady whom, he was sure, returned his affections, but while he was absent she married someone else. Zossima was insulted and immediately challenged her husband to a duel. But, waking on the morning of the duel, he looked out and saw a fresh, clean beauty on all of God's world and he remembered his dying brother's exhortation: love all of God's creatures. He leaped from his bed, apologized to a servant whom he had beaten the night before and made plans for his duel. He would allow his opponent to take the first shot; afterward, Zossima would drop his pistols and beg the man's forgiveness. This he did. But the officers accompanying Zossima were shocked by the strange behavior. They questioned him and were even more surprised at the explanation: he had, he said, decided to resign his military commission and enter a monastery.

Zossima fast became the talk of the town and one night a mysterious stranger visited him. He begged to hear the motives that prompted Zossima's actions. Zossima talked at length to the man and for many nights afterward. Then, after hearing the whole of Zossima's story, the man made a confession of his own: years ago he killed a woman out of passion and someone else was blamed for the deed. The man in question, however, died before he was tried. Now the perpetrator of the deed has wife and children and has become one of the most respected philanthropists in the community. But, he moans to Zossima, he has never found happiness for himself. In spite of an apparently successful life, he has always needed to confess. This, in fact, he finally did, and in public, but no one believed him; they merely thought that he was temporarily deranged. Not long after his confession to Zossima, the man falls ill. The elder visits him and is thanked greatly for his guidance. Zossima, until now, has never revealed the man's secret.

The elder pauses and begins to speak to Alyosha of what it has meant to be a monk. Zossima feels that the Russian monk is, of all persons, closest to the Russian folk and that ultimately the salvation of Russia will come through these common people who, he feels sure, will always remain orthodox in their belief. He also talks of the equality of all people and hopes that everyone can someday be truly meek and can accept a servant as an equal and, in turn, function as a servant to others.

True equality, he says, is found only in the "spiritual dignity of man." As an example, he tells of an old servant's giving him a sum of money for the monastery. This, the elder reveals, is the ideal reversal in action; a master-servant relationship exists no longer.

Zossima admonishes his listeners to love all of God's creatures and to take on the responsibility of all men's sins. He explains that often God expects many things that we cannot understand with human logic. Man, for example, should not judge his fellow men — even criminals — says Zossima; man must pray for those who are outside the church, for there does not exist a material hell. There is only a spiritual hell, he says. He then collapses to the floor and reaches out as though to embrace the earth. Joyfully he gives up his soul to God.

Commentary

The final views of Father Zossima are presented in this book and, because of their positive quality, Dostoevsky inserts them next to the questioning disbeliefs of Ivan Karamazov. They act somewhat like a counterbalance to the many ideas presented in Book V.

Unlike Ivan, Zossima is didactic – the most didactic character in the novel, perhaps in all of Dostoevsky's writings. His ideas are too abstract to be presented as Ivan's were; his ideas are too profound to be presented in any other way than by simple exhortation.

Parts of Zossima's philosophy have, of course, been discussed in earlier books but here almost all of his tenets are gathered together and presented either by examples from his own life or through exhortations and miniature sermons. In one sense, Zossima is an extension of earlier Dostoevskian characters but, because of his personal history, he is much more than a mere abstraction of the author's ideas. Surprisingly, Father Zossima is a rather robust character, one who undergoes many and diverse experiences before dedicating his life to the monastery. There are reasons for his convictions; he is no conventional saint.

Concerning the amount of background material that Zossima gives, it is most important that we see him against such relief. If the elder's theories are to be accepted as valid, we cannot view him as an isolated or even as a repressed person who turns to religion in order to escape the world's rejection. Zossima was not an introvert; his youth was wild and reckless, filled with "drunkenness, debauchery, and devilry." He was popular with his fellow officers and with people in general. His conversion and his subsequent religious dedication, therefore, are grounded in motivated reality.

The account of the duel and Zossima's actions show him to be a person of physical courage as well as of moral courage. It is significant that the conversion was brought about by his remembering some of his dead brother's ideas about loving life and respecting all things in this world. From this time onward, these ideas become more and more central to Zossima's final philosophy of life.

Concerning suffering, Zossima's explanation of why he bowed down to Dmitri has its roots deep in Dostoevskian philosophy. In *Crime and Punishment*, for example, the protagonist bows down before a prostitute because he sees in her "the suffering of all humanity." Suffering, Dostoevsky felt, was the genesis of retribution. Only through great suffering can a man be purified of his sins and it is this process that Zossima sees within Dmitri.

In speaking of his love for the Bible, Zossima says that the book's basic lesson is this: one must realize the vast love that God has for mankind. At first, admittedly, such a realization is not easy. It is difficult to accept God giving his beloved Job to the devil for no other reason than to boast to his opponent. But the value of the parable, says Zossima, lies in the fact that it is a mystery, "that the passing earthly show and the eternal verity are brought together." This, of course, is diametrically opposed to what Ivan believes. He refuses to accept any idea that cannot be comprehended by earthly logic. But for Zossima, the greatness of God lies in the fact that man cannot comprehend God's ways and that some things of earth must remain a mystery. Only with such a mystery does man realize the full extent of God's glory. If man could comprehend all, then God would lose his sense of majesty. And, again in contrast to Ivan (who loves humanity but cannot accept the idea of suffering that God imposes upon man), Zossima says "one who does not believe in God will not believe in God's people. He who believes in God's people will see His Holiness too, even though he had not believed in it till then." The elder insists on practicing active love for mankind; only through love will one come to believe in God. For the present, Ivan would disagree. He spends his time intellectualizing over abstruse problems; he has no time left for active love.

With the appearance of the mysterious stranger, Zossima is put to his first test. It would have been easy to tell the stranger that he has suffered enough and that there is no need for him to ruin his life and his family's life by making an open confession. But Zossima is quietly persuasive in his efforts to get the stranger to recognize his errors. There is no attempt at coercion, but simply a quiet plea for him to perform that which his conscience tells him must be done.

As Zossima confides his wisdom to Alyosha, the reader should be aware that the elder's views are essentially those by which Dostoevsky himself tried to live, or at least, wished to live by. Particularly, Dostoevsky was interested in these concepts:

1. *The Russian monk and his possible significance.* — Zossima believes that the salvation of Russia would come from two sources — the Russian monks and from a vast, idealized section of the Russian population that he referred to as the Russian people, or the Russian folk. The monks, however, were even more important than the folk if the regeneration of Russia was to be accomplished. From the monks would come the energy and ideas of purity and love. The monk, Zossima believes, practices obedience, fasting, and prayer, believing that these three

disciplines will accomplish for him the only true freedom: sacred freedom. Such freedom is forever denied the man who exists in contemporary society, the slave to mechanical and material frivolities; he will never attain the freedom needed for a pure understanding of life's meaning. He is too involved with life to be able to contemplate life. Only the monk, a man who has "freed himself from the tyranny of material things and habits" can conceive great ideas and serve them. In essence, this is the elder's answer to the question posed by the Grand Inquisitor and Ivan. Only in freedom can man conceive of ideas great enough to make life worth preserving.

And after the monk gives birth to example and philosophy, the renascence begins and, within the Russian folk, a new Russia is nourished. The folk, of course, can never hope to completely emulate the life of the monk but, because of their living close to the soil and to basic matters of life, they can most easily assimilate the wisdom of the Russian monk. Of course Zossima realizes that the average peasant sins occasionally, but he also believes that the peasant realizes that he is wrong in his sinning. This realization will be his salvation, for man must first recognize righteousness as the supreme virtue; this the folk do. One must not despair of the peasant, Zossima counsels, for even in his sinfulness and in his ignorant ways, "salvation will come from the people, from their faith and their meekness," an idea very often advocated by Dostoevsky. He uses, for example, Sonia in *Crime and Punishment* as such a type, the so-called passive redemptive character, and suggests that through the passive acceptance of faith and by extreme meekness, salvation will be achieved. The folk are Zossima's hope, for they believe basically as does the monk. The elder says that "an unbelieving reformer will never do anything in Russia. Even if he is sincere in heart and a genius, the people will meet the atheist and overcome him." But if one considers the widespread atheism that followed the Communist revolution in Russia, Dostoevsky perhaps never wrote anything that proved to be so absolutely incorrect as this prophecy of Father Zossima.

2. *Of masters and servants, and of whether it is possible for them to be brothers in spirit.* — Zossima advocates an absolute equality for all men. True dignity does not come from the possession of great material wealth. Dignity, the elder says, is derived only from an inner sense of personal worth; it is able to respect another person without envying that person. When man attains such dignity he creates a unity, a brotherhood in which a master may associate with a servant without losing either self-respect or dignity. This is Zossima's utopia, founded upon "the grand unity of man," preserved by men who long with all their heart to be the servant of all.

3. *Of prayer, of love and of contact with other worlds.* — Zossima admonished his adherents to pray for others, even those who have sinned. God, he says, will look favorably upon any sinner who stands before Him, proving that someone is offering up a prayer for that sinner. And again the elder re-emphasizes to those assembled his strong belief in the power of positive love. "Love a man even in his sin, for that is the semblance of Divine Love and is the highest love on earth. Love all God's creation, the whole and every grain of sand in it. Love every leaf, every ray of God's light. Love the animals, love the plants, love everything. If you love everything, you will perceive the divine mystery in things." By loving, man gains new respect for everything in God's world. Thus "we must love not occasionally, for a moment, but for ever."

One of Zossima's principal ideas that particularly touches Alyosha is the elder's view of man's responsibility for another's sins. Zossima maintains that everyone must make himself "responsible for all men's sins . . . for as soon as you sincerely make yourself responsible for everything and for all men, you will see at once that it is really so and that you are to blame for every one and for all things." If one carries this idea to its logical conclusion, then, we see that Alyosha must eventually take partial responsibility for the murder of his father. This he indeed does, finally realizing that man must become an active participant rather than a passive observer of life.

Concerning man's limitation of understanding all that is holy, Zossima says that man is given a mystic sense of his loving bond with the other world. Like Ivan, the elder admits that man cannot understand the mysterious ways of God, but, for Zossima, the very existence of something so mysteriously unexplainable is proof that man owes love and allegiance to a higher power. Zossima takes Ivan's premises, therefore, for his proof of God's existence. "On the final judgment," says the elder, "man will not be asked to account for things which he cannot comprehend, but only for those things he understands."

4. *Can a man judge his fellow creatures?* — Zossima believes that no one can judge a criminal. First, one must recognize that no man is only a criminal and perhaps more than all other men, the seemingly innocent, and not the allegedly guilty, is most to blame for whatever crime has been committed. Alyosha uses such a theory when he refuses to judge Dmitri; furthermore, during his brother's trial, he forgives him. From a realistic point of view, Zossima's views on the criminal are too ideal. Zossima would allow a criminal to go free and hope that he would come to condemn his acts. Such idealism is touchingly naive.

And with the same sort of idealism, Zossima advocates kissing the earth, "love it with an unceasing, consuming love." Love of the mother earth, one might note, is central to many of Dostoevsky's novels. In *Crime and Punishment*, the murderer Raskolnikov is told to go and bow down to the earth which he has defiled because of his crime. And, in the poem from Schiller that Dmitri often recites, there is a hymn of praise for the earthly existence. In total loving then—loving even the earth—Zossima says that man can realize an ecstasy which is a "gift of God," not given to many but certainly to the elect. The ideal of a spiritual elite is foreign to Ivan's thinking, but Zossima believes in such a minority and stresses that they should be proud of being elect; their examples will lead others to God's light.

5. *Of hell and hell fire, a mystic reflection.*—Zossima's views on this subject do not conform with the orthodox views of the church and later Ferapont will allude to this fact when he drives the devils from Zossima's cell. Zossima absolutely does not believe in a material hell fire, one that burns and punishes. To him, hell is spiritual agony, growing out of the inner conscience of the damned. If there were material punishment, he says, it would alleviate the spiritual punishment because of its intense physical pain. The greater punishment, the spiritual punishment, is the sinner's recognition that he is forever separated from God. Zossima strays even further from the teachings of the church by his prayers for the condemned. He prays for them because "love can never be an offense to Christ."

PART THREE

BOOK VII

Summary

As soon as Father Zossima's body is prepared for burial, it is placed in a large room and, news traveling fast, the room is quickly filled. As soon as they hear of the elder's death, large numbers of people gather, expecting a miracle. There is no miracle, however, only this: Zossima's corpse begins to putrify almost immediately and the odor of decay is soon sickening to all of the mourners. All present become nauseated and begin to grow fearful because they believe that the decay of a body is related to its spiritual character. It seems an evil omen that Zossima's corpse would rot so soon after death, for the elder was popularly believed to be on the verge of sainthood.

Discontented monks and enemies of Father Zossima are not long to act. Quickly they announce that the decaying body is proof that the elder was no saint; at last the doctrine he preached is proved to be incorrect. The townspeople are confused. Tradition and superstition are embedded in their nerves. They have expected something awesome but certainly not a portent that points to Zossima's being a possible disciple of Satan. Not even Alyosha escapes the fear that grips the community. He cannot understand why God has allowed such disgrace to accompany the elder's death.

Father Ferapont, the fanatical ascetic, rushes to Zossima's cell and begins to exorcise devils out of all the corners, and elsewhere there is also madness — the entire monastery is torn by confused loyalties and uncertainties. Finally, the extreme Ferapont is ordered to leave. But shortly thereafter there is another departure from the monastery. Alyosha leaves also; he wishes to find solitude to grieve and ponder.

Alone, he again questions the justice of all that has happened. Instead of receiving the glory that Alyosha believed was Zossima's due, his mentor is now "degraded and dishonored." Alyosha cannot doubt God, but he must question why He has allowed such a dreadful thing to occur.

Alyosha is interrupted in his thoughts as the seminarian, Rakitin, who earlier mocked Alyosha, ridicules his grief and makes contemptuous remarks about Zossima's decaying body. He tempts Alyosha with sausage and vodka, both of which are denied a monk during Lent, and Alyosha suddenly accepts both. Rakitin then goes a step further and suggests that they visit Grushenka and again Alyosha agrees.

Grushenka is astonished at her visitors but regains her composure and explains that she is waiting for an important message to arrive. They are curious about the message and she tells them that it comes from an army officer whom she loved five years ago and who deserted her. Now he has returned to the province and is sending for her.

Grushenka notices Alyosha's dejection and tries to cheer him by sitting on his knee and teasing him, but when she learns that Father Zossima has died only a few hours earlier, she too becomes remorseful. She upbraids herself and denounces her life as that of a wicked sinner. Alyosha stops her, speaking with great kindness and understanding, and the two suddenly exchange glimpses into each other's souls. Love and trust are given, one to the other, and Grushenka unabashedly speaks to

Alyosha of her problems; she no longer feels ashamed of her life. As for Alyosha, Grushenka's genuine expressions of sympathy lift him out of the deep depression he has felt since Zossima's death. Rakitin cannot understand this sudden compassion between them and is spiteful and vindictive, especially after Grushenka confesses that she had paid Rakitin to bring Alyosha to her. The message arrives from Grushenka's lover and she excuses herself and leaves, asking Alyosha to tell Dmitri that she did love him — once, for an hour.

Very late Alyosha returns to the monastery and goes to Zossima's cell. He kneels and prays, still troubled by many things, then hears Father Paissy reading the account of the wedding at Cana in the Gospel of St. John and, because he is exhausted and because of the sweet lull of the Father's voice, Alyosha dozes. He dreams that he is at the marriage in Cana, along with Christ and the other guests. Zossima appears and calls to Alyosha; he tells him to come forth and join the crowd, reminding him that man should be joyful. Even today, he says, Alyosha has helped Grushenka find her path toward salvation.

Alyosha wakes and his eyes are filled with tears of joy. He goes outside and flings himself on the earth, kissing and embracing it. His heart is filled with ecstasy over his new knowledge and his new understanding of the joy of life.

Commentary

Dostoevsky has been preparing the reader throughout the novel for this single crisis in Alyosha's life. There have been many hints that a miracle is expected to accompany Zossima's death, but one of the central points of Ivan's Grand Inquisitor tale is that man must believe freely in the teachings of a person without the benefit of either divine manifestations or miracles. A person's beliefs, furthermore, can be greatly strengthened by emerging triumphantly from a period of great doubt. And, in this chapter, Dostoevsky presents Alyosha's tests — corollaries of Christ's tests in the wilderness. If Alyosha emerges successfully, he will then be qualified to move within society and to influence it.

Alyosha, of course, does not need miracles for himself. But he recognizes the need of others for them and with no miracle and because the body is decaying, he knows that spiteful rumors will rise around Zossima's memory. He cannot endure the holiest of holy men exposed to jeering and mockery. Such indignity and humiliation of premature decay are unnecessary.

Alyosha's questionings align him closely with his brother Ivan. Ivan also asked about God's justice and, like his brother, Alyosha does not question God; he is concerned only about His justice. When the seminarian appears, Alyosha even echos Ivan's arguments by saying, "I am not rebelling against my God; I simply don't accept His world." But Karamazovs are concerned with justice, not God Himself.

Alyosha, of course, realizes that Christ went through such jeering and mockery. But, for a moment, he gives way to temptation and, in this way, he becomes human and not semi-divine; he becomes believably mortal. He can later be more deeply admired for his courage in resisting temptation. Alyosha questions and by his questions one realizes the value of doubting. A serene acceptance of all — with no questioning — is neither courageous nor admirable; it is merely shallow, immature. Alyosha, when he defies his vows and accepts the sausage and vodka and goes to see Grushenka, has a temporary spiritual revolt, but emerges a much stronger adherent of faith.

In terms of a larger perspective within the total action of the novel, one should remember that Ivan leaves town on the day that Zossima dies. Ivan catches the train about the same time that Alyosha arrives at Grushenka's. Also, it is later this evening that Fyodor's murder takes place and it is also later this evening that Alyosha rediscovers his faith and rededicates himself to the principles advocated by Father Zossima.

Ironically, Alyosha's transformation initially results from his encounter with Grushenka. He goes there in defiance of his monastic orders and Grushenka, for her part, hopes to seduce Alyosha's innocence; his purity is threatening. But when they meet, Alyosha sees in Grushenka a woman he cannot condemn; he sees "a loving heart" that can compassionately respond to the suffering Alyosha is undergoing. In his confession to her, he admits that he came hoping only to find an evil woman. Such honesty is infectious and transforming. Grushenka says, "He is the first, the only one who has pitied me...I've been waiting all my life for some one like you. I knew that some one like you would come and forgive me." And, unlikely as it seems, perhaps in a way like the miracle that all expected, carnality and purity create new love and compassion. The explanation, however, is far from being that of a miracle. Alyosha has only followed Zossima's teachings. He has loved Grushenka; he has not damned her and he, and she, suddenly rediscover themselves.

At the end of this scene, Rakitin, who could not understand the attraction between Alyosha and Grushenka, feels that Alyosha dislikes him for taking twenty-five rubles from Grushenka. But the point is this: Alyosha does not judge him; Rakitin leaves because he judges himself and finds himself guilty.

When Alyosha returns to the monastery, he feels such mixed emotions that there is a "sweetness in his heart." By this single experience with Grushenka, he has found the value of much that Zossima has preached. He has seen how responding to even such a person as Grushenka has changed his entire view of life. Suddenly, he feels himself at peace with the entire world.

Alyosha listens to the monk read of the marriage in Cana and realizes that Christ came to give people pleasure in this world; he came to preach a message of joy and love. This is exactly what Father Zossima advocated. In his dream, he sees his beloved elder in the presence of Christ and knows that the message they both preached is far more important than any "miracle." With love, he embraces the earth and is quietly filled with new understanding of all Zossima has said. He leaves the monastery with new conviction. He is ready at last to take his place in the world as Zossima has said that he must.

BOOK VIII

Summary

Dmitri feels that there is still a possibility that Grushenka may accept him as her husband, but his problem is that if she does accept him, he cannot rightfully carry her away until he repays the money he owes Katerina Ivanovna. In a desperate effort to find a solution, then, he contrives a fantastic scheme. He goes to old Samsonov — Grushenka's previous protector — and offers him the rights to some property that he believes the law courts might take away from Fyodor and give to him if the old merchant will immediately give him 3,000 rubles. The merchant, of course, refuses and plays a trick on Dmitri: he sends him off to the country to see a merchant named Lyagavy, who is bargaining with Fyodor for this very property.

Dmitri pawns his watch, hires transportation to the neighboring town, and finds the merchant. Unfortunately, the man is thoroughly drunk. Dmitri tries to sober him up, but is unable to, so waits until the next day. The merchant remains in a stupor, so Dmitri returns to town, hoping to borrow money from Madame Hohlakov. Madame Hohlakov, however, tries to convince him that he should go off to the gold mines if he wants money; she absolutely refuses to lend him anything.

Dmitri next goes to claim Grushenka, but finds that she is not at home. The servant is no help; she pretends that she does not know where Grushenka has gone. Dmitri is outraged. He picks up a brass pestle and dashes to his father's house. Then he sneaks into the garden and peers through a lighted window. He is sure that Grushenka has finally come to the old man. He is disappointed, however; he sees only his father pacing the floor. But to make certain that Grushenka is not there, Dmitri taps the secret signal. The old man opens the window and Dmitri is greatly relieved. Grushenka is not with his father!

Meanwhile, Grigory, the old servant, awakens and goes into the garden for a breath of air. He sees Dmitri leaving the garden and tries to stop him, but Dmitri, confused and distraught, fights off his attacker and finally strikes him on the head with the pestle. The servant crumples to the ground and Dmitri stops a moment to see if the man is dead. He tries to stop the puddle of blood; then, in panic he tosses the pestle away and flees.

He returns to Grushenka's house and forces the servants to reveal where Grushenka has gone. The answer is agonizing: she has gone to rejoin her first lover. Dmitri knows now that he can no longer claim the girl. He must step aside and leave her to her happiness. But he passionately wants one last look at Grushenka. After that, he will kill himself; his future holds nothing without Grushenka. He goes to retrieve pistols from Perhotin, a minor official who lent Dmitri money and kept the pistols as security. Perhotin is amazed to see Dmitri, who is now carrying a large bundle of money and blotched with blood. He goes to a nearby store with young Karamazov and remains while Dmitri buys three hundred rubles worth of food and wine and makes arrangements to go where Grushenka is rumored to be staying. After Perhotin watches Dmitri leave, he decides to do some detective work.

Dmitri is in luck: Grushenka is indeed staying where he was directed. He rushes to her rooms and greatly shocks Grushenka but she recovers and welcomes him. Until now the celebration has been very gloomy and restrained. Dmitri's wine helps liven the spirits and soon Grushenka and her officer friend and Dmitri are all playing cards together. All does not go well, however. The Polish officer begins to cheat and tosses out disgusting, cynical remarks. Grushenka recoils. She realizes that she can never love such a man. Dmitri senses Grushenka's pain and when the officer finally turns his insults on her, Dmitri forces him into another room and locks him inside. Then a real celebration ensues and Grushenka knows that she can love only Dmitri.

Dmitri is not quite so lucky. He is troubled because he has struck Grigory, perhaps killed him; he also owes money to Katerina Ivanovna. He talks with Grushenka of their future together but they are interrupted. A group of officers arrive, charge Dmitri with the murder of his father, and place him under arrest.

Commentary

Until now, the novel has moved with a sure, slow deliberateness as Dostoevsky depicted the intellectual conflicts in Ivan, the philosophy of Zossima, and the mystic affirmation of life by Alyosha. Now, however, this section, devoted to Dmitri, rushes along with breath-taking speed as it records Dmitri's frantic efforts to save both his life and his love.

Dostoevsky is a master at depicting the torment of despondency within a character who has no money and desperately needs it in order to salvage some remnant of his honor. Dmitri has spent most of the money that Katerina Ivanovna has lent him and, although we know that he has the rest concealed on him, he still feels that he cannot elope with Grushenka until the entire sum is repaid. He must secure the money so that he can begin a new life with Grushenka and still retain his integrity. If he were to use Katerina's money to elope with Grushenka, he feels that this would be his absolute lowest, most degrading act. And, looking forward, when he decides to step aside and allow Grushenka to return to her first love, one should realize that by this time, he has decided to end his life. This resolution should be kept in mind when Dmitri shows few qualms about usurping the money; it is not that he considers it any less dishonorable but, because he intends to take his life, he will not have to face the dishonor.

Dostoevsky does not present an entirely admirable character in Dmitri. He continually lets the reader know that Dmitri's financial predicament is due to his irresponsibility with money. Consequently, his frantic search for someone who will lend him money and his absurd proposals reveal his lack of acumen. He is also unable to realize that the old merchant, Samsonov, is making fun of him and sending him on a wild goose chase. It takes two days for Dmitri to come to his senses, but even then he still tries to convince Madame Hohlakov that she should lend him money. Were he more rational he would know that the lady thoroughly detests him. These scenes of begging, then, show to what degree of desperation Dmitri will go in his need for money. This alone casts suspicion upon him concerning his father's murder.

Remember, too, that Dostoevsky arranges his plot in such a way that it is natural and logical for the reader to assume on first reading that Dmitri is the murderer. Every detail in this chapter attests to the incriminating evidence that will be accumulated against Dmitri. Furthermore, even Dmitri's thoughts cast suspicion upon him. As he goes to see Madame Hohlakov, for example, he thinks "...his last hope...if this broke down, nothing else was left him in the world but to rob and murder some one for the three thousand." Such evidence, coupled with his distraught emotions, allows the reader to assume that Dmitri is indeed guilty of his father's murder.

Ironically, one small lie contributes most of all to Dmitri's arrest. Fenya, Grushenka's servant, lies to him; she says she does not know of Grushenka's whereabouts, thereby forcing Dmitri to go to his father's to search for her. Had the servant told the truth, then Dmitri would not have been present at the scene of the murder; nor would he have been covered with Grigory's blood.

Dmitri's resolve to commit suicide is quite believable. On the road to Mokroe to meet Grushenka, he fully intends to see her, then kill himself. Indeed, the mere fact that he is now spending the rest of Katerina Ivanovna's money and the fact that he has left old Grigory to face possible death from his wounds all suggest that Dmitri has no longer any concern about the future. During the ride, he knows that he cannot stand in Grushenka's way but he wants to see her once more. He is in agony; he even asks the peasant driver, as one might ask a priest, to forgive him all the sins of his life. Incidentally, with this last act, he echoes one of Zossima's ideas concerning the repudiation of master-servant distinction and the responsibility of all men for one another.

Dmitri fully intends to kill himself and his prayer, most of all, reveals the anguish in his soul. "Lord," he pleads, "receive me with all my lawlessness and do not condemn me. Let me pass Thy judgment—do not condemn me for I have condemned myself...for I love Thee, O Lord. I am a wretch, but I love Thee. If Thou sendest me to hell, I shall love Thee there and from there I shall cry out that I love Thee for ever and ever." In this prayer is Dmitri's most redeeming value; it holds the key to Dmitri's character—that which Zossima recognized. Dmitri is one of the "folk" of whom the elder spoke. He is one of those who may sin, but who still love God. That love, said Zossima, leads to salvation; such deep love the elder recognized early in his relationship with Dmitri. Henceforth young Karamazov calls upon this love and its strength as he begins the slow journey toward regeneration and redemption.

BOOK IX

Summary

Perhotin's curiosity is overwhelming. He cannot but be suspicious of Dmitri, so decides to investigate the truth of Dmitri's explanations. He goes to Grushenka's maid and learns about the brass pestle, then goes to Madame Hohlakov's to confirm Dmitri's story about the money. Madame Hohlakov is annoyed at being awakened so late at night, but on hearing the reason, she excitedly declares that she has never given anything to Dmitri.

Perhotin has no choice; it is his duty to report all that has happened to the police. But when he arrives, he finds that others also have news to report to the police. Marfa has sent word to them that Fyodor has been murdered.

An investigation follows and it is decided that Dmitri Karamazov must be immediately apprehended. Dmitri is arrested and pleads that he is innocent of the crime but no one, of course, believes him—not even Grushenka, who bursts into the room crying that she drove him to commit murder but that she will love him forever. On cross-examination, Dmitri confesses that he is guilty of hating his father but maintains that in spite of this, he did not murder the old man. His guilt, however, now seems more definite to the authorities. Eventually more admissions are made by Dmitri and he confesses that he did know of the 3,000 rubles that his father had. And he admits that he was indeed in desperate need of that exact sum to repay his debt to Katerina Ivanovna. He does not try to conceal facts that seem to implicate him in the murder, and the knot tightens. Questioned more carefully about his activities on the night of the murder, Dmitri accounts for all his moves, including the visit to his father's house. He even admits taking the pestle with him but cannot give an explanation as to why he did. He is completely honest—on all but one matter: the origin of the large sum of money he had when arrested.

Dmitri is ordered to undress and submit to a thorough search. The officers go through his clothes, searching for more money, and find additional blood stains; they decide to retain his clothing as evidence. Dmitri is then forced to realize the seriousness of his situation and tells where the money came from. He explains about the orgy with Grushenka and reveals that he actually spent only half of the 3,000 rubles Katerina gave him; the other half he has saved. But, having decided to commit suicide, he saw no value in the money any longer and decided to use it for one last fling.

Other witnesses are called in and all agree that Dmitri has stated several times that he spent 3,000 rubles on the orgy and needed 3,000 to replace the sum.

When Grushenka is brought in for her testimony, Dmitri swears to her that he is not the murderer. She, in turn, tries to convince the officials that he is telling the truth, but she is sure that they do not believe her.

The officials complete their examination of witnesses, then inform Dmitri that they have arrived at a decision: he must be retained in prison. He is allowed to say goodby to Grushenka, however. Deeply apologetic for the trouble he has caused her, Dmitri asks her forgiveness and Grushenka answers by promising to remain by him forever.

Commentary

In this book all of Dmitri's past lies and braggadaccios coalesce and smother his pleas of innocence. Logically, one could say that Dmitri had the motive for the murder and was, as confessed, even at the scene of the crime. The conclusion seems obvious. Dostoevsky has carefully arranged the details and the circumstances in such a manner that the case against Dmitri is wholly convincing; the man is guilty. But there is another dimension to the investigation. As the officers review Dmitri's life, Dmitri also reviews his life and begins to realize the nature of his past and its meaning. It is this realization that greatly aids his reformation. Only in the light of such dire circumstances is it possible for someone like Dmitri to evaluate all his acts and take full responsibility for them.

Grushenka has never spoken with Father Zossima, but the wisdom of the elder is a part of her newly discovered self. She tries, for example, to take the blame — to take Dmitri's sins upon herself — by crying out that she is responsible for the crime. She played with the passions of an old man and his son and, as a result, murder was committed. Later, when Dmitri swears to her that he is innocent, she is convinced of the truth of what he has said. She needs no other proof; this alone illustrates the extent of her love for Dmitri. This is the deeply transforming love that Zossima taught.

At first, Dmitri thinks it only a matter of time before he will be able to convince the officials of his innocence, but as the questions and the evidence begin to mount and tighten around him, he begins to see the seriousness of his position. It is then that he undergoes a change. He realizes the need for a transformation. He confesses almost every detail of his life and is bitterly ashamed. And because the officials are writing down the sorry details of his past, he is even more deeply ashamed.

He is quick to see that he is not guilty of the murder but that he is indeed guilty. So often he boasted of killing his father and so often he wished for his father's death; now all that is on trial and he stands, literally, naked before the probing magistrates. The shame of his entire life is revealed in all its disgusting corruptness.

In many of his novels, Dostoevsky is concerned with the actions of police — how officials conduct investigations. Dostoevsky especially details what questions are asked. And throughout the interrogation of Dmitri Karamazov, Dostoevsky does not distort the processes of justice. The officials are depicted as honest and penetrating men, finally arriving at a reasonable conclusion. Dmitri is not tried by brutally caricatured sadists. The logic of the evidence exists.

There is a bit of irony in Dmitri's consideration of Smerdyakov. He is positive that the murder could not have been committed by the cook. He is, according to Dmitri, "a man of the most abject character and a coward."

Perhaps Dmitri's most redeeming act is this: he judges himself and finally welcomes the suffering to be imposed upon him. He assumes his share of the guilt for the murder of his father and he assumes the responsibility for all the deeds of his past. Exclaiming to the officials, he says, "I tell you again, with a bleeding heart, I have learnt a great deal this night. I have learnt that it's not only impossible to live a scoundrel, but impossible to die a scoundrel."

Dmitri's dream is further proof of his redemption. When he dreams that he is crossing the steppes on a cold winter day, passing through a burned village, a gaunt peasant woman holds a crying baby in her arms and Dmitri's heart overflows with anguish and sympathy for such poor people. He is overcome with compassion and love for these and for all humanity. Thus when he wakes he is ready to accept his suffering and exclaims, "By suffering I shall be purified." He is ready to undergo a period of trial and emerge a new and responsible character.

PART FOUR

BOOK X

Summary

Kolya Krassotkin, a widow's only child, is a mature and independent thirteen-year-old with a reputation for being exceptionally daring and imprudent. He is also the boy whom earlier Ilusha stabbed with a penknife; but, good-naturedly, Kolya has never held a grudge. At present he has been training a dog, Perezvon, to do complicated tricks.

On the day before Dmitri's trial, young Kolya is staying with two children of his mother's tenant. He feels uneasy because he has an urgent errand to attend to and leaves as soon as the servant returns. His errand turns out to be a visit to Ilusha. Kolya knows that Alyosha has arranged for other boys to visit the dying Ilusha every day, but until today Kolya has never visited the boy.

He arrives at Ilusha's with a friend, Smurov, and asks him to call Alyosha outside; he has a great curiosity to meet Alyosha. The two meet and immediately become good friends, especially because Alyosha treats Kolya as an equal. Kolya explains to his new friend about Ilusha's background and tells him that once they were fast friends, but when Kolya heard that Ilusha fed a dog a piece of bread with a pin in it, he tried to punish the boy. The punishment backfired, however, and Kolya was stabbed with the penknife. Since this happened, however, Ilusha has come to feel very bad about the dog, Zhutchka.

Alyosha takes Kolya inside and Ilusha is overjoyed to see his old friend again. Kolya, however, begins to tease Ilusha about the dog; then, before anyone can stop him, he calls in the dog he has been training. It turns out to be Zhutchka. Everyone is delighted and the dying Ilusha sheds tears of happiness. Kolya explains that, until now, he has stayed away so that he could train the dog for Ilusha.

A doctor from Moscow, whom Katerina has sent for, arrives to examine Ilusha and the visitors reluctantly leave the room. As they wait outside, Kolya explains his views of life to Alyosha and Alyosha listens carefully, understanding the boy's real motives. He wants to impress Alyosha with his hodgepodge of other people's philosophies. Alyosha is sympathetic to him, though, and especially drawn to the young boy when he confesses his weaknesses.

As the doctor leaves, it is quite apparent that Ilusha has not long to live. Even Ilusha is aware that he is dying. He tries to comfort his father, and Kolya is deeply affected by this scene between father and son. He promises Alyosha that he will now come often to visit the dying boy.

Commentary

Some critics have complained that in a novel of such extreme complexity and length, Book X does not contribute to the novel's unity. The section has often been said to be superfluous and a flaw in construction. A reader, they say, is anxiously concerned about Dmitri at this point, not about Ilusha. But, because of the heavy chapters of violence and passion and murder, this section can be explained in terms of Dostoevsky's inserting a healthy bit of youthful fresh air. The reader is relieved from the strain of contemplating Dmitri's fate.

This relief, however, does not explain all the charges leveled against this section of the novel. It does not, for example, explain an obvious change in tone. Here, Dostoevsky inserts the most overt sentimentality in the entire novel. He seems to play with the reader's emotions and much of the pathetic background material of young Kolya's life is not central to the novel except in the very large perspective of establishing him as the person whom Alyosha will train and who will become one of Russia's future citizens, entrusted with the ideas of Father Zossima.

Perhaps, however, the real purpose of the section is this: Dostoevsky is showing Alyosha as he moves among Russian youth, quietly influencing their lives as a living example of Father Zossima's philosophy. The hope of Russia lies in the young and in the common people and Alyosha teaches Kolya much in this section. He meets him as an equal and offers him understanding and trust; he teaches Kolya that one cannot judge Ilusha's father, saying that there are people of rare character who have been crushed by life. The buffoonery of Ilusha's father, he says, is only the man's way of being ironic toward those who have humiliated and intimidated him for years.

Alyosha also instructs Kolya in what a man can learn from another. And because Alyosha accepts all as equals, even Kolya, he kindles a responsive chord of love. By his quiet examples, Alyosha corrects immature views without arousing animosity. He is, for example, careful not to denounce Kolya's potpourri of philosophy; instead, he simply explains that although he disagrees, he does not have contempt for Kolya's ideas. By the latter's response, it is obvious that he will become one of the strongest disciples of Alyosha.

BOOK XI

Summary

During the two months since Dmitri was arrested, Grushenka has been ill and now, as she begins to recover physically, there are also signs of a major spiritual recovery, of a complete "spiritual transformation in her." Also, there is another change: she and Alyosha have become fast friends, and she confides to him that she and Dmitri have quarreled again. In addition, she fears that Dmitri is once again falling in love with Katerina Ivanova. What most concerns her, however, is that Dmitri and Ivan are concealing a secret from her. She pleads with Alyosha to discover what the secret is. Again, Alyosha promises to help a human being in trouble.

On his way to question Dmitri, Alyosha stops and visits Lise, whom he finds feverish and excited. She tells him that she longs to be punished and castigated by God, and says that she regularly prays to suffer torture, for she can no longer respect anything nor anyone. She continuously feels possessed with a terrible urge to destroy. The young girl becomes hysterical as she confesses her secret thoughts, then suddenly sends Alyosha away. And, after he leaves, she does a curious thing: she intentionally slams the door on her fingers and calls herself a wretch.

When Alyosha arrives at the prison where Dmitri is being held, he notices that Rakitin, a seminarian acquaintance, is leaving. He asks Dmitri about Rakitin's visit and is told that the seminarian hopes to write an article proving that Dmitri is the victim of an unhappy environment and that he could not help killing his father. Dmitri then explains to the puzzled Alyosha that he does not take Rakitin seriously, that he tolerates him only because he is amused by his "advanced ideas." More seriously, Dmitri confesses that he now understands his responsibility for his past life and sins and that he is ready to suffer and do penance for his sins. He is sure that there can still be a full and rewarding life for him. Only one thing troubles him, however—Grushenka. He is afraid that the authorities will not let her accompany him to Siberia and he fears that without Grushenka he will be unable to face his years of punishment and thus will never be redeemed.

Dmitri also tells Alyosha that Ivan has come to the prison and has given him a plan for escape. Of course, Dmitri says, Ivan believes him guilty of murder. He then turns to Alyosha and asks his brother's opinion. Never before has he had the courage to speak so candidly with Alyosha and when he hears the young many say, "I've never for one instant believed that you were the murderer," Dmitri is greatly relieved. He feels the power of a new life rising in him.

Alyosha leaves Dmitri and goes to Katerina shortly thereafter. He finds Ivan just leaving but his brother remains long enough to hear what Alyosha says concerning Dmitri. When Ivan leaves, Katerina becomes highly emotional and insists that Alyosha follow him; she is convinced that Ivan is going mad.

Alyosha rushes to rejoin Ivan and learns yet another piece of news. Ivan says that Katerina has a "document in her hands...that proves conclusively" that Dmitri did indeed murder their father. Alyosha denies that such a document could exist and Ivan then asks who the murderer is. Alyosha tells him, "it wasn't you who killed Father," explaining that he is aware that Ivan has been accusing himself, but that God has sent Alyosha to Ivan to reassure him. Ivan is sickened by Alyosha's religious mysticism and leaves him abruptly.

Ivan's nausea, however, is not due wholly to his brother's mysticism; the sickness begins earlier, almost simultaneously with his first visit to Smerdyakov. The servant is recovering in the hospital and maintains that his epileptic seizure on the night of the murder was real. He says further that he understood that Ivan went to Moscow because he suspected a murder was about to be committed and wanted to be far from the scene of the crime. Ivan answers that he will not reveal to the authorities that Smerdyakov is able to sham an epileptic seizure and Smerdyakov counters by promising to say nothing of a certain conversation, their last before the murder.

During Ivan's second visit with Smerdyakov, he demands to know what Smerdyakov meant by his strange statement about their last conversation prior to the murder. Smerdyakov explains that Ivan so desired

his father's death, in order to come into a large portion of the inheritance, that he planned to leave and thereby silently assented to Fyodor's
murder.

Ivan leaves, bewildered, half realizing that he must share the guilt
if Smerdyakov murdered Fyodor. He goes to see Katerina and explains
his complicity and his guilt and Katerina is able to temporarily alleviate
some of his anxiety. She shows him a letter that Dmitri wrote to her saying that, if necessary, he would kill Fyodor in order to repay the money
he stole from her. This letter puts Ivan's mind at ease; Dmitri, not
Smerdyakov, is surely the villain.

Ivan does not see Smerdyakov again until the night before the trial
but by this time the Karamazov servant is tired of all pretense. He
openly admits that it was he who killed Fyodor. He stoutly maintains,
though, that he did not act alone; he acted only as an instrument of Ivan,
saying, "It was following your words I did it." He then explains in great
detail how he accomplished the murder, continuously referring to the
dual responsibility for the murder. Smerdyakov furthermore recalls all
the philosophical discussions the two men have had and accuses Ivan
of having given him the moral justification that made it possible. All
this Ivan did, he says, besides leaving town and permitting the act.

Stunned, Ivan returns to his lodgings; he plans to reveal at the trial
next day all that Smerdyakov has told him, but in his room he finds a
devil. The apparition is dressed like a rather shoddy middle-aged
gentleman and is full of cynical criticism. He forces Ivan to face the most
terrifying aspects of his inner secrets, taunting him with his private
fears and weaknesses until finally Ivan goes mad with rage and hurls a
cup at the intruder. At that moment he hears Alyosha knocking at the
window. His brother brings the news that Smerdyakov has just hanged
himself. Ivan is so upset by his "devil" that when he tries to tell Alyosha
about the experience, he cannot. Alyosha discovers to his horror that
Ivan is suffering a nervous breakdown. He stays the night to nurse
his brother.

Commentary

This book is concerned primarily with depicting Ivan's guilt and
with detailing his duplicity in the murder of his father. Particularly,
Dostoevsky emphasizes the three interviews with Smerdyakov (solving
for the reader, on the plot level, the mystery of Fyodor's killer) and

Ivan's conversation with his imaginary devil. Dostoevsky manipulates the attention of the reader away from the plot question of legal guilt and confronts him with the intricacies of Ivan's dilemma about metaphysical guilt.

Also, in Book XI, Dostoevsky provides necessary background concerning what has happened during the two months that Dmitri has been in jail and it is most important to the author's total view that one know that Grushenka has lain ill following the arrest of Dmitri. One of Dostoevsky's prime concepts, prominent in all his novels, is that crime (or involvement with crime) is often accompanied by illness. And, besides Grushenka's falling ill after she realizes her role in the Karamazov crime, Ivan also falls desperately ill upon his realization of his involvement in the murder. Thus, besides coupling crime and illness, Dostoevsky is structuring a much more important tenet. Because Grushenka is ill and suffers, she becomes regenerated. Knowledge through suffering is one of the novel's prime equations. And to underscore his presentation, Dostoevsky, as a contrast to the sensitive Grushenka, records the mincings of the whimsical and impish Lise. This young lady maintains that she needs to suffer in order to learn and that she likes to make other people suffer, but she is both shallow and superficial. Suffering, for example, is defined by her as punishing children by eating pineapple compote before them. She punishes herself by slamming the door on her finger!

This destructive girl turns Dostoevsky's theories inside out and delights in reviling everyone and everything. Her perversity functions as a vivid contrast to the more healthy and sound soul of Grushenka.

In Chapter 4, the continued regeneration of Dmitri is recorded. Currently, he ponders Ivan's offer of escape and the finances necessary to accomplish it. Earlier he might have impulsively fled; now, however, he has developed into a type of Zossima-man. He feels that he is "responsible for all." "I go for all," he says, "because one must go for all. I didn't kill Father, but I've got to go. I accept it." Furthermore, he now believes that life is full of enjoyment even if one must live imprisoned. His dilemma therefore is this: he wants to accept his suffering and he looks forward to salvation through suffering but he knows that he cannot withstand suffering unless Grushenka is beside him, serving as his inspiration. If he accepts Ivan's plan for escape, might he be rejecting his own salvation?

Dmitri seeks help and explains to Alyosha that Ivan has planned the escape because he believes Dmitri to be guilty. Alyosha reassures his brother that he never believed him to be the murderer. Alyosha then searches for Ivan and finds that he is on the verge of a mental breakdown.

During the first of Ivan's interviews with Smerdyakov, Ivan is told by the cook that he ran away because he already knew that violence was readying itself in the Karamazov house and Smerdyakov further reminds Ivan that the two of them are very much alike. Neither of these ideas Ivan accepts, but he broods on them and as he leaves he feels that there is "an insulting significance in Smerdyakov's last words." It is this ambiguity that brings him back for a second interview.

During this next interview, Smerdyakov accuses Ivan outright of desiring his father's death. "You had a foreboding," he says, "yet went away." This was, in effect, Ivan's open invitation for Smerdyakov to murder Fyodor. Ivan recoils and threatens to expose Smerdyakov to the police, but the servant is wily. He reminds Ivan that he also will be disgraced in the public eye and will be accused of being an accomplice. Ivan realizes the possibility of the cook's threat and slowly concedes that he is indeed guilty. Literally, technically, Smerdyakov is the murderer, but he, Ivan, must share the guilt. This realization weighs heavily on Ivan and before long he is driven to despair. Then he reads the letter that Dmitri has written Katerina telling of his plans to murder his father and is even more confused. His anxiety finally subsides, but he cannot be sure now that Smerdyakov murdered Fyodor. He returns for a third interview.

Now both Ivan and Smerdyakov are ill and no longer talk in riddles. Smerdyakov openly tells Ivan, "You murdered him; you are the real murderer; I was only your instrument, your faithful servant, and it was following your words I did it." Smerdyakov also reminds Ivan of the philosophy that "everything is lawful if there is no immortality" and that Ivan consented by going away. "By your consent to leave, you silently sanctioned doing it," he says. Ivan still cannot accept Smerdyakov as the murderer, however; as the facts stand, he is guilty, *even* if the servant did commit the deed.

Ivan faces his own conscience that night in the form of a tormenting devil. The doppleganger is a witty, urbane, and clever aberration. He affirms nothing for the distraught Ivan and at Ivan's every question, he merely asks another, often ridiculing Ivan's most private fears.

At the end of Book XI, Alyosha arrives with the news of Smerdyakov's death but Ivan is little concerned with the cook's fate. The realization of his own guilt has so shamed and confused him that realities have almost wholly dissolved.

BOOK XII

Summary

The day of Dmitri's trial arrives and the courtroom is filled with curious visitors from distant parts of the land; the trial has aroused much interest. Besides the gruesome details of parricide, which will be discussed, Dmitri is being defended by the celebrated criminal lawyer, Fetyukovitch, who has come from Moscow to undertake the defense and, it is noted, the jury is made up of mostly peasants. Can such country people understand the subtleties of the much-discussed case?

Dmitri enters the courtroom exquisitely dressed in a new frock coat. The judge then reads the indictment against him and asks for his plea. Dmitri responds, "I plead guilty to drunkenness and dissipation... to idleness and debauchery... but I am not guilty of the death of that old man...." Most of the people in the courtroom, however, even those who are partial to Dmitri, believe that the case against him is a strong one, for much of the evidence and nearly all of the witnesses' statements seem to indicate Dmitri's guilt.

Fetyukovitch is an exceptionally skilled trial lawyer. He has grasped all the various aspects of the case and as Grigory, Rakitin, Captain Snegiryov, the innkeeper from Mokroe, and others are called to testify, he skillfully discredits the testimony of each of them, pointing out inconsistencies in their statements and creating doubts about the integrity of their motives.

Later, when three medical experts are called to testify about Dmitri's mental state, each doctor suggests a different cause for Dmitri's behavior and thus, with the medical evidence so contradictory, there is no firm support for either the prosecution or the defense. There is a minor exception, however; the local doctor, Herzenstube, tells several interesting stories about Dmitri's childhood and creates some new sympathy among the listeners.

Alyosha proves to be an asset for his brother because he is well known for his integrity, and during his testimony, he is able to recall an incident with Dmitri, one that happened just before the murder. It proves that Dmitri did have a large sum of money on him and that he did not murder Fyodor for the 3,000 rubles. This fact impresses most people and convinces them that Dmitri has not stolen old Karamazov's secret fund.

Following Alyosha in the witness stand is Katerina, who tells of Dmitri's saving her father from ruin and then refraining from blackmailing and thereby seducing her. Her story is heard with mixed interest, but Dmitri feels that she need not have told the tale because it is a severe blow to her integrity. Now it is publicly known how thoroughly she has humiliated herself for Dmitri. Grushenka is able to add little to Dmitri's defense except for her passionate outcries that he is innocent.

Ivan has not yet testified. His testimony has been postponed because of his illness but suddenly he appears at the trial and at first he is unable to speak sense. He can give no evidence. Then, as he is about to leave, he turns and shows the court the 3,000 rubles that Smerdyakov gave him. He reveals that Smerdyakov is the murderer and that he allowed the servant to perform the act. He becomes so excited that he says that he has a witness for everything he has said—a devil who visits him at night. Hysterically, he asserts the truth of his testimony but is finally dragged from the courtroom, screaming incoherently.

The trial has one more surprise before it recesses. Katerina reverses her statements and shows the court the letter that Dmitri wrote, stating that he might be forced to kill his father. She defends Ivan because she knows that he is suffering from mental illness. Grushenka then accuses Katerina of being a serpent and an uproar follows. When order is finally restored, the lawyers give their concluding speeches.

Once more, Kirillovitch, the prosecutor, describes the murder and analyzes the members of the Karamazov family, emphasizing Dmitri's passionate and undisciplined personality and reviewing in detail Dmitri's activities and his statements during the days preceding to the murder. He insists that Dmitri is exactly the sort of man whose violent disposition would drive him to seek a solution to all his problems through crime. Kirillovitch then dismisses Ivan's theory that Smerdyakov is the murderer by pointing out that the servant did not have any of the qualities of a murderer's personality; he had no motive and, further, was incapacitated on the night of the crime. Dmitri, on the other hand, did have a motive—his hatred for his father—and he had a great need for money. All this, plus the letter he wrote to Katerina, says the prosecutor, is conclusive proof that the crime was premeditated and was, in fact, committed by Dmitri Karamazov. He concludes by making a stirring appeal to the jury to uphold the sacred principles of justice and the moral foundation on which Russian civilization is built by punishing this most horrible of all crimes—the murder of a father by his son.

Fetyukovitch begins his defense by emphasizing that all evidence against Dmitri is circumstantial. No fact withstands objective criticism if examined separately. He also points out that there is no real proof that a robbery took place; the belief that Fyodor kept 3,000 rubles, he says, is only based on hearsay and there is no reason to disbelieve Dmitri's explanation of where the money he spent at Mokroe came from. He also reminds the jury that the letter Dmitri wrote to Katerina was the result of extreme drunkenness and despair and cannot be equated with premeditated murder. Then, after reviewing all the evidence, he makes this final and important point: Fyodor's murder was not that of parricide. The man was never a father to Dmitri, nor was he a father to any of his sons. It is true that Fyodor's sensuousness resulted in Dmitri's birth, but Fyodor was a father in that respect only. After Dmitri was born, Fyodor continually mistreated the boy and from then on, neglected all his parental duties. He, in fact, abandoned the boy. All his life Dmitri endured mistreatment and now, if he is convicted, the jury will be destroying his only chance to reform and to make a decent life for himself. The lawyer asks for mercy so that Dmitri can be redeemed. He reminds the jury that the end of Russian justice is not to punish ...ner, it is pronounced so that a criminal can be helped toward salvation and regeneration.

The audience is overcome with sympathy and enthusiasm and breaks into applause. The jury retires. The general consensus is that Dmitri will surely be acquitted but such is not the case. When the verdict is read, Dmitri is found guilty on every count.

Commentary

Recorded in detail, in this book, is Dmitri's trial and here is massive evidence of Dostoevsky's long interest in the proceedings of the Russian courts and of the psychology practiced by lawyers. Dmitri's attorney, Fetyukovitch, for example, is able to undermine and cleverly discredit the testimony of every witness. He is particularly masterful as he points out that Grigory, unused to drinking, had been imbibing on the night of the murder and could have seen "the gates of heaven open up." Likewise, with all witnesses, Fetyukovitch discovers and enlarges a loophole in their statements so that truth becomes extremely tenuous.

The trial, which up to a certain point has been shaped by the incisive intelligence of Dmitri's lawyer, takes on a new turn as Ivan comes forward to give his testimony. He desires to tell all he knows and to confess his own part in the murder but he rages incoherently and, most of all, finally suffers a nervous collapse. This, in turn, forces Katerina to admit evidence that ultimately convicts Dmitri. The confused young girl, in her attempt to save Ivan from disgrace, produces the letter written by Dmitri announcing his plan to murder his father, if necessary, to pay back the money he owes. More than any other factor, this letter condemns Dmitri.

The final section of Book XII covers the long speeches of the prosecutor and the defense attorney in which each summarizes the arguments of the trial and offers his interpretation. Actually, nothing new is revealed in these speeches. They serve chiefly to illustrate the nature of the legal minds emerging in Russia during this period.

EPILOGUE

Summary

After Dmitri's trial, Alyosha goes to Katerina's, where Ivan is ill, unconscious, and burning with high fever; in spite of gossip, Katerina has ordered that he be brought to her house. When Alyosha arrives, she confesses her deep regret over what she revealed during the trial, but says that already Dmitri's escape is being planned. She explains further that more help is needed; Alyosha must aid his brother and bribe the appropriate officials. Alyosha agrees, but forces Katerina to promise that she will visit Dmitri in prison.

Alyosha then goes to his brother and tells him that Katerina will also come, but Dmitri has weightier problems troubling him. He explains his craving desire to repent and, through suffering, to become a new human being. He fears only one thing: that he will be unable to carry out his intentions if the authorities do not let Grushenka accompany him. Alyosha explains the plans that have been made for the escape and, reluctantly, Dmitri agrees to them. He makes one stipulation, however; he escapes only for the present. Someday he must return to Mother Russia.

Katerina then enters and she and Dmitri ask each other for forgiveness. Peace though is not so easy, even now, for Grushenka unexpectedly arrives and although Katerina begs her for forgiveness, Grushenka still feels too bitter toward her former rival to acknowledge any pleas.

Meantime, little Ilusha has died and Alyosha leaves Dmitri to go to the young boy's funeral. After the burial, Alyosha talks with the many school friends of Ilusha and asks them to remember forever their friendship at the present moment. He, in turn, promises that he will never forget any one of them. The boys are deeply affected by Alyosha's sincerity and all cheer, "Hurrah for Karamazov."

Commentary

In a sense, the epilogue conforms to the nineteenth-century custom of tidying up the end of a novel. Here the final fates of all characters are revealed and the reader is relieved from any speculating. Dmitri accepts Ivan's plan for escape, but only after he has Alyosha's sanction. As for Alyosha, he conforms to the directives of the late Father Zossima. He does not condemn his brother nor does he object to the escape. In short, he refuses to judge Dmitri.

Even in his escape, it is important to note that Dmitri feels that he will suffer immensely. He has been depicted as being closely attached to Russia and to be exiled to America—to be separated from the soil from which he takes his strength—this is an extreme form of punishment for him. His plans are to return to his country as soon as possible and then to live anonymously in some remote region. This lasting love for Russian soil, of course, reflects Dostoevsky's passion for his native land.

In the novel's final pages, all concern is with Alyosha and the young school friends of Ilusha. The ex-monk has had little success with adults in Russian society, but with children he is unexcelled. The boys eagerly gather around Alyosha and are openly responsive to his speech about love and devotion—a message quite clear: Dostoevsky believes that youth, nurtured on the wisdom of Father Zossima, will be the salvation of Russia.

CHARACTER ANALYSES

FYODOR KARAMAZOV

The father of the Karamazov brothers is a disgusting sensualist. He has virtually no redeeming qualities. He is a self-centered man—corrupt and immoral—and is cynically dedicated only to the fulfillment of his bestial appetites. He has married twice for selfish reasons and has treated each wife with total disrespect. Little wonder, however, for a man who has no respect for himself can respect no one else.

As pointed out during Dmitri's trial, he was never, in the truest sense, a father to any of his sons. When they were young, he was oblivious of their presence and relieved when relatives took them away. Later, he refused to give any of them money, and although the matter is not stated definitely in the novel, all indications suggest that he cheated Dmitri out of a large portion of his mother's inheritance.

Fyodor's vulgarity is part and parcel of his every action; he lives the part of the vulgar buffoon, delighting in embarrassing anyone who is in his presence. Not unsurprisingly, his degeneration leads indirectly to his death; it was his seduction of the village idiot, "stinking Lizaveta," which produced Smerdyakov, the strange epileptic who grew up as his father's servant, then dispassionately slaughtered him.

DMITRI

Dmitri, the oldest Karamazov son, and the only son who grows up with the expectation of coming into property, can be considered the pivotal figure of the novel. The novel revolves around his guilt, in connection with the murder of Fyodor Karamazov, and Dmitri is the person who undergoes the most significant change during the course of the novel.

Dmitri does not have the intellectual pretensions of Ivan and cannot understand his brother's metaphysical concerns, nor is Dmitri as spiritual as his brother Alyosha, although he basically accepts God and immortality. He is, in fact, best represented as being caught midway between a sort of "Madonna-Sodom" opposition; he fluctuates between two poles of existence. Coursing through him are impulses for honor and nobility, side by side with impulses toward the low and the animal. This duality is partly explained by Dostoevsky's belief that the typical Russian is able to love God even while he sins. Dmitri, for example, declares that he will love God forever, even if God sends him to hell.

A particularly crucial scene and one that shows Dmitri's contradictory personality is his manipulation of events in order to force Katerina to come to his room so that he can seduce her. When she arrives, Dmitri cannot carry out his scheme. The better part of his nature has gained control of him.

Compounding Dmitri's confusion is his realization of being raked by these polar extremes. He says, at one point, that "beauty is a terrible and awful thing," meaning that a beautiful woman can arouse sensual desires, yet can also, and at the same time, inspire noble and elevated thoughts. He is the victim of opposite extremes of passion yet cannot comprehend their origin, their dimensions, or their purpose.

When Dmitri is cornered with a serious accusation, of which he is innocent, he begins to face the consequences of all his past acts. Up to now he has lived with no regard for consequence. He has spent money without discretion and has bragged about his intention to rob his father; now his character is forced to change. And it is after his interrogation that he begins to emerge as a tragic figure. He realizes that his past life is not free of guilt and duplicity and, although he is innocent of his father's murder, he is willing to accept another's punishment. This suffering will reform his life and for the first time there exists genuine hope for his resurrection.

IVAN

Ivan's basic nature is defined early in the novel when he is depicted as being a very independent child. He is, in contrast to his brother Alyosha (who freely accepts help and aid from other people), unable to receive freely any act of generosity.

By nature Ivan is a very studious person who has strong intellectual inclinations, qualities that later completely dominate his personality. As a result, we come to know Ivan through his thoughts rather than through his actions; in other words, his intellect defines his essential nature.

As an adult, Ivan seldom speaks and then only to individuals who seemingly are intellectually capable of understanding his complexities. When he accompanies the others to the monastery, for instance, he is quiet and reserved; he waits to talk until someone begins to discuss Ivan's article, written while he was still at the university. This article is a key to Ivan's makeup; he is an atheist, yet concerned with the fate of mankind on this earth; all of his studies have led him to a deep compassion for the sufferings and tribulations of earthly man. But he cannot, honestly, accept religious matters on faith alone. That which does not conform with human logic is totally unacceptable to him. Unlike Alyosha, he cannot accept the abstract theory of God's mercy and goodness because he has seen too many examples of injustice and suffering in the world. He refrains from questioning the existence of God, but refuses to accept this world as being God's world. Ivan feels that a God who is infinitely good and just should have created a world where there was no innocent suffering. Nor can he accept the idea that all innocent suffering is a part of a great plan because God gave unto man a human mind and any theory concerning God's justice must be understood by this God-given mind. Sadly, logic cannot explain the long history of human suffering.

From his questionings, then, Ivan has developed a long prose poem entitled, "The Grand Inquisitor," in which he envisions Christ returning to earth. He is again threatened with death, but this time He is indicted by the church. Christ's second death is demanded because the cardinal explains that mankind is too debased to accept the ideas advocated by Christ. The church, consequently, has taken away the freedom that Christ promised man and for man's good, it has enslaved him. In this poem, Ivan reveals the depths of his compassion for mankind, creatures who he feels do not have the strength to follow the strenuous demands made by Christ.

Ivan supports a general acceptance of Christian morality because he feels that if the average man does not have some type of dictate to follow that an era of lawlessness ensues. Faith in immortality and a healthy fear of retribution are great deterrents to crime, Ivan believes, for with no immortality, then logically "anything is allowed." And it is this statement which Ivan expresses to the servant Smerdyakov that leads to the murder of Fyodor Karamazov. Smerdyakov, convinced that anything is permissible if there is no divine retribution, feels free to commit any act; he chooses parricide.

ALYOSHA

The youngest son of Fyodor Karamazov embodies most of the positive actions in the novel. From his early years onward, we learn that he was an easy-going youth whom everyone seemed to love. Unlike his brother Ivan, he is totally unconcerned with accepting charity or gifts from others. Dostoevsky depicts him as the sort who would quickly give away any money that he might possess.

Alyosha is no stock Christ-figure, however; of all the so-called good characters in Dostoevsky's fiction, Alyosha seems to breathe the most life. This is partly due to the fact that he constantly moves among people and performs quiet acts of kindness and love, even though he is not always successful.

When we first meet Alyosha, he is a member of the monastery and a special disciple of the religious elder, Father Zossima. And, as the story progresses, he becomes the living embodiment of all of Zossima's teachings. Every action of his reflects the qualities that he learned from his elder. For example, he refuses to condemn, he has an unusual ability to love all, and he has great faith in the basic goodness of man.

Alyosha, however, did not come to this faith easily. His credibility as a character is equated with his struggles to keep from losing his belief in God's justice. Particularly after Zossima dies, he questions a God that would allow such a holy man as Zossima to be disgraced by a rotting corpse, putrid and repulsive to his mourners. He rejects a justice that would dishonor a noble man for no logical reason. Then, after Alyosha begins his questionings, he is tempted away from his monastic vows by eating forbidden food, drinking vodka, and being induced to visit Grushenka, reputedly a sensuous, loose-moraled young woman. After the visit, however, Alyosha discovers the great power of all that Zossima has preached. He feels deep compassion for Grushenka and because he refuses to condemn her, he restores her belief in herself and in others. And, more important, Alyosha rediscovers his own faith in all its encompassing magnitude.

Adding to Alyosha's credibility is his failure to convince adults of Zossima's message. His role is not that of an all-perfect, all-successful young missionary. He has his share of failures. His successes, though, are therefore all the more important. In particular, his dealings with young boys are remarkable. He treats them as equals and they respond as equals, and we are led to believe that Alyosha will preach and lecture and that Russia will learn young Karamazov's wisdom. Thereupon, Dostoevsky seems to be saying, the destiny of the country will be the result of Alyosha's message of faith and love.

GRUSHENKA

By the end of Dostoevsky's long novel, Grushenka comes to represent the Slavophillic Russian Woman. She is the female counterpart of Dmitri, the personification of the ideal Russian, whose typical beauty does not immediately attract attention.

When she is first introduced, it is true that she is capricious and willful, but she has suffered a desertion by her former lover, and has finally made herself financially independent so that she can be a "free-spirit."

Grushenka's change of character begins with her captivating both father and son in the Karamazov family. As a coquette and as a tease, she dangles both men and causes them to become bitterly jealous of each other. When she realizes the consequence of her irresponsible nature, however, she assumes her share in the guilt surrounding Fyodor's murder. Perhaps one of her greatest values lies in her faithfulness. As she had previously been true to her first lover, when she finally realizes her love for Dmitri, she vows to remain forever constant and faithful to him. Furthermore, she also accepts her involvement with the murder and willingly seeks to share the guilt with Dmitri. All these factors help redeem her in spite of all her capricious past.

CHRONOLOGICAL CHART

DAY BEFORE MURDER

ALYOSHA	IVAN	DMITRI
Leaves the monastery. Visits his father, goes to see Katerina, meets the boys, and is bitten by Ilusha.	Goes to Madame Hohlakov's house in order to talk with Katerina.	Goes to Samsonov's to borrow money. Is sent by Samsonov to see Lyagavy (Gorstkin).
Goes to Katerina's house and talks with Madame Hohlakov and Lise. Upstairs, he tries to unite Ivan and Katerina.	Explains his position and love for Katerina in Alyosha's presence. Leaves to look for Dmitri.	Pawns watch and borrows money from landlady.
Is sent by Katerina to Captain Snegiryov's house with money; learns Ilusha's identity.		Travels to neighboring town to find Lyagavy.
Returns to Madame Hohlakov's house; finds Katerina in hysterics. Leaves to find Dmitri.	Leaves message with Smerdyakov for Dmitri to meet him in the restaurant.	Finds the priest who tells him that Lyagavy is some miles out in the country.
Hears from Smerdyakov that Ivan is in a restaurant waiting for Dmitri.		Walks the miles to find Lyagavy.
Goes to the restaurant, discusses the idea of suffering with Ivan and hears Ivan recite the poem on the Grand Inquisitor.	Calls to Alyosha to join him in the restaurant. Discusses God, immortality, and the idea of innocent suffering; recites his poem on the Grand Inquisitor to Alyosha.	Arrives at the cabin of a forester. Finds Lyagavy drunk.
Returns to the monastery and listens all night to Father Zossima's last words.	Returns home but cannot sleep before 2 A.M.	Sleeps at the cabin in the hope of borrowing money from Lyagavy when he wakes and sobers up.

DAY OF THE MURDER

ALYOSHA

After talking all night, Zossima dies early in the morning and Alyosha remains with the elder's body.

At 2 P.M., the body begins to smell, Alyosha is in despair.

Rakitin discovers Alyosha and tempts him.

Alyosha agrees to go to Grushenka's house.

He arrives at Grushenka's and hears of her ex-lover's return.

Watches Grushenka leave to join her ex-lover.

Alyosha returns to the monastery.

At the monastery, he has the dream of the wedding in Cana and also undergoes his mystical experience.

IVAN

Awakens at 7 A.M. and begins to pack.
Tells Fyodor that he will tend to some of his father's business in the neighboring town.
At 2 P.M., he catches a carriage to take him to the train station. Before leaving, he tells Smerdyakov of his change in plans.

Arrives at the train station.

Catches the train.

On the train, Ivan calls himself a wretch for leaving as he did.

DMITRI

Awakens to find Lyagavy drinking again. Gives up hope and seeks transportation back to town.

Arrives in town; takes Grushenka to Samsonov's. Pawns his pistols with Perhotin.

Goes to Madame Hohlakov's to borrow money from her.
Has his futile talk with Madame Hohlakov and leaves her.
Encounters Samsonov's servant, who tells him that Grushenka did not stay at Samsonov's house.
Sees Fenya (Grushenka's servant), who pretends not to know where Grushenka is.
Rushes to Karamazov's house; sees his father. Tries to leave and is hindered by old Grigory. Strikes the servant aside and returns to Grushenka's house. Redeems pistols and orders food and wine, and heads for Mokroe.

REVIEW QUESTIONS

1. Compare the basic differences in the personalities and philosophies of Alyosha, Ivan, and Dmitri.

2. State briefly Fyodor Karamazov's personality and indicate his relationship with each of his three sons.

3. How does Fyodor's relationship with Smerdyakov differ from his relationship with his legitimate sons?

4. What influence does Ivan have upon Smerdyakov? What is Ivan's relationship to his other brothers?

5. How does Ivan's story of the Grand Inquisitor relate to his general views throughout the novel?

6. How is Ivan's concern for suffering humanity related to his story of freedom and security in the "Grand Inquisitor" section?

7. Compare the philosophical views advanced by Ivan with those maintained by Father Zossima.

8. How is Alyosha an embodiment of Father Zossima's teachings?

9. Write an essay justifying Dmitri as the main character of the novel.

10. How is Dmitri's repentance and desire for suffering and regeneration a reflection of Zossima's teachings?

11. Contrast the roles and personalities of Grushenka and Katerina.

12. How does Alyosha's relations with the young boys function in the total scheme of the novel?

SELECTED BIBLIOGRAPHY

BERDYAEV, NICHOLAS. *Dostoevsky: An Interpretation*. New York: Meridian, 1957. Berdyaev uses *The Brothers Karamazov* to show that it is the culmination of all of Dostoevsky's ideas. He relates each idea to an earlier expression in previous works.

CARR, EDWARD HALLET. *Dostoevsky, 1821-1881: A New Biography*. New York: Macmillan, 1949. Carr sees *The Brothers Karamazov* as Dostoevsky's first active proclamation of his faith to the world. In this novel, Dostoevsky has worked out to his satisfaction the link between sin and suffering and has resolved the conflict between faith and reason. Carr also treats the religious, romantic, and masochistic elements that formed Dostoevsky's doctrine of suffering.

GIDE, ANDRE. *Dostoevsky*. New York: New Directions, 1926. By selecting illustrative passages from his works, Gide discusses various ideas appearing in Dostoevsky's works and also explores the superman idea which pervades much of Dostoevsky's writings. The volume is perhaps most important as an expression of a great twentieth-century writer about a great nineteenth-century writer.

GIFFORD, HENRY. *The Hero in His Time: A Theme in Russian Literature*. New York: St. Martins, 1950. Gifford relates Dostoevsky's "heroes" to the typical movements and ideas during Dostoevsky's times.

IVANOV, VYACHESLAV. *Freedom and the Tragic Life: A Study in Dostoevsky*. New York: Noonday, 1952. Ivanov uses the "Grand Inquisitor" section as a focal point in explaining Dostoevsky's views about freedom and security.

LAVRIN, JANKO. *Dostoevsky*. New York: Van Nostrand, 1947.

MAGARSHACK, DAVID. *Dostoevsky*. New York: Harcourt, 1963. Magarshack presents a very readable account of Dostoevsky's life, but makes little or no effort to interpret the artistic achievements.

MIRSKY, DMITRI. *History of Russian Literature*. New York: Harcourt, 1963.

PACHMUSS, TEMIRA. *Dostoevsky: Dualism and Synthesis of the Human Soul.* Carbondale, Ill.: Southern Illinois University Press, 1963.

REEVE, F. D. *The Russian Novel.* New York: McGraw Hill, 1966. Reeve has an excellent section discussing the problems confronting Ivan and relates Ivan's ideas to the conflicts faced by Dostoevsky.

SEDURO, VASSILY. *Dostoevsky in Russian Literary Criticism.* New York: Columbia University Press, 1957.

SIMMONS, ERNEST J. *Dostoevsky: The Making of a Novelist.* London: Oxford Press, 1950. Mr. Simmons' book is perhaps the best treatment of Dostoevsky found in English. He sees *The Brothers Karamazov* as an expression of Dostoevsky's ideas and illustrates how each character functions as an embodiment of an idea.

Stravogin's Confession with a Psychological Analysis of the Author by Sigmund Freud, ed. VIRGINIA WOOLF and S. S. KOTELIANSKY. New York: Lear Publishers, 1949. The interest in this lies in Freud's psychological analysis of Dostoevsky.

WASIOLEK, EDWARD. *The Brothers Karamazov and the Critics.* San Francisco: Wadsworth, 1967.

WELLEK, RENE (ed.). *Dostoevsky: A Collection of Critical Essays.* New York, Prentice Hall, 1962.

YARMOLINSKY, AVRAHM. *Dostoevsky, a Life.* New York: Criterion, 1934. An interpretative analysis of Dostoevsky's novels in relation to his life.

NOTES

NOTES

NOTES

CRIME AND PUNISHMENT

NOTES

including
- *Introduction*
- *Chapter Summaries and Commentaries*
- *Character Sketches*
- *Critical Notes*
- *Study Questions and Theme Topics*

by
James L. Roberts, Ph.D.
Department of English
University of Nebraska

INCORPORATED

LINCOLN, NEBRASKA   68501

Editor

Gary Carey, M.A.
University of Colorado

Consulting Editor

James L. Roberts, Ph.D.
Department of English
University of Nebraska

ISBN 0-8220-0328-7
© Copyright 1963
by
C. K. Hillegass
All Rights Reserved
Printed in U.S.A.

1990 Printing

Cliffs Notes, Inc.   Lincoln, Nebraska

CONTENTS

CRIME AND PUNISHMENT

LIFE AND BACKGROUND OF THE AUTHOR

DOSTOIEVSKY was born of lower middle class parents in 1821 and lived until 1881. This period covers one of the most active and changing periods in Russian history until the communist revolution. Dostoievsky's father was a stern righteous man while his mother was the opposite extreme. His early education included an Army Engineering school where Dostoievsky was apparently bored to death with the dull drill and unimaginative life. After two years in the Army, he launched on a literary career at the age of 25, and his first novel, *Poor Folk,* became an immediate success, highly acclaimed by the critics. This novel showed Dostoievsky's first emphasis on the psychological analysis of inner feelings of the soul and the workings of the intricate mind. He penetrated deeply into every aspect. After this work the only important thing he wrote for many years was *The Double,* which treats a split personality and therefore suggests the conception of the character of Raskolnikov.

The most crucial time of Dostoievsky's life occurred after the publication of *Poor Folk.* Using the influence won from this literary achievement, he became involved in political intrigues of questionable nature. At this time in his life he was influenced by all the new and radical ideas entering Russia from the West. Like Raskolnikov, Dostoievsky became addicted to these new ideas and became dangerously involved in certain liberal movements. He was part of a group which was out to revolutionize Russia and to prove that Russia should catch up with the ideas of Western Europe. He began writing and publishing contraband articles on various political questions. These articles were illegal because at this time printing was controlled and censored by the government.

The group was arrested in 1849 and placed in prison. After due investigation, fifteen of the revolutionaries, including Dostoievsky, were condemned to be shot before a firing squad. A few days later, the entire group were bound and placed before the firing squad. As all the horrible preparations were being completed, and the victims were actually ready to be shot, a messenger from the Tsar arrived with a reprieve. (Actually, the Tsar had never intended to have them shot; he was merely using this method to teach them a lesson.) But this soul-shaking, harrowing encounter with death created a strong never-to-be-forgotten impression that haunted Dostoievsky for years to come.

After the commutation of the death sentence, Dostoievsky was sent to Siberia for five years. These were the years in which Dostoievsky changed his entire outlook on life. During this time, amid horrible living conditions — stench, ugliness, hardened criminals, and filth — he began to re-evaluate his life. Here, he also had his first epileptic seizure. Here, he began to reject a blind acceptance of new ideas that were filtrating into Russia. Thus Raskolnikov's view of new ideas and their influence received its origin here. And here was the beginning of his views as a Slavophil. He came to believe that the salvation of the world was in the hands of Russia and that eventually Russia would rise to dominate the world. Therefore, each person must contribute his utmost to the development of Russian ideas and culture. These Slavophillic ideas are later expressed by Porfiry. Likewise, Dostoievsky formulated his thoughts about the necessity of suffering. Suffering, for him, became a means by which the soul is purified and expiated all its sins. Suffering became the means of salvation.

When Dostoievsky was released from prison, he took up his literary career where he left it years before and rapidly rose to become one of the great spokesmen in Russia. But the final years of his life were not easy ones. His first marriage was to a tubercular young widow with a young son by her previous marriage (a somewhat similar position to Katerina Ivanovna's), but this marriage terminated soon in her death. He lost his jobs as editor and was constantly forced to write in order to pay off huge debts that he had accumulated with impatient creditors.

At the end of his life he was considered Russia's greatest novelist and today stands as one of the world's greatest writers.

CAST OF CHARACTERS FROM
CRIME AND PUNISHMENT

NOTE ON PRONUNCIATION

If the reader will remember to give strong stress to the syllable marked with an accent in this list, to give the vowels their "continental" value and pronounce the consonants as in English, a rough approximation to the Russian pronunciation will be obtained. The consonant "kh" sounds rather like the Scottish "ch" in "loch"; the "zh" represents a sound like "s" in measure; and the final "-v" is pronounced "-f."

THE RASKOLNIKOV FAMILY

RODIÓN ROMÁNOVITCH RASKÓLNIKOV
A poverty-stricken student who conceives of a theory of the superman or extraordinary man as a justification or rationalization for his crime.

RÓDYA, RÓDENKA, AND RÓDKA
Nicknames for Rodion Romanovitch Raskolnikov.

AVDÓTYA ROMÁNOVNA RASKÓLNIKOV
His devoted sister who was previously Svidragailov's employee and who is engaged to Luzhin. She arrives in St. Petersburg at about the time of Raskolnikov's crime.

DÓUNIA
Nickname for Avdotya Romanovna Raskolnikov.

PULCHÉRIA ALEXÁNDROVNA RASKÓLNIKOV
His mother.

THE MARMELADOV FAMILY

SEMYON ZAKHÁROVITCH MARMELADOV
A dismissed government clerk who is alcoholic and who is the

father of Sonia by a previous marriage. Presently married to Katerina Ivanovna.

KATERÍNA IVÁNOVNA
Marmeladov's wife who had been previously married to an Army officer by whom she had three children. Socially, she was born into a higher rank than was Marmeladov.

SÓFYA SEMYÓNOVNA MARMELADOV
Marmeladov's daughter by a previous marriage who is compelled to enter into prostitution to support the family.

SÓNIA
Sofya's nickname.

PÓLENKA, LYÓYA, KOLYA
Katerina Ivanovna's children by a previous marriage.

SVIDRIGÁILOV, ARKÁDY IVÁNOVITCH
Dounia's former employer who follows her to St. Petersburg.

MÁRFA PETRÓVNA
His wife who leaves Dounia three thousand rubles in her will.

LÚZHIN, PYOTR PETRÓVITCH
Engaged to Dounia and employed by the government.

RAZUMÍHIN, DMÍTRI PROKÓFITCH
A student and friend of Raskolnikov's who later becomes attached to Dounia.

LEBEZIÁTNIKOV, ANDREY SEMYÓNOVITCH
A roomer in the same house that the Marmeladovs live in and who calls himself an "advanced liberal."

PORFÍRY PETRÓVITCH
An official of the investigating department who is in charge of the "crime."

ALYÓNA IVÁNOVNA
A moneylender.

LIZAVÉTA IVANÓVNA
Alyona Ivanovna's sister and also a friend to Sonia.

PRASKÓVYA PAVLÓVNA
Raskolnikov's landlady who complains to the police about Raskolnikov's failure to pay his rent.

NASTÁSYA
Her servant and a friend to Raskolnikov.

AMÁLIA FYODORÓVNA
The Marmeladov's landlady who is particularly disliked by Katerina Ivanovna.

KAPERNAÚMOV
Sonia's landlady.

ZÓSSIMOV
A doctor who attends Raskolnikov during his illness, and also a friend of Razumihin.

NIKODÍM FOMÍTCH
Chief of the police.

ZAMÉTOV
A clerk in the police station and friend of Razumihin.

ÍLYA PETRÓVITCH
A loud and boistrous police official.

NIKOLÁY and DMÍTRI
Painters who were working at the scene of the Crime.

RUSSIAN NAMES
The middle name of all male characters end in "—vitch" and of all female characters in "—ovna." This ending simply means

"son of" or "daughter of" the father whose first name is converted into their middle name. For example, Rodion and Avdotya's father was named *Roman* Raskolnikov. Thus, their middle name, Rodion *Romanovitch* and Avdotya *Romanovna,* means Rodion, son of Roman and Avdotya, daughter of Roman.

PLOT SUMMARY

Raskolnikov, an impoverished student, conceives of himself as being an extraordinary young man and then formulates a theory whereby the extraordinary men of the world have a right to commit any crime. To prove his theory he murders an old pawnbroker and her step-sister. Immediately after the crime, he becomes ill and lies in his room in semi-consciousness for several days. When he recovers, he finds that a friend, Razumihin, had looked for him. While he is recovering, he receives a visit from Luzhin, who is engaged to Raskolnikov's sister Dounia. Raskolnikov insults Luzhin and sends him away because he resents Luzhin's domineering attitude toward Dounia.

As soon as he can walk again, Raskolnikov goes out and reads about the crime in all the newspapers of the last few days. He meets an official from the police station and almost confesses the crime. He does go far enough in his ravings that the official becomes suspicious. Later he witnesses the death of Marmeladov, a minor government official, who is struck by a carriage as he staggers across the street in a drunken stupor. Raskolnikov assists the man and leaves all his money to the widow. When he returns to his room, he finds his mother and sister who have just arrived to prepare for the wedding with Luzhin. He denounces Luzhin and refuses to allow his sister to marry him. About the same time, Svidrigailov, Dounia's former employer, arrives in town and looks up Raskolnikov and asks for a meeting with Dounia. Previously Svidrigailov had attempted to seduce Dounia and when Raskolnikov had heard of it, he formed a violent dislike for the man.

Raskolnikov hears that the police inspector, Porfiry, is interviewing all people who had ever had any business with the old pawnbroker. Therefore, he goes for an interview and leaves thinking that the police suspect him. Since he had met Sonia Marmeladov, the daughter of the dead man that Raskolnikov had helped, he goes to her and asks her to read to him from the Bible. He feels great sympathy with Sonia who had been forced into prostitution in order to support her family while her father drank. He promises to tell her who murdered the old pawnbroker.

After another interview with Porfiry, Raskolnikov determines to confess to Sonia. He returns to her and during the confession, Svidrigailov is listening through the door. He uses this information to try to force Dounia to sleep with him. She refuses and he kills himself later in the night.

Porfiry informs Raskolnikov that he knows who murdered the pawnbroker. After talking with Sonia, Raskolnikov fully confesses to the murder, is sentenced to eight years in a Siberian prison. Sonia follows him and, with her help, Raskolnikov begins his regeneration.

STRUCTURE

The general structure of the novel must be seen in terms of the main character, Raskolnikov. We must keep in mind his dual personality as the controlling idea behind the murder and behind his punishment. Raskolnikov is used as a representative of the modern young Russian intellectual whose fate is intricately bound up in the fate of Russia herself. Therefore the story is a parable of the fate of a nihilistic and skeptical youth in nineteenth century Russia, whose materialism and revolutionary opinions Dostoievsky hated and feared. (See general background on Dostoievsky's imprisonment.) This book was to be a vision of the ultimate error and moral sufferings of those who had so cut themselves off from established authority and morality that they lost all respect for human life. Therefore, the life and aims of Raskolnikov became in some ways the fate of the young Russian intellectual.

But Dostoievsky loved Raskolnikov. The entire story is presented from Raskolnikov's viewpoint and most of the actions and most of our views are seen through his eyes. Dostoievsky, as author, seldom leaves Raskolnikov except when, in some short scenes, his thesis demands attention elsewhere.

The plot of the novel presents a double conflict, one external and one internal: the one conflict between the estranged individual and his hostile universe, the other a clash between an isolated soul and his ethical or esthetic consciousness. Since the plot is a double conflict, the first general structural problem is to understand Raskolnikov's dual personality. There are several ways of seeing this. In its broadest view, Raskolnikov fluctuates between the ideas of (1) complete self-will and power, and (2) extreme meekness and self-submissiveness.

Actions in the novel which seem to be contradictory are a result of Raskolnikov's fluctuation between these two aspects of his personality; therefore, the first part of the novel deals with a crime committed by this young intellectual. The crime was a result of a theory he conceived about the nature of man's abilities; that is, some men have abilities which make them extraordinary while others possess no abilities. It was this intellectual aspect of his character which caused him to conceive and execute his crime. He wanted to see if he had the *daring to transcend* conscience. His punishment comes about as a result of the *transcendence of conscience*. Therefore, one aspect of his character is a cold, inhumane, detached intellectuality which emphasizes the individual power and self-will. The other aspect is the warm, compassionate side, revealed in his charitable acts and his reluctance to accept credit.

The problem in the novel, therefore, is to bring these two opposing parts of Raskolnikov's personality into a single functioning person. To do this, Dostoievsky opens with the crime which is handled rather quickly so as to get to the punishment. The murder is the symbol of Raskolnikov's thinking. It is the result of having cut himself off from authority, from love, from men. But since Raskolnikov is a dual personality, Dostoievsky also felt the need of creating two additional characters who, taken separately, represent the two opposing aspects of his nature. Thus, Sonia is the warm human, compassionate, charitable aspect of Raskolnikov's character. She is the meek and submissive personality. Svidrigailov is the detached cold manifestation of the self-will and power and intellect. Consequently, so often in the novel, when Raskolnikov is attracted to Sonia, he is repulsed by the depravity of Svidrigailov. Likewise, when he is talking or going to see Svidrigailov, he is disgusted with and repulsed by Sonia's tears and weaknesses.

With Raskolnikov's character established as a dual one, and with these two characters, Sonia and Svidrigailov, representing the two alternating aspects, the general pattern of the novel is to bring Raskolnikov back into one functioning character. Thus we must have *two redemptive* characters. Here the importance of Sonia's role is seen. As she represents one aspect of Raskolnikov's personality, so must she function as the person who is to redeem that aspect. Therefore Sonia is the redemptive figure for Raskolnikov's humane personality. Through her suffering, she makes him realize the importance of a love for humanity, that a human being cannot be a louse or a parasite sucking the life from other human beings. But it should be emphasized that Sonia does not accomplish her purpose by overt action. She is the passive figure whose simple presence serves to inspire Raskolnikov's actions.

The other redemptive figure is Porfiry. Here is the intellectual man who has used his intellect for the good of man. Here is the man who sees in Raskolnikov the potential of a great being who made up a theory and then was ashamed that it broke down. Porfiry is the man who recognized that the theory is base but that Raskolnikov is far from being base. His purpose, therefore, is to make Raskolnikov see the difference between the baseness of the theory and the ever present potential in himself. What Porfiry realizes is that any idea, if it is conceived of for the benefit of humanity, must be a human idea and must be executed by a humane person. He tries to make Raskolnikov see that the idea is base because it views a large portion of mankind as base.

Thus Raskolnikov in the beginning of the novel is a dual personality with the two aspects of his personality represented by Sonia and Svidrigailov, then the problem is to bring this personality into an integrated whole. This task is assigned to Sonia and Porfiry. The emphasis is that man cannot separate the humane aspect of his life from his other endeavors. Whatever man does must be done in terms of general humanity.

Raskolnikov's punishment, that is, the general suffering he undergoes, is a result of this split personality. It was one aspect that murdered, but it is the other humane side that then must suffer.

PART AND CHAPTER ANALYSIS

PART ONE

CHAPTER ONE

Summary
On a hot evening in July, a young student, Rodion Romanovitch Raskolnikov, is seen on his way to visit an old pawnbroker, Alyona Ivanovna. He is in a confused state in which he avoids contact with his landlady and all other associations. Upon arriving at the pawn-broker's, he seems to be disgusted with the entire procedure and finds it all to be loathsome and degrading. After transacting his business with the pawnbroker, he leaves in a state of extreme agitation.

Comment
A. Note Raskolnikov's state of mind, his "sick frightened feeling," his isolation, and his need to avoid all company.

B. The physical description of Raskolnikov in this first chapter is the only one in the entire novel. He is described as being excep-tionally handsome, slim "well-built with beautiful dark eyes and dark brown hair." This description should be emphasized. Too often, illustrators depict Raskolnikov as physically depraved and/or deformed. Dostoievsky wanted to emphasize his physical attractive-ness as to remove any possible view that the crime was based on physical deformity. The physical beauty of the character contrasts with the ugliness of the crime.

C. Even here in the first chapter, Raskolnikov's plans are far from being complete. He notices that the most trivial detail could spoil the entire plan. Thus, this is the first indication that the crime has not yet been worked out completely in all detail. This fact, seemingly insignificant at this point, becomes central to Raskolnikov's redemption when he tries to explain his crime to Sonia at the end of the novel.

D. Note the very careful preparation for the crime, such as counting the number of steps from the house; yet in the midst of this careful planning, he is also suddenly troubled with the loathsomeness and ugliness of the crime; that is, that it is atrocious and degrading. And even though the thought of it repulses him, he continues to proceed toward its completion.

E. The visit to Alyona Ivanovna's shows Raskolnikov's confusion and disgust with the whole episode even as he prepares for its execution. The visit also shows that Raskolnikov is not the hardened cold criminal.

PART ONE

CHAPTER TWO

Summary

After his visit to Alyona Ivanovna's, Raskolnikov feels the need for a drink, so he stops in a tavern. Here he meets Semyon Marmeladov who tells him about his life. Marmeladov had been in the government service but lost his position because of his alcoholism. However, he had recently been reinstated as a clerk in a government office. But he has been drinking for five days and is now afraid to go home. He tells of his marriage to Katerina Ivanovna, a widow of a higher class than he who married him out of destitution. Before he was reinstated in his position, he tells how his daughter, Sonia, had to enter into prostitution in order to support the family, because he refused to quit drinking. Five days ago, he stole all the money the family had and spent it on drink. Now he is afraid to go home. Raskolnikov helps to take Marmeladov home, and when there sees the abject poverty in which the family lives. His sympathy prompts him to silently leave them some of his money.

Comment

A. Of greatest importance in this chapter is the beginning of the establishment of Raskolnikov's *dual* character. That is, we shall see later that Raskolnikov functions at times as (1) a warm, compassionate, humane individual and (2) as a cold, detached, intellectual being. At the beginning of this chapter, he has avoided society of late but suddenly feels the desire to be with someone. Then at the end of the chapter, his humanitarian impulses cause him to leave his only money with Katerina Ivanovna, but immediately, he changes his mind and "would have gone back."

B. In his meeting with Marmeladov, we have our first introduction to Sonia and to the entire Marmeladov family and also to Lebeziatnikov. Marmeladov's story reflects upon Raskolnikov's condition. The discussion of hopelessness, "when one has no one, nowhere else one can go," becomes one of the dominant motifs throughout the rest of the novel. This discussion forces Raskolnikov to consider the hopelessness of his own life. Later, after the murder, Raskolnikov remembers the impassioned cry of "having nowhere to go."

C. Marmeladov's story is one in which he as a human being is seen as an alcoholic whose family is starving while he drinks, whose daughter had to enter into prostitution in order to support the starving family, and whose life has been one of degradation. Since Raskolnikov's murder will be based partially on the rationale that certain people fit into a category of being a louse, then this story should indicate to Raskolnikov that his theory should apply directly to Marmeladov, especially when Marmeladov cries out, "Dare you assert that I am not a pig." But rather than despising Marmeladov as a louse, Raskolnikov feels great sympathy for him and for his suffering, thus contradicting his own theory.

D. As Raskolnikov is attracted to Marmeladov because of Marmeladov's suffering, he is likewise attracted to Sonia immediately because of her suffering state of existence. And just before his confession to Sonia, he acknowledges his attraction to her because she represents "the suffering of all humanity."

E. Raskolnikov's sympathy for Marmeladov makes him doubt the validity of his theory: "What if man is not really a scoundrel... then all the rest is prejudice."

PART ONE

CHAPTER THREE

Summary
After his experience with the Marmeladovs, Raskolnikov sleeps until late the next day. Upon awakening, he is disgusted with the poverty of his room and thinks that his cramped quarters have contributed to his depression of late. Nastasya, the maid in the boarding house, brings him some tea and tells him that Praskovya Pavlovna, the landlady, means to complain to the police because Raskolnikov has not paid his back rent. She then gives him a letter from his mother. Raskolnikov is very excited to receive the letter, kisses it and reads it with intensity. His mother writes that his sister, Dounia, has been working as a tutor at the home of the Svidrigailovs. After a while, Svidrigailov formed an attachment for Dounia and tried to seduce her. Marfa Petrovna, overhearing a conversation, thinks that it is Dounia's fault and spreads ugly rumors about Dounia all through the countryside. Later Marfa Petrovna discovers her error and goes to extreme measures to correct the harm. At about the same time, Dounia received a proposal of marriage from a kinsman of Marfa Petrovna named Pyotr Petrovitch Luzhin who seems to want a wife with a good reputation but without a dowry so that his wife will be indebted to him. Finally, his mother tells him that they will soon be in St. Petersburg so that Dounia will be able to join Luzhin.

Comment

A. The announcement that the landlady means to complain to the police is important because Raskolnikov forgets about this, and the summons actually arrives the day after the murder causing Raskolnikov to think that his crime is discovered.

B. The letter from his mother excites Raskolnikov with devoted feelings for her, emphasizing his compassionate nature.

C. The account of Dounia's relation and trouble with Svidrigailov prepares the reader for viewing him as an evil person.

D. The account of Dounia's engagement with Luzhin reveals that Luzhin is a selfish, petty, and egocentric person.

PART ONE

CHAPTER FOUR

Summary

The letter from his mother upsets Raskolnikov and he goes out for a walk in order to think about it. He decides that his sister, Dounia, is marrying Luzhin in order to provide help for him. He feels that she is sacrificing herself for her family by entering into marriage with a man whom she does not love. While he is thinking about her plight, he observes a young fifteen year old girl staggering down the street as though she were either drunk or drugged. This young girl is being followed by a "young dandy" whose intentions seem to be unmistakable. Raskolnikov interferes and calls a policeman to aid him in protecting the young girl until she can get home. He offers his last twenty copecks for a cab, and then just as suddenly decides that he is interfering in something that does not concern him, and so leaves the scene. At the end of the chapter, he decides to go see one of his school mates, Razumihin.

Comment

A. Raskolnikov's love for his mother and sister compels him to view Dounia's forthcoming marriage with horror and disdain because she is marrying such a petty man as Luzhin. He makes the analogy that her marriage to Luzhin is a type of legal prostitution like Sonia's and may be even worse because Sonia's was for necessity and Dounia's could be for luxury. During these thoughts about the degrading influence of this marriage, Raskolnikov is still contemplating the degrading murder.

B. What we might call the "Marmeladov motif" ("Do you understand, sir, do you understand what it means when you have absolutely no where to turn") returns to Raskolnikov's mind at this time because his present situation is also desperate and hopeless. He feels that Dounia is sacrificing herself for him, and he can do nothing to alleviate the situation.

C. Haunted by the thoughts of Dounia's sacrifice, Raskolnikov's encounter with the young girl, who has been abused and who is being followed by another person with evil designs upon her, prompts the humanitarian side of his character into action. In an attempt to protect the girl, Raskolnikov calls the man a "Svidrigailov" since this name now is the embodiment of evil.

D. Raskolnikov's humanistic and compassionate nature is further revealed in his attempts to protect the young girl. He gives almost all of his scarce money in order to send for a cab. Then note the *sudden change*. He reverses his views and says to "let them be." That is, suddenly the cold intellectual superman aspect of his personality takes over and Raskolnikov maintains that such trivial happenings do not concern him.

E. Raskolnikov unexpectedly wants to see Razumihin so as to escape from that awful feeling of having "nowhere to turn."

PART ONE

CHAPTER FIVE

Summary

Raskolnikov suddenly changes his mind and does not go to see Razumihin, but promises himself that the day after *it* that he will go.

Instea^{...}e goes into a tavern, has a glass of vodka, and goes to a park w...ere he immediately goes to sleep. He dreams that he is back in his childhood, seven years old, and as he is walking with his father he sees a drunken peasant trying to make his old horse pull a heavy wagon full of people. When the crowd laughs at this ridiculous spectacle, the peasant gets angry and begins beating the horse. He beats the horse so ferociously that he kills it. The boy, feeling great compassion for the stricken and dead mare, throws his arms around the beast and kisses it. Upon awakening from the dream, Raskolnikov renounces that "accursed dream of mine." Then as he walks through the Hay Market, he overhears a conversation in which he finds out that Lizaveta, the sister to the old pawnbroker Alyona Ivanova, will be out on an errand at exactly seven o'clock in the evening.

Comment

A. As Raskolnikov calms down, he no longer feels the need to see Razumihin but thinks that he will go after he has committed the crime.

B. The dreams in this novel are usually symbolic. The dream of the peasant, Mikolka, beating the horse to death is a repulsive and degrading dream. When Raskolnikov awakens, he wonders if he can actually "take an axe, split her skull open, tread in the sticky blood and hide." He ends by "renouncing that accursed dream of mine," thus symbolically rejecting his plan to murder Alyona Ivanova. In the dream, we see again Raskolnikov's dual nature at work. He is both the Mikolka who cruelly beats the horse to death and also the boy who feels great compassion for the horse. Thus the waking Raskolnikov rejects the Mikolka aspect of his nature by renouncing the dream. Other ideas developed later are present in the dream. The idea of property being the responsibility of the owner is touched upon. This relates to the pawnbroker's immense amount of property and her right to dispense with it as she pleases. Also the idea of the innocent suffering as the horse must suffer is implicit. The horse has been interpreted as being "mother Russia" since later when Raskolnikov confesses, Sonia tells him to bow down and kiss the earth that he has defiled.

C. After the dream, the overheard conversation in which it is revealed that Lizaveta will be absent at seven o'clock the next night forces Raskolnikov to consider this as a perfect opportunity to commit the crime. Of extreme importance is this *favorable circumstance* which *compels* or *forces* Raskolnikov to commit the crime. Later Raskolnikov will attempt to justify the idea of the crime and maintain only that he executed it before the idea was completely formulated. But at this point, the destitute poverty, the emotional letter from his mother, and the favorable circumstance of Alyona Ivanovna's being alone all combine to *push* the actual act into immediate execution.

PART ONE

CHAPTER SIX

Summary

There is a six week flash-back in time in which Raskolnikov remembers a conversation that he overheard. This conversation was between two young officers who had recently had business with the old pawnbroker, Alyona Ivanovna; they were talking about the benefits to be achieved from killing the old woman, but both admit that they would not do the *actual* killing. After recalling this conversation, Raskolnikov begins to make preparations. He sews a noose into his overcoat in which he will conceal the ax, he wraps a pledge up very securely so that the old pawnbroker will have trouble untying it, he goes to steal the ax from the kitchen and finds the kitchen locked, so he is forced to steal the ax from the porter. These preparations delay him and it is *seven-thirty* before he reaches the pawnbroker's. As he arrives, he notes that there is an empty flat under the pawnbroker's and that there are painters there painting it. He climbs to Alyona Ivanovna's flat and rings. It seems as though he has to ring many times before she opens, and he is almost in despair by the time she finally opens her door.

Comment

A. The conversation that Raskolnikov overhears concerning the justice of murdering Alyona Ivanovna occurs six weeks back in

22

time, but this conversation came at exactly the same time that Raskolnikov was considering the same idea. The idea expressed here is the foundation for the Hegelian view of the superman (or extraordinary man). Here the motives for killing the old pawn-broker are altruistic: (1) the murder will remove a harmful "thing" from society, (2) this creature has actually been doing evil, (3) her money, rather than being wasted in a monastery, can be used to save families from destitution, (4) the person who murders her can then use the money and devote himself "to the service of humanity and the good of all." Therefore, "one tiny crime" would "be wiped out by thousands of good deeds." But there is only one catch: who is to do the *actual killing*. If *everyone* is not willing to perform this murder, then "there's no justice about it."

B. This chapter reveals that Raskolnikov has only conceived of the *general* outlines of his plan and has not worked it out in detail. Therefore his difficulty later occurs because he "put off trifling details, until he could believe *in it all.*" Thus, we see that he committed the murder before he had completely solved all the details.

C. Raskolnikov's thoughts about crime and psychology reveal his theory that the failure of any crime lies not so much in the impossibility of concealing the crime, as in the criminal himself. Every criminal has a failure of the will when he most needs prudence and caution. Thus, later we see that Raskolnikov, after murdering Alyona Ivanovna, has this failure when he leaves the apartment door wide open.

D. Note that even though he knows Lizaveta will be absent at *seven* o'clock, it is *seven-thirty* before he arrives at the flat.

PART ONE

CHAPTER SEVEN
Summary
In the midst of great confusion, Raskolnikov finally obtains an entrance into the pawnbroker's apartment. He gives her the pledge

which he had wrapped so carefully, telling her that it is a silver cigarette case. As she laboriously unwraps the package, he removes the ax and, while her back is turned to him, he "brought the blunt side down on her head." As she sank to the floor, he dealt her another and another blow with the blunt side of the ax on the same spot. Then, he lays the ax down by the body and begins to search through her pockets for keys. While searching for the keys, he notices that Alyona Ivanovna wears two crosses, one of cypress wood and one of copper. He takes the keys and also a small leather purse which is stuffed very full. As he searches the rooms, he suddenly hears footsteps in the entrance way. He comes upon Lizaveta staring at her murdered step-sister in horror. Raskolnikov immediately takes the ax and hits her one heavy blow "with the sharp edge just on the skull and splits at one blow all the top of the head." This second unexpected murder makes him think of abandoning the entire project. After the second murder, he begins to clean the blood from his ax and from his hands and clothes. As he is ready to leave, the door bell rings. There are two people outside who had appointments with Alyona Ivanovna and as they try the door they realize that it is locked from the inside. One leaves to go get the porter and then when the other leaves for a moment, Raskolnikov slips out and hides in the empty, new-painted room below the pawnbroker's flat. When the murder is discovered, he slips out unnoticed and returns to his own room, where he replaces the ax in the porter's lodge and then falls into a state bordering on unconsciousness.

Comment

A. In the *dual* murder scene, note that Alyona is murdered with the blunt side of the ax and that Lizaveta is murdered with the sharp side of the ax. In this dual murder, he has killed one person who is mean, wicked and cold (Alyona) and a second, Lizaveta, who is warm, friendly, humane and compassionate. Thus, in a figurative manner, the two murders represent the two aspects of Raskolnikov's character. The importance here is that later Raskolnikov seldom thinks of the murder of Lizaveta, but is always troubled about the murder of Alyona.

B. As soon as the murder is completed, the first thought that comes to his mind is confession. Since the novel ends with a confession by Raskolnikov, this first thought is of *extreme importance*. Until the actual confession in the end, this same thought of confession serves as a recurring motif and motivates most of Raskolnikov's actions.

C. Note the two crosses, one wooden and one copper, which show up in Sonia's possession later, and which she will pass on to him as he accepts his guilt. Also note the elaborate cleansing ritual that Raskolnikov undergoes before leaving the flat. This finicky concern for touching the blood of the murdered woman contrasts well with the cold deliberation of the murder.

D. When he is trapped by Koch and the other visitor, he thinks of confession for the *second* time. This thought is motivated by the fear created in him when the doorbell rings.

E. Note that as he escapes, he hides in a room that has been freshly painted. Later, when his landlady has him summoned to the police office, the smell of fresh paint there contributes to his fainting spell.

PART TWO

CHAPTER ONE

Summary

After the murder, he collapses into a deep sleep. When he awakens, he immediately remembers the items he had stolen and realizes how foolish it was of him not to lock his door and not to hide these things. As he hides them he begins to wonder if his punishment is not already "coming upon me." After he hides the "loot" in a hole in his room, he falls into a heavy troubled sleep to be awakened by the knocking of Nastasya and a police officer, who gives Raskolnikov a summons to the police office. As he dresses, he is repulsed at the thought of having to wear the bloody socks, but since he has no others, he is forced to do so. On the way to the police station, he thinks he might just confess it all and be done with it. When he reaches the station, the first impression he receives is that of the "sickening smell of fresh paint...from the newly decorated rooms." The interview at the police station is the result of Raskolnikov's landlady suing for back rent. As Raskolnikov is told of his offense, he goes into rather lengthy explanations of his relationship to his landlady and of his previous engagement to his landlady's daughter. The police instruct him to sign an I.O.U., and he is to be released from custody. As he signs the paper, he overhears the police discussing the murder of Alyona Ivanovna and Lizaveta, and he faints. When he recovers, he hurries home thinking that the police suspect him of the murder.

Comment

A. It should be noted that in a novel of six parts and an epilogue, only one part is devoted to the crime and the remainder of the novel is devoted to the punishment. His punishment first begins with his hatred of the blood on his clothes, and the loss of his ability to retain complete control over all of his faculties.

B. When he receives the police summons, his mind is in such a state of agitation that he forgets that Nastasya had told him that his landlady was going to have him summoned.

C. Note again Raskolnikov's repulsion when he is forced to put on the bloody socks. Symbolically, he is forced to live with (or wear) his murder. This scene should be compared with the later scene when he is splattered with blood from the death of Marmeladov. In the latter scene he has no qualms about touching blood *per se*.

D. The third thought of confession—"If they question me, perhaps I'll simply tell...I'll go in, fall on my knees, and confess everything"—is prompted by the summons to the police station.

F. At the police station, he *needs* to confess something; therefore he tells of a most intimate event in his past life, i.e., the engagement to his landlady's daughter. This is for the *fourth* time, a type of confession. Shortly after this his *fifth* thought of confession follows when he thinks that he should confess everything: "to get up at once, to go up to Nikodim Fomitch, and tell him everything." These thoughts of confession are prompted by the tenseness and fear of being summoned to the police station.

G. Raskolnikov's fainting spell is a result of the tension caused by the summons, the oppressive smell of the new paint which reminds him of the murder scene, and finally the discussion of the murder of Alyona Ivanovna. This fainting spell later becomes a caused of suspicion and is used by Porfiry.

PART TWO

CHAPTER TWO

Summary

Upon returning home from the police station, Raskolnikov realizes the need to hide the "loot" in some safe place in case the police ever search his room. He goes to a park and hides it under a large rock. Then he remembers his promise to himself that he will visit Razumihin the day after the murder and goes to his room. Raskolnikov says that he has come to ask for lessons, but then suddenly changes his mind and leaves amid Razumihin's entreaties to know where he is going and where he is living. Raskolnikov walks absent-mindedly toward the river and is almost run down by a coach and is actually struck with a whip by the coachman. As he stands rubbing his back, he suddenly feels someone thrust money into his hand, because he looked so much like a beggar. He immediately throws the money away. When he returns home he dreams that the police officer Ilya Petrovitch is beating his landlady. He is awakened by Nastasya who realizes that he is sick and who goes to get him some water just as he collapses into unconsciousness.

Comment

A. Note that in hiding and concealing all the trinkets and money that he had stolen, that he had never examined the items in order to determine their value. This failure suggests that the murder was not committed either for need of money or for the purpose of helping mankind by using the money.

B. In going to Razumihin's house, Raskolnikov felt the need for human contact. We later find out that part of Raskolnikov's theory about crime is that it isolates one from human contact. But once there, Raskolnikov recognizes this need for society to be a *weakness*, that the extraordinary man *must* be able to stand completely alone. He must be above and beyond wanting or needing or receiving any sympathy or help. It was a weakness on his part to go, and, as he recognizes this weakness, he immediately leaves Razumihin's room.

C. The pathetic and confused state of Raskolnikov's condition is illustrated by his stumbling in front of a coach and being struck with a lash and then being mistaken for a beggar. This beating and charity function as ironic contrasts to Raskolnikov's theory. It shows him to be one of the weak who are subjected to these indignities rather than one of the extraordinary men who are above the need of help.

PART TWO

CHAPTER THREE

Summary
After several days, Raskolnikov recovers consciousness and discovers a stranger present in his room; Raskolnikov also discovers that Razumihin has been taking care of him during his illness. The stranger wanted to deposit with him 35 rubles that his mother had send. Raskolnikov tries to refuse but Razumihin makes him sign the note. Razumihin reveals that he has been able to coerce and cajole the landlady into being of great service to them. He also tells how Raskolnikov has been almost neurotic about clutching his dirty socks while he was unconscious. As Raskolnikov goes back to sleep, Razumihin takes some of the money and goes out to buy new clothes for Raskolnikov.

Comment
A. Raskolnikov's state of illness, his psychotic desire to hold to the *bloody* sock, and his delirium indicate the beginning of his

punishment. This illness supports Raskolnikov's theory (Part I, Chapter 6) in which he states that either disease gives rise to crime or crime is always accompanied by something akin to disease.

B. Raskolnikov's attempt to refuse the money sent him by his mother is a feeble effort to assert his independence.

C. The easy and affectionate way in which Razumihin is able to handle Raskolnikov's landlady again emphasizes Raskolnikov's isolation and abnormality because of his failure to see with what ease he could have controlled her, thus obviating the summons from the police.

D. The recovery from the illness and the new clothes symbolically suggest that Raskolnikov will now begin his path toward redemption.

PART TWO

CHAPTER FOUR

Summary
Zossimov, the doctor, appears to check on Raskolnikov's progress. Razumihin tells of the arrival of his uncle, Porfiry Petrovitch, who is head of the Investigation Department. Zossimov and Razumihin talk of the arrest of two painters for the murder of Alyona Ivanovna and Lizaveta. Razumihin is very firm in his stand that the painters could not have committed the crime and makes an elaborate defense of their innocence. Zossimov notices that the discussion excites Raskolnikov and thinks that this interest in the crime suggests that he is regaining an interest in life.

Comment
A. Note that Razumihin and Zossimov's discussion of the arrest of the house painters for the murder excites Raskolnikov immensely. Razumihin's strong defense of the painters is later regretted when the painter confesses to the murder.

B. The fact that Raskolnikov shows such an intense interest in the murder but is lethargic about everything else later raises suspicion as to his guilt.

PART TWO

CHAPTER FIVE

Summary

In the midst of the discussion of the crime, Pyotr Petrovitch Luzhin appears to make his introduction to Raskolnikov. Luzhin makes feeble and awkward attempts to explain who he is, while Raskolnikov remains sullenly silent. When Luzhin tells of the living accommodations he has made for Dounia and Pulcheria Alexandrovna, everyone immediately recognizes the apartment as "a disgusting place—filthy, stinking, and what's more, of doubtful character." Then when Luzhin tells that he is living with Lebeziatnikov, a name that Raskolnikov had heard from Marmeladov, the trend of the conversation returns to the murder. Razumihin announces that the police are "examining all who have left pledges with her there." As soon as the conversation can be turned to Luzhin's engagement, Raskolnikov accuses him of trying only to make Dounia feel indebted to him. Luzhin protests that Raskolnikov's mother has misrepresented him. At this point, Raskolnikov threatens to "send him flying downstairs" if he ever mentions his mother again, and orders him to "go to hell." As Zossimov and Razumihin notice this sudden outburst, they also notice that Raskolnikov takes no interest in anything except the murder.

Comment

A. The appearance of Luzhin at this particular time (that is at the end of Raskolnikov's illness and at the end of the narration about the crime) plus Raskolnikov's previous established dislike for Luzhin and Luzhin's cheapness in getting rather disreputable living quarters for Pulcherina Alexandrovna and Dounia, help precipitate the violent quarrel between them.

B. Note also that Razumihin reveals Porfiry is examining all who have left pledges. This makes Raskolnikov realize that he must take the initiative and go himself to Porfiry.

C. At the end of the chapter, further suspicion is aroused by Raskolnikov's intense interest in the crime.

PART TWO

CHAPTER SIX

Summary

As soon as his company leaves, Raskolnikov feels the need to leave his room. He goes for a walk in the direction of the Hay Market; there he feels strangely attracted by the singing and the human fellowship in the saloons. Raskolnikov enters a saloon and immediately attracts attention by giving money to a young girl but asks nothing in return. He then remembers the horror of being confined to living on a square yard of space all his life and resolves to live life whatever it may be. He leaves and enters a clean restaurant where he asks for the newspapers of the last five days. While reading the papers, he meets Zametov, a minor official of the police and friend to Razumihin.

As the two begin a conversation, Raskolnikov begins to taunt Zametov with his (Raskolnikov's) activities and motivations. He tells him that he came to the restaurant solely for the purpose of reading about the murder of the old pawnbroker. In fact he *confesses* his extreme concern about the entire episode. When Zametov explains how the police are all wrong in the way they are conducting the case, Raskolnikov begins to resent the implication that the crime was obviously performed by an amateur. As a result of this resentment, he offers what he thinks would be the perfect way of committing the crime and how one should go about hiding the money and jewels. His explanation follows exactly the same steps that he had taken himself in committing the crime. The end of the explanation finished, Raskolnikov asks "And what if it was I who murdered the old woman and Lizaveta?" This question is temporarily disturbing to Zametov, but he quickly dismisses the discussion as an aftermath of Raskolnikov's illness. Almost immediately, Razumihin appears, and Raskolnikov tells him of his annoyance at being followed. "I don't want your benevolence...I may be ungrateful, I may be mean, only let me be, for God's sake, let me be! Let me be, let me be!" Razumihin is so shocked at his outburst that he allows Raskolnikov to go his own way and then immediately realizes that the outburst is part of Raskolnikov's illness. After Raskolnikov has escaped, he goes to a bridge where he is a witness to a woman's attempt to drown herself. He realizes that he was going to attempt the same thing and then became disgusted with himself for even thinking about it. He then returns to the scene of the crime. He is amazed to find the entire apartment being repainted. It no longer looks the same as when he was last in it. He then goes to the door-bell and begins to ring it, listening and remembering the "hideous and agonizingly fearful sensation he had felt when he was trapped after the crime." When the painters demand to know what he is doing there, he tells them to come with him to the police station and he will tell everything. At the end of the chapter, he is fully resolved to go to the police himself and confess everything.

Comment

A. Raskolnikov's thoughts about "living throughout eternity confined to a square yard of space is better than immediate death" becomes a motif which he rejects or accepts according to his desire to live.

B. In the meeting with Zametov, Raskolnikov thinks of *confession* for the *sixth* time. This time, however, it is a type of real confession; but the way the confession is made makes Zametov see it only as a result of Raskolnikov's delirium and sickness. The confession, however, is not readily dismissed by Zametov, and later he uses it as part of his suspicion against Raskolnikov.

C. In his recovery, Raskolnikov again rejects Razumihin's friendship because it is necessary for him to establish his own independence.

D. Raskolnikov's observing the woman's attempt to drown herself reminds him again of existing on "the square yard of space ..." and again there is the *seventh* thought of confession which is motivated this time by the attempted drowning.

E. Raskolnikov's return to the scene of the crime supports the theory that crime is partly a disease since it is a neurotic desire that draws him back to the scene. At the scene he offers to take the workmen to the police station and confess all to them—an *eighth* thought of confession.

F. Standing at the crossroads, for the *ninth* time he contemplates confession. This time he resolves to go in order to end the torment of doubt as to whether or not he should confess.

PART TWO

CHAPTER SEVEN

Summary

As Raskolnikov is on his way to the police station, he witnesses a drunken man who stumbles in the way of a carriage and is killed. Raskolnikov immediately recognizes him as Marmeladov and offers money to anyone who will help carry him home. When they arrive, Katerina is beside herself with grief and anxiety. Raskolnikov offers consolation and tells her that he will pay for the doctor and other expenses. A priest is sent for and also Sonia. When the doctor arrives, he announces that Marmeladov will die immediately. He tries to make some apologies to Katerina and to Sonia who has just arrived dressed in the gaudy finery of prostitution. When Raskolnikov first sees Sonia, he "recognized her crushed and ashamed in her humiliation...meekly awaiting her turn to say goodby to her dying father." As Raskolnikov leaves, he gives his money to Katerina Ivanovna and then meets Nikodim Fomitch, the police official, who exclaims that Raskolnikov is splattered with blood. Polenka follows Raskolnikov at Sonia's request to find out his name and to thank him. Raskolnikov tells her his name and asks her to pray for him. He then resolves that life is still before him and he rejects any thoughts of confessing to the crime. With this thought, he goes to Razumihin and apologizes for his bad temper. Razumihin walks home with him, and tells him of Zossimov's suspicion that perhaps Raskolnikov is going insane. When they reach Raskolnikov's place, they find his mother and sister waiting for him.

Comment

A. Raskolnikov's confession is prevented *only* by his witnessing the death of Marmeladov. Note his immediate emotional response; that is, his intellectual rejections are always a result of a deliberate struggle on his part—his emotional responses are spontaneous.

B. Raskolnikov's first sight of Sonia reveals her as a person of great suffering and shame. The absurd finery and gaudy dress required by prostitution contrast vividly with her demure and humiliated self.

C. Note that Raskolnikov's compassion causes him to give his last twenty rubles to Katerina for help. This is the money that he has just received from his mother. Again, even though Raskolnikov can intellectually rationalize a murder, he cannot stand the sight of others suffering, indicating the tremendous poles of his existence.

D. While helping with Marmeladov, Raskolnikov becomes splattered with blood. Whereas the blood on his person after the murder was a part of the cause of his delirium and was repulsive to him, this blood from helping Marmeladov makes him re-determined to live. "Life is real! haven't I lived just now? My life has not yet died with that old woman!" But with his affirmation of life, he renews his acquaintance with Razumihin so as to have excuse for going personally to Porfiry rather than to the police station.

PART THREE

CHAPTER ONE

Summary

Amid a joyous family reunion, in which everyone seems embarrassed and feels the tension of not knowing what to say first, Raskolnikov suddenly throws a dark cloud over the gathering by announcing that he is violently opposed to Dounia's marriage — "I won't accept the sacrifice." Razumihin attributes this outbreak to Raskolnikov's delirium, but Raskolnikov is firm in his objections, even though he is exhausted and needs rest. His mother refuses to go, but Razumihin insists that it is best for the present to leave Raskolnikov alone. He also insists that Dounia can't be alone in the dreadful lodgings that Luzhin has secured for them. Therefore, he escorts them to their lodgings, promising to return himself and later to bring the doctor to them so that they can hear from him about Raskolnikov's improvement. During all this time, Razumihin has developed a sudden infatuation for Dounia.

Comment

The immediate attraction that Razumihin develops for Dounia, combined with his willing desire to look after the family, leaves Raskolnikov free from practical worries about his family so that he can concentrate upon his own actions and his own guilt.

PART THREE

CHAPTER TWO

Summary

Razumihin gets up early next morning in order to check with the doctor about Raskolnikov's progress and then to go to Dounia and her mother with the news. The doctor is satisfied with Raskolnikov's progress and Razumihin goes immediately to Pulcheria Alexandrovna. He tells them all he knows about Rodya for the last two years; that at times Raskolnikov fluctuates between two characters. "He has been suspicious and fanciful. He has a noble nature and a kind heart. He does not like showing his feelings and would rather do a cruel thing than open his heart freely. Sometimes he is not at all morbid, but simply cold and inhumanly callous." Razumihin tells of Raskolnikov's past engagement to the landlady's daughter who was an invalid, queer and positively ugly. Pulcheria Alexandrovna shows Razumihin the letter she received from Luzhin requesting that Raskolnikov not be present at their first interview. When they arrive at Raskolnikov's room, Pulcheria Alexandrovna is so frightened to see her son that she can hardly stand up.

Comment

A. Note Razumihin's description of Raskolnikov in which the

split personality or dual character is described: "It's as though he were alternating between two characters."

B. The mention of Raskolnikov's desire to marry the ugly, queer, invalid daughter of his landlady illustrates Raskolnikov's predilection for the weak and downtrodden, and helps to explain his later attraction for Sonia.

C. Note Luzhin's attempt to cause dissension between Raskolnikov and his mother by suggesting that Raskolnikov gave money to Sonia rather than Katerina, and his demand that Raskolnikov *not be* present at the interview. Both are attempts to alienate Raskolnikov from his family, thus making them more dependent on Luzhin.

PART THREE

CHAPTER THREE

Summary

Raskolnikov has just awakened and can't understand all the generous care that Zossimov has given him. It troubles him. Pulcheria Alexandrovna is so pleased to see him better, that she narrates with emotion their fear upon arriving in St. Petersburg since Luzhin was unable to meet them. She asks if he knows what it is like to be utterly alone. Raskolnikov tells that he has given all of the money she sent him away to a poor woman whose husband was just killed. Raskolnikov begins to feel impatient with his mother even though he remembers how much he loves them in their absence. He is afraid that he will never be able to speak freely to them again. But immediately he tells of his affair with the landlady's daughter and then insists that Dounia not marry Luzhin: "I do not withdraw from my chief point. It is me or Luzhin. If I am a scoundrel, you must not be. One is enough. If you marry Luzhin, I cease at once to look on you as a sister." Dounia makes an elaborate justification of her engagement and then suddenly Raskolnikov withdraws his objections saying "Marry whom you like!" Dounia shows him Luzhin's letter, and Raskolnikov is amused by it and simply comments that Luzhin wants "to slander me and to raise dissension between us." Dounia insists that Raskolnikov come to the interview. She also invites Razumihin.

Comment

A. Note the reappearance of the Marmeladov motif, this time spoken by Pulcheria Alexandrovna as she asks if you know what it is like to be "alone, utterly alone." The effect of this utterance on Raskolnikov is profound since he has just recovered from the same emotions and the same desperation.

B. Raskolnikov has the sudden realization that the crime, rather than proving to him that he is free and above the ordinary man has, quite to the contrary, imprisoned him and isolated him from others: "It became suddenly plain and perceptible that he would never again be able to speak freely of anything to anyone."

C. Note the juxtaposition of Raskolnikov's dual personality. At one moment he renews his objections to Dounia's marriage to Luzhin: "If you marry Luzhin, I cease to look on you as a sister." This is his compassionate, humane side speaking. Then only a few seconds later there is the sudden reversal. "What am I making such a fuss for? Marry whom you like." Of course, this particular reversal from compassionate to intellectual is brought about by Dounia's terribly convincing justification of her marriage. "If I ruin anyone, it is only myself. I am not committing a murder." This statement forces Raskolnikov to realize that his murder was committed so as to see if he would be able to stand apart and above other human beings; therefore, he must assume this air of not caring whom Dounia marries.

D. As Raskolnikov reads Luzhin's letter, he easily sees through the purpose of the letter, and pretends not to be upset by its comments.

PART THREE

CHAPTER FOUR

Summary

The family reunion of the Raskolnikovs is interrupted by the appearance of Sonia. Rodya offers her a seat and tells her to sit between his mother and his sister. She has come to invite him, in fact to entreat him for Katerina Ivanovna's sake, to be present at the funeral and afterwards at a funeral lunch. Suddenly, Sonia feels extremely embarrassed because she realizes that due to the poverty of his room that Raskolnikov must have given them everything. Dounia and her mother must leave and Raskolnikov is left alone with Sonia after he tells Razumihin that he wants an interview with Porfiry. But immediately Sonia has to go, only to meet Svidrigailov who has been checking to see where Raskolnikov lived. As Raskolnikov and Razumihin are on their way to see Porfiry, Raskolnikov begins teasing Razumihin of being in love with Dounia and of acting like a Romeo because he has shaved and bathed and has "Pomatum" on his hair. They enter into Porfiry Petrovitch's flat laughing loudly.

Comment

A. Note that upon Sonia's appearance Raskolnikov has her sit with his mother and sister. This is a tremendous breach of the social class, and when Raskolnikov does so, he is partially aware, at least subconsciously so, that Sonia is his means of salvation.

B. Note the sudden appearance of Svidrigailov. He *does* live next door to Sonia, and this nearness allows him the chance to listen to Raskolnikov's confession to Sonia.

C. Note the deliberate joviality that Raskolnikov provokes so as to deceive Porfiry. This event shows the return of Raskolnikov's calm rational powers.

38

PART THREE

CHAPTER FIVE

Summary

After arriving, Raskolnikov maintains a sense of joviality for several minutes before he is introduced to Porfiry. Raskolnikov then tells Porfiry that he had left Alyona Ivanovna some small items which were not worth much but to which he attached great sentimental value, particularly a watch left him by his father. Porfiry announced that he had been expecting Raskolnikov and knew all about the pledges, which had been wrapped carefully by the old pawnbroker and dated. Porfiry subtly lets Raskolnikov know that he is aware of Raskolnikov's sickness, of his meeting with Zametov, of his presence at Marmeladov's death. Raskolnikov feels that he is being played with and thinks possibly of telling the the whole truth. Raskolnikov is completely surprised when he hears that an article of his on crime has been published, and furthermore, that Porfiry has read the entire article. Porfiry asks Raskolnikov to explain parts of the theory in more detail, which Raskolnikov undertakes to do. His theory involves the extraordinary man as opposed to the ordinary man. After his explanation, Porfiry subtly wonders if Raskolnikov might have thought of himself as being "extraordinary" while composing or formulating this particular theory. Raskolnikov maintains that even if he did think that, he would not tell Porfiry. Then Porfiry tries to return to the business of the pledges and asks Raskolnikov if he remembers seeing some painters at work there. Raskolnikov tells him that he doesn't recall seeing any but that someone was moving out. Razumihin reminds Porfiry that the painters were only at work on the day of the murder and that Raskolnikov's last time there was several days before the murder. Porfiry pretends to have been confused and offers Raskolnikov his apologies.

Comment

A. In this chapter, Porfiry's age is given as "five and thirty." But earlier it was stated that he was sixty-five (see Part Two,

Chapter Four), and later, he is depicted as a man about to retire, whose life, as he tells Raskolnikov, is about over. But regardless of his age, he seems to be an excellent opponent for Raskolnikov.

B. The essence of Raskolnikov's theory about crime, and the ordinary versus the extraordinary man is here presented.

1. Perpetration of a crime is always accompanied by illness.

2. All men are divided into "ordinary" and "extraordinary."

3. Ordinary men have to live in submission and have no right to transgress the law because *they are ordinary*.

4. On the contrary, the extraordinary man *has the right* to commit any crime and to transgress the law in any way because he is extraordinary, that is, not an official right, but an inner right to decide in his own conscience whether or not to overstep the law (or any obstacle that stands in the way of the practical fulfillment of his idea).

5. All great men would (or should) have the right to eliminate a few men in order to make their discoveries known to all of humanity.

6. All great men capable of giving something *new* (some "new word") must not submit to the common law, or they will cease to be great. Being great means breaking from the common rut of ordinary laws.

7. In conclusion, men are divided into two categories (a) the inferior (ordinary) who can only reproduce their kind and (b) "men who have the gift or talent to utter a *new word*."

What is new, really new and original, in Raskolnikov's theory (thus being new makes him one of the extraordinary) is that he "sanctions bloodshed in the name of conscience." That is, the great man is obligated to give to the world his new word and if it means killing a few ordinary men in order to do so, then the great man must do that.

C. As Porfiry wonders if the great man will suffer, Raskolnikov maintains that the really great will suffer in their own conscience and that "Pain and suffering are always inevitable for a large intelligence and a deep heart." This aspect of the theory partially justifies the suffering that the Raskolnikov has been undergoing.

D. If there seem to be contradictions in parts of Raskolnikov's theory, such as maintaining that the great will suffer and also later, that the great must be above sympathy and dependence on the ordinary, these contradictions are not unintentional on Dostoievsky's part. Instead, it must be emphasized that Raskolnikov at the time of the murder had not worked out his theory in complete detail. The contradictions exist so that later Raskolnikov will have to justify them when he is trying to explain his crime to Sonia.

E. Note that Porfiry tries to apply Raskolnikov's theory to Raskolnikov by asking if he didn't think of himself as an extraordinary person because he has uttered a *new word*. If Raskolnikov's theory is believed in, then Raskolnikov *must* have considered himself extraordinary, even though he denies it to Porfiry.

F. Note that Porfiry tries intentionally to trap Raskolnikov by asking for some detail that Raskolnikov could only have known if he was present at Alyona Ivanovna's on the *day* of the murder. Raskolnikov's perception of this trap again shows the return of his rational powers.

PART THREE

CHAPTER SIX .

Summary

As Raskolnikov and Razumihin leave Porfiry's, they discuss the implication of the conversation. Raskolnikov is certain that he is suspected of the crime. Just as they reach the rooming house where his mother and sister are staying, he parts from Razumihin promising to return shortly. He flees to his room and again searches to see if he might have left some scrap of evidence but can find nothing. As he is leaving his room, a mysterious stranger appears and calls him "Murderer!" This episode leaves Raskolnikov visibly agitated and confused, and he returns to his room and sleeps. He begins to examine the basis of his theory. He still believes in the nobility of the theory but worries about whether he might not have destroyed some of its nobility by practicing it on a disgusting object like the old pawnbroker. Furthermore, he feels that he must be one of the lice and thinks of the possibility of confession. He falls asleep and dreams that he is again striking the old pawnbroker but this time she refuses to die. When he awakens from this dreadful dream, he notices a person standing in his doorway. It is Svidrigailov.

Comment

A. Note the appearance of the man who mysteriously calls Raskolnikov a murderer. He is the man who was present when Raskolnikov returned to the scene of the crime. He is later present when Raskolnikov returns to Porfiry's office and is the "hidden" fact that Porfiry keeps referring to.

B. After being forced to defend his theory to Porfiry, and after being called a murderer by the stranger, Raskolnikov is so agitated that he is prompted by his own confusion to attempt to re-examine his theory. This examination reveals that he still believes strongly in the theory but he does see, for the first time, that he was not good enough for it. In this intellectual examination, he feels little remorse for the actual murder (or death), but instead, *resents* the old pawnbroker. His reasoning is that if his theory is noble, then it should have been tested on a noble object. The old pawnbroker was in herself so detestable, so vulgar, and so insignificant that her murder cheapened (and almost ruined) the nobility of the theory.

C. This *tenth* thought of confession is motivated by his alternating love for his mother, yet his inability to be near her. He fears that his theory—that crime isolates a person—is working on him and he is definitely feeling a sense of estrangement from his family.

D. At the end of the chapter, he wonders why, when he thinks of the murder, he always thinks of Alyona and not of Lizaveta whom he also murdered. The reason is that Alyona's murder stands for the theory. It was deliberately conceived and executed as a part of the theory. Therefore, his intellectual being is at stake with the murder of Alyona. But Lizaveta's murder was done out of desperation and fear and does not fit into the premeditated theory. Thus, her murder is no threat to his existence.

E. After these thoughts, it is significant that he dreams again of murdering the old woman, but this time he fails. And in failing, he would have nothing to confess. At the end of this awful nightmare, Svidrigailov, the symbol of evil, appears to Raskolnikov.

PART FOUR

CHAPTER ONE

Summary

Svidrigailov announces his purpose in coming to see Raskolnikov. He first of all wanted to meet him, and secondly, he wanted Raskolnikov to help him obtain an interview with Dounia. Raskolnikov tells him immediately that he will not aid him. During the course of the conversation, Svidrigailov reveals himself freely and openly to Raskolnikov by telling of many of the intimate events of his life such as the times he beat his wife, Marfa Petrovna. In the midst of the conversation, Svidrigailov points out that he and Raskolnikov have a great deal in common. Raskolnikov rejects this idea. Finally, Svidrigailov announces that he wants to make Dounia a present of ten thousand rubles so as to aid in her rupture with Luzhin. If she does not accept this gift, she will be taking money from Luzhin anyway. And again, Svidrigailov emphasizes that "there is something about you like me." As he is leaving, he tells Raskolnikov that Marfa Petrovna left Dounia three thousand rubles in her will.

Comment

A. Part four of the novel opens with the appearance of Svidrigailov. He will rapidly emerge as the Nietzsche superman — that is, as a person interested mainly in the gratification of his own appetites and desires and in the assertion of his own will. He uses his intellect only so as to aid him in obtaining sensual pleasures. Therefore his request to see Dounia is rejected by Raskolnikov because Raskolnikov fears this aspect of Svidrigailov. Even though Svidrigailov says that he wants to give Dounia ten thousand rubles so she won't have to marry Luzhin, Raskolnikov still refuses. It should be noted here, that Svidrigailov makes the same point about Dounia's marriage that Raskolnikov had made earlier, that is, that Dounia is selling herself by marrying Luzhin.

B. Note that Svidrigailov readily admits that he has a natural propensity to be vulgar whenever it pleases him.

C. Svidrigailov's emphasis that there is something in common between him and Raskolnikov repulses Raskolnikov; but still Raskolnikov recognizes some type of affinity toward Svidrigailov, especially since the latter has made the identical point about Dounia's marriage that he had made earlier. But more centrally, the thing in common is that both men will try to assert their own *will* above that of others.

PART FOUR

CHAPTER TWO

Summary
After Svidrigailov leaves, Raskolnikov meets Razumihin and they go to the interview with Luzhin. Raskolnikov tells Rasumihin to help him guard Dounia from Svidrigailov because he is "Afraid of that man." At the meeting, Luzhin relates some additional stories about Svidrigailov. One is about his supposed seduction of a fifteen year old deaf and dumb girl who later hanged herself. Another is about Svidrigailov's servant who hanged himself as a result of Svidrigailov's beatings and mockery. When Raskolnikov refuses to tell all about his interview with Svidrigailov, Luzhin takes it as a personal affront and pretends that he has to go. Dounia asks for an explanation of Luzhin's behavior. As he is trapped in several inconsistencies, he threatens Dounia about leaving and she accepts the challenge. She turns him out the door and asks that he never return.

But he does not leave before he holds it up to Dounia that he accepted her in the midst of scandal. This final insult is too much, and Razumihin is about to thrash him when Raskolnikov orders him from the room.

Comment
A. The two stories about Svidrigailov's rape of the girl and the death of the servant help to establish Svidrigailov as an amoral sensualist.

B. Note that Dounia's rupture with and dismissal of Luzhin leads to the scene in which he later tries to frame Sonia in order to get back in favor with Dounia.

PART FOUR

CHAPTER THREE

Summary
After Luzhin's dismissal by Dounia, he resolves to find some method by which he can work his way back into her favor. He is determined to do anything so as to have Dounia as his wife. Raskolnikov then tells his sister that Svidrigailov wants to see her and make her a present of ten thousand rubles. This offer puzzles them, and they decide to avoid all contact with Svidrigailov. Razumihin offers a plan whereby they can all profit from the three thousand rubles left Dounia by Marfa Petrovna. He wants to open a small printing firm which will cater to publishing translations. In the midst of these plans, Raskolnikov announces that he must leave. He asks pardon of his mother but insists that he is not well and needs peace and quiet. As he leaves, Razumihin follows him in the hope of some further explanation of his behavior. Raskolnikov is able to communicate a dreadful, strange secret by "some hint," and Razumihin allows Raskolnikov to go, indicating that he (Razumihin) will take care of Dounia and Pulcheria Alexandrovna.

Comment
A. Raskolnikov's sudden announcement to his family that he

must be alone emphasizes again the truth of his theory that crime isolates one from society, and that crime contributes to illness: "I feel ill, I am not at peace... I will come afterwards, I will come of myself. Leave me, leave me alone... I want to be alone; forget me altogether, it's better. Don't inquire about me. When I can, I'll come of myself or... I'll send for you... but if you love me, give me up... else I shall begin to hate you." This impassioned plea indicates the extent to which his crime has isolated him not just from society but also from his own family.

B. Note that when Razumihin follows Raskolnikov, he is able to make Razumihin know that he is implicated in the crime in some fashion. Here, then, Razumihin's function in the novel becomes important. His presence there enables him to look after Raskolnikov's mother and sister, thereby leaving Raskolnikov free to depart and work out his own guilt.

PART FOUR

CHAPTER FOUR

Summary
After Raskolnikov bids farewell to his family, he goes straight to Sonia's house. His appearance there agitates and frightens Sonia. Raskolnikov questions Sonia about her past life and her relationship to Katerina Ivanovna. In doing so, he paints a rather despairing picture of life and existence to Sonia. He taunts her with the thought that Katerina will soon die and that the children will be left without anything. He taunts her with her inability to save any money. He taunts her with the thought that Polenka will probably have to enter also into a life of prostitution. To all of these taunts, Sonia responds with despair and dismay, and maintains that "God will not allow it to be so." To Raskolnikov's taunt that perhaps there is no God, Sonia's suffering increases because she cannot conceive of life without God. At this point, Raskolnikov suddenly bows down to Sonia and kisses her foot, and says: "I did not bow down to you, I bowed down to all the suffering of humanity." But even now he continues to taunt her with the possible courses of action open to her in the future. He then asks her to read to him

the story from the New Testament of the raising of Lazarus. She reads it to him from a Bible that Lizaveta had given to her, and admits to Raskolnikov that she was a good friend of Lizaveta's, that she even had a requiem service for her. After she finishes reading the story, Raskolnikov tells Sonia how much he needs her and asks her to join him and go the same road with him because they both have transgressed against life—that is, Sonia has transgressed against her own self. As he is about to leave, he tells Sonia that if he comes tomorrow he will tell her who killed Lizaveta. The chapter ends with the revelation that Zvidrigailov had been sitting in the next apartment all during the interview listening to the entire conversation.

Comment

A. Raskolnikov's visit to Sonia in her lodgings is in preparation for his later confession. Dostoievsky's theory that "Suffering leads to salvation" and that through suffering man's sins are purified (or expiated) are now brought into the foreground. It now becomes apparent that Raskolnikov goes to Sonia because he sees in her the symbol of "all the suffering of humanity." Since she is a symbol of "great suffering," he seems to torment her with taunts such as the death of Katerina, the possibility that Polenka will be forced into prostitution, and the distressing state in which she now lives. These taunts are used to test her ability to suffer, and to see if she will be capable of withstanding Raskolnikov's confession, consequently, taking his suffering upon herself and helping him to "bear his own cross."

B. Note that Raskolnikov asks Sonia for the story of the raising of Lazarus. Earlier in the novel, Porfiry had asked Raskolnikov if he believed in this particular story. Thus, the two principal redemptive figures, Porfiry and Sonia, are both connected through this same biblical episode. A further note of coincidence is that the story is read from the Bible that belonged to Lizaveta, the woman he did not intend to murder. The story of Lazarus is pertinent mainly in the general outline rather than in the specific detail. Raskolnikov, like Lazarus, died one type of death as a result of the crime; in other words, his crime isolated him from society and from his family to the point that he is figuratively dead. Through Christ, Lazarus was raised from the dead and became again one of the living. Now through Sonia Raskolnikov hopes to again assume his place among the living. Therefore, both stories are of people who were separated from the living and through some incredible miracle were restored to the living. The incredible aspect of the Lazarus story also appeals to Raskolnikov. The raising of Lazarus is considered the greatest miracle that Christ performed. In a lesser aspect, that story is one of suffering, of great suffering that was alleviated by the miracle of restoring life. Therefore, if Sonia can restore Raskolnikov to life, his suffering will be alleviated. And finally, note that Lazarus had been dead for four days before Christ performed the miracle. Likewise, it has been four days since Raskolnikov's crime.

C. Raskolnikov sees in Sonia one who also transgressed against life and asks her to join him so that we "may go our way together." In asking even Sonia to join him, he symbolically breaks out of his isolation caused by the crime. Also he begins to deny that aspect of this theory that advocated the extraordinary man must stand alone and apart from all other people. But still, he has one reservation: Sonia is too much of a "religious fanatic."

PART FOUR

CHAPTER FIVE

Summary

The day after his interview with Sonia, Raskolnikov goes to the police station to see Porfiry. He goes with intense dread in his heart because he hated Porfiry "with an intense, unmitigated hatred, and was afraid his hatred might betray him." Porfiry receives Raskolnikov very cordially and acts as though it is a pleasant social visit. Raskolnikov is determined to keep the meeting formal and business-like; in fact, he keeps threatening to leave unless Porfiry comes to the point and examines him in an official way. Instead, Porfiry seems determined to talk about all types of subjects, including theories about crime and crime detection. As he talks, he paces swiftly around the room and stops frequently at a door and listens to see if perhaps someone is still there. The interview continues for so long that finally Raskolnikov loses his patience and tells Porfiry that he realizes he is suspected of being the murderer of "that old woman and her sister Lizaveta." He demands to be arrested immediately or allowed to leave. At this time, Porfiry reveals that he knows many unusual things about Raskolnikov, such as his trip to the scene of the crime when he rang the doorbell and asked to see the blood. This revelation amazes Raskolnikov so much that he sits quietly and listens to Porfiry proclaim that he likes Raskolnikov and wants to help him as much as possible. And as Raskolnikov demands to be released, Porfiry tells him he has a surprise behind the door and begins to unlock it, but he is suddenly interrupted by "a strange incident."

Comment

A. From Sonia who will redeem Raskolnikov through her simple suffering, Raskolnikov goes to Porfiry, who will try to redeem Raskolnikov intellectually. This second redemption is more difficult since Raskolnikov's existence now is based on the validity of his theory.

B. Note that Porfiry knows more than he reveals. He could arrest Raskolnikov at any time but doesn't. Why? (1) Because he does have a "sincere liking for" him and (2) if he arrested Raskolnikov now, Raskolnikov would never come to a self-realization about the error of his theory. Porfiry tries to make Raskolnikov admit (or confess) on his own the error of his theory. This function of Porfiry's will become clearer at the next interview.

PART FOUR

CHAPTER SIX

Summary

Later when Raskolnikov remembers the scene, he recalled hearing noises, and he recalled the unexpected arrival of several of subordinates. The prisoner Nikolay (who was the house painter at the scene of the crime) was brought in and he confessed to the murder of Alyona Ivanovna and Lizaveta. This confession is an overwhelming surprise to both Porfiry and Raskolnikov, neither of whom expected it. In fact, Porfiry is so vexed that he refuses to believe it, but recovering quickly, he dismisses Raskolnikov and promises to see him again later. Raskolnikov leaves and goes home where the strange man who had once so mysteriously appeared and called him a murderer comes and explains that he was hidden in the closet in Porfiry's office. He apologizes for calling Raskolnikov a murderer and for the trouble he has caused him. With the confession by Nikolay and the apology of the stranger, Raskolnikov resolves to make a new struggle for life.

Comment

A. During the middle of the interview, the house painter, Nikolay, confesses to the murder. Ironically, this confession is a result of Nikolay's desire to suffer, the exact thing that Porfiry had recommended for Raskolnikov.

B. After the porter comes to apologize for accusing Raskolnikov, he decides to "make a fight for it"—a new determination to live and surpass the stupidity of his crime.

PART FIVE

CHAPTER ONE

Summary

Luzhin and Lebeziatnikov discuss some of the dominant ideas now important in Russia. Then the discussion comes around to Sonia, whom Luzhin wants to see. Lebeziatnikov goes and gets her, and Luzhin insists that he remain during the interview. Luzhin questions Sonia about the financial condition of the family and tells her he would like to try to get some type of fund started for the widowed Katerina. To show his good intent, he gives Sonia a ten ruble note. After she goes, Lebeziatnikov emphasizes that he *saw* everything.

Comment

Essentially this chapter is a digression. Regarding the development of the plot, this chapter merely sets up the proper machinery for Luzhin's attempt to frame Sonia. But of slight importance is Dostoievsky's depiction of Lebeziatnikov as both an advanced liberal and also as a comic rube. This picture shows Dostoievsky's extreme dislike and distrust for the radical young men who are too readily influenced by new ideas. The foolishness of Lebeziatnikov is supposedly the foolishness of any person who adheres so closely to the "advanced ideas."

PART FIVE

CHAPTER TWO

Summary

At Katerina Ivanovna's, the funeral party is just beginning. The dinner was given so as to "do like other people." The party far exceeds Katerina's means to pay, but she insisted on inviting everyone, even her landlady whom she disliked intensely. When Katerina noticed that many people, especially the more genteel and influential lodgers, turned down her invitation, she blames it on her landlady and begins to act disdainful and haughty around her. Then as the party progresses, Katerina becomes openly critical and then hostile toward the landlady as though she were responsible for all the misfortunes in Katerina's life. Finally, the insults break into an open fight that is prevented only by the entrance of Luzhin.

Comment

This chapter simply prepares the reader for Katerina's irrational and emotional actions that lead to her eviction and death.

PART FIVE

CHAPTER THREE

Summary

As Katerina begs Luzhin to protect her, Luzhin stands disdainfully apart from her and avoids her as much as possible. Then

Luzhin addresses Sonia and tells about how he had exchanged some securities for rubles, and that when she left the room after their interview, a one hundred ruble note was missing. He carefully explains that he had just counted the money and one of the notes is now missing. He accuses Sonia of black ingratitude and demands that she return the money. Sonia denies the charge and Katerina immediately comes to her defense. Luzhin threatens to send for the police, but tells Sonia that if she will return the note he will forget everything. Katerina then becomes enraged and screams for someone to search her. As Katerina begins frantically to turn Sonia's pockets inside out, hundred ruble note falls out of one of the pockets. Sonia still denies the theft and the landlady orders them from the house. As Luzhin says he will carry the incident no further, Lebeziatnikov steps forward and accuses Luzhin of being vile. He tells how he saw Luzhin slip the hundred-ruble note into Sonia's pocket while she was standing in his room. Luzhin denies this accusation, and Lebeziatnikov is at a loss to explain why Luzhin acted as he did. At this time, Raskolnikov steps forward and explains how Luzhin was rejected by his sister and how he tried to alienate Raskolnikov from his family by implicating Sonia. At this time, Luzhin leaves as quickly as possible. As he leaves, someone throws a glass at him. The glass misses Luzhin but hits the landlady who in turn orders Katerina out of the house. Raskolnikov leaves and is going to see Sonia who left before Luzhin escaped.

Comment

Luzhin's attempt to frame Sonia is revealed here as his desperate attempt to disgrace her only so as to cast aspersion upon Raskolnikov, thereby hoping to prove to Dounia that he was right in his judgment about Raskolnikov's relationship to Sonia.

PART FIVE

CHAPTER FOUR

Summary

As Raskolnikov goes to Sonia, he wonders if he *must* tell her who killed Lizaveta. When he arrives, Sonia immediately pleads with him not to talk to her the way he did yesterday – "there is misery enough in the world." But Raskolnikov ignores her plea and immediately reminds her of the things that he said yesterday, especially because of the attempted efforts of Luzhin prove that Sonia could very easily be in jail herself now. Raskolnikov then asks her the hypothetical question – that is, if she had to decide who was to die, Katerina or Luzhin, whom could she choose. But Sonia refuses to answer such a question and maintains that "I can't know the Divine Providence." As Raskolnikov talks to her, Sonia, perhaps realizing his suffering, keeps asking him what is the matter. Raskolnikov then reminds Sonia that he promised to tell her today who killed Lizaveta. To Sonia's frightened response, he tells her to "Take a good look." At this moment, all of Sonia's suffering suddenly becomes magnified, and she shrinks from Raskolnikov in the same manner as did Lizaveta. Recovering immediately, she sees that Raskolnikov is suffering and she quickly becomes compassionate and sympathetic to him – "There is no one – no one in the whole world now so unhappy as you." A sudden feeling long unfamiliar to Raskolnikov floods his heart and softens it, as he asks Sonia not to leave him. She responds that she will follow him to Siberia. At the mention of Siberia, Raskolnikov recoils, and his haughty attitude returns. Sonia asks how he could bring himself to do such a thing. Raskolnikov offers explanations ranging from his poverty to his extraordinary man theory. Each of his reasons is rejected so that Raskolnikov never successfully explains his crime. Finally Sonia requests him to "Go at once, this very minute, stand at the cross-roads, bow down, first kiss the earth which you have defiled and then bow down to all the world and say to all men aloud, "I am a murderer." She also says that he should "suffer and expiate" his sin. Then suddenly in the midst of their conversation, Raskolnikov felt that Sonia's love for him was "burdensome and painful." As he is about to leave, Sonia asks him to take a cross made from cypress wood, but Raskolnikov refuses for the present and promises to take it at a later date. At this moment, Lebeziatnikov arrives.

Comment

A. Raskolnikov increases Sonia's suffering first by pointing out that Katerina and the children are now homeless. Then, he prepares her for the confession of the murder.

B. By way of preparation for his confession, he asks Sonia the hypothetical question: to decide whether Luzhin or Katerina should live. Note that Sonia's refusal to answer is based upon her reliance on Divine Providence; hence, she simply will not entertain such an idea. In other words, Sonia's meekness would not allow her to ever assert her own will.

C. After many attempts and thoughts of confession (at least ten) Raskolnikov finally makes an open confession, but not with words. During the scene, all that Sonia is aware of is that Raskolnikov is suffering tremendously, emphasizing again the idea of suffering as a way of expiation.

D. After the confession, Sonia promises that she will follow him to Siberia. This is not just an idle promise but is fulfilled later; therefore, she takes part of Raskolnikov's suffering upon herself. But as soon as Sonia mentions Siberia, note that Raskolnikov recoils with hostility against formal punishment.

E. Note that as Raskolnikov attempts to explain or rationalize or justify the murder, each attempt is also rejected by him as soon as he offers it. As pointed out earlier, he was forced by circumstances to commit the murder before his theory was completely formulated. Now as he attempts to explain it, he realizes how incomplete it really was. This realization is seen in the fact that as soon as he offers a reason, he then rejects it with the words: "No, No, that wasn't it." This is repeated so often that it functions as a thematic motif throughout the scene.

1. Raskolnikov attempted to say it was merely for plunder, but then he rejected this idea: "That's not the real thing." Furthermore, the reader knows the crime was not committed for plunder because Raskolnikov not only did not use the money, he did not even look at it.

2. Secondly, he offered the reason that he wanted to be a

54

Napoleon—that is, to see if he could overstep an obstacle in his way the same as Napoleon did. He rejected this by saying "That's all nonsense."

3. He resolved to get the money in order to keep himself in school without being a burden to his mother; then he rejected this reason "that it's not right."

4. He only killed a louse, and to Sonia's cry "a human being—a louse!" Raskolnikov also rejected this idea: "that's not it, you are right there...there were quite, quite other causes for it."

5. He accused himself, as a way of justification of being "vain, envious, malicious, base, vindicative," with a tendency to insanity. Then he rejected this idea: "No that's not it! Again I am telling you wrong!"

6. He wanted to see if he had the daring to do it: greatness is vouchsafed only to those who have the daring to take it. He wanted to find out whether he "was a louse like everybody else or a man." He proved only that he also was a louse, that he murdered himself more than he did the old woman.

F. Sonia's advice to Raskolnikov is to *suffer* and expiate his sin, "to go at once to the Crossroads" and confess. Raskolnikov rejected this because he feared the laughter of men who would call him a coward and a fool, a coward because he couldn't live by his ideas, and a fool because he would follow the advice of a prostitute. Sonia also wanted him to wear her wooden cross, but he rejected it until a later date because he was not quite prepared to acknowledge completely his crime.

PART FIVE
CHAPTER FIVE

Summary
Lebeziatnikov had come to Sonia to tell her that Katerina has been thrown out of her apartment and is now wandering madly

around the town after having dressed the children in rather absurd clothing and making them beg from strangers. After Sonia left, Raskolnikov suddenly feels repulsed by Sonia and wonders why he had come to her. When he reaches his room, he finds Dounia waiting for him. She explains that she better understands his situation because Razumihin explained how he is troubled by the police on false suspicions. Raskolnikov longs to tell Dounia the truth but cannot bring himself to do so. Then, in wandering aimlessly through the city, he comes upon Katerina who has simply gone out of her mind. She is forcing the children to beg, arguing with people on the streets, forcing her way into houses, making the children sing. Then as she runs through the streets, she stumbles, falls, and cuts herself. A doctor is sent for, but Katerina is dying. She maintains that she needs no priest or doctor, and as she dies, Svidrigailov shows up and volunteers to undertake all the arrangements. He says he will use the money that he was going to give to Dounia to take care of the children and will give Sonia a large amount also. He then subtly reveals to Raskolnikov that he was present at Madame Resslich's and overheard the confession to Sonia.

Comment

A. Note that Raskolnikov, after having made his confession to Sonia, is now suddenly repulsed by her; and part of this repulsion is due to the fact that he dislikes her ideas about suffering and going to prison.

B. Note Raskolnikov's desire to confess his crime to his sister. The idea of confession has been constantly with Raskolnikov ever since the murder.

C. The death of Katerina leaves Sonia responsible for the children. Note also that Katerina rejects the intervention of a priest because she has *suffered* so much that God must accept her because of her suffering.

PART SIX

CHAPTER ONE

Summary

As Raskolnikov is sitting alone in his room, Razumihin comes to accuse him of being a monster for treating his family the way he has. As Razumihin is railing against Raskolnikov, Dounia's name is brought up and Raskolnikov tells him how much Dounia likes him. He also tells Razumihin to look after them. As soon as Razumihin leaves, Porfiry arrives for a visit.

Comment

A. Note the emphasis in this chapter on the need of fresh air. Here is the re-emergence of this motif which in the earlier parts of the novel was suggested as a reason for Raskolnikov's illness.

B. With the appearance of Razumihin, Raskolnikov makes a further dispensation for the care of his family, which leaves him free for the actions he is about to take.

C. Note that Raskolnikov in earlier meetings with Porfiry had been frightened of him. But now with his appearance, he was "scarcely afraid of him." The point of this chapter is that Raskolnikov has now made contact with humanity again through his confession to Sonia and therefore is no longer so afraid of being trapped.

PART SIX

CHAPTER TWO

Summary

Porfiry announces that he has come to be honest with Raskolnikov, because in their last interview, he perhaps acted unfairly. He explains to Raskolnikov that he is attracted to him because he believes Raskolnikov possesses a noble soul and elements of magnanimity. Likewise, he wants to explain all the various circumstances which led him to think Raskolnikov the murderer: the pledges, the theory, the illness, the return to the scene of the crime, etc. Then he explains why Nikolay the painter confessed to the crime. The painter happens to belong to an old religious order which believed that man should suffer and to suffer at the hands of authorities is the best type of suffering. At the end of the narration, Porfiry then explains how Nikolay could not have committed the murder. Instead, he tells Raskolnikov that "you Rodion Romanovitch, you are the murderer." After making this accusation, Porfiry tells him that he will not arrest him for several days because he wants Raskolnikov to come of his own volition and make the confession. To arrest him "is not to my interest." Porfiry then tells Raskolnikov why he likes him and advises Raskolnikov to learn to love life, not to scorn the possibility of a mitigation of sentence. Likewise, he advises Raskolnikov to suffer because suffering is a good thing. Porfiry announces before he leaves that he has no fear Raskolnikov might be tempted to run away; therefore, he is quite safe in letting him remain free until he confesses.

Comment

Porfiry's explanation of the crime and refusal to arrest Raskolnikov show that he does sincerely like Raskolnikov, but more important he also believes in Raskolnikov's greatness. Porfiry's true purpose and mission becomes clear in this chapter. First, we must understand that Porfiry, like Dostoievsky, was a Slavophil (see background and introductory material for novel). In other words, Porfiry believed so strongly in the greatness of Russia that he is constantly searching and helping those who he thinks will be the future leaders of Russia or who will be able to contribute to Russia's greatness in other ways. Therefore, he views Raskolnikov as a man of noble character, one of the young intellects of Russia who could be of great service to the state if he learns to reject his radical ideas. Porfiry attempts to force Raskolnikov to acknowledge that his theory is wrong, and from this confession to go on and face life and become one of the important minds of Russia. If Porfiry were to arrest Raskolnikov immediately, it would ruin Raskolnikov's intellectual redemption through self-realization. But if Porfiry gives

Raskolnikov time enough to confess on his own (and thus realize and acknowledge to himself his own error), then Raskolnikov will achieve a greatness in his own right. Therefore, it would be no advantage to arrest Raskolnikov unless it is for simple punishment; but Porfiry has greater views of Raskolnikov.

   B. Note that as Sonia is trying to redeem Raskolnikov by asking him to take up his cross and suffer, so does Porfiry emphasize this same concept of suffering. This idea of suffering accounts for Nikolay's confession, but Porfiry emphasizes the importance of suffering as a means of expiation, "for suffering, Rodion Romanovitch, is a great thing."

   C. Porfiry also emphasized the need of fresh air. The spirit has been cramped by the crime and needs freedom.

PART SIX

CHAPTER THREE

Summary
   After Porfiry leaves, Raskolnikov hurries to Svidrigailov. He feels some strange attraction for Svidrigailov now that he does not understand. At the same time, he feels some repulsion toward Sonia and thinks that he must go his own way or hers. As he is walking toward Svidrigailov's house, he sees him through the window of a restaurant. Svidrigailov appears to be hiding or trying to avoid Raskolnikov but finally calls and invites Raskolnikov to join him. Raskolnikov warns Svidrigailov to desist in his attempts to see Dounia and threatens to kill him if he tries again. Raskolnikov emphasizes that, due to the overheard confession, Svidrigailov should know that he is capable of murder and will certainly carry out his promise. Svidrigailov pretends to be interested only in becoming better acquainted with Raskolnikov and in learning from him about the new ideas and new ways of enjoying oneself. Suddenly Raskolnikov feels oppressed by Svidrigailov's presence and begins to leave.

Comment

A. Note that at the beginning of the chapter, Raskolnikov is drawn to Svidrigailov without realizing that Svidrigailov represents one aspect of his character. Note also, that as he is attracted to Svidrigailov, he is repulsed by the thought of Sonia. "He was afraid of Sonia...he must go his own way or hers." But Raskolnikov is also convinced that his and Svidrigailov's "evil-doings could not be the same kind."

B. Svidrigailov tries to conceal himself from Raskolnikov because he has his interview with Dounia shortly and does not wish to be interfered with.

PART SIX

CHAPTER FOUR

Summary

As Raskolnikov is about to leave, Svidrigailov talks him into remaining for a while longer. Svidrigailov tells Raskolnikov all about his past life with his wife Marfa Petrovna and about his interest in Dounia. He maintains that Dounia had shown signs of liking him and pitying him; moreover, she had actively interceded between Svidrigailov and servants during some quarrels. From Svidrigailov's description of Dounia, Raskolnikov concludes that he still has evil designs on Dounia. Svidrigailov tries to contradict him by singing the praises of the young sixteen year old girl whom he is engaged to. His narration of his engagement prompts Raskolnikov to realize what a "vile, nasty, depraved, sensual man" Svidrigailov really is. At this point they both leave the restaurant.

Comment

In this interview, Raskolnikov is finally able to see what it is in Svidrigailov that disgusts him and sets him apart. It is his vile sensuality which leaves him depraved and vulgar.

60

PART SIX

CHAPTER FIVE

Summary
As they leave the restaurant, Raskolnikov is determined to follow Svidrigailov because he fears that Svidrigailov "has not given up his designs" on Dounia. Svidrigailov is disgusted and annoyed because the time is running out on him. Therefore, he begins to bring up the subject of the murder and to quiz Raskolnikov about it. The disgust of being around Svidrigailov soon gets the better of Raskolnikov and he leaves. As he walks away, he meets Dounia but is so preoccupied that he does not see her. At the same time Dounia sees Svidrigailov waiting for her and she hurriedly goes to meet him. Svidrigailov tricks Dounia into his room by hinting to her strange things about Raskolnikov and also by assuring her that all the neighbors, including Sonia, will be present. Once in his room, he reveals to her all that he has heard about Raskolnikov's confession. He explains how Raskolnikov committed the crime to support some theory of his. Dounia believes him because she read the article that Raskolnikov published about this same theory. After convincing her of Raskolnikov's guilt, Svidrigailov then reveals that only she can save her brother by submitting to seduction. Dounia quickly rushes to the door and finds it locked. Svidrigailov then reveals that the other tenants, including Sonia, are away and will not return until late that night. Svidrigailov implores Dounia to submit to the seduction even though he points out how easily it would be for him to overpower her: she would not be able to complain without implicating her brother. At this time, Dounia pulls out a gun. Actually the gun belonged to Svidrigailov; Dounia had taken it long ago when she was a governess. Svidrigailov begins to approach Dounia. She shoots once and misses. She shoots once again and the bullet grazes his hair. Svidrigailov does not rush Dounia; instead, he gives her all the time she needs in order to reload the pistol. He is willing to let Dounia kill him. After she has the pistol reloaded, he approaches her again; this time at three paces, Dounia can hardly miss, but she can't fire and she drops the

pistol. Svidrigailov feels that this is a good sign. He takes her in his arms and asks her if she can love him. To her response of "Never," he then gives her the key and tells her to take it, go, but make haste and leave.

Comment

A. Raskolnikov is confident that Svidrigailov has plans to seduce Dounia and resolves to follow him, but he is suddenly disgusted and repulsed by the man, especially since Svidrigailov brought up the subject of Raskolnikov's crime.

B. The scene with Dounia is the most crucial in Svidrigailov's life. Prior to this scene, Svidrigailov had functioned as a man completely self-sufficient, needing no one. Like Raskolnikov, he thought that his aims and desires were above those of ordinary man. Likewise, in the past, whenever Svidrigailov wanted something, he simply took it and defied all consequences. He lived with the idea that he needed no one, that he could withstand all things. Now, he finds that he not only wants Dounia, but also, and more important, he wants Dounia to *want him.* Here then, is the failure of the Nietzsche superman, the *impossibility of man's being able to exist completely alone.* If it were only the sensual pleasure derived from seducing Dounia, Svidrigailov could have easily raped her. If it were a matter of simply asserting his self-will and power, he could have easily done that. Previously Svidrigailov had dared to face life alone—that is, to measure his *will* against all things. In doing this, he has been *utterly alone*—in complete solitude (like Raskolnikov). He has committed evil so that he might know whether some power beyond him could punish him. And he has not been punished. So there is nothing for his unconquerable will to will any more. His is a loneliness that is more than he can bear. He then turns to Dounia knowing that she dislikes him, yet hoping there may be a *spark* of love behind all the loathing which would show him he is not alone. Twice she fires at him. He remains and allows her to fire so as to see if he can be punished. But before she fires a third time, she drops the pistol. So one last hope for himself is aroused. "A *weight* seemed to have rolled from his heart...it was the *deliverance from another feeling, darker and more bitter,* which he could not himself have defined." This feeling is the hope that Dounia's

62

dropping of the gun means that she can give freely of herself to him; he asks if she loves him or can ever love him. Never. That hope is destroyed, and he is again completely alone. He has crossed the bounds of all human experience in his desire to find whether the burden of life rests on his will alone or whether there is something beyond, and he has found nothing. Death then is the only thing that he has left untried—the only thing he has not willed. It is for him finally to will his own death.

PART SIX

CHAPTER SIX

Summary

After Dounia leaves, Svidrigailov walks for a long time. Upon returning to his room, he gives Sonia three thousand rubles. Sonia tries to refuse, but when Svidrigailov tells her of Raskolnikov's two alternatives (a bullet through the head or prison), she gratefully accepts. Svidrigailov then goes to see his young fiancee and leaves her a large amount of money. Returning to his room, he dreams of finding a young five year old girl whom he picks up and takes to his room. In the dream, this girl suddenly grows older and assumes the role of a depraved French prostitute. Svidrigailov then gets up and wanders to the park where he takes out his revolver and puts a bullet through his head.

Comment

A. After Dounia vowed she could never love Svidrigailov, he then realized that he needed more than sensual pleasures; he also needed human warmth and affection. Svidrigailov's entire life was based on the theory that he was completely self-sufficient and self-contained, that he needed no one, that whatever he wanted he would simply take and ignore any consequences, and that his will was stronger than anything else. Suddenly with his realization that he needed but could not *will* the human warmth Dounia could supply, he saw himself as the failure and sham of his previous existence. With this insight, he simply cannot return to his previous mode of existence which he realized to be false. Likewise, he cannot change.

The only thing he has not willed so far is his own death. Immediately after these realizations, he has the dream about the little girl whom he picked up and who, under his touch, turns into a shameless prostitute. Thus, these realizations lead him to suicide. There is for him no other place to go and nothing else in the world for him to will except his death.

B. Svidrigailov's suicide is part of Dostoievsky's thesis that no man can set himself apart from humanity. There can be no superman who transgresses the law. Sooner or later every person needs human warmth and companionship.

PART SIX

CHAPTER SEVEN

Summary

On the day that Svidrigailov commits suicide, Raskolnikov pays his last visit to his mother. She refuses to question him about his absences and tries to understand. But as Raskolnikov is about to leave, he asks his mother to pray for him. Promising to come to her again very soon, he takes leave from his mother and returns to his room where he finds Dounia waiting for him. She has been all day with Sonia waiting for him. Dounia now knows of the crime and agrees that Raskolnikov is a contemptible person "but ready to face suffering." She also believes that he expiates his crime "by facing the suffering." Still Raskolnikov cannot bring himself to admit the crime as evil. He sees instead that he was not the person to commit the crime. But he assures Dounia that he is ready to take his suffering even though he can see no value to it. When they part, Raskolnikov is heading for Sonia's house.

Comment

In Raskolnikov's last talk with Dounia, his sister also emphasizes the saving quality of *suffering*. But note that Raskolnikov revolts against this idea. He still has intellectual belief in the idea which provoked the crime. His only regret is that he has disgraced the nobility of the idea because he, as a person, is cowardly and contemptible.

64

PART SIX

CHAPTER EIGHT

Summary

Sonia had been waiting in anxiety all day for Raskolnikov to to come. When he does arrive she is overjoyed. He immediately asks for the cross and tells her that he is now going to the cross-roads as she had recommended. He refuses to go to Porfiry because he is sick of him. Sonia then gives him a wooden cross, saving the copper one until a later date. As he goes to confess, he does not understand Sonia's grief since he is doing what she had asked. But he refuses to allow her to accompany him, so she falls back and follows discreetly at a distance. When he remembers her advice about kneeling at the cross-roads, he does this and kisses the ground. Immediately there is a roar of laughter from all who were around him; therefore, he desists. When he reaches the police station, he has a few moments of qualms before he goes in. Once inside, he asks to see Zametov; Raskolnikov overhears that Svidrigailov has shot himself. Without making his confession, he turns to go out and once on the steps he sees Sonia standing in the distance. He turns and goes back and tells the official: *"It was I who killed the old pawnbroker woman and her sister Lizaveta with an ax and robbed them."*

Comment

A. Raskolnikov, having recognized the need for "human fellowship" goes to Sonia to "take up his cross." In Raskolnikov's suffering, he also sees that Sonia suffers. As he goes to make his confession, he remembers her words to "Bow down to the people, kiss the earth, and say aloud, I am a murderer." As he begins to do these things, he immediately provokes laughter. The difficult thing for Raskolnikov at this point is his fear of being laughed at because he still has a strong belief in the validity of his theory.

B. At the police station, he hears that Svidrigailov has shot himself. This news causes Raskolnikov to leave the station without making his confession. As he leaves the station, the sight of Sonia, the symbol of suffering humanity, causes him to return. And with his confession, the novel comes to a thematic close. The confession is a culmination of the many attempts at confession that he has contemplated since his murder of the pawnbroker and her sister.

EPILOGUE

Summary

The fact that Raskolnikov made a voluntary confession, that he had never counted the money, that he was on the verge of a mental breakdown, that he didn't profit personally from the crime, that many witnesses testified to his unusual behavior and also to the general nobility of his character and that he had often performed many charitable acts all combine to soften his sentence. Raskolnikov's mother fell ill during the trial and was never informed of her son's crime and his sentence. Raskolnikov was sentenced to eight years in Siberia. With the money left by Svidrigailov, Sonia is able to make preparations to follow him to Siberia. Two months after the trial, Dounia and Razumihin are married.

In the prison, Raskolnikov is sullen and distant. He will have nothing to do with the other prisoners. He is antagonistic about Sonia. Then suddenly, he is taken ill and put into the hospital. He re-examines his theories and still considers them to be right even though he blundered. He has not seen Sonia for a long time. When, however, he finds out that Sonia is ill and unable to leave her apartment, he is finally able to see her again. He realizes how much she means to him. At this time, he realizes also that even though he still has seven more years of suffering ahead of him he will have even more years of infinite happiness ahead of him with Sonia.

Comment

Most critics and readers of this novel consider the end of Part Six to be the most logical place the novel to end. All the motifs and symbols suggest that Raskolnikov is now on his way toward becoming the full integrated personality. The Epilogue seems to be a device used to satisfy the average to below-average reader and is essentially superfluous to the novel. In the typical fashion of the nineteenth century novel, the Epilogue simply "tidies up" the loose ends. For example, Dostoievsky tells us in the Epilogue that Dounia and Razumihin are married and that Sonia follows Raskolnikov to Siberia. These two facts were quite apparent to the most average readers without being told again in the Epilogue. Also we find out that Sonia brings about Raskolnikov's final redemption simply by her quiet unassuming presence and her willingness to serve him and suffer with him. But this also we know from the interviews that Raskolnikov and Sonia had together. Thus the formal structure of the novel ends with Raskolnikov's confession at the police station.

EXTRAORDINARY MAN THEORIES

Raskolnikov's views about the ordinary man versus the extraordinary man are based on two philosophers and can be divided into three separate sections. that is, parts of the theory are based on Hegel, parts on Nietzsche, and parts are Raskolnikov's own thinking. Therefore, if the theories seem to be contradictory at times, it is not a result of Dostoievsky's carelessness; quite the contrary, Dostoievsky intentionally made the theory contradictory at times. The point is that Raskolnikov had to commit the murder before he had completely formulated the theory. Dostoievsky wanted to show the young intellectual being influenced by various theories and then using these theories before he had had a chance to analyze them. For example, a typical contradiction would be that Raskolnikov will at one time maintain the murder was committed to benefit mankind; but then he will in turn maintain that the extraordinary man must be above mankind and not be concerned with what mankind will think of him. Such an incomplete understanding of his own thoughts and such contradictory statements are the rationale which leads Raskolnikov to the possibility of redemption. A careful analysis of the various ideas will show what aspects of the theories are borrowed and what aspects are the result of Raskolnikov's own thinking.

THE HEGELIAN SUPERMAN

Hegel, a German philosopher, had written in many of his works on the general nature of superman. His ideas were never formulated into one consistent thesis. But generally extracted from various parts of his philosophy, his views may be consistently stated. In its broadest statement, the Hegelian superman exists for noble purposes in the view that if the ends are noble then the means can be justified. The emphasis is always on the *ends* rather than the *means*. As applied to Raskolnikov's crime, the theories have relevance in the following ways:

1. The old pawnbroker is an evil person who is actually harming society by her vile and cynical grasp on the poor people who come to her for pawning. According to Hegel, any harmful segment of society should be removed. Therefore, Raskolnikov reasons that by murdering the old pawnbroker, he will be removing a harmful "thing" from society.

2. If the *ends* are noble then the *means* can be justified. The old pawnbroker has a lot of money which will be "wasted" upon useless masses and requiem services after her death. With this money, Raskolnikov will be able to complete his education without being cramped and then can devote himself to the service of humanity.

3. One small crime can be wiped out by thousands of good deeds. Raskolnikov could use the money that the old pawnbroker is squeezing out of the poor people, and by distributing it among families, hundreds of people would be saved from ruin and destitution.

The Hegelian superman is one that stands above the ordinary man, but works for the benefit of all mankind.

THE NIETZSCHEAN SUPERMAN

Dostoievsky probably first heard of the Nietzschean superman theory when he visited Germany about five years before writing *Crime and Punishment*. These ideas which are attributed to Nietzsche, therefore, are not as a result of Dostoievsky's reading of the published works but rather, they came to him from the intellectual ideas that were "in the air" at the time of the writing of the novel.

The Nietzschean superman *does not* exist for the benefit of society. Instead he exists for his own personal gratification. His aims are not prompted by any type of nobility. His most important aim in life is self-gratification. This type is represented in the novel by Svidrigailov. It is not necessary to go into all of Nietzsche's reasoning behind his superman theories, but we should see those aspects which affect Svidrigailov's actions.

Through a complex reasoning process, the Nietzschean super-man and also Svidrigailov come to the conclusion that God is dead. Svidrigailov would reason thusly:

> Since there is no Will (or Power) beyond that of my own, then I must completely assert my own Will until it is totally free of all restraint against it. Since there is no Power beyond me which functions to punish, I am free to assert completely my own Will. The question is which shall pre-vail? The "I" (is, the individual Self) which is known to me OR some power which no one knows or understands.

Therefore, the Nietzsche superman is the one who possesses the strongest will and is able to make his desires and his power dominant over others. The superman refuses to recognize any will beyond that of his own will. Consequently, Svidrigailov can rape a thirteen-year-old girl so as to satisfy his will, he can be the instru-ment causing the death of a servant or his wife, and he can pursue Dounia without any fear of some power punishing him. He asserts his own will in order to gratify his own desires.

The test of this type of superman is that he must stand com-pletely alone and must not allow his will to be influenced by the wishes of others. Thus, this assertion of the will isolates man from society. It leaves him in complete solitude. Consequently, when Raskolnikov attempts to assert his will, he finds himself cut off from the rest of humanity. It is this dreadful solitude which Raskol-nikov cannot stand and which makes him confess so as to become again a part of humanity.

THE RASKOLNIKOV EXTRAORDINARY MAN

Raskolnikov took various aspects of the above two theories and added certain touches of his own. For Raskolnikov, all men are divided into two categories (1) ordinary and (2) extraordinary. The ordinary man is inferior, and he can do nothing but reproduce his own kind. The ordinary man has to live in submission and has no right to transgress the law because *he is ordinary*.

On the contrary, the extraordinary men *have the right* to commit any crime and to transgress the law in any way because they are extraordinary. They are extraordinary because they are the men who have the gift or talent to utter a *new word*. It is the extraordinary men who forge civilization onward to new heights of achievements. Since these achievements are important and ultimately benefit all mankind, the extraordinary man has this inner right to decide in his own conscience whether or not to overstep the law or any obstacle that stands in the way of the practical fulfillment of his idea.

All great men capable of giving something *new* to society must not submit to the common law because if they do they cease to be great. Being great means breaking from the common rut of ordinary laws. Great men create new laws by their discoveries and therefore should have the right to eliminate a few men in order to make their new discoveries known to all of humanity. Therefore if a man is really great, and has something really new to communicate to mankind, he *should* or he is obligated to make this known to mankind regardless of the consequences. Thus, Raskolnikov *"Sanctions bloodshed in the name of conscience."*

Raskolnikov constantly uses Napoleon as a point of reference. Such a man as Napoleon is above the common laws of humanity, because he had the daring to commit various acts in order to complete his plans.

But again it should be emphasized that, at the time of the murder, Raskolnikov had not worked these three theories into a consistent whole. All the individual parts were there, but some of the connecting details were missing. Therefore the murder was committed to see "Do I *dare* commit this murder and therefore prove myself to be a man by proving that my will is strong." Am I a real man of power? (This idea is partly from Nietzsche.) Then from this premise, Raskolnikov reasoned that a man may commit a crime if it serves a noble end. (Here he takes part of Hegel's idea.) Then he chooses his victim from the ordinary class of people — that is, he chooses what he considered to be a louse, the old pawnbroker.

CHARACTER REVIEW

RODION ROMANOVITCH RASKOLNIKOV

Raskolnikov is best seen as two characters. He sometimes acts in one manner and then suddenly in a manner completely contradictory. These actions compel one to view him as having a split personality or as being a dual character. Perhaps the best description of Raskolnikov occurs in Part Three, Chapter Two when Razumihin tries to explain to Raskolnikov's mother and sister how he has been of late: "He is morose, gloomy, proud and haughty, and of late — and perhaps for a long time before — he has been suspicious and fanciful. He has a noble nature and a kind heart; he does not like showing his feelings and would rather do a cruel thing than open his heart freely...It's as though he were alternating between two characters." These two characters are best represented as (1) his cold, intellectual, detached side which emphasizes *power* and *self-will* and (2) his warm, humane compassionate side which suggests self-submissiveness and meekness. The intellectual side is a result of his deliberate and premeditated actions; that is, when he is functioning on this side, he never acts spontaneously, but instead, every action is premeditated and thought out. It is this aspect of his personality which enabled him to formulate his theories about crime and to commit the crime. In order to emphasize this dual character, Dostoievsky created two other characters in the novel who represent the opposing sides of his character. These characters are Sonia and Svidrigailov.

Svidrigailov represents the cold intellectual side which emphasizes self-will. All of Svidrigailov's acts are performed so as to give him pleasure and to place him above common morality. This is not to imply that Svidrigailov is an intellectual; but rather it implies that he does not allow minor human actions or morality or law to prevent him from having his way. Thus, as Raskolnikov could commit a murder because of his theories, so can Svidrigailov rape a thirteen year old girl for his own satisfaction.

Raskolnikov's intellectual side is intricately bound up in his theory of the extraordinary man. If Raskolnikov is to be one of the extraordinary, he must be able to stand alone, without needing human companionship or without being influenced by the actions of others. He must rely on no one and he must be completely self-sufficient. When he performs charitable acts, he is temporarily violating this intellectual side of his nature.

The other side of his character is the warm compassionate side. It operates without an interceding thought process. His first and immediate reaction to any situation represents this aspect of his personality. Consequently, he will often act in a warm, friendly, charitable or humane manner, and then when he has had a chance to think over his actions intellectually, he regrets them. For instance, when he spontaneously gives the Marmeladovs his last money, then shortly afterwards regrets that he has given them the money. If left to his immediate reactions, Raskolnikov would always act in a charitable and humane manner; he would always sacrifice of himself for his fellow man.

Sonia represents Raskolnikov's humane side. As Raskolnikov would often sacrifice his own money or self for the benefit of others, so does Sonia go into prostitution in order to benefit her family. Sonia represents the suffering of humanity, and Raskolnikov turns to her in order to help him with his suffering.

Therefore, actions in the novel that seem to be strange and contradictory are rather the result of the two aspects of Raskolnikov's personality. When he refuses at one moment to allow Dounia to marry Luzhin and then tells her to marry whom she pleases, this reversal is an example of the humane side not wanting his sister to enter into an undesirable marriage and then the intellectual side contending that it must not concern itself with the insignificant problems of others.

SONIA SEMYONOVNA MARMELADOV

Sonia functions in the novel as one aspect of Raskolnikov's character and also as the passive redemptive figure. She is the meek and self-submissive figure. And her function is to help redeem Raskolnikov. But her redemptive role is a passive one. This means that she does little in an active way to make Raskolnikov confess or change his way. Rather she is simply available whenever Raskolnikov needs her. Then the question arises as to how can she be redemptive. She is redemptive because through her suffering she becomes for Raskolnikov the symbol of all the suffering humanity of mankind. And through her compassionate nature and ability to love, she touches deeply one side of Raskolnikov's character. Her life is one of simple expediency for existence. No one is less fit for a life of prostitution than is Sonia, but this was the only way in which she could help support the family; therefore, she became a prostitute but feels intensely the degradation and shame of her profession. But in spite of this profession, she has never lost touch with God. Her simple faith in God is part of her strength. She attends church as much as possible and has the basic faith in the goodness of Divine Providence. She could never assert her own will to the degree that the will of Divine Providence would be put into question.

ARKADY SVIDRIGAILOV

Svidrigailov has one function in life — to satisfy his sensual desires. To do so often takes strange ways and means. He represents a type of Nietzsche superman. This type feels that the world is essentially an evil place; therefore to be in tune with this universe, one must essentially be evil. Since there can be no divine providence whose will is stronger than man's, then each individual must assert his own will and power. Since the universe is meaningless and directionless, man's main course of action is the complete gratification of the appetite. Therefore, for Svidrigailov, his pleasure and gratification are all that matter. How they are achieved is unimportant. Svidrigailov admits to Raskolnikov that he has a "natural propensity" for the vulgar. He has no scruples about getting his own way. His life has been constructed on the idea that his own feelings and pleasures are more important than anything else; therefore, he can rape a mute thirteen year old girl and upon hearing that this girl has hanged herself, will have no feelings of remorse. He simply shrugs the shoulders. It is also strongly implied that he was the cause of the death of Petya, his servant, and that he actually poisoned his wife Marfa Petrovna. At least when Raskolnikov accuses him of the latter, he makes no defense against the accusation. Of equal importance are Svidrigailov's acts of seeming charity. If he does do good, it is not because he sees the act as a good action, but simply because the impulse of the moment gives him pleasure. Likewise in his kindness to the Marmeladov family, he is hoping to deceive Raskolnikov and Dounia into believing that he has reformed from his previous evil ways.

At last, even Svidrigailov realizes that he cannot live completely alone and isolated from the rest of humanity. When he realizes that he can not have Dounia, he then is forced to commit suicide. Suicide is the only thing left that he has now left to will for himself. His old manner of living has now been denied him by his realization that he can't live alone and there is no new method left to him. Therefore, he takes his life as the only course of action open to him.

PORFIRY PETROVITCH

Whereas Svidrigailov was working for the gratification of the self, Porfiry is working for the betterment of mankind and more especially for the betterment of Russia. Porfiry is a person who believes that Russia is destined to become the great nation of the world and is to guide the world into a new era based on love and understanding. Consequently, he feels that any person who has intellectual potential should be serving mother Russia in order to attain these goals. He sees in Raskolnikov a potentially great man who has deceived himself by adhering too much to new and radical intellectual ideas that have come from outside of Russia. Porfiry believes that when Raskolnikov finds his true self, he will then become a man with potential greatness and a man who can do a great service for Russia. If he were to play the part of the average policeman or investigator and concern himself only with trapping the criminal immediately, Porfiry would have arrested Raskolnikov very early in the novel. But Porfiry's aim is not so much to see the criminal locked behind bars as it is to help rehabilitate the criminal and make him into a useful member of society. Therefore, he taunts Raskolnikov with the theories, he challenges certain points, he tries to trick him and confuse him with certain facts that he possesses in order to make Raskolnikov realize the error of his way. He knows that if he were simply to arrest Raskolnikov, then Raskolnikov would never come to a self-realization about the error of his theory, and thus would never be a useful member of society. Therefore, in the final interview, Porfiry gives Raskolnikov a few more days in order to confess because a free confession would mitigate the sentence. Through all of their interviews, Porfiry shows himself to be one of the advanced thinkers of Russia through his use of psychology and through his use of new methods and through his belief in the possible rehabilitation of criminals into useful members of society.

MOTIFS

Motif is the recurring idea or thought which acts as a unifying idea and sometimes develops as a commentary on characterization or on the thesis of the work. Sometimes the motifs recur so frequently that they enhance the meaning of the novel and often rise to symbolic importance. Each reading of the novel suggests additional motifs for the experienced reader. But the purpose here is to suggest only a few of the most dominant motifs, most of which have been pointed out in the analysis.

THE MOTIF OF CONFESSION

Perhaps the most frequent motif running throughout the novel is that of confession. From the moment that Raskolnikov commits the crime, he immediately thinks of confessing this act. Various motivations cause him to consider confessing. Sometimes, as with his earliest thought, the idea of confession is prompted by fear of being discovered. Each motivation for confession is a comment on some aspect of the novel. For example, when his thoughts of confession are motivated by a fear of being discovered, the emphasis on fear (the basic realization that Raskolnikov is afraid) is a type of comment on his inability to perform the role of the extraordinary man. If he were the extraordinary man, he would never show such a weakness as is seen when he is prompted to confess by his fear of being discovered. This weakness is a good contrast to the strength needed for him to be one of the extraordinary.

But the confession motif becomes more important as a comment on his theory when the confession impulses are motivated by his terrible sense of isolation and estrangement. His theory suggests that the extraordinary man should have the strength to stand alone, that he should not become involved with petty society. Consequently, when Raskolnikov wants to confess, this indicates that he cannot exist in the solitude demanded of an extraordinary man. He cannot live completely cut off from all human contact. The confession is prompted by his realization that his crime has isolated him from humanity, and by confessing he will at least be drawn back into the stream of humanity.

And finally, the various attempts or thoughts of confession that occur early in the novel act as a kind of symbolic foreshadowing that he will eventually *have* to make a confession. Consequently, this confession motif leads to and prepares for the climactic scenes in which Raskolnikov first confesses to Sonia and then to the police. In view of the many previous attempts and thoughts of confession, the final confession is fully motivated. All the various fears are brought together and the novel is brought to its close with the confession.

THE "ALL ALONE" MOTIF

In the second chapter of the novel, Marmeladov cries out to Raskolnikov: "Do you understand, sir, do you understand what it means when you have absolutely no where to turn?" This concept of man being completely alone, totally isolated from his fellow man and being left all alone with nowhere to turn becomes one of the dominant motifs of the novel. It is this cry which makes Raskolnikov sympathize with Marmeladov rather than to dismiss him as a louse.

This concept is of importance later because we find that in formulating his theory of crime that Raskolnikov maintains crime isolates one from society. Even though the superman should be able to withstand this isolation, Raskolnikov finds that part of his punishment is being confined to this state of solitude. Of course, in the first part of the novel, we find that Raskolnikov has voluntarily isolated himself from all human contact. As a result of this, such things as the landlady's protest are lodged against him. Furthermore, the crime originated out of his solitude; therefore, he must also suffer in solitude.

The murder is a symbol of Raskolnikov's thinking. He had intentionally cut himself off from all authority, from love, from all associations, from humanity. As a result of this isolation, he feels that he himself is nothing and if so, others are also nothing, thus one can kill with impunity.

But this motif appears more consistently during the novel. After hearing Marmeladov make his impassioned cry, Raskolnikov returns to his room where he finds a letter from his mother. In the letter he hears how his sister is sacrificing herself in a marriage. Here the thought of having no place to go returns to him. He would like to prevent this marriage but he has no way, no money, and no person to turn to for help. Thus this cry applies directly to his present situation. The murder was supposed to supply him with money with which he could find a way to turn.

Then after the murder, his mother and sister arrive in St. Petersburg. His mother had been frightened the day before because Luzhin had not met them at the station. When she utters the cry to Raskolnikov, "We were alone, utterly alone," he realizes that they had no one to turn to, no place to go. The desperation of their situation sits heavily upon Raskolnikov, because he had just felt the same terrible sense of confinement due to his crime.

Raskolnikov's thoughts have been so much with this concept of being alone, utterly alone, and having no place to turn, that his approach to Sonia and his ultimate confession is directly correlated to this motif. First, he sees and comments upon Katerina's eviction from her lodgings and tells Sonia that Katerina has no place to go. He predicts a horrible future for Polenka because she will have no other choice than to enter into prostitution. And finally, he taunts Sonia with the thought that she will ultimately have no place to turn. All of these taunts are prompted, however, by Raskolnikov's realization that he has no place to turn.

The final confessions to Sonia and to the police, and the motivation of many of the earlier thoughts of confession are directly correlated to Raskolnikov's recognition of his confinement to solitude, of having no place to go. He confesses to Sonia so as to enter back into the stream of life and humanity. As he acknowledges her to be the symbol of all of suffering humanity, he confesses to her because he can no longer stand to be confined outside of and isolated from humanity. His crime has wielded its drastic punishment by restricting his ability to communicate with his fellow man. Therefore, in order to be restored to humanity he must confess his crime.

This motif has been one of the dominant ideas controlling much of the action throughout the novel. From the theory that crime will isolate, to the perpetration of the crime which was partially a result of his isolation, to the realization that he is forced to exist outside of humanity, this motif permeates most of the central actions of the novel. And finally, the resolution of the novel as seen through the confession to the police was effected by the realization that he cannot live alone.

THE MOTIF OF THE SQUARE YARD OF SPACE

Early in the novel, Raskolnikov tries to evaluate his life in terms of the amount of space or freedom that he possesses as a result of the crime. After his illness, Raskolnikov feels the need of being with people and he goes to a bar. Once there he remembers reading somewhere "that some one condemned to death says and thinks, an hour before his death, that if he had to live on some high rock, on such a narrow ledge that he's only room to stand, and the ocean, everlasting darkness, everlasting solitude, everlasting tempest around him, if he had to remain standing on a square yard of space all his life, a thousand years, eternity, it were better to live so than to die at once! Only to live, to live and live. Life whatever it may be." These thoughts were prompted by Raskolnikov's need to escape from his solitude. But the solitude was caused by the crime, and the crime has confined him to a square yard of space because, as in the above motif, he cannot communicate, he cannot join in the stream of humanity.

Throughout the novel, whenever Raskolnikov considers the thoughts of suicide, this thought of the square yard of space returns to him. Often he is so plagued by fear of discovery, by the tedium of being alone, and by his sense of estrangement, that he contemplates suicide as a logical way out of his predicament. For example, when he is on the bridge, and sees a woman attempt to commit suicide, he had also been contemplating suicide. Then a sudden reversal shows him that life is still worth living, is better than ending even though he is confined to this square yard of space.

Of course, the confinement is due to the theory which prompted the crime. Here, this motif suggests that too great a reliance on the intellect, too great a dependence on intellect at the sacrifice of the humane elements in one's personality leads a person to a type of imprisonment. This concept is further supported by the fact that when Raskolnikov performs some charitable or humane act, he has a greater sense of life and remembers his thoughts of being confined and rejects them. The humane act gives him the realization that life is still full of many potential hours of happiness outside the square yard of space.

And finally, after Raskolnikov has been sentenced to prison in Siberia, he realizes that the square yard of space that he had felt confined to was not an actual thing. In prison he begins to feel a sense of freedom because he has, through his confession, re-entered life.

THE MOTIF FOR SUFFERING

Raskolnikov's salvation is directly dependent upon his ability to suffer. This does not imply that he has not already suffered. In fact, the motif is of importance because he has shown such a great capacity to suffer. Ultimately Dostoievsky's thesis is that suffering, great suffering, leads to salvation, that through suffering man's sins can be expiated.

But to return to the earlier problems, immediately after his crime Raskolnikov falls ill and is unconscious for several days. This illness is a thematic sign of his suffering. This concept is important because earlier, Raskolnikov had written in an article that crime is always accompanied by illness. He had also written that a great personality, the extraordinary man, by his very nature is capable of suffering and *will* suffer intensely for any crime or infringement of the law. If this is Raskolnikov's theory, then by obverse logic, that is, by the fact that he does suffer intensely, Raskolnikov must be seen to be an extraordinary man by his own suffering. But to take a position diametrically opposed to the above, it could be maintained that the reason Raskolnikov suffers is that his disgrace at the realization he is not an extraordinary man makes him suffer. If this view is maintained, the suffering could be said to be a result of the failure of the crime rather than a regret over the crime.

But the important thing to remember is that Raskolnikov does suffer and that his suffering begins immediately after the crime. Now this motif of suffering is not confined to Raskolnikov alone. His sympathy for Marmeladov is partially due to the fact that Marmeladov does suffer, even though he is the cause of the family's destitution. Likewise, Sonia's ability to suffer in a submissive silence makes her the apt person for Raskolnikov to confess to. And previous to Raskolnikov's confession, Nikolay also confessed so as to subject himself to suffering.

In addition to these, Katerina maintains that she does not need a priest to absolve her of her sins because her suffering purified her so that God would have to accept her as she is.

And whereas these people suffer, others recommend suffering as a means of salvation. Porfiry and Sonia, the two redemptive figures of the novel, suggest to Raskolnikov to suffer and "expiate your crime." Dounia tells her brother that his willingness to suffer alleviates the severity of his crime.

The motif of the need of suffering, therefore, acts as one of the strongest unifying devices in the novel. But more important, Raskolnikov's suffering which begins immediately after the crime makes the reader sympathize with him. If he did not suffer, the reader would be tempted to dismiss him as a monstrous and horrible pervert. However, his intense suffering and his willingness to sympathize with others who are suffering mitigate the severity of his crime. And finally, it is through his suffering that he is led to his confession and then to his redemption.

MOTIF OF FRESH AIR

It should be apparent that what is said about one motif depends heavily upon what is said about another. Rather than being repetitious on Dostoievsky's part, this interdependence of motif is a strong unifying device. In such a novel as this where so many ideas are at play and so many divergent themes and motifs are suggested, it is a mark of the novel's greatness that each motif is entwined inextricably with another. Thus we see that the idea of the need for fresh air is entwined with the idea of solitude, with the need of confession, and it contributes to Raskolnikov's suffering, contrasts to being confined on a square yard of space.

This motif begins as soon as Raskolnikov has a visitor to his room. The first comment or observation of every visitor concerns the cramped or close confines of his room. When we look back at some of Raskolnikov's earlier action and thoughts we see that he often looked with hatred at his room. "It was a tiny cupboard of a room about six paces in length. It had a poverty stricken appearance." Often when he leaves the room, it is because these cramped quarters have cramped his soul, and he needs room in which to expand. It can even be suggested that the cramped quarters cramped his thinking so much that he was forced to commit a murder. At least, his mother attributes part of his illness to the poverty of his surroundings and living quarters. Dostioevsky emphasizes this aspect of his living quarters because when he goes to prison, his living quarters are no larger than his room. But he doesn't feel cramped in prison. The reason is that due to the confession, and to the surrounding countryside in Siberia, he has found ample "fresh air."

The motif of fresh air is also emphasized by several other characters. The doctor, Zossimov, recommended fresh air to Raskolnikov as a cure for his illness and as a preventive against future attacks. Ironically, Svidrigailov suggests the need for fresh air. And Porfiry announced several times that fresh air has a curative power. In each of these suggestions, there is a sense that Raskolnikov's soul has been cramped by the crime and needs the fresh air in which to expand and develop.

STUDY QUESTIONS AND SUGGESTIONS

1. Consider the proposition that fundamentally Raskolnikov progresses from adherence to theory and ignorance of self to knowledge of self and rejection of theory. What important developments in his character does this formulation fail to include? (See discussion on Structure and the discussion of the confession and suffering motifs.)

2. What concepts of law are prominent in *Crime and Punishment*. (See Introduction and Background, and discussion of Porfiry.)

3. What concepts of Christianity are prominent in *Crime and Punishment?* (See discussion of Sonia, also analysis of Part Four, Chapter Four, and the motif of suffering.)

4. Stage briefly the rationale by which Raskolnikov considers himself a superior man. (See the discussion of the Extraordinary

Man and Superman theories. Also see analysis of Part One, Chapter Six, and Part Three, Chapter Five.)

5. What are the laws governing a superior man? (See same as in question four.)

6. How might Raskolnikov answer the objection that his theory is only an attempt to justify unrestrained self-will. (See analysis of Part Five, Chapter Four.)

7. How does Dostoievsky forestall the reader's assuming that his central character is simply mad? (See motifs and character analysis.)

8. What qualities of Raskolnikov does Svidrigailov lack or pervert? (See the many chapters in Analysis where Raskolnikov and Svidrigailov encounter each other. Also see structure and character analysis.)

9. Why does Svidrigailov commit suicide? (See analysis of Part Six, Chapter Five; also the character analysis and the structure.)

10. How do dreams function in the novel? (See Part One, Chapter Five.)

SUGGESTED THEME TOPICS

1. What does Dostoievsky gain artistically by representing Sonia as a prostitute? What biblical character did he likely have in mind?

2. Choose the incidents which seem to be major crises in Raskolnikov's life and determine what each contributes to his development.

3. Examine carefully the scene in which Sonia reads to Raskolnikov the story of Lazarus. How does Raskolnikov's condition resemble that of Lazarus?

4. What irony and what value are there in making Sonia the principal outside agent of Raskolnikov's redemption?

5. What is the relationship of Raskolnikov's confession to Sonia and his confession at the police station?

6. The structure of the novel allows Raskolnikov to have alternate interviews with Sonia and Svidrigailov. How does this structure reflect thematic development?

7. What difference would there be in the novel if the Epilogue were omitted?

8. Most of Raskolnikov's important decisions occur on a stairway. How does this reflect a significant thematic meaning?

SELECTED BIBLIOGRAPHY

Berdyaev, Nicholas. *Doestoevsky: An Interpretation,* New York: Meridian, 1957.

Carr, Edward Hallett. *Dostoevsky, 1821-1881: A New Biography,* New York: Macmillan, 1949.

Gide, André. *Dostoevsky,* New York: New Directions, 1926.

Gifford, Henry. *The Hero in his Time: A Theme In Russian Literature,* New York: St. Martin's, 1950.

Ivanov, Vyacheslav. *Freedom and the Tragic Life: A Study in Dostoevsky,* New York: Noonday, 1952.

Krieger, Murray. *The Tragic Vision,* New York: Holt, Rinehart & Winston, 1960.

Lavrin, Janko. *Dostoevsky,* New York: Van Nostrand, 1947.

Magarshack, David. *Dostoevsky,* New York: Harcourt, 1963.

Mirsky, Dmitri. *History of Russian Literature,* New York: Knopf, 1949.

Pachmuss, Temira. F. M. *Dostoevsky: Dualism and Synthesis of the Human Soul,* Carbondale, Ill.: Southern Illinois, 1963.

84

Seduro, V. *Dostoevsky in Russian Literary Criticism,* New York: Columbia, 1957.

Simmons, Ernest J. *Dostoevsky, The Making of a Novelist,* London: Oxford, 1950.

Vivas, Eliseo. *Creation and Discovery,* New York: Noonday, 1955.

Wasiolek, Edward, (Editor). *Crime and Punishment and the Critics,* San Francisco: Wadsworth, 1961.

Wellek, René, (Editor). *Dostoevsky: A Collection of Critical Essays,* New York: Prentice Hall, 1962.

Yarmolinsky, Avrahm. *Dostoevsky, A Life,* New York: Criterion, 1934.

Here's a Great Way to Study Shakespeare and Chaucer.

Cliffs Complete Study Editions

These easy-to-use volumes contain everything that a student or teacher needs for an individual classic. Each attractively illustrated volume includes abundant biographical, historical and literary background information. A descriptive bibliography provides guidance in the selection of additional reading.

The inviting three-column arrangement offers the maximum in convenience to the reader. Shakespeare's plays are presented in a full, authoritative text with modern spelling. Each line of Chaucer's original poetry is followed by a literal translation in simple current English. Adjacent to the complete text, there is a running commentary that gives clear supplementary discussion. Obscure words and allusions are keyed by line number and clarified opposite to where they occur.

Your Guides to Successful Test Preparation.

Cliffs Test Preparation Guides

Efficient preparation means better test scores. Go with the experts and use **Cliffs Test Preparation Guides**. They'll help you reach your goals because they're: • Complete • Concise • Functional • In-depth. They are focused on helping you know what to expect from each test. The test-taking techniques have been proven in classroom programs nationwide.

Recommended for individual use or as a part of formal test preparation programs.

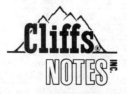

FATHERS AND SONS

NOTES

including
- *Life and Background*
- *A Note on Russian Names*
- *List of Characters*
- *General Plot Summary*
- *Chapter Summaries and Commentaries*
- *Character Analyses*
- *Structure of* Fathers and Sons
- *Review Questions*
- *Selected Bibliography*

by
Denis M. Calandra, M.A.
University of Nebraska

and

James L. Roberts, Ph.D.
Department of English
University of Nebraska

INCORPORATED

LINCOLN, NEBRASKA 68501

Editor

Gary Carey, M.A.
University of Colorado

Consulting Editor

James L. Roberts, Ph.D.
Department of English
University of Nebraska

ISBN 0-8220-0470-4
© Copyright 1966
by
C. K. Hillegass
All Rights Reserved
Printed in U.S.A.

1990 Printing

Cliffs Notes, Inc.   Lincoln, Nebraska

CONTENTS

FATHERS AND SONS

LIFE AND BACKGROUND

Ivan Sergeyevitch Turgenev was born of wealthy parents in the city of Oryol, central Russia, on October 28, 1818. He spent most of his childhood on the family estate under the instruction of tutors until he enrolled at the University of Moscow in 1833. Before a year had passed he transferred to the University of Petersburg, from which he graduated in 1837.

Turgenev traveled for some time in Europe, especially Germany, and chiefly studied philosophy. In 1843, he accepted a minor post in the Ministry of the Interior and also made the acquaintance of Pauline Viardot, a sophisticated French singer whom he would remain devoted to for the rest of his life and for whose sake he would often remain abroad for long periods of time.

After retiring from the service, he went to France, spending summers on the Viardot's estate and winters in Paris. This French period proved to be a very fertile one in his literary career, for it was here that he wrote most of the pieces which later (August, 1852) were to comprise his *A Sportsman's Sketches*. Turgenev had witnessed the February Revolution in Paris (1848) and his subsequent connection with reform groups in Russia and his eulogy of the recently deceased but highly "suspect" Gogol in 1852 led to his arrest and one-month imprisonment in Petersburg.

By the mid-1850's, he was spending as much time in Europe as in Russia, and in 1857 Pauline Viardot gave birth to a child allegedly Turgenev's. In August of 1860 on the Isle of Wight, he conceived the idea for his *Fathers and Sons;* he finished the novel in July of 1861 in Russia.

In 1863, he was summoned to answer charges of having aided a London group of expatriates, but was soon exonerated, bought land at Baden near the Viardots and settled there. In 1869, he ran into financial difficulties and had to sell his newly built villa, but remained there as a tenant while he prepared an edition of his collected works. Some of those finished to date were *Rudin* (1855), *A Nest of Gentlefolk* (1859), *On the Eve* (1860), and *Smoke* (1867), and several dramas.

During the next ten years, Turgenev worked on his novel, *Virgin Soil*, and several more plays, spending time in Baden, Paris, Great Britain, and Russia. In 1879, his brother Nikolai died, and upon Turgenev's arrival in Moscow, he was celebrated by the liberals. This same year he received an honorary degree from Oxford and began to prepare another collection of his works. Always a great admirer of Pushkin, he took an active part in the Pushkin festival of 1880. In 1882, he was taken seriously ill, but continued to work, dictating "Fire at the Sea" and "The End." He died in France on September 3, 1883, with Madame Viardot and her children about him. The year before his death, he published a sheaf of what he called "an old man's jottings" under the title of *Poems in Prose*.

A NOTE ON RUSSIAN NAMES

The middle names of all male characters end in "-vitch" and of all female characters in "-ovna." This ending simply means the "son of" or "daughter of" the father whose first name is converted into their middle name. For example, Nikolai's father was named "Petro." Thus, both Pavel and Nikolai have the name "Petrovitch" for their middle name. This middle name is called the *Patronymic*. All Russians have three names and might be called by any one or any combination of these names.

The spelling of the Russian name might differ slightly from one translation to another because a transliteration must be made, and since English cannot reproduce absolutely exactly certain Russian graphemes, an approximation must suffice. In pronouncing these names, if the reader will remember to give the vowels their "continental" value and pronounce the consonants as in English, a rough approximation to the Russian pronunciation will be obtained. The consonant "kh" sounds rather like the Scottish "ch" in "loch"; the "zh" represents a sound like "s" in "measure"; and the final "v" is pronounced "f".

LIST OF CHARACTERS

Nikolai Petrovitch Kirsanov
A small landowner in a rural part of Russia who has attempted to keep up with modern ideas.

Arkady Nikolayevitch Kirsanov
His son, who has been studying in St. Petersburg and who has come under the influence of a new philosophy called nihilism.

Pavel Petrovitch Kirsanov
Nikolai's brother, who believes strongly in preserving the aristocratic mode of life.

Fenichka
Nikolai's housekeeper, the mother of his young son, and eventually his wife. She is almost always referred to by her nickname, Fenichka. Her real name is Fedosya Nikolayevna Savishna.

Mitya
Nikolai and Fenichka's young son.

Yevgeny Vassilievitch Bazarov
A friend of Arkady's who professes a philosophy of nihilism.

Viktor Sitnikov
An acquaintance of Bazarov's who tries to attach himself to popular causes.

Avdotya Nikitishna Kukshina
A friend of Sitnikov's who professes to be a liberated woman.

Anna Sergeyevna Odintsova
A wealthy widow who is reputed to be quite advanced and liberal.

Katerine Sergeyevna Lokteva (Katya)
Madame Odintsova's sister, who attracts the attention of Arkady, and is eventually married to him.

8

Vassily Ivanovitch Bazarov
Bazarov's devoted father, who is a retired army doctor and who has tried to keep up with the latest advancements in medicine.

Arina Vlassevna Bazarov
Bazarov's mother; the traditional conglomeration of sentiment, superstition, and doting love for her offspring.

Princess Abdotya Stepanovna
Madame Odintsova's old and aristocratic aunt.

Matvei Ilyich Kolyazin
The "uncle" whom Arkady visits in a neighboring province.

Porfiry Platonovitch
Madame Odintsova's neighbor who often comes for conversation and cards.

Father Aleksei
The priest in Bazarov's home town.

Prokofitch
A servant at Marino who adheres to the old principles of the Russian aristocracy.

Piotr
Another servant at Marino; emancipated and "modern."

Dunyasha
A servant at Marino who is fond of Bazarov.

Timofeich and *Anfisushka*
Two of Vassily Ivanovitch Bazarov's servants.

GENERAL PLOT SUMMARY

Arkady Kirsanov has just graduated from the University of Petersburg and returns with a friend, Bazarov, to his father's modest estate in an outlying province of Russia. The father gladly receives the two young men at his estate, called Marino, but Nikolai's brother, Pavel, soon becomes upset by the strange new philosophy called "nihilism" which the young men advocate.

Nikolai feels awkward with his son at home, partially because Arkady's views have dated his own beliefs, and partially because he has taken a servant, Fenichka, into his house to live with him and has already had a son by her.

The two young men remain at Marino for a short time, then decide to visit a relative of Arkady's in a neighboring province. There they observe the local gentry and meet Madame Odintsova, an elegant woman of independent means who invites them to spend a few days at her estate, Nikolskoe.

At Nikolskoe, they also meet Katya, Madame Odintsova's sister, who attracts Arkady. They remain for a short period and Bazarov is more and more drawn toward Madame Odintsova, until he finally announces that he loves her. She does not respond to his declaration, and soon after, Arkady and Bazarov leave for Bazarov's home.

At Bazarov's home, they are received enthusiastically by his parents. Bazarov is still disturbed by his rejection, and is difficult to get along with. He almost comes to blows with his friend Arkady. After a brief stay, they decide to return to Marino, and circle by to see Madame Odintsova, who receives them coolly. They leave almost immediately and return to Arkady's home.

Arkady remains for only a few days, and makes an excuse to leave in order to see Katya. Bazarov stays at Marino to do some scientific research, and tension between him and Pavel increases. Bazarov enjoys talking with Fenichka and playing with her child, and one day he gives her a quick, harmless kiss which is observed by Pavel. The older man feels it is his duty to defend his brother's honor, and he challenges Bazarov to a duel. Pavel is wounded slightly, and Bazarov must leave Marino. He stops for an hour or so at Madame Odintsova's, then continues on to his parents' home. Meanwhile, Arkady and Katya have fallen in love and have become engaged.

At home, Bazarov cannot keep his mind on his work and while performing an autopsy fails to take the proper precautions. He contracts typhus, and on his deathbed, sends for Madame Odintsova, who arrives in time to hear Bazarov tell her how beautiful she is.

Arkady marries Katya and takes over the management of his father's estate. His father marries Fenichka and is delighted to have his son home with him. Pavel leaves the country and lives the rest of his life as a "noble" in Dresden, Germany.

SUMMARIES AND COMMENTARIES

CHAPTER 1

Summary

Nikolai Petrovitch Kirsanov and his servant Piotr are waiting the arrival of Arkady, Nikolai's son, who has recently finished his studies at the University of St. Petersburg and is returning to his country home for a visit. Nikolai is a landlord with a moderate estate. He is the son of a Russian general who had achieved a degree of fame in the front lines of 1812. Unlike his brother Pavel, who excelled in military service, Nikolai "could never distinguish himself by his courage." Later the two brothers shared an apartment in St. Petersburg, where Nikolai finished his studies at the university.

Nikolai married the daughter of his landlord in spite of the objections of his father, and settled in the country, where Arkady was born. His wife died prematurely, leaving Nikolai lonely and isolated. When Arkady came of age, his father went with him to St. Petersburg and remained there with him for three school years while Arkady pursued his studies. The final winter, Nikolai was unable to remain with Arkady and is now nostalgically recalling the past while waiting for the arrival of his son. During his daydreaming, the coach carrying Arkady arrives and the father and son lock in an embrace.

Commentary

Turgenev was a writer intently interested in social reforms, and as a realistic novelist, he set his works in contemporary Russia. Thus, the background and the social changes going on in Russia at the time do function in his novel. Ultimately, Bazarov must be seen as one of the rising new middle class which will dominate the scene in Russia for the next generations. Previous to the 1840's and 1850's, the middle class was virtually nonexistent as a social power, but during these decades, this class began to produce its own intelligentsia which asserted itself in many areas of Russian life. The contrast between a member of the old school such as Pavel with Bazarov, the new middle class, will be developed at length later in the novel.

The relationship between the great landowner and the serf was undergoing a tremendous change also. The situation in Russia during this time is analogous to the conditions found in the southern states of America in the 1840's and the 1850's. The serfs were actually similar to the black slaves in that they lived completely at the mercy of the wealthy landowner. In 1862, the serfs were granted complete freedom, but before that time, most of the more advanced landowners and thinkers had voluntarily freed their serfs in the manner that Kirsanov and Bazarov had done. Earlier, a person's wealth was often evaluated in terms of the number of serfs he owned, and thus we have the expression that the estate was valued at two hundred "souls." By the time of this novel, the word "souls" was used satirically as "baptized property." Turgenev is aware of the basic contradiction involved in recognizing the serfs as Christian souls and some landowner's personal property at the same time.

Thus the first chapter gives us an indication that this was a time of change. Turgenev refers to Piotr as one of the "new, emancipated servants."

Early in the first chapter, we are introduced to a technique that Turgenev employs often. In this case, he interrupts the narrative briefly and addresses the reader directly in order to give us some background information. Later realists will not enter so directly into the narrative. Turgenev uses both the traditional nineteenth-century technique of speaking directly to the reader and the more recent technique of presenting scenes directly without author intrusion.

In the background information, we discover that Nikolai has spent a great deal of time in St. Petersburg while Arkady was enrolled in school there and has in the past had a close relationship with his son. This must be kept in mind when we observe the tension that will soon develop between the father and son. We are also made aware of a certain romantic bent in Nikolai's nature as we observe him dreaming of his past happiness. As soon as Arkady appears, Nikolai will rapidly learn to conceal his romantic thoughts.

Keeping in mind the title of the novel, we realize then the importance of Turgenev's building and expressing directly the exact nature of the father's personality so that he will be seen in contrast to his son's newer and more advanced ways of thinking.

CHAPTERS 2, 3

Summary

Arkady has brought a friend from the university with him whom he introduces as Bazarov. Nikolai is pleased to receive any friend of his son and asks to be informed of his "christian name and patronymic," which is Yevgeny Vassilievitch. Bazarov is tall and thin with a peaceful smile which suggests a degree of self-confidence. He holds himself aloof and does not strike one as being overly friendly on first glance.

Arkady and his father get in the buggy while Bazarov must ride in another conveyance and they depart for the farm. On the way home, Arkady is filled with joy at being reunited with his father again, but he keeps the conversation on a prosaic level so as to discourage his father from becoming over-emotional. Thus, they discuss only the more mundane subjects and Arkady tells Nikolai how important his friendship with Bazarov is. Arkady is convinced that Bazarov is an intellectual giant and wants great care taken of him.

As they drive home, they discuss the problems which Nikolai has encountered during the year that they have been separated. Nikolai has been changing his farm system, trying to remove the serfs and establish them as tenant farmers (or a type of share cropper.)

Nikolai is very sentimental about the farm and the place where his son was born, but Arkady cuts him by saying that it makes no difference where a man is born, indicating an anti-romantic view. Nikolai is somewhat astonished by his son's statement and does not immediately recover.

Nikolai tries to warn his son that one of the servants is now living in the house — the young Fenichka — and tries to apologize for living with this person of "inferior rank." Nikolai expects his son to be shocked, and is surprised when Arkady expresses himself so liberally as to give the impression of not caring in the least that his father has taken a mistress. Nikolai wonders if this fact won't embarrass their guest, Bazarov, but Arkady assures him that Bazarov is a person not to be anxious about.

As they reach the farm, Arkady notices that the place has fallen into a state of degeneration. Soon they arrive at the farmhouse, which Nikolai calls "Marino."

Commentary

The extent of devotion between Nikolai and Arkady is seen in their greetings. There is no tension between them at the present moment and later we will observe that the tension that does develop will be caused largely by Bazarov.

To understand the meaning of Nikolai's question "May I know your Christian name and patronymic?" see the section on the meaning of Russian names.

Note again that Piotr follows his role of the emancipated servant because he refuses to kiss his master's hand in the fashion of the older servants and only bows to Arkady.

At the beginning of the novel and the ride to the estate, Bazarov is separated from Arkady and Nikolai, and must ride in a separate vehicle. Thus at the beginning, Nikolai and his son are together while Bazarov is the outsider. But gradually through the next chapters, we will see a growing separation between Nikolai and Arkady and a closer connection between the two young people. Ultimately, however, Arkady and his father will emerge as the true companions.

On the ride back to the farm, we see the portending separation between father and son. For example, Nikolai thinks that Arkady should be very excited to be returning to his old birthplace, but Arkady cuts his father by saying that it makes no difference where a man is born. After this interchange, there is silence for a long part of the journey. The technique of this small scene is also important. It is presented objectively and dramatically with no author comment or intrusion.

Nikolai brings up the important subject of Fenichka. Arkady's reaction is important because his father is over-apologetic about this somewhat unorthodox relationship, but Arkady feels that he has advanced beyond such insignificant moral discriminations and is filled "with a half-secretive feeling of superiority towards his good, softhearted father."

Turgenev continues to build this contrast between the two generations as Nikolai, the father, looks at the landscape and begins to quote from a Pushkin poem. Pushkin was the father of Russian romanticism and is later the butt of ridicule by Bazarov. Thus, Nikolai is grounded not only in romantic poetry but in the cultural past of Russia, while the young people want to discard all the past.

CHAPTER 4

Summary

Upon arrival at Marino, they are met by Prokofitch, who is described as a simpering old servant. He fawns over the young son of the master and conducts himself in an obeisant manner. Nikolai orders a meal to be prepared immediately and Arkady wants to clean up, but before he leaves, his uncle Pavel appears. He shakes hands with Arkady in a European fashion and then embraces his nephew three times in the Russian fashion.

After Arkady and Bazarov leave to go to their rooms, Pavel asks about the "hairy" creature who is visiting with Arkady.

Bazarov immediately begins to mock Pavel as soon as they are parted. He finds Pavel to be terribly affected for some one living so far out in the country, and in contrast, he finds Nikolai to be very likable. During dinner, Arkady pours himself an extra glass of wine and drinks much more than he usually does.

After returning to their room that night, Bazarov comments about Pavel's affectations and his unique European demeanor. In Pavel's room, long after others have gone to bed, Pavel stays up dressed quite properly and stares about the room. In another room, Fenichka is also awake, but she keeps herself out of sight. In a motherly fashion, she constantly looks in upon her child.

Commentary

Chapter 4 presents the arrival home, but Turgenev lets us know that the event is different from what it would have been in the past. Before the new ideas came into prominence, all the servants would have been gathered around to greet the arrival of the young master, but now this form of activity is frowned upon as being archaic. We do see that Fenichka peeks out of the window and then disappears. More important is the contrast between the two types of servants represented by Piotr and Prokofitch. As noted earlier, Piotr is the new liberated type of servant, but Prokofitch belongs to the old school. Therefore, the latter comes forward and kisses his young master's hand.

We meet Arkady's uncle for the first time. He will stand in contrast to everything that Bazarov represents. Pavel consciously affects European habits of dress and actions. He is an elegant and aristocratic man, immediately repulsed by Bazarov's appearance. Pavel delights in throwing out French phrases and makes every effort to appear Europeanized. One should be aware that during a certain period of Russian history, the educated Russian did correspond mainly in French and used Russian only in communication with the serfs or other low-class servants. In fact many Russians could not read and write the Russian language and knew only the necessary minimum to be able to communicate with the serfs.

We notice for the first time that Arkady is uneasy over his return home. He has outgrown childhood, but now returning to the scene of his past, it is difficult to assume his new role. Arkady is drawn between two loyalties: one to his home and his background and the other to his new friend with the advanced ideas. Arkady tries to defend his uncle, whom he respects in many ways and dislikes the fact that Bazarov refers to him as an "archaic phenomenon."

As much as Arkady tries to deny it objectively, we see that he and his father are essentially alike. He acknowledges that his father is a timid man, but the reader also knows that Arkady is himself rather timid.

The chapter ends on Fenichka as she looks at her sleeping baby. Without knowing it at present, we are being prepared for the fact that the child is actually Arkady's half brother even though his father is not married.

CHAPTER 5

Summary

The next morning, Bazarov arises before anyone else and goes out to catch some frogs for scientific experiments. He notices the broken down condition of the land, and talks freely with a couple of the peasants. Meanwhile, at the house, Nikolai feels compelled to explain in more detail his association with Fenichka. He tells Arkady about their peculiar relationship, and Arkady responds with an air of indifference saying: "Well, you know my philosophy of life, and I would hardly want to interfere with your life or your happiness." Arkady felt that "he was being magnanimous."

Arkady leaves his father abruptly in order to go and greet Fenichka and discovers that she has a child. In a joking sort of manner, he berates his father for not having told him about his new brother.

Pavel then asks Arkady about his friend Bazarov, and hears that he is a nihilist. Both Nikolai and Pavel are astonished by this term and try to figure out what it means. They know that it comes from the Latin word *nihil,* which means "nothing." Upon further discussion, Pavel maintains that a "nihilist" must be one who respects nothing.

Shortly after this, Fenichka arrives to serve cocoa, and we see that she is a rather pretty person who is uneasy in the presence of others. Soon, Bazarov returns from the swamps, all bespotted with mud from his excursion after frogs. He is greeted sarcastically by Pavel as "Mr. Nihilist."

Commentary

The beginning of the chapter informs us about Bazarov's character. He is a scientist and a rationalist who believes that the workings of human beings aren't much different from the workings of a frog. He approaches everything with as much scientific objectivity as possible and will ultimately maintain that human feelings and concepts should be viewed either as nonsense or as only so much weakness in the human body.

The conflict between Arkady and Nikolai increases when Nikolai tries to explain his relationship with Fenichka, and Arkady assumes the role of the more advanced person who could not be disturbed by any form of unorthodox social relationship. Nikolai does not know how to accept these foreign ideas and is thrown into confusion by them. We should note here that Russia of the nineteenth century was strictly divided into definite social classes. Fenichka was a member of the lower class who would not be accepted by the wealthy class to which Nikolai belonged. In the true sense of the word, he married a *servant,* who is socially inferior to him. The point is that the old aristocratic order is so firmly embedded in Nikolai's mind that he can't really justify his relationship with Fenichka as proper, and thus he is thrown into confusion when his son so calmly accepts the fact. We should also be aware that when Arkady is being so magnanimous, he is consciously aware that he is doing so.

We first hear the word *nihilist* in this chapter. Even though this word is common now, it was first coined by Turgenev to describe the type of person represented by Bazarov. When the subject first comes up, Bazarov is not present and the meaning of the term is explained by Arkady. A nihilist is a person who "examines everything from a critical point of view....a person who does not bow to any authorities; who doesn't accept any principle on faith, no matter how hallowed and how venerated the principle is." In contrast, Pavel is proud and arrogant that he is one of the representatives of the old century. He believes that without principles it is impossible to exist.

With the presentation of these ideas, Turgenev introduces one of his main themes, which is the conflict between the romantic past and the realistic present. Pavel stands for the old traditional and romantic past and he can never break away from this past to become a functional man of the present world. He insists on maintaining old views, even though he never bothers to examine the underlying truths of these beliefs. In contrast, Bazarov will reject all things of the past without examining to see if they might possess some values. In their own ways, both of them are mistaken.

Fenichka appears for the first time. She feels insecure because she is not officially married and is furthermore conscious of her inferior social position. Likewise, she is aware that Nikolai has not accepted her as an equal; thus she makes a point of remaining in the background.

Two small details humorously indicate the difference between Pavel and Bazarov. Bazarov notes that Pavel insists on using fancy English washbasins, while at the same time the doors to the house don't work. Pavel notes that Bazarov "doesn't believe in principles, but he believes in frogs."

Summary

Bazarov joins the others at tea, and Pavel begins interrogating Bazarov about his beliefs. Pavel makes derisive comments about Bazarov's admiration for the German scientists. Bazarov tells Pavel that he doesn't "believe" in anything, whether it be science, art or human institutions, but he does pay special attention to science because it "gives him the facts."

Pavel and Nikolai leave to go talk with the overseer, and both are upset over what they have heard from the young people. They can't understand why youth has rejected so much that the old people hold valuable. They are both perplexed, but of the two Pavel is angrier.

When the two of them are alone, Bazarov asks his friend Arkady if Pavel always acts the way he just has. He makes several derogatory comments about Pavel. Arkady defends him, maintaining that Pavel's life story demands some sympathy; then he proceeds to tell Pavel's life story.

Pavel was, in his youth, a "remarkably handsome" person who made women lose "their wits over him," and provoked men to call him a fop. He won fame for his daring feats and dexterity in athletics. Even though every woman in the country was at his feet, he once met an enigmatic noble lady who could never give herself to him entirely. She was not a particularly witty person nor exceptionally beautiful, but she did possess a bizarre and haunting appeal. Pavel was entranced by her, and after a prolonged affair, the mysterious lady grew tired of him. After she left him, he followed her through most of Europe, and for a short time they resumed their relationship. But when they separated this time, it was for good. For some time, Pavel mourned his loss. He resigned his position in the army and finally retired to his brother's farm, where he has lived ever since.

Thus, Arkady feels that one must judge Pavel with special consideration because his life has been so frustrated. Besides that,

Pavel had been most generous in helping Nikolai financially whenever the need arose. Bazarov, rather than being sympathetic, is quite sarcastic and maintains that any person who allows himself to stake his life "on the card of women's love" is not a man but simply a "male animal." Arkady tries to explain that Pavel grew up in a different time, but Bazarov cynically maintains that "It's all romanticism, nonsense, rottenness, art." He prefers to go and look at some frogs or beetles.

Commentary

The reader should be highly aware of the visual images presented in the first part of chapter 6. The intent is to continue the development of the antagonism between Pavel and Bazarov. The visual image is that of Bazarov, who has just returned from collecting frogs in the marshes, extremely dirty and soiled as contrasted with the immaculately clean and precisely dressed Pavel. The sight of the filthy Bazarov entering the house is basically repulsive to the fastidious Pavel, whose "aristocratic nature was revolted by Bazarov's completely free and easy manner."

The argument between Pavel and Bazarov is a result of their basic views. Pavel dislikes Bazarov's lack of patriotism in paying too much homage to German scientists and not enough to Russians. Bazarov likes the Germans because they are scientific and rational, and far superior to the Russians on this count. Each encounter reveals how set and determined both Pavel and Bazarov are. This is about the only quality that they have in common: that is, that each is unbending in his view and each is determined that his way is the correct one.

There has been nothing in Pavel's past life which will enable him to understand Bazarov's point of view. Pavel has always accepted the value of art and music, and when he hears a young man saying that art is meaningless, he practically foams at the mouth with ire. Bazarov doesn't even believe in science as a general principle; only the individual objective experiment is important. Thus, up until now, Bazarov is the complete nihilist who *believes* in absolutely nothing.

Nikolai, like Pavel, is also disturbed, but he does not react as violently against the young people and instead, accepts the fact that the world is changing and that perhaps "the young people are cleverer."

When Bazarov later begins to attack Pavel as useless and aristocratic, Arkady tries to defend Pavel by narrating and explaining his uncle's background. Arkady wants Bazarov to feel some compassion for Pavel, a compassion built upon understanding why Pavel has developed into the type of person he now is. This ability to feel compassion for people and later to enter into wholesome relationships with people is a major point of distinction between Arkady and Bazarov.

Note again how Turgenev interferes in his story by addressing the reader directly, telling him that he will find Pavel's story in the next chapter. Thus, in chapter 6, the main narrative is again interrupted in order to go into the background of one of the characters.

Chapter 7 tells the story of Pavel's life, and we see that he was a dashing young man. Because of a woman, or more accurately, because of a woman's rejection of him, he has suffered a great deal in his earlier life. This information is emphasized because later we will see that Bazarov has the same problem with Madame Odintsova. In fact, the description of the woman Pavel loved is quite similar to that of Madame Odintsova. Both women are enigmatic figures, perfectly pleasant during the day, but wracked with anguish when left to their own thoughts.

After hearing Pavel's story, Bazarov is cynical and ridicules any man who will allow himself to be so dominated by a woman. He has absolutely no sympathy for this type of man, thus the important consideration is that both Pavel and Bazarov have a similar type of experience with a similar type of woman, and both are affected in almost the same way by rejection.

Arkady tries to understand his uncle's position and through this understanding have some type of sympathy for the individual. But Bazarov maintains "that a person who stakes his whole life on the card of a woman's love, then withers and sinks to the point of becoming incapable of anything when that card is trumped — a person like that isn't a man, isn't a male." But ironically, Bazarov will stake almost his entire existence on the love of Madame Odintsova and when rejected will wither away to the point that he cannot work and cannot find himself in life. Arkady, on the contrary, will be seen to have sympathy for both Pavel's and Bazarov's plight. This is a basic difference developing between the two young men.

CHAPTERS 8, 9

Summary

Nikolai and Pavel go to speak to the overseer; Pavel realizes that his brother is not handling the farm correctly but is unable to point out any errors in the management. Even though he has in the past been able to supply money for running the farm, at the present moment he has no extra money to spare and therefore he leaves his brother. Pavel goes to talk to Fenichka, but she is afraid of the cold and distant "aristocratic gentleman."

Pavel wants to see the child and Fenichka goes to bring it. Pavel notes that Fenichka keeps a very neat and orderly house. When she returns with the child, Pavel admires it and Nikolai arrives. Pavel immediately leaves Nikolai, who remembers how he had met his mistress. He had once stopped for an evening at an inn and found it exceptionally well kept and neat. He asked the innkeeper's domestic servant to come and be his housekeeper. The woman agreed and brought her young daughter, Fenichka, with her. After a few years, the woman died of cholera, leaving the young girl alone. Nikolai, who had grown fond of Fenichka, asked her to remain and be his companion.

Meanwhile, Pavel has returned to his study, where he stares at the ceiling "with an almost desperate expression."

The same day, Bazarov also meets Fenichka. He is out in the arbor with Arkady and notices that Fenichka is a very pretty girl. Arkady is pleased for his father's sake, because as Bazarov says, Nikolai is no fool for attaching himself to this girl. Bazarov plays with the child and enjoys it very much.

As Bazarov and Arkady leave, they discuss the miserable condition of the farm. They discuss various views of nature, and Bazarov rejects the romantic conception of nature being a temple, and calls it instead a workshop in which man can work and educate himself. As they approach the house, they hear someone playing Schubert's "Die Erwartung" on the cello, and when Bazarov discovers that it is Nikolai playing it, he bursts out laughing over the incongruous fact of a country farmer in a distant province playing such a piece of classical music.

Commentary

Fenichka's character is developed in these two chapters. Turgenev interrupts the story again in order to give her background, which allows the reader to understand something of the social distinction between her and Nikolai. Fenichka is described in terms of the clean and wholesome Russian peasant, and is in many ways similar to Bazarov's mother in her attention to the basic womanly duties. She is completely subservient to the man who has taken her as his mistress. Perhaps we can say she has yielded with dignity.

The story of Fenichka is presented in contrast to Pavel's story. Thus, we see immediately how far apart the two are. It is at first glance a condescending step for Pavel to go to Fenichka's room, but ultimately, we discover that Pavel is attracted to Fenichka because she bears a strange resemblance to the lady Pavel once loved. Thus, in this chapter we have subtle hints about Pavel's true feelings when Turgenev writes that Pavel looked at Fenichka almost sadly. Fenichka is so simple and basic that she can never perceive Pavel's true feelings and Pavel is too much of a gentleman to reveal them. Thus, later, when Pavel fights the duel with Bazarov, he does so not just to protect his brother's honor, but because he cannot tolerate the idea of Bazarov kissing a woman whom he also admires.

Chapter 8 ends with Pavel sitting alone in his room with his elegant carpets and his distressing loneliness. The description is that of a lost man from the romantic world pathetically clinging to his illusions in an entirely too "real" world.

Bazarov seems to have a natural talent with the peasants and with anyone who cannot contradict his opinions. When he meets

Fenichka and her baby, she allows him to handle the child, but when Arkady tries to handle the baby, it puts up a fight. The touching and "sentimental" scene in which Bazarov idly plays with a child is perhaps intended to give us a hint that even the supremely aloof Bazarov has a hidden spring of tenderness dormant within him. Certainly we can credit Turgenev with subtly preparing us for the breakdown of Bazarov's cold exterior when he is confronted with Madame Odintsova.

Bazarov's nihilism is again revealed when he ridicules Arkady for feeling that Nikolai should marry Fenichka. Arkady actually thought he was being very advanced by advocating such a marriage, but Bazarov is even more advanced or liberal by believing that marriage is just a ridiculous institution that has no meaning. After this discussion, we note a trace of hostility between the friends.

Bazarov is also scornful of the fact that Arkady's father plays classical music on the cello. He finds it highly ridiculous that a forty-four year old father living in a distant Russian province should read classical literature and play classical music.

The reader should now begin to evaluate Bazarov and his views. We should see that Bazarov attacks almost everything about Arkady's family and estate. Basically, he is impolite and intolerant of things in Arkady's family. We should then, be constantly aware of the reactions of each of the young men, both to his own parents and to the other's parents. That is, Arkady could make criticisms later on of the type of people the Bazarovs are, but refrains from doing so. Bazarov makes no effort to conceal his contempt for Arkady's relatives.

At the end of chapter 9, we have another hint that Arkady is not pleased with his friend. After Bazarov has been so critical of Pavel and Nikolai, Arkady feels a slight degree of separation. This will continue until Katya points out at the end that Arkady has finally broken completely from the influence that Bazarov exerted over him.

CHAPTER 10

Summary

After two weeks, everyone except Pavel grew used to the two young men. Pavel, however, came to hate Bazarov "with all the strength of his soul." He regarded Bazarov as arrogant, insolent, and cynical, and suspected that "he all but had contempt for him." The only other person who did not like Bazarov was old Prokofitch who, as a servant, was "just as much an aristocrat as was Pavel."

Arkady and Bazarov often went on long walks and had arguments which Arkady usually lost, even though Bazarov said very little. One day, as they were returning from a walk, Nikolai overheard the two talking when Bazarov was saying that Nikolai is a "very good fellow...but he's on the retired list, his song is sung." Bazarov mentions that Nikolai even reads the poet Pushkin.

Nikolai is so upset by this overheard conversation that he reports it to his brother Pavel. Actually, Nikolai has read constantly in an attempt to keep up with the new generation, and is somewhat disappointed that he is considered so out of date. Furthermore, one day when he was reading a Pushkin poem, his son Arkady came up and gently replaced the book with one by a German entitled *Stoff und Kraft*. Nikolai still remembers his German well enough to read it, but he cannot see any value in this book. Pavel decides that they must have a discussion with Bazarov.

That same day, Pavel had his opportunity to discuss things with Bazarov when the young man referred to a neighbor as a rotter and a petty aristocrat. Pavel objects to both and defends the rights of the aristocrat. Ultimately, after some discussion, Bazarov asks Pavel what benefit he is to mankind, but Pavel merely defends the concept of the aristocrat as a part of the heritage of the world.

After Bazarov tears down all the things that Pavel believes in such as art, poetry, culture, etc., Pavel wonders if nihilism means only to tear down. He asks if "it is necessary to build up." Bazarov explains that it is not their business to build up, but only to "clear the site." Bazarov further explains that the "nihilist" respects no authority and no tradition: he rejects all talk of values as being mere platitudes, and reviles everything.

Pavel wonders how they can tear down when they don't even know why they are destroying. Bazarov explains that "We break things down because we are a force," and a force does not have to "render any account." There is nothing that Bazarov respects; he finds faults with everything. Throughout the discussion, Arkady enthusiastically agrees with his friend. Bazarov ends the discussion by saying that Pavel needs time to think over these things and examine if anything has any value; in the meantime he will continue to dissect frogs.

After they leave, Nikolai reminds his brother that when they were young they thought that their parents were old fashioned, but then admits that he is confident that their values are better than those of the young nihilist.

Commentary

In chapter 10, Turgenev gives us another slant on the character of Bazarov. Note that for all his sarcasm and condescending manner he is basically well liked by all the servants except Prokofitch, who is in his own way "as much an aristocrat as Pavel." Turgenev does not want to present a completely negative picture of Bazarov, but wants the reader to see him as a vividly real person. In terms of literary development, this ability to make his characters into real vivid personalities is one of Turgenev's main contributions to the rise of the realistic novel.

In contrast to many of the realistic techniques, Turgenev also uses a number of devices which smack of the romantic. For example, Nikolai just happens to be situated in a place where he overhears a conversation between Bazarov and Arkady. This technique of an accidentally overheard conversation is artificial and associated with romanticism. From it, Nikolai learns that he is now considered to be "on the retired list." For some fathers, this would be reason enough for complete alienation from the son. The fact that it does not have that effect here allows Arkady and Nikolai ultimately to join together by the end of the novel.

Bazarov had ridiculed Arkady's father for reading Pushkin, so the next time Arkady sees his father reading Pushkin, he replaces it with Buchner's *Stoff und Kraft*. (The book is actually entitled *Kraft und Stoff* [*Force and Matter*] and concerns a materialist view of the world.) The fact that Arkady gives his father this book indicates how much he is still under the control of Bazarov.

Nikolai did try to read the book, and decides that either the contents are rubbish or he is just a stupid man. Since we have seen that Nikolai is cultured (he speaks several languages in addition to knowing classical literature and music), the reader might be led to believe his view that the book *is* so much trash. Pavel's reaction is that Bazarov is being a presumptuous egotist for suggesting this book. This is highly ironic coming from a man who is himself extremely egotistical.

In this chapter, we hear more about the concept of "nihilism." Nikolai and Pavel try to argue that any philosophical concept must have a *positive* end, but Bazarov insists that the "nihilist" is only interested in "clearing the site" by destroying the corruption which presently exists. The older generation cannot understand a concept that stands on totally negative principles. Until all things can be destroyed, the nihilist must revile and undermine all things. They act not for the sake of any values, but merely because they are a force. It does not even matter if they understand why they destroy as long as they *do* destroy. Consequently, there is nothing that the nihilist will respect. The Russian land, country, family, government, church are all equally ridiculous and must be destroyed. What is not brought out in the novel, but is embedded in the concept of "nihilism," is the fact that if "nihilism" were carried to its extreme, it would mean finally that after everything is destroyed, man then must destroy himself. No nihilist can ever build anything because a subsequent adherent of "nihilism" would come along and feel the need to destroy that.

As the discussion between Pavel and Bazarov becomes very heated, Nikolai tries to interpose to prevent a serious disagreement. But there is not much danger of this happening because Bazarov doesn't care enough to get too upset, and Pavel, at this point, feels it would be beneath his aristocratic dignity to become angry with an inferior person. Yet, these types of conflicts prepare us for the approaching duel scene between Bazarov and Pavel.

This chapter also reinforces a wider ranging theme in the novel —the natural antagonism which exists between succeeding generations, between fathers and sons of all periods of history. Nikolai tries to justify his son's different views by reminding Pavel that when they were children, they too thought their parents old fashioned. Basically, Turgenev is suggesting that any two different generations will always fail to understand each other. Pavel, however, only feels that in this particular case the older generation is decidedly the one with truth on its side.

CHAPTER 11

Summary

After the discussion about the "nihilists," Nikolai realizes that despite all his efforts he is more alienated from his son than ever before. He muses on the beauty of nature and poetry and is disappointed that the younger generation has rejected all of this. He dreams of his past happiness and of his wife; he further laments that he can't relive these individual happy moments; that they cannot be extended for an eternal, immortal life.

Suddenly, Fenichka brings him back to reality by calling to him to come to the house. On his way back he meets Pavel who also seems preoccupied. Pavel, not born a romantic, is not capable of dreaming like Nikolai, and thus lives in a more barren world.

The same night, Bazarov suggests that they take up Nikolai's suggestion and go visit Arkady's uncle who is a privy-counselor for a neighboring town. They leave the next day, and "the younger people at Marino were sorry to see them go,...but the elders breathed more easily."

Commentary

Unlike Pavel, who point-blank rejects all the ideas of the younger generation, Nikolai has made some effort to understand the point of view of the young people He did live with them in St. Petersburg and has read what they have read, but he has still failed to understand the modern point of view.

He is trying to see what good can come from their ideas. He wonders if their value can be that they have "fewer traces of feudalism" than the older generation. This is an important point because Nikolai is freeing his serfs and trying to discard the old feudalistic method of managing his land.

Nikolai's final puzzlement is how could the young people reject totally the arts and poetry and all literature. Of course, this would be Turgenev's point of view, since he is creating literature and immediately after having Nikolai query about the nihilist rejection of poetry, Turgenev gives us a magnificently poetic passage describing the area surrounding the arbor. But as we progress in this chapter and as Nikolai loses himself in daydreams about past happiness, Turgenev is slightly critical of Nikolai. If we look closely at Nikolai, we see that he is sadly lacking in the practical sense it takes to run a farm. He needs someone to help him break from the romantic dream world and come to terms with the real world. Thus, Turgenev criticizes both the "nihilist" who rejects everything and the romantic like Nikolai who lives so much in a romantic world that he allows himself to be subdued by the practical considerations of everyday life. His utter romanticism is seen as he ends his reveries with tears in his eyes, and we are reminded of the contrast by the statement that these tears in Bazarov's view would be "a hundred times worse than the cello."

In contrast to Nikolai, the romantic dreamer, Pavel, who was not "a born romantic" in the sentimental sense of the term, is seen as possessing an "exquisitely dry and sensual soul." The comparison leaves Nikolai the more admirable figure of the two.

At the end of the chapter, we see the two young people about to leave Marino to visit Arkady's uncle. Arkady is delighted to do this but "considered it his duty to conceal his feelings. Not for nothing was he a nihilist." Again this gives us a hint that Arkady is not and can never be the true "nihilist."

With the departure from Marino, we have the end of the first cycle of the novel. We now move to a different scene and see the young "nihilists" in other surroundings. The reader should keep in mind a touch of sentimentalism appearing in Bazarov in his reasons for going to visit his parents. And we should also remember Bazarov's relationship with Arkady's father and compare this later with his relationship with his own father.

CHAPTERS 12, 13

Summary

Matvei Ilyich Kolyazin was a vain but good-natured man. He had no particular intellect, but was capable of handling his own affairs. He receives Arkady with good nature and invites him obliquely to a ball that the governor is giving in his honor. Arkady returns to the inn and tells Bazarov, who agrees to meet the governor and "take a look at the gentry." On returning from the governor's house, where they go to pay their respects, they meet Viktor Sitnikov, and old acquaintance of Bazarov's.

Sitnikov suggests that they go and meet a progressive woman named Avdotya Nikitishna Kukshina, who according to Sitnikov, will provide them with a real feast. Bazarov is at first reluctant to go but ultimately agrees to accompany them just out of curiosity.

The three companions arrive at Kukshina's house and are received by the lady who advances the most liberal views. She immediately begins to talk about a variety of typical subjects and demonstrates a superficial knowledge of many contemporary authors and opinions. Throughout the conversation she tries to get Bazarov to agree with her, but he militantly maintains his own individualistic opinions.

Madame Kukshina does mention another person of the neighborhood who shares many of her advanced opinions, a Madame Odintsova, who is a widow and a large landowner. While they are there, a large breakfast is served and with it four bottles of champagne are consumed. After a time, Arkady can stand no more and wants to leave. When the three men are alone, Sitnikov seems proud of having been instrumental in providing his friends with good food and champagne, but his companions give him no credit for his accomplishment.

Commentary

Chapters 12 and 13 function essentially as transitional chapters. Turgenev takes the opportunity to satirize the Russian official who maintains that he is an advanced liberal, but is in reality as much a despot as any of the older officials are.

The characterization of Sitnikov is also satiric. He is the psuedo-intellectual who attaches himself to the fringe of any movement which seems advanced. He is an "idea-taster." He does not comprehend the movement but acts as a parasite so as to gain the attention of people obviously greater than he. In the final chapter, we hear that this absurd person is trying to continue Bazarov's "work" after the latter's death.

Kukshina is also satirized as the advanced and liberated woman. The most cutting remark about her is in the next chapter when she appears at the ball dressed in soiled gloves and dances after everyone else has departed. Kukshina and Sitnikov seem to remain with one another out of desperation in trying to find other companions.

Kukshina's attempt to show off her knowledge of all the contemporary writers in Europe and America indicates the superficiality of her knowledge, since she apparently has not penetrated beneath the surface level of any of these authors.

CHAPTER 14

Summary

At the governor's ball, Arkady's uncle shines like a true French courtier—amiable to all present and especially favorable to the ladies. Endless swarms of people dance and many speak an affected French. Kukshina arrives, but is not appropriately dressed, her gloves being dirty and her dress extremely disheveled.

Suddenly Sitnikov stops and announces the arrival of Odintsova to Arkady, who is immediately impressed and wants to meet her. When introduced, Odintsova acknowledges that she has seen Arkady's father and has heard about him. He becomes completely enraptured with her and chatters on as though he were a stage-struck school boy. She asks him who his companion is, and he rhapsodizes about Bazarov. His enthusiasm for Bazarov moves Madame Odintsova to express her wish to meet the friend. Arkady promises to come for a visit and bring Bazarov with him.

Arkady speaks to Bazarov about Odintsova, but his companion is very cynical about this grand lady. Bazarov's sarcasm annoys Arkady. Kukshina is also annoyed because no one paid any attention to her. The ball ended at four a.m. with Sitnikov and Kukshina dancing a polka-mazurka.

Commentary

Chapter 14 serves to introduce the reader to Madame Odintsova and to satirize the type of provincial Russian ball where the participants ape western culture by their mannerisms and affected French.

The first appearance of Madame Odintsova emphasizes her physical attractiveness. "She carried her bare arms beautifully to set off her graceful figure." Since Bazarov will at first be attracted only by her bodily attributes, it is apropos that Turgenev introduces her with emphasis on her physical beauty. The other quality emphasized is her coldness and severity. Arkady is immediately attracted to her and wonders if she dances. Vaguely, it is suggested that dancing is not an art which a nihilist would practice, and Bazarov does not participate in any of the dances. But when Arkady asks Madame Odintsova *if* she dances, he is unconsciously associating her with the nihilist viewpoint which is opposed to dancing, but she thinks that he is referring to her age.

At the end of the chapter, Bazarov tries to cover up his attraction for Madame Odintsova by saying derogatory things about her and by emphasizing how attractive her body is.

CHAPTER 15

Summary

Bazarov agrees to call upon Madame Odintsova at her hotel. When they are admitted to her rooms, they find that she is dressed very simply in a morning frock. Arkady introduces his friend and secretly notices that Bazarov is embarrassed in the presence of this beautiful aristocratic woman. Even Bazarov is annoyed to find himself "afraid of a woman."

Anna Sergeyevna Odintsova is the daughter of a landowner who educated his daughter in the best way possible and when he died left her only a small estate to manage for herself. A very rich man somewhat older than she saw her and asked for her hand in marriage. She accepted and when he died six years later, she became an immensely wealthy woman. She traveled a good deal throughout Europe, but finally returned to settle in Russia. She was not liked in the province, since she has always been somewhat distant. In fact, there was quite a bit of nasty gossip about her.

When she meets Bazarov, she expresses her delight in knowing a person "who has the courage not to believe in anything." Whenever she brings up a subject for discussion which Bazarov does not like, she immediately changes to some other topic which suits him. As they are leaving, she extends both of them an invitation to visit her at her estate. Both agree to come, even though Bazarov pretends indifference.

After they leave, Bazarov shocks Arkady by emphasizing only the physical beauty of Madame Odintsova. Two days later they leave for her home, Nikolskoe. Bazarov mentions that it is his "day of my angel" and explains that his parents are expecting him but they will have to wait a while longer.

Commentary

For the first time, we see Bazarov in a situation where he is uncomfortable. He is in the presence of a person who has a personality as strong as his own and this disconcerts him. Formerly every time we have seen him he was in control of the situation by being coldly aloof and austere, but here Madame Odintsova is the cold and withdrawn one. She seems to be the controlling factor, not Bazarov.

We must also remember that Madame Odintsova is somewhat older than either Arkady or Bazarov, and she has lived more extensively then either student. Arkady is astounded as he for the first time notices a form of contradiction in his friend; Arkady is shocked to see Bazarov in a situation where he blushes. As they leave, to cover up his embarrassment, Bazarov again returns to the subject of Madame Odintsova's beautiful body. He feels on safer ground talking about a woman's anatomy and even wishes, ironically and ridiculously, that he had her body in the dissecting room.

This chapter follows Turgenev's technique of interrupting the narrative to give some background information about a character. We learn that Madame Odintsova has lived a varied life filled with many experiences and finally decided to return to this Russian province to settle down. Furthermore, we hear that she is not liked by the other people. This causes Bazarov later to ask her if she is disturbed by the rumors in the town.

CHAPTER 16

Summary

Arkady and Bazarov are received in the very stately home of Madame Odintsova. When they are alone, Bazarov remarks very curtly that Madame Odintsova is a duchess who is condescending to receive a future doctor or a doctor's son; he feels that she is simply indulging in a whim.

At tea, they learn that Madame Odintsova lives with her aunt and sister. The aunt is an elderly noblewoman tolerated mainly because of her high birth. The sister is a shy girl of eighteen. Madame Odintsova suggests to Bazarov that they argue about something. He calls to her attention a book of some drawings of Switzerland and explains that he is interested only in the geological aspect of the sketches. She wonders how he can get along in life without any artistic appreciation and asks if he doesn't want to understand people. He replies that "people are trees in a forest; no botanist would study every individual birch tree." Furthermore, the difference between a clever and a stupid person is the same as that between a healthy and sick person. If one could reform society, there would be no cause for sickness.

Odintsova asks Arkady what he thinks of these ideas, and Arkady obsequiously agrees with all that Bazarov has said. The aunt arrives and we *do* see that she is just tolerated by everyone. In fact, no one pays any attention to her except to adhere to the proper obeisances. Porfiry Platonovitch, a neighbor to Odintsova, arrives to play cards. While they are playing, Odintsova suggests that Arkady accompany her sister Katya to the piano. Arkady feels slighted because he senses that Madame Odintsova is dismissing him.

As Katya plays, he is struck by the beauty of Mozart's music despite his feelings of anti-romanticism and his advocation of nihilism. Arkady asks her to explain why she chose this particular piece of music, and Katya, naturally reticent, fails to respond to the question.

Odintsova suggests that Bazarov take her for a walk in order to teach her the Latin names for the various field plants. When he wants to know why she feels the need to know the Latin names, she replies that "one must have order in everything."

Bazarov and Arkady alone at night discuss the two sisters. Arkady praises Madame Odintsova, while Bazarov points out that the real marvel is not the Madame but Katya. That same night, Madame Odintsova is also thinking about her guests. She is intrigued by Bazarov and is fascinated by the sharpness of his opinions. Furthermore, she is confused by her own ambiguous feelings.

The next morning, Madame Odintsova and Bazarov go off to study botany while Arkady remains at home with Katya. When they return, Bavarov greets Arkady "as though they hadn't seen each other that day."

Commentary

When Bazarov and Arkady arrive at Madame Odintsova's estate, she immediately notes the difference between the two men by promising music as entertainment to Arkady while observing that Bazarov would not be tempted by such entertainment. Again, we note that there is an essential difference between the two friends in that Arkady does care for many of the things which the "nihilists" and Bazarov depreciate.

Madame Odintsova openly wants Bazarov to tell her some of his ideas. She wonders how Bazarov can get along without an appreciation of art. He explains that he was looking at some pictures of Switzerland not for the romantic scenery but instead for the geological structure of the land. Madame Odintsova feels that one must have an artistic nature in order to understand people, but Bazarov feels that "individual personalities are not worth the trouble." "People are like trees in the forest; no botanist will stop to study every birch separately." What Bazarov fails to understand is that a botanist *would* indeed study the various types of trees (birch, elm, oak, etc.) and would also be interested in the differentiating characteristics among each separate birch tree, or oak tree, etc. To suggest that all people are the same as every birch tree is the same as an employment of a shoddy analogy and exhibits a gross misunderstanding of human nature.

Madame Odintsova makes the separation between the four people. She sends Arkady to sit with Katya and listen to the piano while she and Bazarov argue. He is struck by the piano music even though a true nihilist would not be. Thus, he is like his father and has inherited from Nikolai an appreciation of music. This mutual appreciation of music will bring Katya and Arkady together more and more until they become engaged.

One of the great contrasts between Madame Odintsova and Bazarov is her emphasis on order. She says that man must "have order in everything." Without order life would be too erratic and too boring. She even wants to know the Latin names for the various plants because these names indicate to her a degree of order. The "nihilist," however, is out to destroy all existing order and to replace it with a type of dominant anarchy. It is significant that Bazarov becomes attracted to a person who believes something diametrically opposed to his way of thinking and, furthermore, to someone whose way of life prevails over him while he remains at Nikolskoe. Later, he even admits that without the order found in Madame Odintsova's house the visit would not have been prolonged so long. The order, in other words, did contribute to the pleasure of their visit.

Madame Odintsova is also attracted to Bazarov because he is so different from her. She is troubled by her own feelings because she has lived for such a long time in an ordered world and here is a person who exudes a certain amount of ambiguity. For her, he represents a degree of disorder entering into her otherwise ordered existence. The reader should be aware of just how far she will allow her sense of order to be violated *before she draws back*.

CHAPTER 17

Summary

Arkady and Bazarov spend a very pleasant two weeks in the "orderly household" of Madame Odintsova. Bazarov at first complains that this strictly regulated existence violates his sense of democracy. Madame Odintsova parries that without order in a country life one would be conquered by boredom.

Apparently unrequited in his feelings for Madame Odintsova, Arkady seeks consolation by spending his time with the young Katya. The two young people play the piano, read stories together, and observe nature, but Arkady is determined that no sentimental emotions will influence him.

Meanwhile Bazarov is maddened by the strange feelings he has toward Madame Odintsova because he realizes that he is totally unable to subdue these emotions. At the same time, Bazarov occupies Madame Odintsova's thoughts constantly. While Bazarov is contemplating his relationship with Madame Odintsova and realizing the futility of it, his father's old retainer, Timofeich, drops by for a visit. Bazarov wonders if his parents have sent the retainer and sends word that he will soon be home for a visit.

That evening, Bazarov surprises Madame Odintsova by announcing his intentions of leaving soon. She recalls to him that he has promised to teach her some chemistry and help her in other pursuits. She assures him that he will be missed and that she will be quite bored when he leaves. Bazarov sarcastically suggests that she can return to her ordered and quiet life and will not be affected by the departure of such an insignificant person. Upon further entreaties, Bazarov asks Madame Odintsova why a woman with "your intelligence, with your beauty," lives in the country. She makes some observations about her life and assures her new friend that she is very unhappy. She has lived so much in the world that she no longer finds many things to interest her. She wishes that she could actually get strongly attached to something, and Bazarov counters by telling her that she is incapable of falling in love. Secretly, he thinks that she is being flirtatious at this moment and is quite disturbed. As Bazarov prepares to leave, she tries to restrain him, but he presses her hand rather hard and quickly leaves.

After his departure, Madame Odintsova sat for a long time before she went to bed. Bazarov, however, walked for two hours before he went to bed. Arkady tries to question his friend about his whereabouts, but becomes so emotionally disturbed that he cannot speak clearly.

Commentary

Note that Bazarov has finally let his guard drop and he is affected by something outside of himself. Anxiety begins to appear and he changes significantly. This is one of the most crucial chapters of the novel because Bazarov's inner nature conflicts with his intellectual nature for the first time. Love in the romantic sense has always been mere tomfoolery to him, but now he seems captured by Odintsova. He lacked the "strength to turn his back on her."

The two pairs of lovers almost seem star-crossed. Arkady thinks that he is in love with Odintsova but more and more he is attracted by Katya's charm. Arkady is as yet still unaware of many things about himself. "Without noticing or confessing to himself that such nonsense interests him too," he is aroused or affected somewhat by the music, poetry, etc. Furthermore, he thinks that he is in love with Madame Odintsova, but feels uncomfortable in her presence. On the contrary, he is quite at ease with Katya.

Intellectually, Bazarov still continues to fight any feelings of love. He still believes that "love in the ideal sense, or, as he expressed it, the romantic sense, was nonsense—an unforgivable stupidity." But nevertheless, "his blood began to burn as soon as he thought of her." His change is even noticed by Arkady, who begins to lose faith in his friend. He noticed that Bazarov spoke more reluctantly, and often looked angry and more than anything else, Bazarov fidgeted and looked ill at ease. Bazarov had always maintained that "If you take a fancy to a woman, try to gain your end or leave her." But with Madame Odintsova, he knows that he can never gain his end, and yet he can't leave her either. Thus, as noted earlier, he is trapped in love in the same way as was Pavel, but the difference between them is that Bazarov condemns himself later almost as much as he condemned Pavel. His failure to see the similarities in the situations is perhaps a flaw in his character.

The more human aspect of Bazarov's nature is seen when the old Bazarov servant comes to inquire about him. Bazarov dismisses the servant as soon as possible, but nevertheless, we see that he is affected by the desires of his parents. If Arkady had shown the same desire to respect the wishes of his parents, Bazarov would have criticized him severely. Thus, gradually, we note more and more of a change in the nihilist.

Philosophically, according to nihilism, Bazarov should be the person who can live totally alone, without dependence on another person. Yet in this chapter, we see that it is more Madame Odintsova who can and who will be able to live without love or human companionship. Suddenly, we realize that in this respect, she is more the nihilist than "Mr. Nihilist" himself, who craves the company and love of Madame Odintsova. But at the same time, her life is also similar to that of Pavel's because she has indeed experienced so many things in the past and has traveled and done so many things that she expects no new adventure. But Bazarov philosophically believes that there is no such thing as a new experience in the same way that he believes that there is no *new* birch tree.

The breach between Arkady and Bazarov is heightened at the end of the chapter as their separation is caused by the two ladies. Arkady is still jealous of the time that Madame Odintsova spends with Bazarov, even though he thoroughly enjoys the hours he spends with Katya.

CHAPTER 18

Summary

The following day, the entire group chooses to remain in the parlor because it is raining outside. Madame Odintsova asks Bazarov to come to the study to point out the chemistry book he had previously suggested she read. Actually, she wants to resume the conversation which was so abruptly broken off the night before.

She tries to discuss happiness and one's purpose in life with Bazarov, but he finds difficulty in discussing such things. "I am not generally accustomed to discussing my feelings and there is such a distance between us." Odintsova presses Bazarov until he is forced to admit what is really happening inside him. She is stunned when he tells her that he is "madly and foolishly" in love with her. When he grabs her and holds her to his chest, she breaks away in complete amazement. The confused Bazarov hurriedly rushes from the room.

Shortly afterward, Bazarov sends her a note requesting permission to stay one more day before he leaves for his visit with his parents. She answers that it is not necessary to go away because the two have not understood each other. Madame Odintsova did not understand her own reaction but thinks that "peace is still the best thing in the world."

Commentary

Madame Odintsova had earlier said that she doesn't know what she wants, and in these chapters seems to be leading Bazarov on to find out his true feelings. It could easily appear and be interpreted that she is acting as a coquette would by suggesting to Bazarov things that she does not mean. But the central point is that she is not content and does not know how to find any type of fulfillment. Thus, she questions Bazarov—the man who has dared not to believe in anything—about his inner feelings in order to try to understand some aspect of her own feelings.

Consequently when Bazarov makes his impassioned declaration of love, Madame Odintsova is entirely taken aback. She was simply not prepared for this. In other words, she has lived an ordered life and is essentially a very self-centered person. She has suffered hardship and has undergone many difficulties; she has now found comfort and does not want to give herself to any person who might interfere with the sense of order and security she now enjoys. After he leaves, she decides that she should not trifle with any commitment because "peace is still the best thing in the world."

In contrast, Bazarov's declaration affects him deeply. It was not something he could easily do. After he declares his love he is visibly affected. "He was gasping; his whole body was visibly trembling.... It was passion struggling inside him, strong and tragic." Thus, Bazarov undergoes a greater change than does Madame Odintsova and consequently violates his entire philosophy of "nihilism."

CHAPTER 19

Summary

Madame Odintsova felt so awkward about her scene with Bazarov that when her neighbor, Porfiry Platonovitch, arrived for cards, she felt greatly relieved. When Bazarov is able to speak to his hostess alone, he explains that now he must leave: there is only one condition which would allow him to remain, and that could never be.

Madame Odintsova feels afraid of herself and of Bazarov, and keeps her sister close to her all day until Sitnikov makes a sudden appearance. Under other circumstances, he would not have been so well received, but he is able to relieve some of the tension.

That night, Bazarov tells Arkady that he plans to leave and Arkady announces his intention of returning to Marino. Before going to sleep, Arkady realizes that he will miss Madame Odintsova, but subconsciously he is more concerned about Katya.

The next morning, Sitnikov offers to let Arkady ride with him so that Bazarov can have the smaller vehicle. After farewells are made in which Madame Odintsova asserts her determination to meet Bazarov again, Arkady leaves with Sitnikov. When they come to the crossroads where they must part, Arkady changes his mind and asks Bazarov for permission to go with him. He leaves Sitnikov, who is confused by this sudden reversal.

In the carriage, Bazarov is very cynical about women and feels that no man should allow a woman to get the best of him. Yet, he feels as though he has "been thrashed" by a woman. By the time Bazarov is through railing against women, they have arrived at his father's house.

Commentary

The change in Bazarov is further emphasized by the fact that he immediately apologizes to Madame Odintsova for his earlier actions. He would never have apologized to anyone for anything at Marino. Consequently, both Bazarov and Arkady are changing, but the significant difference is that Arkady's change is simply a reversion to his basic nature and Bazarov is changing against his intellectual convictions or nature. When he announces his intentions to leave, he explains that it is because he knows that Odintsova does not love him and never can. Thus, the Bazarov who ridiculed Pavel for such romantic nonsense as love is now a victim of the same passion. Madame Odintsova can say nothing to this declaration and only thinks that she is "afraid of this man" because he might destroy her sense of order. We should also remember that in the end Madame Odintsova does make a marriage of convenience — one that will not effect the order she has established for herself.

The arrival of Sitnikov serves to alleviate a delicate situation. He acts as a buffer to many warring emotions. Besides the tension between Bazarov and Madame Odintsova, Arkady and Bazarov are becoming less friendly. "For some time past a hypocritically free and easy bantering had been going on between the two young men, a trick that always indicates secret dissatisfaction or unexpressed suspicions." The difference between the young friends is again emphasized when Arkady decides temporarily not to visit Bazarov's family because "I'm afraid of making them, and you, feel awkward." Yet, Bazarov intentionally made Arkady's family feel awkward. In this comparison, we see that Arkady, in spite of his attempts at "nihilism," is still basically a more humane and tactful individual.

The two friends are not yet ready to part company. The presence of Sitnikov makes Arkady realize that there is much more value in the friendship with Bazarov than in the acquaintance with Sitnikov. Thus, on the spur of the moment, Arkady decides to accompany his friend to the Bazarov home. During the trip Bazarov's frustration is indicated by the cynical remarks he makes about man becoming the slave of a woman only if he is an educated man. The peasants beat their wives and are happy, but the intelligent man is always defeated (or beaten) by a lady.

CHAPTER 20

Summary

As the two friends step down from the coach, Vassily Ivanovitch Bazarov and his wife Arina Vlassevna smother their son with kisses and embraces. The mother is so overjoyed at seeing her son for the first time in three years that she can hardly control herself. The father tries to calm her so as not to make Bazarov feel uncomfortable. Arkady is introduced to the parents and taken to his room in the "humble military home." Vassily Ivanovitch is very apologetic about the house, but Bazarov thinks this is affected and explains that they are not nobility but only good simple people.

Bazarov's father tries to impress his son by relating his attempts at reform on the farm and by expressing an interest in the latest scientific and medical discoveries. He explains that he no longer practices medicine, but he does give free advice and often administers to the peasants. Arina Vlassevna treats the two young men to a magnificent feast accompanied with champagne.

When they retire for the night, Vassily Ivanovitch comes to speak with Bazarov, but his son dismisses him because of his preoccupation with his recent experiences with Madame Odintsova.

"Arina Vlassevna was a true lady of the olden days; she should have lived two hundred years ago in the days of old Moscow." She is a very kind, devout, simple, and superstitious woman who dotes upon her son.

Commentary

Bazarov makes everyone feel uncomfortable except Madame Odintsova. Even Bazarov's parents feel intimidated by their son, who apparently cares very little about how sensitive they are. Bazarov comments about his own father in the same way that he commented about Nikolai. He scorns his own father in almost the same way that he laughed at Nikolai. Both fathers have attempted to keep up with modern developments and Bazarov cannot appreciate the efforts. Bazarov's father mentions some medical theories that he has recently read, but Bazarov says that he scorns all medical theories and pays no attention to any authority. Of course, part of his behavior toward his parents may be due to his disappointment with himself as a result of his unrequited love for Madame Odintsova.

Bazarov's mother is similar to Fenichka, that is, the old Russian who is concerned with the household and with looking after her husband. She is ripe with superstition and peasant customs and her sole concern is keeping her family happy. Sadly, Turgenev notes that "Such women are disappearing now. God knows whether one should rejoice over that."

CHAPTER 21

Summary

On arising the next morning, Arkady saw Vassily Ivanovitch working in the garden. The father is anxious to hear as much about his son as he can. Arkady tells Vassily Ivanovitch that Bazarov is "one of the most remarkable people" he has ever known.

Furthermore, he is confident that "a great future awaits" Bazarov in some way. He then tells the history of their meeting and friendship. Vassily Ivanovitch knows that Bazarov does not like a great show of feelings and suggests that they try not to interfere with him too much. Bazarov appears just in time to join them for breakfast and to advise his father about a patient who is suffering from jaundice.

At noon, Arkady and Bazarov are stretched out in the shadow of a small haystack. Bazarov tells something of his earlier life and affirms that his parents have been very good to him. He is pleased that his folks have been able to adjust so well to their old age, but for himself, he feels so insignificant in view of all eternity. He feels very bitter about life and is still suffering something of the self-humiliation resultant from his defeat by a woman. Arkady, not knowing about Bazarov's relationship with Madame Odintsova, cannot understand his friend who continues to be extremely cynical and negative. They disagree on several subjects, particularly whether a man should have any principles or not.

Just as the argument is about to get out of hand, Arkady suggests that they take a nap. A little later, Arkady makes an observation about a dry maple leaf resembling a butterfly in flight. Bazarov tells Arkady not to talk so foolishly, and asserts that Arkady seems determined to follow in the footsteps of his idiot uncle. Arkady feels that this is an insult that he cannot tolerate, but Bazarov does not stop. He goads Arkady further by sarcastically stating that only a stupid man feels the need to defend his family. Arkady wants to stop the discussion before they quarrel too seriously. Bazarov, however, would like to have one good quarrel "to the death, to annihilation." He suggests that he could seize Arkady's throat and destroy him. At this moment, the fight is prevented by the lucky appearance of Vassily Ivanovitch. The father explains that a local priest is going to dine with them, and since he knows his son's anti-clerical views, he hopes that he will not be offended by the priest. Bazarov asserts that he does not object so long as the priest does not eat his share of the food.

That night after supper, the group played cards and the priest proceeded to win some money from Bazarov. During the course of the evening, Bazarov's mother sat solicitously beside him offering him various things to drink.

The next day Bazarov announces his intentions to leave because he is bored and can't get any work done. He wants to go back to Marino, where he can at least accomplish something. Vassily Ivanovitch is greatly disappointed, but does not dare question or rebuke his son. After his son leaves, he is comforted by his wife in the loss.

Commentary

Whereas Bazarov was abrupt and critical of both Arkady's and his own parents, Arkady conforms to his true nature and is exceptionally considerate of the Bazarovs. He is polite to the old man and takes delight in talking with Bazarov's mother. He discusses their son with them and makes him out to be a greater person than Bazarov actually is. It is, however, highly ironic that Arkady says that Bazarov is "hostile to all effusive feelings," since his friend has just been very effusive with Madame Odintsova. Arkady tells Vassily Bazarov that his son is destined to become a great man some day. This comment is additionally ironic in view of the fact that Bazarov will soon be dead.

The scene between the two friends offers additional views of Bazarov. He is still feeling humiliated for expressing his inner feelings to Madame Odintsova and speaks with extreme malice and hatred. He attacks Arkady relentlessly and mentions the *reductio ad absurdum* of the nihilist theory: "Having decided to mow everything down, then mow yourself down too." Also, he is ready to fight with his friend "to the death, to annihilation." The fight with all its portending viciousness is interrupted by the appearance of Bazarov's father, but at the moment he appeared, Bazarov was indeed ready to destroy his friend totally. Ironically, Vassily Ivanovitch immediately admires the physical appearance of the two young people and comments about how much strength is in each one, but does not know that this same strength was about to be used to destroy each of them.

CHAPTER 22

Summary

The two friends leave the next day, and instead of going to Fyodot's, they follow an impulse and go to Madame Odintsova's, even though they both know that they are indulging in a bit of "foolishness." They realize the impropriety of their actions when they arrive and find Madame Odintsova somewhat cold and nonreceptive to their sudden return visit.

Arkady realizes that he had wanted to see Katya as much as he had wanted to see Madame Odintsova, but the younger sister never emerged from her room during the entire day. They leave Nikolskoe and return to Marino, where they are received with open arms.

Things have not been going well for Nikolai: the hired laborers are giving him trouble, the new machinery has proved ineffective, and the peasants are squabbling among themselves. All Pavel can do is to admonish his brother to remain calm at all costs. Arkady is sympathetic, and Bazarov chooses not to get involved with any of the family problems.

Arkady thinks about Nikolskoe constantly and is surprised to find that he feels bored under the same roof with Bazarov. Under the pretext of studying the organization of Sunday schools in the area, he gallops off to Madame Odintsova's. He is delighted that the first person he meets is Katya, and soon overcomes his uneasiness when Madame Odintsova greets him rather warmly.

Commentary

The opening scene is somewhat comic when we consider that these two are supposed to be adult and intellectual "nihilists." Both of them realize that in terms of their code they are being foolish in even considering a return visit to Madame Odintsova's. As they hedge the question they appear more like two immature school boys than adults, and the decision is finally just a whim which both later regret. Arkady finally makes the decision, and as he does so, he is suddenly aware that he wants to see Katya as much as he ever wanted to see Madame Odintsova. This is for him a momentous step in separating himself from Bazarov.

Important in this chapter is the ineffective romantic who cannot manage to control his help and allows the farm to deteriorate. All the "aristocratic" Pavel can do is say, *"Du calme! Du calme!"* Nikolai simply does not know how to manage the farm, and Pavel is too wrapped up in his own little world. Bazarov is also seen as an ineffective person because he refuses to become involved in any of the problems. The hope lies with Arkady, who assimilates the romantic and the practical, the ideal and the real.

Symbolically at the end of the chapter, Arkady strikes off on his own for the first time. Never before could he have conceived of being bored under the same roof as Bazarov, but now, he is beginning to establish his own identity and he returns to Nikolskoe, not to see Madame Odintsova but to find Katya.

CHAPTER 23

Summary

After Arkady leaves, Bazarov is possessed by a fever to work on his experiments. Except for a few brief clashes, Pavel and Bazarov are able to avoid each other. Both Nikolai and Pavel do take pleasure in observing the young man in his laboratory. The only person at Marino who Bazarov really responds to and gets along with is Fenichka. Fenichka likewise responds to Bazarov. Perhaps it is because she does not consider him of noble birth and could therefore feel more at ease around him.

One day as Bazarov was returning from a walk, he found Fenichka sitting on a bench in a secluded part of the arbor. She thinks that the heat is making her sick, but after Bazarov takes her pulse, he announces that she shall live to be a hundred. They laugh and talk together about his studying and his occupation. She later tells him that the drops he had given her earlier for the baby were very beneficial. Bazarov jokingly said that he has to be paid, but he doesn't want money. He asks for one of her roses. As they are joking, Fenichka thinks she hears Pavel in the vicinity. She expresses her fear and dislike for the man. Bazarov then jokes with her some more and tells her to smell the rose. He leans forward to smell it with her and uses this opportunity to kiss her fully on her parted lips. At this moment, Pavel appears and greets them. Fenichka runs away immediately, and after Pavel leaves, he walks for a long time before he returns to the house in a highly disturbed state of mind.

Commentary

Bazarov is still attempting to forget his unrequited love by devoting himself to work: "he was possessed with a fever to work." Also, we see in the first part of the chapter how much Pavel continues to despise the young "nihilist."

This chapter presents Bazarov as a most likable and most human person by his conversation and relationship with the honest and simple Fenichka. She feels very comfortable in his presence "because she unconsciously felt that Bazarov lacked all the qualities of a nobleman, lacked all the superiority that both attracts and repels." There is a common bond of friendship developing between them and through this relationship, we see more into the essential nature of Bazarov than we did when he was discussing things with Madame Odintsova. He does possess a type of natural charm and easy manner with Fenichka. Furthermore, after his disappointing attempts to find love with Madame Odintsova, he is able to become attracted more easily to Fenichka's simple but sincere charms.

The fact that Pavel saw the two kissing prepares the reader for Pavel's insistence upon a duel in the next chapter. The difference between the two men is seen in the fact that Fenichka reacts strongly to Bazarov but when Pavel appears, she freezes into almost immobility. Pavel, however, will be gentleman enough never to tell Nikolai that he saw Bazarov kissing Fenichka.

CHAPTER 24

Summary

Two hours later, Pavel calls on Bazarov and asks about the latter's views on dueling. Bazarov says that theoretically duels are absurd, but that they can serve a practical purpose. Much to Baza-rov's amazement, Pavel challenges him to a duel for the ostensible reason that he finds Bazarov detestable and superfluous at Marino. They agree to fight with pistols at eight paces and without benefit of seconds at six a.m. the next day. Bazarov insists that they have a witness and suggests Nikolai's valet, Piotr, who "stands at the peak of civilization" for the role. Once Pavel leaves, Bazarov laughs to himself about the idiocy of the entire affair, about the meaning-less kiss he gave Fenichka, and Pavel's asinine gallantry. "What a comedy we played," he muses, "like trained dogs dancing on their hind legs."

Bazarov starts a letter to his parents, but tears it up thinking that if something happens to him, they will hear about it soon enough. He finally decides that nothing is going to happen to him anyway. He goes in search of Piotr and tells him to report to him early the next morning for some urgent business. That night he has many strange dreams concerning himself, Madame Odintsova, Pavel, and Fenichka.

Piotr wakes them up at four and they leave for the dueling place. Piotr is frightened when he learns the true purpose of the trip. Bazarov sees some workers who are also up this early and feels how useless his trip is compared to the workers who are going to do something worthwhile.

Up to the last minute, Bazarov jokes about Piotr's abject fear and the absurdity of the entire episode. But Pavel is in the deepest earnest about the duel. Pavel fires and the bullet barely grazes Bazarov's ear. He returns the shot and hits Pavel in the thigh. When Pavel reminds Bazarov that each is entitled to another shot, Baza-rov dismisses him and assumes the role of the doctor tending to Pavel's wound.

Bazarov must first calm Piotr in order to send him to the house after help. Pavel is impressed with Bazarov's honorable ac-tions. Piotr returns with Nikolai, who is dreadfully upset. Pavel gal-lantly assumes full responsibility for the duel and insists that he insulted Bazarov in such a way that Bazarov was forced to fight.

Later, the household is totally disrupted, and Fenichka makes every possible attempt to avoid Bazarov. Nikolai apologizes for Pavel's action, but he never discovers the real cause of the duel. Bazarov stifles Pavel's attempts to be magnanimous and as he departs, he calls back "damned feudalists," over his shoulder.

While Pavel is convalescing, there is a great deal of tension in the house. Fenichka can hardly face Pavel, and only the old retainer, Prokofitch, who remembered duels from the old days, is not disturbed by the event. Pavel finally calls Fenichka to his room and asks her if she feels no guilt about what she has done. Fenichka answers that it was not her fault and that she could not stop Bazarov from doing what he did. She maintains that she loves Nikolai very much and would die immediately if he thought she was unfaithful. At this point, Nikolai enters and is surprised and pleased when Fenichka openly throws herself into his arms.

After Fenichka leaves the room, Pavel tells his brother that he should do his duty to Fenichka by marrying her and making their relationship decent. Nikolai is astonished at his brother whom he has "always considered the most inflexible opponent of such marriages." Nikolai is overjoyed at this change in Pavel and warmly embraces his brother.

Left alone, Pavel's eyes are moist and he decides that he must go away as soon as he regains his health. "Illuminated by the glaring daylight, his handsome, gaunt head lay on the white pillow like the head of a dead man — and he was, in effect, a dead man."

Commentary

This chapter presents the duel between Bazarov and Pavel. It should be noted that some months earlier, Bazarov would never have consented to the duel. Because it implies standing up for one's honor or principles a duel is in direct opposition to anything a nihilist could advocate. Besides this, dueling for the sake of honor is the height of romanticism. Bazarov, then, accepts out of a sense of boredom and disquiet. However, he does refuse to go so far as to carry a letter in his pocket blaming himself, because "it is just a little like a French romance." As an alternative, he suggests using Piotr.

Thus, we see now why Turgenev has emphasized that Piotr is the emancipated servant because only as such could he possibly function in the role of a witness. Note also that after Pavel leaves, Bazarov admits how foolish it all was, but feels that under the circumstances, it was impossible to refuse Pavel. Furthermore, he knows that the cause of the duel resulted from the fact that he was seen kissing Fenichka. For a "nihilist," this reason only adds to the absurdity of the event.

The next day, Piotr proves not to be as "emancipated" as he thought himself: the duel virtually terrifies him. While waiting, Bazarov, who has always emphasized the value of the practical in life, notices that some other men are up that early, but acknowledges that the others are going to some useful employment. Again, he feels the incongruity of his actions and his views.

After Pavel is wounded slightly, he tries to maintain the right for Bazarov to shoot again as was earlier agreed upon. Bazarov refuses and assumes the role of doctor. For the first time, Pavel realizes that a man as different from him as Bazarov can still be an honorable man. He is now impressed with what an honorable person Bazarov is. It is ironic that Bazarov had to participate in something so romantic and so alien to his beliefs as a duel before Pavel could see any worthy quality in him. That is, Bazarov had to perform something in Pavel's world before Pavel could evaluate Bazarov's importance.

Bazarov's main regret about the duel is that his work is now interrupted, and he expresses his disgust when he leaves by referring to the entire household as "damned feudalists." After he leaves, Pavel calls Nikolai to insist that he do "the right thing" and marry Fenichka. This move is made not because he has shifted from his aristocratic ideas of the impropriety of such a marriage, but because he is probably in love with Fenichka, and knows that she loves only Nikolai. He then is left alone without even the ability to dream. It was as though "Pavel was indeed a corpse."

CHAPTER 25

Summary

At Nikolskoe, Arkady spends all his time in the presence of Katya. He is surprised at first when she mentions how much he has changed and indicates that it is for the better. She suggests that he was too much under Bazarov's influence, and admits that she found Bazarov alien to her personality. She says: "He's a wild animal, and you and I are domesticated." Arkady is impressed with Katya's power of observation and her ability to discern the truth of situations in spite of the fact that she has lived alone so much of her life. She explains that she likes the simple life and wouldn't even want to marry a rich man. Arkady sees that Katya is far superior to her sister and in a moment of excitement tells her that he wouldn't exchange her for anyone in the world, and then he leaves her quickly to conceal his embarrassment.

Returning to his room, he finds Bazarov, who has thus far kept his presence a secret. He tells Arkady about the duel with Pavel; Arkady hears the story out, but feels horrified and ashamed. Bazarov wants to leave immediately because he thinks that Arkady is there only to have an affair with Madame Odintsova. Arkady denies this emphatically, and suggests that the lady would want to see Bazarov.

Madame Odintsova does learn of Bazarov's presence and requests an interview with him. Bazarov immediately explains that he has come to his senses since their last meeting and apologizes for his past stupidities. They forget the past and talk of the present. Bazarov tells her that he is sure Arkady is in love with her, but she thinks that he is mistaken. Arkady, in the meantime, had been sitting alone without the slightest trace of jealousy over the fact that Bazarov was alone with Madame Odintsova.

Commentary

In action and in thought, Arkady's romantic tendencies are now emerging. He is with Katya and is happy that he can express himself in "pretty language" without becoming defensive about it or without being scorned for it.

Katya is now seen to have a certain strength of her own. Previously we had seen that she remained in the background and said or did very little, but now with Arkady, she expresses herself openly and cleverly. These two, the two most admirable characters in the novel, proceed to discuss some of the other characters, especially Odintsova and Bazarov. Katya's keen insight emerges when she evaluates Bazarov as being a "bird of prey" while she characterizes herself and Arkady as "tame." She also notes that her sister values her independence and her "order" too much.

Katya's maturity is seen in her explanation of a woman's role. She maintains that the woman must be able to preserve her self-respect while at the same time being perfectly ready to yield. Odintsova could never yield and could never approach saying anything like this. The older sister's excessive pride would prevent her from ever giving herself completely to another.

Bazarov returns and is still upset over the trouble he had previously had with Madame Odintsova. In this scene between the two young friends, Bazarov is more hostile than he has ever been. This is because he thinks that Arkady actually came to see Madame Odintsova and is jealous. Furthermore, it shows the growing dissatisfaction that the two friends feel toward each other.

Bazarov sums up their relationship as follows: "A romantic would say: I feel that our paths are beginning to divide but I simply say that we have grown tired of each other." From Arkady's viewpoint, this is a good change because we know that Arkady's true nature cannot emerge as long as he is under Bazarov's influence. Arkady's complete change is noted in the last sentence when he realizes that Madame Odintsova is sitting with Bazarov and he feels no quirk of jealousy. In other words, Arkady has now found his love with Katya and is no longer concerned with the older lady.

CHAPTER 26

Summary

The day after Bazarov's arrival, Arkady and Katya are sitting alone in the garden. He tries to tell her how much he has changed and credits her with being a good influence upon him. He wants to tell her something that will surprise her, but he gets twisted up in his speech so badly that Katya has to tell him that she does not know what he is trying to say.

At this time, they both overhear the voices of Madame Odintsova and Bazarov. These two are discussing whether or not Arkady has an attachment to Madame Odintsova. Bazarov is still certain that he is right, but Madame Odintsova doubts it. She is pleased with the brotherly manner of Arkady toward Katya. At this time, the couple pass out of the hearing range of Arkady and Katya.

After overhearing this embarrassing conversation, Arkady immediately confesses his love for Katya and discovers to his astonishment that she also loves him. The couple are then united "innocently weeping and laughing."

The next morning, Madame Odintsova shows Bazarov a letter from Arkady asking for Katya's hand in marriage.

Bazarov lends his support to the marriage, but announces his intention to rejoice at a distance. He plans to leave that day and return to his father's house. Madame Odintsova bids him goodbye, convinced that they shall meet again.

Bazarov congratulates Arkady and explains that marriage is good for certain types. He feels that Arkady was not meant to live the rough and difficult life demanded by "nihilism." Bazarov refuses to say anything sentimental in parting and only wishes his friend good luck. They embrace and part.

That evening in the presence of Katya, Arkady soon forgot his old companion. Madame Odintsova took great delight in observing the happy lovers, who were spending all their time together and avoiding everyone else's company.

Commentary

Even after Bazarov's arrival, Arkady still chooses to spend most of his time in the presence of Katya. In their talks, Arkady finally admits how much he has changed and how much Katya has been instrumental in his transition. Thus, from the beginning of the novel, we have observed the change that has taken place in Arkady until now he has become a responsible member of society desiring a wife and family.

As Arkady tries to propose to Katya, Bazarov, and Madame Odintsova pass close by, talking about the young couple. This is another example of Turgenev resorting to an artificial technique in order to develop his story. As in an earlier chapter, this technique carries little that is convincing in the realistic sense and strikes the reader as being false. But the overheard conversation does serve to prompt Arkady to make his proposal openly and directly.

The next day, when Bazarov hears about the marriage, he announces at the same time that he is leaving. It is almost too much for him to bear, since he has been so disappointed in his own efforts to earn the love of a woman. As he leaves, Madame Odintsova tells him that she is convinced they will meet again. The irony involved of course is the fact that they *will* have but one more meeting—at Bazarov's deathbed.

Bazarov does analyze Arkady's character correctly as he is leaving. He tells his friend: "you haven't either the audacity or malevolence...you were not created for our bitter, caustic, solitary life." In their final embrace, there seems to be a recognition that they have traveled along some good paths together and that they will never see each other again. There is finally no bitterness or regret, just a parting.

After Bazarov leaves, Madame Odintsova reiterates her earlier position that her peace is better than getting involved in his type of life. No one else missed Bazarov or noted his absence, especially Katya and Arkady, who by this time were oblivious to everything but each other.

CHAPTER 27

Summary

The old Bazarovs are extremely pleased to have their son home again. They promise to keep out of his way as he works. After a few days of hard work, Bazarov grew tired of his routine and became bored. His father thinks that he is embittered, but doesn't know what to do for him. Finally, he finds release in helping his father practice medicine, much to the delight of old Bazarov.

Later, Bazarov helps in an autopsy on a person who had died of typhoid and during the operation, he cut his finger. The doctor whom he was assisting had no antiseptic, thus Bazarov feels that he will probably contract the disease in a few days. His father is distressed beyond comprehension when he hears the news.

Three days later, Bazarov comes down with fever and must be tended by his father. Old Bazarov continues to tell himself that it is only a slight chill which will pass, but Bazarov tells him directly that he has typhoid fever. He is brutally frank with his father and tells him that he hadn't really expected to die so soon. Bazarov wants a message sent to Madame Odintsova telling her that he is dying. The old man promises to do so immediately.

Another doctor arrives and suggests that perhaps the fever will pass and that the patient will recover. Bazarov is not deluded and reminds the doctor that no patient has ever recovered from this condition.

Bazarov steadily grew worse, even though for a few hours at a time he would appear to be better. At one point, Old Bazarov asks his son to allow a priest to come to him, but Bazarov refuses for the present time.

Madame Odintsova arrives bringing with her a German doctor. Vassily Ivanovitch feels that she is a benefactress and that the German doctor will be able to save his son. While they are consulting, Odintsova goes in to see Bazarov. He is most appreciative that she came. He tells her how beautiful she is but warns her not to come too close to him. He talks to her more about their relationship and wants her to forget him as soon as he is dead. The next day he is dead.

58

Bazarov is back with his parents, but he is possessed by the gloom and melancholy of a lovelorn romantic. We see that he tries to work but boredom and anxiety overtake him. His father also notices the peculiar behavior of his son. We can assume that his encounter with Madame Odintsova has affected the nihilist more than he is willing to admit.

Bazarov, himself a doctor, takes unnecessary chances in performing the autopsy as though he simply did not care whether he caught the disease or not. When he does know that he has the disease, he merely offers the sardonic comment that it really is unpleasant to die so soon. Then he assumes an extremely romantic role: he sends a note off to Madame Odintsova that he is dying. We then see the nihilist faced with death. In life he could negate everything, but no man is able to negate death, so Bazarov must now face this unpleasant fact.

As long as Bazarov is conscious he refuses the ministrations of the church and thus remains true to his beliefs in this respect. But he does comfort his father by reminding him that the last rites can be administered to an unconscious man.

During the death scene, Bazarov gives in to romantic inclinations when he talks with Madame Odintsova. He tells her how beautiful she is — a compliment that Bazarov would have earlier called a lot of romantic twaddle. As he becomes delirious, he says things which contradict his earlier views. He even recognizes that certain *types* of men are needed by Russia, and he, Bazarov, is not one of them.

CHAPTER 28

Summary

Six months later, Nikolai is giving a farewell dinner for Pavel. During the preceding week, Arkady married Katya and Nikolai married Fenichka. At the party, "Everyone served everyone else with comical attentiveness as if they had agreed to act out some kind of naive comedy." Pavel thanks everyone, embraces his brother, and bids them all farewell in English. Katya suggests to Arkady that they offer a secret toast in memory of Bazarov.

Turgenev briefly informs the reader what each of the characters has done with his life. Odintsova enters into a marriage of convenience with a lawyer and lives in great harmony and "perhaps love" with him. At Marino, the affairs are straightened out as Arkady takes over the farm and Nikolai tends to settling the arguments between the liberated serfs.

Pavel establishes himself in the highest circles of society in Dresden where he is know as "der Herr Baron von Kirsanov." Sitnikov roams around St. Petersburg and claims to be continuing the "work" of Bazarov. In a remote corner of Russia, there is a cemetery where one can sometimes observe two old people visiting the grave where young Bazarov is buried.

Commentary

There is very little to be said about the last chapter, since Turgenev says it all. That is, Turgenev uses the traditional nineteenth-century technique of rounding out the history of all of his characters.

The final chapter does make it clear that Arkady's transition is complete and he becomes the practical man of business who still adheres to many of the more advanced ideas but will not reject all the classical values found in art and literature and music. His father, then, is freed to arbitrate in disputes arising among the peasants and hired help.

Thus, the novel ends with a sense of all things having come to the right end and with everything in the proper perspective.

CHARACTER ANALYSES

Yevgeny Vassilievitch Bazarov

Bazarov is most often considered the central figure in the novel. He inculcates the central idea of "nihilism" and acts as the representative force of the new generation against which the older characters of traditional beliefs can react.

Bazarov is a nihilist of humble background whose life-view involves a rejection of anything that has previously been accepted as valid. The "nihilist" refuses to take anyone's word for anything; he can have no alliances and no emotions; he cares no more for one country than for another and accepts only that which is scientifically proven.

The purpose of the nihilist is to destroy all the existing institutions and values. He considers himself and his kind as a type of pure force whose purpose it is "to clear the site" of traditional values without any consideration of rebuilding or of replacing them with new ones. The ultimate end of the nihilist would seem to be self-destruction, because he can never let stand that which someone else has built and when all is destroyed, he must then turn inward.

When we first meet Bazarov, he adheres strictly to his philosophy of nihilism. In brief arguments with Pavel and others, he spurns art, literature, music, and even loyalty to one's country because none of these things have any meaning to him. As for love and romance, he feels that Pavel or any man who allows himself to be influenced by a woman is idiotic. He believes that if a woman appeals to you that you should have your way with her or leave her.

The first person who ever challenged Bazarov's views was Madame Odintsova. She believed in a type of "order" in her life, whereas the concept of "order" is in direct violation to the nihilist's way of thinking. Bazarov begins to sway in the presence of this grand lady. He knew very soon that he would never have his way with her and at the same time, he did not have the strength to leave her. He finds himself in a situation similar to the one he ridiculed Pavel for being in. Thus, a man who had previously ridiculed emotion and love, makes an empassioned declaration of love and after he realizes that he has made a fool of himself, he cannot return to his past security within the limits of his nihilistic philosophy.

Bazarov never abandons his earlier views, but they do become somewhat modified toward the end of the novel. His response to Fenichka and to his own parents indicates a slight change in his character. Furthermore, when he is dying, his romantic last desire to see Madame Odintsova suggests the degree to which he has strayed away from the concepts of pure "nihilism."

Arkady Nikolayevitch Kirsanov

Arkady undergoes the greatest development during the course of the novel. At first an immature young man, obsequiously following his friend Bazarov and the ideas fostered by him, Arkady eventually finds the strength to assert himself intellectually and emotionally.

He has a strong trace of his father's romanticism in his nature, but until he musters the strength to break from Bazarov and "nihilism" he keeps this side of himself in severe check. As Katya—his beloved and future wife—points out, he is not a nihilistic bird of prey, but rather a domesticated, good-natured creature.

Arkady's relationship with people seems a great deal more wholesome than Bazarov's—he loves and admires certain aspects of his father, he fulfills himself with Katya, and understands his uncle Pavel well enough to offer a good defense of Pavel's character.

Arkady has always been acting somewhat against his nature by following the concept of the nihilist. Basically, he enjoys good music, especially as played by Katya, good art, and the value of tradition. But he also likes to be as modern and as liberal as possible. Thus, one can easily see in this character a positive force in the novel which combines some of the valuable "practical" ideas of the new generation without stripping life to a barren wasteland by abolishing all forms of art, belief, and love. In the final scenes, we see that Arkady was able to make a success out of the deteriorating farm and became a contented married man conducting his farm in keeping with the latest progressive ideas.

Anna Sergeyevna Odintsova

Madame Odintsova is twenty-nine years old, but during her short life she has experienced much and seen a great deal of the world. She had earlier married a very rich man who was considerably older than she. She accepted him because of his age and his ordered way of life. When he died and left her a rich lady, she traveled through various parts of Europe before deciding to return to the provinces to settle down.

Madame Odintsova is not liked in the province because she is a woman with too many liberal ideas. When she meets Arkady, she asks about Bazarov because she wants to know a person who has had the courage "not to believe in anything." This desire to meet Bazarov is a result of Madame Odintsova's cold and austere personality. She has decided to remove herself from all the anxieties of life, and in meeting Bazarov, she hopes to see what someone else's different and unique response is to the problem of living.

For Madame Odintsova, the ultimate concern is to maintain peace and order. She runs her household and estate in a precise orderly fashion, and virtually never strays from the bounds she has imposed upon life. She believes that "without order, life would be too boring." Her reluctance to become attached to Bazarov is actually based upon the fear of being taken away from her ordered existence and led into unknown seas. For her, "peace is after all the best thing in life." Thus, she remains cold and austere even to the end.

Pavel Petrovitch Kirsanov

Pavel is a "dated" aristocratic gentleman who belongs to a rapidly fleeting era in Russian history. He is caught in the dilemma of having to witness the facts of social change without being able to accept them either emotionally or intellectually. Needless to say his reaction to Bazarov and the new "nihilism" is fierce.

Pavel is the true fop, meticulous about his dress and general deportment, but totally hollow in his adherence to the ideals of the aristocracy, and ineffective in all of his actions. For all of his gentility and correctness, he serves no useful function in this life. The only advice he can offer Nikolai when the latter's estate is falling into ruin is *"Du calme! Du calme!"* But our judgment of Pavel is not really too harsh. At times we cannot help pitying this man who has experienced a tragically sad love affair and who sees his way of life crumbling about him. Also, he does exhibit something of a magnanimous spirit when he finally condones, if he doesn't actually approve, the marriage between his brother Nikolai and the servant girl Fenichka. By the end of the novel he has not changed in the least, however, and we leave him playing the role of an aristocratic, bored nobleman in Dresden.

Nikolai Petrovitch Kirsanov

Nikolai is the romantic father of Arkady, who has tried his best to keep up with modern ideas in an effort to remain close to his son. But when Arkady returns home bringing with him a nihilist with whom he apparently agrees, Nikolai feels that there is a great gulf now between the two generations.

Nikolai has very little of the practical in his nature. It is very difficult for him to tend to the business of running the farm. To keep abreast of the most recent ideas, he has freed all of his serfs and is trying to run the estate on a rental basis, but he cannot make it work. Slowly the farm is deteriorating.

While the farm sinks into neglect, Nikolai is often seen dreaming of his past life and remembering events of long ago. He also spends much time reading the romantic Pushkin and playing music on the cello. His greatness lies in his generous and expansive nature and his appreciation for beauty, but his flaw is that he lives too much in an impractical dream world. Unlike Pavel, he does not judge the younger generation too harshly, and by his patient waiting, is finally rewarded by being reunited with his son.

STRUCTURE OF *FATHERS AND SONS*

In many of Turgenev's novels, it is difficult to detect a discernible structure. His greatness often lies with the individual scenes rather than with the total work. The Russian literary critic Avrahm

Yarmolinsky says that "the total effect of *Fathers and Sons* does not measure up to that of individual scenes, so that the whole is less than the sum of its parts." This critic does not mean to imply that Turgenev had no structure, but that the greatness of the novel is best found by the manner in which individual scenes are rendered so powerfully.

The overall structure of the novel is seen through the journeys which the young students make. Furthermore, if we keep the title constantly in mind, we see that the author is building these journeys around the fulcrum of each of the two sons in relationship with his father. Thus there is a type of structure which involves Arkady and Bazarov meeting Arkady's father, and then leaving to meet Bazarov's father. This allows the reader to perceive large and sweeping contrasts.

The purpose of the journeys also influences the development of the structure. We have two types of students or young men. We want to see their basic philosophy of nihilism in action in many types of situations. Thus the novel opens by showing how nihilism evokes certain responses in the older landowning family of the Kirsanovs. Furthermore, here Bazarov comes into conflict with a representative of the old school of romanticism. In the opening portions of the novel, we observe drastic conflicts of opinions. Following this, Turgenev must move to another scene in which we can observe the same nihilistic theories in practice in another environment.

The confrontation with the second set of parents must be withheld until we see Bazarov and Arkady on some neutral ground. This leads them to the house of the liberal and intelligent Madame Odintsova. Here we see that Bazarov is not as adamant in his philosophy as he was in the presence of the romantic Nikolai or the effete Pavel Kirsanov.

The novel eventually moves to a confrontation with Bazarov's parents. During the scenes in the Bazarov house, we note a striking difference between the two young people. Thus, Turgenev has chosen a structure which allows his characters to reveal certain aspects of their personality and their philosophical views dramatically by bringing them into contact with many different aspects of life. After the visit to the Bazarov house, note how Turgenev symbolically presents the rift between Arkady and Bazarov by having each one go off on a separate voyage of his own.

In general, Turgenev has utilized a structure of movement back and forth in order to develop his theme of the new and radical in confrontation with the old and the traditional. To embody this theme, it is necessary for the main characters to move from one place to another in order to come into contact with various ideas in juxtaposition with which their own ideas are tested and evaluated.

REVIEW QUESTIONS

1. Consider briefly what each of the central characters' definition of the term "nihilism" would be.

2. What seems to be Turgenev's judgment of the philosophic concepts of "nihilism"?

3. What alternatives does Turgenev offer to the new generation's philosophy?

4. How do such general motifs as the idea of the *bildungsroman* (the development of a young man) and the traditional conflicts between successive generations function in the novel?

5. How does Turgenev make use of humor to present his themes in the novel? For example, satire, parody, humorous and dramatic situations. Does his use of humor enhance the story?

6. What kind of judgment can we assume Tugenev is making about Nikolai's romanticism and Romanticism in general?

7. What assumption can be made about Arkady's and Bazarov's characters by observing the manner in which they treat their own parents and each other's parents?

8. How does Madame Odintsova contradict Bazarov's nihilistic views?

9. How does Fenichka function in the novel? How would the novel be different if she were omitted?

10. What is the function of Sitnikov and Kukshina? How effective is Turgenev's presentation of these characters?

11. What is the difference between Piotr and Prokofitch as servants?

12. What are the central events which bring about Arkady's change?

SELECTED BIBLIOGRAPHY

Freeborn, Richard. *Turgenev: The Novelist's Novelist.* New York: Oxford University Press, 1960.

Gettmann, Royal A. *Turgenev in England and America,* "Illinois Studies in Language and Literature," V, 27, No. 2. Urbana, 1941.

Granjard, Henri. *Ivan Tourguenev et les courants politiques et sociaux de son Temps.* Paris, 1953.

Wilson, Edmund. "Preface" to *Literary Reminiscences and Autobiographical Fragments.* New York: Vintage Press, 1958.

Yarmolinsky, Avrahm. *Turgenev: The Man, His Art and His Age.* New York: The Orion Press, 1959.

– – –. "Turgenev: A Reevaluation," Introduction to the *Vintage Turgenev.* New York: Vintage Books, 1960.

NOTES

NOTES

NOTES

NOTES

NOTES

NOTES

NOTES FROM UNDERGROUND

NOTES

including
- *Life and Background*
- *List of Characters*
- *Introduction to the Novel*
- *General Plot Summary*
- *Summaries and Commentaries*
- *Character Analyses*
- *Review Questions*
- *Selected Bibliography*

by
James L. Roberts, Ph.D.
Department of English
University of Nebraska

INCORPORATED

LINCOLN, NEBRASKA 68501

Editor

Gary Carey, M.A.
University of Colorado

Consulting Editor

James L. Roberts, Ph.D.
Department of English
University of Nebraska

ISBN 0-8220-0900-5
© Copyright 1970
by
C. K. Hillegass
All Rights Reserved
Printed in U.S.A.

1990 Printing

Cliffs Notes, Inc.   Lincoln, Nebraska

CONTENTS

CHARACTER ANALYSES

REVIEW QUESTIONS

SELECTED BIBLIOGRAPHY

Notes from Underground

LIFE AND BACKGROUND

Fyodor Mikhailovich Dostoevsky was born in 1821, the second of seven children, and lived until 1881. His father, an army doctor attached to the staff of a public hospital, was a stern and self-righteous man while his mother was the opposite — passive, kindly, and generous — and perhaps this fact accounts for Dostoevsky's filling his novels with characters who seem to possess opposite extremes of temperament.

Dostoevsky's early education was in an army engineering school, where he was apparently bored with the dull routine and the unimaginative student life. He spent most of his time, therefore, dabbling in literary matters and reading the latest authors; his penchant for literature was obsessive. And almost as obsessive was Dostoevsky's preoccupation with death, for while the young student was away at school, his father was killed by the serfs on his estate. This sudden and savage murder smoldered within the young Dostoevsky, and when he began to write, the subject of crime, and murder in·particular, was present in every new publication. Dostoevsky was never free of the horrors of homicide and even at the end of his life, he chose to write of a violent death — the death of a father — as the basis for *The Brothers Karamazov*.

After spending two years in the army, Dostoevsky launched his literary career with *Poor Folk*, a novel which was an immediate and popular success and one highly acclaimed by the critics. Never before had a Russian author so thoroughly examined the psychological complexities of man's inner feelings and the intricate workings of the mind. Following *Poor Folk*, Dostoevsky's only important novel for many years, was *The Double*, a short work dealing with a split personality and containing the genesis of a later masterpiece, *Crime and Punishment*.

Perhaps the most crucial years of Dostoevsky's melodramatic life occurred soon after the publication of *Poor Folk*. These years included some of the most active, changing phases in all of Russian history and Dostoevsky had an unusually active role in this era of change. Using influences acquired with his literary achievements, he became involved in political intrigues of questionable nature. He was, for example, deeply influenced by new and radical ideas entering Russia from the West and soon became affiliated with those who hoped to revolutionize Russia with all sorts of Western reforms. The many articles Dostoevsky wrote concerning the various political questions, he published knowing full well that they were illegal and that all printing was controlled and censored by the government.

The rebellious writer and his friends were, of course, soon deemed treasonous revolutionaries and placed in prison, and after nine months a number of them, including Dostoevsky, were tried, found guilty, and condemned to be shot by a firing squad.

The entire group was accordingly assembled, all preparations were completed, and the victims were tied and blindfolded. Then, seconds before the shots were to be fired, a messenger from the Tsar arrived. A reprieve had been granted. Actually the Tsar had never intended that the men were to be shot; he merely used this method to teach Dostoevsky and his friends a lesson. This harrowing encounter with death, however, created an impression on Dostoevsky that he never forgot; it haunted him for the rest of his life.

After the commutation of the death sentence, Dostoevsky was sent to Siberia and during the four years in prison there, he changed his entire outlook on life. During this time, in horrible living conditions – stench, ugliness, and filth – he began to re-examine his values. There was a total change within the man. He experienced his first epileptic seizure, and he began to reject a heretofore blind acceptance of the new ideas which Russia was absorbing. He underwent a spiritual regeneration so profound that he emerged with a prophetic belief in the sacred mission of the Russian people. He believed that the salvation of the world was in the hands of the Russian folk and that eventually Russia would rise to dominate the world. It was also in prison that Dostoevsky formulated his well-known theories about the necessity of suffering. Suffering became the means by which man's soul is purified; it expiated sin; it became man's sole means of salvation.

Dostoevsky married a young widow while still in exile. After his exile, he served four more years as an army private, was pardoned, and left Siberia to resume his literary career. He soon became one of the great spokesmen of Russia. Then, in 1866, he published his first masterpiece, *Crime and Punishment*. The novel is the story of Raskolnikov, a university student who commits a senseless murder to test his moral and metaphysical theories concerning the freedom of the will. The novel exhibits all the brilliant psychological analyses of character for which Dostoevsky was to become famous and incorporates the theme of redemption through suffering.

After finishing *Crime and Punishment*, Dostoevsky married again and went abroad, hoping to find peace from numerous creditors and also hoping to begin a new novel. The peace of mind Dostoevsky longed for he never found; instead, he discovered the gaming tables of Europe—and accumulated even more guilt in addition to his ever-mounting debts. The novel Dostoevsky composed abroad was *The Idiot,* the story of a wholly good and beautiful soul. In his notes, Dostoevsky sometimes called this hero Prince Christ; he hoped to create a man who could not hate and who was incapable of base sensuality. The novel is one of his masterpieces, a fascinating, intense study of the destructive power of good.

Dostoevsky's last novel, *The Brothers Karamazov,* was his masterwork and is a masterpiece of Western literature. Only a year after its publication, Dostoevsky was dead but already he was acknowledged to be one of Russia's greatest writers.

LIST OF CHARACTERS

The Underground Man

The unnamed paradoxical narrator of the story who is addressing an imaginary audience.

Liza

The prostitute whom the Underground Man befriended and then cruelly rejected.

Anton Antonich Syetochkin

The Underground Man's immediate superior from whom he borrowed money and whom he visited when he needed to "embrace humanity."

Simonov

Practically the only schoolmate the Underground Man has seen since graduating from school.

Zverkov

A good-natured schoolmate whom the Underground Man detested because of his social success.

Trudolyubov

A distant relative of Zverkov's, a rather inoffensive and undistinguished person.

Ferfichkin

A sycophant who hung onto Zverkov's coattails.

Apollon

The Underground Man's servant whom he hated and also feared.

Olympia

The most desirable of the prostitutes; Zverkov claimed her for himself.

GENERAL PLOT SUMMARY

The narrator introduces himself as a man who lives underground and refers to himself as a spiteful person whose every act is dictated by his spitefulness. Then he suddenly admits that he is not really spiteful, because he finds it is impossible to be anything—he can't be spiteful or heroic; he can only be nothing. This is because he is a man of acute consciousness and such a person is automatically rendered inactive because he considers too many consequences of any act before he performs the act and therefore never gets around to doing anything. In contrast, a person who is not very intelligent can constantly perform all sorts of actions because he never bothers to consider the consequences.

The man of acute consciousness finds that he cannot even commit an act of revenge because he never knows the exact nature of the insult. Such a man is plagued with an active imagination which causes him to exaggerate any type of insult until it becomes fantasized out of all proportion to the original insult. By this time it is ridiculous to try and perform any act of revenge.

It is easy for other people to classify themselves, but the Underground Man knows that no simple classification can define the essence of one's existence; therefore, he can only conclude that he is nothing. Yet in society, the scientists and the materialists are trying to define exactly what a man is in order to create a society which will function for man's best advantage. The Underground Man objects to this trend because he maintains that no one can actually know what is man's best advantage. Such a society would have to be formulated on the theory that man is a rational being who always acts for his best advantage. But the history of man proves that he seldom acts this way.

The Underground Man then points out that some people love things which are not to their best advantage. Many people, for example, need to suffer and are ennobled by suffering; yet, the scientist and the rationalist want to remove suffering from their utopian society, thereby removing something that man passionately desires. What the Underground Man wants is not scientific certainity, but the freedom to choose his own way of life.

The Underground Man concludes that for the man of conscious intelligence, the best thing to do is to do nothing. His justification for writing these *Notes from Underground* is that every man has some memory which he wishes to purge from his being, and the Underground Man is going to tell his most oppressing memory.

Sixteen years ago, when he was twenty-four, he lived a very isolated and gloomy existence with no friends and no contacts other than his colleagues at work. To escape the boredom of this life, he turned to a life of imagination. There he could create scenes in which he had been insulted and then could create ways of revenging himself. But he never fulfilled his dreams.

When his isolation became too unbearable, he would visit his immediate superior at his home. Once, however, feeling the need to "embrace humanity," he was driven to renew his acquaintance with an old schoolmate, Simonov. Arriving at the house, he found Simonov with two old schoolmates discussing a farewell party they were planning for Zverkov. The Underground Man invited himself to the party even though he had always hated Zverkov and had not seen him since their school days.

At the party, the Underground Man unknowingly arrived an hour early (the time had been changed) and, during the course of the evening, created a repulsive scene. When the others left to go to a brothel, he begged for some money from Simonov so that he could go too. He was ashamed and horrified at what he had done, but he followed his companions to the brothel.

When he arrived, he was determined to slap Zverkov, but he could not find him; he was relieved to discover that everyone had already retired. Then he met Liza, a prostitute with whom he retired. Later, he awakened and told her in high-flown language about the miseries of prostitution. He knew he was doing so partly for effect and partly because he felt rejected by his friends. Upon leaving, he gave Liza his address and told her to visit him. She promised to do so.

During the next day and for days afterward, the Underground Man was horrified that Liza might actually show up. He knew that he could not keep up the pretense of the previous night. And, one night as he was having an absurd argument with his servant, she did arrive. He was embarrassed that she should see him in such poverty and in such an absurd position. He went into hysterics, and she comforted him. Later, he insulted her and told her that he was only pretending about everything he said. Crudely, he gave her five roubles for her services, but before she left, she crumpled the five-rouble note and left it on his table. He ran after her to apologize but could not find her. His shame over his conduct still troubles him.

INTRODUCTION TO THE NOVEL

Notes from Underground is perhaps Dostoevsky's most difficult work to read, but it also functions as an introduction to his greater novels later in his career. The ideas expressed in *Notes from Underground* become central to all of Dostoevsky's later novels, and therefore this work can be studied as an introduction to all of Dostoevsky's writings. One reason that the work is so difficult is that Dostoevsky included so many ideas in such a short space, and thus the ideas are expressed with extreme intensity and are not elaborated upon. The student who has read other of Dostoevsky's works will immediately recognize many of Dostoevsky's ideas in this work.

Notes from Underground is composed of two parts: a confession to an imaginary audience in Part I, and then, in Part II, an illustration of a certain episode in his life entitled "A Propos of the Wet Snow." First of all the confession itself is a dominant technique in Dostoevsky's writings. As a monologue or a confession, the man from underground can use it to reveal directly his innermost thoughts. These thoughts are made more dramatic by the fact that he is addressing them to an imaginary audience which is opposed or hostile toward his views and toward him. Therefore when he ridicules, or laughs at, or becomes spiteful about, some idea, he is doing so in terms of an imaginary audience reacting against him.

The novel can act as a rebuttal to a novel published the year before, 1863, by Chernyshevsky, entitled sometimes *What Shall We Do?*, or sometimes translated as *What Is To Be Done?*. This particular novel advocated the establishment of a utopia based upon the principles of nineteenth-century rationalism, utilitarianism, and socialism. Such a rationalistic, socialistic society, Dostoevsky thought, would remove from man his greatest possession: human freedom. Dostoevsky therefore becomes the champion of the freedoms of man: the freedom to choose, the freedom to refuse, the freedom to do anything he wants to do. For Dostoevsky, then, man's freedom was the greatest thing that he possessed and Dostoevsky thought that in a scientific, rationalistic, utilitarian society man's freedom would be replaced by security and happiness. This is what Chernyshevsky and other socialists were advocating: that if man is given all the security he needs, then man will automatically be happy.

Dostoevsky attacked these ideas because he believed that if man were simply *given* security and happiness, he would lose his freedom. To him science, rationalism, utilitarianism, or

socialism were equated with the doctrines of fatalism and determinism, which contradict man's freedom to control or determine his own fate.

When the Underground Man says that twice two makes four,
this is a scientific fact. But man does not always function merely
by scientific fact. For Dostoevsky the rational part of a man's
being is only one part of his makeup. That is, man is composed
both of the rational (two times two makes four) and the irrational.
It would be nice to think sometimes that twice two makes five.
This would be, in Dostoevsky's words, "a very charming idea
also." The point is that if man functions solely as a rational
being, then man's actions are always predictable. Dostoevsky's
point is that man's actions are *not* predictable. There are even
some men who enjoy suffering and are only happy when they
suffer. Consequently in a socialistic society where man's security and happiness is being assured, this would deny the fact
that men — some men — want to suffer and are improved by their
suffering.

Thus one of the great ideas throughout all of Dostoevsky's
fiction is the idea that through suffering man achieves a higher
state in the world. That is, through suffering man can expiate all
his sins and become more closely attuned with the basic
elements of humanity. Consequently if a utopia removes suffering, then it is removing one of the essential ingredients by which
man improves himself and becomes a greater person.

In another image in the novel Dostoevsky is afraid that if
man lives in this utopian society then he will end up like a
mechanical being — the "organ stop," as Dostoevsky puts it.
Man is meant to be more than an organ stop or a piano key; he
is meant to be more than a mechanism in a well-regulated clock.
The freedom to choose was, for Dostoevsky, the greatest thing
that man had. The freedom to choose, if he wished to, suffering. The freedom to choose religion. The freedom to choose,
sometimes, those things which are destructive to man. Take
away this freedom and man ceases then to be a man. He becomes,
as in another image, an ant. Man deserves something better than
to die upon an ant heap.

In a later novel, *The Brothers Karamazov*, Dostoevsky makes perfectly clear his ideas in a passage called "The Grand Inquisitor." In this later novel the grand inquisitor offers man security and happiness; Jesus reappears upon the earth offering man total freedom. Dostoevsky believed that the voluntary choosing of Christ, the freedom to choose Him at whatever expense, is the greatest gift given to man. And man's freedom then becomes central to all of Dostoevsky's novels.

SUMMARIES AND COMMENTARIES

PART I

The Footnote

Summary

In a footnote, Dostoevsky asserts that while the diary and the narrator are imaginary, such a person as the narrator not only exists, but that he *must* exist because he represents many people who are forced by the circumstances of society to live, as he does, underground.

Commentary

Dostoevsky's footnote makes it clear that the Underground Man is not an absolute anomaly, is not an exception, but that in such a strict, scientific society as that of the nineteenth century, such a man *must* exist or else society would become a single, collective, mechanical robot. He is *not* a "representative man" or an "active man" who consents to the scientific determinism being perpetrated in nineteenth-century society; instead, he is that important and significant holdout against a scientific acceptance of life. Therefore, in a purely scientific-oriented society, he represents the man of consciousness who refuses to accept and to yield to the discoveries of science. Consequently, we must assume that in a mechanistic society, such a person as the narrator must exist, metaphorically, underground; that is, contrary to the general trend of the rest of society.

Summary

The narrator immediately reveals that he is a sick, spiteful, and unattractive man who believes that his liver is diseased. He refuses to consult a doctor about his liver, out of spite, even though he knows that he is hurting only himself by his spite. He is now forty years old and has been a spiteful person ever since he began working for the government twenty years ago. Throughout his employment, he never accepted a bribe, but he did delight in making any petitioner feel uncomfortable and unhappy, even though most of the petitioners were timid and poor.

The narrator confesses that the real motive for his spitefulness lies in the fact that he is really neither a spiteful nor an embittered man. He simply amuses himself, like a boy scaring sparrows, by being spiteful. Furthermore, he says, he was lying when he said he was a spiteful man; he was lying out of spite because even if he wanted to, he couldn't really become a spiteful man. Furthermore, he cannot become anything. Even though he is aware of many opposing elements within himself, he can't become anything—neither hero or insect, honest or dishonest. He will live out his life in his small corner because an intelligent man can't do anything; only a fool can. "A man of character, an active man is pre-eminently a limited creature." A man living in the nineteenth century is morally obligated to be a creature without a character.

To become older than forty, the narrator tells us, is "bad manners, is vulgar, immoral." And he has a right, he feels, to say this because he plans to go on living for many, many years past forty. As for the reason he joined the civil service, he says that he did so only to have something to eat. When a distant relative died, leaving him 6,000 roubles, he immediately resigned and settled down in his "corner"—a wretched, horrid room on the outskirts of St. Petersburg. He has a servant, a stupid, ill-natured country woman, and he knows that he could live more cheaply elsewhere, but he refuses to leave, even though the climate in St. Petersburg is bad for his health.

Commentary

In introducing himself as a sick, spiteful, and unattractive man, the Underground Man sets the tone for the entire narrative. He describes what is now commonly called the "anti-hero"; that is, a person whose traits and actions are not considered heroic or even admirable — a person who might even be common and ordinary, but one with whom we can align ourselves in one way or another because his ideas strike us as proper and reasonable or, at least, understandable whether or not we agree with those ideas. The use of the term "anti-hero" has become prominent in twentieth-century literature and here, in *Notes from Underground,* is one of the germinal ideas for this type of character.

The Underground Man is one who is sick and spiteful, and we acknowledge that here is a man who is sick mainly because he cannot accept the ideas currently popular in his society. He is spiteful because he resents the direction of development he finds in his society, and his revolt against these unacceptable trends render him, in the eyes of his contemporaries, a spiteful being. But he is also physically sick and won't consult a doctor, out of spite. And he is also spiritually sick, as we find out in Part II, because he can't accept love.

Dostoevsky conveys these ideas dramatically by having the Underground Man address an imaginary audience who is, he assumes, antagonistic to his ideas. Part of the paradox, then, is that the "spiteful" narrator constantly interrupts his narration in order to try and seek the approval of his audience and to justify his own behavior. He intentionally identifies himself as being spiteful because he knows that his audience will characterize him as a spiteful person; therefore, he anticipates his audience by admitting that he is spiteful.

Dostoevsky offers yet another paradox when he has the Underground Man admit that he was lying when he said that he was spiteful, then confessing that he could never become spiteful. This type of contradiction is characteristic of the Underground Man and is further realized when he admits that "I am well educated enough not to be superstitious, but I am superstitious." These ideas lay the groundwork for presenting his later ideas or beliefs in the necessity of man's contradictory nature.

The contradiction introduces us to several important aspects of Dostoevsky's writing. First, as noted, Dostoevsky is always concerned with the sense of duality present in every man. *Crime and Punishment*, the novel that he wrote after he finished *Notes from Underground*, depicts a character with a split personality. Here, Dostoevsky was attempting to illustrate the complexity inherent in human nature and to show how contradictory impulses inhabit the same personality. Second, we should note that this entire work is in the form of a long confession. This obsession for confession characterizes a large portion of Dostoevsky's mature writing; throughout his major novels, characters constantly confess all types of vagaries. Finally, Dostoevsky introduces the concept, to be developed more fully later, of the relationship between honesty and self-evaluation. For example, the Underground Man is attempting to be honest with both his readers and with himself, but as he suggests in Section 11, there are some things that one will never admit — even to himself.

Part of the narrator's difficulty lies in his realization that he can do nothing and can become nothing because an intelligent man will always consider the complexity of anything for so long that often he ends up doing nothing. In contrast, the average or normal man can perform actions, but only because he is a limited creature who hasn't the intelligence to evaluate the intellectual ramifications of his actions.

Throughout the narrative, a central problem involves determining how "spiteful" the Underground Man is. To determine this, one must deal with layers of paradoxes. Basically, as noted above, he is spiteful mainly because he is going against the main trend of his society. However, when he says "I am a spiteful man" and then contradicts himself by saying he was lying when he said he was spiteful and then adds that he "was lying from spite," we are then confronted with a double paradox and must conclude that the Underground Man is actually a spiteful man; but the problem continues in that we basically agree with what this disagreeable man says and, while we tend to dislike him as a person, we are forced to accept most of his views.

As factual history, the Underground Man is the same age (forty) as Dostoevsky was when he wrote this novel, and he also lived in St. Petersburg (now Leningrad), the capital of Russia until 1917. St. Petersburg was built by Peter the Great on land which had once been marshland and was reclaimed; the references the Underground Man makes to the unhealthy climate of St. Petersburg refer to this fact.

Section 2

Summary

The narrator tells us why he could not become an insect even though he has wished many times to become one. He is too acutely conscious, which, he says, is a real "thorough-going illness." The flaw in any cultivated man is that he possesses a higher level of consciousness than is necessary. It would be better to possess only the amount given to "direct persons and men of action" who seem to have the correct dosage.

He does not mean to brag about his illness (i.e., his over-dosage of consciousness), but it is fashionable to brag about one's diseases. He is, however, convinced that every type of consciousness is a disease. For example, often when he feels "every refinement of all that is 'good and beautiful,'" he also feels and does very ugly things. "The more conscious I was of goodness and of all that was 'good and beautiful,' the more deeply I sank into my mire. . . ." Thus, he feels that depravity might perhaps be the normal state of man. Until now, he has always felt ashamed of this condition—especially after he had just completed a loathsome act and then began to feel a positive, real enjoyment from his depravity. This enjoyment, he says, has always been directly correlated to his "too intense consciousness of [his] own degradation" and has stemmed from his awareness that he could never become anything else and probably will never want to change.

The worst aspect of the narrator's sickness is that it is in agreement with the "normal, fundamental laws of overacute consciousness." He concludes that one is not responsible for being a scoundrel and wonders if that is any consolation to the person who realizes that he is a scoundrel.

There have been moments in his life when he would have enjoyed being slapped in the face. His consciousness forces him to admit that he is to blame for every insulting thing that happens to him, but the humiliation is that his blame is due to no fault in himself, but is in accordance with the laws of nature which control him. Thus, if he were insulted, he would probably not seek revenge because he could never decide what to do. He could not seek revenge because his acute consciousness forces him to realize the impossibility of his being anything different from what he is.

Commentary

Section 2 introduces in germinal form many more ideas that are both central to this work and prominent throughout Dostoevsky's fiction. The narrator continues his attack against scientific rationalism by asserting, paradoxically, that one of the main flaws in mankind is an over-developed consciousness. This acute awareness is a most dreadful illness. The paradox of these views works on many levels. In any society, especially one given to scientific rationalism, a man's education and intellectual achievements are to be lauded in the highest sense. These are the qualities which define man's humanity and separate him from the beasts. Yet, the Underground Man sees them as an illness because these very attributes, that is, "acute consciousness" and "intellectual awareness," are the very things which make it impossible to accept scientific rationalism. To be able to accept the prevalent society of his day, the Underground Man asserts that a person must be a non-thinking man of direct action. A high level of consciousness will always cause a man to reject his society; thus, man's greatest attribute becomes his worst illness.

The Underground Man finds in his society that it is fashionable for people to brag about their diseases. So, since he is persuaded that a high level of consciousness is a disease, he will be fashionable and brag about his disease — the paradox being that his disease is that which is desired by all intelligent people and it is a disease only in terms of a scientific society. The idea of a man's acute consciousness being a detriment to living in a scientific society is used here in only a paradoxical sense, but Dostoevsky makes extensive, serious use of this idea later. In subsequent novels, he develops the point more fully that the greater the intellect, the more that the intellect must suffer. The ignorant are simply not aware of the complexities and imperfections in the world, but the great intellect suffers intensely for all of mankind. In other words, the great intellect is aware of wars and holocausts, of innocent suffering, of starvation in all parts of the world, of disease and poverty, and of all the trials of mankind; therefore, the great intellect suffers for all of the ills of society, whereas the limited intellect or "the man of direct action" is concerned only with matters of the moment.

Concering the duality of man's nature, the Underground Man says that in a scientific society, man's nature must be consistent, but he, the Underground Man, views man as a highly inconsistent being. He uses as an example the fact that people, while in the midst of contemplating "the good and the beautiful" also allow ideas of depravity and vulgarity to intrude upon their thoughts. Again, this idea is developed more fully in later novels and receives its climactic form in Dmitri Karamazov's discussion in *The Brothers Karamazov*. Following publication of this later novel, this idea was often referred to as the Madonna-Sodom opposition, meaning that radical and diametrically opposed feelings exist at the same time within a person. Dmitri Karamazov says, "I can't endure the thought that a man of lofty mind and heart begins with the ideal of the Madonna and ends with the ideal of Sodom. What's still more awful is that a man with the ideal of Sodom in his soul does not renounce the ideal of the Madonna." Dmitri wallows in his emotional quagmire but, at the same time, longs to imbue his life with utmost purity. He is especially attracted to purity as represented by the Madonna image but, at the same time, finds himself helplessly trapped in a life of orgies. These orgies he equates with the city of Sodom, destroyed by God because of its corruptness.

Further, Dmitri Karamazov says, when he sinks "into the vilest degradation," he always reads Schiller's "Hymn to Joy." In the very depths of that degradation he makes such pleas as: "Let me be accursed. Let me be vile and base, only let me kiss the hem of the veil in which my God is shrouded. Though I may be following the devil, I am Thy son, O Lord, and I love Thee, and I feel the joy without which the world cannot stand."

The acute consciousness referred to by the Underground Man is ultimately related to a "self-consciousness." The average man, "the man of direct action," functions on instinct and never stops to evaluate his actions. He is close to being an animal which responds instinctively and does not consider, much less contemplate, the ramifications of his actions. Therefore, the "direct man" can perform an act of depravity and not be troubled by it. However, the Underground Man is always intensely conscious of any act of depravity, and consequently, takes pleasure from his depravity by being aware of it. This awareness renders him inactive in that he constantly evaluates every aspect of any act in such depth that there can be no clear lines for direct action. Thus, knowledge and self-consciousness have given him an omniscience that seems (or would seem so to his scientific-oriented audience) to be a liability, one that renders him a spiteful, inactive man.

Section 3

Summary

The direct man (or the man of action) is often possessed by feelings of revenge and may carry out that revenge quickly and effectively. Such a man is, of course, stupid, but he *does act* whereas the man of acute consciousness can *never* carry out any revenge. Instead, like a mouse, he will retreat to his hole, or corner, where he relives the insult, intensifying it, questioning and doubting it until his convictions are totally warped. Wallowing in his self-humiliation, he remains isolated in his own spite until his death.

A stone wall is the only thing that will stop the direct man of action if he is bent on revenge, but the Underground Man resents the implications of the stone wall; to him, the wall represents mathematics and deductions of natural science. The Underground Man dislikes both the laws of science and the direct man's ready acceptance of them. The direct man, for example, accepts unquestioningly the "proof" that man is "descended from a monkey." The Underground Man recognizes that it is better "to understand it all, to recognize it all" but he refuses to be reconciled to conclusions. His rebellion is painful.

Commentary

Proof of the idea that acute consciousness renders a man inactive is illustrated in this discussion of revenge. The direct person, the man of action, can revenge himself without any thought processes; he never considers the various implications concerning the act of revenge — he just accomplishes it. Thus, revenge can be performed only by the stupid person who in this society is the "normal" person. The man of acute consciousness, however, considers and weighs all the various aspects of revenge; then, after all the contemplation, it is too late, it is too impossible, and it is too absurd. The paradox is that the normal or direct man considers revenge his due when he is insulted; the man of acute consciousness sees revenge, upon deliberating about it, as an act of a savage. Yet, paradoxically, the Underground Man, for not committing revenge, is considered a savage by his audience. The paradox deepens when the Underground Man with his intense self-consciousness and finely-honed sensitivity realizes the futility of confessing to an unsympathetic audience composed of men of direct action (savages). In using the idea of revenge, Dostoevsky undoubtedly had Hamlet in mind, in that Hamlet was prevented from taking revenge by thinking too long about it and by considering all the variant alternatives.

Now we understand why the Underground Man can never become anything, not even an insect. The only experiences he can have are those which he creates in his own mind. For example, when he returns to his hole and relives an insult, he tortures himself with imaginary insults until they become authentic.

This section also introduces two images which the Underground Man will later use as thematic motifs in commenting upon the nature of a scientific world. In the "stone wall" and the "twice two makes four" images, the Underground Man says that nothing will stop the direct man unless he runs into a stone wall. The "stone wall" is equated with the "laws of nature, the deductions of natural science, mathematics." The Underground Man, however, refuses to accept as binding the various conclusions of science. In contrast, the direct man *can* accept the idea that we are descended from apes, but the man of acute consciousness rebels against such conclusions. As an individual, he reserves the right to ignore the idea that twice two makes four. This, however, forces him into inertia and boredom.

Section 4

Summary

The Underground Man maintains that there is even some type of enjoyment in a toothache. For example, why does a person moan with a toothache? If he did not find enjoyment in moaning, he would not moan. First of all, the moaning represents the intellect's inability to understand the aimlessness of pain. But as the ache continues for days, the moans become a desire to force others to suffer as you are suffering and the moans become "nasty, disgustingly malignant." Also, he knows that the audience for whom he is moaning only loathes him for his efforts, and from these recognitions comes a perverse pleasure. He wonders if, ultimately, a man of acute consciousness and perception can ever respect himself.

Commentary

Scientific rationalism, according to Dostoevsky, tries to categorize everything, place everything into its proper slot. Yet the Underground Man, in using the idea of the toothache, illustrates the fallacy of such attempts. When his imaginary audience ridicules him by laughing, saying "you will be finding enjoyment in a toothache next," the Underground Man develops this idea so as to show that science cannot predict a human being's reaction to pain or to anything else. Since all people universally agree that a toothache is unenjoyable, the Underground Man shows how the pain can be enjoyable, how the person enduring the pain enjoys wallowing in his own misery. This again points to the Underground Man's theory of man's contradictory nature, a nature which prevents him from fitting into the scientific mold which the rationalists have fashioned for him.

The idea of a man's moaning over a toothache carries also metaphysical implications. The moans are a protest against the futility and aimlessness of pain. The stupid person, or the man of direct action, simply accepts pain as a part of the everyday aspect of living, but the man of acute consciousness searches for some reason or some purpose to the pain. He moans at his inability to comprehend any valid purpose for his being inflicted with pain. The more the pain continues, the more fully he recognizes the discrepancy between enduring pain and the capricious inflicting of pain upon him. His increased moans, hopefully, will force others to see the absurdity of pain and man's inability to cope with it.

The Underground Man, having come to his realization about the aimlessness of pain, and having forced others to despise him because of his moans, then asks: can a man of acute consciousness (acute perception) ever respect himself? In other words, if the introspective man of self-consciousness constantly analyzes himself and his functions, he understands himself so thoroughly that it is impossible to respect himself. But, as he will later point out, few people have the courage to analyze themselves in any depth.

The idea of the function of pain and more particularly of innocent suffering receives Dostoevsky's fullest treatment in his later novels. For example, Ivan Karamazov investigates the idea that pain and suffering might have a function in God's total purpose for the universe, but since God didn't give us an intelligence sufficiently complex to understand it, he rejects the idea that the innocent must suffer and questions God's justice.

With these ideas about the pleasure in pain, we could wonder if the Underground Man finds pleasure in writing these *Notes from Underground* and, especially in the second part, if he receives pleasure from intentionally inflicting mental pain upon the prostitute, Liza?

Section 5

Summary

Continuing with his question, the narrator wonders if a man who takes pleasure from degradation can ever respect himself? And where does respect enter into emotion? Many times, he says, he has simply pretended to be offended, but as he relives the situation, he comes to the point of being really offended. And what is the cause of this play-acting? "It was all from ennui," because the man of acute consciousness is prevented from action; therefore, he becomes bored and inertia is his constant state. In contrast, the "direct" person, or the "man of action," is "active just because he is stupid and limited." Before beginning to act, a man's mind must be totally free of doubt and the man of consciousness can never remove doubt from his mind. The active man can revenge himself because he uses justice as the primary cause of his revenge, but the Underground Man can see neither justice or virtue in revenge because his acute consciousness knows the complexities of the nature of justice.

Even if the man of consciousness were to abandon himself, to act "without reflection," to accomplish something—to actually hate or to actually love—he would end by despising himself for having consciously deceived himself.

Commentary

When Sigmund Freud was investigating man's psychological impulses and behavior, he constantly turned to literature to illustrate his various points and the writings of Dostoevsky proved to be exceptionally fruitful for his investigations. (See Freud's book on Dostoevsky.) In this chapter, for example, the Underground Man records one of the quirks of human nature— that is, the penchant to over-exaggerate the degree of insult which a person feels, and then, later, relishing the insult to such a degree that one actually feels offended. This, the Underground Man believes, happens most frequently to a person of acute consciousness since the man of direct action is too involved, too busy even to have the time to allow such imaginary feats to occur. Consequently, the Underground Man realizes that his own boredom and inertia are the direct result of his being a man of acute consciousness; conversely, just the opposite is true in that "all direct persons and men of action are active just because they are stupid and limited." Again he emphasizes that action is correlated with stupidity, and inaction is the result of a self-conscious awareness.

The Underground Man maintains that action can occur only when a man's mind is completely without doubt. The intelligent man, however, is never without doubt; therefore, he can never act. Revenge requires a firm sense of the nature of justice and no intelligent man would ever assume to know anything conclusive about the true nature of justice. The intelligent man is aware, for instance, that the philosophical concept of "justice" has been under constant investigation since the time of Socrates. Therefore, he is aware of the subtle distinctions concerning this concept and consequently he is rendered inactive. The ironic paradox is that if a man is able to complete an action which he initiates, then that man is stupid. But, then, not even the

Underground Man wholly accepts this idea because it would be, as he says in the next section, too easy an excuse for being inactive.

Section 6

Summary

The narrator wishes that he could simply say that he is a sluggard or that he is lazy. This would at least be a quality and he could then be positively defined as "a sluggard." He says that he once knew a man who prided himself on being a connoisseur of Lafitte. The man died in tranquility believing that being a connoisseur of Lafitte was a great virtue. Thus, logically, being lazy could also be considered a career. By having been both a sluggard and a glutton, yet possessing "sympathies for the good and beautiful," he could have occupied his entire life with offering toasts to everything good and beautiful. And then he could die with dignity. In such a negative age, he says, it would be good to have something definite to say about oneself.

Commentary

In this section, the Underground Man is attempting to define his own personality and, more important, he is trying to define his own existence. For the introspective person, one of the great difficulties of life lies in trying to define the nature of one's own existence. This has been a central problem of twentieth-century philosophy and has been the crux of the school of philosophy called Existentialism, particularly as expounded by Jean Paul Sartre. At this point, the reader should be aware that modern existentialists returned to much of Dostoevsky's writings in order to express much of their philosophy. Like the Underground Man, the existentialists believe that too many people define their own existence by what *others* think of them. Also, too many people try to define themselves by assigning a title or a definition to themselves.

The Underground Man says that he knew a man who lived contentedly throughout his life simply because he defined himself as a connoisseur of Lafitte. To be an expert, however, the narrator says, does *not* define one's essence or one's existence. To believe so is to live in self-deception. But the "connoisseur of Lafitte" took the definition of himself from what *others* thought of him or how others defined him. And, therefore, the Underground Man realizes that it is impossible for him to define himself as a sluggard, even though it would definitely mean that he was "positively defined; it would mean that there was something to say about" himself. But he knows, as a man of acute consciousness, that he could never really accept such a superficial classification and live meaningfully with it. But it would be very pleasant to be able to be stupid enough to do so.

Section 7

Summary

The Underground Man wonders who first proposed this theory: that man's evil acts are performed from a mistaken knowledge of his own best interests and that if he were only educated he would at once become good and noble because he would then understand his own advantages. If this were so, the Underground Man wonders what is to be done with the millions of intelligent people who have consciously acted against their own self-interests — who have *deliberately* chosen a path that is contrary to their best self-interests? Furthermore, who can define "advantage" sufficiently so that it is clearly understood? Some people, he says, do perform acts with the full consciousness that the act is harmful to them because wealth and freedom and peace are not necessarily "advantages" to them.

Men are not all mathematicians and man is made up of more than intellect. A certain friend of the Underground Man has been known to explain why he is about to do something in clear, lucid arguments, and then suddenly turn about and do just the opposite, and therefore illogical, thing. Thus, there must be something more important "to almost every man than his greatest advantages." Whatever it is, it functions to break down classifications. The intellect alone cannot improve man, the narrator tells us, and to prove his point, he compares the barbarous ages to the present time. Obviously man has still not learned "to act as reason and science would dictate." What man really needs is the freedom to choose whatever course he may desire. This independent choice is more advantageous than always, rationally, choosing something because of its "advantage."

Commentary

In Section 7, Dostoevsky broadens his attack against scientific rationalism, utilitarianism, and against all of the assumptions of modern civilization concerning the establishment of utopias. Historically speaking, Dostoevsky is attacking the ideas expressed in a novel by Nikolai Chernyshevsky entitled *What To Do?* (1863) (sometimes translated as *What Shall We Do?* and *What Is To Be Done?*) Chernyshevsky, a radical socialist and revolutionary, had popularized ideas found in Jeremy Bentham's (1748-1832) philosophy of utilitarianism and in (François Marie) Charles Fourier's (1772-1837) socialistic doctrines. In his novel, Chernyshevsky had presented a utopian, socialistic society based upon the concept that man, basically good, always searches after his own enlightened self-interest and that through science and rationalism man can arrive at an incontrovertible truth. His conclusion was that if society were reformed along purely scientific lines, an earthly paradise could be achieved.

Using a series of images and employing several paradoxes, the Underground Man attacks and disproves Chernyshevsky's assumptions. First, he exposes the fallacy in the proposition that man always acts in his own best interests. Only an innocent (that is, an ignorant) child could believe such nonsense because throughout history man has consistently and *consciously* acted in a way contrary to his best interests. "Millions of facts . . . bear witness that men, *consciously* . . . have rushed headlong to meet peril and danger," knowing full well that they might be killed. Can such acts be considered "in man's best interests," he wonders.

The Underground Man also investigates the definition of the word "advantage." What type of man in this world is to decide or define exactly what is man's "best advantage" because what is an advantage to one man might be detrimental to another. Furthermore, some men will always, intentionally, break away from their "best advantage" simply to assert their own freedom.

For the Underground Man (and Dostoevsky), freedom to choose one's actions is one of the most prized rights of mankind. If we are provided with a logical and scientific society, man would lose his freedom to choose. Our freedom therefore allows man to often choose that which is *not* to his best advantage. Consequently, man often performs acts for no reason other than to prove that he is free to perform those acts.

The Underground Man then attacks the proposition that if a man is educated and civilized, he will become an ideal person by using his intellect to choose that which is good and advantageous. To disprove this idea, the Underground Man reminds his audience that civilized man still commits as many blood-thirsty actions as did barbarians. In spite of all the knowledge and science, individual man has not improved; in fact, "civilization has made mankind if not more bloodthirsty, at least more vilely, more loathsomely bloodthirsty." Consequently, merely because a society is organized on a scientific, rationalistic basis, it cannot change the basic nature of man because what man most wants "is simply *independent* choice."

Throughout his fiction, Dostoevsky constantly asserts the importance of freedom and his greatest expression on the subject is found in *The Brothers Karamazov* in the legend of the Grand Inquisitor. For Dostoevsky, man can have freedom on the one hand or else he can have security and happiness on the other. It is impossible to have both freedom and happiness. Therefore, Dostoevsky sees that a socialistic, rationalistic society is offering man security and happiness, but at a high price: man would have to relinquish his freedom. Thus, all socialistic utopias are a way of imprisoning man, of taking away his freedom to choose a capricious or illogical course of action.

Summary

The Underground Man realizes that some people will object to his ideas by saying that choice and freedom of will can be reduced to a mathematical formula. But, he explains, if things are explained scientifically, then man will cease to feel desire, for if reason and desire should conflict, man would be compelled to follow reason and this would lead to a senseless, mechanistic existence. One could then calculate one's entire life for thirty years beforehand and have nothing more to do but follow a mechanical existence. The prospect of such a life is repulsive. Man is made up of both reason and impulses, and thus man's life is made more meaningful by wanting to respond with all his capacities and not with just his capacity for reasoning. This caprice and these non-rational desires are in reality a great advantage to man because they are what define his personality and individuality.

The Underground Man argues further that the history of the world proves that man is not rational. The whole of man's life consists of "proving to himself every minute that he is a man" and not a predictable cog in a logical mechanism.

Commentary

The Underground Man continues his attack against a utopian society in which man would become a mechanistic robot. In such a scientific society, even choice and freedom of will would be reduced to "two times two makes four." If everything is known beforehand, if everything can be predicted with mathematical certainty, the Underground Man points out that under such conditions, man will lose certain valuable aspects of his basic humanity. For example, if it is pointed out with mathematical and scientific certainty that when desires and emotions conflict with logic, then man must "cease to feel desire, and instead perform the logical act, and if man's acts can thus be predicted with logical certainty, life would then be dull and boring, and man would become a mechanistic peg in a large machine. He would become an "organ-stop" or a "piano key," and thus lose part of his humanity. "For what is a man without desires, without free will and without choice, if not a stop in an organ."

The point the Underground Man is leading to is that the nature of man is not defined by his intellectual achievements alone. Thus, a scientific society would be catering to and satisfying "only the rational side of man's nature." Instead, the entirety of man is made up of part reason and part impulse (or caprice). A scientific, rational society would then satisfy only one's capacity for reason and not one's capacity for life in its entirety. Such a society, rather than benefiting man, would deny an essential part of his nature; that is, his irrational impulse, desire, emotion, or caprice.

For the Underground Man, freedom of choice, the freedom to commit irrational acts, is the very quality which defines man's personality and his individuality. Without this quality, man becomes a mechanical robot performing routine acts. Consequently, man often deliberately performs irrational acts, deliberately encounters chaos and destruction for no other purpose than to assert his individuality and prove that he *is* free.

Section 9

Summary

The Underground Man asks his audience: even if it were possible to reform men to act "in accordance with science and good sense," is it desirable to do so? Do "man's inclinations need reforming?" and would it be a benefit to man? Recognizing that man is essentially a creative person, he asserts that the act of creating is more important than the final product. It may be that man's "passionate love for destruction and chaos" is because he is afraid of attaining his object. Man, unlike a race of ants which dies in an ant-heap, is frivolous and unpredictable, and thus loves the game of living even though the act of living is filled with uncertainties. If life were a mathematical certainty, then all the mystery of living is done away with and the act of living becomes "the beginning of death." Man likes the "process of attaining," but not the final product. Consequently, mathematical certainty is intolerable. And, even though two times two makes four is good logic, two times two is five "is sometimes a very charming thing too."

Man, perhaps, does not want a mathematical calculation for his well-being—because, perhaps, suffering is just as great a benefit for him. Some men do passionately love suffering and this fact stands in opposition to the idea that man should logically work only for his well-being. Man will never renounce real suffering because, through suffering, man's consciousness is heightened and consciousness is "infinitely superior to two times two makes four."

Commentary

To disprove the rationalist's attempt to force man into a scientific pattern, to make man no more than an organ stop, the Underground Man continues presenting examples which prove the duality of man's nature. As noted earlier, man's duality is central to all of Dostoevsky's writings. For example, in *Crime and Punishment*, the work following *Notes from Underground*, the plot is built on the duality of its main character, Raskolnikov.

Still attempting to prove that the utopia proposed for man would relegate man to a mechanized existence, the Underground Man uses in this section the image of the ant-heap. Ants are industrious insects admired by the utilitarians for their predictable nature. Unlike man, they are not frivolous and incongruous. The Underground Man continues the image by pointing out that if man imitates the ant in joining a socialistic community, then man will end up in an ant-heap. But, he emphasizes, the nature of man should transcend that of an ant and mankind deserves something better than ending up on an ant-heap.

Speaking of man's duality, the Underground Man further illustrates man's conflicting desires to create and to destroy.

"Man likes to make roads and to create, that is a fact beyond dispute. But why has he such a passionate love for destruction and chaos also?" Because of man's duality, the narrator says, man enjoys the process of attaining rather than the actual object or goal. It is the process of living with all of its uncertainities which man finds attractive. In contrast, "mathematical certainity is . . . something insufferable." Thus, the Underground Man despises and rejects any organized society of robots and prefers a life filled with uncertainities and freedom. When he says "twice two makes four," he means that this is a mathematical certainity. But he adds, "Twice two makes five is sometimes a very charming thing too," meaning that it is often pleasant to contemplate the absurd, the unpredictable, or the irrational.

The Underground Man's insistence that suffering is valuable is central to all of Dostoevsky's writing. The Underground Man attacks the utopian society as a place where suffering would cease to exist. The paradox is that man is "sometimes extraordinarily, passionately, in love with suffering," and if suffering ceases to exist, then man loses something he deeply desires. The value of suffering is that it increases one's consciousness and, in doing so, makes the idea of a socialistic society loathsome.

Section 10

Summary

The Underground Man is afraid of such an edifice as the "Crystal Palace," a place which can never be destroyed. For, if it were not a palace, and if he were caught in a rainstorm, he would then creep into it to avoid getting wet. But he rejects the Crystal Palace because it would be a place where one would not dare stick out his tongue. The narrator's desire is to always have the right to stick out his tongue if he wishes; and one's desires should not be eradicated. He would even let his "tongue be cut off" if he were to lose "all desire to put it out." This is the way he is constructed. Thus he wonders if he was so constructed so as to realize that he was cheated in his construction.

Commentary

The reader will be disturbed by the total confusion of this section. In Russia, there has always been strict censorship, both in Dostoevsky's time under the Tsar and later under the Communist regime. Therefore, everything that Dostoevsky wrote had to be submitted to a censor for approval, and when the censor finished with this section, it was so badly mutilated that, as it now reads, it makes little sense. On March 26, 1864, Dostoevsky wrote to his brother Mikhail (Michael) complaining about the censored parts. He was incensed at the "swine of a censor who approved the passages where I jeered at everything and blasphemed everything" and yet the same swine "suppressed all the passages where I drew conclusions that faith in Christ is needed."

Why Dostoevsky never restored the passages or left no indication of the meaning of the censored passages is still a mystery. However, we can safely say that this section offered some positive solution. From his other writings, we can assume that the solution was probably in terms of a voluntary choice to follow Christ in spite of the pain and suffering such a choice would entail.

In the passages left in, we see that the Underground Man is still using images to attack the socialistic utopia. In addition to the ant-heap of the last section, he now uses the images of the "henhouse," the "block of tenements," and the "Crystal Palace." The main image, the Crystal Palace, refers to the building in London made of glass and iron, which was thought of as a magnificent and monumental architectural feat. The Underground Man, however, uses it as an image of scientific advancement which is supposed to replace man's inner needs, desires, and emotions. He cannot look upon this palace and be satisfied. He cannot respect science at the expense of a spiritual hunger that needs to be satisfied.

Section 11

Summary

The Underground Man concludes that, in the final analysis, to do nothing—to be consciously inert—is the best thing an intelligent man can do. Even though he envies the normal man, he would not change places with him. For the present, a life underground is more advantageous, even though he admits that he thirsts for something different. And he would feel better if he believed what he has written.

He knows that his audience will object that he is being ridiculous in writing these things if he never intends to let anyone read what he has written. But he counters this objection by asserting that every man has some memories which he would tell only to his friends; and there are some memories which one would tell no one except himself; and, finally, there are some which one will not admit even to himself. Furthermore, the more decent a person is, the more secrets he has which he represses from himself. Only lately, says the Underground Man, has he decided to remember some of his early adventures. He says that a true autobiography can never be written because any author will always lie about himself (so as to impress his readers), yet the Underground Man's autobiography will be honest because he is writing only for himself. The reason he addresses an imaginary audience is that this form of writing is the easiest for him. And it is necessary to get his ideas written down so that he can criticize himself more objectively and gain some type of relief from writing. At present, he is particularly oppressed by one memory which he hopes to rid himself of by narrating it. And besides, he is bored; writing will give him something to do.

Commentary

In this final section of Part I, the Underground Man returns to his earlier credo: a man of acute consciousness can do nothing—"conscious inertia" is best for an intelligent man. He does not mean that inertia is that which an intelligent man should seek; instead, in such a scientific society, it is forced upon him. As in Section 10, the Underground Man is seeking "something quite different, quite different, for which I am thirsting, but which I cannot find." That "something different," we know from his other writings, is a re-emphasis upon the basic teachings of Christ which were being rejected in favor of scientific rationalism.

When the Underground Man questions the validity of everything he has written—"I feel and suspect that I am lying like a cobbler"—he introduces a problem central to Dostoevsky's view of writing and one which characterizes Dostoevsky as a forerunner to the modern novel of psychological investigation. The statement "I am lying" should *not* be taken as a rejection of what the Underground Man has said, but as a philosophical questioning as to whether any writer is capable of presenting the reality of one's thoughts and of one's psychological motivations. Unlike such realists as Turgenev or Balzac, Dostoevsky was not concerned with presenting external reality—that is, depicting a scene from life with such verisimilitude that no one would ever question its accuracy. In contrast to this type of fiction, he wanted to plunge into the depths of a reality hidden from ordinary sight, to investigate the validity of contradictory human impulses and hidden psychological drives.

But if this is a confession, how can we know that the Underground Man is telling the truth? Because unlike Rousseau in his *Confessions,* who lied in order to impress people, the Underground Man is writing only for himself, and there is no need to lie to one's self. The paradox is that many people, however, do lie to themselves. The Underground Man parries this psychological fact with the counter argument, later supported by Freud, that only decent people lie to themselves and repress unpleasant things about themselves. In fact, "the more decent one is, the greater the number of things" repressed. Paradoxically, then, since the Underground Man is not decent, is indeed spiteful, then we can accept his version as being close to the truth. Furthermore, the story related in Part II stands as proof that he is not lying because no "decent" person would reveal it if he acted

38

as degradingly and as spitefully as does the Underground Man. Finally, as Freud recommended as a treatment, the Underground Man thinks that by writing out his experiences, he can view them with more critical objectivity. Thus, the next part will narrate a reminiscence which oppresses the narrator, but which, by writing it down, he hopes to purge himself of.

PART II

Section 1

Summary

Even at age twenty-four, the Underground Man says, he lived a gloomy and solitary existence with no friends or companions. At the office where he worked, he constantly imagined that his colleagues looked upon him "with a sort of loathing." He could never understand why the other workers were so oblivious to their appearance while he was always so self-conscious about his own. Even workers who had pock-marked faces or who wore dirty, disgusting clothes never seemed disturbed, but he was constantly aware of his own shortcomings. In fact, he hated his own face and was convinced that the other clerks also hated it.

In turn, however, he hated his fellow clerks, yet was also afraid of them. When he saw one of them staring at him, he would try to stare back, but "was always the first to drop my eyes." He was morbidly sensitive but concluded that "every decent man of our age must be a coward and a slave."

Having no friends, he spent most of his time reading, but he was often so bored that he longed for some type of adventure or excitement. To compensate, he "indulged in filthy vice" and frequented various obscene haunts. While returning one night from one of his visits, as he passed a tavern, he saw a man being thrown out of a window. He was in such a strange mood that he envied the man being thrown out.

Entering the tavern, he stood by a billiard table and became highly incensed when an officer "moved me from where I was standing and passed by as though he had not noticed me." This slight nagged at his very existence, since the officer ignored the Underground Man's humanness and treated him as an object. He wanted to start a quarrel but instead sneaked away. It was not from cowardice, however. He says that he has never been a coward at heart, only in action. It was an "unbounded vanity" that drove him away; it was not a lack of physical courage but a lack of moral courage.

His resentment over this insult built until he wanted to return to the tavern and begin a quarrel except that it would be necessary to use literary language and he realized that as soon as he began speaking in literary terms, the other people would begin laughing. This would be too humiliating. Instead, for several years, he stared spitefully at the officer and even wrote a satire on him. It was rejected by the publisher.

Two years after the insult, the Underground Man composed a splendid letter, asking for an apology and hinting rather plainly at a duel. Fortunately, the letter was never sent. Then suddenly he conceived a plan whereby to gain revenge: he often strolled along the Nevsky, the main street of St. Petersburg and had frequently seen the officer strolling there also. While strolling, the Underground Man would always step aside to make way for any important personage or well-dressed stroller. He hated himself for doing so, but was overly-conscious about the shabbiness of his clothes. Like the narrator, the officer would also step aside for people of higher rank. But when he met people less well-dressed and of lesser rank, he would walk indifferently past them, forcing them to move out of his way.

To get revenge, then, the Underground Man decided to force the officer to step aside for him. But to accomplish this required great preparations. First, he would have to be dressed as a person of dignity. That would be no easy matter; he was forced to get an advance on his salary. Still, however, he didn't have enough and had to borrow from his superior (Anton Antonich Syetochkin) in order to buy a new beaver fur collar for his overcoat.

Having made all the preparations, he went to the Nevsky and, before he knew it, he encountered the officer. But he stepped aside for him. Again and again, his courage failed at the last minute, and the officer simply stepped over him. Afterwards he would be feverish and delirious. Then, one day, unexpectedly, the officer was three feet from him. He closed his eyes and did not budge an inch. They bumped into each other, and even though the officer pretended not to notice, the Underground Man knew better. Elated, and singing Italian arias, he was at last able to get home feeling triumphant and exhilarated.

Commentary

The title of this second part, "A Propos of the Wet Snow," becomes the dominant image throughout the rest of the novel. We are constantly reminded of the wet, falling snow. The image is also related to the Underground Man's state of mind during the narration of the events. He is living in a barren, frigid world where he is unable to communicate with other people; and, even in episodes like those with Liza, he uses cold and snow and wetness to describe funerals and other unpleasant episodes.

At the end of Part I, the Underground Man is reminded of the story of Liza as a result of the falling snow and he must purge this memory from his consciousness. To do so, he must relive the episode which occurred when he was twenty-four years old, one which has haunted him for these sixteen intervening years.

As noted in the commentary to Part I, the reliving or retelling of an unpleasant or repressed event in the past has, in the twentieth century, become the basis of much modern psychoanalysis. Thus, the entire *Notes from Underground* can function as a type of confession from a disturbed personality, and can be seen as the forerunner of one of the main trends in twentieth-century literature.

The opening of this section shows the Underground Man to be a person overly self-conscious and overly sensitive. This intense awareness causes him to believe that others view him in the same way as he views himself. For example, he says that he hated his own face and therefore assumed that everyone else hated his face. But we know from Part I that thoughts such as these emanate only from the man of acute consciousness; thus we become increasingly aware that one of the Underground Man's major drawbacks is his over-sensitivity and his dual nature. His duality is present in almost every action and thought. For example, he says that he "alternated between despising [his fellow workers] and thinking them superior" to himself. At least, he could never help but drop his eyes first when he caught someone staring at him. The Sartrean existential hero would not be the first to drop his eyes; he would "stare down" the other person. The Underground Man's acute self-awareness, in contrast, has rendered him almost totally useless in society.

The realization that he was different and unlike most other people prevented him from acting as he would like to. This same realization is made by Rousseau in the opening section of his *Confessions* and becomes the subject and the rallying cry of romanticism, freeing the romantic man from the shackles of restraint. And even though the Underground Man says that Rousseau lied in his *Confessions* (see Part I, Section 11), the same realization about his own uniqueness renders him inactive rather than liberating him.

This self-awareness causes him, and any "decent man," to become a coward and a slave. As expressed in Part I, the full realization of the consequences of any act renders the intelligent man inactive. The Underground Man insists that the man of acute consciousness is not a coward at heart, but that he is a coward in action. To prove his point, he narrates his encounter with the officer in the billiard parlor.

Note, however, that before he sees the officer that he is plagued with guilt feelings for having been to a house of prostitution. Thus, when he envies the "gentleman thrown out of the window," this expresses something of a subconscious desire to be punished for his dissipation of the evening.

The episode with the officer illustrates many of the abstract matters discussed in Part I. Since the Underground Man brooded so long, we see his inability to become a "man of action." He broods upon a subject, but can't act. To perform even the most minimal action, he must adopt the existing social standards and buy clothes which will imply that he is a superior person because of the clothes he wears. Even when he does bump against the officer, it is an action which occurs almost by accident. That is, he is hardly aware of the officer's presence and cannot take time to think about his own decision. This illustrates that, for the man of acute consciousness, simple revenge is impossible.

Section 2

Summary

The Underground Man's periods of dissipation would be followed by periods of deep remorse. And then to escape the sickening feeling of remorse, he would resort to daydreaming which would totally occupy him for long periods of time, even up to three months. After a particularly lurid spell of dissipation, his dreams would then be more "sweet and vivid."

Whereas in real life the Underground Man was merely anonymously miserable, in his dreams he could either ride the apex of fame and honor, or else grovel in utter debauchery; "there was nothing in between." But even when he was dreaming of himself as heroically good and beautiful, he was always aware of compelling, sensuous desires. Being a dream hero, however, allowed him to surround himself with imaginary dream people who would excuse his shameful deeds and thoughts, as they kissed him and wept. He was a fascinating, Manfred-like dream hero to all his friends; even his shameful deeds had something about them that was "good and beautiful."

In his dreams, he inherits untold millions and immediately contributes them to the benefit of mankind while he goes among the people "barefoot and hungry preaching new ideas." A new millennium will occur: a universal amnesty will be declared; the pope will resign and go to Brazil, and Lake Como will be transferred from northern Italy to Rome for a grand ball. Finishing his discussion of dreams, the Underground Man admits that he could never stand more than three months of isolated daydreaming before he would be forced to seek the society of other men.

Plunging back into society meant visiting his superior, Anton Antonich Syetochkin. But he could go see Anton Antonich only on Tuesdays, the day his superior received visitors. Thus, if the Underground Man's passionate "desire to embrace humanity" fell on any other day, he had to curb that passion until Tuesday. The Underground Man did have one other acquaintance, an old school friend of a sort, Simonov. He didn't particularly like Simonov, though, and had a strong suspicion that Simonov had an adversion for him. But, on one occasion, when he was especially lonely, he decided to go see his old schoolmate.

Commentary

This section shows the Underground Man's fluctuation between reality and illusion. He can live for only so long in a dream world before he is forced to face reality again. The dichotomy between the two worlds is worth noticing. In his dream world, he is a lover of all that is good and beautiful, he is the champion of the people, and he is filled with love for all of humanity. But in reality, he cannot tolerate the individual person and becomes a spiteful man in the presence of others.

This dichotomy is directly related to the Madonna-Sodom concept discussed in Part I. Since the Underground Man's periods of dissipation force him to retire from the world, he then goes to the opposite extreme where he dreams of being the poet and hero, and where all his friends cluster about him and will even forgive him his shameful deeds when he confesses them. This love-of-humanity-and-hatred-of-neighbor idea is one which Dostoevsky further developed in the character of Ivan in *The Brothers Karamazov*. For someone like Ivan or the Underground Man, it is much easier to love mankind in the abstract than it is to love one's next-door neighbor.

The duality in man's character is expressed in the fact that the Underground Man cannot bear dreaming for a long period any more than he can stand dissipating for a long period. So, after "three months" of dreaming, he confesses that he was forced again to seek the company of mankind. It is ironic (and humorous) that when this desire to embrace humanity overtook him, he could not do so immediately but had to wait until his superior at the office had his open house on Tuesday afternoon.

The puzzling aspect of the Underground Man's compulsive nature is that at the end of this section, he is convinced that his old schoolmate Simonov does not like him, yet he is determined to put himself "into a false position." This drive will later involve him in the episode concerning Liza.

Section 3

Summary

When the Underground Man arrived at Simonov's, he found two other old schoolmates there. He was disgusted that all three completely ignored his entrance even though Simonov seemed positively surprised at his coming. The three were planning a farewell dinner for a comrade called Zverkov whom the Underground Man also knew and had hated during their school days. Zverkov had inherited an estate while still in school and even though he was good-natured and generous, the Underground Man still found reasons for disliking him.

Simonov's two visitors were Ferfichkin, a Russianized German who had been the Underground Man's bitter enemy since early school days and Trudolyubov, a distant relative of Zverkov's. The three decided that for twenty-one roubles (seven each), they should be able to provide a good farewell dinner for Zverkov at the Hotel de Paris. Abruptly, the Underground Man invited himself by asserting that his seven roubles would make a grand total of twenty-eight. The other three men tried to convince the Underground Man that he had never been on good terms with Zverkov, but he insisted on being invited; the party ended and Trudolyubov left puzzled and vexed.

After the others were gone, Simonov paused, then asked the Underground Man if he could pay his share now. Suddenly, the

Underground Man panicked as he realized that not only was he broke, but also that he had owed Simonov fifteen roubles for some time. Simonov tactfully told him that it could all be settled after the dinner tomorrow.

Strolling along the street, the Underground Man could not understand what possessed him to insist upon attending a party for such a detestable scoundrel as Zverkov. Furthermore, he didn't even have any money, especially if he were to pay his servant's wages. He knew he should write a note and send his regrets, but he knew that he would definitely attend the dinner.

Having renewed his acquaintance with one of his school-mates, the Underground Man suffered through a serious of hideous nightmares at night. In his dreams he relived the miserable days when his relatives sent him off to boarding school where he was a quiet, timid boy unable to form any friendships. He hated his schoolmates and they repaid him by ignoring him. To get revenge, he studied hard and forced himself to the top of the class. The Underground Man did develop one friend, but he became so possessive and demanding in the relationship that his tyranny drove his friend away. Then, as soon as the Underground Man graduated, he gave up the special position he had been trained for so that he could divorce himself completely from his schoolmates.

The morning after his horrible dream, he says that he slipped away from his office two hours early in order to be ready for the dinner. When he began to dress, however, he was horrified over his threadbare clothing and knew that he would become the subject of derision. Furthermore, he knew that a yellow stain on one knee of his trousers would deprive him of nine-tenths of his personal dignity. He was in despair when he thought how coldly, disdainfully, and rudely the others would glare at him. He dreamed of "getting the upper hand" by means of his superior wit and intelligence so that Zverkov would be left isolated and then later they would be reconciled and drink to an eternal friendship. Finally noticing the time, he hailed a sledge, spent his last rouble, and arrived at the Hotel de Paris in grand style.

Commentary

The Underground Man has already discussed the subject of duality in a man's personality. This chapter offers a concrete picture of this theory, of how opposite, conflicting emotions and actions can function within the same person. The entire section, in fact, is a masterful description of contradictory actions and emotions which are difficult to define. Dostoevsky's theory of realism was to make the reader recognize in the bizarre actions of others something in his own personality which heretofore he has refused to acknowledge. Observing the actions of the Underground Man, we feel a horror for him, followed by uncomfortable, comic feelings. At every word the Underground Man utters, we sense how deeply he is trapping himself in a situation which he has no real desire to be a part of.

For example, he did *not* like the company and he definitely detested Zverkov, for whom the dinner was being given. Yet he invited himself. He insisted on being allowed to help pay for a dinner he could not afford. Then, afterward, his inability to pay caused him even more distress and, as the dinner neared, he felt himself pulled further and further toward an abyss from which there was no escape.

The flashback into the Underground Man's youth and schooling is a literary technique often used by Dostoevsky. As with many authors, Dostoevsky utilized personal events in his own life for dramatic or literary purposes. Unlike the Underground Man, he was *not* an orphan, but he *was* sent to schools in which he had no interest and, according to reports, which he hated. Also in this section, his description of Ferfichkin as a Russianized German and as a despicable person parallels Dostoevsky's intense dislike and prejudice toward Germans.

The Underground Man states that as much as he desired friends, he was never able to develop a friendship. The one time he tried, he became a tyrant. This idea lays the groundwork for his failure at the party in the next section and also for his failure in the relationship with Liza where he is able to humiliate and ridicule her, but unable to respond to her as a decent human being. Already we see that the Underground Man is unable to accept people unless he can absolutely dominate them.

Section 4

Summary

When the Underground Man arrived at the hotel, not only did he have difficulty finding his comrades, but he also had trouble finding the room. After many inquiries he discovered that the dinner had been re-scheduled for an hour later, at six o'clock. He sat sullenly and brooded about not being informed. When the others arrived, however, he was not angry; instead of being offended he was overjoyed to see them. He had especially expected Zverkov to make some insipid jokes, but was taken aback when he did not. In fact, Zverkov treated him with courteous cordiality.

Everyone was surprised to learn that the narrator had been waiting for over an hour. They all laughed and the blame was finally placed on Simonov. Zverkov was astounded that the Underground Man didn't at least order a drink for himself while he was waiting. When they were seated, Zverkov asked the Underground Man some questions about his job but, for the narrator, each question seemed to carry a taint of superiority. And, when queried about his salary, the Underground Man felt that he was being cross-examined. But he told his salary anyway. Noting that it was indeed a rather miserable sum, Zverkov and the others commented on the salary. This caused the narrator severe agony; he became offended and loudly announced that he was paying his own way. He continued, spouting a few more spiteful remarks, then was told, "You invited yourself to join us, so don't disturb the general harmony."

After this, no one paid any attention to the Underground Man, who sat silently and broodingly while Zverkov narrated an episode about how he almost got married. The Underground Man was almost determined to get up and leave the others without a word, but he knew that he could not do this. When Zverkov mentioned the name of a famous prince, the Underground Man was certain that Zverkov was "name-dropping," so offered an impertinent and rude remark. Zverkov merely looked at the narrator as though he were an insect. Later, the Underground Man attempted to make a speech and since he was unused to drinking and spirits, he became confused and insulting. The others, regretting that he was present, tried to ignore him and after dinner, they did not invite him to join them on the sofa. Instead, the Underground Man paced loudly back and forth on the other side of the room for three hours, while the others ignored him.

When they were about to leave to visit a brothel, the Underground Man approached Zverkov and apologized to him for having insulted him. Zverkov responded that it was impossible for such a person as he to ever be insulted by the Underground Man. Then everyone left except Simonov who stayed behind to tip the waiters. The Underground Man decided he wanted to go with the others to the brothel and tried to borrow six roubles from Simonov. Simonov hesitated, but felt so embarrassed by his friend's begging that he finally gave him the money.

Commentary

The Underground Man's arrival an hour early for the party sets a tone of tension for the entire evening. Ultimately, it is his own fault for the initial confusion since he *did* intrude upon the private party and also because, having had nothing to do with the group, they did not know his address, thus could not inform him of the change in plans. However, with his over-sensitive awareness, his acute consciousness, and his sense of shame over his "threadbare" clothes, he feels that he is the epitome of ridiculousness for having waited an entire hour. When the others fail to understand why he didn't order something to drink, he cannot tell them that he spent his last rouble to arrive in style for their sake — an hour early. Thus, only the Underground Man is aware of the absurdity of his situation. He feels that he is ludicrous, so takes offense at every statement; even when the others try to bring him into the conversation, he is painfully aware of what they are doing.

As a man of acute consciousness, the Underground Man cannot perform any direct action. Throughout this scene, he was aware that he should take his hat and simply leave. But this would be a positive action — one beyond the scope of a man of acute consciousness. Instead, he remained and became more and more absurd and created more and more disorder.

The absurdity of his position is represented by the fact that he stomped up and down the room while the others were talking. He was fully aware that his actions were an attempt to draw attention to himself, and therefore he became more incensed when "they paid no attention" to him. As he confessed in the preceding section, he has always needed to dominate or tyrannize any relationship; therefore, we now see that he cannot enter into any normal conversation or relationship with these people so does everything to dominate the situation. It is a vicious circle: when he is ignored, he becomes more and more determined to bring a climax to the relationship.

Section 5

Summary

On the way to the brothel, the Underground Man compared what happened at dinner with his dreams of the pope, Lake Como, and the grand ball. The memory of how he cringed before Simonov begging for the six roubles made him double up in shame. He was determined to make everything right, but realized that probably everything he tried would be futile; the others would never get on their knees and beg his pardon. Therefore, his only alternative was to slap Zverkov in the face. He pictured the scene in the drawing room of the brothel where Zverkov would be sitting with the prostitute, Olympia. The Underground Man then decided that not only Zverkov should be punished; if necessary, he would also pull Olympia's hair.

The Underground Man knew that Ferfichkin and Trudolyubov would probably beat him, but he didn't care so long as they were "forced at last to see the tragedy of it all." He also knew that the slap would lead to a duel and although he had no idea where he would find pistols and a second before sunrise, he would absolutely be forced to duel. In the midst of these wild imaginings, he recognized the disgusting absurdity of his plans to wreak revenge. It would probably be better simply to go home and forget it all. He knew this, yet he urged the driver on.

Another thought occurred to him: perhaps the others would have him arrested! He conceived of a prison sentence lasting fifteen years; then, released, he would find Zverkov, would offer him a pistol and moments before the duel he would forgive his enemy. As he thought of the grand gesture of nobility, the Underground Man was on the point of tears — when he suddenly remembered that the exact, same scene had been written about in Romantic literature. He knew now, for a certainity, that he would have to slap Zverkov.

When he arrived at the brothel, he found himself alone. Everyone else had retired. So, being spared the task of slapping Zverkov, the Underground Man felt extremely relieved, as though he "had been saved from death." Then he noticed he was no longer alone; a girl had entered. She was very quiet, very simply dressed, and very well developed. The Underground Man felt something loathsome stir within him and was also secretly pleased that he must seem repulsive to the prostitute.

Commentary

The Underground Man, who had just emerged from isolation after three months, felt as if he were embracing real life as he rushed from the Hotel de Paris to join his dinner companions at the brothel. How different this was from his dream world in which the pope abdicated and a ball was held on Lake Como in Rome. Yet the paradox is that his concept of the real world is as fantastic as his dream world. In other words, his belief that he will be able to make his four companions "go down on their knees and beg" for his friendship has no relationship to reality. It is as absurd as his dreams. For the Underground Man, stark reality is often converted into dream fantasy. This scene is concrete; it illustrates his contention in Part I: direct action is impossible for the man of acute consciousness. Note, for example, how utterly relieved he is when he discovers that Zverkov and the others have already gone, thus removing the need for him to slap Zverkov. His relief is as great as being "saved from death."

Furthermore, unlike the Underground Man, the man of action would not be troubled or plagued by the implications inherent in previous actions, but the Underground Man is so horrified over the disgraceful manner in which he begged for six roubles from Simonov and is so plagued by the remembrance of Simonov's reaction to him that he "tumbled into the sledge like a sack."

The image of the wet snow dominates the action of this section, reminding us again of the cold, frigid approach the Underground Man has toward life and toward human relations. His delight at the end of the section that the prostitute (he thinks) finds him repulsive underscores his own view of himself.

Throughout this section, we see that the Underground Man, while attempting to actually perform some definite act is constantly confronted by so many alternatives that any act becomes impossible. Even as he conceives of some fantastic plan in which he will return from fifteen years in prison in order to forgive his enemy, he must also admit that he is not even original in his dreams — that Romantic writers of the previous decade have already depicted such scenes. His awareness forces him to admit that he often tries to make his own life conform to that found in literature, and he is thus disgusted with his own commonplace thoughts.

Section 6

Summary

Suddenly at 2 A.M., a noise awakened the Underground Man out of his half-conscious state. When he was fully cognizant of his surroundings, he noticed two eyes observing him. He and the prostitute gazed at each other for awhile, then he asked her name. She told him that it was Liza and that she came from a town called Riga. She had been in the house of prostitution for only two weeks.

The Underground Man questioned her about other matters and then stopped as he suddenly remembered a scene he had observed the day before: a coffin of a prostitute was being dragged from the basement of a filthy, debris-littered house. He turned to Liza and told her what he had seen, recalling how the grave diggers had to stand in water and how the corpse was buried in an icy, watery grave. He then launched upon a discourse about death and the nature of dying. Liza merely listened to him, strangely, asserting at intervals that she was not concerned about dying. The Underground Man then painted a depressing picture of how a person could not last long leading a life of prostitution. He even suggested that in another situation, she could find a husband and live a happy, married life. Liza, however, knew that being married was not synonymous with being happy.

The Underground Man continued to torment Liza with his tales of the horrors of prostitution. He told her that she would never be able to buy her freedom and would get deeper and deeper in debt to the madam. He used himself as an example of how hideous prostitution is: they came together and said not one word and it was hours afterward before they spoke. This can hardly be considered love.

Liza then became involved in what the Underground Man was saying and he, in turn, began taking new pleasure in being able to completely control her responses and emotions. He continued talking about prostitution versus the advantages of family life. He confessed that he had no family and thus this was part of his problem. Liza countered by saying that some families "are glad to sell their daughters." The Underground Man then realized that Liza had been forced to enter prostitution. Only in a family where there is no love and no God could such a thing happen. He continued talking about family happiness and mutual love, courage, and respect, and when he had finished, Liza looked at him and told him that he spoke "like a book."

Commentary

The scene between the Underground Man and Liza is highly typical of Dostoevsky's writing. In its subject matter, in its character delineation, and in technique are the kernels of what one thinks of as "typical Dostoevsky." In terms of subject matter, a confrontation between an intelligent, troubled man of awareness and a simple, passive prostitute is the subject matter of his next major novel, *Crime and Punishment*. Throughout his writing, in fact, Dostoevsky created many climactic scenes involving people of opposite attributes who react against each other. Nowhere else in literature can we find such scenes of sustained mental and emotional agony between opposites. Yet the unlikelihood of such encounters are made realistically believable by Dostoevsky's genius in giving verisimilitude to his characters.

Liza is only one of many down-trodden, shy, passive, and oppressed women found throughout Dostoevsky's novels. Like Sonia in *Crime and Punishment*, Liza says very little other than to answer, cursorily, questions put to her by the Underground Man. Instead, her very passivity, her simple presence, evokes from the protagonist varying responses and reactions. But ultimately we feel that in Liza there is a greater love of humanity and a greater responsiveness to life than there ever can be in the Underground Man. Whereas his suffering carries an imposed artificiality about it, her suffering seems real and intrinsically sincere.

The sordid story which the Underground Man relates concerning the degradation inherent in a life of prostitution is a masterpiece of narration. The entire scene is permeated with images of wetness, of morbidity, and of decay. The depiction is a seemingly accurate one of the horrors of prostitution, but we must ask what was the Underground Man's motivation for describing such a depressing scene to Liza. Out of his own misery, one could easily maintain, he wanted others to suffer. Also, having just been rejected by his former schoolmates, he was determined to make another outcast feel rejected. In a sense, then, he desperately needed Liza, but was unable to respond to her except by being superior and tyrannical.

The Underground Man enjoys hearing his own voice, especially in view of his recent rejection, and he enjoys the sense of power he feels in giving his "sermon" and in totally captivating his listener. There is a certain degree of honest intent in his narration, but there is also hypocrisy since he knows he is partly showing off his superior rhetoric and knowledge. And he knows that he will never be able to fulfill the expectations he has created in Liza. But, becoming involved in his own rhetoric, he cannot stop and compulsively continues. In the same way that he was earlier driven to embrace humanity, now he cannot stay this impulse to talk and to tyrannize.

Section 7

Summary

The Underground Man continued to describe horrendous scenes of prostitution. He also told Liza that in another place, at another time, it would have been highly possible that he could have fallen in love with her and would even have considered it an honor to be betrothed to her. But here, in a house of prostitution, he has only to whistle and she must come to him whether she wishes to or not: her wishes are insignificant—only his are important.

Furthermore, to practice prostitution is not just to sell one's body, but also to sell one's soul. This is a more horrible loss because now she can never really fall in love with anyone. Even if she were allowed to have a lover, he would have to be of such a type—such a brute—that he would not be worth her love.

The Underground Man then reminded Liza that she was sacrificing her health and that when she was twenty-two, she would look thirty-five. Then she would begin moving from one house to another until she ended up in the worst possible house in Haymarket Square. To prove his point, he told about a prostitute who was once turned out in Haymarket and by 9 o'clock in the morning, she was already "drunk, dishevelled, half-naked, and covered with bruises." And, eight or ten years ago, this very wreck was exactly like Liza today. Many prostitutes, he continued, die of consumption—a strange disease because until the last, each victim thinks that she will recover. Instead, she is usually dumped in the "filthiest corner of the cellar, in the damp and darkness," so that her moans and cries will not disturb the customers.

All at once, the Underground Man realized that he had worked himself to such an emotional peak that it was difficult for him to continue. He also knew that he had so skillfully exercised his rhetoric that Liza was deeply disturbed. Never before had he witnessed such total despair. Liza lay on the bed, sobbing into her pillow, "clutching it in both hands. Her heart was being torn to pieces." The Underground Man tried to calm her but he could not stop her weeping until he found some matches and lit a candle. Only then did Liza begin to calm down. The Underground Man effusively asked her forgiveness then invited her to his address. She promised to come visit him.

Before he left, however, she ran to fetch something for him. It was a letter which a young medical student had written to her. A few days ago, at a dance where no one knew anything about her background, she had danced all night with this young man and, afterward, he had written this letter. It was in a respectful and sincere style and exposed his tender feelings for her. The Underground Man knew that she would keep this letter always; it was her treasure.

Commentary

The Underground Man continues to torment Liza with the reality of her deplorable condition, painting her situation in the bleakest, most horrible images he can conceive. This type of

scene foreshadows Dostoevsky's later writings in that Raskolnikov in *Crime and Punishment* also described to Sonia (a prostitute) the horrors of her profession and pointed out how she was
destroying her life. This type of scene is a favorite device of
Dostoevsky.

One of Dostoevsky's greatest attributes as a writer is the
manner in which he can depict scenes of degradation and expose
all the abject horror inherent in that situation without ever destroying the reality or verisimilitude of the situation. The Underground Man merely points out some of the degrading aspects of
prostitution – that men come to Liza only when they are drunk,
that they are later ashamed of their actions, that she must be a
slave to the man and come at his whistle, that she is destroying
not only her body but also her soul, and that in a few years when
her health begins to fail, she will be shifted from house to house
and will die of consumption in some forlorn, cold, dark cellar
only to be dumped into the first water-filled grave that is
available.

Whether or not Liza is aware of the truth of the Underground
Man's statements prior to this night is not as important as the fact
that after his description, she is earnestly desirous of escaping
the trap she is in. For she is not a prostitute by choice or desire;
she was sold into the trade by her parents and cannot escape
until her debts are paid off. But, being trapped as she is, the
Underground Man's speech serves only to torture her since there
is no possibility of escape.

The intensity of her desire to escape is seen in her revealing
the existence and contents of the letter from the smitten medical
student. This is her most prized possession. To show it to the
Underground Man affirms the power of his speech on her. The
irony of the situation, however, is that the letter shows that she
can evoke genuine feelings for love from others, whereas the
Underground Man is incapable of communicating with another
person. As the Underground Man leaves, Liza is left alone with
her prized treasure, but the Underground Man is also alone –
exhausted and bewildered and solitary, he must walk home
through the snow.

Summary

Walking home from Liza's, the Underground Man recognized a "loathsome truth," but he did not want to recognize it, so he tried to put it out of his mind. Later he was surprised at the sentimentality he expressed with Liza. He is aghast that he would give her his address. Too many thoughts have crowded his mind, so he decided to think of something more immediate: he had to redeem himself with Simonov for last night's behavior. And, in order to repay the money, he must go to his superior, Anton Antonich. After borrowing the money, he sat down and wrote Simonov a long letter blaming the wine, and lying further as he explained that he had had several drinks before the others arrived. Having finished the letter, he began to consider himself rather aristocratic and good-humored. Thus he tucked in the six roubles he had borrowed from Simonov, and then dismissed the entire episode.

He was not long at peace. He began to worry that Liza might show up at his lodgings. He was horrified that she should see the way he lived. Yesterday he was a hero to her, but what would he be after she saw the poverty he lived in? What was even worse, he would have to pretend again and "put on the dishonest, lying mask again." Even now, as he writes this confession more than fifteen years later, he says that he can still remember how Liza looked when he struck the match and saw her face. He is haunted by her pale, distorted features; and he is still more than a little impressed how a few words can suffice to completely alter a human life.

Days passed and every evening after 9 o'clock, he felt safer, surer that she would not come. Gradually he began to create scenes between himself and Liza. She would come and listen to him and fall in love with him and, finally, would — all trembling and sobbing — fling herself at his feet declaring her everlasting love for him. They would begin living together and perhaps go abroad. At the same time he was having these dreams, he

58

recognized that the dreams were vulgar. Furthermore, he knew that a prostitute would not be allowed to leave her house during the evening. But he was still frightened that someday she might actually appear at his door.

During these difficult days, his servant Apollon was very trying and rude. Apollon had been the bane of the Underground Man's existence for years, and he hated his servant, but could do nothing about it. He knew that Apollon looked down on him and despised him. And he had sometimes tried to withhold Apollon's seven roubles, which constituted his salary, until the servant would come and humbly request his wages. The plan had never worked; instead, he would come into the Underground Man's room and stand staring at him, then would reappear later and continue staring. The Underground Man broke under such treatment; he had never been successful at playing the master. He would scream and rail and curse his servant and one time he even demanded that Apollon send for the police. During this scene, when the Underground Man was screaming at his servant, Liza suddenly appeared in the entrance way. He rushed to his room, but Apollon followed and quietly announced the presence of the young woman.

Commentary

The mysterious "loathsome truth" that the Underground Man is reluctant to recognize is that he needs Liza and is, at the same time, frightened at the prospect of entering into a close relationship with another person. We know already that he can endure a friendship only if he can be a tyrant in that relationship. In reviewing his behavior on the night before, he is shocked at his sentimentality; he is horrified that Liza might actually visit him, and tries his best to dismiss the entire affair as though "it didn't matter." Paradoxically, it does matter—as evidenced by his extreme nervous apprehension.

To escape his haunting thoughts about Liza's impending visit, the Underground Man composes a letter to Simonov, including the six roubles he had borrowed. The letter is another of his attempts to escape facing the reality of his shameful behavior. He blames his actions on wine which he had not drunk and, after composing a letter filled with "aristocratic playfulness," he feels that the episode is closed.

He cannot, however, escape so easily from the tormenting thoughts about Liza. Knowing that he needs her and knowing that through his rhetoric that night he succeeded in impressing her as a man of distinction and compassion, he is horrified of her seeing that in actuality he is not compassionate but spiteful and tyrannical, and that he is not distinguished, but frightened and insecure. Furthermore, to rise again to such rhetorical heights would be too emotionally demanding. Liza's appearance would also involve him in a responsibility for which he is not prepared and which he is unable to cope with. As a person who lives underground, who lives in a world of dreams, the reality of actually meeting Liza again would be almost more than a man of acute consciousness could endure. It is for him much easier to create in his dreams imaginary scenes and situations involving the two of them than it would be to meet her again face to face.

Apollon, his servant, functions as his main distraction to keep his mind off Liza's possible visit. The fact that he does become involved in such an outrageously ridiculous argument with his servant is more proof of how troubled he is. And the final irony is that in the midst of the most absurd behavior, Liza actually does arrive and witnesses the Underground Man's wild ravings.

Section 9

Summary

Standing before Liza completely confused and embarrassed by his ragged dressing gown and his obvious poverty, the Underground Man finally asked her to sit down. Then he immediately began to justify and defend his poverty, asserting that he was an honorable man, in spite of his poverty. Even though Liza refused his offer for tea, he ran out of the room to ask Apollon to run to the restaurant and fetch some tea and something to eat. For a while, Apollon ignored both the seven roubles salary, which the Underground Man had just given him, and also his master's presence. But, after a bit, he agreed to go on the errand.

Returning to his room, the Underground Man started screaming about the necessity to kill Apollon who had become such a torturer to him. Then he burst into hysterics and even though his attack was a genuine one, he delighted in making it sound even worse. Liza brought him water and, at the same moment, Apollon arrived with the tea.

Alone with Liza, the Underground Man gave her some tea and decided that he would not speak to her, and for five minutes there was total silence. During this time, the Underground Man was aware of the "disgusting meanness of [his] spiteful stupidity." When Liza hesitantly announced that she wanted to escape from her employment, the Underground Man allowed another five minutes to pass without saying a word. And even though his heart ached for Liza, "something hideous suddenly stifled all compassion" in him.

After Liza volunteered to leave, the Underground Man broke his silence and began a hysterical attack on the girl, demanding to know why she came. He told her that he was laughing at her that night in the brothel. He explained that he had been insulted just before he arrived and so he had wanted to insult someone in return. He spoke very fast, knowing that Liza would not understand all of it, but he also knew that she would get the general gist of it.

He ridiculed Liza for allowing him to treat her the way he did that night. All he wanted was power over her, and he used sentimental talk to gain this power. He then confessed that he was horrified by the thought that she would actually come to his apartment and see him in a "wretched, torn dressing-gown, beggarly, loathsome." He can never forgive her for having seen him this way and for having been present during his hysterics.

Suddenly, when he stopped, he observed that Liza had understood much more than he thought she was capable of. She realized that the Underground Man was dreadfully unhappy. She jumped up from her chair, rushed to him and embraced him. The Underground Man then collapsed into "genuine hysterics" which lasted at least fifteen minutes. But even in the midst of these hysterics, lying face down on the sofa, he was fully conscious that the hysterics could not last forever and that he must soon face Liza again. Suddenly he hated her because she now had mastery over him. Yet, while hating her, he was also drawn to her. She merely looked at him and embraced him.

Commentary

This section fully illustrates the spite and the spiritual void of the Underground Man. His inability to love or communicate with another person renders him a pathetic case. Such a man whose intellect is so powerful that he cannot function as a human being becomes the epitome of moral bankruptcy. Dostoevsky continued to use this intellectual type in later novels. For example, Raskolnikov in *Crime and Punishment* and Ivan in *The Brothers Karamazov* are both characters who commit horrible acts because they are dominated by intellect rather than human compassion. The Underground Man is an early study of this type.

This section also offers the concluding proof that the Underground Man cannot love because of his desire to dominate and tyrannize the other person — "I cannot get on without domineering and tyrannizing over someone." As seen in later Dostoevsky characters, to love and to commune with another person involves revealing one's weaknesses. The Underground Man has an inordinate fear of being ridiculed because of his weaknesses. He is horrified that Liza sees him in ragged clothes, in a poor apartment, and in a ridiculous argument with his servant. "I stood before her crushed, crest-fallen, revoltingly confused." His immediate attempt to justify his poverty reveals his absurdity in that there should be, in reality, no need to justify oneself before a prostitute.

That the Underground Man needs an emotional outlet is illustrated by the hysterics which he engages in and which he even exaggerates. Yet, his duality forces him to hate Liza because she has witnessed this weakness in himself. The Underground Man spoke of contradictory impulses inhabiting the same person in Part I, and now we see his own contradictory nature in action. For example, his own compulsive desire to be punished is partly the rationale behind his spiteful behavior toward Liza.

The Underground Man's fear of Liza is partly due to his realization that she is more in touch with basic humanity than he is. In this scene, she intuitively responds to his agony in a compassionate manner which is more genuine and sincere than all his emotions. Her simple love and human warmth far exceed his intellectuality. His ambiguous reaction toward her— "How I hated her and how I was drawn to her"—contrasts to her simple, warm, and compassionate response to him.

Section 10

Summary

Fifteen minutes later, the Underground Man peeked through a screen to see what Liza was doing. She was on the floor with her head leaning against the bed. The Underground Man was pleased that she had been so thoroughly insulted. Finally, he had made her understand that his outburst of passion was merely a method of getting revenge.

For the Underground Man, love means tyrannizing and dominating a person and once he has subjugated the person, he no longer loves that person. Instead, by then he hates the person. But, as he peeks at Liza, he does not overtly hate her as much as he is simply oppressed by her presence. He wanted her to disappear so that he could return to the peace of his underground world. Real life is so oppressive that he could hardly breathe.

A few minutes later when she emerged and told him goodbye, he seized her hand, forced something into it, and dashed away to another part of the room. He confesses to us that he stuffed money into her hand—out of spite. The act was not an impulse from the heart; it was conceived in his evil brain. Almost immediately he rushed to the door to catch her before she disappeared but there was no answer to his calls.

Returning to his room, he wandered aimlessly about until he noticed a crumpled five-rouble note lying on the table. It had to be the same note he had tried to force on Liza. Being an egotist, he was not able to imagine doing her such a thing. Immediately, he flung on his clothes, rushed out into the streets, but was unable to find her.

He then began to question why he was searching for her so frantically. His answer was that he wanted to "fall down before her, to sob with remorse, to kiss her feet to entreat her forgiveness!" He knew that if he did not find her, he would begin to hate her the next day. Perhaps it would be best for her to keep her resentment of the insult. He has never seen Liza again.

Even now, after so many years, this is still an evil memory. And, in writing these notes, he has felt shame, partly because these scribblings aren't literature but a type of self-punishment. Why should anyone want to read about a man who has ruined his life by spite, through divorce from reality, and through moral disintegration? A novel needs a hero, and he admits that he is an anti-hero. Furthermore, the public itself is afraid to read of real life and prefers stories and novels. Yet by being honest, the Underground Man contends that he has faced life more acutely than do his readers.

Commentary

This final section shows concisely how thoroughly spiteful the Underground Man is. After this section, we wonder what qualities are left him. He still possesses his intellectual honesty and there is a quality of sincerity in his narration, especially since few people would have the courage to admit to performing such spiteful, horrible acts. But sincerity in such a hateful person is a questionable quality.

The Underground Man's original purpose in narrating this second part was to purge himself of all guilt feelings concerning his relations with Liza. He thought that by confessing his disgraceful behavior that he would purify himself. Instead, however, he now understands that he can only enter into a relationship by "tyrannizing and showing [his] moral superiority." Thus this idea of his inability to enter into a relationship without dominating that relationship has become the central theme of Part II.

In Section 9, the Underground Man comes to realize that he cannot achieve a real domination over Liza. Through her simple and innocent approach to life, she possesses a "moral superiority" to the Underground Man simply because she intuitively understands and responds to his agonized suffering and gives herself freely to him out of human compassion. There was no subtle intellectualizing connected with her actions. She responded to the Underground Man as a human being who was in distress and who needed affection. This basic response makes her morally superior.

If, therefore, the Underground Man cannot dominate her by "moral superiority," there is only one course open to him: he must spitefully subjugate her and force her to see that he was using her and ridiculing her and that his every act, even his screaming hysterics, were intentionally dramatic enough to create an effect.

To subjugate her completely, he forces a five-rouble note into her hand, an act performed out of spite to remind Liza that she is nothing but a prostitute. He admits that the act "was not an impulse from the heart, but came from [his] evil brain." This contrasts to Liza's impulse earlier when she "warmly and rapturously embraced" the Underground Man. Her action was that of responding compassionately; his was malicious spite.

The Underground Man, however, still fails to subjugate Liza since she, quietly and unknown to the Underground Man, leaves the five-rouble note on the table. This act reaffirms her basic goodness and reveals the Underground Man as a spiteful and malicious creature.

The final conclusion of the Underground Man is that even though he has the qualities of the anti-hero, he is no more divorced from life than anyone else. He, at least, has faced life more realistically than most, because he has dared look at the unpleasant side of his own life. Thus, the *Notes from Underground*, as Dostoevsky himself points out, ends with a paradoxical twist.

CHARACTER ANALYSES

THE UNDERGROUND MAN

The Underground Man is a spiteful man whose ideas we may agree with and admire, but whose actions we hate and deplore. These contradictory reactions to him suggest something of the duality of his own nature. For example, he resents being insulted and yet consciously places himself in a position where he cannot avoid being insulted. Throughout Part I, we are exposed only to the Underground Man's ideas; they are the thoughts and conclusions of an intelligent man, no matter of what age or century. In contrast, Part II depicts the Underground Man's actions in relationship to other people, and they are spiteful and deplorable acts.

To return to Part I, we admire a man who refuses to accept scientific rationalism when an acceptance involves the destruction of man's individuality; we agree with him that human freedom — that is, the freedom to choose one's own way of life regardless of the consequences — is more important than the life of a robot. We accept his idea that only the individual can choose what is to his best advantage. We acknowledge the validity of his view that while science has improved living conditions, it has not changed the basic desires of man; and we are aware that the human personality is composed of both rational and irrational desires. Furthermore, we enjoy and concur in his criticism of scientific utopias, of progress, of utilitarianism, and of other assumptions made by modern civilization. As humanists, we are in accord with almost every proposition he advocates in Part I, even though he argues them in a spiteful manner.

By contrast, in Part II, we are repulsed by almost every action undertaken by the Underground Man. As an intellectual advocate against scientific rationalism, he was a voice arguing in a void and we could concentrate on the validity of the arguments without confronting directly the warped and distorted personality of the speaker. However, in Part II, we see directly his failure to function as a human being in his own society.

The Underground Man told us in Part I that, in his dreams, he could take an unintentional slight and magnify it into an outrageous insult. In Part II, we see that his fragmented personality will allow him to experience things only vicariously; contact with real life is impossible because of his extreme fear of reality.

Ultimately, his fear of being ridiculed, rejected, or scorned causes him to demand complete domination and even tyranny over any friend or any person in any relationship. He could be friends with Zverkov only if he can dominate Zverkov, an impossible task. This need to tyrannize others results from feelings of inadequacy caused by his over-refined sensibility and his over-acute intellectual awareness. The Underground Man's intentional attempts to subjugate Liza show his spiteful, twisted, despicable nature.

Finally, even though we agree with his ideas in Part I, the final view of this refugee from humanity is that of a twisted deranged soul who deserves no compassion and who should exist in an underground hole.

LIZA

Liza is one of a long string of quiet, meek, passive, downtrodden women who inhabit Dostoevsky's novels. Through her, the Underground Man has the possibility of coming into touch with real humanity, but being unable to escape from his own ego, he needlessly and viciously insults Liza. However, she remains the morally superior person.

Through her own sufferings, which are real (instead of imagined, like the Underground Man's), she has developed a compassionate nature and an ability to love. We are deeply touched because the Underground Man is so callous in his feelings. Her life is one of simple expediency — she was sold into prostitution and feels the degradation and shame of her profession. Her feelings are intensified as a result of the Underground Man's depiction of the horrors of such a life. Yet, she seems to possess a simple faith and honesty that she can escape, that she won't be doomed to this type of life forever.

Even though Liza cannot "talk like a book," like the Underground Man, and even though she is simple and uneducated, she nevertheless possesses qualities which Dostoevsky considers more important than intellect or education. She is still in touch with basic humanity, she can understand the meaning of suffering, she can communicate with others, and even though the Underground Man has insulted and humiliated her, she forgives him because she intuitively perceives his torment and unhappy existence. Therefore, her simplicity and understanding, her sympathy and compassion place her as a morally superior person, in spite of her profession.

ZVERKOV

In Part I, the Underground Man spoke of the "man of direct action" as being diametrically opposite to the "man of acute consciousness." We have seen that the Underground Man is so hyper-conscious that he must examine every action so thoroughly that, as a result, he is rendered inactive. His acute consciousness prevents him from ever accomplishing anything. Zverkov is the complete opposite of the Underground Man. Zverkov functions in society with success, he has a coterie of acquaintances (maybe even friends), and he is admired by many; he is the man of action. By the standards set up by the Underground Man (that is, the man of action is of necessity stupid), Zverkov can perform any action without being hindered by introspection, but at the same time, he probably has little or no true understanding of the action he commits.

REVIEW QUESTIONS

1. What significant correlations are there between Parts I and II?

2. What are the reasons for the title of Part II, "A Propos of the Wet Snow"?

3. What various meanings can be attached to the title?

4. Liza says very little and yet emerges as the strongest person in Part II. How does Dostoevsky accomplish this?

5. How effective would the novel be if Parts I and II were reversed?

6. What are the Underground Man's objections to scientific progress? Are these same objections valid today?

7. Using the Underground Man as an example, offer a definition of the "anti-hero."

8. What is gained dramatically by having the Underground Man address an imaginary audience in Part I?

9. Part II is narrated theoretically to purge the Underground Man of his guilt feelings. Do you think that the narration will have a cathartic effect?

10. If you have read other novels by Dostoevsky, choose one idea from *Notes from Underground* and relate its development in the later novel.

SELECTED BIBLIOGRAPHY

Books

BERDYAEV, NICHOLAS. *Dostoevsky: An Interpretation.* New York: Meridian, 1957.

CARR, EDWARD HALLET. *Dostoevsky, 1821-1881: A New Biography.* New York: Macmillan, 1949.

IVANOV, VYACHESLAV. *Freedom and the Tragic Life: A Study in Dostoevsky.* New York: Noonday, 1957.

MAGARSHACK, DAVID. *Dostoevsky.* New York: Harcourt, 1963.

TROYAT, HENRI. *Firebrand: The Life of Dostoevsky.* New York: Roy Publishers, 1946.

WELLEK, RENE (ed.). *Dostoevsky: A Collection of Critical Essays.* New York: Prentice Hall, 1962.

Essays

FAGIN, N. B. "Dostoevsky's Underground Man Takes Over." *Antioch Review,* XIII (Spring 1953), 23-32.

MATLAW, RALPH E. "Structure and Integration in *Notes from Underground.*" *PMLA,* LXXIII (March, 1958), 101-09.

NEIDER, CHARLES. "Introduction." *Short Novels of the Masters* New York: Rinehart, 1948.

TRASCHEN, I. "Dostoevsky's *Notes from Underground.*" *Accent,* XVI (Autumn 1956), 255-64.

NOTES

NOTES

NOTES

ONE DAY IN THE LIFE OF IVAN DENISOVICH

NOTES

including
- *Life and Background of the Author*
- *The GULAG System*
- *Article 58*
- *Brief Plot Synopsis*
- *List of Characters*
- *Preface to the Original Edition*
- *Critical Commentaries*
- *Critical Essays*
- *Questions for Review*
- *Suggested Theme Topics*
- *Selected Bibliography*

by
Franz G. Blaha, Ph.D.
Professor of English
University of Nebraska

Cliffs Notes

INCORPORATED

LINCOLN, NEBRASKA 68501

Editor

Gary Carey, M.A.
University of Colorado

Consulting Editor

James L. Roberts, Ph.D.
Department of English
University of Nebraska

ISBN 0-8220-0960-9
© Copyright 1986
by
C. K. Hillegass
All Rights Reserved
Printed in U.S.A.

1990 Printing

Cliffs Notes, Inc.   Lincoln, Nebraska

CONTENTS

CRITICAL ESSAYS

QUESTIONS FOR REVIEW

SUGGESTED THEME TOPICS

SELECTED BIBLIOGRAPHY

ONE DAY IN THE LIFE OF IVAN DENISOVICH

Notes

LIFE AND BACKGROUND OF THE AUTHOR

Alexander Isayevich Solzhenitsyn was born in Kislovodsk, a small resort town in the Caucasus mountain range on December 11, 1918, six months after the death of his father in a hunting accident. Shortly afterward, Solzhenitsyn's mother moved to Rostov-on-Don, a city some 600 miles south of Moscow. Life was extremely difficult there; the young mother and son had to live in thatched huts and, at one time, even in a stable.

Solzhenitsyn attended school there, and in 1938, he entered Rostov University as a student of mathematics and physics. He claims that he chose these fields of study only because of the financial security which they would provide him, but that even at this time, literature was the greatest attraction in his life, a fact that was recognized by his teachers. Thus, he enrolled in a correspondence course in literature from the University of Moscow and even tried to get a role on stage as an actor while pursuing his science studies.

Following his marriage in 1940 and his graduation in 1941, he joined the Red Army immediately after Nazi Germany's invasion of Russia and became an artillery officer. He was promoted to captain in the Battle of Leningrad, but was arrested in February of 1945 for veiled but unmistakable criticism of Stalin in some letters to a friend, in which he alluded to the dictator as "Whiskers," the same allusion used in *One Day in the Life of Ivan Denisovich.*

When he was only twenty-seven, Solzhenitsyn was thrown into prison because of "counterrevolutionary activity" and was sentenced to eight years of forced labor and exile by one of Stalin's infamous *troikas,* courts consisting of three military judges. After first serving in a correctional labor camp and then in a prison research institute near Moscow, the author was finally sent to a special camp in the mining region of Kazakhstan, because, as he claims, he would not make moral compromises with the secret police. It was there, in Siberia, that he conceived of the idea of writing *One Day in the Life of Ivan Denisovich;* like the hero of the novel, Solzhenitsyn had to wear his prison number stamped on the areas of the forehead of his cap, as well as on the heart, the knees, and the back of his uniform.

After serving out his complete eight-year sentence, plus one month, and having had a cancer operation, which he miraculously survived, Solzhenitsyn was released but was forced to live in Siberia, where he found a position as a high school mathematics teacher.

In 1957, Solzhenitsyn was permitted to return to European Russia in connection with a decree of the Twentieth Congress of the Russian Communist Party. He settled down in Ryazan, some 100 miles south-east of Moscow, and continued to teach physics and mathematics until the publication of *One Day in the Life of Ivan Denisovich* in the November 1962 issue of the literary magazine *Novy Mir (New World)*. The novel catapulted him to national and international fame.

The reason for the Soviet regime's acquiescence to the publication of *One Day* was Premier Nikita Khrushchev's attempt to expose some of the horrors of Stalin's reign of terror in order to assert himself in the power struggle following the dictator's death. It was during this brief period of the so-called Khrushchev "thaw" that Solzhenitsyn was allowed to publish his works in the Soviet Union.

The end of 1964 marked the end of the de-Stalinization efforts of Khrushchev, and it also signaled the end of Solzhenitsyn's being officially tolerated. The praise for *One Day* and for his other popular short prose piece, "Matryona's Home," soon turned to criticism and to threats. His candidacy for the Lenin Prize, the most prestigious literary award in the USSR, was defeated, and after he had managed to smuggle a manuscript of his novel *The First Circle* out of the country, his private papers were confiscated in 1965 by the secret police. Subsequently, after much controversy and many debates inside the Soviet Union and in the West, Solzhenitsyn was expelled from the Union of Soviet Writers – thus, in practice, withdrawing all publication privileges from him and forcing him to publish his work abroad by smuggling the manuscripts out of the country. *The First Circle, Cancer Ward, August 1914,* and *The Gulag Archipelago* were published in this fashion.

In 1971, Solzhenitsyn was awarded the Nobel Prize for Literature, but he decided not to go to the award ceremony in Stockholm for fear of not being allowed back into the Soviet Union. While the international fame of having won the Nobel Prize probably saved him from being arrested and imprisoned again, his continued refusal to compromise with the political system, and his steady criticism of his own and some fellow dissidents' treatment, finally led to his forcible deportation to West Germany on February 13, 1974.

Since this time, Solzhenitsyn has made his home in the West, changing his permanent domicile frequently. He continues to criticize the Soviet regime, but he is convinced that any change in Russia will come from within, gradually brought about by the triumph of the inherent goodness of the Russian people, rather than by a violent overthrow of the government. The author has been increasingly critical of the West for not taking a stronger political, moral, and military stance against Soviet international aggression. In addition, he is a vociferous opponent of "detente," since he believes that it will weaken the Russian people's resolve to resist and subvert the Communist regime.

THE GULAG SYSTEM

One Day in the Life of Ivan Denisovich takes place in a "special" camp run by the Chief Administration of Corrective Labor Camps and Settlements, better known by the Russian acronym: GULAG. The new rulers of Russia after the violent overthrow of the Czars dealt very harshly with their former, as well as with their new, political adversaries, and, rather than sending their enemies to prison, they began sentencing offenders to "corrective labor" soon after the revolution of 1917. In the following years, concentration camps were built and were combined with corrective labor camps in Siberia, under the administration of the secret police. It is estimated that by 1929, there were already more than 1 million prisoners in these camps, mainly for political reasons.

The establishment of the Five-Year Plans for the economic reconstruction of the Soviet Union created heavy demands for workers to achieve this drive toward changing the Soviet Union from an essentially agricultural society to an industrial society, and it was difficult to find willing and qualified workers for the construction of canals, railroads, highways, and large industrial centers. Thus, from 1929 on, the Soviet rulers began to depend more and more on forced labor. There were hardly any traditional jail terms handed out any longer; instead, criminals and political enemies were sent to labor camps. These sentences, initially for three-year terms, were based mainly on convictions for violations of the infamous Article 58 of the 1926 Criminal Code (see the essay on Article 58).

The first large wave of forced laborers consisted mainly of *kulaks,* disowned farmers who had resisted collectivization, but soon religious believers of all denominations, members of minority groups and nations, socialists, and engineers (who failed to perform their assigned industrial tasks and were classified as industrial saboteurs) followed them to the camps. It is estimated that in 1940, over 13,000,000 (thirteen million) people slaved in these forced labor camps. In 1937, when many Russians had believed that an amnesty would be declared to celebrate the twentieth anniversary of the Revolution, Stalin instead increased the length of the sentences from ten years to fifteen and twenty years, a procedure which was repeated for the thirtieth anniversary of the Revolution, when the twenty-five-year sentences became standard, and ten-year terms were reserved for juveniles.

During World War II, many soldiers believed to be responsible for the initial Red Army defeats were sent to these camps – as were soldiers like Ivan Denisovich, who had allowed himself to be taken prisoner, and men like Solzhenitsyn who had made critical remarks about Stalin or the Communist Party, and many civilians who had lived "in contact with" the enemy during the Nazi occupation. After the war, they were joined by soldiers who had had contact with the Allies, now the enemy. Captain Buynovsky, whose crime was that he had been assigned as a liaison officer to the British Navy and had received a commendation for his services, is one such example in *One Day in the Life of Ivan Denisovich.* In addition, members of former independent countries like Latvia, Lithuania, and the Ukraine, all of whom were now satellite republics of the USSR, as well as other ethnic and national minorities, were interned in these labor camps in large numbers.

Solzhenitsyn describes the history, the methods, and the structure of these forced labor camps in great detail in his long, multi-volume work, *The Gulag Archipelago.* While Article 58 was repealed in 1958 in the course of a complete revision of the Penal Code, Solzhenitsyn maintains that the GULAG still exists and has, with the addition of the sentences to psychiatric clinics, grown even more vicious.

ARTICLE 58

Article 58, which deals with what are described as counterrevolutionary crimes, is included in the part of the Criminal Code which deals with crimes against the state; offenders of this article are not considered "political" offenders, however. (These are dealt with in another section of the Code.) There are fourteen sub-sections, all of them formulated so broadly that practically any action (or even non-action) could be, and was, interpreted as "a crime against the state."

Section 1: deals with any act designed to overthrow, undermine, or weaken the authority of the power of the state. This was applied to workers, even in prison camps, who were too sick or too weak to meet their quotas; it also covers Ivan Denisovich's "crime" of allowing himself to be taken prisoner. It should be noted that this particular section not only included proven acts of "treason," but, by way of another article of the Code, also included "intent to commit treason."

Section 2: covers armed rebellion, especially with the aim of forcibly separating any part or territory from the USSR. This was broadly applied to all members of annexed nations, such as the Ukraine, Lithuania, Estonia, and Latvia.

Section 3: assistance, rendered by any means whatever, to a foreign state at war with the USSR. This made it possible to send to a labor camp virtually any Russian who had lived in occupied territory during World War II.

Section 4: rendering assistance to the international bourgeoisie. This sent thousands of Russians to the camp who had left the country long before the Criminal Code was passed and who were captured by the Red Army or turned over to it by the Allies upon request.

Section 5: inciting a foreign state to intervene in the affairs of the USSR.

Section 6: espionage. This was interpreted so broadly that it included not only proven acts of transmitting information to enemies of the state, but also included "suspicion of espionage," "unproven espionage," and "contacts leading to suspicion of espionage." Any person who knew or had recently talked to a person accused of espionage could be arrested under the provisions of this sub-section.

Section 7: subversion of industry, transportation, trade, monetary exchange or the credit system. Failure to meet agricultural quotas, allowing machines to break down, and allowing weeds to grow too high were also crimes punished under this section.

Section 8: terrorist acts. This included hitting a party member or a policeman and was also broadened by "threat of" or "expression of intent."

Section 9: sabotage—that is, the destruction of state property.

Section 10: This was the most often and most broadly used section of Article 58. It covers "propaganda or agitation containing an appeal to overthrow, undermine, or weaken the Soviet regime, or to commit individual counterrevolutionary crimes, and also the distribution, the preparation, or the conservation of literature of this nature." Such propaganda and agitation included not only the printing and dissemination of subversive material, but also conversations between friends, letters, and private diaries. Solzhenitsyn's letter to his friend about the "Whiskered One" was such "subversion."

Section 11: This section covered and aggravated any of the previous activities when they were found to have been committed not by individuals, but by "organizations." The minimum number for an organization was two people, as evidenced by the exchange of letters between Solzhenitsyn and his friend. Both were sentenced under Section 11.

Section 12: failure to report reliable knowledge of preparations for, or commission of, a counterrevolutionary crime. Denunciation was elevated to a duty to the state.

Section 13: crimes committed in the service of the Czarist regime, particularly as a member of the Czarist secret police.

Section 14: counterrevolutionary sabotage—that is, deliberate nonfulfillment by anyone of duties laid down, or the willfully careless execution of those duties with a view to weakening the authority and functioning of the state. Many prisoners received second and third terms under this provision.

Virtually all the inmates of the "special" camp described in *One Day in the Life of Ivan Denisovich* have been sent there because of a violation of some provision of Article 58. It is obvious that even the most innocent word or action could have been and, when convenient, was found to be a "counterrevolutionary crime," or, as Solzhenitsyn puts it, "Wherever the law is, crime can be found."

BRIEF PLOT SYNOPSIS

One Day in the Life of Ivan Denisovich describes the daily routine – from reveille at 5 A.M. to lights out at 10 P.M. – in a "special" prison camp in Siberia. The protagonist of the novel is Ivan Denisovich Shukhov, a former carpenter, who has been in several of these camps for the past eight years, serving a ten-year term for "treason."

The novel – one could better call it a short novel or a novella – narrates the events of this day without chapter divisions, recording Ivan's progress through the eyes of an omniscient, third-person narrator who sometimes places himself into the protagonist's mind, recording his thoughts and feelings as Ivan himself would express them (see the chapter on "Style and Narrative Perspective").

When the prisoners are awakened by the sound of a hammer clanging against a steel rail, Ivan does not get up immediately, as is his usual practice. Instead, because he feels feverish, he stays in bed, thinking about the possibility of getting on the sick list. A guard pretends to take him to the punishment cells for his tardiness, but he really only wants Ivan to mop the floor of the guardroom.

After performing this task rather superficially, Ivan has a meager breakfast, and then he goes to the camp hospital, where a young poet-medic checks his temperature and then sends him to work. After picking up his bread ration in his barracks and hiding half of it in a hole in his mattress, Ivan joins the rest of the prisoners for the daily roll call and the frisking, which precedes their march to the worksite.

Ivan's "gang" has been assigned to continue building a power plant, and at the heavily guarded construction site, the prisoners try to find a warm place while the gang bosses negotiate the daily work assignment and the work quota which will determine their food rations. Ivan and his work brigade will lay bricks on the second story of the plant after they prepare the tools and the mortar. This is a job that will fill up the hours and the minutes until their noon break.

During lunch, Ivan is able to trick the kitchen staff into giving his gang two extra bowls of mush, one of which he is allowed to keep for himself. He also picks up a piece of steel which he thinks might be useful later on, and he succeeds in buying himself a cigarette.

After the noon break, Ivan becomes so involved in his task as a bricklayer that he loses track of time and eventually he delays the return of the whole prison detachment because of his feverish perfectionism. After the march back to the camp, the prisoners line up for the regulation body search before reentering the camp. Ivan discovers that he is still carrying the piece of steel he found, which, if discovered by the guards, could lead to severe punishment, possibly death. He panics, momentarily, but once again, he is lucky. He manages to smuggle the piece of steel past the guards.

Later, in return for standing in line for one of his wealthier fellow prisoners, one who has received a food package from home, Ivan is given the man's evening meal ration. After dinner, Ivan is able to buy some good tobacco in another barracks, and he is even lucky enough to receive additional food for guarding a gang member's food parcel during the evening check.

After evening inspection is over, Ivan returns to his bunk and discusses God and the efficacy of prayer with Alyosha, a Baptist prisoner with whom he also shares some of his unexpected "wealth." After a second inspection and roll call, Ivan begins to fall asleep, feeling "almost happy" because of all the "good fortune" which has befallen him during this day.

LIST OF CHARACTERS

MAJOR CHARACTERS

Ivan Denisovich Shukhov

Prisoner S-854, who is the protagonist and focal point of the novel. He has been sentenced to ten years of hard labor and has spent the past eight years in a number of prison labor camps. Given above is his full name, which consists of his first name (Ivan), his patronymic (Denisovich = son of Denisov), and his last name (Shukhov). His last name is reserved for use by the bureaucracy, and in the novel, only the prison authorities apply it to the main character. Personal acquaintances would use the first name, plus the patronymic (Ivan Denisovich), as the title of the book suggests, and very good friends might use the first name, or a diminutive of it – that is, Ivan or Vanya.

Tyurin

The boss of Ivan's "gang," or work brigade. A big, tough man who has already spent nineteen years in prison camps and who knows all the rules and all the ruses. He manages to get the best quotas and work assignments for his men. He began to take an interest in Ivan during their days in the camp at Ust-Izhma. Tyurin is not afraid to stand up to Der, the foreman.

Alyosha the Baptist

A mild-mannered prisoner in Ivan's gang who has been sent to the camp for his religious beliefs. He considers his prison term a blessing because it affords him time to pray and to think about his soul. His religiously oriented code of ethics contrasts with Ivan's existential code of behavior.

Captain Buynovsky

Prisoner S-311 has been in the camp only three months and still has much to learn if he is to survive. Sentenced to twenty-five years of hard labor for illegal contacts with the enemy, he is, nevertheless, a faithful Communist and naively believes in Soviet law.

Caesar Markovich

A rich prisoner and a former film director whose packages provide the work gang with a vital means of bribing themselves into better work assignments. He is an intellectual who feels no common bond between himself and his fellow inmates.

Prisoner Y-81

An anonymous prisoner whom Ivan admires because of his dignified, stoic behavior; he serves as a model for the existential behavioral code which Ivan is trying to live by.

Fetyukov

Once a supervisor in an office, he has chosen scrounging (scavenging) as his method for best surviving the work camps. Ivan considers Fetyukov's behavior debasing and counterproductive in the long-term struggle for survival.

Kuzyomin

Ivan's first gang boss in 1943. He took it upon himself to teach Ivan the methods necessary to survive his ten-year sentence by formulating his "Law of the Jungle."

MINOR CHARACTERS

Pavlo

The assistant gang boss who carries out Tyurin's orders in an impartial and impersonal way.

Ivan Kilgas

A Latvian bricklayer in Ivan's gang; a good worker who respects Ivan for his work ethic. He looks healthy and well-fed since he gets two packages a month from home.

Gopchik

A young prisoner from the Ukraine in whom Ivan takes a fatherly interest.

The Two Estonians

Two prisoners strongly bonded by their common fate as members of an annexed nation. They share everything equally and are inseparable.

Senka Klevshin

A deaf member of Ivan's gang who was an inmate in the Nazi concentration camp at Buchenwald; he led an underground movement there and was cruelly tortured. On his return to Russia, he was sentenced to hard labor for "contacts with the enemy"—in other words: treason.

Nikolay Semyonovich Vdovushkin

The young medic in the prison hospital without any background or experience in medicine. He has been chosen for this task by the prison doctor who fancies himself a patron of the arts and wants to give the young poet "a chance to write." Vdovushkin is generally self-centered and has little sympathy for his fellow prisoners.

Stepan Grigoryevich

The new prison doctor who has established bureaucratic methods for determining who is sick and who is healthy. He believes in work as the best medicine for sick prisoners. Only two prisoners per day are allowed to be ill.

Der (Prisoner B-731)

The sadistic foreman at the construction site. He is reputed to have once worked in a high post in Moscow and is now trying to rise to the position of an engineer in the camp. Without any knowledge of bricklaying, he criticizes Ivan's conscientious work.

Lieutenant Volkovoy

The officer in charge of prison discipline. He has only recently stopped lashing prisoners with his whip. His name is derived from the Russian word for "wolf." He forces the prisoners to give up extra articles of clothing before they march to the construction site in sub-freezing weather.

The Thin Tartar

A cruel prison guard.

Big Ivan

An easygoing, compassionate guard.

Clubfoot

A mess-hall orderly; an "invalid" criminal.

Shkuropatenko

Prisoner B-219; a worksite guard.

It should be mentioned that, contrary to the conventional treatment in prison fiction or concentration camp fiction, the Camp Commandant is mentioned only briefly. He never makes a personal appearance.

PREFACE TO THE ORIGINAL EDITION

One Day in the Life of Ivan Denisovich had been completed in manuscript form in 1958, but Solzhenitsyn did not submit it for publication until 1961, when Nikita Khrushchev's continued policy of "de-Stalinization" gave the author some hope that the political climate was right for getting his short work printed. He sent the novel to Alexander Tvardovsky, the editor-in-chief of the influential literary magazine *Novy Mir*, who made the bold decision to bypass the official Soviet censorship authorities and to submit the work directly to Premier Khrushchev. This astute politician immediately recognized the potential propaganda value which the novel could provide for his de-Stalinization policies and had twenty copies of the work sent to the members of the Politburo of the Communist Party.

Khrushchev later claimed that it was his personal decision – against some so-called "opposition" in the Politburo – to let *Novy Mir* proceed with the publication of the novel. Thus, *One Day in the Life of Ivan Denisovich* was published in the literary journal on November 21, 1962, in an edition of 100,000 copies. It created a literary sensation and sold out on the first day, as did a second printing a short time later.

In spite of the limited scope and the relative simplicity of the novel, Khrushchev – through the persona of Tvardovsky – did not want to leave any reader in doubt about the intention and meaning of the work, and so the editor of *Novy Mir* added a preface to the first edition, entitled "Instead of a Foreword," which has been reprinted in almost all editions of the novel.

Tvardovsky explains that the topic of *One Day in the Life of Ivan Denisovich* is unusual in Soviet literature because it describes the "unhealthy phenomena" of Stalin's personality cult (Stalin's name, however, is never mentioned explicitly) – thus saying, in effect, that it is now possible to deal with any and all aspects of Soviet reality "fully, courageously, and truthfully."

Tvardovsky also says that it is the purpose of the novel and of its mentor, Nikita Khrushchev, to "tell the truth to the Party and the people" (note the order of importance of the two terms), in order to avoid such things from ever happening again in the future.

Tvardovsky goes on to affirm that the novel is not a "memoir," or a recounting of personal experiences by the author, but a work of art which is based on personal experience, and which, since it is based on "concrete material," conforms to the aesthetic theory of Socialist Realism.

Because the theme of the novel is limited by the realities of time and place – a Siberian labor camp of the 1950s – Tvardovsky insists that the main thrust of the work is not a critique of the Soviet system but that, instead, it is a painting of an exceptionally vivid and truthful picture about the "nature of man." The novel, the editor stresses, does not go out of its way to emphasize the "arbitrary brutality which was the consequence of the breakdown of Soviet legality," but instead, it describes a "very ordinary day" in the life of a prisoner without conveying to the reader a feeling of "utter despair." Thus, Tvardovsky claims, the effect of the novel is cathartic – that is, it "unburdens our mind of things thus far unspoken [and] thereby strengthens and ennobles us."

It may be unfair to call this preface "political hackwork." Evidence indicates that Tvardovsky was sincere – both in his belief in Khrushchev's liberalization policies and in his disgust at Stalin's personality cult. It is clear, however, that he avoids any outright critique of the Soviet system by insisting that *One Day in the Life of Ivan Denisovich* does not level any criticism at the Soviet social and political realities, but rather, it attacks only the excesses of the Stalin regime, a temporary "breakdown of Soviet legality."

This contention was certainly expedient at the time of the publication of the novel, but it does not hold up under close scrutiny. Solzhenitsyn was, and still is, a firm critic of the Soviet system of government, regardless of the regime in power, and he has reaffirmed this conviction countless times since the publication of this novel. In fact, as late as the 1980s, the author commented that the passing of the Stalin era did nothing to do away with the GULAG system. Indeed, it is the author's contention that the prison camp system has been expanded rather than phased out, and that it now envelops more people than ever before.

It is interesting to note that Tvardovsky, at the end of the preface, apologizes to his readers for Solzhenitsyn's use of "certain words and expressions typical of the setting in which the hero lived and worked"— in other words, for Solzhenitsyn's use of some rather vulgar language, which was typical of the language used in such labor camps. Obviously, the editor feared that he might offend some readers. Authoritarian regimes, both left-wing and right-wing, are notorious for their puritanical prudishness, particularly as regards the descriptions of bodily functions and sexual activity. The prolific use of profanity and the vivid descriptions of sexual activity in modern Western art and literature are seen by many Soviet critics as yet another sign of the increasing decadence and the impending decline of the West. It is ironic that Tvardovsky decided to print the offensive words and phrases, whereas many English editions, in fact, edit or omit them entirely.

Tvardovsky's preface is of interest to the Western reader not so much for its critical astuteness, as it is for its revelation of the political difficulties surrounding the publication of the novel. The editor attempts to justify the critical picture of Soviet life by insisting that the novel focuses on a "temporary aberration," thus trying to steer readers into a very limited interpretation of the work.

Political reality, however, has shown that Khrushchev's liberalization and de-Stalinization policies were a temporary aberration and that the publication of *One Day in the Life of Ivan Denisovich* coincided with the end of the "great thaw." Immediately following the publication of the novel, Khrushchev came under pressure from the conservative, pro-Stalin wing of the Communist party and had to make large concessions to this group in order to survive politically; one of these concessions was the withdrawal of his patronage from Alexander Solzhenitsyn and the eventual exile of the author in 1974.

CRITICAL COMMENTARIES

One Day in the Life of Ivan Denisovich is difficult to classify in terms of traditional literary genres. Solzhenitsyn himself has remarked on the disappearance of the traditional boundaries between genres and the lack of interest in "form" within contemporary Russian literature. Commenting on the form of the work, he states that it is a mixture, something between a short story (Russian: *rasskaz*) and a story (Russian: *povest*). A *povest* is defined as "what we frequently call a novel: where there are several story lines and even an almost obligatory temporal expanse." *One Day,* on the other hand, is more of a short story in the sense that it concentrates mainly on one protagonist and on one episode in his life, but the fact that this one day is seen as being typical of a large segment of Ivan's life, as well as being a description of a number of different human fates, also places the work in the genre of the novel.

In keeping with its short story form, there is no formal subdivision into chapters, but we can distinguish twenty-four distinct episodes which make up Ivan's day. *These episodes have been given "titles" in this set of Notes for the sake of easy reference to any of the twenty-four episodes.*

The episodes are arranged thematically around the three main areas of concern for a typical prisoner: food, work, and the eternal battle against the cruel camp authorities. Formally, the episodes – one might properly call many of them vignettes – are arranged in such a way that scenes describing the harsh camp environment which is a threat to Ivan's survival alternate with episodes which depict his overcoming these threats, showing Ivan's small triumphs over the inhumane prison system.

An Unexpected Trip to the Commandant's

The novel begins with a description of Ivan's waking up to the sound of a hammer being banged against a metal rail, the sound muffled by a thick crust of heavy ice on the windows. Usually, Ivan gets up immediately to begin his battle for survival by doing odd jobs which will bring him extra food, but on this particular day, he feels ill and stays in his bunk.

He listens to the noises of the awakening barracks, afraid that the rumors of an impending reassignment of duties for his work gang might be true. He hopes that Tyurin, his gang boss, can bribe the authorities to let them keep their current work project, since reassignment could mean working without shelter on a bare field for at least a month, and without being able to make a fire. A new assignment could also mean grave illness or death to him and his fellow gang members.

As Ivan makes up his mind to go to the infirmary and put himself on the sick list, he is surprised by the arrival of a sadistic guard, nicknamed the Thin Tartar, who announces that Ivan will have to spend three days in "the can," the prison blockhouse, for not getting up immediately. Ivan is relieved. At least he will get hot food, and he won't be forced to go outside to work. Protesting all the while, however, Ivan follows the Thin Tartar to the Commandant's office, sure that his comrades will keep his breakfast for him.

Solzhenitsyn chooses to open his story at reveille in a labor camp in Siberia, describing his protagonist as he is being awakened. This seems to be a logical place to start an account of a typical day in such a camp, but we must remember that several masterpieces of modern literature use the same technique for their opening scene. In Franz Kafka's enigmatic existentialist novel *The Trial*, the protagonist Josef K. awakens to find himself being arrested for having committed a crime which is never explained. In Kafka's story *The Metamorphosis*, Gregor Samsa awakens from uneasy dreams to find himself transformed into a gigantic, odious insect, without ever finding out explicitly for what reason. Other authors place their protagonists into this state between sleep and waking, where the character and the readers have difficulty deciding whether or not the events to follow are a dream or reality.

On one level, *One Day in the Life of Ivan Denisovich* is certainly a story about the nature of man, defined by his inability to make sense of the universe, surrounded and threatened by forces which he is unable to control or even explain. At this level of meaning, the work aligns itself with those of other existential writers who see human beings trapped in a monotonous daily routine very similar to that of Ivan's labor camp (see the essay on "*One Day* as an Existential Commentary").

This impression is reinforced by the use of numbers instead of names—Ivan is called S-854 by the Thin Tartar—a technique used by many modern writers; for example, it is used by Elmer Rice in his play *The Adding Machine,* and by Karel Capek in *R.U.R.* Interestingly, Solzhenitsyn had originally chosen the title *S-854* for the novel.

Ivan's day begins on a negative note in this first episode. He feels ill, which does not happen often; he remembers the work reassignment, which is possible; and he is surprised by the Thin Tartar, who has come on duty instead of Big Ivan, a humane and lenient prison guard (he is associated with Ivan, the protagonist, because of the similarity of their names). Finally, Ivan is sentenced to three days in "the can," but even here, the counterswing of the pendulum begins: Ivan's sentence is "with work as usual," words which are important to Ivan, because not being allowed to work would be real punishment for him. Ivan is not worried about losing his share of the food allotment: the ethics of survival dictate that his comrades will keep his breakfast for him. We should also note that Ivan, while trying against hope to persuade the Thin Tartar to change his mind about the punishment, does not grovel in a demeaning manner but only protests because it is part of the game.

This opening episode establishes some of the ground rules in the camp – a camp which is, in many ways, a paradigm for Soviet Russian society. Improved conditions can be attained only by bribery. Ivan hopes that his gang boss can bribe the chief clerk not to change their work assignment. This means, of course, that some less fortunate gang will be assigned to the job and exposed to its hardships. Ivan does not waste much sympathy on these fellow prisoners. The struggle for survival demands *some* human decency, of course, but *ultimately*, the law of the jungle prevails.

Ivan remembers Kuzyomin, his first gang boss in another camp, reminding some newcomers that the first one to die is always the prisoner who licks out bowls, puts his faith in the infirmary, or turns into an informer.

Mopping the Guardroom Floor

Following the Thin Tartar across the frozen prison compound, Ivan discovers that he is being taken to the Commandant's office. He is led to the guardroom, where he is told that he does not have to serve his three-day sentence, and he is given orders to mop the guardroom floor instead, which makes him forget about his aches and pains immediately. On his way to get a bucket of water from the well, Ivan observes some of the gang bosses trying to read the camp thermometer: if it reads lower than 41 degrees below zero, the prisoners don't have to march to work, but it is commonly assumed that the thermometer does not work properly.

The fear of getting his boots wet reminds Ivan of a pair of new boots which he lost because of a petty bureaucrat's whim to change prison regulations, an event which he describes as the most devastating blow in his eight years in the camps.

Meanwhile, he does a very superficial job of mopping the floor, and the guards treat him with contempt and – worse – as if he were sub-human. When his task is completed, Ivan begins to ache again, and he decides to go to the hospital after joining his work gang for breakfast in the mess barracks.

Note that in this section, when Ivan discovers that the real purpose of his punishment is to clean the guardroom floor, he is relieved; significantly, his body stops aching as soon as he is assigned work, even though his attitude to the mopping of the guardroom floor is not on the same level as his attitude to his bricklaying is, later on in the story.

Much of the moral force of *One Day* is derived from the matter-of-fact way in which Solzhenitsyn describes the inhuman conditions in the camp. There are no adjectives of indignation or protest in his sober statement that the prisoners do not have to work when the temperature sinks below 41 below zero, and the reader should be horrified to hear the narrator describe without commentary that the water in Ivan's bucket was steaming and that he had to hack through a crust of ice to be able to get the bucket into the well.

The guards, addressing Ivan in dehumanizing terms, complain about his careless mopping performance, not realizing that for Ivan "There's work and work. It's like the two ends of a stick. If you're working for human beings, then you do a real job of it, but if you work for dopes, then you just go through the motions." Ivan does not take any pride in his mopping, since he does not, in this instance, work for "human beings"; when he works for his own satisfaction and for the benefit of his whole work gang, as when he later lays bricks, then he will do a "real job." Even so, this work makes him feel better right away, and his aches return only when the mopping is done.

The guards, faceless and nameless lackeys of the system, have one chance to redeem themselves and show some humanity. When they ask Ivan whether he remembers his wife washing the floor, he responds that he has not seen her since 1941 (the novel takes place in January of 1951; ten years have passed), and he says that he does not even remember what she looks like. For any decent human being, this remark might have at least prompted a rough response from the guards about his wife's looks, anything to show a trace of human interest and compassion. But the guards only continue to berate Ivan's work and to belittle him further. Their chance to prove their humaneness has passed.

Breakfast

Ivan joins his gang in the mess hall, remarking on the routine surrounding the daily meals. Fetyukov, the scrounger, is guarding Ivan's breakfast and is clearly disappointed when the latter shows up to claim it. For the next ten minutes, Ivan concentrates only on his food, even though it has gone cold while he has been away. He eats slowly and carefully, since the time spent eating – ten minutes at breakfast, five minutes at lunch, and another five minutes at supper – is the only time which the prisoners have to themselves. When he has finished his poor meal – cottage gruel, boiled fish bones, and mush (made of "Chinese" oatmeal) – he goes to the hospital block.

Note in this episode that as Ivan pushes his way into the mess hall to claim his breakfast, he comments on the fact that it is sometimes necessary to use physical force to push other prisoners out of the way. As we can see in other episodes, Ivan is capable of aggressive or even rude behavior, even though he is basically a gentle and non-violent man. Yet there are clearly times when physical force is necessary for him to assert himself in his fight for survival. These acts are not committed maliciously or even with premeditation; they are instinctive actions performed either for self-preservation, or else because they are part of the camp ritual.

On his way to a table, Ivan observes a young man crossing himself before eating his meal, and briefly he ponders the loss of religious customs in Soviet Russia. Solzhenitsyn repeatedly calls this suppression of religion in Soviet Russia one of the worst offenses of the Soviet regime and believes that a revival of traditional Russian religiosity and the eventual overthrow of the regime will go hand in hand. It is interesting to see Ivan, himself not a man of traditional Christian faith, comment somewhat sadly on the decline of religion in Russia.

In this episode, the reader becomes acquainted with Ivan Denisovich's personal code of behavior, which is a mixture of sound advice from experienced prisoners, his personal adaptation to the work ethic, and certain guidelines derived from his background as a superstitious Russian peasant. He accepts without comment the camp code that allows fishbones to be spit onto the table, wiped off, and then ground into the floor, but forbids the prisoners to spit the fishbones directly onto the floor. He eats slowly and carefully, even when he is very hungry or when the food is not very good, and he eats the eyes of the fish in his soup, but only when they are still in place, not when they are loosely floating around in the soup. He has also come to the realization that all prisoners, despite their uniform outer appearance, are different individuals, with different roles and talents; he accepts without misgivings the fact that he himself does not count for very much in his work gang, but he is proud of the fact that there are jobs which are even beneath him and which the other members of his gang will not ask him to do.

A Sicklist Attempt Fails

In this novel, Solzhenitsyn rarely gives us lengthy descriptions of a person's character or of his background. Instead, information about the protagonist and his fellow prisoners is given in small installments as the story progresses and as it becomes important for the reader's understanding of the protagonist. Thus, we have found out so far that Ivan has been away from home for ten years, that he has a wife, that he has spent some time in a camp near Ust-Izhma (where he was sick with scurvy), that he has a vitamin deficiency disease, and that he has lost some of his teeth. But we still do not know why he is a prisoner.

In this episode, we are told that Ivan is now in a "special" camp, a prison camp with particularly harsh conditions. This is Solzhenitsyn's phrase for camps which are designed mainly for opponents of the Soviet regime; these men were sentenced under Article 58 of the Soviet penal code (see "The GULAG System").

Ducking behind some barracks to avoid being caught unsupervised, Ivan makes his way to the prison hospital. On the way, he considers buying some tobacco from a Latvian prisoner who has received a package from home, but he decides to try the hospital first. The young medic, Nikolay Semyonovich Vdovushkin, has no medical background at all; he is a student of literature whom Stepan Grigoryevich, the new prison doctor, has taken under his wing.

As Ivan enters, Vdovushkin is copying out a long poem he had promised to show the doctor and from which he does not want to be distracted by Ivan. After explaining that the maximum daily number of prisoners (two) have already been put on the sicklist, he puts a thermometer into Ivan's mouth and continues to write.

Ivan dreams about the luxurious possibility of being "just sick enough," for three weeks, not to have to work. But then he remembers the new prison doctor, whose therapy for any illness is work; clearly, this doctor does not care about the health of the prisoners at all. By the time the young poet-turned-medic tells Ivan that he has a temperature of just under ninety-nine degrees, Ivan is resigned to go to work, commenting that a person who is cold cannot expect any sympathy from a person who is warm.

In this episode, then, we see Ivan on his way to the hospital, considering changing his plan for getting on the sicklist in favor of buying some tobacco from a fellow prisoner. The reader learns that some lucky camp inmates receive packages from home, a fact of prison life which is investigated throughout the novel.

The person from whom Ivan wants to buy the tobacco (and later on, he does) is a Latvian—that is, he comes from one of the small Baltic countries which the Soviet Union annexed after World War II. The camp population is a cross section of the oppressed peoples of contemporary Russia, and most of the ethnic minority groups are represented. In addition to the Latvians, there are also Ukrainians and Estonians, as well as a Moldavian.

The Vdovushkin episode is one of the most interesting episodes in this novel, since Ivan comes in contact here with a creative writer. Young Nikolay was arrested at the university, presumably for reading or writing seditious material. As an idealistic student-poet here in the camp, however, he has forsaken all of his political ideals. He has, to some degree, become a "tool" of the system, in exchange for an untroubled work time. He follows instructions, copies out a long, probably unimaginative poem ("he was writing in neat, straight lines, starting each line right under the one before with a capital letter and leaving a little room at the side") to please his loudmouthed, know-it-all benefactor. He shows no compassion at all, nor any initiative to ease the lot of the prisoners because he fears losing his privileges. He slavishly defends the inhumane rules of the doctor.

Ivan realizes that if one is cold, he should not expect sympathy from one who is warm—that is, from "an ordinary person" who is warm. But, from a poet, a creative humanist, seemingly, one should be able to expect *some* sympathy.

Vdovushkin is Solzhenitsyn's portrait of the contemporary Russian writer who has abdicated his ideals for small conveniences and who now writes long, unimaginative works in prison as a trustee. Solzhenitsyn is particularly harsh with the young poet because he himself has made it his dangerous task to demonstrate what path contemporary Soviet writers should take.

Morning Search and Departure

Ivan Denisovich returns to his barracks and waits for the morning roll call along with the rest of his work gang. Pavlo, the assistant gang boss, hands him his bread ration, which Ivan immediately realizes is half an ounce short of the regulation one-pound loaf of bread. He decides to take half of it with him to the worksite; the other half he hides in the sawdust of his mattress, then he sews up the hole.

While the prisoners wait to be frisked in the freezing cold yard, Ivan makes his way to one of the artist-prisoners to have the faded numbers on his prison uniform repainted. When he returns to his gang, Ivan notices that one of the fellows in his gang, Caesar Markovich, is smoking a cigarette, and Ivan is reminded of his own lack of tobacco. Fetyukov, the scrounger, begs Caesar for "one little drag," but Ivan does not beg; he stands by silently. Significantly, it is Ivan who is rewarded; he receives the rest of the cigarette.

Gang 104, Ivan's gang, is about to arrive at "the friskers," just as Lieutenant Volkovoy, the feared disciplinary officer, orders the guards to search the prisoners. Camp rules forbid wearing any extra clothing or carrying anything out of camp; this law exists in order to thwart prisoners from wearing civilian clothes under their camp uniforms and carrying food out with them, hoping to escape. Because of this rule, the inmates have to undo their coats – even in freezing weather.

Captain Buynovsky, a former Navy officer and a newcomer to the camp, is caught with a non-regulation jersey on and is forced to take it off. He protests that this procedure violates the Soviet criminal code, and he accuses the guards of not being true Soviet people, as well as being "bad" Communists. This brings him a sentence of ten days in solitary confinement, a punishment which very few prisoners survive.

After repeated body counts (the guards are personally responsible for every single prisoner and will be sentenced to take a missing prisoner's place themselves), the prisoners finally begin their march to the different worksites, heavily guarded by armed guards and dogs. As Ivan marches along, he tries to stop himself from thinking about his aches and his hunger, and he begins to daydream about his wife and the village which he comes from.

If we look back at the beginning of this episode, we should focus first on Ivan's return to his barracks. Note that when he receives his bread ration, he is immediately aware that half an ounce is missing. Every food ration, we learn, is short. Why? Because the authorities and trustees charged with food distribution always save some for themselves in order to survive a little better. However, Ivan realistically admits to himself that the people who cut up the bread would not last long if they gave every prisoner honest rations. Food, then, is the most important item in the prisoners' battle for survival.

Ivan keeps one hand on his piece of bread, even while he takes his boots off with the other hand. Any edible item left unattended will be stolen immediately – if not by a prisoner, then surely by an orderly or a guard. Ivan accepts this condition as a reality. There are no misgivings; Ivan simply takes the appropriate precautions. Note, however, that he is not afraid that Alyosha the Baptist, who has the bunk next to him, will steal from him. He knows that the man's religious beliefs won't allow him to become a thief. Later in the story, in one of the key episodes of the novel, Ivan and Alyosha will have a serious discussion about religion and the meaning of life.

After it becomes official that Tyurin, Ivan's gang boss, has successfully bribed the officials into letting Gang 104 keep their former work assignment, Ivan has his prison uniform number repainted. The uniform numbers are mentioned over and over; together with the animal terminology which is applied to the prisoners, the numbers serve to emphasize the dehumanizing conditions in the camp. The counting and recounting of the prisoners before they leave the camp is on a literal level – that is, it is standard precautionary procedure. On a symbolic level, however, the counting and recounting signify the existence of the prisoners not as human beings, but as digits.

The cigarette butt episode continues and reinforces the theme of Ivan's code. Ivan wants the cigarette as badly as Fetyukov does, but he does not demean himself, as the latter does. Fetyukov literally drools and begs for the butt. Caesar Markovich, an upper-class intellectual who feels no great allegiance to any of his fellow prisoners, finally gives Ivan the cigarette butt, but he does so because he dislikes Fetyukov more than he likes Ivan. Ivan, however, is pleased to have bested the scrounger. It is a vindication for the code which he learned from his former gang boss, Kuzyomin.

The frisking episode demonstrates the senseless, cruel camp rules.

To make the prisoners take off extra underclothing in the freezing cold is absurd since it diminishes their effectiveness at work.

Captain Buynovsky is a former Navy officer who has only recently been sent to this "special" camp. He is still used to giving commands and has not understood that survival in a prison camp is not possible by insisting on "rules and regulations." His protest that Lieutenant Volkovoy's frisking orders are a violation of the Soviet Criminal Code is sincere but nonsensical in view of the provisions of that same Criminal Code which sent him to this camp in the first place. Volkovoy (his name means "wolf" in Russian) can tolerate an appeal to legality, but he cannot stand being accused of being a "bad" Communist.

The Captain's quixotic protest nets him ten days of solitary confinement, a punishment that he has little chance of surviving. Ivan is better prepared to survive the brutal rigors of the camp. He realizes that vocal or physical protest is self-defeating, and thus, he lets more powerful people, like Tyurin and Pavlo, look out for his rights.

Ivan also realizes that there are moral limits to the struggle for survival. He believes that when one acts in a demeaning way in order to receive favors (whether it's for a cigarette butt or a place on the sicklist, or a reprieve from punishment), it leads to a loss of self-respect and, eventually, to losing the will to live. Ivan's healthy sense of self-preservation, which is not necessarily always based on being considerate and mild-mannered, refuses to adopt demeaning behavior, and, as a result, Ivan has gained a measure of respect from his fellow prisoners. By adhering to his own "code" of behavior, Ivan has kept himself alive for eight years.

Daydreams of Home and of the *Kolkhoz*

Hungry and still feeling ill, Ivan daydreams about a letter that he considers writing to his wife – while all the time marching along, automatically, toward the power plant, his gang's worksite. He is allowed to write two letters yearly, but there is not much he can write about that might interest his wife. The letters that he has received from her have left him puzzled.

According to her letters, his former *kolkhoz*, the collective work farm of the Soviet agricultural system, is in total disarray. Many of the men did not return to the *kolkhoz* after the war, and those who did return only "live" there; they earn their money somewhere else. Most of the young people have left the *kolkhoz* to work in the towns and in the factories. The agricultural work is done almost entirely by women. Carpentry and basket weaving, once the specialities of his village, have been abandoned in favor of painting cheap commercial carpets from stencils. The collective farm is suffering because everybody is earning easier and better money with these carpets. There is a great demand for them, since most Russians cannot afford real carpets. Ivan's wife hopes that he'll return and become a carpet painter.

Ivan does not like these new developments, and he resents his wife's urging him to take up carpet painting after his release from prison. He wants to work with his hands, either making stoves or doing carpentry. But then he remembers, just as his column arrives at the gates of the worksite, that he cannot go home – even after his release from camp. Nobody will hire a man "convicted with loss of civil rights."

At this point, it is obvious that almost all of *One Day in the Life of Ivan Denisovich* will be concerned with life in a prison labor camp. Very little is mentioned about life in Soviet Russia outside of the camps. This particular episode, therefore, is important because, in it, Solzhenitsyn gives detailed attention to one of the prized institutions of the Soviet system – the collective farm, or *kolkhoz*. Here, the author uses Ivan's daydreams during the march to the worksite as a device to show the depressing facts of an institution which has been deserted by the people charged with making it the mainstay of Soviet agricultural production. Most of the older men have not returned to the *kolkhoz* after the war, and the younger men prefer to work in the towns or in factories, and so the collective farm, administered by corrupt and incompetent officials, is left to women and old men.

The pride which the Russian rural population once had in quality craftsmanship has given way to the desire to make easy money with cheap commercial products – in this case, the three kinds of stenciled carpets, for which there is such a heavy demand because the general population cannot afford quality craftsmanship any longer.

Ivan, like Solzhenitsyn, deplores this disappearance of traditional Russian pride in honest quality work and is determined not to follow the modern trend after his release. But then he remembers that he will be, at best, a "free worker" – that is, a former prisoner who, after serving his sentence, is not allowed to return to his former place of residence.

He will have a hard time finding work, due to the "loss of civil rights" which is included in his sentence. Solzhenitsyn mentions "free workers" several times in the story; there are settlements of such workers close to the camp, with only minimally greater comforts than those available to the camp inmates.

This brief episode is the author's only comment on the deteriorating collective farm system. The subject, however, was of deep concern to Solzhenitsyn, who considered the traditions of the rural Russian population vital to any change in the political system. His story "Matryona's Home" (1963) is devoted solely to the topic of rural life and the innate goodness of the Russian people, a goodness which is slowly but surely being undermined by the corrupt Soviet system.

Some Thoughts on Comrades and Bread

Ivan's gang arrives at the worksite and begins to settle into the daily routine. Meanwhile, Ivan ponders about Alyosha's faith, which allows him to survive without extra food rations. He also thinks about the importance of a good gang boss for the survival of the gang members. Tyurin, his assistant Pavlo, and Caesar Markovich, who has a privileged position in the gang because his two packages per month furnish material for bribing the camp officials, go to the office to get the work assignments for the day, while the rest of the gang seeks shelter around a stove in a repair shop. Ivan, still feeling a little ill, begins to nibble the bread ration which he saved from breakfast, thinking about his wasteful eating habits before he was sent to the camp.

While he eats, Ivan observes some of his fellow gang members: the two Estonians who are inseparable and whom he likes, and Senka Klevshin, a deaf prisoner who was sentenced to jail after having survived the concentration camp at Buchenwald.

When Tyurin returns, he hurriedly hands out work orders to the gang members; they will finish a power plant which they worked on in the fall. Ivan and Kilgas, a Latvian, will lay bricks in the afternoon, but they are first ordered to find some material to cover the three big windows in the generator room, where the gang will mix the mortar. Ivan enjoys the prospect of working with Kilgas; they respect each other as skilled workers.

Soon, they manage to retrieve some roofing-felt which Kilgas had hidden illegally, and they plan to use it now to cover the windows.

This pleases the gang boss, and so he assigns them the important tasks of fixing the stove and the cement mixer.

Of significant note in this episode is Ivan's decision: whether or not he should eat his half bread ration. He remembers how thoughtlessly he once filled his stomach with food back in his village, and how wrong he was to do so. Prison life has taught him that food is to be treated thoughtfully and with respect; he is proud of how much work he has done in the last eight years on so little food.

While Ivan eats, he thinks about some of his fellow prisoners. He likes the two Estonians for their camaraderie and for their support of each other; he thinks that he has never met a bad Estonian. Ivan appreciates most of the minority groups whom he meets in the camp, and he makes negative comments only about Russians, referring presumably to the population in the European part of the Soviet Union.

He accuses these people of having abandoned traditional Russian values and having become corrupted by the system. He praises the minority groups for their unwavering support of each other, for their preservation of their folk traditions, and for their good manners, as well as for having retained their religious beliefs. Later in the novel, Ivan will comment on the fact that the two Estonians see where he hides his food, but he feels sure that they will neither steal from him nor reveal his secret hiding place.

Deaf Senka Klevshin illustrates the absurdity of Article 58 of the penal code; he was taken prisoner by the Germans and was thrown in the concentration camp at Buchenwald, where he led a resistance movement. After the war, however, he was sentenced to ten years' hard work for "allowing himself to be taken prisoner" and for "collaborating with the enemy."

After reflecting on Alyosha's religious faith, Ivan thinks about the god-like power of the gang boss. This thought association is not accidental: in Ivan's world, the gang boss replaces Alyosha's God as the omnipotent authority. As Ivan will state in a later conversation with Alyosha, his (Ivan's) world is based on existential principles, in which metaphysical authorities do not operate. In Ivan's world, the gang boss makes all decisions, and these decisions directly affect the all-important food rations. In comparison to this situation, even the Camp Commandant is unimportant, and, significantly, we never even see this supposedly powerful figure. We see only his lackeys.

While the men wait for the work assignments, they discuss the fact that there has not yet been a blizzard this winter which would prevent them from marching to work. It should be noted, though, that a blizzard could hardly be much worse than the sub-zero temperatures and the winds which they have to endure on this particular day; in addition, they have to make up all lost working days by working on Sundays. Significantly, however, any break in the boring routine is welcome.

After another brief look at the unadaptable Buynovsky and at the disgusting Fetyukov, we observe the gang receiving their work orders. Ivan Kilgas (the Latvian) and Ivan Denisovich Shukhov, both named Ivan, are teamed up. Their identical first names are an indication of their parallel backgrounds as skilled, conscientious workers. While neither one of them is important in terms of the bureaucratic hierarchy of the gang—Caesar Markovich's packages carry more weight there—they are respected for their skill and for their practical problem-solving ability. They may not be fortunate enough to be able to provide food to bribe officials, but they assure the well-being of the gang by appropriating material to keep the bitter cold out of the workroom and by assuring the fulfillment of the work quotas by fixing the stove and the cement mixer. In this sense, they are of equal, or greater, worth than Caesar, the rich intellectual, who has been able to bribe himself out of doing hard work altogether.

The GULAG Work Ethic

This short episode contains a discussion of the work ethic in the camps. Clearly, the system is designed to make the prisoners keep each other working hard in order for the whole group to survive. Tyurin has assigned the Captain and Fetyukov to work together carrying sand because that particular job does not need intelligence; here, we should realize that Solzhenitsyn is being satiric: the Captain has been a Navy officer and Fetyukov has been "a big shot" in a government office.

The work makes the men animated, and they even joke about what they will charge for doing such an excellent job. For awhile, Ivan works with Gopchik, a young Ukrainian whom he likes, and time passes very quickly as they prepare for the bricklaying ahead. After one of the very few, directly sarcastic comments about the Soviet government—which has decreed that when the sun is directly overhead, the time is 1 P.M. – Ivan has to undergo some good-natured ribbing about the fact that his ten-year sentence is almost up, which leads to his reflecting about the reason for his being in this "special" camp.

In this episode, Solzhenitsyn deals with the old question of why prisoners work so hard – rather than doing sloppy work or even sabotaging some of the work projects. In this particular scene, we see that the work quota system has been designed so that food rations are tied to the fulfillment of the assigned work. Thus, each prisoner is anxious for all of his gang members to work hard, because he is the beneficiary of the results and will suffer if, due to a lack of effort on the part of any single gang member, the work quota is not completed. The work quota, however, only encourages quantity, not quality of work.

Other, more sophisticated reasons, are given in the course of the story to explain Ivan's hard work. First of all, only meaningful work – that is, work which influences the food rations – is done well: the mopping of the guardhouse floor does not fall into this category, and Ivan does a sloppy job. In addition, it becomes clear that work, any work, is better than no work at all.

In this episode, we hear no more of Ivan's aches and pains after he is given a meaningful task; all thoughts of going on the sicklist are forgotten. Work, as we see later in the story, serves to bolster an individual's self-esteem, and work well done (Ivan's brick wall) gives an otherwise unimportant, faceless prisoner an individual identity. This is also the reason why Ivan actually does his job well, when it might be enough to make it look as if it had been done well. Fetyukov, not used to doing manual labor, has to be forced to work and, accordingly, he performs his tasks unwillingly. Small wonder that he is a scrounger and a bowl licker.

Also in this episode, we discover a special relationship between Ivan and Gopchik, a young Ukrainian. Gopchik, in many ways, serves as Ivan's surrogate son (Ivan's only son died young), and Ivan is trying to pass on some of his knowledge to the young man. He does not even mind that Gopchik does not share any of the packages he receives from home, but, instead, eats the contents secretly at night. Just as Tyurin picked out Ivan upon his arrival at the other "special" camp, Ivan now adopts Gopchik in a fatherly way.

When Ivan looks up at the sky, he notes that it is almost noon, and this leads to a sarcastic criticism about the Soviet bureaucracy.

Prisoners are not allowed to carry watches; they have to judge the time of day by the position of the sun. But when Ivan deduces that it is noon because the sun is directly overhead, the Captain remarks that the observation is an outdated superstition: the Soviet Government has passed a law that decrees that when the sun is directly overhead, it is 1 P.M. Ivan wonders naively whether the sun now falls under Soviet law, too.

While most days seem to go by quickly with hard work, the end of Ivan's prison sentence does not seem to come any closer. Ivan, who has already served eight years of his term, is teased about having "one foot already out of the camp."

This teasing is done mostly by prisoners sentenced after 1949 (after the "good old days"), when the previous ten-year prison sentences were converted to automatic twenty-five-year terms. Ivan cannot understand how anybody could survive twenty-five years in a "special" camp, but he also does not really believe that he will be released in two years. He remembers many prisoners with original three-year sentences, who had five years added on at the end of their first term. He would not be surprised to have another ten years added to his term. The best he can do is not to think about the end of his sentence and to accept whatever is in store for him. During this good-natured joking about his impending release, Ivan begins to daydream again, this time about the reason for his being in the camp.

Ivan Considers his "Treason"

In February of 1942, Ivan's unit had been surrounded by the German army, without food or ammunition, so Ivan and some of his fellow soldiers had surrendered. A few days later, he and four others escaped from the Germans and made their perilous way back to the Russian lines, with Ivan and one other Russian being the only survivors. On their return, the two were arrested on suspicion of having been sent back by the Germans to spy on their comrades. Thus, Ivan is in the prison camp for "treason." During his interrogation, he confessed. We are told that he confessed because he knew that if he did not, he would be shot on the spot.

A brief discussion of the differences between a "regular" camp and a "special" camp follows. Ivan thinks that life in their "special" camp is easier, because their camp schedule is a regular schedule, whereas in the other camps that he has been in, mainly logging camps, the prisoners have to work until the quotas are filled, regardless of the time of day. The rations are higher in "special" camps, and the numbers which the prisoners have to wear on their uniforms "don't weigh anything," according to the deaf Klevshin.

In this episode, the reader is again confronted with the absurdity of Article 58 of the Penal Code. Ivan has been sentenced to prison camp for treason, his offense having been not only to "allow" himself to be captured by the Germans – but for having had the audacity to escape and rejoin his forces. Thus, Ivan is guilty under both Sections 1 and 3 of Article 58. But, had Ivan remained a German POW and survived, he would have been sentenced for Senka Klevshin's "crime." This is a true Catch-22 situation.

In the rest of the episode, Solzhenitsyn dispels the notion that a "special" camp is much worse than the hundreds of other "regular" camps; in fact, Ivan comments that the only thing that might be considered worse in their camp is the obligation to wear numbers on their uniforms. In return, the food ration is higher, the work schedule more regular, and the numbers are not really a burden. Ivan and his comrades are not singled out for a particularly harsh fate; many hundreds of thousands of their compatriots in "regular" camps suffer the same fate – or worse.

The Midday Meal Caper

The gang suddenly realizes that they have been so preoccupied with their work and talk that they will be late in the food line for the midday meal. Half the day has gone by, and they have not even begun their assigned work. Pavlo, Ivan, and Gopchik secure bowls for the rest of the gang, and Ivan manages to swindle two extra portions of oat mush (a delicacy, compared to the usual magara weed they are served). Although Ivan is responsible for the extra portions, he must wait for Pavlo's decision. (Tyurin never eats with the rest of the gang, a sign of his privileged position.)

Pavlo finally gives Ivan one of his extra portions (every gang boss gets double portions), and he asks Ivan to take one of the extra portions to Caesar Markovich, who has bribed himself into an office job and thinks it beneath him to eat with the rest of the gang. Captain Buynovsky – ten days of solitary confinement ahead of him – is given the other extra portion.

In this episode, the author also gives us an exact account of the food portions served to the prisoners. There are exactly two pounds of groats – crushed oats for each gang, which makes each man's portion miniscule. However, this amount is reduced by cuts for the cook, for the mess hall orderlies, and for the "sanitary" inspector, a double portion for the gang boss, and extra cuts for the bowl washers and for the friends of the cook. And the groats are considered a delicacy; frequently, they are replaced by magara, a Chinese grass substitute. The author does not bother to state what the actual size of a prisoner's portion is after these reductions.

Once again, this episode concentrates on the daily fight for food and on the power which the gang boss has over his crew. Ivan, who has managed to cheat the cook out of two extra portions, does not even think about keeping one for himself. Instead, he hands both to Pavlo, who makes him wait for his reward until he has finished his regular portion. In the meantime, Solzhenitsyn shows us the Captain, who has been in the camp for only a short time, slowly changing – from being a loudmouthed naval officer, used to commanding – into a cagey and cunning camp inmate. The change, however, is probably too late, in view of his impending punishment. In spite of all the impersonal ritual he has to perform, Pavlo, the assistant gang boss, shows that there is still a trace of humanity left in him when he assigns the other portion of the groats to Captain Buynovsky.

A Discussion of Art

Ivan enters the office to bring Caesar Markovich his bowl of now-cold mush and finds Caesar engaged in a conversation with prisoner K-123, an old man who has already served twenty years. The two are hotly debating the artistic merits of Sergei Eisenstein's famous film *Ivan the Terrible*. Caesar defends the film as a work of genius while the other man condemns it for its vindication of a one-man tyranny, something that would have pleased Stalin very much. When Caesar objects that Eisenstein had to make compromises to get his work past the censors, K-123 violently objects to Caesar's calling Eisenstein a genius: "a genius does not adapt his treatment to the taste of tyrants."

In this very brief scene, Solzhenitsyn gives his critique of a masterpiece of Russian art, Eisenstein's film *Ivan the Terrible*. At the same time, he deals with all his fellow artists who have been willing to compromise with the Stalin regime. In this sense, the episode is a continuation and an intensification of the theme begun in the episode focusing on the young poet Nikolay Vdovushkin (Episode 4). Here, however, Caesar Markovich is an artist and an intellectual; he despises manual labor and has made art his quasi-religion in the camp. Accordingly, the discussion between him and K-123 takes on the sense of being a religious debate (remember, the two contestants are sitting in a comfortably warm office); the debate proves much too sophisticated for Ivan, the naive witness to the conversation. Caesar is not interested in any "political message" that might be in the film; instead, he admires the artistic concept and its masterful execution, and thereby, he insinuates that an artist has no political responsibility. This enrages K-123, who criticizes the film for its vile political praise of a one-man dictatorship. He denies the title of genius to any artist who "adapts his treatment to the taste of tyrants."

K-123 is clearly a mouthpiece for Solzhenitsyn, who, in many letters and speeches to the Soviet Writers' Union, insisted on the personal and political morality of the artist and expressed his open contempt for all of those Russian writers who compromised or collaborated with the Stalin regime in order to get their works past the censors. As will also happen in a later episode, Ivan Denisovich is an uncomprehending bystander here, one who simply waits around to see whether or not Caesar will give him a little tobacco or some of the mush; in many ways, Ivan's simple, traditional, naive values are far superior to those of Caesar, whom both Ivan and Solzhenitsyn view with distrust.

Tyurin's Story

Returning to his workplace, Ivan picks up a small piece of steel, for which he may have some use later, and he puts it into his pocket. Tyurin has managed to get them better work rates, which means more bread for the next five days. Before the signal to return to work after their meal break, the men huddle around the two stoves, listening to Tyurin tell a story.

In 1930, Tyurin was dishonorably discharged from the army for being the son of a *kulak,* a member of the land-owning middle-class who had fallen into disfavor with the Soviet regime for resisting the collectivization of their farms. Ivan borrows a cigarette from Eino, one of the Estonians, and listens to the continuation of his gang boss' story.

After his dismissal from the army, Tyurin says, he managed to get on a train which would take him home. Since train tickets were available only by voucher, he secretly boarded a train and got to his hometown with the help of some girls who hid him under their coats. He later met one of them again, in a labor camp, and he was able to return the favor which she had done for him. Then, when he got home, he took his young brother with him to the south of Russia and put him into the care of a group of street thugs, who would teach the child how to survive. He never saw his brother again. He himself ended up in prison soon afterward, during a wave of arrests directed at the *kulaks.*

This episode could rightly be entitled "Tyurin's Story." It serves to direct interest away from the protagonist for a short time and to demonstrate how many Russians of all backgrounds have been sent to the camps during the Stalin regime. Tyurin's only crime is that he is the son of a *kulak,* a farmer who had understandably resisted the government takeover of his private farm. Rather than expose his young brother to the inevitable wrath of the Stalin regime, he gives him into the care of a street gang, where he might learn the necessary techniques for survival. The power of Tyurin's story, like much of *One Day in the Life of Ivan Denisovich,* lies in the matter-of-fact way in which it is told – with no attributes of anger or sorrow accompanying Tyurin's account of his own fate and that of his brother. Indignation is really impossible because Tyurin's story is not extraordinary at all. It has been experienced by all of his listeners in the camp and by uncounted Russians outside.

There is also a brief glimpse of Ivan's basic, uncalculated humanity when he gives the butt of his cigarette to the deaf Senka Klevshin, whom he pities for not being able to follow the boss' story; before that, he even considers – momentarily – giving the butt to the scavenger Fetyukov, because he feels sorry for him.

The Art of Bricklaying

After his story is finished, Tyurin orders his men to work, although the official signal has not yet been given. Ivan, Kilgas, and Klevshin begin to lay bricks on the second story of the unfinished power plant. Once he begins to work, Ivan does not focus on anything except the task in front of him. For these short hours, he is his own "boss," proud of his skills and eager to win the friendly competition he has with the people who are supplying him with bricks.

Ivan proves to be a master bricklayer, building his wall perfectly straight. Meanwhile, Fetyukov begins to wilt under the strain of work, while the Captain gets better and better, a fact which Ivan acknowledges with small, jocular compliments. Alyosha the Baptist also turns out to be a good worker, good-naturedly following the commands of the Captain. This period of concentrated and united work is interrupted by Der, the construction foreman.

The emphasis in this episode is primarily on work. On Tyurin's orders, the gang immediately begins their daily work – although no official command has been given. Once again, this demonstrates the power of the gang boss who, in Ivan's words, "fed you [and who] wouldn't make you work if you didn't have to." Most of the prisoners to whom the author attributes positive qualities (Ivan, Kilgas, Tyurin, Klevshin, and Alyosha) symbolically work on the upper level of the building, while Fetyukov and the others labor below.

Ivan really becomes immersed in his work. Work is his equivalent to Alyosha's religion and Caesar's art, and he is equally fanatic about it. Indeed, the whole description of Ivan at work can be compared to the description of a religious ritual, of a priest performing a sacred task, aided by some minor attendants. The whole gang seems reduced to providing Ivan with material for his work at the right time.

In stark contrast to Ivan's quasi-religious work ethic is the stance of the foreman who has come to check on the defective electrical hoist. He stands by and watches one of his underlings tinker with the motor. And in contrast also, Ivan thinks only of how much more efficiently he could perform his work if the hoist were repaired.

Foreman Der Is Put to Shame

Der, the construction foreman, who wants to be promoted to engineer, is enraged about the theft of the roofing-felt which Ivan and Kilgas used earlier in the day to cover the windows of the generator room so that the gang and the mortar would be protected from the freezing wind. He threatens Tyurin with an additional sentence for condoning the theft, but the gang boss is not afraid. He warns Der that he will lose his life if he utters a word about the roofing-felt. The rest of the gang, including Ivan Denisovich, is ready to use physical violence to protect their boss. Der becomes afraid and backs down, and as he leaves, Tyurin berates him about the non-functioning hoist and demands that the gang be given better work rates for having to carry the mortar and the bricks to the second story by hand. As the foreman leaves, he weakly criticizes Ivan's bricklaying, but he is cleverly repudiated by Ivan, continuing to shout for more mortar.

Der, the focus of this episode, is a prisoner himself; he was once, however, an official in a government ministry, and he considers himself superior to the rest of the prisoners, even the gang bosses. He has no practical knowledge of the work which he is supervising, and so he tries to improve his position by tyrannizing the inmates. Ivan comments that one should be able to build a house with one's own hands before one hopes to be called an engineer.

Again, Solzhenitsyn contrasts the educated but impractical bureaucrat with the uneducated but handy workman, and he clearly takes the side of the simple man. The former bureaucrat proves as useless as his successors in the Soviet government bureaucracy. The burden of keeping the country going is on the shoulders of peasants, tradesmen, and craftsmen like Ivan, who contemplates that he is, by trade, a carpenter, and yet he can (and easily does) learn a dozen more practical trades, if necessary. In *One Day in the Life of Ivan Denisovich* and in many of his subsequent works, Solzhenitsyn shows his deep distrust of intellectuals and bureaucrats; he indicates that any hope for a regeneration of Russia will have to be found within the common, rural Russian population.

Ivan's Zealous Perfectionism

Reflecting on the run-in with Der, Ivan concludes that machines cannot be trusted, because they always tend to break down. Meanwhile, the work is proceeding fast, and there is more mortar left than the gang can reasonably use before their return to camp. The other gangs at the worksite have already handed in their tools and are getting ready for their return, but Ivan is unwilling to quit. He works furiously, trying to use up the rest of the bricks and the mortar, and his enthusiasm infects his comrades. Finally, Tyurin has to order Ivan's trowel to be taken away from him, but Ivan continues to work with his own trowel, one which he had stashed away secretly.

The rest of the prisoners are ready to be counted for the return march, but Ivan will still not quit. Finally, after taking one last satisfied look at his work, he hides his trowel and runs to the roll call.

This episode is the climax of the story. Ivan's furious absorption in his work makes him *virtually a free man* for a few hours. He is reluctant to let go of this sense of freedom and individuality, and his enthusiasm is shared by some of his fellow prisoners for awhile. But they do not feel Ivan's deep, unique sense of personal fulfillment. When it is time to quit, they are pulled back into the grim reality of prison life much sooner than Ivan, who wants to finish his work properly, "even if the guards would set their dogs on him." Ivan's work reaffirms his worth as a human being in spite of the inhuman conditions under which he has to live. As he lovingly takes a last look at the straight lines of "his" wall, he is reassured that "his hands were still good for something."

Ivan Speculates about Faith and Astronomy

Ivan and Klevshin are greeted by derision and curses from the men whom they have kept waiting in the cold. As the ritual of the counting of the prisoners begins, Ivan reveals in a conversation with the Captain that he is indeed a simple, superstitious Russian peasant: he believes that the moon which they see rising is a new one every month and that the old one is broken up into stars by God. New stars, according to Ivan, are constantly needed because the old ones fall from the sky. Yet, in spite of these rather pagan opinions, Ivan asserts that he believes in God.

The head count reveals that a man is missing; it turns out to be a prisoner from another gang who has fallen asleep in the repair shop, and the five hundred men whom he has kept waiting for half an hour hurl abuses at him and even assault him physically, because he has deprived them of precious minutes of comparative leisure back in camp. Finally, the column begins its long march home.

Here in this episode, the reality of preparing to go back to camp is an anticlimax to Ivan's frenzied happiness while he was at work. Slowly, reality begins to overtake him, and the battle for survival which had been suspended for a few hours must be fought again.

Ivan's simple-minded statements concerning the lunar orbit reveal his naive faith in a pantheistic God, and he is looked at with disbelief by the educated Captain. To Ivan, God is revealed in nature. Note in particular that the Captain's sneering about Ivan's ignorance does not disturb Ivan at all. As in his later discussion with Alyosha, Ivan reveals an instinctive faith which needs no sophisticated theological argument. He is full of old Russian peasant superstitions, and Solzhenitsyn considers such faith to be superior to an adherence to the superficial rules of the Russian Orthodox church or to Alyosha's impractical Baptist beliefs.

Solzhenitsyn's distrust of intellectuals is once again shown. Here, in the discussion between the Captain and Caesar Markovich about *Potemkin,* another film by Sergei Eisenstein, Ivan overhears the part of the discussion which deals with a graphic visual scene in the film, in which the sailors on the battleship *Potemkin* are fed rotten meat, crawling with maggots. While the two connoisseurs discuss the artistic merit of this scene and other scenes in the film, they conclude, as an afterthought, that the prisoners in their own camp would eat such meat if it were served to them, presumably without revolting, as the sailors on the *Potemkin* eventually did. The reality of prison camp life, however, is far harsher than the "artistic imagery" of a film or a book; this may be a comment by Solzhenitsyn about the fact that even a starkly realistic work like *One Day in the Life of Ivan Denisovich* is incapable of adequately describing the grim reality of an isolated, freezing cold Siberian prison camp.

An Unexpected Race Homeward

Now that the men know that they will be the last ones back in camp and the last ones to eat the evening meal, their march homeward is slow and melancholy. Ivan remembers that he had been trying to get on the sicklist that very morning; he decides that it is a waste of time to try again.

Suddenly, another column of prisoners comes into view, and the remainder of the trip home turns into a race, trying to beat the other prisoners back to camp, since they know that the other gang comes from the tool works and are given an especially thorough frisking. They manage to win the race, and Ivan offers to go to the package room to look for a parcel that might have come for Caesar Markovich. Of course, he hopes to be rewarded for his troubles.

In this episode, note that the prisoners march slowly in order to get even with the guards for keeping them waiting for so long; they are exercising this tiny bit of power by "getting even." When they sight the other column of prisoners, however, their competitive spirit is aroused, and their once-slow march turns into a race, a change of mind which no official command could have achieved.

During this episode, we find out why the Captain is in the "special" camp. He had been detached, at one time, as a liaison officer to the allied British navy during World War II, and the British admiral to whom he had been assigned sent him a little gift after the war, with the inscription "In gratitude." The result of this innocent little gift was a twenty-five-year sentence for "rendering assistance to the enemy" – in spite of the fact that Great Britain was Russia's ally during the war.

Toward the end of the march, Ivan deplores the lack of solidarity among the prisoners; he states that the worst enemy of a prisoner is "the guy next to him. If they did not fight each other, it'd be another story." It seems that Solzhenitsyn's statement here is meant to apply not only to Ivan's prison camp, but to Russia as a whole. In his opinion, the Stalinist regime can stay in power only because the Russian population is divided against one another. If this were not so, the author indicates, Russia's fate might be vastly different.

The Risky Search

Just before he is to be searched prior to his entry back into camp, Ivan discovers the piece of steel in one of his pockets, the piece of steel that he picked up at the worksite in the morning. If the guards find it on him, it will mean ten days in solitary confinement. He is undecided whether or not to throw the incriminating potential weapon into the snow or to try and smuggle it through the search and, later, turn it into a small, valuable tool. His practical sense conquers his fear, and he hides the piece of steel in one of his mittens. He is lucky enough to have the guard miss it when he is frisked.

This is the third time that Ivan has exposed himself to the potential anger of the authorities. First, he was lucky not to be punished more severely for sleeping in late; then he took a chance in taking too long to finish his brick wall, and he made the guards wait for him. Now, he risks severe punishment by smuggling in a piece of steel, which could be defined as a weapon. Interestingly, this is the only time that we see Ivan pray to God. Later, he ungratefully expresses doubt in the efficacy of prayer. In any case, however, his prayer is answered, and he passes the inspection. The potential gain in his fight for survival – that is, he will be able to use the piece of steel to make extra money by using it as a knife or a tool – outweighs the risk of being caught.

At first, the importance of all three of these episodes might seem trivial: staying in bed a few moments too long, leaving work late, and accidentally pocketing a small piece of steel. These are hardly earth-shaking events in the world of the average reader, but, for Ivan, they are events which could be the difference between life and death. He is indeed lucky to escape all three incidents unscathed. The Moldavian, who fell asleep in the repair shop, and the Captain who voiced a rash but justified protest, were not so lucky. They may not survive the consequences of ten days in solitary confinement with reduced rations.

Markovich's Package

After his close call with the authorities, Ivan hurries to the package room to see if he can do Caesar Markovich a worthwhile favor by standing in line for him. As he waits, he remembers that in the Ust-Izhma camp, he received packages a couple of times. Since not much was left by the time the parcels reached him (many of the contents of these packages disappear when they are opened for "inspection"), Ivan has since instructed his wife not to send him any more parcels, particularly since he knows that his family back home has nothing to spare. Still, he sometimes hopes that a package will arrive for him unexpectedly. During his wait, he also finds out that the authorities will make the prisoners work on Sunday of next week, news which depresses Ivan, although he had expected it.

When Caesar finally arrives, he virtually disregards Ivan and begins a conversation about Moscow art events with another prison intellectual who is waiting for a package. They use a language which sounds foreign to Ivan, who has nothing but contempt for Moscow intellectuals. He suppresses his dislike for Caesar's intellectual snob-bery and asks him if he can bring him his supper, but Caesar, as Ivan had hoped, lets him have his portion as a reward for waiting in line.

This part of the story contrasts Ivan, a have-not, with the wealthier prisoners who are lucky enough to receive additional food in packages from home. Even the supposedly egalitarian Soviet system has not eliminated "privilege," and the camp is a reflection of society as a whole. Ivan does not begrudge anybody the packages – some of the people he likes receive them. That is, Kilgas and Gopchik receive packages, but Ivan has decided that his own family cannot spare any food from home. Therefore, he has considerately forbidden his wife to send him any parcels. He knows that he can supplement his food rations by skill and cunning, and he enjoys his little rewards, like the extra bowl of mush at midday, more than if he were receiving food which he would know that his family could not spare.

Solzhenitsyn again shows his contempt for Caesar and his fellow intellectuals. In the scene in which Caesar ignores Ivan, who is doing him a favor, and engages in a lengthy discussion of the latest theater productions in Moscow, we see the black irony of the situation. That is, in the midst of starving men, such a discussion of "theater productions" (which none of the men will ever see) is absurd. But neither Caesar nor his fellow art connoisseur feel any affinity with the other prisoners and their fate. They themselves are well fed and can debate the latest issue of the *Moscow Evening News,* while Ivan has to struggle to survive. Soon afterward, Caesar has to rely on Ivan's cunning and loyalty – and on his hunger – to keep possession of the food in his package. In this scene, however, Caesar condescendingly lets Ivan have his supper – a morsel for a beggar.

Supper Rations

When Ivan returns to his barracks, there is a commotion because somebody's bread ration has been stolen while they were at work. Ivan finds his own bread intact in its hiding place and runs to the mess hall to join his gang for supper. In the mess hall, the manager and his orderlies are trying to keep order by using force when necessary. The fight for food is ruthless, and the otherwise meek Ivan brutally shoves a smaller prisoner out of the way when he needs a tray for his gang.

The food rations at supper are measured according to work output, and Ivan is rewarded for his good work by receiving a bigger bread portion than the others. In addition, he also has Caesar's portion, and so he contentedly settles down to his usual meal ritual. While he eats, he watches Y-81, a tall, old prisoner, and he thinks about what he has heard about the man, who has become a legend in the prison camps. After his meal, Ivan sets out to buy some tobacco from a Latvian in another barracks, a plan he put off in the morning on his way to the hospital.

In this episode, then, we see that after the elation of his brick-laying work and the joy of his luck at the search point, the depressing facts of camp life again fill Ivan's mind. Some bread (luckily, not his) has been stolen from his barracks, and the mess room orderlies, prisoners themselves, tyrannize the inmates by exercising the miniscule amount of authority given to them by the authorities. Here, Solzhenitsyn uses a theme which has been used in many works that are set in prisons, prisoner-of-war camps, and in mental hospitals: that is, the oppressed make the best oppressors. Other examples of this can be found in Ken Kesey's *One Flew Over the Cuckoo's Nest,* in Henri Charriere's *Papillon,* and in Tadeusz Borowski's concentration camp novel, *This Way for the Gas, Ladies and Gentlemen.*

In this episode, Ivan is shown as less than perfect when he brutalizes a smaller and weaker prisoner in a fight for a food tray. In fact, there are a number of small incidents in the story which show Ivan in a less than saintly way, but this is the most negative one. Solzhenitsyn did not intend to make Ivan a "perfect" human being. Yet, in spite of all his shortcomings, Ivan is still the model of the average Russian "common man": kindhearted without being a saint, religious without being a bigot, wise but not intellectual, cunning but not devious, practical and resourceful, yet not coldly calculating.

From the moment that he sits down to his "grand dinner" – two bowls of thin gruel and a double bread portion – until the end of the day, Ivan feels content. He even forgets about the extra work on Sunday and about the two years which he still has to serve. But then he comes face to face with his alter ego of the future: prisoner Y-81.

According to prison lore, Y-81 has been in prison longer than anybody else. Whenever one of his sentences has run out, another one has been added on to it, and yet his back is still as straight as a ramrod. He has lost all his hair and his teeth (Ivan has lost many of his own teeth), and he takes no interest in anything or anybody around him. He is determined never to give in, and he has developed his own rigid code of behavior. His eating habits are impeccable; he does not put his bread on the filthy table, but lays it on a clean rag. We are reminded that Ivan has begun to establish similar habits: he does not eat loose fish eyes (only when they are still in the sockets); he has never bribed anybody or taken a bribe. Solzhenitsyn insinuates that, like Y-81, Ivan will not leave the prison camp, but he will not give in. And he will survive because of his strength of will and his refusal to compromise his human dignity.

Buying Tobacco

Ivan goes to Barracks 7 to buy some tobacco, thinking about the differences between the "special" camp and the previous camps he has known. In the "special" camp, prisoners do not get paid, while in Ust-Izhma, he was given at least thirty rubles a month. Here, Ivan makes extra money by doing odd jobs, such as making slippers for two rubles, or patching up jackets. He uses the money to buy tobacco at inflated prices from prisoners who get packages from home.

In the barracks of the Latvian from whom he buys his tobacco, Ivan listens to a conversation about the Korean War before he approaches his supplier. Then, he craftily haggles for as much tobacco as he can get into his shaving mug, the standard measure for such transactions. In between, he overhears other prisoners making derogatory comments about Stalin, and he contemplates the fact that the inmates of "special" camps are allowed much more freedom of expression than those in a "regular" camp, where such a remark would have been severely punished. There is, however, not much spare time to use this "freedom."

When Ivan gets back to his own barracks, he sees Caesar Markovich spread out the contents of his package on his bunk. Caesar has received some sausage, canned milk, a large smoked fish, sugar, butter, cigarettes, and some pipe tobacco – an unimaginable treasure for Ivan. Caesar generously lets Ivan keep his (Caesar's) supper bread ration, and Ivan is happy with this gift. He rationalizes to himself that packages create quite a bit of trouble for the people who receive them. They have to share their good fortune with many others – the guards, the gang boss, the barber, and the doctor. Ivan considers all this a mixed blessing. He is happy that he does not rely on other people. He does not envy Caesar, as many of the other prisoners do.

Here, the tobacco episode shows Ivan, once again, to be a crafty, practical man; he is clever enough to avoid being taken advantage of in any transaction. While he was paid rubles in the other camps, he was not able to use the money the way he would have liked to. Here, he has to do extra work to make a few rubles, but he can buy much better tobacco on the camp's "black market." As usual, Ivan is able to see the positive side of his situation and does not dwell on the disadvantages, another strong weapon in his survival arsenal.

Without comment, Solzhenitsyn introduces another conversation into this episode, this time about the Korean War and the possibility of its widening into a worldwide war after the Chinese intervention. Ivan, who has come for a practical purpose – to buy tobacco – is not at all interested in this topic. It is as irrelevant to his personal struggle for survival as a debate about Eisenstein films or the latest Moscow theatrical productions. The Korean War or, for that matter, a world war, will not change Ivan's situation substantially. Talking about it is a waste of precious spare time.

The comment by a prisoner about "that old bastard in Moscow with the mustache [who] wouldn't give a damn about his own brother" is the author's only direct reference to Stalin in the whole work. It is claimed that Khrushchev, through the editor of the first edition of *One Day in the Life of Ivan Denisovich*, wanted at least one direct, negative comment made about Stalin, whose policies he was trying to undo. This passage was Solzhenitsyn's way of complying with this request. Significantly, he chooses to refer to Stalin as "that old bastard in Moscow with the mustache," almost literally the same expression which he himself used in his correspondence with a friend; earlier, his correspondence and this reference were the reasons for Solzhenitsyn's imprisonment. Here in camp, however, the authorities don't even bother to punish such irreverence – a meaningless leniency which Ivan naively interprets as "freedom of speech." We must remember, however, that the Captain will spend ten hard days in solitary confinement for a more innocent and a more justified remark. In addition, there is not much time in this "special" camp to engage in "free speech," and Ivan considers any abstract discussion a waste of time.

Back in his barracks again, Ivan demonstrates that he is a reasonable, practical man. He looks at the assortment of Caesar's riches without envy and even realizes that such packages are a mixed blessing. He himself is able to provide the small luxuries he needs for himself by craftiness and hard work, and thus, he does not have to bribe anybody or defend and share his "wealth." In addition, he has seen ample evidence that packages do not come regularly enough to be relied on. He has observed many of these privileged people scrounging when their parcels did not show up. Ivan is content with Caesar's extra bread ration, and the extra food he has been able to get on this day, as well as some tobacco. His self-reliance will guarantee his chance for survival. But what will Caesar and the others do if their packages from home do not arrive?

Ivan Reviews the Day

Ivan settles down for a few small moments of relaxation before the evening roll call and lights-out. He considers several ways that he can use the little piece of steel which he has smuggled in. Then he hides it in a safe place.

Fetyukov comes into the barracks crying. He has been beaten up by somebody, probably for scrounging, and although he dislikes the man, Ivan feels sorry for him because he is certain that Fetyukov will not survive the camps.

Caesar Markovich still has the contents of his package spread out on his bunk when he asks Ivan for his little illegal knife so that he can cut some meat. He doesn't share his food with Ivan, though; he shares his food with the Captain, the only man in the gang whom he considers his equal. This meal, however, is only a short reprieve for Buynovsky, who is led away shortly afterward to the punishment block.

When the signal for the evening roll call is given, Caesar does not know what to do with his package. It is certain that most of it will be stolen by a prisoner or a guard while he is outside in the line-up. In spite of the fact that Caesar has treated him condescendingly all through the day, Ivan feels sorry for him and shows him a way to protect his food.

After the tedious daily routine of the roll call, Ivan and the other prisoners return to their bunks, find a place to dry their boots, and settle down for the night. Ivan, however, does not feel like sleeping; he is too elated about the many good things which have happened to him during the day. He is grateful that he has not ended up in a cell like the Captain and that he can even enjoy sleeping on his sheetless, sawdust mattress.

Ivan's day, then, is coming to a close on an upbeat note. He has successfully braved all the difficulties of the work day. More than that, he has been able to acquire some small luxuries which will help him during future days. The little piece of steel will allow him to make additional money, he has bread left over for the next day, and he has enough tobacco for awhile. Best of all, he has acquired all these benefits without having to compromise his dignity. In this generous mood, he even feels sorry for the scavenger Fetyukov, whom he sees humiliated and crying.

Ivan's generosity and basic good nature is further shown by his offer to assist Caesar Markovich, who considers himself so much better than the simple peasant Ivan. It is that same "simple peasant"

Ivan, however, who must come to his aid when the contents of Caesar's food package are threatened; knowledge of "art" and an upper-class background are of no practical use within the grim reality of the prison camp. Caesar's preoccupation with art may provide a temporary escape from prison life, but only Ivan's pragmatism and level-headedness can guarantee survival.

How close they all are to annihilation is demonstrated by the Captain's being led away to the prison block. And even at the last moment, he reveals that he is not as well prepared to survive as Ivan. If he could have stalled a little longer, he might have had at least a temporary reprieve. Instead, he responds immediately to his name being called.

The rest of the prisoners, while feeling sorry for him, are unable to provide him with more than trite encouragement – because, here, but for the grace of God, they all go.

The battle for survival even extends to the drying of the boots; it is every man for himself when they try to find a place close to the stove for their footwear; the unlucky ones will have to brave a day in damp boots and the danger of frostbite. It is bitter irony to hear Ivan thank God for his having had such a "good day" as he prepares for sleep, still giddy with joy over his several "successes" during the day.

Small but Important Triumphs

Alyosha the Baptist hears Ivan's mumbled "Thank God" and asks him why he does not pray more often. Ivan answers that he does not believe in the efficacy of prayer. His pragmatic nature does not place much stock in matters of the spirit, and his personal acquaintance with a worldly and corrupt priest of the Russian Orthodox church in his home village have made him cynical about organized religion. He again affirms his belief in God, but he expresses his skepticism about the outer trappings of religion and its complicated, dogmatic points. Religion does not provide him with a satisfactory explanation for his fate. Consequently, he has no use for it.

When the prisoners are called out for a second roll call, Caesar Markovich shows that he has learned his lesson. He gives Ivan cookies, sugar, and some sausage for his help in protecting his package. When they return, Ivan voluntarily shares some of it with Alyosha and thinks about what he will do with the rest. As he falls asleep, he recounts the triumphs of this day:

(1) he has not been put into solitary confinement;
(2) his gang has not been reassigned to a new, harder worksite;
(3) he has managed to get an extra bowl of mush at lunch;
(4) Tyurin has gotten them good work rates;
(5) he has smuggled a valuable piece of metal into camp;
(6) he was given extra food by Caesar in the evening; and
(7) he was able to buy some tobacco.

This has indeed been an extraordinarily happy day, and as Ivan drifts off into sleep, he recalls that there are 3,653 days in his sentence; the extra three are due to leap years.

A contented Ivan explains why he rejects organized religion. He compares prayers to the complaints which the prisoners are allowed to put into boxes set up for this purpose in the camp. Either there is no answer, or they come back marked "Rejected." Alyosha tries to persuade Ivan with dogma, but the pragmatic Ivan is unprepared to accept the symbolism of mountains moved by prayer. His literal mind equates the "daily bread" of the Lord's Prayer to the prison rations, and he cannot imagine God moving any mountains in spite of Alyosha's intensive prayers.

When he confronts Alyosha with the cruel facts of worldly, corrupt priests, the young man winces. There is very little he can respond with, except to say that the Baptist church is less corrupt than the Russian Orthodox church. Alyosha's final argument – that his imprisonment is cause for rejoicing because it gives him a chance to contemplate and strengthen his faith – is met with a resigned silence by Ivan. What he wants is an explanation for his being imprisoned. Alyosha can take solace in the fact that he is a martyr for his faith, but Ivan is here, in the prison camp, because Russia was not prepared for World War II in 1941. She sent him to the front lines ill-equipped, to be taken prisoner by superior German forces, and then punished him for that. For Ivan, religion provides no satisfactory answers for such anguished questions as "Why am I here?" and "Was it my fault?"

At some point, Ivan even expresses doubt that he still wants to regain his freedom. First of all, he does not know whether he will really be released at the end of his term. Second, he doubts that he will be allowed to go home and rejoin his family, even if he is released.

Third, and most depressing, he does not know any longer *where* he would be better off.

It is easy to understand that a prisoner, after eight years, would have many doubts concerning whether or not he would be able to readjust to life outside the camp. The stable prison routine, despite all its cruelty, could begin to seem like a safe, comfortable place.

Ivan's Code of Survival

The final paragraphs of this short novel are the most memorable ones. After our initial horror at the inhumane conditions of life in a "special" camp, the reader gradually begins to see Ivan's day through the eyes of a man who has become used to much of this horror and, unlike the reader, is no longer angry, or even dejected, about his condition. Such emotions would be a waste of time and would detract from his efforts to survive and, if possible, to improve his lot. Thus, Ivan takes most of the outrages of camp life for granted; he spends his energy trying to cope with unexpected dangers. Finally, even the reader adopts Ivan's stance. If one accepts the everyday camp conditions as natural and unalterable, as Ivan does, then the protagonist has indeed had an "almost happy" day.

CRITICAL ESSAYS

LEVELS OF MEANING IN THE NOVEL

• **A Prison Novel.** Most worthwhile pieces of literature operate on multiple levels of meaning. One of these is the literal level – that is, a level on which one requires only an understanding of the basic denotation of the terms and concepts employed by the author. Expressed simply, on this level the author communicates with the reader in a "realistic," non-symbolic fashion. The reader has to transfer very few terms and concepts to a non-literal, symbolic or allegorical level.

One Day in the Life of Ivan Denisovich is literally a prison story, and thus, it takes its place in a long list of similar works which deal with conditions in prisons, labor camps, concentration camps, mental hospitals, or POW camps. As such, it deals with many of the same problems that works like *The Survivor* by Terrence des Pres, Pierre Boulle's *The Bridge on the River Kwai*, Borowski's *This Way for the Gas,*

Ladies and Gentlemen, Henri Charriere's *Papillon,* and many German, French, and British POW novels attempt to come to grips with.

Like all of these works, *One Day in the Life of Ivan Denisovich* deals with the struggle for survival under inhumane conditions. What must a man or a woman do to get out of such a camp alive? Is survival the only and most important goal, or are there limits to what a person can and should do to stay alive? Is religious faith necessary or vital for survival? All of these are questions which this work attempts to answer on a literal level.

Solzhenitsyn, who has first-hand experience of the camp conditions which he describes in this story, relates the actual experiences of millions of his compatriots, and his Russian readers could not help but ponder the real possibility of their being confronted with Ivan Denisovich's situation.

Like the authors of other prison novels, Solzhenitsyn concludes that it is the duty of a human being not to resign and give up the struggle for survival. However, it is wrong to concentrate on what one must do to survive. It is better to establish a personal code of behavior which dictates *what one will not do* just to preserve one's physical existence.

Existence without dignity is worthless – in fact, loss of human dignity will also diminish the will and the capacity to survive. Compromises are certainly necessary, but there is a vast moral gap between Ivan and Fetyukov: Fetyukov will do anything for a little more food, and he is properly referred to as a scavenging animal; Ivan, in contrast, will swindle and bully, at times, but basically, he relies on his resourcefulness to achieve the same goal. He does not lick bowls, he does not give or take bribes, and he is deferential when necessary, but he never crawls. With some improvement in his habits of personal hygiene, he will probably, eventually, become what might be termed "the ideal prisoner," represented by Y-81, the meticulous old camp inmate whom Ivan admires.

Survival is a task which needs Ivan's constant, simple-minded attention. Abstractions, esoteric discussions on religion or on art are irrelevant and counter-productive. Caesar Markovich can survive only as long as his packages arrive. The Captain, if he survives solitary confinement, will have to give up his unrealistic ideas about communism and his overbearing manner if he wants to live. Alyosha the Baptist is, by the very nature of his faith, more interested in an afterlife than he is in physical survival during this lifetime. Clearly, Fetyukov and most of the informers will not live long.

Only Ivan combines all the qualities necessary to survive: he works for himself and for his comrades, but not for the authorities; he does not rely on outside help, but on his own skill and craftiness; he is used to obeying sensible orders and circumventing absurd ones; he has faith, but it is a faith designed to help him cope with the realities of this life, not one which exhausts itself in dogmatic theological debate. Ivan believes in the strength and the dignity of the simple Russian worker and peasant without being a doctrinaire Communist. He is, with some lapses, a compassionate human being who looks at his fellow prisoners with sympathy and understanding. Most of them appreciate this attitude and treat him with the same respect.

• **A Social Commentary.** The population of Ivan's prison camp contains a cross section of Russian society. There are prisoners representing virtually every professional, social, and ethnic group in the Soviet Union: we find artists, intellectuals, criminals, peasants, former government officials, officers, Ukrainians, Latvians, Estonians, and gypsies (Caesar Markovich), just to name a few. If one looks, therefore, beyond the literal level of the novel, it becomes clear that Solzhenitsyn not only wanted to give a realistic description of life in a Siberian prison camp, but that he also wanted the reader to understand that the camp – on an allegorical level – was a representation of Stalinist Soviet Russia.

In an interview, Solzhenitsyn once stated that he had been interested in a statement made by Leo Tolstoy, who said that a novel could deal with either centuries of European history, or with one day in a man's life. (This statement by Tolstoy may have also been the reason why Solzhenitsyn changed the title of this work from *S-854* to *One Day in the Life of Ivan Denisovich.*) During his own prison term, the author made up his mind to describe one day of prison life, one day in the life of Ivan Denisovich Shukhov, whose fate Solzhenitsyn once called "the greatest tragedy in Russian drama."

Read on this level, the novel becomes a scathing indictment of the Soviet system during the Stalin era. Solzhenitsyn would now certainly extend this indictment to the Soviet system as a whole. There are chronic food shortages, except for a privileged few who can bribe advantages out of corrupt officials. There is vandalism and bureaucratic inefficiency, leading to waste and sabotage. To dispel any doubt that all this applies only to camp life, Solzhenitsyn introduces Ivan's thoughts about the collective farm from which he comes ("Daydreams of Home and of the *Kolkhoz*"), which is barely functioning. The men there have bribed the officials to relieve them from farm work so they can paint the profitable, sleazy carpets. In addition, there is also the constant spying and informing activities which are typical of Soviet society, and Solzhenitsyn deplores them most of all, for they create distrust among people who should cooperate against the authorities rather than against themselves. A prisoner, he says, is another prisoner's worst enemy, not the authorities. It is interesting to note that, in spite of serving ten- or twenty-five-year sentences, all of the prisoners seem to be serving life terms. Nobody is ever released from the larger Soviet prison; when one term ends, another one is added on.

It was probably an accident that *One Day in the Life of Ivan Denisovich* was published exactly one hundred years after *Letters from the House of the Dead,* Dostoevsky's famous account of his own experiences in prison under the Czar. But certainly, many Russian readers would immediately recognize the connection between the two works and realize the irony inherent in the comparison: prisons under the hated Czars were, by far, more humane than those under Stalin, and far fewer people were imprisoned in them.

What can be done to overcome these wretched social conditions? It is clear that Solzhenitsyn sees as little possibility for a successful, violent overthrow of the Soviet regime as he does for an armed revolt in Ivan's camp. The real hope is that the corrupt, inefficient system will destroy itself from within, and that Russia will return to a system which is founded on the qualities which Ivan represents: hard work without too much reliance on technology.

Here, Solzhenitsyn follows Dostoevsky's anti-Western, anti-technological attitude. He calls for (1) a revival of the old Russian folk traditions, (2) a simple, mystic faith without the dogmatic bureaucracy of any established church, (3) cooperation between the multitudes of ethnic and social groups in Russia who are now divided and, thus, "their own worst enemies," and (4) an attitude of non-cooperation and non-violent undermining of the bureaucracy and the authorities.

Even if it appears that conditions will not change soon (another prison term may be added on), the actions of the Russian people should be designed to survive with dignity and pride, not with groveling and crawling. It should be noted that Solzhenitsyn does not expect any leadership from intellectuals, churchmen, or artists in this struggle. Their love for abstractions and endless discussion is shown as not producing practical results.

• **An Existential Commentary.** Beyond the literal and the social level, we can detect in this work a theme which aligns it closely to many works of modern fiction. Its theme is the fate of modern man who must make sense of a universe whose operations he does not understand. Thus, the level of meaning which addresses the questions "How is one to survive in a prison camp?" and "How is one to survive in the Soviet Union, which is like a prison camp?" is extended to this question: "According to what principles should one live in a seemingly absurd universe, controlled by forces which one can't understand and over which one has no control?"

Ivan's fate closely resembles that of Josef K. in Franz Kafka's *The Trial.* Josef K. is arrested one morning without knowing why, and he attempts to find out the reasons. In his search, he encounters a cruel court bureaucracy which operates according to incomprehensible rules; lawyers and priests cannot provide him with reasonable answers for his fate, and so he finally concludes that he must be guilty. Accordingly, he willingly submits to his execution.

Ivan is also arrested and sent to prison camps for absurd reasons, and so are most of his fellow inmates. He does not understand the legalities of his case. He is, after all, only a simple worker, and he never encounters the highest authorities who might provide him with an answer. He meets only cruel, minor officials of the system, who only obey orders but do not give explanations. The intellectuals around him do not seem to have the right answers, and the religious people, like Alyosha the Baptist, are very similar to the comforters who try to explain to Job the reason why he must suffer so cruelly. Their arguments are dogmatic; they are not logical or practical.

A man who finds himself in such a situation has several options. One is despair, a passive acceptance of whatever fate has in store for him. This, as Camus indicates in *The Myth of Sisyphus,* is unacceptable behavior for an intelligent human being. An extension of that option is suicide, an alternative that is not even mentioned in *One Day in the Life of Ivan Denisovich.*

Another alternative is to search for a system of thought which will provide an explanation for such a basic existential question as "Why is all this happening to me?" These could be philosophical, religious, or political systems of thought, most of them having spokesmen who seemingly are able to give answers. Unfortunately, they all require that a person accepts at least one basic point of dogma *on faith* — that is, one must not ask for proof. And that is unacceptable to many practical, logical people like Ivan. Therefore, Ivan must ultimately reject Alyosha the Baptist's interpretation of the universe.

Despite the fact that Ivan does believe in God, albeit a pantheistic pagan god, his answer to the existential question of modern man is fundamentally that of Jean-Paul Sartre and other Existentialists. He decides to adopt a personal code of behavior similar to that of Hemingway's so-called "code heroes," whose highest satisfaction is derived from demonstrating "grace under pressure." Rather than adopting other people's behavioral codes (for example, the Ten Commandments), Ivan establishes his own set of morals, which are designed to help him survive with dignity. Since nobody can give him a logical explanation for his fate, he abandons all attempts at finding such an explanation and structures his life by the premise that there is, in fact, none. This allows him to concentrate on gaining satisfaction from following the standards he has set for himself. He does not have to please anyone about practical matters. This is graphically demonstrated by Ivan, particularly in his sense of self-reliance and in his "grace under pressure" behavior. He is a prototype of what Sartre calls a man "living in good faith," as well as a prototype for the common Russian, in whom Solzhenitsyn puts his hope for a better future.

STYLE AND NARRATIVE PERSPECTIVE

The choice of a protagonist created a problem of narration for Solzhenitsyn. Ivan is certainly not *un*intelligent, but his educational background is not suited for narrating a lengthy story. On the other hand, it would not have been suitable to have a highly educated narrator tell us about Ivan, because the educational and emotional distance between the two would have been too great. First-person narration by Ivan and third-person omniscient narration were therefore not possible. Solzhenitsyn uses a form of narration in *One Day in the Life of Ivan Denisovich* which is an ingenious variation of a traditional Russian narrative form, the *skaz*. This technique, employed widely in Russian folk tales, establishes an anonymous narrator who is on the same educational and social level as the protagonist and is able to transmit the main character's actions and thoughts, using the third-person singular, and sometimes the first-person plural, but giving the impression to the reader that the story is being told in first person by the protagonist. Indeed, in *One Day,* the reader has the impression that Ivan is the narrator, and only a closer look reveals that most of the story is told in third person. The reader sees through Ivan's eyes, although Ivan is *not* the narrator.

In addition to the *skaz* narrator, Solzhenitsyn employs another narrator who could be an educated fellow prisoner – the persona of the author – who is used only when the story has to deal with concepts which are clearly beyond the intellectual and linguistic grasp of both Ivan and the anonymous *skaz* narrator.

In yet other instances, this anonymous alter ego of Ivan's is present, but unable to penetrate into Ivan's mind. In these cases, we are told Ivan's thoughts in the third person, but in Ivan's own words; this perspective is mainly used for Ivan's daydreams.

We can thus discern three different narrative perspectives in *One Day in the Life of Ivan Denisovich*:

1. a prisoner (*skaz*) narrator who is on Ivan's intellectual level, but who has a greater gift for narration; he uses mainly third person, but will fall into first-person plural (we, us) when he wants to stress communality between Ivan, the other prisoners, and himself.

2. an omniscient, educated narrator, who is more or less the mouthpiece for the author's philosophical views.

3. Ivan himself, though using third person, mainly describing flashbacks and daydreams.

Once the reader is aware of these differences in point-of-view, it becomes easy to differentiate between the narrators.

> "Some fellows always thought the grass was greener on the other side of the fence. Let them envy other people if they wanted to, but Ivan knew what life was about."

This is clearly the *skaz* narrator speaking, characterized by the informal language and the choice of words.

> "With the same swift movements, Shukhov hung his overcoat on a crossbeam, and from under the mattress he pulled out his mittens, a pair of thin foot-cloths, a bit of rope, and a piece of rag with two tapes."

This is obviously the educated, omniscient third-person narrator.

> "What was the point of telling them what gang you
> worked in and what your boss was like? Now you had
> more in common with that Latvian Kilgas than with your
> own family."

This is Ivan marching along to the worksite in the morning, thinking about the letter which he will probably *not* write to his wife.

The most important function of this separation of points-of-view and the reason why Solzhenitsyn did not want to present the events in first person, through Ivan's eyes, is his intention of giving an "objective" picture of this day in Ivan's life, a goal that would have been diminished by the use of the highly subjective first-person point-of-view. Had Ivan told his own story, the reader might dismiss much of what is stated as opinion, lack of insight, or outright bias. Solzhenitsyn's method allows us to see Ivan objectively from the outside through the eyes of two anonymous fellow prisoners—one educated, the other on Ivan's peasant level—but still sharing the inner thoughts and feelings of the protagonist.

QUESTIONS FOR REVIEW

1. What is the significance of the scenes in which Caesar Markovich discusses films by Sergei Eisenstein with other intellectuals?

2. Consider the fact that the reader is never given a view of the Camp Commandant. What may be the reasons for the absence of this stock figure of prison novels?

3. What is Solzhenitsyn trying to say when he states that "the prisoner's worst enemy is the guy next to him"?

4. What is the purpose of having so many different factions of Russian society represented in the camp?

5. What is the relationship between Ivan Denisovich Shukhov and prisoner Y-81?

6. Why does Ivan forbid his wife to send him packages with food? Is there another, more important reason than the one given by Ivan himself?

7. Why is Captain Buynovsky in this "special" camp? Is his reason for having been jailed substantially different from the other prisoners?

8. What is the deeper meaning of the fact that most prisoners have new sentences added on when their original ones expire?

9. Why are escape attempts from the camp not only hopeless but also absurd?

10. What is Ivan's (Solzhenitsyn's) attitude toward intellectuals and artists? Do you think it is justified? Only in Russia, or elsewhere as well?

SUGGESTED THEME TOPICS

1. *One Day in the Life of Ivan Denisovich* can be read on three different levels of meaning. Give a coherent review of each, providing examples from the work and show how the three levels are related to each other.

2. *Cancer Ward* is another work by Alexander Solzhenitsyn which deals with life in a Soviet prison. Show the similarities and dissimilarities in the two works.

3. Leo Tolstoy has said that a novel can deal with either centuries of European history or with one day in one man's life. Show how this short novel deals with both one day in Ivan Denisovich Shukhov's life and with a piece of European history at the same time.

4. Compare *One Day in the Life of Ivan Denisovich* with one or more prison or POW novels (some titles have been suggested in this text).

5. Give a brief, interpretive comparison between the award-winning play and motion picture *Stalag 17* and *One Day in the Life of Ivan Denisovich*. Is it possible to imagine a humorous treatment of Solzhenitsyn's theme?

SELECTED BIBLIOGRAPHY

BAUER, DANIEL J. "An Existential Look at Solzhenitsyn's Ivan Denisovich." *Fu Jen Studies: Literature & Linguistics.* Taipei, Taiwan, Republic of China 12:17–38, 1979.

CISMARU, ALFRED. "The Importance of Food in *One Day in the Life of Ivan Denisovich,"* in *San Jose Studies* 9/1 (1983), pp. 99–105.

ERICSON, EDWARD E. *Solzhenitsyn: The Moral Vision.* Grand Rapids, 1980.

FEUER, KATHRYN, ed. *Solzhenitsyn: A Collection of Critical Essays.* Englewood Cliffs, 1976.

KODJAK, ANDREJ. *Alexander Solzhenitsyn.* Boston, 1978.

LUPLOW, RICHARD. "Narrative Style and Structure in *One Day in the Life of Ivan Denisovich." Russian Literature Triquarterly,* Ann Arbor, Michigan, 1(1971): 399–412.

MATTHEWS, IRENE J. "A. Solzhenitsyn's *One Day in the Life of Ivan Denisovich,"* in *The Humanities Association Review.* 23/ii (1972), pp. 8–13.

MOODY, CHRISTOPHER. *Solzhenitsyn.* New York, 1976.

RUTTNER, ECKHARD. "The Names in Solzhenitsyn's Short Novel, *One Day in the Life of Ivan Denisovich,"* in *Journal of the American Name Society.* 23(1975), pp. 103–11.

SCAMMELL, MICHAEL. *Solzhenitsyn: A Biography.* New York, 1981.

NOTES

NOTES

NOTES

WAR AND PEACE

NOTES

including
- *Life of Leo Tolstoy*
- *Synopsis of* War and Peace
- *List of Main Characters*
- *Summaries and Commentaries*
- *Character Analysis*
- *Structure, Themes, Technical Devices*
- *Questions for Discussion*
- *Selected Bibliography*

by
Marianne Sturman

Cliffs Notes

INCORPORATED

LINCOLN, NEBRASKA 68501

Editor

Gary Carey, M.A.
University of Colorado

Consulting Editor

James L. Roberts, Ph.D.
Department of English
University of Nebraska

Cliffs Notes, Inc.   Lincoln, Nebraska

CONTENTS

War and Peace

LIFE OF LEO TOLSTOY

Leo Nicolaevich Tolstoy (1828-1910) was the next to youngest of five children, descending from one of the oldest and best families in Russia. His youthful surroundings were of the upper-class gentry of the last period of serfdom. Though his life spanned the westernization of Russia, his early intellectual and cultural education was the traditional eighteenth-century training. Lyovochka (as he was called) was a tender, affection-seeking child who liked to do things "out of the ordinary." Self-consciousness was one of his youthful attributes and this process of self-scrutiny continued all his life. Indeed, Tolstoy's life is one of the best documented accounts we have of any writer, for the diaries he began at seventeen he continued through old age.

In 1844 Leo attended the University of Kazan, then one of the great seats of learning east of Berlin. He early showed a contempt for academic learning but became interested enough at the faculty of jurisprudence (the easiest course of study) to attend classes with some regularity. Kazan, next to St. Petersburg and Moscow, was a great social center for the upper class. An eligible, titled young bachelor, Tolstoy devoted his energies to engage in the brilliant social life of his set. But his homely peasant face was a constant source of embarrassment and Tolstoy took refuge in queer and original behavior. His contemporaries called him "Lyovochka the bear," for he was always stiff and awkward.

Before his second-year examinations, Tolstoy left Kazan to settle at his ancestral estate, Yasnaya Polyana (Bright Meadow), which was his share of the inheritance. Intending to farm and devote himself to improve the lot of his peasants, Tolstoy's youthful idealism soon vanished as he confronted the insurmountable distrust of the peasantry. He set off for Moscow in 1848 and for two years lived the irregular and dissipated life led by young men of his class. The diaries of this period reveal the critical self-scrutiny with which he regarded all his actions, and he itemized each deviation from his code of perfect behavior. Carnal lust and gambling were those passions most difficult for him to exorcise. As he closely observed the life around him in Moscow, Tolstoy experienced an irresistible urge to write. This time was the birth of the creative artist and the following year saw the publication of his first story, *Childhood*.

Tolstoy began his army career in 1852, joining his brother Nicolai in the Caucasus. Garrisoned among a string of Cossack outposts on the borders of Georgia, Tolstoy participated in occasional expeditions against the fierce Chechenians, the Tartar natives rebelling against Russian rule. He spent the rest of his time gambling, hunting, fornicating.

Torn amidst his inner struggle between his bad and good impulses, Tolstoy arrived at a sincere belief in God, though not in the formalized sense of the Eastern Church. The wild primitive environment of the Caucasus satisfied Tolstoy's intense physical and spiritual needs. Admiring the free, passionate, natural life of the mountain natives, he wished to turn his back forever on sophisticated society with its falseness and superficiality.

Soon after receiving his commission, Tolstoy fought among the defenders at Sevastopol against the Turks. In his *Sevastopol* sketches he describes with objectivity and compassion the matter-of-fact bravery of the Russian officers and soldiers during the siege.

By now he was a writer of nationwide reputation and when he resigned from the army and went to Petersburg, Turgenev offered him hospitality. With the leader of the capital's literary world for sponsor, Tolstoy became an intimate member of the circle of important writers and editors. But he failed to get on with these litterateurs: he had no respect for their ideal of European progress, and their intellectual arrogance appalled him. His lifelong antagonism with Turgenev typified this relationship.

His travels abroad in 1857 started Tolstoy toward his lifelong revolt against the whole organization of modern civilization. To promote the growth of individual freedom and self-awareness, he started a unique village school at Yasnaya Polyana based on futuristic progressive principles. The peasant children "brought only themselves, their receptive natures, and the certainty that it would be as jolly in school today as yesterday." But the news of his brother's illness interrupted his work. Traveling to join Nicolai in France, he first made a tour of inspection throughout the German school system. He was at his brother's side when Nicolai died at the spa near Marseilles, and this death affected him deeply. Only his work saved him from the worse depressions and sense of futility he felt toward life.

The fundamental aim of Tolstoy's nature was a search for truth, for the meaning of life, for the ultimate aims of art, for family happiness, for God. In marriage his soul found a release from this never ending quest, and once approaching his ideal of family happiness, Tolstoy entered upon the greatest creative period of his life.

In the first fifteen years of his marriage to Sonya (Sofya Andreyevna Bers) the great inner crisis he later experienced in his "conversion" was procrastinated, lulled by the triumph of spontaneous life over questioning reason. While his nine children grew up, his life was happy, almost idyllic, despite the differences which arose between him and the wife sixteen years his junior. As an inexperienced bride of eighteen, the city bred Sonya had many difficult adjustments to make. She was the mistress of a country estate as well as the helpmate of a man whose previous life she had not shared. Her constant pregnancies and boredom and loneliness marred the great love she and Tolstoy shared. In this exhilarating period of his growing family, Tolstoy created the epic novels, *War and Peace* and *Anna Karenina* while Sonya, rejoicing at his creative genius, faithfully turned his rough drafts into fair copy.

Toward the end of 1866, while writing *Anna Karenina,* Tolstoy entered on the prolonged and fateful crisis which resulted in his conversion. He recorded part of this spiritual struggle in *Anna Karenina.* The meaning of life consists in living according to one's "inner goodness," he concluded. Only through emotional and religious commitment can one discover this natural truth. Uniquely interpreting the Gospels, Tolstoy discovered Christ's entire message was contained in the idea "that ye resist not evil." This doctrine of "non-resistance" became the foundation of Tolstoyism, where one lived according to nature, renouncing the artificial refinements of society. Self-gratification, Tolstoy believed, perverted man's inherent goodness. Therefore property rights — ownership by one person of "things that belong to all" — is a chief source of evil. Carnal lust, ornamental clothing, fancy food are other symptoms of the corrupting influence of civilization. In accordance with his beliefs, Tolstoy renounced all copyrights to his works since 1881, divided his property among his family members, dressed in peasant homespun, ate only vegetables, gave up liquor and tobacco, engaged in manual work, and even learned to cobble his own boots. Renouncing creative art on account of its corrupt refinements, Tolstoy wrote polemic tracts and short stories which embodied his new faith.

But the incongruity of his ideals and his actual environment grieved Tolstoy. With his family, he lived in affluence. His wife and children (except for Alexandra) disapproved of his philosophy. As they became more estranged and embittered by their differences, Sonya's increasing hysteria made his latter years a torment for Tolstoy.

All three stages of Tolstoy's life and writings (pre-conversion, conversion, effects of conversion) reflect the single quest of his career: to find the ultimate truth of human existence. After finding this truth, his life was a series of struggles to practice his preachings. He became a public figure both as a sage and an artist during his lifetime and Yasnaya Polyana became a mecca for a never-ceasing stream of pilgrims. The intensity and heroic scale of his life have been preserved for us from the memoirs of friends and family and wisdom seeking visitors. Though Tolstoy expressed his philosophy and theory of history with the same thoroughness and lucidity he devoted to his novels, he is known today chiefly for his important contributions to literature. Although his artistic influence is wide and still pervasive, few writers have achieved the personal stature with which to emulate his epic style.

SYNOPSIS OF *WAR AND PEACE*

PART I

We are introduced to the major families through the vehicle of a soirée at the Anna Pavlovna's home, a name-day celebration at the Rostovs, and a description of the isolated existence of the Bolkonskys at their country seat. Prince Andrey and Pierre discuss their futures and what they seek in life, both young men idealizing the "man of destiny" who is soon to invade Russia. Old Count Bezuhov dies, leaving Pierre wealthy, titled, and the most eligible bachelor in Petersburg.

PART II

Nikolay Rostov and Prince Andrey undergo their first war experience at the battle of Schöngraben. They each discover the ineffectuality of the individual in a mass situation. Nikolay accepts being a "cog in a machine" and Andrey rejects being part of the administering forces, choosing, instead, to fight at the front.

PART III

Pierre marries Ellen; Anatole unsuccessfully courts Marya. Andrey attends the war council on the eve of Austerlitz and wishes to be a hero.

He is wounded during the battle. Compared to the limitless sky, which symbolizes death, Napoleon seems to Andrey petty and insignificant.

PART IV

Nikolay, with Denisov, is home on leave and he ignores his sweetheart Sonya. Pierre wounds Dolohov in a duel over Ellen's alleged infidelity. Liza Bolkonsky dies giving birth to a son, leaving Andrey with a deep sense of unassuageable guilt. Dolohov falls in love with Sonya, avenges her rejection of him by fleecing Nikolay during a card game. "Intensity" is the keynote of this section, shown by incidents of love and hate, life and death.

PART V

Separated from his wife, Pierre devotes himself to "goodness," by joining the masons and by an inept reforming of his estates. He and the retired Andrey have a discussion about the meaning of life and death and Andrey is inspired with new hope. The significance of their exchange points out the contrast between Pierre and Andrey. Meanwhile Nikolay has rejoined his starving regiment and Denisov faces court-martial for stealing food for his men. Nikolay asks the tsar for Denisov's pardon and witnesses the meeting between Napoleon and Alexander, a meeting between the old and new orders of government. His petition rejected, Nikolay decides the sovereign knows best and submits to "higher authority."

PART VI

This is an account of "real life," as opposed to politics, where the "inner man" is more significant than the "outer man." Andrey becomes involved with Speransky's circle of reformers, but when he falls in love with Natasha these activities pall for him. Pierre becomes disillusioned with masonry, while Princess Marya is made more unhappy by her father. The Rostovs' financial problems increase, and Andrey goes to Switzerland.

PART VII

With the wolf hunt, the sleigh ride, Christmas celebrations, and family harmony, the Rostovs enjoy the last period of their "youth." Natasha's restlessness increases during Andrey's absence, the family is almost bankrupt, and there is foreboding of hard times to come as the children enter adulthood.

PART VIII

Natasha meets Anatole during the opera and is almost abducted by him. During her near-nervous breakdown, Pierre emerges as her comforter and their love is implied.

PART IX

The life-and-death struggle against France begins, with Napoleon depicted as a glory-seeking fool. Andrey turns away from his past and commits himself to the men in his regiment, who adore him. Nikolay refrains from killing a Frenchman and is decorated for bravery because he took a prisoner. Natasha slowly recovers, aided by religious faith. Petya joins the army out of a youthful patriotism which Pierre also shares. The Russians respond massively to the national threat, and Pierre feels within him an "ultimate mission" involving his love, the comet, Napoleon, the war itself.

PART X

The French penetrating Russia march toward their doom in the "irresistible tide" of destiny. The old prince dies and Marya moves her household to Moscow, but the war looms closer. Despite the national upheaval, the Petersburg salons remain the same. Marya and Nikolay have a romantic first meeting, while Pierre visits the death-marked Andrey on the eve of Borodino. The battle is described as a death duel, with the Russians winning morally, if not physically. This marks the turning point from defeat to victory for Russia.

PART XI

Tolstoy discusses mass activity as a combination of "infinitesimal units of activity" and provides a short summary of past and future events. Moscow's abandonment and burning is the great deed that saves Russia and the moment-by-moment details of the event are discussed, including Rastoptchin's last-minute bid for glory at the expense of the cause he pretends to further. The Rostovs leave Moscow, their caravan including the mortally wounded Prince Andrey. He is reunited with Natasha, who nurses him. So close to death, Andrey understands the quality of divine love. Truth results from a life-death confrontation. Pierre conceives the plan to assassinate Napoleon, but other incidents show he is destined to fail.

PART XII

Nikolay and Marya meet again in the provinces, and Marya travels to see her brother. She and Natasha are with him when he dies. Pierre is nearly executed by the French, who accuse him of incendiarism. He experiences a "rebirth" in prison through Karataev, an almost mythic figure symbolizing the unity of love and hate, life and death.

PART XIII

End of war is in sight as the French retreat more and more rapidly. Their retreat is the "fruit" of "unconscious activity" rather than the will of Napoleon. Pierre discovers an intense freedom in prison.

PART XIV

This period of guerilla fighting involves Denisov, Dolohov, and Petya, who gets killed. A surprise attack led by Denisov and Dolohov frees Pierre and other prisoners. In a flashback we learn how Karataev died, what Pierre suffered and overcame during the death march. Death and decay are part of the processes of life and growth.

PART XV

Natasha and Marya are recalled from their mourning into active life: Marya by her household responsibilities, Natasha by exercising love to comfort her bereaved mother. As the war history is over, Kutuzov's career ends. A new era begins to disclose itself with Russia's entrance into international leadership. Tolstoy apotheosizes Kutuzov. Pierre and Natasha meet again.

FIRST EPILOGUE

Tolstoy details the "happy ending" of the careers of his fictional characters in scenes to show the domestic happiness of Nikolay and Marya Rostov, Natasha and Pierre Bezuhov. The cycle of life begins anew as Nikolinka, Andrey's son, comes of age and desires to be like Pierre and like his father.

SECOND EPILOGUE

This is the philosphical exegesis wherein Tolstoy shows that "free will" is a mere construct which historians use to explain the movements of nations and people. Causality is impossible to descry when we regard the pattern of historical events, and the concept of "free will" prevents deep understanding of the nature of history. The paradox, however, is inescapable: we need to maintain the illusion of free will in order to carry on our daily lives, for our hopes, our basic beliefs depend on this notion of an inner consciousness; at the same time we are victims of innumerable and infinitesimal constraints of necessity which spell out our destiny and we are not "free" at all.

LIST OF MAIN CHARACTERS

BOLKONSKY FAMILY

Prince Nikolay Andrei[vi]tch Bolkonsky

Scion of an ancient and honorable family, now an old man, who clings more and more to the values of an outdated feudal society.

Prince Andrey Bolkonsky

His son and heir, who is an intensely intellectual, basically egotistical young man who seeks to exchange his sense of alienation for a sense of being at one with the world. His quest affirms his nihilism.

Princess Marya Bolkonsky

A plain, graceless young woman who sustains her lonely life by a strong Christian piety.

Mademoiselle Bourienne

Marya's companion, an orphaned Frenchwoman of a frivolous and opportunistic nature.

Nikolushka, later *Nikolinka*

Prince Andrey's son, who attains adolescence by the end of the novel.

Princess Liza Bolkonsky

Andrey's wife, a silly, chattering society girl who never grows up and who dies in childbirth.

BEZUHOV FAMILY

Count Kirill Vladmirovitch Bezuhov

An old man, once a grandee in Catherine's court, who dies early in the novel after legitimizing his oldest son, to whom he leaves vast wealth.

Pierre Bezuhov

The hero of the novel and the old count's son, whose spiritual development is the best expression of Tolstoy's philosophy.

ROSTOV FAMILY

Count Ilya Rostov

A gregarious, good-natured, and generous family man whose interest in maintaining his family's pleasures contributes to his financial ruination.

Countess Natalya Rostov

His wife, a typical Russian noblewoman, whose main interests center within the family.

Natasha Rostov

The heroine of the novel and a bewitching young girl whom Tolstoy regards as the creature-manifestation of love, nature, and femininity.

Nikolay Rostov

The oldest son, who is an officer in the hussars and who later marries Marya Bolkonsky. He is an unimaginative young man who believes that doing one's duty is the highest virtue of the individual.

Vera Rostov

The eldest child, who marries Alphonse Berg, an opportunistic youth of German descent.

Petya Rostov

The youngest child, whose vivacity is closest to that of Natasha and who dies prematurely near the end of the war.

Sonya

The Rostov's poor relation whom they raise with their own children. She devotes her life to loving Nikolay but never marries him.

Boris Drubetskoy

Son of a friend of Countess Rostov who has been educated with the Rostov children. Boris becomes important in court circles and is a career-man in the army.

KURAGIN FAMILY

Prince Vassily

A well-practiced courtier whose life is a series of political and social maneuvers to maintain prestige.

Ippolit Kuragin

His dull-witted son, who would like to compromise Andrey's wife, Liza.

Anatole Kuragin

An avowed hedonist whose handsomeness attracts both Princess Marya, whom he would like to marry for her fortune, and Natasha, whom he all but seduces.

Ellen Kuragin, later Countess Bezuhov

A beautiful sensualist who married Pierre and who becomes a celebrated *salonniere*.

MAJOR HISTORICAL FIGURES

Napoleon

Tolstoy uses him as the outstanding example of the "great man" who is so deluded by his own mystique he cannot see himself as history's unwitting tool.

Kutuzov

Commander-in-chief of the Russian forces, whom Tolstoy apotheosizes as the "Russian of Russians" whose intuitive power and humble self-image contribute to the victory.

Alexander I

Tsar of the Russias whose divine-right function denies his personal existence. He is depicted as a noble figurehead.

Speransky

The intellectual young secretary of state whom Tolstoy treats ironically. Speransky believes his motives are to liberalize and enlighten the operations of government, whereas his real motives are to belittle others.

Wintzengerode, Pfuhl, Weierother, and others

Prussian generals whom Tolstoy makes fun of for their mechanistic and "scientific" interest in war.

Prince Bagration

General hailed as the "hero of Austerlitz." Tolstoy shows that in reality he was a passive leader in the midst of numerous, separate events which compose the battle of Austerlitz.

OTHER CHARACTERS

Platon Karataev

More symbolic than real, this peasant is Pierre's fellow prisoner and the inspiration of Bezuhov's conversion.

Vaska Denisov

Captain of Nikolay's regiment who falls in love with, and is rejected by, Natasha. He is Nikolay's mentor in battle and performs the same function later for Petya Rostov.

Dolohov

Penniless cardsharp, notorious as a bully. His cruelty and bravery play a part in various incidents in the novel.

Anna Pavlovna Scherer

Celebrated St. Petersburg hostess who constantly schemes to maintain her prestige in court circles.

SUMMARIES AND COMMENTARIES

PART I

CHAPTERS 1-6

Summary

Anna Pavlovna talks with Prince Vassily Kuragin, the first guest to arrive at one of her soirées in 1805. "Chère Annette" is a forty-year-old spinster who runs one of the most celebrated salons in Petersburg, and as usual, her manner of speaking expresses enthusiasm whether she feels it or not. She speaks of Napoleon as the Antichrist scourging Europe, asserting that the lofty-souled Alexander I must save them all against the "hydra of revolution" Bonaparte represents. Easily changing the subject, she tells Prince Vassily how charming his three children are, and that she knows a wealthy heiress to match with his profligate son, Anatole. The lady is Princess Marya Bolkonsky, who lives in the country and is dominated by her old father. Her brother Prince Andrey will appear here this evening with his wife Liza. Annette promises to speak to Liza about this matter.

With all her guests arrived, Anna Pavlovna supervises them smoothly, making sure each conversation group avoids controversy as well as boredom. The "little princess," Liza Bolkonsky, chatters eagerly. Although visibly pregnant, and once considered the most seductive young woman in Petersburg, she still makes every man she speaks to feel successful and masculine. But when she addresses her husband in the same coquettish manner she uses for casual acquaintances, Prince Andrey turns away with an involuntary grimace. His bored expression is a vivid contrast to the liveliness of his little wife. Anna Pavlovna is uncomfortable when Pierre Bezuhov arrives, for he is bound to be rude. This is his first appearance in society since his return from abroad. An illegitimate son of Count Bezuhov, a celebrated dandy in the days of Catherine, Pierre's tall stout figure and his "clever, though shy, observant and natural look" distinguishes this mild, bespectacled young man. Prince Andrey's handsome face lights up for the first time when he sees Pierre, and from their greeting, it is obvious they are good friends. Prince Vassily's daughter, the beautiful Ellen, now arrives. She wears a radiant, unvarying smile as if to acknowledge her awareness of the splendid beauty barely hidden by her décolleté. As she and her father leave, an elderly lady accosts Prince Vassily, begging him to petition the emperor so her son Boris can transfer to the Guards. She is Anna Mihalovna Drubetskoy, a member of one of the best families in Russia. Now that she is poor and out of touch with her former connections, she appears uninvited at the soirée expressly to beg Prince Vassily's favor. Wearily the elderly courtier agrees to petition for her son.

When the guests talk of the assassination of the Duc d'Enghien, Anna Pavlovna's worst fears are realized. Pierre shocks everyone by his earnest defense of Bonaparte, who, he says, saved France from anarchy. Prince Andrey joins in, defending Napoleon's action. The tension subsides when Ippolit, Prince Vassily's dull-witted son, tells a pointless story. The mystified guests do not know whether to regard Ippolit as a clown or a wag.

After the party, Pierre and Andrey spend the evening together. Bezuhuv must choose a career, but he refuses to join the army to help fight against "the greatest man in the world." Bolkonsky admits he is going to war merely to escape his wearisome life at home. Liza joins them now and makes a scene because her husband is so changed to her and treats her as if she were a child, she tearfully says. While they dine alone, Bolkonsky offers Pierre some advice. First off, he says, never marry, or you will be forever imprisoned in the enchanted circle of soirées, balls, gossip. Society women like Liza cannot live without this silliness and vanity and through them everything becomes trivial. Second, Andrey goes on, Pierre should no longer associate with Anatole Kuragin and his dissipated set of bachelor friends. Bezuhov readily agrees but cannot resist the drinking party Kuragin invited him to that night. The drunken evening ends in scandal when Pierre and his friends tie a police officer to a live bear and toss both into the river.

Commentary

Like a host welcoming strangers to his town, Tolstoy throws a cocktail party to introduce us to most of the people in his novel. At Anna Pavlovna's we meet the main characters as we usually meet people in real life: we are given a minimum of biographical detail and our attention is drawn to a person's features, his smile, the look in his eyes, his way of looking or not looking at another person. We first learn of Pierre, for instance, when Anna Pavlovna greets him with the nod she reserves for her lowest-ranking guests. This harmless-appearing, massively built, bespectacled youth must possess a special power if he can threaten the equanimity of a large soirée. Our awareness of his latent power is our first indication of Pierre's importance in the novel.

Prince Andrey is introduced to us through his lively little wife, with Tolstoy emphasizing her charm and appeal to the male guests. This charm has no effect on Andrey, who turns away in disgust when he arrives and turns eagerly to Pierre. Clearly we observe how their naturalness and spontaneity distinguish Pierre and Andrey from the other guests and that Tolstoy favors this distinction.

Sketching in other details like Ellen's unvarying smile and her décolleté, Liza's seductiveness despite her pregnancy, Anna Pavlovna's constant enthusiasm, and Ippolit's storytelling, Tolstoy provides us with a penetrating first impression of the "enchanted circle" of Petersburg life.

We learn more about Pierre and Andrey from their conversations after the party. As they both regard Napoleon as their hero, we can see their youthful desires for fame, glory, love of men. While these desires for power are basically the same that motivate the social climbers at Annette's salon, the egotism of Pierre and Andrey represents no more than a phase of their maturation and not its end. Indeed, Tolstoy spends a large part of *War and Peace* showing how self-conscious and selfish interests lead to disillusion and how self-aware heroism turns to powerlessness. Besides denying the greatness and power of Napoleon, Tolstoy carries Pierre and Andrey through experiences that make each conclude the nothingness of personality and the greatness of soul.

The little we know of their heritage is already a key to their destiny. Because Pierre is illegitimate, his search for identity is unencumbered by personal history; in effect, he is without history. Prince Andrey, however, bound by strong family ties as well as by marriage, must escape his past in order to find his purpose in life. Bolkonsky's past already foredooms him, whereas the freer Pierre will find a meaningful way of life.

By introducing Pierre and Andrey at the beginning of their careers, Tolstoy indicates to us that the novel will deal with their personal development. Having observed the microcosm of Russian aristocracy at Anna Pavlovna's salon, we learn that Tolstoy will discuss society as a whole. With Napoleon being the personal hero of Pierre and Andrey as well as the "Antichrist" threatening the world of the ruling classes, we recognize that history itself is the unifying investigation of *War and Peace*.

CHAPTERS 7-21

Summary

After Prince Vassily gets Boris Drubetskoy his commission in the Guards, Anna Mihalovna returns triumphant to Moscow, where she lives with the Rostovs, her rich relatives who have supported Boris and educated him with their children. Countess Rostov and her daughter—who both have the name Natalya—are celebrating their name-day at this time. The guests are busy gossiping about Pierre Bezuhov's scandalous conduct during the drinking party in Petersburg even while his poor old father lies on his deathbed. They also wonder whether Prince Vassily, the old man's nearest legal relative, or Pierre will inherit the immense fortune.

Suddenly the children invade the drawing room, led by the irrepressible thirteen-year-old Natasha. Boris Drubetskoy and Nikolay Rostov follow her, with sixteen-year-old Sonya (the Rostov's niece who lives with them) and Petya Rostov, the youngest child. The children's gaiety and high spirits are in vivid contrast with the small talk of the adults.

The dark-haired Sonya, with the shyness and softness of a half-grown kitten, loves Nikolay and is jealous when he flirts with Julie Karagin. Nikolay swears he loves only Sonya. Natasha and Boris are also in love, and they promise to marry each other when she is older.

Dinner is held up until Marya Dmitryevna Ahrosimov arrives. Known for her frankness as *le terrible dragon*, the old lady has won the respect and fear of Moscow and Petersburg society. She congratulates her goddaughter and the countess and turns to scold Pierre for his behavior with the police officer.

The men talk about war and the emperor's proclamation that he will defend Russia and her allies against Napoleon. Excited by the discussion, Nikolay cries out that the Russians "must die or conquer" and everyone applauds his youthful patriotism. From the children's end of the table, Natasha's voice rings out as she impudently asks what dessert shall be. Everyone pretends to be horrified at her interruption, although her pertness amuses the guests. After dinner the men play cards, then there is dancing. Feeling very grown up, Natasha asks Pierre to dance, and Count Rostov and Marya Dmitryevna perform a complex écossaise.

While the Rostovs blithely celebrate, Count Bezuhov suffers another stroke. Doctors and undertakers arrive at the immense house. A priest administers extreme unction. A deeply moved Pierre hastens to his father's side, shadowed by Anna Mihalovna, who has last-minute hopes for part of the inheritance. To Pierre, the old man seems unchanged; he has the same leonine head and strong healthy features. But a shudder passes through the body to show the nearness of death. Perhaps at the horrow-struck expression on his son's face, perhaps as comment on his own helplessness, the old man suddenly smiles. Then he lapses into a coma.

Everyone prepares for the vigil. Prince Vassily, Anna Mihalovna, the count's eldest niece Katish, and Pierre are together in the next room. Katish and Anna Mihalovna have a vulgar argument about the inheritance portfolio. During the brief scuffle they learn that the old count has just passed on.

Commentary

As a counterbalance to the first scenes, Tolstoy takes us to a family party in Moscow with Marya Dmitryevna's frankness and warmth as counterpoise to Anna Pavlovna's superficiality and coldness. Joy, affection, youth, generosity, and spontaneity characterize the name-day celebration, with Natasha as the radiant focus for these qualities. We recognize her potential intensity and intuitive force immediately. Her emotional freedom and readiness to love identify her as the female protagonist, and we see, as they dance, the first connection between Pierre and his future bride. With Nikolay's patriotism stirred, with Natasha's singing and with her father and godmother dancing, Tolstoy provides a sense of the fullness of life as the party is in full swing.

Now we are ready to learn of death. Without irony, Tolstoy tells us that as the Rostovs dance the "sixth anglaise" Count Bezuhov suffers his sixth stroke. This is but one of many ways that the author devises to emphasize a favorite idea: we cannot know life without knowing death. At this early juncture, however, the statement merely prefaces what Tolstoy considers a basic investigation in the novel. The youthful characters of *War and Peace* have yet to discover the awesomeness of life before this death can deeply touch them. Here, the loss of the old count shows the symbolic passing of the old order while the new generation blooms on this name-day. We have yet to see the intensifying throes of maturation and the actual tension between generations to come later.

CHAPTERS 22-25

Summary

At Bleak Hills, the estate of Prince Nikolay Andreivitch Bolkonsky, everyone awaits the arrival of Prince Andrey and his wife Liza. Besides the old man, nicknamed the "Prussian king," the household includes Princess Marya, her orphaned companion Mlle. Bourienne, the prince's architect Mihail Ivanovitch (whom the old man admits to the table to show that all men are equal), and numerous servants. Once a commander-in-chief, the old man was banished from Moscow by Paul; although reinstated by Catherine, he still lives in exile, declaring that anyone who wishes to see him can travel the 150 versts from Moscow. Secluded in the country, the old prince has many occupations — mathematics, woodworking, gardening, writing his memoirs, managing the estate — each of which fills an apportioned place in his unwavering daily schedule, where even meals must be served at a precise moment. Human vices derive from idleness and superstition, proclaims the prince, and energy and intelligence are the only virtues. With this in mind, he educates his daughter in algebra and geometry and maps out her life in uninterrupted occupation.

Princess Marya suffers each day during her father's lessons, her misery and fear blocking her comprehension. Each day he dismisses her in anger and she goes to work out the problem in her room. Today she turns to her correspondence with her childhood friend, Julie Karagin. Julie's letter contains news of the name-day party and of the splendid Nikolay Rostov who is going to fight the "Corsican monster." Julie writes that Pierre Bezuhov inherited the immense fortune and title of his father and warns Marya that Prince Vassily intends to marry her to his son, Anatole. In answer, Princess Marya expresses her profound religiosity: killing one's fellow man even in war is a crime, Pierre deserves pity for being exposed to new temptations from his sudden wealth, and if God ordains wifehood and motherhood for her destiny she will submit to His will. Stolid and plain-faced, the twenty-eight-year-old Marya becomes beautiful when her large, deep, luminous eyes express, as now, her soulful intensity.

Prince Andrey and Liza arrive later that day. Though they hardly know each other, the sisters-in-law tearfully embrace and Andrey feels uncomfortable at the unnecessary emotion. Quickly cheerful, Liza begins to chatter about society trivia. Marya asks about her pregnancy and the little princess bursts into tears; she is frightened of childbirth.

Andrey greets his father with eager and reverential eyes, and the old man hides his delight at the meeting by mocking the new military men of the time. Liza is awed by her father-in-law, especially as he rudely interrupts her patter of small talk to continue his favorite theme. The old man loves to censure the modern politicians who do not know how to stand up to that "scheming upstart" Bonaparte, as a "real Russian" would. But Napoleon is a splendid tactician, Andrey argues, and his father cites all the blunders the Frenchman committed. Despite his isolation, the old man accurately judges current affairs.

Getting ready to leave the following evening, Prince Andrey is packing in his room when his sister comes to talk with him. Marya begs him to lessen his "pride of intellect" and above all, to show their father more respect. She also asks him to understand Liza's pitiable plight, being separated from the town social life she depends on. Marya now presents her atheist brother a silver talisman engraved with Christ's image and Andrey promises to wear it faithfully.

He goes to take farewell of his father, who gives his son a letter of commendation to his friend and commander-in-chief, Mihail Ilarionovitch Kutuzov. Only serve if the position does honor to you, counsels the proud father. The old prince promises to care for Liza during her confinement, even agreeing to send for an obstetrician from Moscow when the time comes. Andrey makes one more request: if he should die his father must raise his little son at Bleak Hills and not with Liza.

Commentary

The scenes at Bleak Hills are excellent examples to show how Tolstoy works his materials on two levels. A bastion of the old order, the Bolkonsky estate seems a working model of the Russian aristocracy, with the old prince as tsar of an isolated Russia that will cease to exist after the coming war. Imperious and rigid though he is, the old man conveys to his children a pride of heritage, personal integrity, and love of the land which are among the Tolstoyan virtues. Princess Marya's religiosity and Prince Andrey's intellectual coldness equally derive from their father's character. Both children are representative types of the Russian temperament.

On the personal level, we see the interaction among the individual members of the Bolkonsky family. Princess Marya provides the sentiment and emotional content in the family relationship that her godless father and brother are too emotionally restrained to express. In this respect she fulfills the Tolstoyan function of the female: to hold the family together and provide it with emotional richness. In her talk with Prince Andrey, we see how her Christian fidelity and depth of feeling contribute to express her familial love. The childlike Liza clearly lacks Marya's emotional intensity.

Another outstanding feature of Tolstoy's technique is his smooth transition between scenes. Although the author brings us deep into the country, he maintains continuity with previous settings through Julie's letter, which contains news of Moscow previously withheld from us — Pierre's inheritance, for instance — and Liza's prattle about Petersburg soirées.

The description of the country routine at Bleak Hills provides us with an overall sense of continuity, for Tolstoy has now completed his introduction of domestic life in contemporary Russia. We have yet to witness the military scene. Although Tolstoy's categorization of the threefold environments of Petersburg, Moscow, and rural life is an important structural device in the novel, these settings provide the moral conditioning of the characters. Petersburg, for instance, is where socially powerful people have the least awareness of social and personal reality. Prince Vassily, Anna Pavlovna, and Liza are most at home here. Less prestigious a setting, Moscow allows for the spontaneity of Natasha and her family, while country life nurtures the "Russian-souled" Prince Bolkonsky and his children.

In all three settings we hear Tolstoy's characters discuss the imminent conflict between Alexander and Napoleon. Of these discussions, Prince Bolkonsky's are the most prophetic, with Tolstoy speaking through the old man, whose "natural" life in the country has made his vision the least clouded. Napoleon is a mere puppet of history, declares the old prince, and the generals in Russia who are cowed by his "military genius" do not understand their nation's destiny. Only a "real Russian" like Suvorov or Potemkin would know how to put down this upstart schemer. Indeed, Tolstoy depicts Napoleon as history's deluded tool and raises Kutuzov to become the hero who saves his nation.

Thus we are given the main themes, the basic setting, the characters, the problems they face, and a foreshadowing of their solutions by the end of Part I. Not only do we see each individual being consecrated to his personal search, but we see how Russia herself must affirm her national destiny. Individuals relating to circumstance and nations to history are part of Tolstoy's investigation. Part I tells us that a huge philosophic treatise will become manifest through the powerful resources of the novelistic mode.

24

PART II

CHAPTERS 1-8

Summary

As an adjutant in Kutuzov's suite, Prince Andrey is lighthearted and stimulated by his work. His alert expression bears no trace of his former ennui. At this time in October 1805, he is privy to the discussions between Kutuzov and his Austrian allies. The Russian general orders an inspection of his men, haggard from a thousand-mile march, to prove to his ally how unfit his troops are for fighting. However, circumstances operate against Kutuzov: the Austrian general Mack suddenly arrives, reporting the utter defeat of his army at Ulm. This means that half the defensive campaign of Austria is lost and the Russians must fight sooner than anyone had planned.

Nikolay Rostov, now an ensign in Vaska Denisov's squadron of hussars, is billeted near Branau, the scene of the next battle. Nikolay and Denisov have become good friends from sharing quarters, the younger man regarding his brave captain as a hero. At this time, Nikolay suffers a conflict of loyalties between his personal honor and that of the squadron. In the presence of other officers, Rostov inappropriately reported a fellow hussar to his colonel for theft. The officer accused Nikolay of lying and Rostov hotly called the colonel a liar. While Nikolay now agrees he was wrong to compromise the regiment's honor in public, he refuses to apologize to the colonel, as his comrades ask him to.

Kutuzov falls back to Vienna, burning bridges as he crosses each river. As his troops now cross the Enns, they see the French encampment on the near side. The weather is mild, the soldiers bored but cheerful. At the moment of the first cannon boom the sun appears from beneath a cloud: the two impressions blend into one "inspiring note of gaiety." Soon only Denisov's squadron remains on the side of the river where the column of blue-clothed French steadily advances. The 600 yards between the two forces seems a barrier between life and death and each hussar is alert. Ignoring the grapeshot falling around him, Denisov gallops back and forth among his men, cheering them on. Rostov feels calmed, almost blissful. As soon as the squadron has safely crossed the bridge, Denisov receives the order to burn it. The men grab straw and go back, and Nikolay is under fire for the first time. Paralyzed with fright, Rostov regards the peaceful eternity of the sunlit sky. But the bridge is fired and Nikolay and his comrades return to the safe side. Their colonel is proud of a successfully accomplished mission. With only two men wounded and one dead, the losses "are not worth mentioning," he says.

Commentary

Tolstoy arranges these chapters to illustrate the pyramidical structure of the military chain of command. First, reproducing some of the men's conversations, he shows us the broad base of the mass of common soldiers. Then he scales to the top as he depicts Kutuzov and the general staff of the Russo-Austrian alliance, including the now-alert Prince Andrey. We discover how the aging Russian general shows primary concern for the welfare of his men as he tries to avoid battle because the troops are exhausted and ill-equipped.

When the troops move toward the front we see how the closeness of death quickens their morale and how each man forgets himself during the critical moment. Tolstoy now individualizes Nikolay Rostov to show how one person becomes part of the whole and takes his place as a smooth-working cog in the military machine. The vehicle for this statement is the incident of the theft where Nikolay asserts his personal honor and then must reconsider his action in terms of regimental honor. Under fire, the need to apologize to the colonel disappears. Having faced death in the line of duty, Nikolay has signified his commitment to the regiment. The pervasiveness of death is symbolized by the indifferent heavens whose sunny peace Rostov envies in that helpless moment on the bridge.

CHAPTERS 9-21

Summary

After numerous retreats and skirmishes, Kutuzov crosses the Danube and successfully engages Mortier's division of the French forces. Despite the victory, a third of the Russian troops are disabled, with the rest more ill-fed and ill-equipped than before. Kutuzov dispatches Prince Andrey to report the victory to the Austrian court at Brünn. Exuberant from participating in battle, Bolkonsky becomes dispirited when the Austrian war minister receives the news with indifference.

At Brünn, Bolkonsky lodges with Bilibin, an acquaintance of his circle known for his wit and urbanity. From his diplomatist friend,

Andrey learns about the behind-the-scenes politicking of the war. The Austrians are dissatisfied, says Bilibin, because Kutuzov allowed most of Mortier's division to escape. Moreover, the Austrians support Russia's troops on their land and Napoleon still occupies Vienna. Bilibin foresees that Austria will make a secret peace with the French and turn against Russia. After Prince Andrey has an audience with the Austrian emperor Francis, he decides to quickly return to fight with the exhausted army, although they will be unable to hold off the French at the next battle. He has seen enough of the gamesmanship attitude of the controlling powers.

At first Kutuzov refuses to allow Andrey to go to the front under General Bagration. We will be lucky if one-tenth of Bagration's men survive, he says. The exhausted army of Prince Bagration must hold off the entire French force while Kutuzov and the main body of men and supplies gain a safe retreat and await fresh reinforcements from Russia. Fortunately, Murat believes Bagration's tiny force to be the whole army and he sues for a three-day truce. Napoleon, however, orders Murat to attack.

As Prince Andrey is first shown around the fortifications, he takes notes in order to make suggestions to Bagration. He overhears a conversation between two officers, one of whom is Captain Tushin, one of the "unsung heroes" of the coming campaign. Tushin expresses Tolstoy's fatalistic view of death. The front lines are so close together that the French and Russian soldiers talk together and share a joke. But their guns and cannon face each other in mute menace.

As Andrey observes Bagration during the barrage, he suddenly realizes the general gives no orders to the officers reporting to him. Rather, he seems to approve of everything they tell him, and the officers return to their men calmer and more cheerful. Marching past Bagration, the troops seem composed and confident, and when the general leads the attack, with a "hurrah" the men gaily plunge down the hill to rout the enemy. This covers the retreat of the right flank. Tushin, whose battery has been overlooked and abandoned in the center, meanwhile sets fire to the town of Schöngraben. The French are kept busy putting out the flames while the Russians gain more time for retreat. Nikolay's regiment, however, is attacked before it can get away. Denisov encourages his hussars, and Rostov joyfully spurs his horse to a gallop. His mount shot out from under him, Nikolay sees the enemy running toward him. He realizes in surprise they intend to kill him— "me whom everyone is so fond of"—and he races back to his own lines.

Meantime Captain Tushin and his gunners are isolated but they maintain a steady fire until Andrey brings orders to retreat. Bolkonsky fights his panic as he remains to help remove the cannon.

As he gathers his officers' battle reports, Bagration holds Tushin in disgrace for abandoning two cannon in the center. The little captain is too humble to explain there were no troops to reinforce him. Prince Andrey offers explanation, saying how Tushin operated with two-thirds of his men disabled and no troops to back him up. We owe our success to Captain Tushin's steadfastness and bravery, he tells Bagration. Then he abruptly leaves the council, feeling bitter and melancholy.

Meanwhile Nikolay huddles over a fire in the woods, lonely and miserable. He recalls the cheerful faces of his family, sees images of soldiers wounded, unwounded, battling, and forlornly wonders why he came to be here.

Commentary

Tolstoy uses the Schöngraben engagement as Nikolay's "baptism of fire," a ceremonial rite initiating him into the world of anonymity and death. His happy childhood is a dream of the past as he abandons himself to the grim presentness of war. By contrast, Prince Andrey sees war as the background for self-assertion and he dreams his life will become significant when he is a hero. Twice he is disillusioned in these chapters. Bringing the news of Kutuzov's victory to the court at Brünn, Bolkonsky's exhilaration vanishes among the cold responses of the politicians for whom war is an instrument of gamesmanship. For the first time he is aware of the gap between the commanders and the men who do the actual fighting. His second disappointment occurs when he bears witness to Captain Tushin's courage, which otherwise would have remained in obscurity. That heroic acts can be undiscovered and unrewarded fills Andrey with bitterness. Bolkonsky has not yet learned that heroism expresses submissiveness and resignation, like that of Captain Tushin, and not egotism and self-assertion. General Bagration understands this, realizing battles are won or lost according to the confidence and tranquility within each soldier and not according to the commander's plans. He does not initiate action himself, but reflects and underscores the best qualities of his men during battle. By submitting to inevitable forces, Bagration, as well as Kutuzov, can gain ultimate victory.

28

Tolstoy thus states an important idea that he repeats throughout the novel: heroism and greatness derive from unselfconsciousness, whereas egotism and intellectuality lead to alienation, weakness, and illusion.

PART III

CHAPTERS 1-5

Summary

Since he has become wealthy and titled, Pierre is one of the most sought-after young men in Petersburg. He even believes, as weak-willed persons do, that he deserves the attention and admiration of the people around him. Prince Vassily, who attaches himself to the young count and helps him manage his suddenly numerous business affairs, succeeds in involving Pierre with his daughter. As they are always thrown together at parties, Pierre is soon overpowered by the accessibility of Ellen's dazzling décolleté and feels fated to marry her. Although uneasy at rumors linking Ellen and Anatole in incest, considering her stupid as well, he forces himself to say the words. Six weeks later they marry.

With his daughter taken care of, Prince Vassily takes Anatole to visit Prince Nikolay Bolkonsky. The old prince dislikes having to entertain this "upstart" and his profligate son, and dislikes the agitation of Princess Marya, Liza, and Mlle. Bourienne at the visit. Carefully dressed for her first appearance by the well-intentioned ladies, Marya looks plainer than ever in her fancy clothes and hairdo; she feels humiliated by her appearance. Moreover, Anatole's handsomeness and grace attract her, and God willing, she would be glad to marry him. Irritated that his child might leave him, the old prince warns Marya that Anatole finds Mlle. Bourienne more attractive. After she sees her suitor and her companion kissing, Princess Marya refuses the marriage offer.

Commentary

While Pierre gives way to his profane desires and marries Ellen, Princess Marya is able to resist profane temptations. Through these parallel incidents we can compare the pattern of Pierre's search for truth with that of Marya. Pierre's weak, undefined nature compels him to go through life's experiences in order to learn from them, while

Marya's deep morality and religious strength allows her to bypass negative encounters.

CHAPTERS 6-8

Summary

The Rostov's are greatly excited with Nikolay's letter telling them of the battle and his injury. They ask Boris to deliver some money and mail to their son. Boris and Nikolay discuss their military experiences with Berg, the young German engaged to Vera Rostov. When Nikolay gets to talk about his participation in the battle against the French, unwittingly embellishing the facts, Prince Andrey enters the room. "Yes, many stories have come out of that engagement," he says with cool contempt. Nikolay hates him and feels humiliated; at the same time he secretly admires the older man's authoritativeness.

Among the eighty thousand men passing in review before the Russian and Austrian emperors, Nikolay falls in love with his youthful tsar. As his throat strains with "Hurrah," he thinks he would be glad to die on the spot were Alexander to smile at him. When he spies Prince Andrey sitting his horse in a "slack, indolent pose," his fury is aroused anew but subsides in a rush of self-sacrifice and forgiveness inspired by his love for the sovereign.

Commentary

After the immature "first loves" of Pierre and Marya, Tolstoy describes the hero-worship of Nikolay for his emperor. The review also provides the author with a vehicle to contrast Rostov's self-abnegation with Prince Andrey's assertive egotism. When Nikolay retells the story of the Schöngraben campaign as he would have liked it to happen, Tolstoy contrasts them again. He shows how someone like Rostov, who acted unconsciously during the battle, has no objective view of it, whereas Prince Andrey, who never forgot himself for a moment during the fighting, knows the facts of the action. We are convinced of the sincerity of each man; both views are truthful. Through the experience of Captain Tushin, however, we must conclude that unselfconscious soldiers, who, like Nikolay, accept anonymity, contribute more heroism to their cause than self-aware men like Bolkonsky.

CHAPTERS 9-19

Summary

Prince Andrey keeps a general waiting while he has an interview with Boris Drubetskoy, who seeks a better position in the army. Boris learns a lesson from this which helps him pursue his opportunism: besides the existing protocol within the hierarchy there operates another and more actual system of subordination which allows a captain and lieutenant to talk while a general respectfully waits.

Prince Andrey attends the council of war prior to the Austerlitz campaign because he has a plan to present to Kutuzov. In a private aside to his aide, Kutuzov predicts they will lose the battle. While the droning voice of the Austrian general Weierother outlines the details of the campaign plan, the old general begins to snore and wakes up when the discussion is over. Prince Andrey never gets the chance to set forth his own scheme. He is unable to sleep that night and paces the floor. Andrey imagines how, at the point of defeat, he will lead his regiment to victory according to his own plan and become a national hero. He realizes he would be glad to sacrifice the love of those he holds dear in order to gain glory and the love of men he does not know. "The only thing I love and prize," he muses, "is...that mysterious power and glory which seems hovering over me in this mist."

That same night, Rostov rides the sleepy round of picket duty. When shouts resound from the enemy encampment he is sent to the French lines to find the cause for the noise. The enemy troops were shouting in response to Napoleon's proclamation encouraging his men to fight bravely. Exhilarated from his gallop and from having been shot at, Nikolay is eager for the battle.

At sunrise, the Russians advance to their positions. They descend into a fog-filled valley where many officers and men get separated during the blind march. Dispirited, the troops sense confusion and mismanagement; indeed they reflect the disagreements between the Austrian and Russian generals about certain dispositions. From the heights where he has a sunlit view of the enemy, Napoleon signals the battle to begin.

Kutuzov is furious when he finds out his sharpshooters have been ordered to change position and he sends Prince Andrey to check. Then the resplendent emperors, Francis and Alexander, with all their staff arrive, restoring confidence to Kutuzov's cheerless retinue. Suddenly the densely massed French appear; they were supposed to be a mile away. As the troops recoil in confusion, Kutuzov turns a tearful face to Prince Andrey. With a weak "Hurrah," Bolkonsky snatches up the flag and rushes forward; a few men follow him. Suddenly Andrey is hit and sinks to the ground. Struggling to keep his men in sight, he sees only the lofty clear sky. The boundless vista promises peace and loveliness and he feels happy. "All is vanity, all is a cheat, except that infinite sky," he thinks, and then loses consciousness.

Not yet called to action, Bagration sends Rostov to get orders from Kutuzov. Nikolay gallops through the gunfire and into the village where the commander is to be found. But the town is entirely French-occupied. Clearly the battle is lost. As Rostov gallops on, he discerns his young tsar standing alone and forlorn in the middle of the field. He is too shy to offer assistance to his beloved Alexander and he sees one of the generals approaching the emperor.

Prince Andrey regains his senses while Napoleon and two adjutants inspect the field of dead and wounded. They stop before him. "A fine death," Bonaparte says, but to Andrey the words are no more than the "buzzing of the flies." His hero seems insignificant compared with the infinite sky above and the feeling in his soul. Prince Andrey next finds himself in an ambulance which the emperor is inspecting. Recognizing him, Napoleon asks how he feels, but Andrey does not reply. As he gazes into his hero's eyes, he muses on "the nothingness of greatness, on the nothingness of life...and on the...nothingness of death...." His delirium is filled with images of Bleak Hills, his future son, that "little, petty Napoleon," and over all, the lofty sky.

Commentary

Prince Andrey strives to attain meaning in his life through being a hero and he imagines how his battle-winning plan will launch him to fame. Being a hero, however, is another way of expressing the youthful needs for acceptance and recognition, and Bolkonsky must first value himself before he can assess his value to the world. Through these conflicting viewpoints—self-esteem versus the esteem of others—Prince Andrey is caught in an "enchanted circle": while depending on the approval of the world for self-definition, he cannot approve enough of himself to recognize the conditions for being unique and outstanding. This dichotomy between Andrey's lack of emotional self-awareness and his highly developed intellectual awareness results in a profound nihilism, a deep desire for the restfulness of death.

Tolstoy invokes images of death when he speaks of the "mysterious power and glory" Bolkonsky feels hovering over him "in the mist," and when the stricken Andrey views the "infinite lofty sky" (which Nikolay viewed in Part II) promising the sought-for surcease from his personal struggles; life, death, individuality combine into nothingness under that eternal expanse.

With this death-oriented insight, Prince Andrey sees Napoleon as insignificant as an insect. Like a parasitic buzzing fly fed on carrion, the great man regards the battlefield corpses as nourishment for his personal needs. Because death has no absolute value for Napoleon, he is deluded about the value of life; this means he is also unaware of his historic significance. Symbolizing Napoleon's nature as that of a fly, Tolstoy projects Andrey into a symbolic state of death. Henceforth Bolkonsky must be "reborn" in order to live, and we foresee a new phase in his life. Andrey's symbolic death, however, is a foreshadow of his ultimate demise.

PART IV

CHAPTERS 1-6

Summary

Early in 1806 Nikolay returns home with Denisov and the Rostov household is lively and gay. Although Sonya is very pretty, Nikolay neglects his sweetheart in order to amuse himself as young men of his station do. Count Ilya Rostov, a generous, good-natured father, has mortgaged all his estates to provide for his family's pleasures. He is now busy preparing a huge banquet in honor of General Bagration, the hero of Austerlitz. While the guests await dinner they exchange news. They are sad at the death of Prince Andrey Bolkonsky and discuss a rumored affair between Countess Bezuhov and Dolohov, Pierre's former drinking buddy.

Despite the superb dinner, Pierre is moody and depressed. Dolohov sits opposite him. Roused to fury by his former friend's sneering manner, Bezuhov challenges Dolohov to a duel. They meet at dawn the next day and Pierre, who never fired a pistol before, wounds his rival. Nikolay drives Dolohov home while the wounded man weeps at having to face his "adored angel" (his mother) and hunchbacked sister. This notorious bully and cardsharp, Nikolay discovers, is the tenderest son and brother.

Meanwhile Pierre believes he has killed his wife's lover. He blames himself for having married a dissolute woman whom he never loved in the first place. Ellen tells him he is a fool and denies her infidelity. A week later Pierre departs for Petersburg alone, having made out more than half his property over to his wife.

Commentary

Besides violence on the battlefield there is also violence on the home front. These chapters of Pierre's "war" within himself complement the previous description of the Austerlitz campaign and illustrate, once more, Tolstoy's handling of his theme on two levels, the individual and the collective. Pierre projects against Dolohov all his anger toward himself and his wife. With one pistol shot he concludes this loathsome, animal-passion marriage and sets off on another route of his life's journey. With this scene of violence, Tolstoy makes a powerful transition from the battlefield of nations to the battlefield within individual souls.

CHAPTERS 7-9

Summary

At Bleak Hills, Liza is expected to deliver her child within days. Marya and the old prince conceal the news from her that Andrey is missing in action, although they both fear he is dead. The "little princess" is frightened and tense when her pains begin and relays of servants stand at the road waiting for the doctor. When the doctor arrives, Prince Andrey also emerges from the carriage; the men met at the train station. Princess Marya is struck by the strangely softened expression on her brother's face. Liza, however, does not realize the significance of Andrey's sudden appearance. Her frightened eyes seem only to reproach him for being unable to relieve her suffering. The birth is not going well; when the inhuman screams suddenly subside and the baby is heard crying, Andrey joyfully rushes into the room. His wife is dead. Her charming face expresses piteous reproach. "I have done no harm to any one," she seems to say, "what have you done to me?" Something is torn out of Andrey's soul; he feels guilty of a crime he can neither expiate nor forget. The baby receives the name of Nikolay Andreitch and Princess Marya is godmother.

Commentary

With Liza's passing, death becomes a poignant, personal crisis for Prince Andrey. Because of her innocent reproach, he is forced to confront his basic guilt and assess the quality of life that placed this guilt upon him.

Liza's existence was but a shadow of life, a series of trivial social affairs without meaning, direction, or moments for self-scrutiny. Prince Andrey is guilty of drawing his doll-like princess into the realities of life by removing her from Petersburg, causing her to face the chancy conditions of pregnancy, and finally, allowing her to die without having known what it is to live.

Liza's death scene demonstrates Tolstoy's powerful manner of stating a moral truth through fictional narrative. The "moral" of the scene, repeated throughout the novel in variations, is that Liza is a poor victim of an empty, corrupt society and dies without having known the substance of life; and that her husband, having married her, has been an unwitting accomplice in this "crime" and feels guilty for it. The illustration for this moral is entirely contained in the reproachful look on the dead princess' face and its soul-searing effect on Andrey. Tolstoy prepares Prince Andrey for this emotional awareness through a characteristic device: "rapid juxtaposition of joy and sorrow…[to show] a state of emotional light and darkness" (quoted in R. F. Christian's *Tolstoy's War and Peace, a Study*). Andrey is agonized at the inhuman cries of Liza in her labor. Overjoyed and relieved at the first cry of his newborn infant, he rushes eagerly into the room only to discover his wife is dead. The simultaneous occurrence of death and birth heightens the dramatic impact of the scene. Tolstoy has set Andrey free of his dull marriage and the hero, armed with a new understanding of life and death, may struggle onward in his search for meaning.

CHAPTERS 10-16

Summary

Count Rostov has managed to hush up the scandal of the duel, and Nikolay, in the meantime, has become friends with Dolohov. In one of their talks, Dolohov states his intense nature: I would give my life to those I love, he says, and crush those who get in my way. For Dolohov, people are either useful or mischievous and almost all women are of the latter. He searches, he says, for a "heavenly creature, who would regenerate and purify and elevate me."

Dolohov falls in love with Sonya but she refuses to marry him even though Nikolay frees her of her promise to him. Sonya says she is content merely loving Nikolay and will demand nothing more from him. Meantime, Denisov, who is spending the Christmas holidays with the Rostovs, is captivated by Natasha.

Vengeful at Sonya's refusal, Dolohov plans a gambling party where he intends to fleece Nikolay of 43,000 rubles (the sum of his and Sonya's ages). Nikolay feels like a trapped mouse in the pitiless paws of a cat as he watches Dolohov's broad-boned hands deal out the fateful cards. His misery is more complete, since he had given his word of honor to his debt-ridden father not to ask for money.

In profound despair and shame, Nikolay enters the house where Sonya, Natasha, and Denisov are grouped around the clavichord. Denisov plays a song he composed for his "enchantress," and Natasha commences to sing it. Her pure untrained voice soothes Nikolay's spirit. As she hits a high note, his soul thrills and soars to a sphere beyond the world of Dolohovs, of losses, of honor. "One might murder, steal, and yet be happy," Nikolay thinks in the ecstasy of the moment.

Confessing his shame to his father, Nikolay bursts into sobs as Count Rostov murmurs words of comfort, none of reproach, to his penitent son. Natasha, at the same moment, is in her mother's bedroom telling the countess that Denisov has made her an offer. "Everyone is in love around here," remarks her mother, thinking Natasha is too young to consider marriage.

Crushed at Natasha's refusal, Denisov leaves Moscow the next day while Nikolay, having paid his debt to Dolohov, joins his regiment in Poland two weeks later.

Commentary

The prevailing spirit in these chapters is intensity, and Tolstoy withholds his more characteristic tone of morality to emphasize this quality. The scenes of love and life-affirmation in the Rostov household not only complement the previous scene of death and birth at Bleak Hills but advance its spirit. Intensity, Tolstoy seems to say, is a quality equally important with moral awareness, for without intense feelings — be they negative or positive — one has no feeling of life. Dolohov's vengeful cat-and-mouse game with Nikolay is the way Tolstoy expresses the "law of intense life" which Dolohov maintains and which he states to Nikolay during their talks. Nikolay sums up this "law": one can be a criminal and be happy because the ability to feel and to be is more important than empty commitment to moral principles. Tolstoy's symbol of feeling and pure being is contained in Natasha's singing, therefore in Natasha herself. This is the quality that enchants Denisov. As the creature embodiment of growth and naturalness, Natasha radiates love as naturally as she pours out her song. At this point, however, she is unready for a mature love affair.

"Intensity" is thus the keynote of the entire Part IV. Each main character—Pierre, Andrey, Natasha, Nikolay—has been brought to a state of fruition and definition and each has a unique destiny to be worked out in future events.

PART V

CHAPTERS 1-14

Summary

At a way station where he awaits fresh horses to take him the rest of the journey to Petersburg, Pierre sits in meditation on what is life for, what must one love or hate, what is right and wrong. The old man who joins him and recognizes him begins to talk on these very problems. Pierre must seek God, the stranger says, and like Adam, strive to comprehend Him. The way is not through wisdom and reason but through the experience of the "inner man." Pierre must give up his parasitic way of life, purify his soul through solitude and self-contemplation, and then devote himself to serving his neighbor. The old man is Osip Alexyevitch Bazdyev, one of the best known Martinists and freemasons in Russia, and he invites the receptive Pierre to become a member of the order. Pierre feels elated and believes freemasonry will provide him with the answers he seeks.

After a week of solitude in Petersburg, Pierre is conducted to his initiation in the brotherhood. Blindfolded, awed, and reverential, he hears the rhetor unfold the mysteries of the order. The object of freemasonry is "to combat the evil paramount in the world" by offering an example of piety and virtue. Despite the unreality of the ceremony, Pierre feels restored and blissful; he is prepared for a life of goodness. When the blindfold is removed, Bezuhov is welcomed into the brotherhood by many acquaintances of his social set.

He now feels as changed and refreshed as if returning home from a long journey. Pierre spends the next few days studying books on masonry and dreams how he will begin a career of "good works" by improving the lot of his peasants. Prince Vassily interrupts his meditations one day, breezily dictating a letter of reconciliation Pierre must write to Ellen. He is shown the door without any explanation.

Meantime Petersburg society speaks contemptuously of the crack-brained Bezuhov, regarding poor Ellen as the victim of an eccentric spouse. At one of Anna Pavlovna's soirées, Boris Drubetskoy, now an adjutant in the suite of a high-ranking official and just returned from an important commission in Prussia, becomes friends with Ellen Bezuhov and often visits her.

With war approaching Russia's borders in the early part of 1807, life at Bleak Hills undergoes changes. The old prince, grown stronger since Andrey's return, is one of the commanders-in-chief appointed to equip the militia and, thus, he is often away touring the three provinces under his command. This frees Princess Marya from her lessons and she devotes most of her time to the baby, little Prince Nikolay. Prince Andrey lives in retirement at his estate in Bogutcharovo, about thirty miles from Bleak Hills. He receives his news through letters from his father and Bilibin. Reporting of Bennigsen's victory over Napoleon at Eylau, his father writes, If a German can beat him, then we will find it easy to do the same if people don't meddle who've no business to meddle. He is referring to the political intrigue that cuts down the efficiency of the military; describing this area is Bilibin's forte. With characteristic irony, the diplomat writes that the whole joke of the war is that nothing is accomplished other than the pillaging of the Prussian countryside as the poorly equipped troops freeload off the inhabitants. But Andrey has little interest in military crises. At this time he is entirely absorbed awaiting his sick child to pass safely through a fever crisis.

Pierre, meanwhile, makes his "good works" tour through the Kiev province where most of his peasants live. He orders hospitals and churches and schools to be built, but has no idea that these "benefits" only add to the already oppressive burdens of the peasants. Moreover, his lack of business sense allows his crafty steward to cheat him at every turn and to misrepresent the actual conditions on his estates. Pierre believes he has done wonders to improve his serfs' lives and in this happy frame of mind, pays Prince Andrey a visit.

They have not met for two years and Pierre is struck by Andrey's lusterless gaze, which belies the smile and words of welcome. They exchange news and then discuss personal matters, Pierre talking of his marriage and his guilt feelings about the duel. Andrey shrugs at this. "Men are for ever in error," he says, "...and in nothing more than in what they regard as right and wrong." But doing good for others is the only source of happiness, Pierre insists, and Andrey differs because his war experience has taught him the emptiness of "glory." "My only aim is to live for myself"; he says, "living for others is a source of evil and error." For this reason he refuses to enter active service again.

As they drive to Bleak Hills that evening, Pierre tells his friend about freemasonry, that the "dominion of good and truth" is the universal expression of God. Even though mankind still exists in a state of darkness and deception, each man shares in the vast harmony of the universe. All forms of life, from inanimate to animate, occupy rungs of an endless ladder that continues further and further, into afterlife where nature is a unity with the free spirits of the air. All of life, of truth, is a manifestation of God. Yes, that's the theory of it, says Andrey, but it is life and death that has convinced me, especially, he bitterly adds, the death of a creature bound to me, to whom one has done wrong, and who suddenly ceases to be. What for? I believe there must be an answer! You feel the answer, Pierre says, there is a future life and God! We must live, we must love, we must believe "that we are not living only today on this clod of earth, but have lived and will live forever there (pointing at the sky) in everything." As he looks up, Andrey suddenly recalls, with the same joyful quickening, the lofty eternal sky he gazed at from the battlefield at Austerlitz. Though this feeling vanishes in his daily life after that, Prince Andrey has it within him, awaiting the moment of growth. Pierre's visit marks a new inner life for Bolkonsky.

Princess Marya is taking tea with her "God's folk" when Pierre and her brother arrive. She regularly receives these excessively devout pilgrims who tell her of fantastic visions and miracles, but Marya is now embarrassed because her brother always mocks these saints. Pierre remains at Bleak Hills for two days and they all remember his visit warmly.

Commentary

An outstanding feature of Tolstoy's writing is that his characters are always "becoming" and not just "being." Even in these static chapters, where there is little external action, the characters are changing. The function of this section, then, is to provide a stock-taking of Pierre's and Andrey's development up to now, to allow the friends to compare their thoughts and ideas, and to act upon each other. By turning this static part of his narrative into a low-keyed turning point in the lives of his heroes, Tolstoy makes unusual dramatic material out of essentially undramatic stuff.

Using the long conversations to chronicle the inward change in Prince Andrey is another device whereby Tolstoy underscores Bolkonsky's basically intellectual and passive nature. From a point of static action, a chain of inner reactions is sparked within Prince Andrey which prepares him to emerge into active life once again.

Mere thoughts and arguments, however, are insufficient to mark inner changes for the more ebullient and sensual Pierre. Bezuhov's "conversion" to freemasonry, therefore, takes place in the more active setting of a journey, a symbolic mode whose image contains Tolstoy's implicit judgment that this is just a passing stage in his hero's life.

From their discussion of life and death, we have another opportunity to contrast Pierre's nature with that of Andrey. Where Pierre is eager to believe the ready answers of the masonic system he has newly embraced, Prince Andrey maintains, with the rigidity reminiscent of his father, the conclusions of his personal experiences. Faithful to his own logic, Andrey has concluded that retirement and "living for oneself" is the only way to avoid disillusion with ideals in life and to avoid the pains of futile death. We see clearly that Andrey does not embrace life with the exuberance and unreservedness of Pierre; that he is too intellectual and aristocratic indicates lack of the intensity with which Tolstoy endows Pierre.

Andrey's future is foretold here with Tolstoy invoking his double-edged symbol of the indifferent sky. To Pierre, the sky is analogous to the limitless power of life and the spiritual infinity of God. Although the same life-affirming vision quickens Andrey's listless spirits and gives him the first glimmer of an inner renewal, the sky echoes the death-wish image of Andrey at Austerlitz. Andrey will rediscover meaning in life, but will eventually succumb to the promise of peace death offers.

Tolstoy thus chronicles the subtle changes wrought in the inner selves of his protagonists. By way of contrast, he provides us with sketches of outward change in the static sphere of Ellen Bezuhov and Boris Drubetskoy as they maneuver within the social hierarchy of Petersburg.

Princess Marya's "holy fools" provide another point of contrast. These zealous half-wits, entirely self-forgetful in their submission to God, are delivered equally from the flux of life and the terrors of death. Between the extremes of the primitive humility of the "God's folk," and the primitive self-indulgence of Ellen Bezuhov are the struggles of Prince Andrey to extend himself and of Pierre to contain himself.

These stock-taking episodes, mainly philosophical, depict the theories of Tolstoy regarding an individual's quest for meaning. These theories—man's need for self-forgetfulness, man's struggles to be self-perfecting, man's relationship in the chain of being emanating from God—are eventually illustrated by the characters' actions and by their final destinies.

CHAPTERS 15-21

Summary

Nikolay returns to his regiment with a great sense of peace. He feels it is as "unchangeably dear and precious" to him as his parental home. As before, Rostov and Denisov share quarters but now their common affection for Natasha draws them closer together. Their regiment, encamped near an utterly ruined German village, loses more men from hunger and disease than from battle. When Denisov waylays a transport delivering food to the infantry in a valiant attempt to feed his hungry men, he is threatened with court-martial for brigandage. To avoid trial, Denisov goes into the infirmary with the excuse of suffering a minor flesh wound. Rostov visits him some weeks later. Humbling his pride, Denisov has composed a petition for pardon to the emperor and asks Nikolay to ride to Tilsit and deliver the letter.

This is the time of truce after the battle of Friedland when Alexander and Napoleon meet at Tilsit to sign their alliance. Boris Drubetskoy is among the suite accompanying Alexander and he welcomes Nikolay to his social circle of high-ranking French and Russian officers. Angered at having to regard his former foes as friends, Rostov avoids Boris' invitations. His main business here is to gain audience with the emperor. Finally a general in Alexander's suite offers to sponsor Denisov's petition and, while Nikolay looks on, he presents the letter to the tsar. The youthful emperor reads the paper, smiles, and shakes his head. The law is mightier than I, Alexander says, and I cannot grant this pardon. Despite his deep disappointment, Nikolay is caught up in the cheering crowd that follows the tsar down the street to the public square.

Now the historic meeting between Alexander and Napoleon takes place, with each monarch flanked by a colorful battalion of guards. Rostov is horrified at the little Corsican's audacious assumption of equality with the divine-right emperor. Napoleon now confers the Legion of Honor to the "bravest Russian soldier," a man chosen at random among the ranks. The following day, Alexander confers the medal of St. George to an equally random choice of the bravest French soldier. Rostov has horrible questions to ask himself now. If this self-satisfied Napoleon and his beloved Alexander are allies, what of those mutilated arms and legs he saw in Denisov's infirmary? What of all the dead and dying on the battlefields? Why is this unknown Russian rewarded for bravery and the valiant Denisov punished? Nikolay forces his thoughts to conclusions during a celebration dinner that night. He decides the emperor and not soldiers like himself must know what is right. Soldiers must only take orders, die if necessary, accept punishment if they are punished. "If we were once to begin criticizing and reasoning about everything, nothing would be left holy to us. In that way we shall be saying there is no God, nothing!" Rostov says. "It's our business to do our duty, to hack them to pieces, and not to think."

Commentary

Ostensibly these chapters reveal the limited nature of Nikolay Rostov as he becomes aware of a conflict between personal goals and the "system." Tolstoy brings Nikolay to question authority for the first time when he appeals to the tsar for Denisov's pardon. What these chapters finally illustrate, however, is the entire ethical system under which feudal Russia operates.

Unlike Pierre and Prince Andrey, Nikolay Rostov does not strive to transcend the "outer" man to achieve freedom and self-definition. In fact, he recognizes no conflict between the demands of the individual and society, between instinct and intellect. Through the incidents that lead up to his petitioning for Denisov, Nikolay reaffirms his place in the fixed order of the universe where God's laws operate through the divine right of the tsar and through the structure of the state. He decides that questioning this structure is a heresy whose end result is anarchy.

Tolstoy does not condemn Rostov for his blind obedience to authority as modern readers would expect him to do. Rather, Tolstoy shows that this "blind obedience" is based on a rational system of ethics which demands the same acquiescence of Alexander as it does of Rostov. Man's highest virtue, according to Nikolay (and the tsar) is in doing one's duty. Sentiment and personal feeling must give way to higher, more universal demands, as manifest in the universal institution of the state. Even Alexander loses his individuality when he chooses to deny Denisov's petition. Although personal sentiment might persuade the tsar to confer the pardon, the demands of universal law impose a higher duty. "The law is mightier than I," speaks the divine-right monarch who cannot, by virtue of his function, express his temporal personal self.

Through Nikolay's conflict, Tolstoy once more expresses a situation on the personal and national level. That code of ethics wherein duty is the highest good has maintained feudal Russia for centuries. It is the system where kings express God's will and where an individual's highest mission is to obey.

Napoleon, however, represents the coming of a new order where the free expression of the individual becomes a higher virtue than obedience to the universal. Thus the confrontation at Tilsit between the revolutionary upstart and the divine-right monarch marks a turning-point in the evolution of western civilization. Demonstrated on a personal level, Nikolay's confrontation of duty with personal sentiment marks a turning-point in his own ethics.

Part V, in total, describes the waning power of a static, ethically based society represented by Alexander and by Nikolay Rostov. Napoleon, as well as Andrey and Pierre, herald the new order where the "free" individual is ascendant. Tolstoy will now prove that the free will of an individual operates under many constraints. He will show the fallacies of Napoleon's assumption of his free individuality, and allow Pierre and Andrey to test their own individual freedom. Eventually he will synthesize the antithetical concepts of "free will" and "necessity" to a conclusion illustrated by the lives of his protagonists.

PART VI

CHAPTERS 1-10

Summary

By 1809 the two emperors are so much in accord that Alexander sends troops when Napoleon declares war on Austria. There is talk of a match between one of the tsar's sisters and Bonaparte. Despite political friendship or enmity, international scheming or wars, Tolstoy says, life, meanwhile—real life, with its essential interests of health and sickness, toil and rest, its intellectual interests in thought, science, poetry, music, love, friendship, hatred, and passions—went on as usual.

Prince Andrey quietly and efficiently frees three hundred serfs by making them "free cultivators," replaces forced labor with a rent system, hires a priest to teach reading and writing to peasant children, and provides midwives. These are among the earliest reforms in Russia. Throughout the past two years he spent at Bogutcharovo, Andrey has kept up with current affairs and knows more about the world than do his city visitors.

In spring of 1809, on the way to inspect his Ryazan estates (his son's inheritance), Andrey spies an ancient gnarled oak whose limbs are yet unadorned with blossoms. He agrees with the grim tree: Let others— the young—yield to the fraud of life, he says, but we who are experienced know life is finished. Bolkonsky pays an obligation-visit to the marshal of Ryazan, Count Ilya Rostov. As his carriage drives down the avenue, Bolkonsky sees a slim girl, running and laughing with some companions. She seems to personify the creature awakening of springtime. In his room later that night, he is unable to sleep. From his open window he hears the rustle of a dress at the floor above and realizes Natasha is silently gazing at the beauty of the soft, clear night. Sonya calls her cousin to sleep but Natasha is too enraptured with the spring air to stir. Suddenly Andrey's soul is again kindled with youthful hopes and ideas. He is so disturbed by this contradiction of his life for the past years he forces himself to sleep.

Homeward bound, Prince Andrey passes the old oak whose gaunt limbs are cloaked now by new leaves. His thoughts change at once and he plans to be active in life again. "Life is not over at thirty-one," Andrey decides and recalls his talk with Pierre, his thoughts of love, glory, and in his memory Liza's dead face no longer expresses reproach.

Bolkonsky arrives in Petersburg in August, 1809, intending to join the service again. Having sent to the tsar his suggestions for certain army reforms, Andrey visits the minister of war by way of follow-up. He becomes a member of the Committee on Army Regulations.

This period of Alexander's reign is a time of liberal reform led by the young secretary of state, Mihail Mihalovitch Speransky. Andrey, being well-received in society, meets this luminary at a soirée and feels flattered when Speransky takes him aside for a talk. They discuss necessary changes in civil service and Prince Andrey believes the young secretary is his ideal of a rational and virtuous man. At a subsequent party in Speransky's home, Bolkonsky admires his practical sense and agrees with everything the great man says. Only vaguely does he discern Speransky's serious faults: his coldness, his contempt for others, his belief in the sovereign power of reason. Through Speransky, Andrey becomes chairman of a committee to revise the legal code.

Actively involved in freemasonry at this time, Pierre begins to feel serious doubts. He discovers that many members are hypocrites, interested not in attaining inner virtue but in bringing distinction to themselves. He finds they are niggardly in contributing to the organization. Pierre decides that Russian freemasonry rests on formal observances and, at the end of 1808, travels abroad to devote himself to the higher mysteries of the order. In the summer he returns and speaks before a large gathering of the lodge. He suggests that masons organize and train members to form a "universal government" — not to interfere with national governments or civil obligations — to carry out the best principles of Christianity. Violence and revolution have no part in this, since wisdom has no need of these measures. The agitated members discuss Pierre's resolutions, but the final word of the Grand Master is a strong rejection. Bezuhov leaves the group.

After days of anger and idleness, Pierre receives a letter from Ellen asking for reconciliation; his mother-in-law also comes to make the same request. Pierre calls on his benefactor, Osip Bazdyev, for advice. Only in midst of worldly cares can you achieve self-purification, peace, love of death, that is, regeneration into a new life, he is told. "Life shows us its vanities only through worldly corruptions," says Osip Alexyevitch. As a result, Bezuhov recalls his wife and once having overcome the pain of this reconciliation, he feels happy and regenerated.

Once established in Petersburg, Countess Ellen Bezuhov becomes one of the most distinguished women in society. Attendance at one of her soirées insures a "certificate of intellect" to an aspiring social climber. Pierre appears as a harmless, contemptible figure as he moves absent-mindedly among his wife's guests. He is always amazed at how her stupidity can be considered the expression of intelligence, how her least remark gains rapt attention.

Since his visit with Bazdyev, Pierre keeps a diary to chronicle his spiritual progress. Here he recounts being the rhetor for Boris Drubetskoy's initiation into the lodge. He notes that Boris, intent on grooming the "outer man," seeks in masonry another connection with influential persons. When they meet, Pierre cannot repress anger and insults Boris. Another entry in Pierre's diary recounts a dream in which Bazdyev talks of "conjugal duties" and later he receives a letter from his benefactor with the same advice. In another dream Bezuhov symbolizes his sexual desire and is terrified by the strength of these base passions within him.

Commentary

Introducing these chapters with an editorial flourish to show the reader that the "essential interests" of "real life" have nothing to do with the gamesmanship of Napoleon and Alexander, Tolstoy steps out of his novel as if to make sure we will understand the "message" of his story. This is our signal that the author is winding up to become more and more instructive. Indeed, Tolstoy becomes increasingly editorial in future chapters.

Thus encouraged to find a moral, we can immediately surmise that Andrey will not be happy as a government official. His "real life" has to do with his springtime awakening and his feelings for Natasha. By the same token, we realize that Pierre's disaffection with freemasonry is less "real" than his internal struggle against low passions. In effect, these experiences restate Tolstoy's discussion of Part V as both Pierre and Andrey discover that institutions which attempt to solve problems for the mass of individuals leave personal needs unsatisfied. "Real life" refers to the individual dynamics of how a human being comes to terms with the conflicts in his own soul.

For Tolstoy, moreover, "real life" is expressed when an individual acknowledges his bond with nature and the instinctive life forces within himself. Thus Prince Andrey's self-comparison with the old oak is significant as a sign of his renascence. When the tree puts out new leaves, Andrey affirms his commitment to life and love.

CHAPTERS 11-26

Summary

Despite having mortgaged the three estates that were to be his daughters' dowries, the financial troubles of Count Ilya Rostov increase.

Yet when Berg becomes engaged to Vera, the eldest daughter, Count Rostov promises 100,000 rubles to his future son-in-law for settlement.

Boris Drubetskoy now becomes attracted by Natasha and often visits the Rostovs. Her mother, however, says Boris is too poor for Natasha to marry and asks the young man to visit them less.

Natasha attends her first grand ball on New Year's Eve of 1810. Sparkling with excitement, aglow with feeling how pretty she is, Natasha seeks out Pierre and finds him conversing with a handsome young officer. This distinguished but conceited fellow, the chaperone tells her, is "hand in glove" with Speransky. When Prince Andrey leads Natasha through a waltz he feels spirited and youthful; her beauty intoxicates him. Watching her dance with other partners he delights anew in her freshness and charm. He surprises himself by wishing to marry her.

Prince Andrey finds work difficult the next morning. He recalls how fresh and original, how "unlike Petersburg" this charming "younger Rostov" was. When a fellow committeeman calls on him, Bolkonsky finds their talk tedious and petty. At Speransky's dinner party that night, he finds the great statesman suddenly unnatural and unattractive. Speranksy's forced staccato laugh rings unpleasantly in his ears. Prince Andrey marvels how unimportant and idle all his pursuits of these past four months now seem.

Calling on the Rostovs the following day, Andrey discovers that Natasha is even prettier in her everyday surroundings. Her singing brings tears to his eyes. In her company he is transported to a world where he forgets his dead Liza, where he can believe in happiness, strength, and freedom again.

Vera and Berg are having their first social evening and they invite Pierre. Their soirée is just as boring and as superficial as every other gathering and the newlyweds are delighted with their success. Pierre notices how dull Natasha seems, and how she becomes radiant when Prince Andrey arrives. Something serious is between them, he thinks to himself, and suddenly realizes his gladness is mixed with bitterness.

Old Bolkonsky is against his son's marrying Natasha. She lacks maturity as well as fortune, he thinks. Mainly he dislikes any change in the routine he has fixed for his old age. By way of compromise, Prince Andrey agrees to defer the marriage for one year. Meanwhile three weeks pass without Natasha having seen Andrey. Depressed and ambivalent, she prefers to remain a "girl-baby" one day, the next day she wishes to marry soon. In one of these childish moods, she confronts Prince Andrey at the door. Count Rostov accepts Bolkonsky's proposal, but Natasha is panic-stricken that she must wait a year for their marriage. Andrey does not wish a formal betrothal, for he leaves Natasha free to break her promise during the waiting period. He is afraid for her, thinking she is too young to know her own mind.

As Andrey visits the Rostovs each day, they come to accept him naturally. Natasha finds more to love and admire in him as they are together and their relationship is close and simple. When Bolkonsky is about to depart, he tells her to regard Pierre as a close friend and to confide in him if she has need. Deeply depressed after Andrey leaves, Natasha takes two weeks to become herself again.

Feebler and more irritable than ever while his son is absent, the old prince vents his anger against Princess Marya, jeering at her piousness and at her devotion to the baby. Only from her brother's letter from Switzerland does Marya learn of the betrothal. Andrey writes that he has never known love until now, that his life is full of value and meaning once more. He asks her to approach their father to cut the waiting period by three months. Dutifully Princess Marya tenders Andrey's request. Her father jeers: what a fine stepmother young Rostova will make for Nikolushka, and her family is so clever and rich besides. Let him marry, says the old man, then I can marry Bourienne and give Prince Andrey a suitable stepmother! He says nothing more on this subject but among other mockeries against his daughter he adds allusions to a stepmother and offers gallantries to Mlle. Bourienne. In her misery, Princess Marya has a recurrent daydream: she would join her "God's folk" on a pilgrimage through the world where worldly troubles and deceptions have no meaning. But she would not leave home, she realizes, for she loves her father and her nephew better than she loves God.

Commentary

Having previously identified Natasha with the springtime, Tolstoy uses her as the means for Prince Andrey's emotional renascence. Natasha's debut at the grand ball provides a fairytale atmosphere where the "princess" enkindles immediate love in the heart of a "prince charming." Tolstoy expands this romantic formula by forcing the heroine to undergo a test before she can prove herself worthy to marry the hero. This mythic beginning for the love relationship between Natasha and

Prince Andrey strikes a note of unreality which foreshadows disaster for the newly conceived romance.

At the same time, his romantic passion provides Prince Andrey with a point of reality. Against his emotional fulfillment, he can measure the value of all his other activities. Suddenly love is Andrey's "real life" and his political business and committee services become mere reflections of life. Compared to Natasha's laughter, Speransky's laugh seems an echo of the deadness Andrey discovers among all the court officials.

Pierre's sense of reality receives a similar shock in these chapters as he begins to see the futility of finding emotional fulfillment through freemasonry. He realizes he has joined the organization to seek answers to his personal disorders, not those of the world. When Pierre discovers that the problems he symbolizes in his dreams—his sexual desires, for instance—are more substantial than the hollow virtues he seeks to achieve through freemasonry, he can already begin toward self-perfection.

Tolstoy has thus turned the concepts of worldly reality into unreality and dream-life and passion of an individual into substantial qualities. "Real life," according to Tolstoy, are the struggles of the "inner man," and these struggles for self-knowledge provide the only means with which to understand the outer world.

Women, however, have fewer problems with a divided self, Tolstoy believes, and he personifies the unity of civilization and nature in Natasha. Responding only to her instincts for love, all her activities radiate from this central truth of her nature. Problems arise for Natasha only when this love-instinct is frustrated, and the threat of this frustration is implicit in the deferred marriage. Princess Marya's womanly instincts are already suffering through her father's enmity, although she somewhat compensates by her maternal attentions to Nikolushka. She realizes that escape into religion will not satisfy her emotional needs; only through worldly involvement with husband and children can she find fulfillment.

Tolstoy has thus set up the pattern for the maturation of his characters. Love provides the inner content of reality in the lives of Andrey, Pierre, Natasha, and Marya. How this quality becomes manifest in their respective lives involves all the future incidents in which each participates throughout the rest of the novel.

PART VII

Summary

Idleness (writes Tolstoy)—the absence of work—was a condition of man's first blessedness before the Fall. Now we are cursed by guilt feelings when we are not working and rarely can we feel we do our duty and be idle at the same time. Tolstoy observes that only during military duties can we approximate this state of "primitive blessedness" and this irreproachable idleness is one source of Nikolay Rostov's contentment as he serves in the now-inactive Pavlograd hussars, a captain of the regiment Denisov used to command. Upsetting and urgent letters from home mar Nikolay's happiness at this time. His mother pressures him to return to Otradnoe to straighten out their pressing financial problems. Finally, when he hears that their properties are to be auctioned off, Nikolay returns home.

He finds his favorite sister basically unchanged despite her engagement, and Sonya, in the full bloom of her twenty years, is as lovely as she will ever be. Nikolay devotes himself to a serious examination of the family's business accounts but cannot make head or tail out of the complicated entries. Helplessly, he contents himself with abusing the crafty steward and then ignores the whole matter, devoting himself instead to the pleasures of hunting, which are carried out on a grand scale at his father's estates.

Tolstoy now indulges in a long, joyous description (six chapters) of a wolf hunt, in which even Natasha and their younger brother Petya participate. Altogether there are more than twenty horsemen and 130 dogs. Nikolay finds nothing more delightful and absorbing than to gallop across the fields chasing his prey. When evening falls the hunting party puts up at the estate of their distant relative whom they call "Uncle." After a splendid dinner Uncle plays his guitar and Natasha abandons herself to a gypsy dance. Still later, the Rostov children, bundled in furs, drive home through the starry night. Sitting side by side, Natasha and Nikolay talk over the day's events. She suddenly gives a musical, causeless laugh. Suddenly serious, Natasha says "I know I shall never be as happy, as peaceful, as I am now." Aloud, Nikolay says, "Nonsense!" but he wishes to himself she would never marry and thinks he will never find another friend like Natasha.

Meanwhile financial troubles force Count Rostov to resign as marshal of the province, a position that demands extravagant entertaining. As debts continue to pile up, the parents only hope to prevent the ruin of their children's fortunes by having Nikolay marry an heiress. Countess Rostov and Julie Kuragin's mother agree to match their children, but nothing comes of it. Natasha meantime becomes visibly depressed, although Prince Andrey is not expected back for another six months. Life at the Rostovs loses its gaiety.

Christmas week restores some of the festive spirit, but Natasha is bored by the third day. "I want *him*," she grimly tells her mother, and nothing interests her. Nikolay, Sonya, and Natasha spend an evening in their favorite corner reminiscing on their childhood. When Natasha begins to sing for the family, the countess cries. She feels there "is too much of something" in her daughter, and it will prevent her being happy.

The arrival of holiday mummers interrupts the singing. Inspired, the children dress themselves in costumes and decide to call on their neighbors. During the drive, Nikolay finds Sonya more attractive than ever and he seeks a private moment to embrace her and renew his promises.

When they return home, Sonya and Natasha discuss their future husbands. They set up mirrors in the traditional manner for divining the future, but Natasha sees nothing. But Sonya says she sees Prince Andrey. He is lying down, she reports to the now pale-faced Natasha. Confused as to the truth of her vision, Sonya says he is not ill, that he looks cheerful. Natasha, however, is too frightened to sleep that night and lies motionless for a long time, staring into the dark.

Nikolay tells his parents he will marry no one but Sonya. The count feels guilty that he cannot afford this happy match for his son, while the countess blames her niece and calls her an "intriguing creature." Sonya has torn loyalties: she wants to make Nikolay happy but realizes she owes a debt to the Rostovs. Natasha's diplomacy finally calms them down, although the countess is quite ill from mental anguish. Nikolay returns to his regiment in January, while his father plans to move to Moscow to sell his estates. Natasha at this time is filled with self-pity and she is angry that her fiancé can enjoy the pleasures of being abroad while she must languish at home.

Commentary

Part VII describes the high point of youth and happiness and a falling-away into adulthood in the lives of the Rostovs. The hunt scene, the joyousness of the Christmas mummery express the joyful radiance overflowing in Natasha, Nikolay, Sonya—a radiance which will soon slip from them. At this high point in their lives, Nikolay loves Sonya, who is now at the peak of her attractiveness. Natasha savors these moments of abandon and innocence with the intuitive foreboding that these are the last she will enjoy.

Particularly in this section we see how Tolstoy integrates nature with human life. The autumn abandon is the autumn of their youth and Sonya, Nikolay, and Natasha try to draw all the power of their common childhood to arm themselves for the wintry future. They even call on supernatural powers to help them, but Sonya's fortunetelling only predicts death for Prince Andrey, despair for Natasha.

As this symbolic autumn passes into "winter," Natasha becomes desperate for Andrey to claim her; she feels as if her spirit is in enforced hibernation. Now that she is ready to give up her claims to childhood, there is no one to claim her, and her restless love can be expected to seek an object for itself. Sonya is also caught in a stormy dilemma: her desire for self-sacrifice to repay her debts to the Rostovs conflicts with her love for Nikolay. The Count and Countess Rostov, who prepare to break up their ancestral properties, feel likewise lost in the harsh climate of circumstances which makes their futures insecure.

In effect, Part VII carries the Rostovs through the paradisiacal innocence of their youth into the alienation and confusion of a grace-denied Fall. Tolstoy provides a pagan atmosphere to celebrate the end of youth. The hunt, the rites of Christmas mummery, the divining session to foretell the future are human activities left over from pre-Christian times. The author invokes the entire childhood of man to show that the Rostovs are giving up their innocence. From a state of "primitive blessedness" they now face the afflictions of adulthood and civilization.

PART VIII

CHAPTERS 1-5

Summary

About the same time that Natasha and Andrey become engaged, Pierre's mentor dies. With Bazdyev's passing, Pierre loses all interest in a religious life and retires to his Moscow home. Assuming his old habits of dissipation—drinking and gambling with his bachelor friends at the English Club—Pierre tries to drown out the meaninglessness and deception of life. Basically he still believes in the possibility of goodness and truth, but all around him he sees only evil and falseness in every human activity. Recalling what is said of soldiers under fire—that they try to find occupation to bear their danger more easily—Pierre imagines all men are like soldiers, using cards, women, horses, politics as a refuge from the mortal danger of life.

When winter begins, Prince Nikolay Andreitch Bolkonsky and his daughter Marya move to Moscow. More feeble than ever, the old man is also more irascible and forgetful, blaming his daughter for every misfortune in his life, and making a great show of affection for Mlle. Bourienne. Princess Marya is lonelier than ever. She misses her God's folk, cannot go about in society because of her father, and finds nothing in common with her friend Julie Karagin, who is now a wealthy heiress engrossed in a whirl of fashionable amusements.

Celebrating his name-day in 1811, the old prince has a small dinner party and invites Boris Drubetskoy and Pierre. Just before the guests arrive, the old prince becomes furious at his daughter and tells her they must live apart from now on. Princess Marya confesses her unhappiness to the sympathetic Pierre. Bezuhov then tells her that Boris is seeking to marry a rich wife, either herself or Julie Karagin. Marya inquires after Natasha, badly concealing her ill-will toward her prospective sister-in-law. Pierre has little to say, other than that Natasha is fascinating.

Boris Drubetskoy soon chooses to marry Julie Karagin and they announce the betrothal.

Commentary

These chapters offer another instance of parallel experience for Pierre and Marya as both find their lives difficult. When Tolstoy has Pierre observe that life is fraught with dangers that men try to avoid thinking about, like men under fire, he prepares us for his further examinations of actual battle conditions as Napoleon invades Russia and as Pierre himself is drawn into the battle front.

Moreover, as he plunges each character into his deepest despair, Tolstoy readies us for the main battle within each soul he bares before us. In order to bring about the final state of inner peace and adulthood of these protagonists, the author now shows each stage of inner war as his characters strive to meet their destiny.

Summary

Count Ilya Rostov moves to Moscow with his family, except for the countess, who is still ill. Until his house is readied for the winter, the Rostovs stay with Marya Dmitryevna Ahrostimov (mentioned in Part I), who is Natasha's godmother. She oversees the selection of Natasha's trousseau and plans diversions for her guests. Marya Dmitryevna keeps telling Natasha what an excellent husband she has chosen and counsels her to visit her in-laws as soon as possible.

Natasha pays her call, certain the Bolkonskys will love her as everyone does, but is unprepared for the cold reception she receives from Princess Marya. She weeps for a long time when she returns home, blaming Prince Andrey for not having arrived soon enough to spare her this humiliation.

Count Rostov escorts Natasha and Sonya to the opera one evening and the girls attract a great deal of attention. While Natasha feels deeply pleased, she feels more strongly a sense of loss for someone to love and admire her. Recognizing her womanly attractiveness, she misses Andrey poignantly at this moment. In this serious mood, Natasha finds the conventions of the theater grotesque and unnatural, even to the point of being embarrassed for the foolish exaggerations of the actors.

Gradually accustomed to the half-naked women of the audience and the brilliantly elegant men, her mood becomes one of intoxication and she has the surrealist desire to leap upon the stage or to tickle Ellen Bezuhov's bare shoulders. At this moment, Anatole Kuragin makes his self-confident entry and his roving glance fixes upon Natasha; their eyes meet. His fearless and intimate look makes Natasha feel she knows him already.

Ellen Bezuhov invites Count Rostov to bring the girls to her box during the intermission. Her beautiful, unvarying smile nearly hypnotizes Natasha, and Ellen says flattering things to her and mentions Prince Andrey favorably. Now the opera no longer seems unnatural to Natasha and she thoroughly enjoys the stagecraft. At the next entr'acte, Ellen introduces her brother to Natasha. In their brief talk, the girl feels fearfully close to this bold, handsome stranger. She feels no barrier of reserve as usually exists between men and women. Thereafter during the opera Natasha is only conscious of Anatole's presence.

Something dreadful is happening, she thinks to herself later, and realizes with dread, she has lost the old purity of her love for Andrey.

Anatole is a man who believes utterly that the world exists for his pleasure. Besides amassing huge gambling debts, his past excesses once forced him to marry the daughter of a well-to-do farmer. He deserted his wife, paid off the father, and has lived as a bachelor ever since. He adores "little girls," he confides to Dolohov and his friend warns him off Natasha.

But Ellen Bezuhov is amused by the idea of bringing her brother together with Natasha and tells the bewitched young girl now Anatole pines away for love of her. At a party, Anatole's kiss confuses and excites Natasha and she wonders whom she really loves.

At the same time that she receives an apologetic note from Princess Marya, Natasha receives a love letter from Anatole. In her reply to Marya, Natasha writes that she is breaking her engagement to Prince Andrey. Sonya discovers Anatole's letter while Natasha is asleep. The cousins quarrel, with Natasha hotly defending the honorable intentions of Anatole. Shocked and grieved at the broken engagement, Sonya determines to watch her friend day and night.

Meanwhile Dolohov and Anatole carefully plan Natasha's abduction. Sixty versts from Moscow an unfrocked priest awaits to perform a fake marriage when they arrive. Their plans are foiled, however, for instead of Natasha, they discover Marya Dmitryevna's huge groom awaiting them at the gate. Anatole and Dolohov barely manage to escape to their sledge.

Dry-eyed and silent, Natasha lies on the sofa heeding no one. Marya Dmitryevna keeps the news from Count Rostov, only telling him his daughter's engagement is broken. She tells Pierre the whole story and Bezuhov is not only shocked about the abduction, but about his wife's encouragement of the affair. Gently Pierre tells Natasha about Anatole's previous marriage, which makes his proposal to her a mockery; she is too shaken to reply. Pierre next searches out Anatole, and his towering rage entirely cows Kuragin, who quickly agrees to leave Moscow immediately.

Prince Andrey returns soon afterward, immediately learning that Natasha broke her promise. When Pierre visits him, he begs his friend to never mention the matter again, but to deliver back to Natasha all her tokens and letters. Theoretically Andrey believes one must forgive a fallen woman, but actually, he knows he can never forgive Natasha.

Returning to Natasha to fulfill Andrey's request, Pierre talks with her. She is confused now, no longer certain about her love for Anatole. Out of her tears, she casts him a glance so full of tenderness and gratitude that Pierre is stirred to his depths. His heart is full as he departs; he considers all men's actions pitiful compared with the tenderness of Natasha's glance. The famous comet of 1812 lights up the sky: a portent, it is said, of all horrors and the end of the world. To Pierre the glorious spectacle coincides with his feelings of harmony and joy in the universe. In his softened and emboldened heart it betokens the new vigor that has blossomed into his life.

Commentary

Her poor affair with Anatole Kuragin is Natasha's uneasy entrance into maturity and she becomes aware, for the first time, that the actions of an adult bear moral consequences. But Tolstoy says a great deal more than this through the vehicle of his heroine's false love affair. In showing what it means to lose one's childhood in civilized society, Tolstoy points out the paradoxical nature of the social order; that society encourages false moral values and then punishes those that transgress.

The beauty of Natasha's nature is her belief in her own emotions and her ability to respond to natural impulses. And, with her characteristic intensity and directness, she discovers that not only is it wrong to give way to her natural impulses but that she can no longer trust them. At once, her entire self is destroyed and there is no way possible for her to replace the loss. Pierre, however, holds out future hope for Natasha as she intuitively recognizes him as the only one she can trust.

The way Tolstoy depicts Natasha's coming-of-age and loss of innocence during the course of an opera is a brilliant exercise in irony. Natasha is fulfilled with a sense of her womanly attractiveness by the attention she receives as she enters her box. At the same time she poignantly realizes her femininity is an empty gesture as long as Prince Andrey is not here to claim it. In this serious mood, the first act of the opera seems to her grotesque and unnatural. But the bare décolleté of the women around her, especially that of the dazzling Ellen Bezuhov whom she meets during the first intermission, and the sensual stimulation of the stagecraft itself soon have an effect on Natasha. By the second act she is intoxicated by the unreality of her surroundings and the opera now seems natural and normal to her. In other words, society has perverted Natasha's pure feelings of love into sexual terms and she is unable to distinguish between truth and illusion. The opera symbolizes this confusion.

Anatole's entrance into the theater and into Natasha's life deepens her confusion of love and sex, and illusion and reality. Just as the opera provides an imitation of life, Anatole provides an imitation of love, and Natasha falls victim to a socially created deception.

In her moral innocence, she believes in her own feelings and with the integrity outstanding in her nature, she follows her inner promptings. When she discovers she has transgressed the moral code, she learns she can no longer trust her own emotions. Natasha's hopeless conclusion is a dead-end: the world is based on deception.

This is exactly what Prince Andrey has always believed. Maintaining his retirement at Bogutcharovo to avoid the deceptive nature of human relations, he has only emerged because of his faith in the purity and naturalness of Natasha's joyous life-force. Natasha's "fall" merely proves his original belief and he cannot forgive her for deceiving him. Losing this last meaningful attachment to life, Prince Andrey will seek to escape into death.

At its lowest ebb, Natasha's spirit must gather its forces before it can surge upward to a new self-understanding. At odds with society which has wronged her, Natasha feels herself imprisoned by inimical forces she has not yet the strength to overcome. In this way she is in the same situation as Russia, which suffers invasion by the superior forces of Napoleon. With her powers temporarily shattered, Russia must gather herself together, discover her own deep-rooted strengths, and then throw off the alien forces to surge onward to a new and stronger sense of self. This audacious transition from Natasha's story to that of Russia is a remarkable *tour de force*. That Tolstoy can carry off such an unlikely parallel between a situation in the life of one human being and an entire chapter in the history of a nation and yet maintain the verisimilitude of both accounts indicates the unique power of his craftsmanship.

Pierre bridges the gap between these two levels in the novel. When Natasha reaches out to him and Pierre is stirred so deeply, we see that Tolstoy is preparing him for a more central role in the story and uses him as a transition figure to carry the personal theme into the realm of the universal. Pierre's identification with the free-wheeling comet lighting up the night sky in 1812 shows us that he is to become the personal focus of Tolstoy's examination of the historical life-and-death struggle between France and Russia which begins in Part IX.

PART IX

CHAPTERS 1-7

Summary

In June, 1812, war between France and Russia begins. Historians who describe the many events leading up to the war still cannot explain its cause, Tolstoy writes. None of the reasons they cite account for the sheer vastness of the event. At best, the author says, we can only describe the numerous coincidences that combine to make up the parts of the fatal event, the course of individual human destinies linked with those of other humans. The more important the human being, the more his actions connect with the actions of others. What may seem to be a free will act of a great man, says Tolstoy, is not free at all, "but in bondage to the whole course of previous history and predestined from all eternity."

Napoleon arrives at the Niemen River, beyond which extend the vast Russian steppes, with Moscow glittering in their midst. Long grown used to the adoration of his men who shout "Vive l'Empereur" wherever he appears, Napoleon believes in his own godlike image. An ecstatic colonel of the Polish Uhlans begs his permission to ford the river; unmindful of the swift current, the officer only desires to shine in the eyes of his hero. Forty men and horses drown in the rushing waters, but each man exults in the chance to die before the emperor.

Meanwhile Alexander and his court spend a month at Vilna, readying the troops. Ellen Bezuhov, currently favored by an important official, travels with the emperor's suite and so does Boris Drubetskoy. Keeping a watchful eye on the tsar even during a lavish ball, Boris overhears Alexander's talk with a minister. He is one of the first to learn of the French invasion.

Demanding Napoleon's withdrawal from Russia, the emperor dispatches his best diplomat, Balashov, to deliver the letter. Balashov finds Napoleon in an affable mood. As the "little corporal" warms to his

58

speech, his words become increasingly unguarded and irrational. To Balashov, the purpose of the talk seems to be to insult Alexander and to glorify himself. Napoleon invites the Russian to dine with him the next day, politely inquiring about Russia with the interest of a tourist who expects to flatter his native host. After Bonaparte refuses to turn back, no further letters are exchanged between the emperors. War has begun.

Commentary

These chapters are a caricature of Napoleon. Tolstoy depicts him as a fool who is so carried away by his own importance that he is blind to reality. This fact, however, does not deny Bonaparte's qualities as a great personality, and Tolstoy provides instances of this charisma by citing the suicidal adoration of the Uhlan colonel and his men. The scene is almost a comedy, as if it is part of a puppet play, where Napoleon believes himself to be the puppeteer. Tolstoy's purpose is to show Bonaparte's illusions of free will; rather than being the puppet master, however, the "little corporal" is just another character playing out a role in history without, of course, being aware of it. Lacking this insight, Napoleon treats human beings as creatures whose purpose is either to live or die for him. This is the attitude he conveys to Balashov, who is astounded at being treated as an already devoted supporter. By depicting Napoleon's self-conceits as ridiculous, Tolstoy shows us a "great man" who, believing in his own free will, cannot recognize himself as a tool of historical necessity.

CHAPTERS 8-15

Summary

Thinking of vengeance, Prince Andrey pursues Anatole to Petersburg but finds his rival has eluded him by joining the army in Moldavia. Meeting Kutuzov in Petersburg, Andrey agrees to accompany his suite to Moldavia, where the general is to take over the command. By this time, however, Anatole has returned to Moscow.

After a brief stay with Kutuzov, Prince Andrey asks to be transferred to the western forces now campaigning in Bucharest. Kutuzov sends him with a commission to Barclay de Tolly. Andrey goes home for a visit, amazed to find Bleak Hills so unchanged after the three eventful years in his own life. He finds a household divided into two hostile camps:

his father and Mlle. Bourienne on one side, Princess Marya, Nikolush-ka, and the nurses on the other. When Andrey defends his sister on one occasion, his father orders him out of the house. Andrey mourns Marya's sufferings, and his father's guilt, of which the stubborn old man is aware, and Andrey wonders what still drives him to seek out Anatole to be further sneered at or perhaps killed. Life seems to Prince Andrey a series of "senseless phenomena following one another without any connection."

In June he reaches Barclay de Tolly's army, and lacking as yet a specific post, Andrey observes the various factions within the high command. Since the emperor is attached to de Tolly's army (Generals Tormasov and Bagration command the other two armies) several parties cluster around Alexander, four of which deserve mention here. One consists of Germans, like Wintzengerode and Pfuhl, who, as rigid military theorists, believe in the science of warfare. Another party favors direct spontaneous action rather than theoretically devised plans. The third group, mainly courtiers, wish to reconcile the first two. Finally, there is the large number of place seekers comprising the fourth party, men guided by selfish motives who chase medals, crosses, promotions.

Accepting the tsar's invitation, Bolkonsky attends the war council and finds the discussions reminiscent of those preceding the Austerlitz campaign four years before. A science of war does not exist, he thinks to himself, for no one can predict the moral strength of the soldiers at the moment of battle. As the generals talk with awe about Napoleon's "genius," Andrey recalls with amusement the smugness of the little man who inspected the dead and wounded men at Austerlitz. An effective leader, decides Bolkonsky, must lack genius; with a narrow outlook a man can work through many conflicting impressions which would confuse a more thoughtful man. A military leader endowed with pedestrian intelligence would be more likely to have the patience required to carry out his plans. At the end of the council, Alexander asks Andrey where he desires to serve. Bolkonsky wishes to be sent to the front.

When Nikolay Rostov learns of Natasha's broken engagement, he is glad of the excuse to be detained with his army because of the coming campaign. Writing to Sonya, he promises to marry her when he comes home again. Rostov's squadron is ordered to the attack long before dawn. Nikolay rides with Ilyin, a young officer who hero-worships him as he himself once admired Denisov. As the galloping hussars drive against the French dragoons, Rostov feels the same freedom and excitement that he felt when coursing the wolf. Overtaking a Frenchman,

Nikolay raises his sword and then confronts the frightened gaze of his foe. Rostov trembles before his prisoner's fear of being killed; he cannot imagine committing such a crime. Suddenly he is overwhelmed by doubts as to the meaning of war, the meaning of men's lives, the meaning of bravery.

Because he has taken a prisoner, Nikolay later receives the cross of St. George for being an officer of dauntless courage.

Commentary

In these chapters, Tolstoy follows the earlier pattern of Part II when he paralleled the actions of Bolkonsky and Rostov during the Schöngraben campaign. Both men have undergone a change in attitude since then and we can measure this change by noting how their present points of view draw close together.

Prince Andrey now realizes that heroism takes place at the battlefront when a man is able to confront and overcome death through his own actions and not by commanding other men according to an abstract grand scheme. Nikolay, who has accepted his lot as part of the universal order designed by his superiors — even though this may involve getting killed — now discovers that "the enemy" consists of men like himself who fear death. With this insight, both protagonists have discovered a sense of individual morality that can only be acted out according to an individual responsibility.

When Andrey asks the tsar to send him to the front, thereby losing his chance for achievement in the world of the court, he is stating the central truth in his life: a human being has a unique value in the harmonious scheme of the universe that is proved when he can face death to fulfill and define his life.

Nikolay's moment of truth occurs when he raises his sword against his enemy and hesitates, trembling, at the enormity of taking a life so like his own. The glorious gallop against the faceless enemy, reminiscent of that carefree race after the wolf, suddenly has moral consequences Nikolay must consider. No longer ruled by a corpsman's sense of duty alone, he must now answer to his conscience as well.

Compared with Rostov's and Bolkonsky's awareness of individual worth, Napoleon's sense of values is as undeveloped as a child's. Like Nikolay's wolf hunt, his desire to conquer Russia is a glorious game that has no significance except to feed his own self-image. This is the point where Tolstoy draws together the divergent parts of the two-leveled story and foreshadows some ultimate conclusions. As individual characters begin to participate in the large affairs of a global war, we see how they derive their life's meanings through the challenge of historic necessity. Napoleon, however, who tries to play with history in a game to further his self-glorification, never recognizes life's necessities. This fatal misunderstanding provides his downfall.

CHAPTERS 16-23

Summary

Having tried to swallow poison, Natasha lies gravely ill. She languishes all through the hot Moscow summer and improves gradually. Unable to sing or laugh without catching a sob, Natasha seems most revived when Pierre is with her. About this time, Natasha finds in religion her greatest solace and she prays daily for repentance.

With his love for Natasha filling each moment of his life, Pierre becomes increasingly restless as she recovers and has less need of his pity. When one of his acquaintances informs Pierre that the beast prophesied in the Apocalypse of St. John corresponds to an anagram of "l'empereur Napoleon," Pierre finds that "l'russe Besuhof" also qualifies. He believes there is a cosmic connection among the factors of his love, the prophecy in St. John, the comet, Napoleon's invasion. He also believes a crisis will develop to lead him to some great achievement and great happiness. Although wishing to enter the army, he decides to await his ultimate mission.

Arriving one day for his usual Sunday dinner at the Rostovs, Pierre discovers Natasha singing her sol-fa exercises for the first time. The fifteen-year-old Petya jumps at him, begging Pierre to get him a place with the hussars, but his parents become angry and indignant. Meantime Pierre becomes uncomfortable in Natasha's blooming presence and feels forced to cut short his visit. She challenges him, asking why he must go. Mumbling something about business and that it is better not to come so often, Pierre looks her full in the eyes, almost speaking his love. Natasha blushes suddenly in dismayed understanding. As he departs, Pierre decides not to visit her again.

Petya resolves to see the tsar himself and ask for a commission. He is among a huge mob of people waiting for Alexander to arrive at the gates of the Kremlin. When he returns home, having been nearly trampled, he threatens to run away if his parents do not let him join the army. Count Rostov gives in and seeks a place where his son shall not be in any danger.

Pierre is among a group of noblemen thronging the halls of the palace where Alexander is to give audience. Many men stand up to make fiery speeches about sacrifice and conscripting peasants and fighting with every ounce for the cause. Pierre feels moved to speak and, in bookish Russian, urges that the group offer counsel to the tsar, that they should consider what is needed before acting. He is shouted down and a near riot ensues. A secretary then informs the gathering that the emperor asks the nobility to furnish and equip ten of every thousand men. When Alexander himself appears and thanks them all, everyone, including Pierre, sheds tears of emotion, feeling nothing except an intense desire to sacrifice everything for the sovereign and the nation.

Commentary

The mass movement of the novel now accelerates as Tolstoy impels his characters to face the imminent national crisis. We see Petya, the coming generation, emerging into an early manhood and eager to participate in saving his nation. As Petya is caught up in the excited mob outside the Kremlin, Tolstoy conveys to us a sense of the tide of history that causes men to forget their immediate problems and unite in a common effort. By the same token, Pierre prevents himself from speaking to Natasha of his love as if postponing his personal life to a time in the future. When he decides to await his "ultimate mission" we realize he is directing his love energies toward a more cosmic goal involving the coming trials of history.

Pierre is again the transition figure as Tolstoy goes from the plane of the personal to the national. He is among the multitude thronging the palace halls, a group of nobles, merchants, and others of the "third estate" gathered together by the tsar to deliberate with the monarch. The mob scene here not only illustrates how men sublimate their personal needs to respond to national needs, but illustrates a subtle change in the ancient system of government.

The divine-right sovereign, in this moment of crisis, has convened even the third estate to advise him—to "deliberate" with him. In other words, the national emergency demands the response of its citizens as free men, not as servants of the king, in order to overcome the threat to their existence. Tolstoy shows how the old order gives way to the new through historical necessity, masses of men who must act as free individuals who define themselves through a mass goal.

PART X

CHAPTERS 1-14

Summary

Neither foresight nor planning has anything to do with the way Napoleon conducts the war with Russia, declares Tolstoy. The unseasonal march of the French into the Russian heartland is by no means an example of Napoleon's "military genius." It would seem obvious to the French to realize they march to their doom the more they advance into the Russian winter. As for the Russians, they should have realized they could do no worse than hinder the French advance; yet this is what they did. When the two forces met, they fought the ill-planned battle of Smolensk. When the outraged citizens burned the town and the fields rather than leave them to the French to despoil, they set the pattern for the subsequent burning of Moscow.

The force of history is blind and unpredictable, concludes Tolstoy. The general busy scheming for his own advancement or Rostov's gallop against the dragoons because he cannot resist the run on a level slope are moments in history whose significance and coincidence with other random events have consequences beyond the event itself. Mishaps and fortuitous happenings neutralize each other often enough so that nothing is apparent except the "irresistible tide of destiny."

Prince Nikolay Andreitch Bolkonsky is ill and he avoids Mlle. Bourienne as well as Princess Marya as a result of his quarrel with Andrey. Never mentioning the war, he lives increasingly in the past. But when Prince Andrey writes an apology to his father, the old man answers affectionately. Andrey warns that the war will come close to Bleak Hills, but his father refuses to believe this. He even sends his servant Alpatitch to Smolensk on an errand. The battle is in progress when the peasant arrives, and he meets Prince Andrey in town. Alpatitch returns with a message from Andrey: they must leave for Moscow right away, for the enemy will arrive at Bleak Hills within a week. When Bolkonsky arrives for a last look at his ancestral estate with the rest of the retreating forces, he hears from Alpatitch that the family left two days ago.

Despite all the changes over the past years, the two principal Petersburg salons remain the same. At Countess Bezuhov's home one evening, the company discuss the incompetence of the old man Kutuzov, whom even the tsar thinks is unfit to command the army. Some days later, the guests discuss with horror that the court council chose Kutuzov as commander-in-chief and the old general made one condition upon accepting the post: that the tsar should not be with the army.

Meanwhile Napoleon pushes on to Moscow, lured by the glory of conquering "the holy city." Three times he tries to engage in battle but the Russians always evade his troops. Owing to various incidents, the opposing armies finally meet at Borodino, 112 versts from Moscow.

Because her father refused to leave Bleak Hills, Princess Marya remained with him, sending Nikolushka and his tutor to Bogutcharovo, thence to Moscow. The old man is so angry at his daughter's disobedience that he suffers a stroke. At the last moment he summons her to his side, calling her endearing names and begging her forgiveness. The dried-up old body, encased in his full dress-uniform, is buried at Bogutcharovo.

Now that the old prince is dead, Marya and Mlle. Bourienne reconcile their past differences. Princess Marya takes charge of her household as her father would have done. Rather than acquiesce in the enemy occupation of her ancestral estates, she prepares to depart for Moscow. She orders all the stored grain to be distributed among the peasants and invites them to follow her to Moscow. The Bogutcharovo peasants are rebellious and savage. No longer serfs, since Prince Andrey made them rent-paying tenants, they regard Napoleon as the Antichrist and and consider themselves entirely free. They refuse to obey Alpatitch's orders to supply Princess Marya with horses and carts for her departure.

With their village elder, Dron, at their head, the rebellious-tempered peasants meet with Princess Marya. They refuse her enslavement, they say, and will neither accept her grain nor accompany her to Moscow. Sternly repeating her orders to Dron to provide horses and carts, Princess Marya retires.

Meantime Rostov and Ilyin gallop merrily to Bogutcharovo, which lies between the two hostile camps. Nikolay hopes to provide provisions for his men before the French reach this place. Alpatitch runs out to the horsemen, begging their help. The peasants are all drunk, he says, and they prevent the mistress from leaving the house.

Angrily Rostov summons the village elder to bring him the leader of the rebellion. Humbled by his authority, the peasants contritely set to work packing and loading the carts. Nikolay's first meeting with Princess Marya is thus tinged with the romance of a rescuing hero and a lady in distress. She is grateful to him, and the expression of her large luminous eyes makes her appear beautiful and noble.

Their meeting impresses them both, with Princess Marya suddenly realizing she has fallen in love with a man whom she may never see again. For his part, Nikolay carries the agreeable impression of her charm, beauty, and soulfulness, realizing as well that her enormous fortune alone recommends her as a suitable wife for him. He wishes he could recall his written promise to Sonya.

Commentary

Beginning to describe the French invasion of Russia, Tolstoy looses in earnest the forces of destiny that carry his characters through the flux of this moment in history. The last bastion of the old order collapses when Prince Nikolay Andreitch Bolkonsky passes on, and the new generation, no longer hampered by the past, comes into power. Besides historical destiny, Tolstoy also maintains a sense of novelistic destiny. As Princess Marya meets her romantic deliverer for the first time, we foresee the marriage of Marya and Nikolay, a sign of the new Russia to emerge from the holocaust.

Tolstoy illustrates the changeover from the old to the new when Princess Marya faces the rebellious peasants. The theme here is that of the enlightened, gentle ruler confronting the blind anarchy loosed by the threat of war. This situation of the peasants against their mistress is analogous to the situation at court, where the tsar's orders are countermanded by the court council that chooses Kutuzov to lead the army. Tolstoy considers this an example of the ascendant will of the mass of people, who instinctively know whom they need in the moment of crisis. Kutuzov is thus the great Russian general chosen by his people, despite their sovereign, and attuned to the necessities of the critical moment. Because he reflects the expressed will of the people rather than his own ambitions, Kutuzov will bow to the manifest forces of necessity and prevail over the ambition-directed Napoleon.

Tolstoy also shows how Prince Andrey bows to historical necessity. Committing himself entirely to his men, who adore him, he avoids his aristocratic acquaintances and acts coldly to his fellow officers. Bolkonsky wishes to break entirely with the past and work through this transition period for the future.

The parallel themes of the domestic novel and the war chronicle that have interwoven throughout the story thus far, now draw closer together as the historic events reach their climax on a personal as well as on a national level.

CHAPTERS 15-25

Summary

Summoned by Kutuzov, Prince Andrey observes the general as he waits to talk with him. Denisov, whom Bolkonsky recalls from his conversations with Natasha, comes to set forth a battle scheme for Kutuzov while the old man looks bored. Another general comes with another plan and Kutuzov barely listens. He despises intellect and knowledge, Bolkonsky thinks to himself, without lacking respect for patriotic sentiment or intellect. Out of his old age, out of his life's experience, Andrey observes to himself, Kutuzov realizes that the forces which control events are called into being by unforeseeable factors at the moment of action.

In a private talk with Kutuzov, Prince Andrey tells him he wishes to serve with his regiment. Counselors are easy to get, the old man answers, we need men in our regiments and they are scarce. "Time and patience are the strongest warriors," Kutuzov tells Andrey, and he owes his victories against the Turks to these factors. Before this war is over, he says loudly, the French will "eat horseflesh," as the Turks did, and counselors will not help us bring that about.

Prince Andrey is reassured by Kutuzov's impersonal approach. He will put nothing of himself into the effort, will contrive nothing, will undertake everything, Bolkonsky thinks. He will hear everything, think of everything, put everything in its place and will not allow anything that can do harm. He knows there is something stronger and more important than his will—"that is the inevitable march of events and he can see them, can grasp their significance . . . can abstain from meddling, from following his own will. . . ."

As if sparked by the nearness of danger, the social round in Moscow is more lively than ever that season. The Drubetskoys, soon to leave

Moscow, give a farewell soirée and Pierre attends. Two items of gossip are outstanding: one is Rostov's rescue of Princess Marya, and the other, which makes Bezuhov blush, is Pierre's being a knight in shining armor to Natasha.

Finding most of his acquaintances have left Moscow, although the Rostovs are still in town, Pierre decides to drive to the army. More and more troops throng the road as he drives along. The more he plunges into the sea of soldiers the more joyful Pierre feels. He believes the qualities of a happy life — wealth, comfort, life itself — can be easily flung away in exchange for the value of "something else," though he does not know what. The object of the sacrifice is unimportant; outstanding is his joy in the sacrifice.

Two days after the Shevardino engagement, the armies fight the battle of Borodino. There is no sense in this engagement, Tolstoy assures us, for the French are now closer to ruination and the Russians closer to the destruction of Moscow, which they fear above all else. The plains of Borodino provide a poor battlefield for both sides, and the Russian forces get reduced by one-half.

Pierre speaks to a doctor he meets who tells him he expects twenty thousand casualties from tomorrow's battle. Pierre goes on, musing about the healthy, sound-limbed young men doomed to die the next day. Arriving on a hilltop overlooking Borodino, Pierre sees a religious procession approach. He watches Kutuzov and his officers kneel and kiss the holy image. Boris Drubetskoy accosts Bezuhov and offers to show him around the camp. Boris belongs to Count Bennigsen's party, the group opposed to Kutuzov. Pierre compares the excitement in Boris caused by thoughts of personal success with the excitement he sees in the faces of common soldiers, faces expressing the problems of life and death. While Kutuzov cordially greets Pierre, Dolohov appears, He begs Bezuhov to forgive their differences and forget their quarrel, since this might be their last day of living. The two men embrace tearfully.

Bennigsen and his suite, Pierre among them, inspect and criticize the disposition of men. Glad to correct an obvious blunder of Kutuzov's, Bennigsen orders the left flank to another position without bothering to inform the commander-in-chief. Bennigsen did not realize these troops were originally placed as an ambush for the enemy.

Prince Andrey feels excited and nervous about the coming battle. With his death perhaps imminent, he recalls the vanity of his past life.

Glory, good society, woman's love, fatherland seem meaningless phrases now. Pierre's arrival interrupts his meditations. Regarding his friend coldly, even hostilely, Andrey seems unwilling to talk privately with Pierre. As they take tea with other officers, Bolkonsky speaks animatedly about the grimness of war. Its sole object is murder, he says, and ideas like magnanimity to prisoners, battling for one's allies makes a polite recreation out of these horrors. Vile as slaughter and mutilation may be, glorifying victory, offering thanksgiving to the dead belies the intensity of the sacrifice. War is not a game of chess; in the heat of battle a pawn is often more powerful than a knight. The outcome of the battle, he says, depends on what each fighting man feels inside himself. Pierre feels this is his last meeting with Prince Andrey and he departs sadly. Unable to sleep that night, Bolkonsky recalls his best moments with Natasha. Where others saw only a fresh young girl, he understood her very soul. The idea of Anatole, alive and happy, angers him anew and he paces up and down.

Commentary

As the battle of Borodino is the turning point in the war between France and Russia, the eve of the event provides a lull-before-the-storm where men take stock of their lives and make peace with their past as if preparing to die. Ambition-ruled men like Bennigsen, who plots to show the incompetence of his rival Kutuzov, and Boris, who is occupied by self-seeking, are set in comparison to Kutuzov as he kneels in prayer, Dolohov, who embraces his former rival Pierre, Andrey, who regards his past life, and Bezuhov, who is on the threshold of discovering life on this eve of death. Even the social round of Petersburg runs a more fevered course at the nearness of danger.

Having seen the faces of soldiers who are close to death, Pierre recognizes the expectation of death in his friend Bolkonsky. He understands Prince Andrey's coldness as part of his turning away from the past in order to accept death with a full sense of immediacy and without misgivings.

In these chapters we begin to learn more about General Kutuzov, the savior of Russia because he is as deeply Russian as Suvorov and Potemkin, old Prince Bolkonsky's heroes. Prince Andrey carefully observes the lack of personal will in this aged veteran who merely acts as a catalyst, allowing the forces of destiny to work through him while he remains unchanged and makes no changes. With intuition and emotion, not sentiment or intellect, Kutuzov understands the state of mind of the Russian troops and can assess its moral force.

Summary

Napoleon's answer to an adjutant is "No prisoners," for he believes the Russians are working their own destruction. When his toilette is finished, he composes his face to simulate tenderness and unwraps a new portrait of his son, called the King of Rome. Then he dramatically asks to have the painting removed, for the tender-aged child should not have to gaze on a battlefield. Having inspected the disposition of his troops, Napoleon draws up an impressive list of orders. These orders seem very competent and military, writes Tolstoy, but not one will be carried out. Some are impossible to begin with, others do not correspond with the situation they were designed for, since unforeseen changes always occur during the heat of battle. Indeed, Tolstoy adds, Napoleon was so far from the scene of the battle that he knew nothing of what was happening. The author shows Napoleon playing the role of military leader when, in fact, such a role is impossible to play once the battle has begun. After a final inspection of his lines, Napoleon declares, "The pieces are on the board, the game will begin tomorrow."

Pierre awakens to the noise of cannons booming and longs to be in the midst of the smoke and the noise. On the faces of Kutuzov and his men, Pierre finds the "latent heat" of patriotism and the composure of men who face death. As the battle waxes, Bezuhov sees the "latent heat" gleam brighter in the eyes of those around him and feels it burning within himself. Soldiers are now falling all about him and cannon balls hit nearby targets. He himself is knocked down by the force of a near explosion. Panicked, he dashes back to the safety of the battery, but the men are gone and the guns silent. All about are corpses. The battle will stop now, Pierre thinks, for they will be horrified at what they have done. But the booming goes on while the sun climbs to its zenith.

By the middle of the day, Napoleon receives reports that all say the same thing: the weak Russians stand steady while the French dissolve and flee. All his officers are asking for reinforcements and he feels suddenly involved in a bad dream. His concern in all previous battles was to choose the various ways of success, but against these Russians — of whom not a single corps has been captured, not a flag or cannon taken in two months — he can only consider the possibilities of failure. From his view on a battlement, he sees his is a massacre not a battle, and, slowly, defeated, he turns back to Shevardino.

Kutuzov has remained in the same place since morning. He issues no orders, but simply assents to or disapproves of whatever is proposed to him. His old age has shown him battles are not won by commanders but by the intangible force called the spirit of the army and he merely follows the force and leads it as far as it lays in his power to lead. When an adjutant-general reports that the battle is lost at all points, Kutuzov becomes furious and quickly pens an order to be sent all along the lines: tomorrow we attack. The weary soldiers pass the message along; feeling confirmed by the highest command in what they wish to believe, they take heart and courage anew.

Prince Andrey's regiment, under heavy fire all day, is ordered to stand by inactive. The men carry off their wounded, close up ranks once more, and await death. A grenade drops among them, and, to set an example, Andrey remains standing. Gazing at the object of his death sputtering a few paces away, Bolkonsky is filled with love for the grass and earth and air. The explosion flings him into the air and he lands in a pool of his own blood.

At the sight of the battlefield heaped with dead and wounded, Napoleon's phantasm of life is momentarily replaced by personal, human sentiment as he imagines the agonies and death for himself. To take personal responsibility or personal interest in that carnage is too much for him; this would admit the vanity of all his strivings. He must return to his comfortable fantasy, consider it significant that five Russian corpses lie for each French one, that he is battling for the welfare of his people and the nations of Europe, and that he controls the destiny of millions.

Borodino has blood-soaked ground for two acres. Thousands lie dead. Borodino is not a physical victory, since half the Russian force is disabled, but it is a moral one. The Russians have stood and barred the way to Moscow, while the French, superior in arms and men, would merely have had to put in a little extra effort to overcome the weak resistance. They could not do this, Tolstoy declares, for their moral force was exhausted in face of the steadfast defenders. Borodino foreshadows the inevitability of the French defeat, now that they meet a foe of a stronger spirit.

Commentary

The long description of the battle of Borodino immerses us completely in the "war" area of Tolstoy's novel. No longer concerned with the personal conflict within the souls of specific characters, Tolstoy extends his writing to include the national struggle and the moral force generated on a national scale. As Prince Andrey and Pierre dispose of their personal past and fuse themselves with the whole of the Russian defending force, so does Tolstoy dispose of the glory and gamesmanship of past battles. In these chapters we find none of the romance and daring of Rostov and Denisov at Eylau, but only the carnage and life-and-death seriousness of the steadfast Russians at Borodino. This is the battle that galvanizes the defenders into a powerful definition of the Russian spirit and presages Napoleon's downfall.

Tolstoy overstates a comparison between Kutuzov's recognition of reality and Napoleon's "artificial phantasm of life" to show how Russia's ultimate victory will come about. Not only does Bonaparte have no control over the events of the battle, but his megalomania (illustrated in Chapter 29) prevents him from understanding the actual insignificance of his role. He is shown to be more helpless in the tide of destiny than any soldier in the ranks. Kutuzov's power, on the other hand, lies precisely in his awareness of being a passive instrument among the play of forces beyond his control.

From this sense of passivity in face of destiny, Kutuzov as well as each soldier he commands, gains an awareness of death that heightens each sense of personal — hence national — being. In this awareness consists the "superior moral force" of the Russians whom the French cannot overcome.

Moral force of an individual or nation, Tolstoy says in many ways, derives from being part of a cosmic whole and submitting to a universal destiny. This is but another version of Pierre's analogy of "an endless ladder of progression" from inanimate life to the free spirits close to God. Where Napoleon is blinded by considering his will free, thus hastening the destruction of his army, the self-forgetful Kutuzov bows to necessity and guides an inspirited Russian force to victory.

PART XI

CHAPTERS 1-12

Summary

Tolstoy introduces this section by showing the error of applying scientific analysis to history. As a mathematician takes arbitrary small units and by integral calculus develops a system of dynamics to understand the continuity of motion, so does a historian take small units of history to understand the continuity of history. But we fall into error, Tolstoy says, when the "unit" we choose to examine is the career of a great man or the effects of a particular political crisis. What we fail to realize, he continues, is that these "units" are made up of still smaller forces operating upon the great man or the political phenomenon. As we establish a unit of "absolute motion," so must we examine the "homogeneous elements" of history: single human beings and their daily lives. For, he says, it is "the sum of men's individual wills [that] produced both the revolution and Napoleon; and only the sum of those wills endured them and then destroyed them." We can never understand the laws of history; but to assume the beginning of an event by citing a historical personality is as mistaken an idea as saying the turning wheels cause the steam engine to move. We must begin to study history by considering the lives of the men within the masses and the infinitesimal activities of each.

Tolstoy now sums up the overall movements of that period. Armies of twelve different nations invade Russia and the Russians fall back, avoiding battle until Borodino. Then the French move on toward Moscow, leaving behind them thousands of versts of famine-stricken, hostile country. As they retreat, the Russians burn ever more fiercely with hatred of their foe; venting this fury at Borodino. For five weeks the French occupy Moscow before they flee while the Russians retreat well beyond the city. As the French flee, their army totally disintegrates, although not a single engagement takes place between the foes.

Kutuzov could never have foreseen this overall pattern, although militarists have criticized him ever since. A commander-in-chief is limited by many factors, says Tolstoy, and he is never present at the beginning of any event. Always in the middle of a changing series of events that unfold moment by moment, he is always unaware of the whole pattern.

When he realizes his troops are too exhausted to fight further, Kutuzov also realizes Moscow is doomed. The safety of Russia lies in her army alone, says Kutuzov to his generals at a meeting; it is better to abandon Moscow and maintain the security of our troops. The generals hear the decision and their council is like a funeral meeting. To himself, Kutuzov expresses bewilderment. "This I did not expect!" he says. Then he shouts in fury, "But they shall eat horseflesh like the Turks!" and strikes the table with his fist. He still believes himself destined to deliver Russia from the French.

The abandonment and burning of Moscow, says Tolstoy, is as irresistible an event as the army's retreating without a battle. Another "irresistible event" is the evacuation of Moscow. More and more swiftly after Borodino the rich people leave the city, then the poor, with the rest burning or destroying what remains. Although exhorted by the governor to remain and fight, the citizens who depart are responding to a deeper patriotism that they feel but cannot express. Despite the vague and varied reasons that prompt each departure, leaving the wealthy city is the great deed that saves Russia. Count Rastoptchin, governor of Moscow, however, fails to recognize the "tide of destiny." Wishing to be considered as his nation's defender, he issues proclamations demanding the people remain and take a last stand against the French invaders, despite his own inner knowledge of the futility of this action. Tolstoy says Rastoptchin acts like an attention-demanding child frolicking about "the grand and inevitable event of the abandonment and burning of Moscow."

Meantime Countess Bezuhov faces a peculiar dilemma. Two of her lovers appear in town at the same time and to each she says, in effect, "If you wish to have a claim on me, why not marry me?" She decides to convert to Catholicism because then her marriage to Pierre would become invalid, since it took place according to the precepts of a "false religion." Choosing one of her lovers as a husband, she writes to Pierre for a divorce.

The sunset over Borodino finds Pierre sharing fried biscuits with some common soldiers. He feels delighted to be among them and in his dreams that night his benefactor, Osip Bazdyev, appears to him. Goodness, his mentor says, is being like *them* (the common soldiers). The voice continues: "No one can be master of anything while he fears death. If it were not for suffering, a man would not know his limits, would not know himself. The hardest thing...is to know how to unite in one's soul the significance of the whole." These are the things Pierre has longed to hear, and these statements seem to answer his most perplexing questions.

When Pierre arrives in Moscow the next morning, an adjutant of the governor tells him Rastoptchin wishes to see him. The messenger informs Pierre of the deaths of his brother-in-law Anatole and of Prince Andrey. In the waiting room, an official he knows tells him how severely Rastoptchin treats "traitors," a group of pacifists who allegedly have circulated Napoleon's proclamation around Moscow. For this crime a youth named Vereshtchagin will be sentenced to hard labor. When

Pierre talks with the governor, Rastoptchin reproaches him for aiding one of these alleged traitors and warns him from further associations with that subversive group of freemasons. Pierre had better leave town, Rastoptchin says in conclusion. When he returns home, Bezuhov discovers Ellen's letter. Rehearsing the ridiculous sequence of events, he falls asleep with various thoughts running through his head: death, suffering, freedom, Ellen's marriage, the petty demagoguery of Rastoptchin. The next morning Pierre disappears and no one in his household sees him again until after the occupation of Moscow.

Commentary

According to his interest in beginning an examination into the course of history through the "infinitesimal activities" of each participant, Tolstoy conveys to us a sense of the overall pattern of events and then closely details some daily particulars of one "arbitrary unit" — Pierre especially — amidst these events. As we see the "irresistible tide of history" enveloping not only Kutuzov but Pierre as well, we see how Tolstoy draws a favorable comparison between these individuals. Just as Kutuzov submits to the conditions of historical necessity by abandoning Moscow, so does Pierre strive to partake of the "significance of the whole" by abandoning his former life. Submission to destiny is the path of victory for the hero of Russia as well as the hero of the novel.

In contrast to the Kutuzov-Pierre parallel, Tolstoy provides us with the comic relief of Ellen Bezuhov's amorous crisis and the dangerous moral hypocrisy of Rastoptchin. The countess and the governor both share a childish, limited interpretation of moral universals. Both pervert human values to their own uses: Ellen travesties marriage and Rastoptchin makes a tragic parody of patriotism and historical necessity.

These "infinitesimal" incidents involving Ellen and Rastoptchin, however, perform a useful function both in terms of the novel and in terms of the history within the novel. With Ellen's faithlessness freeing Pierre from his marital ties and Rastoptchin's banishment freeing him from civic ties, Bezuhov is liberated from society into the mainstream of the events to follow. He is now free to follow his destiny toward self-attainment through plunging into the "tide of history."

CHAPTERS 13-29

Summary

The Rostovs finally get set to leave Moscow one day before the French enter the city. As civilians stream out of town, the wounded soldiers are carted in and Natasha, in midst of packing, offers some disabled officers hospitality. Count Rostov comes home with the announcement that the police have left Moscow and the countess, terrified at the idea of uncontrolled violence, orders the servants to frenzied occupation. With a sudden burst of vigor, Natasha sets to work and organizes the packing. Late at night, while the housekeeper is still working, a wounded officer in a closed carriage is driven into the yard. Stifling a shriek, the housekeeper recognizes Prince Andrey.

In the morning, as their thirty carriages are being loaded, Vera's husband Berg drives up in his sleek carriage. He asks Count Rostov to send some servants to help him move some abandoned furniture to his new house. At this effrontery of his son-in-law's badly concealed looting, Count Rostov throws up his hands in confusion and leaves the room. The Rostov's street is full of wounded soldiers, begging a ride out of Moscow. Natasha calls to her father to order some carriages unpacked so they can convey a few disabled men out of town. Her demand re-establishes the humane instincts lost when Berg arrived, and after much rearranging and unpacking of carts, only four carriages remain loaded with the Rostov possessions. At the last minute, Sonya learns the identity of the wounded officer in the closed carriage; she and the countess agree to keep the news secret from Natasha. Prince Andrey's conveyance leads their procession out of Moscow. As she drives along, Natasha recognizes Pierre walking on the street. They are able to exchange a few hasty words as they pass each other.

During the previous days, Pierre has been secretly living in Osip Bazdyev's house, sorting the papers of his dead benefactor. Besides Gerasim, the butler, and Osip's besotted half-mad elder brother, no one else lives there. In his solitude, Pierre conceived the fantastic idea of assassinating Napoleon upon his entrance to the city tomorrow. With this purpose in mind, accompanied by Gerasim, he is on his way to purchase a pistol when Pierre meets the Rostovs.

Napoleon poses on the hill and looks down at Moscow; the goal of his ambitions awaits him. He will convene the nobles, and in a stirring speech he has prepared, will convince them of his peaceful intentions and of his interest in the welfare of his new subjects. As Napoleon awaits the expected deputation, his adjutants are too ashamed to inform him that the city is empty, except for drunken mobs in the streets. Finally, Bonaparte enters Moscow. Tolstoy likens the great city to a deserted beehive that looks inhabited and healthy from the outside, but is totally defunct within.

Because Rastoptchin interfered with the tide of destiny, he caused great harm to his country's cause. Besides Moscow being the only city during the war where rioting occurred, valuable food stores, equipment, church relics, and other necessities helpful to the army were left behind because the governor, eager to exercise power, refused to abandon the city in time. An eager mob, convened at his earlier orders, forms outside his palace willing to fight a last stand against the French. But Rastoptchin has lost heart and realizes his mistake. Rather than admit his miscalculations to the people, he decides to throw them a victim and subdue their excitement. He pushes the prisoner, Vereshtchagin, into their midst and rouses the mob to beat this youth to death. Rastoptchin consoles his guilt feelings by convincing himself he acted in the public welfare. But the echo of the crime in his soul shames him forever.

Warily at first, because they expect resistance, the French troops march into Moscow. When they see it is safely deserted, they disperse, faster and faster, among the houses like water in a beach of dry sand. With so many strangers lighting cooking stoves and smoking pipes, fire is inevitable. Moscow was not burned out of hostility from the invaders or defenders, Tolstoy says, but because fire usually breaks out in a town of empty wooden buildings. The real reason for the burning of Moscow lies in the desertion of the city by its inhabitants.

As he broods in solitude over his wild idea to assassinate Napoleon, Pierre is not quick enough to catch Osip's mad brother as he enters the room and runs away with Pierre's pistol. While the old butler, Gerasim, struggles with the madman, some French officers arrive at the door. The madman aims his pistol at the officer. Pierre intercedes just in time and the gun goes off harmlessly. "You have saved my life," declares the enemy captain, concluding with unique logic, "You are French." Pierre answers he is a Russian. The Frenchman, Ramballe, makes himself at home over a dinner and many glasses of wine, and he is so good-natured and full of gratitude that Pierre listens to his stories with interest. After Ramballe describes many adventures and amorous escapades, Pierre finds himself confessing to his unsuccessful marriage, his love for Natasha. Late that night the two new friends walk in the clear air. Though the glare of a distant fire is visible, Pierre only sees the lofty starlit sky and the bright comet. A tender joy stirs within him, but when he recalls that he must kill Napoleon tomorrow, he becomes dizzy and leans against a fence for support.

Commentary

The various incidents in these chapters are variations on the basic theme of humaneness, a theme in harmony with Tolstoy's larger investigation of virtue and submission to destiny. The Rostovs giving up their possessions to free carts in order to convey disabled soldiers out of town and Pierre's saving the life of the enemy captain are natural and spontaneous acts of humanity. By comparison, Rastoptchin's vindication of personal failure by sacrificing Vereshtchagin and the parallel scapegoat idea of Pierre's intended assassination of Napoleon are examples of unspontaneous and unnatural acts that, by being egotistically generated, lead to dehumanization. In both situations, Pierre and Rastoptchin operate on the fallacious assumption that one man is responsible for historical acts: the governor tells the mob Vereshtchagin is a traitor to his nation and Pierre wishes to destroy the man who caused the war. These incidents all resolve on a note of love, hope, life itself as Pierre's emotions focus on the starry peaceful night sky and the comet.

Tolstoy illustrates obvious truisms through these incidents: when one acts according to his natural instincts for goodness, his acts are humane; when one acts out of self-consciousness and quells his sense of conscience, his acts are destructive. Unselfish motives generate acts that follow the necessities of destiny, whereas selfishly motivated acts introduce a destructive chaos to the overall pattern of destiny.

CHAPTERS 30-34

Summary

With the road so crowded, the Rostovs are able to travel only five versts out of Moscow and they stop for the night among some huts in a small village. An ever-brightening glow shines from Moscow, and the servants who sit outside the hut mourn and pray for "our mother, the white city" doomed to burn.

In his fever and pain, Prince Andrey is constantly delirious. Trying to order his thoughts, he recalls the experience of loving the man he hated. When he was in the hospital tent getting treatment for his wound, Anatole Kuragin had just suffered a leg amputation. Prince Andrey wept in tenderness and sympathy for the man he hated. Close to death then, he suddenly felt what divine love is: the kind of love that never changes. He shared for a moment God's universal love for every human soul, whether friend or enemy. Recalling Natasha now, he realizes he loves her and has always loved her despite his momentary hatred of her as well. He wishes he could tell her this. Suddenly an unidentifiable white shape hovers at the door like a dream and approaches his bedside. Andrey realizes at last his wish has become a reality. Smiling, he holds his hand to her and she drops to her knees beside him. From then on, Natasha refuses to leave his side and the doctors admit she has unusual skill and fortitude in nursing the sick man.

Pierre walks across Moscow, armed with the pistol and dagger with which he intends to kill Napoleon. On his way, he rescues a child from a burning building and defends a young woman against a Frenchman. The scuffle attracts the attention of some Polish Uhlans who are scouring the city in search of incendiaries. Because Pierre carries weapons, they arrest him and he is placed under strict guard.

Commentary

Because of his humanity, Pierre is sidetracked from his goal of murder. Being equally motivated toward saving life as well as destroying life, containing within himself the power of life and death, Pierre is prepared by Tolstoy for a major revelation. The same is true for Prince Andrey and Natasha as they are united in love during the last death-shadowed moments of Andrey's life. The intense mingling of living with dying generates the "salvation" and moment of truth that ultimately defines Tolstoy's characters.

PART XII

CHAPTERS 1-13

Summary

Petersburg society has hardly changed during these critical times, and the aristocrats still hold balls, levées, theater parties, and they are still concerned with court politics. They rejoice at the victory of Borodino and discuss the battle with the same emotions they talk of Ellen Bezuhov's sudden heart ailment. At Anna Pavlovna's soirée some days later, the guests exchange commiserations on account of the death of Countess Bezuhov. After Moscow is abandoned, the grief-stricken emperor declares he will stop at no sacrifice to save his country and will himself lead the peasants to battle if the army fails.

Despite the war, despite all the self-sacrificing, people carry on their personal lives. Tolstoy says that these daily human interests and activities are more important than the public ones we hear so much about. Those who are concerned with their immediate problems, he writes, play the most useful role in history, while those who strive to grasp the general course of events, and try by heroism and self-sacrifice to take a hand in it, are the most useless in society. "It is only unself-conscious activity that bears fruit," he says, "and the man who plays a part in an historical drama never understands its significance. If he strives to comprehend it, he is stricken with barrenness." In the remote provinces people bewail the fate of Russia and of Moscow and in Petersburg society-minded persons talk only of war and self-sacrifice; but the men in the army are silent on these issues and, as they gaze on the flames, their thoughts are not on revenge but on their next pay check or on the next halting place. Their silence comes from an implicit understanding of what they must do, whereas the discussions of those far from the battle scene come from a lack of understanding and a lack of experience.

Nikolay has orders to purchase horses in the district of Voronezh and he departs a few days before Borodino takes place. After the first day, with the horses chosen and contracted for, Nikolay is free to pursue his social life and attends a ball. He also calls on an aunt of Princess Marya and tells her what is in his heart: that he has promised to marry his penniless cousin Sonya, that he admires Marya but will not marry her for her wealth. The aunt promises to be tactful about the whole matter, especially since her niece is still in mourning.

Two days later, Nikolay and Marya have an impressive meeting. Filled with love and joy at his presence, she becomes transformed into a lovely woman whose face reflects the beauty of her soul; on his part, Nikolay regrets his promise to Sonya. At this point he gratefully receives a letter from home. Sonya writes to free him of his promise, and his mother tells him that Andrey is traveling with them, nursed by Natasha and Sonya. With this news of her brother, Princess Marya regards Nikolay almost as a kinsman.

Pierre believes he is sentenced to death along with the other incendiaries with whom he has been imprisoned for a week. Because he has refused to divulge any information about himself, he is sent to General Davoust, a man known for his cruelty, for further questioning. Here Pierre tells his name and states he is not a spy. At one point during the interview, he and Davoust exchange a long look. At once a relationship springs between them; their look is an acknowledgment of their common humanity. Led to the firing squad among five other prisoners, Pierre is ready to die and watches as each man is methodically shot. But he himself is led away. That he has again the gift of life means nothing to him now; he feels himself dead inside, with all his faith in human life destroyed by that disciplined machinery that has had the other innocent prisoners killed.

Later, when he is in the barracks with other prisoners of war, Pierre learns he had been officially pardoned. A caressive sing-song voice addresses him and the words penetrate Pierre's numbness. "Ay, darling, don't grieve," says an old man from the corner, "Trouble lasts an hour, but life lasts forever." The man sits hunched over his knees, a dog next to him, and the round peasant face characterizes the roundness of his entire aspect. This is Platon Karataev, whom Pierre remembers for the rest of his life while he hardly recalls the other prisoners. Influenced by his new acquaintance, Pierre's soul finds a new world to replace the one destroyed at the firing squad—a world of new beauty which rests "on new foundations that cannot be shattered."

The four weeks Pierre spends in the shed are brightened by Platon's presence. The other prisoners, too, regard the old man with warmth and the dog follows him everywhere. When Karataev goes to sleep he ends his prayers with a special appeal to the "Saints Frola and Lavra," the horses' saints. "For one must think of the poor beasts too," Platon explains. Platon, energetic and strong, is over fifty years old. His face bears the innocent expression of a child, and childlike, everything he utters is spontaneous and genuine. He speaks with caressive epithets like a peasant woman which (Pierre thinks) he invents as he goes along and never knows beforehand what will come out. When hearing stories from the soldiers, Platon asks questions and repeats details to emphasize the moral beauty of what is told. Lacking special attachments, Karataev loves every creature equally: the French, his comrades, the dog, his neighbor. Pierre feels that Karataev, despite his deep affection, would never suffer a moment's grief at parting from him, and Pierre begins to have the same feelings toward Platon. Neither actions nor words seem to hold any significance for the old man; they exist only as part of a sentence or an event that expresses, for the moment, an incomprehensible force, his life itself. And Karataev regards his life meaningful only because it is part of a whole of which he is conscious at all times.

Commentary

The moments he spends watching the firing squad and feels death upon him are the moments of Pierre's turning point in life. Because this is such an important moment, Tolstoy has carefully foreshadowed this death-to-life movement and has provided once more a brief but significant incident to illuminate the qualities of humanity and inhumanity.

Having refused to even give his name, Pierre has no other identity except that of a human being. To have an excuse for killing him, his captors have labeled him as a spy or an incendiary. Pierre realizes himself a victim of an impersonal machinery already set in motion and realizes as well that this trick of dehumanizing a person is the only means whereby an innocent individual can be executed. When Pierre and Davoust look at each other in the face, this impersonalizing machinery is reversed and Pierre becomes an individual with the right to live. As his fellow "incendiaries" are methodically fired upon, Pierre feels himself dead. His soul has been "killed" from an intense awareness of the facility with which individual human beings become impersonal objects of execution. Tolstoy must now bring his hero back to life.

The scene of rebirth is as symbolically rich as the scene of dying. The darkened shed that imprisons Pierre is like a womb. Karataev, endowed with feminine sympathy, is his midwife and he offers Pierre some simple food (potatoes) for his first nourishment. Karataev's "roundness," itself suggestive of the womb, is like the wheel of life in which every human soul is part of God and the spirit of God part of each soul. As a living symbol of life's unity and universal love, Karataev is the means for Pierre's renewal.

Platon Karataev exemplifies that person whose "unselfconscious activity bears fruit." The "activity" Tolstoy means is the moment-by-moment business of life lived with spontaneity and simplicity of soul. The "fruit" of such activity is life itself with its implicit awareness and acceptance of death and suffering by which life is defined. Platon embodies the love that Prince Andrey felt when he confronted Anatole in the hospital: a love universal and unchanging like God's love to all creatures. Each activity of Karataev, whether speaking, listening, or breathing, expresses the cosmic unity that guarantees significance and continuity to each organic and inorganic component of the universe.

Platon Karataev is Tolstoy's creation wherein all opposites are resolved. From the "roundness" of his aspect, Tolstoy implies the solution to all the conflicts he illustrates in his novel. Karataev is the symbol of the universe where all things come full circle; personal love and impersonal love, age and youth, sagacity and naivete, immediacy and eternity, imprisonment and freedom, life and death — all are concepts to describe unities, not polarities.

CHAPTERS 14-16

Summary

Princess Marya makes the two-week journey to see her brother for the last time. Her love for Nikolay provides her with the spiritual strength she needs to encounter the dying Andrey. Greeted tenderly by the Rostovs, pitying Count Ilya Andreitch, who now seems aged and bewildered, Princess Marya feels warmth for Natasha. As she sees Natasha's face expressing boundless love for Prince Andrey, Marya embraces her and the two women weep together. Natasha describes a "sudden change" in Prince Andrey and says he has lost his hold on life.

Andrey's manner to Marya is cold, his impersonal conversation shows he is absorbed by inner thoughts that a living person cannot conceive, and he seems to blame his sister for being healthy and alive. He barely shows interest in his son, now a serious-eyed seven-year-old.

The "sudden change" Natasha speaks of is the result of Andrey's rejecting love and life and choosing death. It occurred two days before when, falling asleep, he suddenly recognized that love is God, that dying is a particle of love, a way of returning to the universal and eternal sources of love. He dreams that death has stolen into the room and he could not prevent it and he has died. Then he awakens. Yes, death is an awakening, he tells himself, and suddenly feels delivered of a heavy bondage. This moral change has left him softened and gentle and Natasha realizes he will die. Remaining at his beside to the last, Natasha and Marya see him slip away into death. It is too soon for them to weep at the loss; rather they weep at the emotion and awe that fills their souls before "the solemn and simple mystery of death accomplished before their eyes."

Commentary

Prince Andrey has always sought for death as the ultimate resolution of the problems of his life. Tolstoy shows how his hero has always suffered his moments of truth when facing death: at the battlefield of Austerlitz, at the death of his wife Liza, in the hospital tent with Anatole, and even during his life-affirming conversation with Pierre when he regards the peaceful sky. On the other hand, Tolstoy shows how Andrey has always suffered disillusion whenever he followed life's beckoning: his dream of being a hero, his work with Speransky and his committee positions, and finally, his despair at Natasha's "fall." In his death scene, where Andrey believes very much like Platon Karataev in the cosmic unity of life and love and death and God, he arrives at an ultimate understanding of himself. At that moment he chooses death, welcoming its deliverance from all his problems of self-definition and resolving his life's futile activities. Andrey's ultimate expression is nihilistic, and this nihilism is the only solution his civilized, intellectual, egotistical nature can provide him.

In working out Andrey's nature to its ultimate conclusion, Tolstoy has neatly provided the end of one thread of his narrative and a point of beginning for two others. Nikolay and Marya are now free to marry, and Natasha, enriched by her awareness of love by the death of her fiancé, will be mature when it is time for her to accept Pierre.

PART XIII

Summary

A close look at historical events, writes Tolstoy, shows us that the heroes of history are controlled by the actions of the multitudes. By showing various incidents of this part of the war occurring through freak happenings (he cites the battle of Tarutino occurring because a Cossack, hunting rabbits, happened upon the French encampment) Tolstoy attributes error to most historians who say Kutuzov is responsible for this or that, or Napoleon's "genius" caused this or that to happen.

Tolstoy describes the secure position of the French army who, with twice the manpower of the Russians, have all the wealth and supplies of Moscow to draw upon if they wish to attack the Russian forces. Despite these obvious advantages, the French neither seek out the Russians nor reserve winter supplies. It is clear, says Tolstoy, that the French themselves do the most damage to their cause, and Napoleon's "genius" cannot prevail over the inevitable course of events.

With the pretext of punishing the Russian army for defeating the French at Tarutino, Napoleon leaves a small garrison in Moscow and orders the army to depart. This simple maneuver begins the headlong flight of the Grande Armée out of Moscow. The army is overloaded with trains of booty-laden wagons—Napoleon has his own collection of treasure—and despite his past experiences, Bonaparte refrains from having the booty burned. Moreover, the army takes the same route out of Moscow as it had entered it, passing again through lands and towns devastated and pillaged and lacking sustenance for the men and horses. Tolstoy says the army is now like a stampeding herd of cattle, trampling its own necessities and approaching nearer to ruin. Napoleon is like a child sitting in the carriage who fancies he is moving it by pulling on the straps. In reality, Tolstoy says, Napoleon is led by his army, which acts in the blind panic of a wounded beast heading straight for the hunter with the gun.

This, then, is the significance of the battle of Tarutino: it signifies the transition from retreat to attack for the Russians, it exposes the weakness of the French, and provides the shock that puts the Grande Armée to flight.

Pierre is regenerated since that day of execution which killed the thoughts and feelings he felt were so important. Stripped of all the superfluities of civilization—his title, his conveniences, his search for self-sacrifice—he has found the inner harmony he has yearned for. His four weeks of hardship create only basic demands for food, cleanliness, and freedom. The men in the barracks like him and respect him. The very peculiarities that used to embarrass him in civilized society—his strength, his disdain for comforts, his absent-mindedness, his good nature—now give him the prestige of a hero among his comrades.

The night of October 6 begins the retreat of the French. Among the drumbeats that drown the groans of the sick prisoners, Pierre begins to feel afraid. *It* is here again—the mysterious, unsympathetic force that drives men, against their wills, to do their fellow creatures to death. *It* is the force he felt at the execution. At the end of the first day of a grueling march, Pierre walks among the campfires. Suddenly he laughs a hearty, good-humored laugh. He laughs at the imprisonment that has freed him, for his immortal soul is still his. Gazing at the sky, at the distant forests and boundless fields, he muses, "All that is mine, all that is in me, and all that is I." And all this they caught and shut up in a shed closed in with boards! He falls asleep still smiling.

When he receives the news that Napoleon has evacuated the entire army from Moscow, Kutuzov weeps for joy at the proof of what he suspected: the doomed French have fled from Moscow and recoil in blind panic from Russian soil. From now on his aim is to avoid losing his men unnecessarily and to avoid, as well, obstructing the French retreat out of Russia. On the other hand, Kutuzov knows he cannot prevent his men from attacking the helpless enemy, for he realizes how eager men and officers are to distinguish themselves in battle. Kutuzov is correct; from now on the French retreat with increasing rapidity. As the army goes along, troops melt away, each man desiring to be taken prisoner and escape the horrors and miseries of his position.

Commentary

These chapters illustrate the inevitable tide of history that engulfs individuals. Tolstoy shows how all the "single wills" of the French troops combine into the huge movement of the retreat from Moscow, with Napoleon, mistaking this inevitable movement as an expression of his own will, carried along by the tide and helpless to avoid the disaster that occurs. That Napoleon is unable to use his military "genius" to avert the self-destruction of the French proves Tolstoy's thesis: that leaders merely follow movements and do not originate them.

Kutuzov resolves the forces of necessity with his free will by submitting to the inevitable tide of history. He will not encourage military victories for his own glory, but will merely supervise the historical forces already unloosed; his aim, therefore, is merely to keep the French moving out of Russia. Kutuzov, like Pierre, is able to use the forces of destiny to gain freedom for his nation.

Contrasting Napoleon's "imprisonment" by the "irresistible tide of history" with Pierre's newly found freedom as a prisoner, Tolstoy underscores his thesis of free will and necessity with a personal example and translates a historical theme into an individual one. Carried along by the movement of the multitude, stripped of its insignia as well — title, conveniences, all the false values that define an individual in society — Pierre discovers his inner self freed from the prison of outer significations. Having no one to command and no one to be commanded by, he is freer than Napoleon; he is left with his own soul and a will free to overcome all physical and emotional obstacles.

PART XIV

Summary

Tolstoy now shows how the events of 1812 violate all the "rules" of history historians write about. Nations are considered conquered, he writes, when the invaders win more battles than the defenders and occupy the enemy capital. The French, for example, who have repeatedly won battles, especially that of Borodino, who then occupy and raze Moscow, lose an army of 600,000 men without fighting in any major engagement after the retreat. Victories alone do not signify conquest, Tolstoy concludes. The force deciding the fate of millions of people resides not in leadership, battles, or armies; it lies in the spirit behind the army. The spirit of the Russians makes them fight desperately to overcome the foe, and they use all means to rout the invaders. This is the part of history when Russian soldiers become guerillas and harry the French constantly. Again rules of warfare are reversed, writes Tolstoy. Usual battle patterns involve a massed front of attackers, with scattered groups retreating. The French, however, retreat in a compact mass and the self-confident Russian attackers advance in small numbers.

Denisov and Dolohov each lead a group among the many troops of "irregulars" which destroy the Grande Armée piecemeal. They plan to combine their bands for an attack on a French transport. A courier comes to Denisov's camp with a message from a general. The soldier is none other than Petya Rostov, now an officer, and he is so excited at the coming attack he begs Denisov to allow him to remain. Petya has an intense desire to be a hero and his foolhardy behavior during a previous battle nearly caused his death. More excited than ever when Dolohov arrives, Petya longs to fight at the side of this hero whose courage and cruelty are famous.

A cold and shivering French drummer boy is Denisov's prisoner and Petya gives the youth some warm food. Dolohov wishes to shoot the prisoner but Denisov protects his charge. Petya's moment of daring occurs when he and Dolohov, disguised as French officers, pass through the enemy lines to spy out their disposition. Denisov is relieved to have the boy return safely and Petya can barely sleep for the excitement of the next day.

Before sunrise, Dolohov's cossacks and Denisov's band attack the French. Petya gallops ahead, eager to sight the enemy. He is shot from ambush and dies instantly. The quick skirmish is successful and liberates many Russian prisoners. Pierre is among the men freed.

Pierre has marched for more than three weeks, suffering intense privations which have killed two-thirds of the other prisoners. Through his ordeal, he has learned there is nothing in the world to dread; man is created for happiness and that happiness lies in itself. Superfluity, not privation, is the force that imprisons mankind. Freedom exists when one learns the limits of suffering, when one can recall soothing memories to overcome physical anguish. This feeling, or avoidance of feeling, is the vitality Pierre discovers every human being can possess.

Platon Karataev grew increasingly weaker from his fever and Pierre began to avoid him. One night at a campfire he listened to a story the peasant had told many times before. The story told of an innocent man imprisoned in Siberia for murder. Telling the tale of his frame-up to his barracks-mates the old man meets the man who committed the actual murder and who begs forgiveness. But when the pardon from the tsar finally arrives, the innocent sufferer is already dead. Karataev's face expressed ecstasy at the end of his tale and the mysterious significance of that gladness filled Pierre's soul with joy. By morning, Karataev was too ill to move, and as some French soldiers advanced toward the sick man, Pierre exchanged a final glance with his friend. He heard the shot and never looked back.

The night before his liberation, Pierre has a dream whose images are all of Platon Karataev. Life is God, his dream tells him, and "to love life is to love God. The hardest and the most blessed thing is to love this life in one's sufferings, in undeserved suffering." That morning of Pierre's freedom is the funeral day for Petya Rostov.

With the onset of frost in late October, the French retreat begins to assume its tragic aspect. Men die from freezing, exhaustion, and starvation. Owing to the incredible rapidity of the desperate flight, the Russians can rarely catch their enemy. Neither army knows where the other is and they often meet by chance. The leaders flee even faster than their men. Still pretending they care for the army, the generals plan battles and give orders, although they mostly care for self-survival. The greatness of Napoleon, for his historians, is still undiminished even as he rides off in his closed carriage with furs wrapped around him. So is the greatness of General Ney, who runs off leaving nine-tenths of his men and all his artillery behind. "And it never enters anyone's head," editorializes Tolstoy, "that to admit a greatness immeasurable by the rule of right and wrong is but to accept one's own nothingness and immeasurable littleness."

Commentary

With the final retreat of the French, with Pierre's discovering a new freedom out of imprisonment and a new joy out of suffering, Tolstoy is preparing us for many conclusions which are, in effect, beginnings as well. The imminent Russian victory begins a new chapter in the history of Russia, just as the premature bloom and death of Petya Rostov marks the new generation. Tolstoy's sensitive depiction of Petya's eagerness and immaturity, and his newly awakened sympathies toward the enemy drummer boy echo Nikolay's early experiences as a novice soldier who cannot kill an individuated human being. This repetition not only shows the passing of time and generation but underscores the continuity of life and the universality of experience.

Because it is prefigured by the death of Platon Karataev, Petya's death is conveyed to us by the author with the same "lack of feeling" Pierre felt at Platon's demise. The "lack of feeling" is not callousness but rather an expression of God's universal, equally extended love. Death is one consequence of the process of growth, Tolstoy seems to say, and Petya's death is another incidental sacrifice to the cause of the war, in itself a mode of national growth.

By comparing the way Petya is sacrificed with the way Napoleon and Ney sacrifice their men to their own self-interests, Tolstoy restates his thesis on the "nothingness and immeasurable littleness" of human beings. In the Tolstoyan sense, men are "immeasurably little" compared to the universe of which they are a part; in the "Napoleonic" sense, they are nothing because they are tools, and this is the fallacy historians accept. Ability to act according to the measure of right and wrong is one of the defining qualities of human beings. With these standards suspended, as they are when historians refrain from judging the actions of "great men," the humanness of man no longer exists. Tolstoy wishes to ask historians why they consider Napoleon a "great man" when what he precisely lacks is this defining quality of humanness.

PART XV

CHAPTERS 1-3

Summary

Since Andrey's death, Princess Marya and Natasha keep to themselves and never mention him. Marya emerges from mourning first, because she has commitments to Nikolushka and to her estate, while

Natasha gives herself up entirely to her thoughts. What rouses Natasha from her morbid lethargy is a resurgence of active loving, this time toward her mother. The countess is hysterical with grief at Petya's death and only the constant presence of Natasha—night and day for three weeks—quiets the mother's frenzy. Countess Rostov emerges from her mourning a spiritless old woman; Natasha emerges exhausted, but her mother's affliction has returned her to the world.

Princess Marya puts off leaving Moscow in order to nurse Natasha back to health. The two women form such a close friendship that each is comfortable only in the presence of the other. Gradually Natasha grows stronger and her life-spirit begins to break out of the mold in which her soul languished.

Commentary

In her isolation, Natasha has tried to focus her thoughts to "penetrate the mystery which her spiritual vision fastened on." This unsuccessful attempt to duplicate the emotions of Prince Andrey, and thus to remain attached to him, is Tolstoy's way of showing the essential life-affirming qualities of Natasha. She cannot reach the understanding of death that Prince Andrey reached because she is a creature of life, of nature, and of love. Here Tolstoy compares Natasha to a flowering plant whose bloom has been injured; her roots are still intact and she must eventually reflower. Love is Natasha's restorative, and with her exercise of love toward her mother, she is able to bloom once again.

CHAPTERS 4-11

Summary

Unable to restrain his troops, Kutuzov unwillingly fights at Vyazma and his troops race after the fleeing French with their pursuit exacting a terrible toll of men and horses. All Kutuzov wishes to do is to follow the enemy and "see them off," but his ambitious generals, anxious to distinguish themselves, order maneuvers and battles the men are not fit to carry out. The generals consider Kutuzov cowardly and incompetent and senile.

Kutuzov was the only leader who judged the events of the war accurately, Tolstoy reminds us. He persisted in calling Borodino a victory, recognized that losing Moscow did not mean losing Russia, and correctly assessed the driving power of his army's spirit. He exerted his powers as commander-in-chief not to kill and maim men but to save them and have mercy on them. His simplicity and greatness is of a different nature from that of the "strutting, vain" figure of Napoleon whom history considers great.

After Vyazma, after the long chase, Kutuzov addresses the troops and tells them Russia is delivered. "We will see our visitors off, then we will rest," he says, counseling them to have pity on their frost-bitten and starving prisoners, for they are men too.

As the French retreat faster and more helplessly than ever, Kutuzov's lack of aggression wins him more disfavor. The sub-commanders openly mock him and treat him as if he were senile. Clearly Kutuzov's day is almost done. At Vilna, where the tsar gives him the highest honors and decorations, Kutuzov's career begins its ebb. Alexander gradually transfers his staff to himself and appoints a new commander; he wishes to carry on the war to liberate Europe and this is beyond Kutuzov's scope. His mission in life is completed with Russia restored to the highest pinnacle of her glory. Kutuzov has nothing left to do, except to pass on.

Commentary

Tolstoy uses these chapters as a eulogy for Kutuzov. Calling him the "Russian of the Russians," Tolstoy echoes Prince Nikolay Bolkonsky's earlier pronouncements about Russia requiring a "true Russian" to lead her, a man who intuitively understands the nature of his country and can act according to its spirit. Like the old prince whose life is outdated, Kutuzov also passes on, leaving a clean slate for the next generation to inscribe.

In many statements, Tolstoy describes Kutuzov by means of the same expressions he uses to describe Platon Karataev. "This old man [he says, by way of an example], who through experience of life had reached the conviction that the thoughts and words that serve as its expression are never the motive force of men, frequently uttered words, which were quite meaningless — the first words that occurred to his mind." Karataev, we recall, also uttered words with the same simplicity and spontaneity.

By comparing Karataev with Kutuzov, Tolstoy illustrates the general's awareness of the universality of experience and the organic continuity of history of which each man is a significant part. This awareness allowed Kutuzov to win the war. Thoughts and words, however, do not reveal this inner truth; rather, by externalizing it they diminish its clarity. Tolstoy thus states a truth he has stated before: words are mere outer manifestations of a sensibility essentially inexpressible, and only actions reveal implicit truths. We shall presently see how Pierre lives his "new life" without philosophizing its significance; his happiness expresses itself in a personal harmony whose roots, like those of Kutuzov and Karataev, grow out of a sense of cosmic unity.

CHAPTERS 12-19

Summary

Although outwardly unchanged, Pierre is inwardly different since his imprisonment. He has become a good listener and everyone who talks to him feels understood and secure. His quiet gentleness encourages people to open their hearts to him and express the best sides of their character. Decisions now come easily to Pierre and no longer is he perplexed by doubts that hampered his judgment in former times.

Three months have passed since the day of his liberation and Pierre crosses the now-bustling city of Moscow to visit Princess Marya. Gazing closely into the stern thin face of Marya's black-clad companion, he suddenly recognizes Natasha. They spend the evening in heart-to-heart discussions. Marya tells about Prince Andrey and how he was filled with understanding when he died. Pierre tells them about his new faith in God, how he feels the omnipresence and infinitude of God in his soul and how the old burning questions have no meaning anymore in his new-found peace and freedom. For the first time, he talks of his imprisonment and his friendship with Karataev and the execution and the forced marches. Natasha describes in detail her last days with Prince Andrey and the depth of her love for him. This is the first time she has mentioned the subject in all these months, and Princess Marya rejoices at the rapport between Natasha and Pierre. Pierre's statement before they all part sums up his belief: "We imagine that as soon as we are torn out of our habitual path all is over, but it is only the beginning of something new and good. As long as there is life, there is happiness." Natasha tells Marya late that night how "clean and smooth" Pierre seems, just as if he has just emerged from a bath, a moral bath.

Commentary

All that is left for Tolstoy to tell is the "happy ending" of his surviving protagonists, and this he leaves for the First Epilogue. Having satisfied the nihilism of Prince Andrey with death, the author discusses the affirmative life-seeking resolutions of Pierre with his newborn soul. Natasha's referring to this baptism when she speaks of Pierre's "moral bath" shows her recognition of a future liberated from the memories of the past. She and Pierre are ready for a new life together, a life founded on the acceptance and understanding of death.

Tolstoy thus defines maturity in these favorite protagonists. Maturity, he seems to say, is an internalization of death as part of the life process. His system of growth is based on the unity of the forces of life with death, of the experiences of the past that are part of the chain toward the future, of the universality of human souls, both living and dead. Andrey's spirit has contributed to the depth of that of Natasha while the spirit of Platon lives within Pierre.

FIRST EPILOGUE

Summary

In the seven years that have passed, Alexander passes from the liberalism of his early reign to a period of reaction, characterized by the Holy Alliance, the restoration of Poland, and the balance-of-power politics beginning in 1820. These then, are the events, and the judgments we make about them are relative, according to what contemporary historians consider to be the good of humanity and what later historians consider good. Standards of good and bad are always changing in light of different viewpoints, says Tolstoy, and if we had an invariable standard of good and bad by which we could assess events as they take place, then the "bad" events could be prevented. If this were the case, no dynamics of human activity would exist. "Once admit that human life can be guided by reason," asserts Tolstoy, "and all possibility of life is annihilated."

If we make limited assumptions about historical phenomena, as we do when we assert, for example, that great men lead humanity to certain ends like the aggrandizement of France or Russia, then we can only explain specific happenings as occurring by chance or through the acts of a genius. But if we admit that events occur for reasons beyond our ken, we will be presented with a unity and coherence among the facts of history. When we recognize that the events which convulsed Europe constitute the essence and end of a series of happenings, then we sense an integrity of individual occurrences, just as we can accept the integrity of the separate parts that contribute to the whole flower without having to explain the cause of each part.

Tolstoy sweepingly describes the career of Napoleon as built upon a series of millions of chances: his spectacular rise to power, his invasion of Africa, his invasion and retreat from Russia, his subsequent ruin and comeback ten years later. Because of the way events unfold among all these chance happenings, Napoleon considers himself great and confers the title of greatness to whatever he does or fails to do. Yet the final aims of historical persons or nations remain unfathomable, says Tolstoy, regardless of what may be described as their aims.

The marriage of Natasha and Pierre in 1813 provides the last happy event in Count Rostov's life and he dies an old, ineffectual man. Nikolay is forced to shoulder the burden of his father's debts and valiantly maintains the household on slender means. He feels guilty before the patient and self-sacrificing Sonya and does not love her.

Later in 1813 Nikolay marries Princess Marya and with Sonya and the old countess they move to Bleak Hills. Within a few years Nikolay repays all his debts, enlarges his estate, and has the means to repurchase his ancestral holdings. His excellent understanding of the peasants causes them to respect and revere him, and his lands bring in abundant harvests. Although Marya does not share his passion for the land, she sustains him in everything he does. They are very happy together and Nikolay thinks it his greatest fortune to marry a woman of such deep-souled nobility. Sonya lives with them like a cat attached to the household itself rather than to the people in it. She accepts her barren position and does small thankless favors for everyone in the family.

By 1820 Natasha has three daughters and an infant son she insists on nursing herself. In the robust-looking young mother one is hard put to discover the slim, mobile girl of former days. Natasha is positively devoted to Pierre and understands everything about him and everything about him is lovely to her. She is boundlessly possessive toward her children and her husband and has no other interests. Pierre allows himself to be henpecked by her because he believes this is the way families operate. Denisov, who spends a week visiting the Bezuhovs, sees only a bad likeness of the Natasha who had once submitted to him, and her constant talk of the nursery bores him.

Nikolinka, Andrey's child, lives with the Rostovs but has no strong affection for Nikolay. He considers Pierre his hero and is delighted to stay up one night while the men talk politics. Pierre and Nikolay have a long argument about the duties of a citizen. Pierre says people should voice disagreement when their government is wrong and Rostov says he believes in loyalty to the state under any conditions. "Would my father agree with you?" Nikolinka shyly asks Pierre, and he is answered, yes. The child gazes with luminous eyes at his idol.

Marya and Nikolay talk over the day's event as they usually do at bedtime. She shows him a diary in which she chronicles the day-to-day moral development of her children. Nikolay is filled with wonder at his wife, whose untiring, perpetual spiritual efforts enhance his life immeasurably. Marya assures her husband that his views on duty to the state are in exact agreement with her own.

Meantime the Bezuhovs talk in their rooms. Pierre remarks how little significance Nikolay finds in ideas, whereas he himself finds nothing serious except ideas. Natasha asks whether Platon Karataev would agree with his view, and Pierre says no. But he would approve of my home life, he tells her, "for he did so like to see seemliness, happiness, peace in everything."

Nikolinka lies dreaming of Pierre, whose image suddenly becomes that of his father and the boy is dissolved in the weakness of love. "I shall study hard," he tells himself, and become someone great and glorious so that even my father would be proud.

Commentary

The life cycle of the personal novel within *War and Peace* is completed; the new generation awakens from a dream of the past and is eager to begin the future. To underscore the movements of the ebb and flow of generations that has occupied a great part of the novel, Tolstoy provides Nikolinka with a dream that seems an echo of Prince Andrey's youthful aspirations to glory and knowledge. Unlike his father, whose hero was Napoleon, however, Nikolinka admires Pierre, whose soul has a spiritual affinity with those of Kutuzov and Karataev. Tolstoy's conclusion sounds a note of youthful striving and optimism: it affirms the best parts of Pierre and Andrey as these qualities distill in the soul of the rising generation.

The staid, middle-aged domesticity of the Rostovs and the Bezuhovs reflects the peace and harmony of people who have matured through their experiences of life. They have passed through the trials of youth—the "war" as the title suggests—and have thus earned the spiritual and emotional peace of their adult lives.

These romantic youthful figures of *War and Peace* have become dull and complacent; after the hazards they have run, after the pain and anguish they have suffered, their quiescent emotions and uninteresting happiness is a disappointment to readers who have been caught up in the sweep and drama of their earlier lives. But Tolstoy's sense of realism forces us to face the dreary truth of adulthood: youthful possibilities of an individual become narrowed by experiences that convey him to his appointed condition in life. The First Epilogue is not merely a brief statement of a lazy author's "and they lived happily ever after"; rather, it is a significant section of the work, which examines how the heroes live out their day-to-day lives once they have solved the burning problems of youth and once their time of adventure has passed.

We see how each character realizes his predestined aim. While Pierre is still fat and good-natured, still dabbles in "causes" and ideas, he has retained, at the same time, the inexpressible sense of God's love and universality. Nikolay has become a conservative but successful country gentleman, unintellectual as ever, but with the best parts of his nature enriched and deepened by his marriage to Princess Marya. Where she was unhappy before, Marya is now content and satisfied, with the same devotion and piety once directed toward her domineering father now directed toward her family. Natasha provides us with a disappointment in her development, for we are modern readers who prefer the bubbling, ever-seductive young girl to the henpecking, fussbudget housewife she has become. Yet Natasha's present nature is of one piece with her previous one, for Tolstoy, guilt-ridden by his own sensuality and sexually threatened by women, can only create heroines whose seductiveness and loving nature expresses itself in child-rearing and in sustaining their husbands. As a creature of nature, Natasha's final flowering is to follow her natural destiny of bearing children and providing happiness for her spouse.

Not content with merely summing up the personal histories of his characters, Tolstoy supplies the discussion between Pierre and Nikolay to suggest national events. Nikolay's conservatism reflects the attitudes of the landowning class in Russia and Pierre's liberalism speaks for the dissenting intelligentsia. Each man represents the political thinking that contributes toward the dynamics of this new historical era.

96

SECOND EPILOGUE

Summary

The life of peoples and humanity is the subject of history, writes Tolstoy, and the writing of history is an attempt to make intelligible the course of human events. But, he asks rhetorically, what is the cause of these events, and what is the force that moves nations? Historians construct answers based on their special viewpoints; some discuss history in terms of the "great men" theory, some in terms of cultural issues, some according to the interplay between nations. Examining each school of historiography, Tolstoy shows how inadequate these separate theories are to explain complex events.

How can the cultural historian explain, for instance, the murder of millions of Frenchmen during the French revolution in terms of what men thought about the equality of man, Tolstoy asks? To do this, the historian must show a propelling force equal to the resultant force, just as the physical scientist explains the thrust of a steam engine in terms of input. Tolstoy argues that a mere "idea" cannot generate such a power.

The biographical historian is equally at fault. To assume that "great men" move nations is as arbitrary as assuming, as did the ancients, that the will of God ordains history. Tolstoy analyzes how these historians explain the decisions of the "great men" who move nations. They cite, for example, Talleyrand's influence upon Alexander, or describe the part Mme. de Staël played in changing the course of government. Naturally it is ridiculous to assume that millions of people submit to whatever Talleyrand or de Staël convinced Alexander.

Tolstoy goes on to discredit the historical construct of "power" as the motive force of events. If the concept of power is valid, he argues, then we must be able to explain its nature and define how it works. If people submit to the power of their government, and if the mass allows its will to be reflected and represented by its leaders, then we can examine what does constitute the will of the masses and how the lives of the people can be represented, or symbolized, by the lives of their monarchs. Tolstoy concludes that we cannot ascribe the activities of millions of men moving from place to place, butchering one another, burning housing and harvests, as a reflection of the actions of some dozen persons who do not kill men or burn property.

On the other hand, events are clearly connected with the will of the leaders. We see that when Napoleon commands, thousands of men march into Russia. To show how "power" is expressed in the relationship between leaders and followers and the conditions under which the leader's will operates—or fails to operate—Tolstoy uses the structure of the military as a working model. His examination concludes that the men issuing the most orders are the farthest removed from the action they are ordering, while those directly involved in the action are the least responsible for directing it. He has already illustrated this principle during the war scenes in the body of his novel.

Tolstoy also examines the kind of power a commander has over the men he commands; it is either moral power or physical power, he says. The physical strength of a leader can only be effective on a small number of men, whereas moral power extends the leader's control to a larger group. Yet history offers many examples of weak and ineffectual leaders who still control the destinies of the men they lead.

Having failed to reveal how the power of a commander is transmitted to his followers, and having failed to describe the nature of this power, Tolstoy adds another argument to discredit the concept of power —the factor of time. Since human beings, he begins, operate within time, and events change according to time, a command can only cover a specific time sequence. Moreover, the commander himself is always in the middle of an event as it unfolds and he can never control all aspects of the event. Tolstoy shows how, out of all the commands given to cover the various conditions of any event, only those that are possible to be carried out will be carried out. No command can produce an event that is not ready to be enacted.

Historians who say that this or that decision caused this or that event to occur are mistaking cause and effect. Tolstoy uses an analogy to illustrate his statement. Consider some men who are about to drag off a log, he says, and each man offers an opinion as to where the log should go. They drag it away, and it turns out to end up where one of them had advised. This is the man, historians would say, who gave the command. All the other commands and commanders are thus forgotten after the event has been enacted. With these analyses, Tolstoy concludes that "power" vested by the mass in one or a few persons, expressed through the followers of a commander, and operating within the constraints of time, can never serve to explain historical causality.

Having thus discredited the various schools of historiography and pointing out the fallacy of general concepts like "power," Tolstoy examines human existence in relation to the forces of destiny. His previous arguments have considered external phenomena only and have overlooked the intrinsic quality of man's freedom of will. Tolstoy now comes to the crux of his argument, which remains an unresolved paradox: freedom of will is as mythic a quality as that of power, but without this concept all human activities become meaningless.

If men have free wills, history would be a series of unconnected incidents, says Tolstoy, who believes nevertheless in historical determinacy. But if we admit that even one man has the power to act freely, he argues, then we cannot formulate any law to explain the actions of men. By the same token, if one law controls the actions of men, then no one is free, all wills being subject to that law.

Tolstoy attacks this problem by hypothesizing two views of man, an "inner" view and an "outer" view: "Looking at man as a subject of observation from any point of view—theological, ethical, philosophical —we find a general law of necessity to which he is subject like everything else existing. Looking at him from within ourselves, as what we are conscious of, we feel ourselves free." This "inner" quality is our consciousness or free will, and the "outer" quality is reason, or necessity. "Through reason, man observes himself," writes Tolstoy, "but he knows himself through consciousness."

Despite our "reason," which accepts the scientific proofs that we are subject to naturalistic constraints as other creatures are, our "consciousness" senses freedom. Without this "meaningless feeling of freedom" life would be insupportable. All the concepts of our existence express this instinct for freedom, Tolstoy says: the notions of wealth and poverty, hunger and repletion, health and disease, are only terms for greater or less degrees of freedom. Our sense of free will can never be reconciled with the immutable laws of necessity; at best, we conclude that men and animals share nervous and muscular activity, but man has, in addition, consciousness.

History does not differentiate between free will and necessity. Rather, it relates how free will has manifested itself in the past and under what conditions it has operated. History is "our representation" of the action of free will, and we regard every event as a proportionate combination of free will with necessity. The more we know of the circumstances under which an act was performed, the less free the act

seems. When a period of time has elapsed, allowing us to see more consequences of a particular act and its relation to previous acts, we see
more and more necessities that determine the nature of the act. Free
will, therefore, is an illusion we maintain because we cannot know all
the factors contributing to the accomplished act.

With our limited knowledge, we can only conclude that human
existence is made up of the "incomprehensible essence of life" and the
"laws that give form to that essence." Our consciousness expresses the
reality of free will, according to this scheme, while our reason expresses
the laws of necessity. When we describe historical events, we express
all the known factors as the laws of necessity, while those unknown we
term free will. For historians to state, however, that free will (like
Napoleon's genius) causes historical phenomena is analogous to as-
tronomers recognizing freedom in the movement of heavenly bodies.
As in science, we must seek to describe in history what can be observed
then state what we know and admit what we do not know.

We cannot describe the essence of the force that moves heavenly
bodies, but we can describe how this "vital force" operates. In history,
this "vital force" is our concept of free will, and to show how it operates, we cite the observable laws of necessity. To approach history as a
science, therefore, we must begin with the necessities: that is, the study
of movements of people and of nations, and not episodes from the lives
of great men. In order to discover historical laws, we must seek the
properties common to all the equal and inseparably interconnected,
infinitesimal elements by which free will is constrained. To be intelligible, history must admit that personality is subject to the laws of time,
space, and motion, just as physics admits the relative movement of the
earth as the basis of its investigations. We do not feel the earth's movements with our senses, neither do we feel our consciousness dependent
on external phenomena. Yet our reason has descried the planet's motion, and our reason must detect the limits of our free will. Only with
this kind of scientific approach can historiography become a credible
discipline, and ultimately, reveal the nature of human life.

Commentary

Most critics regard Tolstoy's philosophical exegesis in the Second
Epilogue as unliterary, boring, and outside the intentions of the novel.
They regard the didactic passages liberally sprinkled throughout the
book as redundant. Yet Tolstoy's interest in history is the most serious
and intense aspect of *War and Peace* and provides the novel with its

underlying unity. The Second Epilogue, therefore, deserves our attention because it reveals Tolstoy's obsessive and passionate search for truth; this quest not only gives force to his major novels, but provided him with the philosophic focus of his life.

Isaiah Berlin has discussed Tolstoy's theory of history in a brilliant essay, and the commentary in these Notes is based on his work with the quoted statements taken from his book *The Hedgehog and the Fox: An Essay on Tolstoy's View of History* (New York: Simon & Schuster, 1953).

Tolstoy's interest in history derives from his desire to penetrate first causes, to answer for himself the burning question of the meaning of human life and death. "History, only history, only the sum of the concrete events in time and space — and sum of the actual experience of actual men and women in their relation to one another and to an actual three-dimension, empirically experienced, physical environment — this alone contains the truth, the material out of which genuine answers — answers needing for their apprehension no special senses or faculties which normal human beings did not possess — might be constructed" (p. 11). Life consists of innumerable events and history chooses only an insignificant arbitrarily patterned part of these events with which to document a special theory as the primary cause of social or political change. What then is the "real" history of human beings?

Tolstoy says that the "inner" events of human beings are the most real and immediate experiences; "they, and only they, are what life, in the last analysis, is made of"; hence the routine political historians who write history as a series of public events "are talking shallow nonsense" (p. 15).

Tolstoy illustrates this difference between written history and actual — or "private" — history throughout *War and Peace* when he shows how the statesmen and commanders highest in the pyramid of authority are far removed from the ordinary men and women whose lives are the "actual stuff of history." In various battle scenes, Tolstoy shows how little control the commanders have over the destiny of the event they believe they command, while the soldiers who do the fighting are the most responsible for its outcome. Andrey discovers this truth when he meets the "important" people who guide their nations' destinies at Brünn, or when he talks with the reformer Speransky; all these men delude themselves into believing that their memoranda, resolutions, councils are the motive factors that determine historical change, whereas they are, in fact, nothing but "self-important milling in the void"

(p. 17). Men of destiny like Napoleon equally with men of science like the German militarists, must be impostors, since no single will or theory can fit the immense variety of "possible human behavior, the vast multiplicity of minute, undiscoverable causes and effect which form that interplay of men and nature which history purports to record."

This then, is the ultimate illusion that Tolstoy attempts to destroy in the course of his novel: "that individuals can, by use of their own resources, understand and control the course of events"; and the men of history who believe this turn out to be hugely mistaken. The real world, on the other hand, does not consist of men who exert their alleged "free will" or who theorize motives for what they do, but it consists of the day-to-day stream of life of men in their everyday existence. Social, political, economic phenomena are not the ultimate realities at all; rather, these are "outer accidents" of the ultimate reality, which consists of the "ordinary, day to day succession of private data" (p. 20).

Tolstoy's mastery of describing the moments of individual subjective experience – the details that compound "real life" – is unsurpassed. Yet he realized that history's task is not merely to describe transitory minutiae but to explain the totality of events without using those "thin disguises for ignorance" like "chance," "genius," or "cause."

Tolstoy believes that the lives of human beings are subject to the control of natural law, along with the entire universe. Men, however, are unable to accept this "inexorable process," and elect to view their existence as regulated by the operation of free choice on the part of individuals of extraordinary capacity for good or ill. These supposed "great men" are in fact quite ordinary persons whose ignorance and vanity induces them to accept responsibility for all of the evils attributed to them. They prefer this role to recognition of their own helpless insignificance in the "cosmic flow" of events which is indifferent to them. Tolstoy excels in presenting this focal idea by means of descriptions of events placed in apposition to the ridiculous interpretation of those events entertained by men carried away by their own egoism. Similarly, Tolstoy's thesis is given forceful expression by those instances of revelation when the reality of human existence is comprehended by "those who have the humility to recognize their own unimportance and irrelevance" (p. 27).

War and Peace contrasts the "universal and all-important but delusive experience of free will, the feeling of responsibility, the values of private life generally, on one hand; and on the other, the reality of inexorable historical determinism, not indeed, experienced directly, but known to be true on irrefutable theoretical grounds" (p. 29). Tolstoy is unable, in the last analysis, to entirely discredit the historiography we know. Although the "important" people in history are less important than they believe themselves to be, neither are they shadows; individuals do have social purposes and they can transform the lives of communities.

Tolstoy's concern with history is not merely to point out the faulty reasoning of historians; his interest stems from a deeper, personal quest, a "bitter inner conflict between his actual experience and his beliefs, between his vision of life, and his theory of what it, and he himself, ought to be, if the vision was to be bearable at all" (p. 35). He desired to discover a single doctrine or law to which the multiple and seemingly unrelated daily events that make up reality belong, and his obsessive interest to discover this unifying truth drove him to this ruthless criticism of all theorists and historians who provide a shoddy, illogical law as the common denominator of multiple experience. This desire generates the philosophical examination of history in *War and Peace* and not a spirit of academic rumination.

The very idea of a unifying moral law to cover all the realities of experience presented Tolstoy with a lifelong paradox: moral life with its sense of "responsibility, joys, sorrows, sense of guilt, achievement," is illusory, since "free will" does not exist if we know — and theoretically we can know — the laws of necessity that govern every phenomenon and human activity. Faced with this paradox of believing in and yet denying free will, Tolstoy, like Prince Andrey, chooses nihilism and regarded the "first causes of events as mysterious, involving the reduction of human wills to nullity" (p. 55).

CHARACTER ANALYSIS

PIERRE BEZUHOV

Perpetually prey to new ideas, a man of strong emotions, although lacking the will to control them, Pierre in many ways represents a typical Russian nobleman. He is the protagonist of the novel and expresses some of Tolstoy's favorite personal beliefs.

Lacking a legitimate father to provide him with a self-image, Pierre's career is a quest for self-definition. Pierre himself provides us with the key to this quest when, in Part I, he values Napoleon as the man who carries out the ideas of the French revolution. His ideas of freeing man from the stultification of class life, ideas implicit in the French revolution, indicate the nature of his search and its resolution. Pierre can find no freedom until he gives up the "outer man," and his quest fails so long as he seeks an answer within his class; that is, when he frees his serfs, joins the masons, observes Borodino as a spectator rather than as a soldier.

When he is an identity-lacking prisoner, and is all but executed for his namelessness, he begins to discover his own nature. Those very qualities that were weaknesses of character in society, become, through the isolation of suffering and imprisonment, his strengths. Baptized by suffering, morally cleansed through the experience of death, Pierre is reborn into a sense of freedom of self, borrowing of Karataev's sole possession of "inner harmony."

Pierre's great weakness, like that of Tolstoy, is his sensuality and his problem is to harness the forces of his nature into the mainstream of nature itself. Domesticity solves this problem, and while Pierre does not become like Karataev, he maintains an ability to actively participate in natural life with its daily vicissitudes and moments of futility and still have the inner harmony that expresses the expectation of death. Once having known the nearness of death, dying holds no terrors for Pierre. He can thus live fully, even sensually, and still follow all the ideas his expansive nature feeds upon. Pierre's final resolution is a compromise, but one that turns his personal foibles into strengths and harmonizes his temporal nature with the infinity of life.

PRINCE ANDREY BOLKONSKY

Like his father, Andrey is the "best of his generation," but is also a product of it. He sees how the rigid standards of his autocratic father isolate the old prince from his closest relations and how he suffers in a world of his own making. From this, the sensitive Andrey concludes that suffering and death are not as terrible as the power that allows people to inflict it, a conclusion that implicitly turns him away from life to seek perfection in death. To overcome the emotional anguish of these observations about his father, Andrey has developed a cold, intellectual approach to life which, by defining experience, also limits it. With his reason constantly pointing out to him the futility of his own life and the lives of those around him, his basic moral values are negative ones. Andrey's career thus becomes a quest to rid his civilized self of the burden of isolation his intellect imposes upon him, just as his father is isolated by the burden of rigid class values.

Primarily seeking a career in which to forget himself, Andrey joins the army, becomes disillusioned with the futility of warfare, and, reaffirmed in his nihilism, retires from active life. Through Natasha, however, Andrey renews his life-commitment, for love promises him the possibility of an ego-dissolving relationship. Her frailty proves to him the imperfection and futility of all the activities of life and impels him to seek perfection in death.

Death, for Andrey is not so much the final affirmation of life, as it is the cessation of being an individual. In death he discovers the release from his possessive egotism, an ultimate reassertion of the natural order where the creature is valueless save as an element in the infinite physical process.

NATASHA ROSTOV

Natasha is Tolstoy's ideal woman. Attractive and bewitching as a child, her expressiveness and spontaneity are the natural outpourings of a creature imbued with life forces. She is compassionate, intense, with a soul responsive to music and dance, Tolstoyan symbols of her emotional spontaneity, and every moment of her being manifests the qualities of "instinctive life." Tolstoy equates her with springtime, Andrey's "renascence," Nikolay's affirmation of the "intensity of life" after his humiliation from Dolohov, and she is, as well, the agency of love for her bereaved mother and the reconciler of family quarrels.

Vehemently opposed to women being sexual objects, Tolstoy sees the feminine destiny entirely constrained within the limits of child-rearing and familial harmony. Sexuality for Tolstoy must be directed toward its natural end of reproduction, else it is decadent and destructive. His own passionate nature attesting to sensual temptations, Tolstoy believed the only "safe" women were those who sublimated their seductiveness into the natural cares of womanhood. Thus Natasha is her author's example of a successful woman: as she grows stout with child-bearing, she directs her enthusiasm and affectionateness toward her household responsibilities. Her femininity is no longer an empty gesture as in the days of Anatole, but now is participant in the biological continuity of life.

NIKOLAY ROSTOV

Very good at saying the obvious, Nikolay is unimaginative and conservative, a man of action rather than of ideas. Although his development does not chart a course of agonized illuminations, as do the careers of Andrey and Pierre, his adulthood maximizes the positive qualities of his personality; thus, with all his shortcomings, he is a "successful" character.

Motivated by utilitarian drives, Nikolay is always straightforward and never masks his intentions by thoughts of "virtue" or "doing for others." While this utilitarianism and lack of hypocrisy cause Nikolay to reject Sonya in favor of marrying an heiress, these very qualities guarantee his marriage. Marya's religious depths provide her husband with an added dimension of soul that he lacks, even as her wealth provides him with the capital he requires. Her submission to Christian virtue is similar to Nikolay's submission to the higher authority of the state. Tolstoy thus approves of Nikolay's self-interest, and makes everything he does fruitful, at the same time disapproving of and rejecting Sonya for her empty selflessness.

HISTORICAL FIGURES

The characters of Napoleon, Murat, Rastoptchin, Speransky, and the other historical persons that appear throughout the novel are remarkable for their static nature. Compared to Tolstoy's fictional heroes, who are always in process of "becoming" and are constantly responsive to personal and environmental challenges, these factually real characters never undergo change. Their purpose in the "moral panorama" of *War and Peace* (to borrow James T. Farrell's term) is to show the limits of individual freedom and the salience of objective necessity. Napoleon and Alexander and the others express what Tolstoy said of "great men": "that they imagine they know what they are doing, and they are doing it for themselves, but that in reality they are the involuntary tools of history, performing a task which is concealed from them, though comprehensible to us" (quoted in Christian's *Study of War and Peace*, p. 93). Except for Kutuzov, whose historical reality is exaggerated to point out his mythic importance, the historical characters are flat and static figures devoid of personal life.

STRUCTURE

War and Peace is of such epic proportions that its endless out-pourings of martial history, personal saga, social document carries the reader along as a helpless spectator caught up in the full tide of life. Percy Lubbock in *The Craft of Fiction* (New York: The Viking Press, 1957) says it is a combination of two stories: "It is like an Iliad, the story of certain men, and an Aeneid, the story of a nation, compressed into one book."

The way Tolstoy combines the personal, Iliad-like novel with the historical, Aeneid-like novel forms the dualistic structure of *War and Peace*. Beyond this duality—in fact beyond the bounds of the novel itself—the unifying focus of the book lies within the mind of its author, in his endless lifetime search to extract a single truth out of the pro-fusion of specific experiences. The unifying element of *War and Peace*, although somewhat disclosed in Tolstoy's philosophic epilogue on the nature of history, is not evident within the material of the novel.

The complexity and sweep of *War and Peace*, lacking the singularity of viewpoint achieved, for instance, in *Anna Karenina*, derives from the tension between two constant and interlocking orientations: the collec-tive and the personal, the events of a nation and the experience of individuals.

Thus the protagonists of the novel have a dual significance. On one plane they reveal individuals in their quest for self-definition, on the other they are participants in a mass movement whose pattern is forever undisclosed to them. By the same duality, public events and public figures reveal basic truths about the nature of private experience, and the relationship between moment-by-moment experiences of in-dividuals and their long-term search for meaning, with the unfolding destiny of a nation, generate the dramatic conflicts and the individual turning points of the novel.

A clear example of the way Tolstoy endows situations and char-acters with dual significance is our introduction to the Bolkonsky family in its country seat. The old prince, like the tsar himself, dominates and leaves his autocratic mark upon each member of his household. The situation we meet at Bleak Hills is a working model of old Russia.

By the same token, Andrey and Marya exemplify the special types of Russian personalities acculturated under the tsars. Marya's religious fervor enables her to accept and forgive the repression under which she lives, and Andrey's heightened understanding of the ravages this repression wreaks in the soul of the man in power—his father, in this case—causes him to develop his intellectual powers as a weapon to blunt the anguish of his observations. In a later situation, where Nikolay argues with Pierre about politics, Tolstoy again uses his personal characters for a similar sociological observation: Nikolay represents the obedient subject, while Pierre tries with reason and emotions to define individuality.

Natasha's career is also invested with dual significance. At the same time that she is a particular adolescent growing into womanhood, her emotional maturation is symbolic of the historic transformation of Russia itself. Natasha's coming-of-age occurs when her personal values conflict with socially imposed values inimical to her nature, while, at the same time, Russia's great period of change occurs when the nation rises up against the foreign invaders. Both "wars"—the historical one involving the nation and the symbolic one Natasha fights—provide the necessities for self-definition.

In the same way individuals stand for more than themselves, events partake of the same dual quality. The evacuation of Moscow provides a good example of this twofold significance. On a private level, the citizens believe they leave the city for various vague and personal reasons, among these being the preference to appear as cowards rather than live under foreign occupation. On a historical level, this is the "deed that saves Russia," for the French arrive finding no one to conquer; thus Napoleon's dream of glory is robbed of all meaning and his conquest is a futile gesture.

Tolstoy's ultimate parallelism, however, is keynoted in his title, with the polar qualities of war and peace providing the physical and emotional settings of incidents that further investigate the duality between collective life and individual life. Events that occur in peacetime are often echoed during the war scenes and the perspective Tolstoy achieves from these twice-told incidents deepens our understanding of the moral truths he wishes to underscore.

When we compare the "peacefulness" of the first campaigns depicted in the novel with the death duel of the battle of Borodino we see how Tolstoy uses this duality to intensify our feelings for the event that forms the turning point of the war. The first cannon boom at Schöngraben coincides with a burst of sunlight that lifts the spirits of the bored, but gay, soldiers. The sunrise over Borodino, on the other hand, illuminates a scene of carnage and desperation while the grim survivors face death every moment.

Numerous minor incidents illustrate how Tolstoy uses the settings of war and of peace to reveal new aspects of particular situations. Pierre, for example, meets Osip Bazdyev during a peacetime journey that sets him on a new moral path. Osip's influence here foreshadows Pierre's ultimate conversion through Karataev, Bazdyev's spiritual counterpart, which occurs during Bezuhov's wartime experiences.

Natasha, to provide another example, has two major meetings and partings with Andrey: the first, during the tranquil days of her youth, the final one during the wartime exodus from Moscow. Prince Andrey's first awareness of death, occurring in peacetime when he sees Liza die, prefigures his own fatal moment on the Austerlitz battlefield.

Moreover, Dolohov, to cite a minor character, exercises his cruelty against Nikolay during a card game, then against the drummer boy whom he wants shot during the last campaigns. The first instance of vengeance is necessary to explain Dolohov's character, whereas the second is another expression of that cruelty which helps Dolohov win battles.

The structural integrity of *War and Peace* thus derives from Tolstoy's two-leveled handling of his material through the vehicles of characterization, narrative, and setting. Individual parts of the novel are integrated into the whole through this parallel plot technique which, moreover, allows the author to enrich the significance of particular incidents by repeating them in another context. This duality enables Tolstoy to compare the nature of private experience with historical events, the "inner" and "outer" states of the human condition, unconscious with conscious motives, and, finally, to illustrate the conflict between "free will" and "necessity."

THEMES

Tolstoy's heroes have a single aim: they search for a way to live life without its transience and want of purpose. Andrey despairs of finding such a purpose when, in Part IX, he says life is a series "of senseless phenomena following one another without any connection." Pierre, on the other hand, discovers that most human beings live life like soldiers under fire, diverting themselves with cards, women, horses, parties, to avoid thinking about the ultimate problem in life, which is death.

Death, therefore, provides the individual with a definition of life, just as suffering provides an understanding of what man's basic needs are, as Pierre discovers in Part XIII. Understanding the existential opposites of life and death are essential to the growth of a human being. Stated in many ways throughout the novel, these opposite values provide the illumination that defines the main characters. Thus Pierre learns freedom through imprisonment, Andrey achieves love through hate and a knowledge of life as he lies dying.

Tolstoy exposes these polar values during the moments of crisis his characters face, and each crisis carries with it a measure of personal growth for the protagonist. The crisis provides the "necessity" – that is, the outer structure – within which the individual must grow and extend himself in order to adjust to the new situation. The crisis is the moment at which the individual must retrench his values through self-reflection, or "consciousness," in order to overcome the forces that threaten him. The rest of Tolstoy's themes, including his interest in history, derive from these ultimate unities of life and death.

War and Peace is in itself an invocation to the forces of life, and in the novel we see the dramatic development of children becoming adults. Tolstoy clearly shows the moments when this maturation takes place. Natasha's love affair with Anatole, Nikolay's guilt when he almost kills a Frenchman, Andrey's disillusion with the politicians at Brünn, Pierre's liberation during imprisonment, and, finally, Nikolinka's dream provide a few examples.

At the same time that Tolstoy depicts with such palpable details the childhood, youth, and adulthood of his heroes, he endows his depictions with such universality that they correspond, roughly, to the same three stages of the evolution of civilization. The Rostov family, for instance, radiates a spirit of joyful paganism as the children unconsciously express the life-forces within them. In their youth they become aware of the social and environmental limitations they are victims of and follow blindly the social conventions. This is that stage where Nikolay, adoring his tsar, becomes a good soldier. Finally, when Tolstoy develops his heroes into adults, they become self-conscious enough to participate in the making of their own destiny. This is the point when Andrey expresses his nihilism, when Pierre and Natasha marry, and when Pierre discovers the strength of his inner life. Through these characters, Tolstoy arrives at the Christian stage of civilization where individuals must come to terms with their own lives in order to prepare for death.

TECHNICAL DEVICES

According to Le Vicompte E. Melchior de Vogüé in *The Russian Novel* (New York: Alfred A. Knopf, 1916), *War and Peace* is "a unique alliance between the grand spirit of an epic and that of minute analysis." This "unique alliance" derives from Tolstoy's careful craftsmanship, only a few significant devices of which we have space here to discuss.

TRANSITIONS

To provide the vast material of *War and Peace* with some semblance of unity, the author must make his transitions between ideas or between settings intelligible to enable the reader to keep up with the movement of the novel. Tolstoy smoothly introduces us to the three settings wherein we first meet the major and minor characters as he takes us from one party in Petersburg to another in Moscow, thence to a family reunion at Bleak Hills. From the general war scene at Austerlitz in Part III, Tolstoy conveys us, in Part IV, to a scene of violence in a duel between Pierre and Dolohov. This marks the transition between the "outer" state of war and the inner turmoil within Pierre. The radiant intermezzo of Part VII shows us the end of youth for the Rostovs and prepares us for Natasha's sad moment of maturation in Part VIII. Within this movement, Pierre appears as the transition figure between the personal events of the novel and the gathering tide of war that engulfs the whole nation. He effects the bridge to convey us from Natasha's heartsick lethargy to Russia's major historic struggle. Many other significant and masterfully executed transitions can be cited besides these examples, but the careful reader can discern these for himself as he studies the novel.

SYMBOLS

Besides formal transitions to carry specific ideas from one context to another, Tolstoy employs symbols to underscore the moral significance of his narrative. His most frequent symbolic devices are naturalistic. For Tolstoy, nature is not merely a background for human destiny but is a partner to it, and images of nature provide him with the physical manifestations of the inner struggles of his protagonists. In this way, the author emphasizes for individuals his major thesis that historical happenings spring from unconscious impulses and from the instincts of the masses. As Tolstoy associates the indifference of nature to death with its unquenchable impulse to life, we see the peaceful sky over Austerlitz promising death to Andrey, and later, during his talk with Pierre, the same sky promises him a renewal of inner life. The comet of 1812 is another example: whereas it symbolizes the apocalypse to most people, Pierre believes it shines as a beacon for his inmost hopes. The old oak tree, to cite another example, is at one point a projection of Andrey's despair, at another it affirms his renascence. The pagan quality of the wolf hunt shows Rostov's youth and recklessness; later when the same spirit carries him at a gallop against the French, Nikolay cannot bring himself to kill another human being. As Tolstoy describes the joys of hunting in the same way he describes the primitive exultation of war, the parallel is a symbolic expression that elemental forces may enrich or submerge the humanity of man.

PHYSICAL DESCRIPTION

Tolstoy's ability to evoke the physical presence of characters is what Merezhovsky calls his gift of "clairvoyance of the flesh." Karataev's symbolic roundness, the podgy hands of Napoleon, the mobile play of Natasha's facial expressions attest to this judgment. Kutuzov's obesity, for instance, becomes symbolic of his passivity in face of destiny, his impassivity at moments of crisis. Ellen Bezuhov's "unvarying dazzling smile" indicates her picture-book beauty as well as her emotional shallowness.

These details of physical description also act as identifying motifs to help us distinguish among the many characters in the novel. Marya's "heavy tread," Dolohov's cold blue eyes, Andrey's bored expression, Count Rostov's characteristic attitude of ineffectuality—his gesture of throwing up his hands—are significant particulars that fix these personalities firmly in our minds.

IRONY

Tolstoy uses irony to express his opinions on certain incidents he portrays. An obvious example is the way he handles Pierre's initiation into the masons and his light treatment of Pierre's methods to better the lot of his peasants. Tolstoy is decidedly satirical when he describes the German theorists who believe in the science of war. The incidents Tolstoy selects from biographies of Napoleon are satirical evidences to show Bonaparte's vanity and showmanship.

INTERIOR MONOLOG

Where narrative devices ... l externalizing inner states of mind are insufficient to show the train of thought of his characters, Tolstoy uses the device of interior monolog. Having his characters talk to themselves, Tolstoy clearly shows us the development of their ideas and their abilities, or lack of abilities, of self-reflection. Andrey's thoughts on the eve of battle and his reflections on Kutuzov, Pierre's notions of right and wrong and his inspiration upon seeing the faces of soldiers at Borodino are a few examples of this device.

QUESTIONS FOR DISCUSSION

1. Discuss what is meant by the statement that "So-called great men serve as visible signs of a process forever concealed." (In your own words, try to restate the discussion from the commentaries on Tolstoy's Second Epilogue.)

2. What does Napoleon symbolize for Prince Andrey and Pierre in Part I? How does this image of Napoleon prefigure their respective careers? (See section Character Analysis as well as commentaries throughout the Notes.)

3. Why did Tolstoy believe that "philosophic principles can only be understood in their concrete expression in history"? (Base your answer on Tolstoy's theory of history throughout the novel as well as in the Second Epilogue.)

4. Discuss how the Bolkonsky family illustrates the two-planed structure of *War and Peace* (See commentary on Part I as well as section on Structure.)

5. Some critics believe that *War and Peace* is an unsatisfactory combination of two novels, the personal novel and the historical novel,

with the one aspect taking away vitality from the other. Discuss whether this judgment is accurate or mistaken.

6. What is the function of the historical characters in the novel? (See section Character Analysis.)

7. Describe the careers of Prince Andrey and Pierre in terms of the dual significance of the title, where "War" (according to Professor Janko Lavrin) means the "state of the isolated individual," and "Peace" equals the "state of depersonalized Christian love." (See section on Structure as well as commentaries throughout the Notes.)

8. Discuss the significance of various nature symbols in *War and Peace*. (See individual commentaries as well as section on Symbols.)

9. What is the significance of Platon Karataev in the novel? Discuss whether you believe he is a credible character. (See commentary, Part XII, but give your own opinion.)

10. Discuss the Tolstoyan relationship between "free will" and "necessity." (Try to synthesize your discussion from the summary and commentary on the Second Epilogue, and formulate the answer in your own words.)

11. What does Tolstoy express by his historically inaccurate "apotheosis of Kutuzov" and by his satirical depiction of Napoleon? (See commentaries throughout the Notes as well as relevant sections in Critical Analysis.)

SELECTED BIBLIOGRAPHY

BERLIN, ISAIAH. *The Hedgehog and the Fox: An Essay on Tolstoy's View of History*. New York: Simon & Schuster, 1953. This essay discusses Tolstoy's view of history as part of Tolstoy's personal quest for meaning.

CHRISTIAN, R. F. *Tolstoy's War and Peace, a Study*. Oxford: Clarendon Press, 1962. An analysis of the novel in terms of genre, themes, structure, dramatic devices, and characterizations.

FARRELL, JAMES T. "Tolstoy's War and Peace as a Moral Panorama of Tsarist Feudal Nobility" and "History and War in Tolstoy's War

114

and Peace," *Literature and Morality*. New York: The Vanguard Press, 1947. Two essays discussing the novel in its social, moral, and historical context, showing how the fictional characters illustrate particular Russian types and how the historical characters connote the historical issues in the novel.

FAUSSET, HUGH L'ANSON. *Tolstoy: The Inner Drama*. London: T. Cape, 1927. A psychologically oriented biography of Tolstoy, part of which discusses *War and Peace* as an expression of Tolstoy's own conflicts.

GORKY, MAXIM. *Reminiscences of Tolstoy*, trans. S. S. Koteliansky and Leonard Woolf. New York: B. W. Huebtsch, 1920. Contains anecdotes about Tolstoy and conversations with Tolstoy that reveal the personal vision and personal greatness of a man of genius and profound isolation.

LAVRIN, JANKO. *Tolstoy, an Approach*. New York: Macmillan, 1946. A biography of Tolstoy with particular insight into the poignant conflicts within Tolstoy and revealed in his works.

LUBBOCK, PERCY. *The Craft of Fiction*. New York: The Viking Press, 1957 (paperback). A structural and analytical approach to literary criticism with the author using *War and Peace* and *Madame Bovary* to exemplify his analyses.

REDPATH, THEODORE. *Tolstoy*. London: Bowes & Bowes, 1960. A general biography of Tolstoy from a social and personal, rather than psychological orientation.

STEINER, GEORGE. *Tolstoy or Dostoevsky: An Essay in the Old Criticism*. New York: Alfred A. Knopf, 1959. An excellent critical analysis of these two authors and their works according to "old-style" criticism of evaluating the novels according to formal literary standards.

DE VOGÜÉ, LE VICOMPTE E. MELCHIOR. *The Russian Novel*, 2 vols., trans. Colonel H. A. Sawyer. New York: Alfred A. Knopf, 1916. A well-rounded introduction to Russian literature when such works were almost unknown in Europe. The book provides insight into the Russian mind and spirit that provides the special character of this national literature.

NOTES

NOTES

NOTES

NOTES

NOTES

NOTES

This is the TITLE INDEX, indexing the over 200 titles available by Series, by Library and by Volume Number for both the BASIC LIBRARY SERIES and the AUTHORS LIBRARY SERIES.

TITLE	SERIES	LIBRARY	Vol
Black Like Me	Basic	American Lit	6
Bleak House	Basic	English Lit	3
	Authors	Dickens	1
Bourgeois Gentleman, The (in Tartuffe....)	Basic	European Lit	1
Brave New World	Basic	English Lit	5
Brave New World Revisited (in Brave New World)	Basic	English Lit	5
Brothers Karamozov, The	Basic	European Lit	3
	Authors	Dostoevsky	2
Caesar and Cleopatra (in Shaw's Man and Superman....)	Basic	English Lit	6
	Authors	Shaw	11
Call of the Wild, The	Basic	American Lit	3
Candide	Basic	European Lit	1
Canterbury Tales, The	Basic	Classics	3
"Cask of Amontillado, The" (in Poe's Short Stories)	Basic	American Lit	1
Catch-22	Basic	American Lit	6
Catcher in the Rye, The	Basic	American Lit	6
Choephori (in Agamemnon)	Basic	Classics	1
Clouds, The (in Lysistrata....)	Basic	Classics	1
Color Purple, The	Basic	American Lit	6
Comedy of Errors, The	Basic	Shakespeare	1
	Authors	Shakespeare	8
Connecticut Yankee in King Arthur's Court, A	Basic	American Lit	2
	Authors	Twain	13
Count of Monte Cristo, The	Basic	European Lit	1
Crime and Punishment	Basic	European Lit	3
	Authors	Dostoevsky	2
Crito (in Plato's Euthyphro....)	Basic	Classics	1
Crucible, The	Basic	American Lit	6
Cry, the Beloved Country	Basic	English Lit	5
Cyrano de Bergerac	Basic	European Lit	1
Daisy Miller	Basic	American Lit	2
	Authors	James	6
David Copperfield	Basic	English Lit	3
	Authors	Dickens	1
Day of the Locust, The (in Miss Lonelyhearts....)	Basic	American Lit	5
Death of a Salesman	Basic	American Lit	6
Deerslayer, The	Basic	American Lit	1
"Delta Autumn" (in Go Down, Moses)	Basic	American Lit	4
Demian	Basic	European Lit	2
Diary of Anne Frank, The	Basic	European Lit	2
"Displaced Person, The" (in O'Connor's Short Stories	Basic	American Lit	7
Divine Comedy I: Inferno	Basic	Classics	3
Divine Comedy II: Purgatorio	Basic	Classics	3
Divine Comedy III: Paradiso	Basic	Classics	3
Doctor Faustus	Basic	Classics	3
Doll's House, A (in Ibsen's Plays I)	Basic	European Lit	4
Don Quixote	Basic	Classics	3
Dr. Jekyll and Mr. Hyde	Basic	English Lit	3

TITLE	SERIES	LIBRARY	Vol
Three Musketeers, The	Basic	European Lit	1
To Kill a Mockingbird	Basic	American Lit	7
Tom Jones	Basic	English Lit	2
Tom Sawyer	Basic	American Lit	2
	Authors	Twain	13
Treasure Island	Basic	English Lit	4
Trial, The	Basic	European Lit	2
Tristram Shandy	Basic	English Lit	2
Troilus and Cressida	Basic	Shakespeare	1
	Authors	Shakespeare	8
Turn of the Screw, The (in Daisy Miller....)	Basic	American Lit	2
	Authors	James	6
Twelfth Night	Basic	Shakespeare	1
	Authors	Shakespeare	8
Two Gentlemen of Verona, The (in	Basic	Shakespeare	1
Comedy of Errors...)	Authors	Shakespeare	8
Typee (in Billy Budd & Typee)	Basic	American Lit	1
Ulysses	Basic	English Lit	6
Uncle Tom's Cabin	Basic	American Lit	2
Unvanquished, The	Basic	American Lit	5
	Authors	Faulkner	3
Utopia	Basic	Classics	4
Vanity Fair	Basic	English Lit	4
Vonnegut's Major Works	Basic	American Lit	7
Waiting for Godot	Basic	European Lit	1
Walden	Basic	American Lit	1
Walden Two	Basic	American Lit	7
War and Peace	Basic	European Lit	3
"Was" (in Go Down, Moses)	Basic	American Lit	4
"Waste Land, The" (in T.S. Eliot's Major Poems and Plays)	Basic	English Lit	6
White Fang (in Call of the Wild & White Fang)	Basic	American Lit	3
Who's Afraid of Virginia Woolf?	Basic	American Lit	7
Wild Duck, The (in Ibsen's Plays II)	Basic	European Lit	4
Winesburg, Ohio	Basic	American Lit	3
Winter's Tale, The	Basic	Shakespeare	1
	Authors	Shakespeare	8
Wuthering Heights	Basic	English Lit	4

This is the AUTHOR INDEX, listing the over 200 titles available by author and indexing them by Series, by Library and by Volume Number for both the BASIC LIBRARY SERIES and the AUTHORS LIBRARY SERIES.

AUTHOR	TITLE(S)	SERIES	LIBRARY	Vol
Aeschylus	Agamemnon, The Choephori, & The Eumenides	Basic	Classics	1
Albee, Edward	Who's Afraid of Virginia Woolf?	Basic	American Lit	7
Anderson, Sherwood	Winesburg, Ohio	Basic	American Lit	3
Aristophanes	Lysistrata * The Birds * Clouds * The Frogs	Basic	Classics	1
Aristotle	Aristotle's Ethics	Basic	Classics	1
Austen, Jane	Emma	Basic	English Lit	1
	Pride and Prejudice	Basic	English Lit	2
Beckett, Samuel	Waiting for Godot	Basic	European Lit	1
Beowulf	Beowulf	Basic	Classics	3
Beyle, Henri	see Stendhal			
Bronte, Charlotte	Jane Eyre	Basic	English Lit	3
Bronte, Emily	Wuthering Heights	Basic	English Lit	4
Brown, Claude	Manchild in the Promised Land	Basic	American Lit	7
Buck, Pearl	The Good Earth	Basic	American Lit	4
Bunyan, John	The Pilgrim's Progress	Basic	English Lit	2
Camus, Albert	The Plague * The Stranger	Basic	European Lit	1
Carroll, Lewis	Alice in Wonderland	Basic	English Lit	3
Cather, Willa	My Antonia	Basic	American Lit	3
Cervantes, Miguel de	Don Quixote	Basic	Classics	3
Chaucer, Geoffrey	The Canterbury Tales	Basic	Classics	3
Chopin, Kate	The Awakening	Basic	American Lit	2
Clark, Walter	The Ox-Bow Incident	Basic	American Lit	7
Conrad, Joseph	Heart of Darkness & The Secret Sharer * Lord Jim	Basic	English Lit	5
Cooper, James F.	The Deerslayer * The Last of the Mohicans	Basic	American Lit	1
Crane, Stephen	The Red Badge of Courage	Basic	American Lit	2
Dante	Divine Comedy I: Inferno * Divine Comedy II: Purgatorio * Divine Comedy III: Paradiso	Basic	Classsics	3
Defoe, Daniel	Moll Flanders	Basic	English Lit	1
	Robinson Crusoe	Basic	English Lit	2
Dickens, Charles	Bleak House * David Copperfield * Great Expectations * Hard Times	Basic	English Lit	3
	Oliver Twist * A Tale of Two Cities	Basic	English Lit	4
	Bleak House * David Copperfield * Great Expectations * Hard Times * Oliver Twist * A Tale of Two Cities	Authors	Dickens	1

AUTHOR	TITLE(S)	SERIES	LIBRARY	Vol
Dickinson, Emily	Emily Dickinson: Selected Poems	Basic	American Lit	2
Dostoevsky, Feodor	The Brothers Karamazov * Crime and Punishment * Notes from the Underground	Basic	European Lit	3
	The Brothers Karamazov * Crime and Punishment * Notes from the Underground	Authors	Dostoevsky	2
Dreiser, Theodore	An American Tragedy * Sister Carrie	Basic	American Lit	3
Dumas, Alexandre	The Count of Monte Cristo * The Three Musketeers	Basic	European Lit	1
Eliot, George	Middlemarch * The Mill on the Floss * Silas Marner	Basic	English Lit	4
Eliot, T.S.	T.S. Eliot's Major Poets and Plays: "The Wasteland," "The Love Song of J. Alfred Prufrock," & Other Works	Basic	English Lit	6
Ellison, Ralph	The Invisible Man	Basic	American Lit	7
Emerson, Ralph Waldo	Emerson's Essays	Basic	American Lit	1
Euripides	Electra * Medea	Basic	Classics	1
Faulkner, William	Absalom, Absalom! * As I Lay Dying * The Bear * Go Down, Moses * Light in August	Basic	American Lit	4
	The Sound and the Fury * The Unvanquished	Basic	American Lit	5
	Absalom, Absalom! * As I Lay Dying * The Bear * Go Down, Moses * Light in August The Sound and the Fury * The Unvanquished	Authors	Faulkner	3
Fielding, Henry	Joseph Andrews	Basic	English Lit	1
	Tom Jones	Basic	English Lit	2
Fitzgerald, F. Scott	The Great Gatsby	Basic	American Lit	4
	Tender is the Night	Basic	American Lit	5
Flaubert, Gustave	Madame Bovary	Basic	European Lit	1
Forster, E.M.	A Passage to India	Basic	English Lit	6
Fowles, John	The French Lieutenant's Woman	Basic	English Lit	5
Frank, Anne	The Diary of Anne Frank	Basic	European Lit	2
Franklin, Benjamin	The Autobiography of Benjamin Franklin	Basic	American Lit	1
Gawain Poet	Sir Gawain and the Green Night	Basic	Classics	4
Goethe, Johann Wolfgang von	Faust - Parts I & II	Basic	European Lit	2
Golding, William	Lord of the Flies	Basic	English Lit	5
Greene, Graham	The Power and the Glory	Basic	English Lit	6
Griffin, John H.	Black Like Me	Basic	American Lit	6

AUTHOR	TITLE(S)	SERIES	LIBRARY	Vol
Haley, Alex see also Little, Malcolm	The Autobiography of Malcolm X	Basic	American Lit	6
Hardy, Thomas	Far from the Madding Crowd * Jude the Obscure * The Mayor of Casterbridge	Basic	English Lit	3
	The Return of the Native * Tess of the D'Urbervilles	Basic	English Lit	4
	Far from the Madding Crowd * Jude the Obscure * The Mayor of Casterbridge The Return of the Native * Tess of the D'Urbervilles	Authors	Hardy	4
Hawthorne, Nathaniel	The House of the Seven Gables* The Scarlet Letter	Basic	American Lit	1
Heller, Joseph	Catch-22	Basic	American Lit	6
Hemingway, Ernest	A Farewell to Arms * For Whom the Bell Tolls	Basic	American Lit	4
	The Old Man and the Sea	Basic	American Lit	7
	The Sun Also Rises	Basic	American Lit	5
	A Farewell to Arms * For Whom the Bell Tolls The Old Man and the Sea The Sun Also Rises	Authors	Hemingway	5
Herbert, Frank	Dune & Other Works	Basic	American Lit	6
Hesse, Herman	Demian * Steppenwolf & Siddhartha	Basic	European Lit	2
Hilton, James	Lost Horizon	Basic	English Lit	5
Homer	The Iliad * The Odyssey	Basic	Classics	1
Hugo, Victor	Les Miserables	Basic	European Lit	1
Huxley, Aldous	Brave New World & Brave New World Revisited	Basic	English Lit	5
Ibsen, Henrik	Ibsen's Plays I: A Doll's House & Hedda Gabler * Ibsen's Plays II: Ghosts, An Enemy of the People, & The Wild Duck	Basic	European Lit	4
James, Henry	The American * Daisy Miller & The Turn of the Screw * The Portrait of a Lady	Basic	American Lit	2
	The American * Daisy Miller & The Turn of the Screw * The Portrait of a Lady	Authors	James	6
Joyce, James	A Portrait of the Artist as a Young Man * Ulysses	Basic	English Lit	6
Kafka, Franz	Kafka's Short Stories * The Trial	Basic	European Lit	2
Keats & Shelley	Keats & Shelley	Basic	English Lit	1
Kesey, Ken	One Flew Over the Cuckoo's Nest	Basic	American Lit	7
Knowles, John	A Separate Peace	Basic	American Lit	7

AUTHOR	TITLE(S)	SERIES	LIBRARY	Vol
Lawrence, D.H.	Sons and Lovers	Basic	English Lit	6
Lee, Harper	To Kill a Mockingbird	Basic	American Lit	7
Lewis, Sinclair	Babbit * Main Street	Basic	American Lit	3
	Babbit * Main Street	Authors	Lewis	7
Little, Malcolm see also Haley, Alex	The Autobiography of Malcolm X	Basic	American Lit	6
London, Jack	Call of the Wild & White Fang	Basic	American Lit	3
Machiavelli, Niccolo	The Prince	Basic	Classics	4
Malamud, Bernard	The Assistant	Basic	American Lit	6
Malcolm X	see Little, Malcolm			
Malory, Thomas	Le Morte d'Arthur	Basic	Classics	4
Marlowe, Christopher	Doctor Faustus	Basic	Classics	3
Marquez, Gabriel Garcia	One Hundred Years of Solitude	Basic	American Lit	6
Maugham, Somerset	Of Human Bondage	Basic	English Lit	6
Melville, Herman	Billy Budd & Typee * Moby Dick	Basic	American Lit	1
Miller, Arthur	The Crucible * Death of a Salesman	Basic	American Lit	6
Milton, John	Paradise Lost	Basic	English Lit	2
Moliere, Jean Baptiste	Tartuffe, Misanthrope & Bourgeois Gentleman	Basic	European Lit	1
More, Thomas	Utopia	Basic	Classics	4
O'Connor, Flannery	O'Connor's Short Stories	Basic	American Lit	7
Orwell, George	Animal Farm	Basic	English Lit	5
	Nineteen Eighty-Four	Basic	English Lit	6
Paton, Alan	Cry, The Beloved Country	Basic	English Lit	5
Plath, Sylvia	The Bell Jar	Basic	American Lit	6
Plato	Plato's Euthyphro, Apology, Crito & Phaedo * Plato's The Republic	Basic	Classics	1
Poe, Edgar Allen	Poe's Short Stories	Basic	American Lit	1
Remarque, Erich	All Quiet on the Western Front	Basic	European Lit	2
Rolvaag, Ole	Giants in the Earth	Basic	European Lit	4
Rostand, Edmond	Cyrano de Bergerac	Basic	European Lit	1
Salinger, J.D.	The Catcher in the Rye	Basic	American Lit	6
Sartre, Jean Paul	No Exit & The Flies	Basic	European Lit	1
Scott, Walter	Ivanhoe	Basic	English Lit	1
Shaefer, Jack	Shane	Basic	American Lit	7
Shakespeare, William	All's Well that Ends Well & The Merry Wives of Windsor * As You Like It * The Comedy of Errors, Love's Labour's Lost, & The Two Gentlemen of Verona * Measure for Measure * The Merchant of Venice * Midsummer Night's Dream * Much Ado About Nothing * The Taming of the Shrew * The Tempest *	Basic	Shakespeare	1

AUTHOR	TITLE(S)	SERIES	LIBRARY	Vol
Shakespeare, William	Troilus and Cressida * Twelfth Night * The Winter's Tale	Basic	Shakespeare	1
	All's Well that Ends Well & The Merry Wives of Windsor * As You Like It * The Comedy of Errors, Love's Labour's Lost, & The Two Gentlemen of Verona * Measure for Measure * The Merchant of Venice * Midsummer Night's Dream * Much Ado About Nothing * The Taming of the Shrew * The Tempest * Troilus and Cressida * Twelfth Night * The Winter's Tale	Authors	Shakespeare	8
	Antony and Cleopatra * Hamlet * Julius Caesar * King Lear * Macbeth * Othello * Romeo and Juliet	Basic	Shakeapeare	2
	Antony and Cleopatra * Hamlet * Julius Caesar * King Lear * Macbeth * Othello * Romeo and Juliet	Authors	Shakespeare	9
	Henry IV Part 1 * Henry IV Part 2 * Henry V * Henry VI Parts 1,2,3 * Richard II * Richard III * Shakespeare's Sonnets	Basic	Shakespeare	3
	Henry IV Part 1 * Henry IV Part 2 * Henry V * Henry VI Parts 1,2,3 * Richard II * Richard III * Shakespeare's Sonnets	Authors	Shakespeare	10
Shaw, George Bernard	Man and Superman & Caesar and Cleopatra * Pygmalion & Arms and the Man	Basic	English Lit	6
	Man and Superman & Caesar and Cleopatra * Pygmalion & Arms and the Man	Authors	Shaw	11
Shelley, Mary	Frankenstein	Basic	English Lit	1
Sinclair, Upton	The Jungle	Basic	American Lit	3
Skinner, B.F.	Walden Two	Basic	American Lit	7
Solzhenitsyn, Aleksandr	One Day in the Life of Ivan Denisovich	Basic	European Lit	3
Sophocles	The Oedipus Trilogy	Basic	Classics	1
Spenser, Edmund	The Faerie Queen	Basic	Classics	4
Steinbeck, John	The Grapes of Wrath *	Basic	American Lit	4
	Of Mice and Men * The Pearl * The Red Pony	Basic	American Lit	5

AUTHOR	TITLE(S)	SERIES	LIBRARY	Vol
Steinbeck, John	The Grapes of Wrath * Of Mice and Men * The Pearl * The Red Pony	Authors	Steinbeck	12
Stendhal	The Red and the Black	Basic	European Lit	1
Sterne, Lawrence	Tristram Shandy	Basic	English Lit	2
Stevenson, Robert Louis	Dr. Jekyll and Mr. Hyde *	Basic	English Lit	3
	Treasure Island & Kidnapped	Basic	English Lit	4
Stoker, Bram	Dracula	Basic	English Lit	3
Stowe, Harriet Beecher	Uncle Tom's Cabin	Basic	American Lit	2
Swift, Jonathan	Gulliver's Travels	Basic	English Lit	1
Thackeray, William Makepeace	Vanity Fair	Basic	English Lit	4
Thoreau, Henry David	Walden	Basic	American Lit	1
Tolkien, J.R.R.	The Lord of the Rings & The Hobbit	Basic	English Lit	5
Tolstoy, Leo	Anna Karenina * War and Peace	Basic	European Lit	3
Turgenev, Ivan Sergeyevich	Fathers and Sons	Basic	European Lit	3
Twain, Mark	A Connecticut Yankee * Huckleberry Finn * The Prince and the Pauper * Tom Sawyer	Basic	American Lit	2
	A Connecticut Yankee * Huckleberry Finn * The Prince and the Pauper * Tom Sawyer	Authors	Twain	13
Virgil	The Aeneid	Basic	Classics	1
Voltaire, Francois	Candide	Basic	European Lit	2
Vonnegut, Kurt	Vonnegut's Major Works	Basic	American Lit	7
Walker, Alice	The Color Purple	Basic	American Lit	7
Warren, Robert Penn	All the King's Men	Basic	American Lit	6
West, Nathanael	Miss Lonelyhearts & The Day of the Locust	Basic	American Lit	5
Wharton, Edith	Ethan Frome	Basic	American Lit	3
Whitman, Walt	Leaves of Grass	Basic	American Lit	1
Wilder, Thornton	Our Town	Basic	American Lit	5
Williams, Tennessee	The Glass Menagerie & A Streetcar Named Desire	Basic	American Lit	6
Woolf, Virginia	Mrs. Dalloway	Basic	English Lit	5
Wordsworth, William	The Prelude	Basic	English Lit	2
Wright, Richard	Black Boy	Basic	American Lit	4
	Native Son	Basic	American Lit	5

INDEX OF SERIES

BASIC LIBRARY (24-0)

THE SHAKESPEARE LIBRARY: 3 Volumes, 26 Titles (25-9)
    V. 1 - The Comedies 12 titles (00-3)
    V. 2 - The Tragedies, 7 titles (01-1)
    V. 3 - The Histories; The Sonnets, 7 titles (02-X)

THE CLASSICS LIBRARY: 4 Volumes, 27 Titles (26-7)
    V. 1 - Greek & Roman Classics, 11 titles (03-8)
    V. 2 - Greek & Roman Classics, 2 titles (04-6)
    V. 3 - Early Christian/European Classics, 7 titles (05-4)
    V. 4 - Early Christian/European Classics, 7 titles (06-2)

ENGLISH LITERATURE LIBRARY: 6 Volumes, 55 Titles (29-1)
    V. 1 - 17th Century & Romantic Period Classics, 7 titles (07-0)
    V. 2 - 17th Century & Romantic Period Classics, 7 titles (08-9)
    V. 3 - Victorian Age, 11 titles (09-7)
    V. 4 - Victorian Age, 10 titles (10-0)
    V. 5 - 20th Century, 10 titles (11-9)
    V. 6 - 20th Century, 10 titles (12-7)

AMERICAN LITERATURE LIBRARY: 7 Volumes, 77 Titles (33-X)
    V. 1 - Early U.S. & Romantic Period, 11 titles (13-5)
    V. 2 - Civil War to 1900, 11 titles (14-3)
    V. 3 - Early 20th Century, 9 titles (15-1)
    V. 4 - The Jazz Age to W.W.II, 11 titles (16-X)
    V. 5 - The Jazz Age to W.W.II, 10 titles (17-8)
    V. 6 - Post-War American Literature, 13 titles (18-6)
    V. 7 - Post-War American Literature, 12 titles (19-4)

EUROPEAN LITERATURE LIBRARY: 4 Volumes, 29 Titles (36-4)
    V. 1 - French Literature, 12 titles (20-8)
    V. 2 - German Literature, 7 titles (21-6)
    V. 3 - Russian Literature, 7 titles (22-4)
    V. 4 - Scandinavian Literature, 3 titles (23-2)

AUTHORS LIBRARY (65-8)

    V. 1 - **Charles Dickens** Library, 6 titles (66-6)
    V. 2 - **Feodor Dostoevsky** Library, 3 titles (67-4)
    V. 3 - **William Faulkner** Library, 7 titles (68-2)
    V. 4 - **Thomas Hardy** Library, 5 titles (69-0)
    V. 5 - **Ernest Hemingway** Library, 4 titles (70-4)
    V. 6 - **Henry James** Library, 3 titles (71-2)
    V. 7 - **Sinclair Lewis** Library, 2 titles (72-0)
    V. 8 - **Shakespeare** Library, Part 1 - The Comedies, 12 titles (73-9)
    V. 9 - **Shakespeare** Library, Part 2 - The Tragedies, 7 titles (74-7)
    V. 10 - **Shakespeare** Library, Part 3 - The Histories; Sonnets, 7 titles (75-5)
    V. 11 - **George Bernard Shaw** Library, 2 titles (76-3)
    V. 12 - **John Steinbeck** Library, 4 titles (77-1)
    V. 13 - **Mark Twain** Library, 4 titles (78-X)

Moonbeam Publications ISBN Prefix: 0-931013-

HARDBOUND LITERARY LIBRARIES

INDEX OF LIBRARIES

This is the INDEX OF LIBRARIES, listing the volumes and the individual titles within the volumes for both the BASIC LIBRARY SERIES (24 Volumes, starting below) and the AUTHORS LIBRARY SERIES (13 Volumes, see Page 6).

BASIC LIBRARY SERIES (24 Volumes)

THE SHAKESPEARE LIBRARY: 3 Volumes, 26 Titles

Vol 1 - The Comedies (12 titles)
*All's Well that Ends Well & The Merry Wives of Windsor * As You Like It * The Comedy of Errors, Love's Labour's Lost, & The Two Gentlemen of Verona * Measure for Measure * The Merchant of Venice * A Midsummer Night's Dream * Much Ado About Nothing * The Taming of the Shrew * The Tempest * Troilus and Cressida * Twelfth Night * The Winter's Tale*

Vol 2 - The Tragedies (7 titles)
*Antony and Cleopatra * Hamlet * Julius Caesar * King Lear * Macbeth * Othello * Romeo and Juliet*

Vol 3 - The Histories; The Sonnets (7 titles)
*Henry IV Part 1 * Henry IV Part 2 * Henry V * Henry VI Parts 1,2,3 * Richard II * Richard III * Shakespeare's Sonnets*

THE CLASSICS LIBRARY: 4 Volumes, 27 Titles

Vol 1 - Greek & Roman Classics Part 1 (11 titles)
*The Aeneid * Agamemnon * Aristotle's Ethics * Euripides' Electra & Medea * The Iliad * Lysistrata & Other Comedies * Mythology * The Odyssey * Oedipus Trilogy * Plato's Euthyphro, Apology, Crito & Phaedo * Plato's The Republic*

THE CLASSICS LIBRARY (cont'd)

Vol 2 - Greek & Roman Classics Part 2 (2 titles)
*Greek Classics * Roman Classics*

Vol 3 - Early Christian/European Classics Part 1
(7 titles)
*Beowulf * Canterbury Tales * Divine Comedy - I. Inferno * Divine Comedy - II. Purgatorio * Divine Comedy - III. Paradiso * Doctor Faustus * Don Quixote*

Vol 4 - Early Christian/European Classics Part 2
(7 titles)
*The Faerie Queene * Le Morte D'Arthur * New Testament * Old Testament * The Prince * Sir Gawain and the Green Knight * Utopia*

ENGLISH LITERATURE LIBRARY: 6 Volumes, 55 Titles

Vol 1 - 17th Century & Romantic Period Classics
Part 1 (7 titles)
*Emma * Frankenstein * Gulliver's Travels * Ivanhoe * Joseph Andrews * Keats & Shelley * Moll Flanders*

Vol 2 - 17th Century & Romantic Period Classics
Part 2 (7 titles)
*Paradise Lost * Pilgrim's Progress * The Prelude * Pride and Prejudice * Robinson Crusoe * Tom Jones * Tristram Shandy*

Vol 3 - Victorian Age Part 1 (11 titles)
*Alice in Wonderland * Bleak House * David Copperfield * Dr. Jekyll and Mr. Hyde * Dracula * Far from the Madding Crowd * Great Expectations * Hard Times * Jane Eyre * Jude the Obscure * The Mayor of Casterbridge*

BASIC LIBRARY SERIES

ENGLISH LITERATURE LIBRARY (cont'd)

Vol 4 - Victorian Age Part 2 (10 titles)
*Middlemarch * The Mill on the Floss * Oliver Twist * The Return of the Native * Silas Marner * A Tale of Two Cities * Tess of the D'Urbervilles * Treasure Island & Kidnapped * Vanity Fair * Wuthering Heights*

Vol 5 - 20th Century Part 1 (10 titles)
*Animal Farm * Brave New World * Cry, The Beloved Country * The French Lieutenant's Woman * Heart of Darkness & The Secret Sharer * Lord Jim * Lord of the Flies * The Lord of the Rings * Lost Horizon * Mrs. Dalloway*

Vol 6 - 20th Century Part 2 (10 titles)
*Nineteen Eighty-Four * Of Human Bondage * A Passage to India * A Portrait of the Artist as a Young Man * The Power and the Glory * Shaw's Man and Superman & Caesar and Cleopatra * Shaw's Pygmalion & Arms and the Man * Sons and Lovers * T.S. Eliot's Major Poems and Plays * Ulysses*

AMERICAN LITERATURE LIBRARY: 7 Volumes, 77 Titles

Vol 1 - Early U.S. & Romantic Period (11 titles)
*Autobiography of Ben Franklin * Billy Budd & Typee * The Deerslayer * Emerson's Essays * The House of Seven Gables * The Last of the Mohicans * Leaves of Grass * Moby Dick * Poe's Short Stories * The Scarlet Letter * Walden*

AMERICAN LITERATURE LIBRARY (cont'd)

Vol 2 - Civil War to 1900 (11 titles)

The American * The Awakening * A Connecticut Yankee in King Arthur's Court * Daisy Miller & The Turn of the Screw * Emily Dickinson: Selected Poems * Huckleberry Finn * The Portrait of a Lady * The Prince and the Pauper * Red Badge of Courage * Tom Sawyer * Uncle Tom's Cabin

Vol 3 - Early 20th Century (9 titles)

An American Tragedy * Babbitt * Call of the Wild & White Fang * Ethan Frome * The Jungle * Main Street * My Antonia * Sister Carrie * Winesburg, Ohio

Vol 4 - The Jazz Age to W.W.II Part 1 (11 titles)

Absalom, Absalom! * As I Lay Dying * The Bear * Black Boy * A Farewell to Arms * For Whom the Bell Tolls * Go Down, Moses * The Good Earth * The Grapes of Wrath * The Great Gatsby * Light in August

Vol 5 - The Jazz Age to W.W.II Part 2 (10 titles)

Miss Lonelyhearts & The Day of the Locust * Native Son * Of Mice and Men * Our Town * The Pearl * The Red Pony * The Sound and the Fury * The Sun Also Rises * Tender is the Night * Unvanquished

Vol 6 - Post-War American Literature Part 1 (13 titles)

100 Years of Solitude * All the King's Men * The Assistant * The Autobiography of Malcolm X * The Bell Jar * Black Like Me * Catch-22 * The Catcher in the Rye * The Color Purple * The Crucible * Death of a Salesman * Dune and Other Works * The Glass Menagerie & A Streetcar Named Desire

AMERICAN LITERATURE LIBRARY (cont'd)

Vol 7 - Post-War American Literature Part 2 (12 titles)
*The Invisible Man * Manchild in the Promised Land *
O'Connor's Short Stories * The Old Man and the Sea *
One Flew Over the Cuckoo's Nest * The Ox-Bow Incident
* A Separate Peace * Shane * To Kill a Mockingbird *
Vonnegut's Major Works * Walden Two * Who's Afraid
of Virginia Woolf?*

EUROPEAN LITERATURE LIBRARY: 4 Volumes, 29 Titles

Vol 1 - French Literature (12 titles)
*Candide * The Count of Monte Cristo * Cyrano de
Bergerac * Les Miserables * Madame Bovary * No Exit &
The Flies * The Plague * The Red and the Black * The
Stranger * Tartuffe, Misanthrope & Bourgeois Gentlemen
* The Three Musketeers * Waiting for Godot*

Vol 2 - German Literature (7 titles)
*All Quiet on the Western Front * Demian * The Diary of
Anne Frank * Faust Pt. I & Pt. II * Kafka's Short Stories
* Steppenwolf & Siddhartha * The Trial*

Vol 3 - Russian Literature (7 titles)
*Anna Karenina * The Brothers Karamozov * Crime and
Punishment * Fathers and Sons * Notes from the Underground * One Day in the Life of Ivan Denisovich * War
and Peace*

Vol 4 - Scandinavian Literature (3 titles)
*Giants in the Earth * Ibsen's Plays I: A Doll's House &
Hedda Gabler * Ibsen's Plays II: Ghosts, An Enemy of the
People & The Wild Duck*

AUTHORS LIBRARY

Vol 1 -Charles Dickens Library (6 titles)
*Bleak House * David Copperfield * Great Expectations * Hard Times * Oliver Twist * A Tale of Two Cities*

Vol 2 - Feodor Dostoevsky Library (3 titles)
*The Brothers Karamazov * Crime and Punishment * Notes from the Underground*

Vol 3 - William Faulkner Library (7 titles)
*Absalom, Absalom! * As I Lay Dying * The Bear * Go Down, Moses * Light in August * The Sound and the Fury * The Unvanquished*

Vol 4 - Thomas Hardy Library (5 titles)
*Far from the Madding Crowd * Jude the Obscure * The Major of Casterbridge * The Return of the Native * Tess of the D'Urbervilles*

Vol 5 - Ernest Hemingway Library (4 titles)
*A Farewell to Arms * For Whom the Bell Tolls * The Old Man and the Sea * The Sun Also Rises*

Vol 6 - Henry James Library (3 titles)
*The American * Daisy Miller & The Turn of the Screw * The Portrait of a Lady*

Vol 7 - Sinclair Lewis Library (2 titles)
*Babbitt * Main Street*

Vol 8 - Shakespeare Library, Part 1 - The Comedies (12 titles)
*All's Well that Ends Well & The Merry Wives of Windsor
* As You Like It * The Comedy of Errors, Love's Labour's
Lost & The Two Gentlemen of Verona * Measure for
Measure * The Merchant of Venice * A Midsummer
Night's Dream * Much Ado About Nothing * The Taming
of the Shrew * The Tempest * Troilus and Cressida *
Twelfth Night * The Winter's Tale*

Vol 9 - Shakespeare Library, Part 2 - The Tragedies (7 Titles)
*Antony and Cleopatra * Hamlet * Julius Caesar * King
Lear * Macbeth * Othello * Romeo and Juliet*

**Vol 10 - Shakespeare Library, Part 3 - The Histories; Sonnets
7 titles)**
*Henry IV Part 1 * Henry IV Part 2 * Henry V *Henry VI
Parts 1,2,3 * Richard II * Richard III * Shakespeare's The
Sonnets*

Vol 11 - George Bernard Shaw Library (2 titles)
*Pygmalion & Arms and the Man * Man and Superman &
Caesar and Cleopatra*

Vol 12 - John Steinbeck Library (4 titles)
*The Grapes of Wrath * Of Mice and Men * The Pearl *
The Red Pony*

Vol 13 - Mark Twain Library (4 titles)
*A Connecticut Yankee in King Arthur's Court * Huckle-
berry Finn * The Prince and the Pauper * Tom Sawyer*